More praise for *A Guide to Biblical Commentaries & Reference Works*:

"Covering both the Old and New Testaments, book by book, Evans offers an update (9th ed. no less!) of his guide to commentaries and reference works, a daunting task, but one he has accomplished with remarkable currency and theological sensitivity. This work is not a dry bibliographical list, but is distinguished by ample and insightful annotations, providing a "guide" in the real sense of the word. Of particular value also is his introduction which contains "Standards for Evaluating Commentaries," an excellent list of "Other Bibliographies," along with the author's assessments, and a most helpful evaluation of the major commentary series. The broad theological range of the works included is a further positive quality of the Guide, which belongs alongside the reference books in the libraries of scholars and preachers alike."

C. Hassell Bullock
Franklin S. Dyrness Professor of Biblical Studies, Emeritus
Wheaton College

"With so many books now in print, we need a guide to lead us through the maze of titles. John Evans is precisely who we need. With a remarkable knowledge of the discipline, Evans has selected the best titles for ongoing study, written annotations for each entry, and the result has been the most thorough bibliography in print. Very highly recommended."

Gary M. Burge, Ph.D.
Professor of New Testament
Wheaton College and Graduate School

"Evans' annotations of the NT commentaries are very impressive. He is well versed in both critical/liberal and conservative views. I rarely found an annotation that I could disagree with. I especially appreciate Evans's even-handed annotations of critical/liberal New Testament commentaries. He notes many positives, but also offers brief critiques based on a conservative/evangelical/Reformed view point. Evans has a very good grasp of the many scholarly issues that are present in New Testament commentaries. He also is concerned to note which commentaries are useful for evangelical pastors. Although knowledgeable about the liberal/critical world, Evans is clearly evaluating the New Testament commentaries from an evangelical/ Reformed perspective. My students and many pastors will appreciate that."

Robert Cara, Ph.D.
Hugh and Sallie Reaves Professor of New Testament
Reformed Theological Seminary

A GUIDE TO BIBLICAL COMMENTARIES
& REFERENCE WORKS

A GUIDE TO BIBLICAL COMMENTARIES
& REFERENCE WORKS
for Students and Pastors
(9ᵗʰ Edition)

by John F. Evans

www.doulosresources.org

A Guide to Biblical Commentaries & Reference Works, 9th edition

Published by:

> Doulos Resources, 195 Mack Edwards Drive, Oakland, TN 38060, USA;
> PHONE: (901) 451-0356; WEBSITE: www.doulosresources.org.

In partnership with:

> Covenant Bookstore, 481 Covenant Lane, St. Louis, MO 63141, USA; PHONE:
> (877) 213-3353; WEBSITE: www.covenantseminary.edu/bookstore.

Please address all questions about rights and reproduction to Doulos Resources, 195 Mack Edwards Drive, Oakland, TN 38060, USA; PHONE: (901) 451-0356; E-MAIL: info@doulosresources.org.

Published 2010

Printed in the United States of America by Ingram/Lightning Source

ISBNs:

978-0-9828715-6-0 (trade paperback edition)

978-0-9828715-7-7 (electronic/digital editions)

Library of Congress Catalogue Number: 2010940351

Cover illustration: "The Library at Alexandria" by O. von Corven (public domain).

"Yehudit" font used with permission from Accordance/Oak Tree Software, 498 Palm Springs Drive, Suite 100, Altamonte Springs, FL 32701 USA; PHONE: (407) 339-5855; E-MAIL: oaktree@accordancebible.com.

www.doulosresources.org

ותפארת בנים אבותם

Proverbs 17:6b

TO THE MEMORY OF MY GRANDFATHER

THE REV. FREDERICK WALTER EVANS

A.B. B.D. A.M. LL.D. D.D.

Moderator of the 1946 General Assembly,

Presbyterian Church USA;

Faithful Minister of the Gospel

For Seventy-Two Years; 1880–1977

AND THE MEMORY OF MY FATHER

THE REV. FREDERICK W. EVANS, JR

B.A. B.D. M.A. S.T.M. D.Min.

Faithful Minister of the Gospel

For Forty-Five Years; 1924–1992

~ Sequar, Etsi Non Passibus Equis ~

I Follow, Though With Unequal Steps

CONTENTS

Contents

FROM THE AUTHOR

Perhaps you are wondering why I have undertaken this project. During my senior year at Covenant Seminary, three fellow students were occasionally asking me for advice about commentaries. Eventually, they suggested that I write up a guide to Old Testament commentaries. That guide was well received, and, as a surprise to me, the OT Department decided to reproduce it for distribution to the students. There was a revised and expanded guide later that year (1989) after Professors Phil Long and Gerard Van Groningen read the paper and made suggestions for its improvement. When New Testament Professors George Knight and Karl Cooper mentioned that they would like to see a NT counterpart, I quickly demurred. After all, there were many NT bibliographies, and Dr. Knight had been giving out his own fine survey for several years. When another faculty member made the same request, I decided to attempt the NT analogue and was able to produce it while completing my course work for a second degree at Covenant.

A few years later (1993) I received several inquiries from friends and Covenant faculty about another revision and decided to make the effort. Revised editions were released in October 1993, June '94, June '95, June '96, July 2001, January '05, and June '09. I am gratified that, again, a revision has been requested and that an up-and-coming publisher has asked to carry it.

You may also be curious about my qualifications. I offer no great erudition in OT or NT scholarship. What I do have is a longstanding interest in theological bibliography, the blessing of a substantial personal library (in part inherited from my father and grandfather), and a sincere desire to help others make full use of the study tools available today.

After seminary I was privileged to pastor Faith Presbyterian Church (PCA) in Morganton, NC for five years. I left the pastorate in 1996 to become a missionary lecturer in Africa and first served at the Theological College of Central Africa (Zambia), eventually as Academic Dean. More recently I have been on faculty at seminaries in Namibia and Kenya. The reader will detect both my pastoral and academic interests. I have often identified myself as "evangelical, catholic, and Reformed" (Nevin) in theology, as a churchman owning the heritage of all Christian history, and as being influenced by both Continental and British Calvinism.

No author profit has, up to this point, ever has been made on this guide; I have sought to be the reader's servant for Jesus' sake (2 Cor. 4:5). Now a portion of the author proceeds will be sent by the publisher to the Scholarship Fund of Nairobi Evangelical Graduate School of Theology, one of the premier theological schools in English-speaking Africa, offering degrees from the bachelors level to the Ph.D.

It is a joy to acknowledge and thank those who have encouraged me and supported this project over the last twenty years. First of all comes my loving family: Elizabeth my wife and our three children, now all grown up, Martyn, Beth, and Daniel. They have sacrificed a great deal over the years for me to have time with the books and are far more precious than all the volumes in the Cambridge University Library (well over 7 million at last count).

Let me add to the list my mother and my brother Bill, for his example of fine theological scholarship and his words of encouragement.

Also deserving thanks are past and present members of the Covenant Seminary faculty, staff, and administration, especially the Librarian, Rev. Jim Pakala, who gave assurances many times that the project was worth the effort. One astonishing kindness of the seminary deserves mention. Only a handful have ever heard the story and it is worth recording here. In June 1989 because of the financial needs of our growing family I had given up hopes of continuing my seminary training beyond the MDiv, despite winning the Honorary Grant for Graduate Theological Studies that year. Some person(s) in the administration discovered I was planning to leave school, and I was called into the Registrar's office. There, with no small amount of mystery attached, I was offered a full scholarship for the next year. God be praised for his kindness to me through his people. What grace!

It is gratifying that the Covenant Bookstore managers kept the Guide in print through eight editions (1989–2009). Thank you, Hugh and Nick. I count it a blessing now to be able to work with Ed Eubanks Jr. of Doulos Resources in producing this 9th edition.

A wonderful English couple, Graeme and Sue Walker, were unfailingly generous and helpful in sharing their rural Cambridgeshire home with my family during the summer of 2010; I owe them more than I can say. Finally I express my gratitude to the Warden, Librarian, and staff of Tyndale House for the opportunity to study in Cambridge for about seven weeks. Much of the revision work was done there. To one accustomed to making do with fewer library resources, Tyndale House is "like the Garden of Eden" (Ezek 36:35).

Please write me with comments or recommendations for improving the guide, either via email (john.evans@negst.edu) or mail to the following addresses.

Dr. John F. Evans
c/o Mrs. F. W. Evans, Jr.
4602 Aldersgate Drive
Carmel, Indiana 46033
USA

Dr. John F. Evans
NEGST/AIU
P. O. Box 24686
00502 Karen, Nairobi
KENYA

ABBREVIATIONS

NOTE: Abbreviations for series of commentaries are listed and annotated in the chapter entitled, "Commentary Series."

ABD	*Anchor Bible Dictionary*
ABRL	Anchor Bible Reference Library
ANE	Ancient Near East(ern)
AsTJ	*Asbury Theological Journal*
AUSS	*Andrews University Seminary Studies*
BAR	*Biblical Archeology Review*
BASOR	*Bulletin of the American Schools of Oriental Research*
BBR	*Bulletin for Biblical Research*
BHS	*Biblia Hebraica Stuttgartensia*
BibInt	*Biblical Interpretation*
BJRL	*Bulletin of John Rylands Library*
BL	*Book List, attached to JSOT and JSNT*
BSac	*Bibliotheca Sacra*
BSB	*Biblical Studies Bulletin (e-journal)*
BTB	*Biblical Theology Bulletin*
CBD	Christian Book Distributors
CBQ	*Catholic Biblical Quarterly*
CBR	*Currents in Biblical Research*
Chm	*Churchman*
CJ	*Concordia Journal*
CRBR	*Critical Review of Books in Religion*
CT	*Christianity Today*
CTJ	*Calvin Theological Journal*
CUP	Cambridge University Press
CurBS	*Currents in Research: Biblical Studies (later CBR)*
CurTM	*Currents in Theology and Mission*
DenvJ	*Denver Journal: An Online Review*
DH	Deuteronom(ist)ic History
DOTWPW	*Dictionary of the Old Testament: Wisdom, Poetry & Writings*
DSS	Dead Sea Scrolls
ed.	edition
EC	*Early Christianity* (journal of Mohr Siebeck, 2010–)
ET	English Translation
ETL	*Ephemerides Theologicae Lovanienses*
EuroJTh	*European Journal of Theology*
Evangel	*Evangel: The British Evangelical Review*
EvQ	*Evangelical Quarterly*
ExpTim	*Expository Times*

F&M	*Faith and Mission*
GNB	Good News Bible (1976)
HALOT	*Hebrew and Aramaic Lexicon of the Old Testament*
hb	Hardback
HBT	*Horizons in Biblical Theology*
HebStud	*Hebrew Studies*
IBT	Interpreting Biblical Texts (Abingdon series)
Interp	*Interpretation* (the periodical)
IVP	InterVarsity Press
JAJ	*Journal of Ancient Judaism*
JAOS	*Journal of the American Oriental Society*
JBL	*Journal of Biblical Literature*
JETS	*Journal of the Evangelical Theological Society*
JHebS	*Journal of Hebrew Scriptures (e-journal)*
JNES	*Journal of Near Eastern Studies*
JR	*Journal of Religion*
JSHJ	*Journal for the Study of the Historical Jesus*
JSNT	*Journal for the Study of the New Testament*
JSOT	*Journal for the Study of the Old Testament*
JSOTSup	Journal for the Study of the Old Testament Supplement Series
JSS	*Journal of Semitic Studies*
JTI	*Journal of Theological Interpretation*
JTS	*Journal of Theological Studies*
KAT	Kommentar zum Alten Testament
LHB/OTS	Library of Hebrew Bible/Old Testament Studies
LXX	Septuagint
MT	Masoretic Text
n.d.	No Date of Publication Noted
NEB	New English Bible (1970)
NIDNTT	*New International Dictionary of NT Theology*
NIDOTTE	*New International Dictionary of OT Theology & Exegesis*
NIV	New International Version (1978, 1984)
NJPS	*Tanakh: The Holy Scriptures: The New JPS Translation*
NovT	*Novum Testamentum*
NRSV	New Revised Standard Version (1989)
NTS	*New Testament Studies*
o/p	Out of Print
OTA	*Old Testament Abstracts*
OUP	Oxford University Press
P&R	Presbyterian & Reformed Publishing Co.
pb	Paperback
PCA	Presbyterian Church in America
PCUSA	Presbyterian Church (U.S.A.)
Presb	*Presbyterion*
PSB	*Princeton Seminary Bulletin*
RB	*Revue Biblique*
RBL	*Review of Biblical Literature* (online, only partially in print)
RelSRev	*Religious Studies Review*

RevExp	*Review & Expositor*
RSV	Revised Standard Version (1952)
RTR	*Reformed Theological Review*
RTS	Reformed Theological Seminary
SBET	*Scottish Bulletin of Evangelical Theology*
SBL	Society of Biblical Literature
SJT	*Scottish Journal of Theology*
SMU	Southern Methodist University
SwJT	*Southwestern Journal of Theology*
TDNT	*Theological Dictionary of the New Testament*
TDOT	*Theological Dictionary of the Old Testament*
TEDS	Trinity Evangelical Divinity School
Them	*Themelios* (e-journal as of 2008)
ThTo	*Theology Today*
TJ	*Trinity Journal*
TPI	Trinity Press International
TynBul	*Tyndale Bulletin*
UBS	United Bible Societies
vol.	volume
VT	*Vetus Testamentum*
WJK	Westminster John Knox Press
WTJ	*Westminster Theological Journal*
ZAW	*Zeitschrift für die Alttestamentliche Wissenschaft*

—щ—

Symbols

‡	A Work Espousing a Critical Theological Position (See Introduction for Further Explanation)
[*M*]	A Work which Espouses a "Mediating" or Mildly Critical Approach to Biblical Interpretation (See Introduction)
✓	An Important Scholarly Work Worth Consulting, But of Debatable Value for a Pastor's Library (See Introduction)
F	A Forthcoming Volume
★	Suggested for Purchase (See Introduction)
☆	A Worthwhile Purchase, But Not a First Priority (See Introduction)
Bold	A Leading Commentary, Influential for Evangelical Scholarly Discussion

—⚟—

INTRODUCTION

So Philip ran to him and heard him reading Isaiah the prophet and asked, "Do you understand what you are reading?" And he said, "How can I, unless someone guides me?" And he invited Philip to come up and sit with him.

Acts 8:30-31, ESV

Meagreness, leanness, and shallowness are too often the main features of modern sermons. ...The churches must be reminded that there can be no really powerful preaching without deep thinking, and little deep thinking without hard reading.

J.C. RYLE, 1862[1]

Over years of ministry twin convictions have grown in me. One is that the greatest longing the Church has is for God himself—to know him, his glorious presence, his power, his loving voice. The other conviction is that the Church longs for her ministers to be full of God and his Word. Building from this, I cannot see any pastoral ministry being effective long-term if not characterized by God's love for his people, prayerfulness, brimming confidence in the power of God's Word, and what Ryle termed "hard reading" in the study of Scripture.[2] Thank God for quality Bible commentaries which help preachers and teachers in their study! The challenge comes in recognizing "quality."

Seminary students often face confusing choices in researching exegetical papers or composing sermons. They stand in the library stacks and ask themselves, "Which of these commentaries or reference works should I consult? Obviously, I can't skim even a tenth of these books on Romans; which ones are important and which ones may I safely pass by? Where should I spend my time?"

Prospective pastors or educators face a greater difficulty while searching for calls and preparing to leave for the fields of ministry to which Christ has called them. Knowing that commentaries are an important resource, the new graduates wonder which volumes deserve a place on the shelf. After all, they may possibly be far from a good theological library and will need an adequate personal collection to spur on their own growth in understanding the Bible. They ask, "Where should I spend my money?"

Pastors with some experience in the ministry usually keep on the lookout for new reference works, scanning booksellers' websites and catalogs a few times a year. They too wonder which commentaries would be a smart buy. This guide has been written to aid both in research and in making purchases for a personal library. It is not written for specialists—they have little need for such a guide as this—but for students and pastors, especially

---

1   J.C. Ryle, "Memoir of Samuel Ward, BD," in Samuel Ward, *Sermons and Treatises* (Edinburgh: James Nichol, 1862), xvi.

2   In pressing the point I add a clarification. The expression "hard reading" does not mean general book learning, but the minister's discipline of work so as to become learned and powerful (or well versed) in the Scriptures (Acts 18:24). One could properly adapt Paul's warning in 1 Cor 4:20 to read, "the kingdom of God does not consist in [book-smarts] but in power."

the evangelical and Reformed. For both students and pastors, the need for guides like this grows more acute with each passing year as the publications multiply.

TWO WARNINGS FOR ORIENTATION

It is necessary to warn the reader at the outset that commentaries should not be used as a crutch. Reading a commentary or two, or even 10, is no substitute for your own thorough initial study of the biblical text. The commentaries cannot do your work for you. They are meant to take you deeper than you have already gone and to help you check the conclusions of your own exegesis.[3] Also, commentary resources are not an excuse for neglecting the Hebrew and Greek languages, which are the best, most direct avenue to understanding and expounding the Bible in a responsible way. Charles Spurgeon said that pastors "should be able to read the Bible in the original," and he went on to explain his thinking:

> Every minister should aim at a tolerable proficiency both in the Hebrew and the Greek. These two languages will give him a library at small expense, an inexhaustible thesaurus, a mine of spiritual wealth. Really the effort of acquiring a language is not so prodigious that brethren of moderate abilities should so frequently shrink from the attempt.[4]

With your seminary training, a willingness to dig, and prayer for the Spirit's illumining grace, you can competently exegete and expound the text. (Frankly, you're likely to do better than some of the commentators listed here.) Please don't cheat yourself out of that exciting learning experience. The use of commentaries apart from a careful study of the text (in the original, if possible) is a misuse of them. They are not written to relieve you of the responsibility to interpret the Scriptures, on the way to fulfilling your calling to declare the word of the LORD (Deut 5:5).

As a second warning, there is an inevitable subjectivity in compiling a selective bibliography. One Bible student is stimulated most by rigorous critical scholarship, while another perhaps views the Reformers, Puritan writings, and other classics as most valuable. It is hoped that this guide may be of some aid to both students. This list betrays my appreciation for both the older works that have stood the test of time and the more recent studies which seriously wrestle with issues of literary criticism, history, and biblical-theological interpretation. Let me elaborate.

I make no apology for emphasizing up-to-date and highly respected scholarly works in this survey. I believe that they usually best meet the needs of the pastor and student. (But see, too, my notes on old commentaries below). Many older works—frequently the Puritans—can be faulted for not paying close enough attention to the message of the text in front of them. It is disappointing to peruse an old volume and discover that the commentator has been distracted from the text itself by some locus of systematic theology hinted at,

---

3   For further reflection on the art and purpose of commentary-writing, see John Nolland, "The Purpose and Value of Commentaries," *JSNT* 29.3 (2007): 305–11; Frederick W. Danker, "Commentaries and Their Uses," in *Multipurpose Tools for Bible Study*, Revised and expanded ed. (Minneapolis: Fortress, 1993), 282–307; Frank H. Gorman, "Commenting on Commentary: Reflections on a Genre," in *Relating to the Text*, edited by J. Sandoval and C. Mandolfo, 100–119 (London: T&T Clark, 2003); and Walter C. Kaiser, Jr., "Appendix B: The Usefulness of Biblical Commentaries for Preaching and Bible Study," in *Malachi: God's Unchanging Love* (Grand Rapids: Baker, 1984).

4   C.H. Spurgeon, *Commenting & Commentaries* (London: Banner of Truth, 1969 reprint), 47. See also John Piper's essay, "Brothers, Bitzer Was a Banker" (pp.81–88), in *Brothers, We Are Not Professionals* (Nashville: Broadman & Holman, 2002); Heinrich Bitzer (ed), *Light on the Path* (Grand Rapids: Baker, 1982 reprint).

perhaps obliquely, in the passage.[5] Calvin's magnificent commentaries are unlike some Puritan works in this regard. The Reformer consciously rejected the Aristotelian method of establishing the meaning of a document by searching out its *loci* (i.e., its definitive concepts), and kept strictly to the task of elucidating the line of thought in the text, saving the discussion of *loci* for his *Institutes of the Christian Religion*.

However, many modern commentaries have, from the pastor's point of view, worse problems. Quite a few technical works reveal little or no interest in the message and theology of the text. Many commentaries have been written with "the assumption that the genetic origins of a text, often terribly hypothetical, are all one has to discover."[6] It is disappointing to spend time and money on a commentary in which the intricacies of such historical critical debate take precedence over interpreting the text as we have it.[7] Also, some volumes hardly do more than catalog the history of scholarly opinion on each crux of historical criticism. Sometimes the scholar leaves you hanging and fails even to draw a conclusion. At the other end of the spectrum, the student or pastor finds many breezy homiletical commentaries that pay no serious attention to the text at all; the author's notions and observations about life in general supplant Scripture's message. How can you avoid such books?

Hopefully this survey will be some help to you, but don't depend entirely on one list. This guide is subjective and reflects my own proclivities (quirks?), which may be different from yours. You may be helped by a book I find dull and pedestrian, or, conversely, you may dislike a commentary I have suggested for purchase. I urge students to use the seminary library as much as possible. Too many students fail to make good use of the library, and upon leaving school they have little idea what commentaries are out there or what kinds of books they like.

An invaluable resource for the commentary buyer is book reviews. Several evangelical journals have been especially helpful to me on account of their frequent commentary reviews: *Bulletin of Biblical Research, Calvin Theological Journal, Evangelical Quarterly, Journal of the Evangelical Theological Society, Themelios*—briefly dormant, now online free[8]—and *Westminster Theological Journal*.[9] I have cited over 3500 reviews, both evangelical and critical, throughout this guide so that you will be able to consult them quickly

---

5   Having said that, I might add that such Puritans' digressions on systematic loci are usually worth reading.

6   Roland E. Murphy, Review of Craig G. Bartholomew, *Reading Ecclesiastes: Old Testament Exegesis and Hermeneutical Theory* (Rome: Biblical Institute Press, 1998), in *CBQ* 61.4 (1999): 735.

7   For long years biblical scholarship was fixated on historical questions, and there were indefatigable efforts both to trace "the text's becoming" (compositional history) and to "get behind the text" so as to reconstruct the religio-historical context of the writing. Often enough those reconstructions contradicted the story presented in the text. From the 1960s onward scholars have become increasingly impatient with this focus, and they have shifted from historical to literary concerns ("the text's being"). They want to study the art, the shape/structure, the rhetoric in the final-form. As one might expect, commentaries reflect this shift. Recommended reading: Craig Bartholomew, *et al* (eds), *"Behind" the Text: History and Biblical Interpretation* (Grand Rapids: Zondervan, 2003); David Firth and James Grant (eds), *Words and the Word: Explorations in Biblical Interpretation and Literary Theory* (Nottingham: Apollos, 2008); and Thomas Olbricht, "Rhetorical Criticism in Biblical Commentaries," *CBR* 7.1 (2008): 11–36.

8   See the digital journal at: <www.thegospelcoalition.org/publications/?/themelios>.

9   In addition to these, some of the best critical journals with reviews are: *Catholic Biblical Quarterly; Expository Times* (often the first review to appear); *Interpretation; Journal of Biblical Literature* (now in the auxiliary annual print publication *Review of Biblical Literature* and at the SBL website: www.sbl-site.org/SBL/Reviews/); *Hebrew Studies; Biblica; Vetus Testamentum; Novum Testamentum; Journal of Hebrew Scriptures* (e-journal at http://www.arts.ualberta.ca/JHS/reviews/jhs_rev.html); *Journal of Theological Studies*; and *Biblical Interpretation* (more monographs than commentaries). Other recommended evangelical periodicals are *Denver Journal* (www.denver-journal.densem.edu); *Reformed Theological Review*; and *Trinity Journal*.

without poring over the indexes. These citations are intended as a check to counter subjectivity in this guide and will be found in a smaller font and in [brackets]. I also hope to save you some eye-strain, which (I laugh) may be a contribution to scholarship. Besides the book reviews students are helped enormously by two publications of the Catholic Biblical Association of America which summarize the latest of both periodical articles and books: *Old Testament Abstracts* and *New Testament Abstracts*.

OTHER BIBLIOGRAPHIES

The pastor or student who desires to build a fine personal library will learn much from consulting other bibliographies. Spurgeon's famous book dates from 1876 and is still quite valuable for its judicious reviews of old commentaries on both testaments. Barber's 3-vol. survey has a wealth of bibliographical data, but often poor judgment in its recommendations. (Anything Dispensational is typically given high marks, regardless of quality.) Now it is quite dated. Barber's pb volume of 2000 is more of a supplement and does not include the huge catalog of commentaries found in the earlier set. Rosscup is now the better Dispensationally-oriented survey. He is similar to Barber in placing a higher value on older works and in consistently recommending a narrower range of commentaries, i.e., those sharing his theology. Kiehl once offered a lot of information, but few will now depend on such an old guide (current through 1986). It was evangelically oriented, and some would say gave too much weight to Lutheran works. For a more recent, conservative Lutheran guide to commentaries, see Brug below. Unfortunately, Stuart's 1990 guide had limited usefulness from the beginning because he made few value judgments.

Two more recent bibliographies merit special attention. The first is Bauer's large guide (2003), which covers a huge amount of ground and, therefore, is more selective. The reviews and recommendations are intelligent (from a Wesleyan and mildly critical stance), but one wonders at points if selectivity or ignorance was at work when he omitted entirely the NIV Application Commentary and the New American Commentary.[10] Excluding his commentary recommendations, this is about the fullest and best bibliographic guide into the whole range of tools available for exegetical research.

Secondly, I am delighted to recommend John Glynn's work in a 10th ed. (2007) [*JSNT-BL* 2009]; at the same time I sadly report that my friend is with the Lord (†2007).[11] Glynn's perspective is unabashedly conservative, yet he covers every significant commentary series, evangelical or liberal. He is well-read and informed in his recommendations. Two possible drawbacks are the brevity of his descriptions or reviews and a strict focus upon recent works. His wide-ranging survey of reference works and theological resources—atlases, dictionaries, hermeneutics textbooks, lexicons and grammars for the languages, introductions, systematics and church history works, etc.—fills a real need. The commentary section is probably Glynn's best. Among up-to-date guides, only Bauer treats a similarly broad range of resources for exegesis. Note, too, that Bauer does not discuss the literature

---

10 A pastor who wants to preach on Gideon or Samson is misled if Bauer does not recommend Block's NAC work on Judges/Ruth. In Zondervan's NIVAC, the pastor is helped immensely by Enns on Exodus, Jobes on Esther, and Duguid on Ezekiel. I could list many additional jewels in other series that he misses: Milgrom on Numbers; Christopher Wright on Deuteronomy; Provan on Kings; Murphy on Proverbs (WBC); Baker Books' 3-vol. set on the Minor Prophets. Once in a while, his "highly recommended" lists make no sense whatsoever, as when he includes the Sanday-Headlam ICC on Romans but not Cranfield. We had better stop here, so a survey of a survey of Bible commentaries does not become silly.

11 There are reports that Dallas Seminary faculty will continue Glynn's project and publish future editions.

in the fields of systematic theology and church history, as does Glynn, and that Glynn is more current.

More than "just in passing," I call attention to a fine set of quick internet guides to commentaries on both testaments. See the Grove "Biblical Studies Bulletin" edited (mostly) by Michael Thompson, Principal of Ridley Hall in Cambridge, England. He engages leading conservative Anglican scholars—with rare exceptions—to make recommendations for pastors. Would you like to know which commentaries Wenham thinks are best on Genesis? He tells you in about two minutes. Hugh Williamson does the write-up for books on Chronicles and on Ezra–Nehemiah. In the area of NT, Peter Head among others has sage advice on the commentaries most serviceable for pastors. Occasionally I select quotes from contributors and mark them BSB with a date.

Among OT annotated bibliographies, Childs' 1977 book, *Old Testament Books*, is excellent but out of print (o/p). He is usually fair and well worth reading cover to cover, but do note that his choices are informed by critical presuppositions. He may discount a work of quality if it is at odds with dominant critical theory, but the discounting is not egregious or severe. Of course Childs misses the flood of works published over the last 30 years. The aging Goldingay/Hubbard list is quite good as well; in the U.K. there is a Goldingay revision. Tremper Longman's survey is clearly the best current bibliography here in the U.S., though all four editions occasionally overlook important works.[12] The 2nd ed. (1995) is not to be discarded, for it had features not included in the 3rd and 4th eds.: (a) reviews of reference works like OT introductions, Hebrew grammars, etc.; (b) an appendix listing "best buys"; and (c) an appendix suggesting which works might be included in "an ultimate reference library." Moving on to an internet resource, I can heartily recommend the Denver Seminary bibliography done by Carroll R. and Hess.

Among the NT bibliographies, Don Carson's must head the list. Years ago we used to read Carson and Ralph Martin's 1984 book—now available free on the internet—side by side. Both were full, wide-ranging, and well done indeed. (Martin's guide was meant to serve as a companion to Brevard Childs'.) Carson, in contrast to Martin, has been repeatedly updated. The most recent edition was released in 2007. Written from a more consistently evangelical perspective, his recommendations have usually been more responsible and discerning than Martin's. It would be a mistake, however, to think that Carson's conservative stance narrows the purview of his survey; he reviews the works of Bultmann alongside the Puritans. As he says, "this survey is a guide to commentaries, not orthodoxy."[13] This means he does not slight works coming out of the critical camp if they are worthy contributions (e.g., he rightly gives high marks to the Anchor Bible volumes on Luke by Fitzmyer). Carson is an excellent guide and worth buying along with Longman. The Denver Seminary list on the internet is updated every year and provides good guidance. These and other notable bibliographies are listed below. Bold print below indicates the more informative or instructive lists.

Aune, David E. *Jesus and the Synoptic Gospels.* Theological Students Fellowship – Bibliographic Study Guides. Madison: IVP, 1980.
Austin Graduate School of Theology: <www.austingrad.edu/Library/LibraryCommentary-3.html>.
Barber, Cyril J. *The Minister's Library.* 3 Vols. Grand Rapids: Baker, 1974–89.

---

12 In the 2003 and 2007 editions, we lacked reviews of Nelson on Deuteronomy; Hawk on Joshua; Schneider on Judges; Davidson on Psalms; the NCB volume on Hosea; Westermann on Lamentations; Macintosh's ICC on Hosea; Wolff on Micah; and all the Abingdon OT Commentaries.

13 D.A. Carson, *New Testament Commentary Survey*, 6th ed. (Grand Rapids: Baker Academic, 2007), 8.

Barber, Cyril J., and Robert M. Knauss, Jr. *An Introduction to Theological Research: A Guide for College and Seminary Students.* 2nd ed. New York: University Press of America, 2000. [*JETS* 12/01]

Barker, Kenneth L., Bruce K. Waltke and Roy B. Zuck. *Bibliography for Old Testament Exegesis and Exposition.* Dallas: Dallas Theological Seminary, 1979.

Bauer, David R. *An Annotated Guide to Biblical Resources for Ministry.* Peabody, MA: Hendrickson, 2003.

Bazylinski, Stanislaw. *A Guide to Biblical Research.* 2nd enlarged ed. Rome: Gregorian & Biblical Institute Press, 2009.

Biblical Studies Bulletin (BSB): <www.ridley.cam.ac.uk/bsb.html>. Edited for a long time by Michael B. Thompson of Ridley Hall, Cambridge.

Brug, John F. (Wisconsin Lutheran Seminary, conservative), "Old Testament Commentaries for the Pastor's Study": <www.wlsessays.net/files/BrugCommentaries5th_0.pdf>. 5th ed. 2005. [Accessed 4/29/2010]

Carson, Donald A. *New Testament Commentary Survey.* 6th ed. Grand Rapids: Baker Academic, 2007. [4th ed. 1993; 5th ed. 2001]

Childs, Brevard S. *Old Testament Books for Pastor and Teacher.* Philadelphia: Westminster, 1977.

Childs, Brevard S. *The New Testament as Canon: An Introduction.* Philadelphia: Fortress, 1985. [See "Excursus IV"]

Danker, Frederick W. *Multipurpose Tools for Bible Study.* Revised & expanded ed. Minneapolis: Fortress Press, 1993, 2003 (with CD).

Denver Journal Bibliographies: <www.denverseminary.edu/article/annotated-old-testament-bibliography-2010/> (Hess, Carroll R., and Dallaire for OT); <http://www.denverseminary.edu/article/new-testament-exegesis-bibliography-2010/> (Klein, Blomberg, and Hecht for NT).

Eves, Terry, and Steven Schlei. "A Guide to Old Testament Commentaries and Reference Works." Revised ed. 1982. Published by Westminster Seminary Bookstore. Philadelphia, PA.

Fee, Gordon D. *New Testament Exegesis.* 4th ed. Louisville: WJK, 2010. [See "Aids and Resources for the Steps in Exegesis"]

Finley, Thomas J. (Talbot Seminary). <www.people.biola.edu/faculty/tomf/OT_Expositional_Tools.pdf>. Accessed 2005. [No longer available]

Fitzmyer, Joseph A. *An Introductory Bibliography for the Study of Scripture.* 3rd ed. Rome: Pontifical Biblical Institute, 1990.

France, R.T. *A Bibliographical Guide to New Testament Research.* Cambridge: Tyndale Fellowship for Biblical Research, 1974.

Glynn, John. *Commentary & Reference Survey: A Comprehensive Guide to Biblical and Theological Resources.* 10th ed. Grand Rapids: Kregel, 2007.

Goldingay, John, and Robert Hubbard. *Old Testament Commentary Survey.* Rev. ed. London: Theological Students Fellowship, 1981. There is a relatively up-to-date, though brief bibliography by Goldingay at <www.theologybooks.com/site/biblio.cfm?tkey=9>.

Goodacre, Mark. <http://ntgateway.com/resource/biblio.htm>.

Harrington, Daniel. *The New Testament: A Bibliography.* Wilmington, DE: Michael Glazier, 1985.

Kepple, Robert J., and John R. Muether. *Reference Works for Theological Research.* 3rd ed. Lanham, MD: University Press of America, 1992.

Kiehl, Erich H. *Building Your Biblical Studies Library.* St. Louis: Concordia, 1988.

Klein, Ralph W. <http://prophetss.lstc.edu/~rklein/> (2008).

Knight, George W., III. "New Testament Commentaries for a Minister's Library." Revised 1993. Privately Produced. (Available from the author.)

Longman, Tremper, III. *Old Testament Commentary Survey.* 4th ed. Grand Rapids: Baker Academic, 2007 (1st ed. 1991; 2nd ed. 1995; 3rd ed. 2003).

Martin, Ralph. *New Testament Books for Pastor and Teacher.* Philadelphia: Westminster, 1984. [The full text of this o/p book can be found at <www.theologybooks.com/site/feature.cfm?tkey=51>.]

Meredith, Don (Harding U. Graduate School of Religion). <www.hugsr.edu/library/researchguides.php> There were several fine bibliographies of bibliographies on this site.

Mills, Watson E. *Critical Tools for the Study of the New Testament.* Lewiston, NY: Mellen, 1995.

Moo, Douglas (ed). *An Annotated Bibliography on the Bible and the Church.* Compiled for the Alumni Association of Trinity Evangelical Divinity School, 1986.

Moore College. "List of Recommended Commentaries and Reference Works": <www.moorebooks.com.au>

Oak Hill College, London (Faculty Recommendations): <www.oakhill.ac.uk/resources/old_testament.html> and <www.oakhill.ac.uk/resources/new_testament.html>. Accessed 2005. [No longer available]

Pakala, James C. "A Librarian's Comments on Commentaries," *Presb* 21.2– (1995–).

Pierce, Jeremy. <http://parablemania.ektopos.com/archives/2006/05/forthcombook.html>

Princeton Theological Seminary. <www.ptsem.edu/Academics/BS/NT/Commentaries%20(Abrgd).htm>. Accessed 2005. [No longer available]

Rosscup, Jim. *Commentaries for Biblical Expositors.* Revised ed. The Woodlands, TX: Kress, 2006.

Scholer, David M. *A Basic Bibliographic Guide for New Testament Exegesis.* 2nd ed. Grand Rapids: Eerdmans, 1973.

Silva, Moisés. "The Silva Mind-Control Method for Buying NT Commentaries." Revised Jan. 1993. Published by Westminster Seminary Bookstore, Philadelphia, PA.

Smick, Elmer B. "A Pastor's Bibliographical Guide to the Old Testament." Revised 1985. Privately Produced at Gordon-Conwell Seminary, South Hamilton, MA.

Southwestern Baptist Seminary: <www.swbts.edu/departments/essentialbooks/theology/index.htm>.

Spurgeon, C.H. *Commenting & Commentaries.* London: Banner of Truth, 1969 reprint (1876 ed.).

Stewart, David R. *The Literature of Theology: A Guide for Students and Pastors.* Revised ed. Louisville: Westminster John Knox, 2003.

Stitzinger, James F. (The Master's Seminary, Santa Clarita, CA) "Books for Bible Expositors" (2007): <http://www.masters.edu/deptpagenew.asp?pageid=2685&minimal=true>. Accessed 5/22/2009.

Stuart, Douglas. *A Guide to Selecting and Using Bible Commentaries.* Waco, TX: Word, 1990.

Stuart, Douglas. *Old Testament Exegesis.* 4th ed. Louisville: Westminster John Knox, 2009. [See "Exegesis Aids & Resources"]

Sugg, Martha Aycock, and John Boone Trotti. *Building a Pastor's Library.* Richmond, VA: Union Theological Seminary, 1991.

Thomas, Derek. *The Essential Commentaries for a Preacher's Library.* Greenville, SC: Reformed Academic Press, 1996.

Thorsen, Donald A.D. *Theological Resources for Ministry: A Bibliography of Works in Theological Studies.* Nappanee, IN: Evangel Publishing House, 1996.

Turner, John. "Bible Commentary Reviews": <www.disciples.org/biblea.htm#Biog>. [No longer available]

United Bible Societies. "Bible Commentaries" >>"List All": <www.ubs-translations.org/>.

Virginia Theological Seminary, "A Preacher's and Teacher's Bookshelf": <www.vts.edu/logue/books.htm>.

Williams, Tyler F. (Taylor University College, Edmonton). "Old Testament Commentary Survey" (current as of 2006) <http://biblical-studies.ca/ot_commentaries/otcom.html>.

Zannoni, Arthur E. *The Old Testament: A Bibliography.* Collegeville, MN: Liturgical Press, 1992.

Here are two final notes: (1) A few commentary series (e.g., New Interpreter's Bible, Abingdon NT Commentaries, and NIV Application Commentary) include annotated bibliographies worth consulting. (2) Baker's "IBR Bibliographies" have value but most do not cover commentaries; two notable exceptions are Porter/McDonald on NT Introduction and McKnight/Williams on the Synoptic Gospels.[14]

---

14 Private correspondence with Rev. Doug Stelzig, a missionary college lecturer in South Africa.

THE GUIDE'S FORMAT

In this guide I have made few changes to the format of previous editions because that layout has been well received and seems well suited to helping the reader quickly survey the books available. I have usually starred (★) about five or six works for each Bible book as suggestions for purchase, allowing myself an extra selection or two for those books a preacher will often turn to (e.g., Genesis, Psalms, John, Romans). The majority of these recommended works emphasize scholarly exegesis and full exposition rather than devotional and sermonic helps, but I have kept in mind the need for a mix. As readers will notice, the mix I prefer includes commentaries which exegete the text in the original languages (e.g., NIGTC, BECNT, ICC); more accessible commentaries using English translations (NICOT, NICNT, NAC); and expositions which are practical in aim, relating the Bible's message to today's world (BST and NIVAC). Series such as NIGTC and BST will be helpful in different ways at different points in sermon preparation.[15] In making recommendations for purchases, I have mainly had pastors in mind; preachers want reliable and accessible tools, focused more on the message of the text. More specifically, I have been thinking of studious pastors, who take seriously the life of the mind and the academic study of Scripture, even if academia is not their calling. (The pastorate is a higher calling in my book.) While making recommendations for purchases, I have not forgotten seminarians' interest in philology, grammar, sophisticated hermeneutical methods, cutting-edge literary analysis, bibliographies, etc. To benefit those students using this guide in their research, I have placed in bold type the authors of the weightier, more influential scholarly commentaries, i.e., those works an evangelical seminary professor would probably like to see consulted in exegetical papers.

The star-outline symbol (☆) designates a valuable commentary or reference work which would be worth buying, but would, in my judgment, be a second priority. The checkmark (British "tick") symbol (✓) designates an important scholarly work that could profitably be consulted for seminary papers, but is either difficult/expensive to obtain or of debatable value for a pastor's library. The symbol (F) indicates a forthcoming volume. It must be said that some of these promised volumes may never be published.

As a rule of thumb, it is unwise to purchase an entire series of commentaries, despite the lure of deep discounts. Some exceptions to this rule come to mind: Calvin's Commentaries, Keil & Delitzsch (OT), perhaps the two Tyndale series and the New International Commentary series (NICOT and NICNT). The basis for this rule is the fact that series are always uneven, some more than others, even when they are the work of only one commentator. Because of different price structures for series on CD-ROM (e.g., Word Biblical Commentary), this rule will not be followed as regularly as it once was. *Please note: in this guide I have not included Keil & Delitzsch or Calvin's NT Commentaries among the purchase suggestions under individual books. Rather I have assumed that many students and pastors will eventually either obtain these for their personal collections or gain access to these classics via the internet.*

---

15 Fred Craddock, the Bandy Distinguished Professor of Preaching and New Testament, Emeritus, at Candler School of Theology, has an interesting system of describing the books on a pastor's bookshelf. He writes of classifying "resources for preaching according to the days of the week, Monday being farthest from the pulpit, Saturday being closest. The technically and critically heavy books…are called Monday books; those less so, Tuesday books. Wednesday books refer to those which are biblically and theologically substantive but which have preachers in mind. Thursday books make suggestions about how to preach their contents, Friday books contain sermon outlines, and Saturday books are collections of full sermons." *Luke*, Interpretation (Louisville: John Knox Press, 1990), vii.

For the student just beginning to build a library, I pass along my late father's excellent advice: as you're able, buy one solid exegetical volume and one suggestive expositional-devotional commentary for each book. I might add that it would be wise to garner the exegetical tools first and to begin with the major books of the Bible, i.e., those on which you will be preaching with some regularity. Another, more long-term system for developing a library collection, used by probably thousands of ministers, is to purchase four to five helpful works for preaching through a book. I did this for my very first sermon series. Planning to do a full exposition of 1 Peter, I purchased Selwyn, Davids, Michaels, Grudem and Clowney. My father encouraged me further by giving me Stuart Briscoe's book of sermons entitled, *When the Going Gets Tough*. The main point is to have a smart plan in mind and keep at it.

STANDARDS FOR EVALUATING COMMENTARIES

A few words are in order about the kinds of commentaries I have recommended.[16] What was I looking for? First, I examined a commentary for exegetical help with the text, especially at the cruxes where help is most needed. Is the commentator learned and sensitive when it comes to language and grammar questions? Is there any analysis of structure, literary art, and rhetoric? Does the author employ traditional diachronic or recent synchronic methods (or attempt an integration of the two)? Does the commentary help me understand the flow of the story or argument (perhaps with discourse analysis)? Does it give evidence of the scholar's patient, hard work with the text, including a good awareness of past research. I count two strikes against scholars who have not kept up with reading in their field. Of course, some scholars give perhaps too much evidence that they read widely. From them, Andrie du Toit humorously says, "one can learn a lot about the art of compilation."[17]

My second concern was for an understanding of the historical and cultural background of the literature. Who was the author? When was it written? To whom and for what reason? What social, cultural, economic, and religious factors, in the milieu of the intended audience or readership, are key for understanding how the message was first received? What may have been the use of the text in the life of the faith community, if we know little or nothing of its author and the circumstances of composition (as with many of the psalms)? Do these facts (or guesses) throw any light on how I ought to interpret the text?

Third, does the commentator provide mature theological reflection (preferably from both the biblical theology[18] and the systematic theology angles) after making well-based

---

16 Some of these concerns and questions were culled from the 1982 commentary guide produced by Steven Schlei and Terry Eves for Westminster Seminary students. I used their list extensively when I began seminary.

17 Andrie B. du Toit, Review of Abraham J. Malherbe, *The Letters to the Thessalonians* (AB 32B; New York: Doubleday, 2000), in *RelSRev* 29.1 (2003): 46. The reviewer adds, "I once heard the late Willem van Unnik warn against writers who draw on nine other publications to produce a tenth."

18 I am among those who believe that a neglect of the biblical theological (or redemptive historical) approach mutes true gospel proclamation in many pulpits today. Moralizing preaching is tiresome—see "A Paper Doll King David" in *Christianity Today* 6/16/97. But it is also dangerous theologically. I implore young seminarians to get well acquainted with IVP's *New Dictionary of Biblical Theology* (2000) and to read and digest books like Sidney Greidanus' *Preaching Christ from the Old Testament* (1999); Graeme Goldsworthy's *Preaching the Whole Bible as Christian Scripture* (2000); and Edmund Clowney's *Preaching and Biblical Theology* (1961), which on p.78 boldly says,

"Preaching which ignores the *historia revelationis*, which 'again and again equates Abraham and us, Moses' struggle and ours, Peter's denial and our unfaithfulness; which proceeds only illustratively, does not bring the Word of God and does not permit the church to see the glory of the work of God; it only preaches man, the sinful, the sought, the redeemed, the pious man,

exegetical decisions? The commentator ought to be alert to theological questions such as: How are themes contained in this passage anticipated earlier in Scripture? How are they developed or fulfilled later in Scripture? Does the text express truths or themes which are emphasized in the theology of the Bible book being studied: say, the New Exodus theme in Ezekiel or Glory in John's Gospel? How is this passage similar to others and how is it different? What is the passage's unique message? What doctrines are taught here? Does the passage shed light on doctrinal controversies? Are there tensions between the teachings in this pericope and others in Scripture which need to be addressed and resolved?

Fourth among the concerns was to look for clarity of expression and economy of words. Books that were full in their discussion, but somewhat unfocused or prolix were sometimes excluded from the list of suggested works—many homiletical commentaries fall into this category. According to Calvin, *perspicua brevitas* is the chief virtue of a commentator. Along the same lines, Professor I. Howard Marshall warned of "a real danger that pastors are going to stop reading modern commentaries simply because they haven't the time to cope with the vast mass of material in them and produce their expository sermons. Students and pastors need something more succinct!"[19] I agree with this but also wish to leave room for big reference works which are more likely to take up technical questions. Hengstenberg once wrote, "There are two kinds of commentaries on Holy Scripture—those that are more adapted for perusal, and those that are more suitable for reference. Both are necessary, and it would not be desirable that either should exclude the other."[20]

Fifth, I look at the price tag. It is astonishing what some publishers ask for a book. Some superb commentaries, like the Davies/Allison ICC volumes on Matthew, are far beyond the reach of the pastor; that 3-vol. hb set with 2400 pages now lists for $156 per volume! Do the math and it's $468.00 for a commentary on a single Bible book.

Sixth, is the work readily available for library use or purchase? It is nonsensical for me to urge readers to purchase books that are long out-of-print.

My seventh concern related to the genre of commentary. If the author set out to write a warm-hearted, devotional exposition with lots of anecdotes and application, I will naturally apply different standards to evaluate it than, say, a volume in the technical series NIGTC. I asked, what kind of commentary did the person set out to write, for what kind of audience, and how well did the author accomplish his or her aim?

Eighth, the pastor asks whether the commentator can suggest ways the text may speak to contemporary issues facing the Church. These days, some fine practical series, such as the "NIV Application Commentary," understand the distinction between homiletical commentaries and published sermons. They seek to lay a reasonably solid exegetical foundation for understanding the meaning of the text in its ancient context before moving on to matters of contemporary application. For application, these commentaries aim to be "suggestive," to present sermon "seed thoughts" for preachers to mull over and develop on their own. They provide guidance rather than pre-fabricated sermons in the guise of commentary. The better series may suggest *multiple* possibilities for proper application of the text's message to the people of God. Other series now in print do not seem to understand this distinction

---

but not Jesus Christ'" (Karl Dijk, *De Dienst der Prediking*, 109).

19 I. Howard Marshall, Review of Rudolf Schnackenburg, *The Epistle to the Ephesians* (Edinburgh: T&T Clark, 1991), in *EvQ* 68.1 (1996): 70. From the OT side, Richard Coggins has spoken of commentaries having suffered "a kind of elephantiasis" (*Joel and Amos* [NCB; Sheffield: Sheffield Academic Press, 2000], vii).

20 E.W. Hengstenberg, *The Prophecies of the Prophet Ezekiel Elucidated*, trans. by A.C. Murphy and J.G. Murphy (Edinburgh: T&T Clark, 1869), v.

between homiletical commentaries and ready-made sermons. We all should look askance when poor quality, edited sermons which offer no serious, sustained engagement of the text are today dressed up as "commentary." What sort of book are preachers looking for? What will help them? The preface to the *New Interpreter's Bible*, in describing the aim of its practically oriented "Reflections" section, expresses the felt need of most ministers I know: "Preachers and teachers want some specificity about the implications of the text, but not so much specificity that the work is done for them. The ideas in the Reflections are meant to stimulate the thought of preachers and teachers, not to replace it."[21]

My comments above on homiletical commentaries may be open to misunderstanding. Books of sermons have done me a world of good; I do not denigrate them. I relish reading in volumes of sermons by the great expositors, including John Calvin, Charles Spurgeon, Campbell Morgan, and Martyn Lloyd-Jones. In this guide I recommend a few of these volumes for purchase, not so much for their application, which often cannot easily or properly be carried over to the present day, but for their penetrating exposition which drives to the theological heart of the text.

It is appropriate to make two additional comments regarding the exegeses and expositions I recommend here. First, I consider almost all the reader-response type works to be of diminished value for students and working pastors. (One of the rare exceptions is Clines on Job.) Too often they seem contrived and even self-indulgent, offering more insight into that particular reader's ideology than into the message of the ancient text. Don't people buy commentaries to understand the text better? In the extreme, such reader-response works may betray a postmodern abandonment of the search for any "determinate meaning" in the text. Second, it is in my recommendations of expositions that my Reformed theological commitments are most obvious.

Another type of commentary, one which I rarely mention in this guide, is the single volume Bible commentary. The pastor or student can sometimes get a wonderful overview of a Bible book using these hefty tools. I give as an example Derek Kidner's 38 pages on *Isaiah in The New Bible Commentary: Revised* (Eerdmans, 1970), later retitled *Eerdmans Bible Commentary* after the publication of the *New Bible Commentary: 21st Century Edition* (IVP, 1994). Other quality single volumes in this category are the *New International Bible Commentary* (Zondervan); *Eerdmans Commentary on the Bible* (2003) [*CBQ* 10/04]; *The HarperCollins Bible Commentary*, produced by members of SBL (1988, revised 2000); *The New Jerome Biblical Commentary* (Prentice Hall, 1990); *The Jewish Study Bible* (OUP, 2004) [*CBQ* 10/04]; *The Oxford Bible Commentary* (2001); *The New Interpreter's Study Bible* (2003); and the *Africa Bible Commentary* (Zondervan, 2006). I have not yet seen Robert Gundry's one-vol. *Commentary on the New Testament* (Hendrickson, 2010), but I suspect it deserves the advance plaudits regarding its learning, wise selectivity in what it treats, and fullness (1100 pages).

David A. Dorsey's single volume on the OT, *The Literary Structure of the Old Testament: A Commentary on Genesis–Malachi* (Baker, 1999), is *sui generis* and worth recommending here. Not everyone can believe that palindromes or chiasms are as common as Dorsey argues, but his 330-page book is fascinating and helpful for pastors and students [*JETS* 9/01]. At times his hermeneutical moves are brilliant. For example, he shows the multiplied verbal links between Job's anguished speeches, especially the lament in ch. 3, and God's response at the close of the book; this proves that God has indeed heard his servant and kept a record (see Job 19:23).

---

21 "Features of the New Interpreter's Bible," *The New Interpreter's Bible*, 12 vols. (Nashville: Abingdon, 1994–2002), xviii.

THE RANGE OF THIS GUIDE— CONSERVATIVES & CRITICS

I have included a full complement of Neo-Orthodox and liberal books in this guide. I might have focused more on evangelical works that are respectful of Scripture's author- ity. However, I have chosen to include (and recommend on occasion) critical materials of note alongside important evangelical contributions. I have done so for several reasons. 1) The inclusion of non-conservative works will best serve the evangelical seminary student who is expected to show some familiarity with critical scholarship. I trust I am correct in assuming a certain level of theological training, sophistication, and especially, spiritual discernment. 2) A few Bible books do not have a technical, recent, in-depth evangelical commentary. 3) Also, frequently many of the strongest commentaries on a given book (us- ing the points of evaluation above) have been written by critics. Wide reading will soon convince you that "good and bad exegesis cuts across doctrinal lines and is represented at both ends of the theological spectrum."[22] 4) You will learn a great deal from the critics as you discipline yourself to read with discernment, measuring their presuppositions, method- ology, and conclusions by the standard of Holy Scripture. The late F.F. Bruce once wrote, "I have sometimes learned most from scholars with whom I have agreed the least: they compel one to think and rethink."[23]

I have taken care to specify critical works listed in this guide (‡, or [*M*] if mildly critical or mediating). I hope this will enable "the fledgling student"[24] to read and make purchases with discernment. Recognizing scholars' faith commitments (in regard to the in- spiration and authority of the Bible) can be helpful for knowing how to approach and digest their work. (This is often especially true where those scholars [naïvely?] deny any personal faith commitment.)[25] So-called higher critical scholarship is often hostile to the evangelical faith. I can illustrate by quoting the liberal OT scholar, John J. Collins, who argues: "His- torical criticism…is not compatible with a confessional theology that is committed to spe- cific doctrines on the basis of faith." It is only "compatible with theology understood as an open-ended and critical inquiry into the meaning and function of God-language."[26] Some critical treatments are more, some less, objectionable to an evangelical pastor or student.

22 Brevard S. Childs, *Old Testament Books for Pastor & Teacher* (Philadelphia: Westminster, 1977), 11– 12.

23 F.F. Bruce, *The Epistles to the Colossians, to Philemon and to the Ephesians* (Grand Rapids: Eerdmans, 1984) xii. Beginning students can feel distress when they encounter attacks upon the Bible and con- tradictions of their beliefs. Here we may listen to the counsel of I. Howard Marshall: "… people who disagree with you may be wrong, even if you can't immediately know how to refute them" (53). See Carl Trueman, "Interview with Professor Howard Marshall," *Them* 26.1 (2000): 48–53.

24 This is a phrase from the "Editorial Preface" of the Word Biblical Commentary series.

25 In one of his defenses against Robert Carroll's attacks on his Jeremiah scholarship, Walter Brueggemann ("Sometimes Wave, Sometimes Particle," *CBR* 8.3 [2010]: 384) protested that Carroll imagines he has no theological commitments himself. "He seems not to realize that in all our interpretation, we are, willy-nilly, exhibiting our own views of God, try as we will for critical objectivity."

26 "Is a Critical Biblical Theology Possible?" *The Hebrew Bible and Its Interpreters* (Winona Lake, IN: Eisenbrauns, 1990), 14. Higher criticism commonly presents two challenges to evangelical, believing scholarship. The first is a "hermeneutic of suspicion" regarding the truth-claims and accuracy of the Scriptures. Michael Fox says, for example, "the willingness *not* to take a text at face value is the essence of critical scholarship" (*Character and Ideology in the Book of Esther*, 2nd ed. [Grand Rapids: Eerdmans, 2001], 148–49). The second challenge is the tendency of the more radical critics to reject the supernatu- ral. Sheffield professor Philip R. Davies could not be clearer about his presuppositions, which amount to methodological atheism: "I don't allow divine activity or any unqualifiable or undemonstrable cause as an arguable factor in historical reconstruction, and, even if I were to accept privately the possibil- ity of such factors, I do not see how I could integrate such explanations into anything recognizable as a historical method" ("Method and Madness: Some Remarks on Doing History with the Bible," *JBL* 114 [1995]: 703). Cf. R. Bultmann, "Is Exegesis Without Presuppositions Possible?" *Existence and*

We must realize that everyone has to deal with the liberal-conservative divide. If some conservatives are often—more than wary—broadly dismissive of all critical scholarship, it is also true that liberals can be rudely dismissive of diligent, erudite evangelical scholars just because they belong to "the gaggle of conservatives." One caveat is for all of us: "The branding as 'liberal' or 'conservative' has too often been mistaken for engagement with the arguments put forward, and has hobbled those from across the theological spectrum who take such an exclusionary position."[27] Even as we recognize theological differences and their ramifications, we want to avoid "theological profiling" which excludes.

BACKGROUND READING

DICTIONARIES OF BIBLICAL INTERPRETATION

Students will find invaluable several major reference works, beginning with the 6-vol. *Anchor Bible Dictionary* (1992). A rival work is the *New Interpreter's Dictionary of the Bible* in 5 volumes (2006–09). Concentrating on historical and contemporary hermeneutical questions are the Coggins/Houlden *Dictionary of Biblical Interpretation* (1990); the 2-vol. *Dictionary of Biblical Interpretation* (1999), edited by John Hayes; and the *Dictionary of Biblical Criticism and Interpretation*, edited by Stanley Porter and published in 2007.

DEVELOPMENT OF HIGHER CRITICISM

Those who feel uninformed and even mystified by the complexities of scholarship and desire some orientation to the climate of critical opinion will find several books helpful. Some OT and NT Introductions include surveys of the 200-year debate over Higher Criticism. A book by the critic R.E. Clements, *One Hundred Years of Old Testament Interpretation* (1976), may be useful to you. Werner Kümmel's volume, *The New Testament: The History of the Investigation of Its Problems* (ET 1973), is quite helpful for understanding theological developments in Germany. Stephen Neill's fascinating work, *The Interpretation of the New Testament 1861–1961*, was revised and expanded by N.T. Wright and covers the period 1861–1986. It gives an especially fine account of developments in Britain. John Riches' *A Century of New Testament Study* (1993) is selective in its coverage, but what it does is quite well done [*CRBR* 1995]. No one remotely conservative rates a mention in Riches. The best book surveying the history of evangelical scholarship in this country and its response to higher criticism is Mark Noll, *Between Faith and Criticism: Evangelicals, Scholarship, and the Bible in America* (Harper & Row, 1986; 2nd ed Baker, 1991). None of these books, however, discusses the newer holistic literary approaches to the text.

HISTORY OF BIBLICAL INTERPRETATION

To dig back further into the history of OT and NT scholarship, students will turn to other works. For the whole history of biblical interpretation, pride of place still goes to the 3-vol. *Cambridge History of the Bible* (1963–70). I believe, however, the ambitious project edited by Hauser and Watson, *A History of Biblical Interpretation*, may eventually take its place, at least in the sense of bringing the discussion up-to-date. Two of four volumes have appeared: "Vol. 1: The Ancient Period" (Eerdmans, 2003), and "Vol. 2: The Medieval

---

Faith (NY: Meridian, 1960), 291–92. Thankfully, Davies' is still a minority view, and many moderately critical scholars would strenuously disagree. Such presuppositions make a huge difference in biblical studies, and my point here is that critical (or conservative) methodological assumptions can be noted as relevant in a guide to commentaries.

27 David W. Baker, and Bill T. Arnold (eds), "Preface" in *The Face of Old Testament Studies: A Survey of Contemporary Approaches* (Grand Rapids: Baker; Leicester: Apollos, 1999), 11.

through the Reformation Periods" (2009); the first is strong on Jewish interpretation but weak on the canon and too brief on the Fathers [*Chm* Sum 08; *VT* 55.1]. Reventlow's full treatment of the *History of Biblical Interpretation* is coming into English translation (2009–), with a total of four volumes expected.

There are two stunningly comprehensive projects focused on but one testament. Magne Saebø edits the *Hebrew Bible/Old Testament: The History of Its Interpretation*, with volumes on I/1: Antiquity (1996), I/2: The Middle Ages (2000), and II: From Renaissance to the Enlightenment (2008). Already the incomplete set can boast of nearly 3000 pages. An enthusiastic welcome is being extended to William Baird's Fortress series, *History of New Testament Research*. Volumes are slowly appearing: Vol. 1: *From Deism to Tübingen* (1992), and Vol. 2: *From Jonathan Edwards to Rudolf Bultmann* (2002) [*JETS* 6/03; *CTJ* 11/04; *EuroJTh* 15.1 (Stenschte)].

Because these reference works are daunting for beginners, I recommend two quick overviews: the basic sketch Yarchin provides in the "Introduction" (pp.xi-xxx) to his *History of Biblical Interpretation: A Reader* (Hendrickson, 2004) [*VT* 57.2], and *A Short History of the Interpretation of the Bible* by Grant and Tracy (Fortress, 1984). I judge the best introduction to be the wise, well-balanced survey of Gerald Bray: *Biblical Interpretation, Past & Present* (IVP, 1996), particularly for its treatment of theological currents. Because of the publisher, I had high hopes for John Court (ed), *Biblical Interpretation* (Continuum, 2004), but you can safely ignore it [*Anvil* 22.1 (Moberly)].

The Shape of Current Scholarship

Those wanting a useful summary of the current *status quaestionis* in various areas of critical scholarship may consult the two volumes of essays produced by SBL: *The Hebrew Bible and Its Modern Interpreters* (1985) and *The New Testament and Its Modern Interpreters* (1989). More recent are the following books of note, on both testaments: *Methods of Biblical Interpretation* (Abingdon, 2004); *To Each Its Own Meaning* (WJK, 1999); and the large *Oxford Handbook of Biblical Studies* (2006) [*NovT* 49.2; *ExpTim* 11/08; *JSOT-BL* 2007; *EuroJTh* 18.1]. On the OT you may consult the Abingdon Press issue, *Old Testament Interpretation: Past, Present and Future: Essays in Honor of Gene M. Tucker* (1995); the WJK volume, *The Hebrew Bible Today: An Introduction to Critical Issues* (1998); and Oxford University Press's *Text in Context* (2000). Moving over to the NT, you will find helpful the collection of essays published in Porter (ed), *Handbook to Exegesis of the New Testament* (Brill, 1997); in Powell (ed), *The New Testament Today* (WJK, 1999); and in *Approaches to New Testament Studies* (Sheffield, 1995), edited by Porter and Tombs. Finally, students should be reminded of the treasures in the *Anchor Bible Dictionary* (see, e.g., the articles on "Form Criticism" by Barton and Robbins) and the *New Interpreter's Dictionary of the Bible*. All the aforementioned works come out of the critical camp.

One asks, what has been produced by conservatives? Readers should note the Zondervan series, *Foundations of Contemporary Interpretation*, now published in a one-vol. collection [*Evangel* Spr 02 (Marshall)]. For those interested in OT studies more particularly, there are two volumes to recommend: the Baker title, *The Face of Old Testament Studies*, 1999 [*EvQ* 10/02; *DenvJ*]; and the collection of essays in vol. 1 of the *New International Dictionary of Old Testament Theology & Exegesis*. For students of the NT, we first have two volumes edited by Dockery and Black: *New Testament Criticism and Interpretation* (Zondervan, 1991); and *Interpreting the New Testament* (Broadman & Holman, 2001). The latter is a revision and expansion of the 1991 issue [*Them* Spr 03]. Secondly, there is *Hearing the New Testament* (Eerdmans, 1995, 2nd ed 2010), edited by J.B. Green. Lastly, the most recent survey is *The Face of New Testament Studies* (2004), which is a magnificent addition to the literature [*Chm* Spr 06; *BBR* 15.1; *Them* 10/06; *TJ* Fall 05; *RelSRev* 4/07; *Anvil* 22.4; *DenvJ* 11/04].

For discussion of individual interpreters, see the McKim edited *Dictionary of Major Biblical Interpreters* (IVP, 2007), which replaced the 1998 *Historical Handbook*; and the *Oxford Dictionary of the Christian Church* (3rd ed 2005). For entries on those conservative scholars missed or ignored in other dictionaries, look up Elwell and Weaver (eds), *Bible Interpreters of the 20th Century: A Selection of Evangelical Voices* (Baker, 1999), and Larsen (ed), *Biographical Dictionary of Evangelicals* (IVP, 2003).

TERMINOLOGY

Some of the terminology used in biblical scholarship and in this guide to describe various hermeneutical approaches may be unfamiliar to neophyte seminarians. "What is this 'tradition-history' you mention? And what does 'diachronic' mean?" Students will find quick help in the *Soulen Handbook of Biblical Criticism* (3rd ed 2001) and the *Westminster Dictionary of Theological Terms*, 1996. For yet more help, see the major dictionaries of biblical interpretation referenced above and the textbooks of exegesis.[28]

Philosophical sophistication is also becoming more and more necessary for high level work in theological fields. It is understandable why an information technology major or physical education major might struggle in a competitive MDiv program. A propaedeutic or quick reference is the slim dictionary, *101 Key Terms in Philosophy and Their Importance for Theology* (WJK, 2004), written by Kelly James Clark, Richard Lints, and James K.A. Smith. Much more in-depth are Anthony Thiselton's superlative *New Horizons in Hermeneutics* (Zondervan, 1992), and *Thiselton on Hermeneutics* (Eerdmans, 2006) [*ExpTim* 6/07; *JTS* 4/09] which discuss the most significant philosophical currents affecting biblical studies.[29] The best counsel I can give at present, though, is to buy and digest well Thiselton's 409-page *Hermeneutics: An Introduction* (Eerdmans, 2009) [*RBL* 6/10]. He is a master teacher, a teacher of teachers, and this is the best introduction to biblical and theological hermeneutics I've found for the bright beginner. For individual hot-topics in hermeneutics, e.g., history, philosophy of language, biblical-theological interpretation, see also the Paternoster/Zondervan "Scripture and Hermeneutics Series" (2001–) [*EuroJTh* 17.1].

OTHER BIBLE REFERENCE WORKS

In past years, several friends have asked me to expand this survey to include a full review of OT and NT reference works, such as atlases, introductions, grammars, histories of Israel, etc. I have rejected that idea for a number of reasons I won't list here. At the end of this guide I have provided a brief list of those works which, to my thinking, could form

---

28 Students have long repaired to such textbooks as John Barton's *Reading the Old Testament: Method in Biblical Study* (Revised 1996); McKenzie and Haynes (eds), *To Each Its Own Meaning: An Introduction to Biblical Criticisms and Their Application* (Revised 1999); Soulen's *Handbook of Biblical Criticism* (3rd ed. 2001); Hayes and Holladay, *Biblical Exegesis: A Beginner's Handbook* (Revised 1987, 3rd ed 2007); or Barton (ed), *The Cambridge Companion to Biblical Interpretation* (1998). More in depth would be the many OT and NT volumes in the Fortress Press "Guides to Biblical Scholarship." For a good overview of the aims of, and an apology for, historical criticism, see John Barton, *The Nature of Biblical Criticism* (2007) [*VT* 59.1]. More conservative overviews are available in Armerding's *The OT and Criticism* (1983) and the Klein–Blomberg–Hubbard *Introduction to Biblical Interpretation* (1993, revised 2004) [*Them* 1/95].

29 I regret that I cannot be as enthusiastic about a newer Thiselton issue: *A Concise Encyclopedia of the Philosophy of Religion* (Grand Rapids: Baker Academic, 2005), which is poorly edited [*SwJT* Fall 04]. A stimulating and sagacious study of the interface of hermeneutics and theology is Thiselton, *The Hermeneutics of Doctrine* (Grand Rapids: Eerdmans, 2007) [*RelSRev* 34.2; *ExpTim* 10/09].

the nucleus of a preacher's basic reference library; see "An Ideal Basic Library for the Pastor." For a more complete listing of OT and NT research tools, please consult Longman's[30] and Carson's commentary surveys; Danker's *Multipurpose Tools for Bible Study* (Revised 1993, 2003); the section "Exegesis Aids and Resources" in both Douglas Stuart's *Old Testament Exegesis* (4th ed 2009) and Gordon Fee's *New Testament Exegesis* (4th ed 2010); the Denver Journal bibliographies; David R. Bauer's *An Annotated Guide*; and John Glynn's *Commentary and Reference Survey*, all of which are cited above.

OLD COMMENTARIES AND FOREIGN LANGUAGE WORKS

OLD COMMENTARIES

I have not mentioned the two famous Puritan commentaries by Matthew Henry and Matthew Poole in the section on individual books. Please don't think of them as relics. Henry, particularly, is still quite useful. Childs counsels,

> I would strongly recommend that pastors secure one of the great English pastors who wrote commentaries on the whole Bible. ...These old books can work as a trap and deception if the pastor is simply looking for a retreat into the past, but if they are correctly used, innumerable riches can be tapped.[31]

Much the same thing can be said for the mountain of rich exposition in the best old sets of sermons; see, for example, the Church Father Chrysostom, Luther, Calvin, the Puritans, Maclaren, Spurgeon, and Campbell Morgan.

For the OT, many pastors once used the Jamieson-Fausset-Brown commentary alongside Keil & Delitzsch (KD). I would not counsel the purchase of J-F-B, which covers the NT too. Though the point can be overstressed (see below), it remains true that, for many of these older commentaries, the best insights were mined out long ago and incorporated in newer works. But if you have inherited J-F-B and have few resources, don't discard it. This set continues to be reprinted. For comments on the KD and Lange sets, see "Commentary Series" below.

Bengel's New Testament Commentary is a great classic (1742), about 2000 pages long. John Bengel was a pioneer exegete for the modern era. I can't say I'd counsel you to buy it, however. Several other older sets on the NT should also be mentioned briefly. *Alford's Greek Testament* (6th ed 1873) and the *Expositor's Greek Testament* (1897) both served past generations well and still have some use. I would not recommend you purchase them unless they were drastically marked down in a second-hand bookstore. A.T. Robertson's *Word Pictures in the New Testament* (1933), though a different sort of work, would fall into the same class.

Two sets of devotional commentaries are of similar age (late 19th century) and usefulness. J.C. Ryle's *Expository Thoughts on the Gospels* is suggestive in seven pb volumes (some editions are without the more detailed notes, which often include excellent quotes from the Church Fathers, the Reformers and Puritans). Part of the set has been included in Crossway's "Classic Commentary" series. The comments are clear, edifying and vigorous-

---

30 Do note that Longman's 3rd and 4th eds. do not contain the thirty or so pages of reference works reviews found in the earlier editions. To read his evaluation of OT Introductions, OT theologies, OT histories, Bible atlases, Hebrew lexicons, etc., look up the 2nd ed. But as you consult that 1995 edition, keep in mind the important tools published in the intervening years. Here are examples: the 2- vol. "study edition" of *The Hebrew & Aramaic Lexicon of the Old Testament* (HALOT); the Provan-Long-Longman *A Biblical History of Israel*; the 5-vol. *New International Dictionary of Old Testament Theology & Exegesis*.

31 Childs, *Old Testament Books for Pastor and Teacher*, 30.

ly Calvinistic. H.C.G. Moule's expositions of the epistles are full of the love of Christ. Usually they have titles like *Colossians Studies*. Moule was a fine scholar as well as preacher. He produced several volumes in The Cambridge Bible for Schools and Colleges and The Cambridge Greek Testament for Schools and Colleges. Both Ryle and Moule were godly Anglican bishops.

I offer two final notes on older commentaries. First, advertisers have spent trillions to convince us that "newer" always means improved, and "older" always means inferior and obsolete. One should believe them when it comes to computers. Wiser seminarians, however, should not buy into such categorizing, when it comes to theological literature and the genre of commentaries in particular. Students should also be apprised that there is a growing movement within biblical studies that takes the history of interpretation more seriously—older books teach us much—and humility should incline us to join that movement.[32] My second note is a recommendation of a Cambridge friend's work on "Pre-20th Century Commentaries on the Old Testament in Cambridge University Library." Dr. Leslie McFall spent years of work using and assessing old commentaries (17th to 19th centuries). The fruit of that labor is a list of recommended works, available free at <www.btinternet. com/~lmf12/Pre20thCenturyCommentaries.html>. While you may not have access to all the Cambridge resources, you may discover some work of interest on the list which you can hunt down closer to home.

FOREIGN LANGUAGE COMMENTARIES

There isn't room in this guide to note important, individual foreign language works. Those who are doing fuller research and can handle the languages may consult those works. Strong volumes are available in French, especially in the series *Etudes Bibliques* (e.g., Spicq on the Pastorals and Hebrews), *Commentaire de l'Ancien Testament*, *Commentaire du Nouveau Testament* (e.g., Bonnard on Matthew), and *Sources Bibliques*. For those with some proficiency in German there are the important series, *Herders Theologischer Kommentar*, and *Regensburger Neues Testament* from the Roman Catholic scholars. Catholics and Protestants collaborated to produce the *Evangelisch-katholischer Kommentar* (EKK). Largely Protestant series include *Kommentar zum Alten Testament* (KAT), *Das Alte Testament Deutsch*, *Das Neue Testament Deutsch*, *Theologischer Handkommentar*, *Zürcher Bibelkommentare*, and, most importantly, *Biblischer Kommentar* (BKAT) for the Old Testament and the constantly revised *Meyer Kritisch-exegetischer Kommentar* (KEK) on the New Testament. There is an abundance of good commentaries in Dutch too (e.g., Aalders on Ezekiel, Beuken on Isaiah); see HCOT below under "Commentary Series." For reviews of continental European works, peruse *RB*, *Ephemerides Theologicae Lovanienses*, *Biblica*, *Etudes Théologiques & Religieuses*, *ZAW* (but not *Zeitschrift für die Neutestamentliche Wissenschaft*), *VT*, *NovT*, and *Theologische Literaturzeitung*.

To put it succinctly, we are being swamped with fine commentaries these days. The publishers have discovered that they sell well, and they are contracting for new volumes and new series all the time. None of us can keep up with the pace. But count your bless-

---

32 Excellent arguments for doing so are made in Dale C. Allison, "Matthew and the History of Interpretation," *ExpTim* 120.1 (2008): 1–7. None of us wants to fall into the category of those Christian moderns chided by Mark Noll as full of "self-confidence, bordering on hubris, manifested by an extreme antitraditionalism that casually discounted the possibility of wisdom from earlier generations" (*The Scandal of the Evangelical Mind* [Grand Rapids: Eerdmans, 1994], 127). See, too, C.S. Lewis' warnings against "chronological snobbery" and his essay "On the Reading of Old Books" (*God in the Dock: Essays on Theology and Ethics*, ed. Walter Hooper [Grand Rapids: Eerdmans, 1970], 200–07).

ings—I bought some "top pick" commentaries just five years ago that are now superseded by a couple better ones.

NOTES ON COMPUTER TECHNOLOGY

The world of biblical scholarship is undergoing revolutionary changes due to developments in computer technology. It is likely that the day will soon be upon us when the serious Bible student will be able to access via the internet the contents of the world's great theological libraries. One gets excited dreaming about what the future holds. But in all your dreaming about tomorrow, you can't afford to miss today's opportunities.

In past editions of this guide, I made recommendations of Bible study software. Because of my last 14 years of missionary service in Africa, I have lost my grasp of developments in the area of software. I won't take the chance of misleading you or embarrassing myself by continuing to make recommendations, except to urge more advanced students using PCs to consider Hermeneutika "BibleWorks 8" [*JHebS* 2009; *Them* 11/09] or Libronix "Logos Bible Software 4" [*Them* 11/09; earlier reviews were *Them* Spr 04; *WTJ* Fall 04; *JETS* 6/05; *BTB* Fall 07]. Mac-users have something just as good, arguably better, in the "Accordance" program [*JETS* 3/05]. Many top scholars choose to use Macs because they love Accordance so much. (Yes, I have Accordance.) The second recommendation is to seek guidance from John Glynn's *Commentary & Reference Survey* (2007), pp.343–64; though that information is rapidly going out-of-date, Glynn still gives one a good idea of the basic strengths and capabilities of different programs.

There is a real need for an up-to-date guide to internet resources. Years ago, we had Patrick Durusau, *High Places in Cyberspace: A Guide to Biblical and Religious Studies, Classics, and Archeological Resources on the Internet*, 2nd ed., Scholars Press Handbook Series (Atlanta: Scholars Press, 1998). I have not seen a 3rd edition. At this point in time, however, we don't need print editions of such guides, only online versions. About the best, brief print edition is, again, John Glynn (2007); see pp.365–68. For leads to discover far, far more that is available on the internet for theological studies generally, read Meriel Patrick, "Disentangling the Web: A Guide to Online Resources for Theology," *ExpTim* 121.5 (2010): 213–17.

If they don't know already, those who love classic works need to know about the major project called "Christian Classics Ethereal Library" <www.ccel.org/>, which is now based at Calvin College. Previously Wheaton College had it. If you look up the site, you can find an amazing assortment of materials: the writings of the Church Fathers, Calvin's Commentaries (19th century ed.), Matthew Henry, ancient Greek texts, the Hebrew OT, etc. The index is already pages long, and new materials are being added on a regular basis.

COMMENTARY SERIES

What is the intended readership of a specific commentary? Some of the best technical commentaries are both unsuitable for, and unusable by, the average church member, even the one who is most eager to understand the Bible. On the other hand, many well-written Bible study guides and commentaries for laypeople are considered too light to offer serious help to the studious pastor. The general reading level of the following series will be indicated by the following symbols: [L] for educated laypeople, such as the Bible study leader; [P] for theologically trained pastors and seminarians; [S] for advanced students and scholars. My rating will sometimes mix these categories, and the first letter has the greater weight. This rating system is an adaptation of the one used by Longman's *OT Commentary Survey.*

AB   ANCHOR BIBLE. ‡ (Doubleday). See AYB. [SM]

ACCS   ANCIENT CHRISTIAN COMMENTARY ON SCRIPTURE. (IVP). A marvelous project headed up by editor Thomas Oden, the ACCS seeks to reacquaint the Church with its rich heritage of ancient commentary on Scripture. Too many biblical scholars pay little attention to anything more than a few decades old. The publisher has released a 28-vol. "series encompassing all of Scripture and offering contemporary readers the opportunity to study for themselves the key writings of the early church fathers." It is my conviction that we fail to honor the Holy Spirit, who has instructed the Church from its beginning, if we neglect the insights of a Chrysostom, an Augustine. Dip into these volumes and discover for yourself the theological and devotional power of the Fathers. (See Christopher Hall's *Reading Scripture with the Church Fathers* [IVP].) The whole canon has now been covered, but keep in mind that some books receive scanty comment (341pp on Exodus–Deuteronomy), while others get a lot (764pp on John). An additional volume on the Apocrypha is expected. The series is now available on CD-ROM. Cf. "The Church's Bible" series. [PS]

ANTC   ABINGDON NEW TESTAMENT COMMENTARIES. ‡ (Abingdon). A series begun in 1996 and now complete which provides compact, critically informed commentaries on the NT. They are competent, non-technical, and written for students and pastors—somewhat like the Tyndale series, but liberal and perhaps more scholarly. You will appreciate the annotated bibliographies appended to most volumes. Credit goes to the editors for keeping the commentaries so uniformly compact; some other series have less to say in twice the pages. The gospels are appropriately allotted a good bit more space. [P]

AOTC   ABINGDON OLD TESTAMENT COMMENTARIES. ‡ (Abingdon). In my 2001 edition, I paid ANTC the compliment of wishing Abingdon would produce a series of similar thrust and quality on the OT. That same year saw the publication of Brueggemann's highly theological exegesis of Deuteronomy in AOTC. One anticipates that many good volumes will follow in this moderately critical series. Patrick Miller of Princeton Seminary is the General Editor. As with the NT counterpart, one should expect a focus on exegesis rather than exposition. In this way it can be contrasted with the Interpretation series. The scholarship in AOTC tends to be less original and more "derivative," in the sense that it draws from others' works and re-presents the more convincing conclusions of (mainly critical) scholarship. [P]

Apollos APOLLOS OLD TESTAMENT COMMENTARIES. (IVP–Apollos). Many eagerly awaited the first installments of this series. Originally, I believe the publishers were announced as Baker in the U.S. and HarperCollins in the U.K., but that did not work out. The wise choice of general editors, Gordon Wenham and David Baker, indicated to me years ago that the series would likely be of high quality and present evangelical, critically-informed exegesis. The first two volumes—McConville on Deuteronomy and Lucas on Daniel—were well-researched, insightful and judicious. (I must state my regret, however, that Lucas follows the critical line on the dating of Daniel. The line-up of contracted authors leads me to believe that Lucas' mediating approach may be more the exception than the rule in Apollos.) The commentaries are intended to be both in-depth and user-friendly for pastors; McConville is a little less user-friendly because so densely-packed. The editors mean for the series to be accessible to "non-experts," but the use of in-text citations may discourage some. Do continue to watch for this series, which has recently added volumes on Leviticus, 1 & 2 Samuel, and Ecclesiastes & Song of Songs. [PS]

AYB ANCHOR YALE BIBLE. ‡ (Yale). As originally conceived, the "Anchor Bible" (AB) was an interfaith project, meant to be accessible to educated laity and to provide lengthy introductions and new translations with up-to-date philological discussion. AB was not intended to be a full-orbed commentary. The series has changed markedly since the mid-1960s and now includes some of the most exhaustive commentary efforts ever attempted (Leviticus, Song of Songs, Jeremiah, Amos, 1 Peter, John's Epistles). The series has been renamed to reflect the change in publisher from Doubleday to Yale. You will find AB/AYB to be rather uneven. Many contributions are quite thin in theological interpretation (particularly the older volumes) and reflect varying critical approaches. A number of the commentaries can be safely ignored, but others are successful efforts and can be put to good use by the discerning, scholarly pastor (e.g., Proverbs, Jeremiah, Ezekiel, Jonah, Thessalonians, Timothy, James). Hebrew and Greek are transliterated. The AYB is both under revision (by Yale since 2007), with replacement volumes appearing regularly, and nearing completion in the sense of covering the entire canon. The series also includes commentaries on the Apocrypha/Deutero-canonical books. It would not be surprising if AYB moves in a more liberal and skeptical direction as the previous moderate Jewish editor, David Noel Freedman, has retired and been replaced by John J. Collins. The bibliographies in the more recent volumes are marvelous. Volumes now appear in pb as well as hb, and an expensive CD-ROM of the yet incomplete set (84 vols.) is available from logos.com [*Them* 7/09]. [SP]

BBC BLACKWELL BIBLE COMMENTARIES. ‡ (Blackwell). This newer series by an Oxford-based publisher offers a reception history approach to the Bible. As stated below in the review of the Judges volume, these can be evocative as they present centuries of much-varied cultural and artistic responses to the biblical literature. I have had hardly any opportunity to use the series and don't plan to say much about them. [PL?]

BCBC BELIEVERS CHURCH BIBLE COMMENTARY. [𝓜], (Herald Press). This pb set is pitched more at a general audience and reads Scripture from the perspective of the historic Anabaptist tradition. So far it has proven to be well written and edited. The stance on higher critical issues varies from author to author; many are conservative and some are more critical. Generally speaking, there is a lot of "heart" and pastoral concern evident in the contributions now available. Martens on Jeremiah and Geddert on Mark are among the best of the lot. [PL]

BCOT BAKER COMMENTARY ON THE OLD TESTAMENT: WISDOM AND PSALMS. (Baker). Tremper Longman edits these expositions of Job–Song of Songs, produced by critically-aware evangelical academics. Readers will find quality exegesis which drives at the theological message of the text. There is a good mix of comment on the Hebrew, literary observations, socio-cultural insights, and theological exposition. While diachronic concerns are not wholly absent (some mild form criticism), the focus is surely on the final-form. Preachers will find good help in all the BCOT volumes, while students will gain more from some entries (Psalms, Ecclesiastes, Song of Songs) than others (Proverbs). We only await the volume on Job. The most critical entry is Goldingay on the Psalms. [PS]

BE THE BIBLE EXPOSITION COMMENTARY. (Victor). Warren Wiersbe, formerly pastor of Chicago's Moody Church and regular radio preacher, was for decades publishing little popular commentaries on the NT and OT. The comments are clear and simple, but not simplistic; the outlines are useful too. He has such a flair for communicating the Bible's message in a practical, warm-hearted way that a pastor might consider buying them to use alongside more in-depth exegetical commentaries. About 20 years ago all the NT volumes—called the "BE books"—were compiled into a 2-vol. set of about 1300pp. Wiersbe has finished the Old Testament, too, and all those little books fill four large hb volumes. The series has a Dispensational orientation. I will not be noting these commentaries below. [LP]

BECNT BAKER EXEGETICAL COMMENTARY ON THE NEW TESTAMENT. (Baker). This series has become well-established and is among the most useful for help in exegesis of the Greek. It picked up where the Wycliffe Exegetical Commentary left off when that project had its demise in the early 1990s. See WEC, and note that there were some reassignments (e.g., Schreiner rather than Moo on Romans). Pastors working with their Greek Testament will find BECNT easier to use than some other series like NIGTC and the ICC (compare, for example, Thiselton and Garland on 1 Corinthians). The series editors are Robert Yarbrough and Robert Stein. Keep watching this solidly evangelical series, which now covers most of the NT! [PS]

BHGNT BAYLOR HANDBOOK ON THE GREEK NEW TESTAMENT. (Baylor University Press). This series is edited by Martin Culy, who has already contributed two volumes (see *Acts* and *I,II,III John*), and is intended to walk the student through the basic lexical and syntactical issues. The scheduled authors are mainly conservative Greek grammarians at American seminaries. It's too early to say how helpful these guides (not "commentaries" in the traditional sense) will be, but there are good signs. [PS]

BHHB BAYLOR HANDBOOK ON THE HEBREW BIBLE. (Baylor University Press). This new series complements the BHGNT (see above), providing a wealth of lexical, morphological, and syntactical information for intermediate to advanced Hebrew students. So far, the few volumes released (Tucker on Jonah, Bandstra on Genesis, Garrett on Amos), though small in page-size, are large enough with regard to number of pages to accomplish some good. BHHB does not offer commentary per se; rather it prints the Hebrew text with a new translation and grammatical analysis. There is some measure of discourse analysis besides. Some of the information can easily be found elsewhere, say in the morphological tagging systems of Bible study software. Overall this is a welcome series. The data (parsing, etc) presented is not perfect but usually quite accurate. [PS]

BKAT   BIBLISCHER KOMMENTAR ALTES TESTAMENT. ‡ (Neukirchener Verlag). Many volumes from this extraordinary, technical series of OT commentaries have been translated from the German into English. BKAT is known for its thoroughness, text criticism, rigorous diachronic exegesis, and often profound theological reflection. Only the English translations will be noted in this guide. See Westermann on Genesis, Kraus on Psalms, Wildberger on Isaiah 1–39, Zimmerli on Ezekiel, and Wolff on several Minor Prophets, all published in the Continental Commentary (ContC) and Hermeneia (Herm) series below. [S]

BNTC   BLACK'S NEW TESTAMENT COMMENTARY. ‡ (Hendrickson). This series was always called "Harper's NT Commentary" here in America and "Black's" over in Britain (using the publishers' names, Harper & Row [now HarperCollins] and A. & C. Black). Though in the late 1980s the American publisher Hendrickson was reprinting these volumes under the title "Harper's," since around 1990 they have gone by the name "Black's" on both sides of the Atlantic. The series is presently under revision, with Henry Chadwick as General Editor. Most of the volumes are moderately critical, models of clarity, and must be used with discernment. The best volumes are written by Barrett, Kelly, Laws, Hooker, Bockmuehl, and Boxall. I will list both the older volumes (usually o/p) and the replacement works using the same indicator, BNTC. Now appearing in pb. [PS]

BO   BERIT OLAM. ‡ (Liturgical Press). The subtitle of this newer series is "Studies in Hebrew Narrative and Poetry." Though the publisher is a Roman Catholic order, it has enlisted several fine Jewish contributors (e.g., Schneider on Judges, Cohn on 2 Kings, Sweeney on The Twelve Prophets) alongside Christians. These studies offer stimulating literary readings of the final form of the text and can be good complements to historically and theologically-oriented commentaries. According to Cohn, "The aim of a literary commentary is not the sources, but the discourse, not the genesis of the text, but 'the text itself as a pattern of meaning and effect' (Meir Sternberg)." For the NT, Liturgical Press publishes "Sacra Pagina," a consistently Roman Catholic series noted below. [PS]

Brazos   BRAZOS THEOLOGICAL COMMENTARY ON THE BIBLE. [*M*], (Brazos). "Causing much inter-disciplinary raising of eyebrows" [*BSB* 6/06 (Briggs)], here is a brave, creative venture which enlists mainly systematic theologians to write expositions of Old and New Testament books. The editor writes that "commentators were chosen because of their knowledge of and expertise in using the Christian doctrinal tradition." Several volumes have appeared, and it is still too early to judge how successful Brazos will be as a series. The list of contributors raises questions about the goals and cohesiveness of this ecumenical project: Yale historian Pelikan (Acts), Peter Leithart of Moscow, Idaho (Kings), TEDS's Kevin Vanhoozer (Jeremiah), Princeton Seminary's Ellen Charry (Psalms), Beeson's Timothy George (James), the Orthodox John Behr (Exodus). Editing the series is R.R. Reno of Creighton University. The series is marketed in the UK as the SCM Theological Commentary on the Bible. [ML]

Broad   BROADMAN BIBLE COMMENTARY. [*M*], (Broadman Press). This 12-vol. set covered both testaments and was mostly critically oriented. Rather dated at this point, BBC was never all that remarkable to begin with and was not used much outside Southern Baptist circles. I will not list the individual contributions to this series in this guide. Because the Southern Baptist denominational agencies, including what is now B&H (Broadman & Holman) Publishing Group, are now controlled by conservatives, their publishing arm is producing another, more evangelical series of Bible commentaries. See NAC below. [P]

BSC   BIBLE STUDENT'S COMMENTARY. (Zondervan). This now defunct project is still worthy of consideration. Translations of the Dutch Reformed series *Korte Verklaring*, these volumes are easy to read and have some fine biblical theological insights. Most of the original Dutch commentaries were published in the early 1950s. BSC stalled after Ridderbos' commentary on Matthew was published in 1987. Only one volume appeared in the NT section (Matthew), and there are eight for the OT, covering Genesis to Ruth, and Isaiah. [P]

BST   BIBLE SPEAKS TODAY. (IVP). These expositions, not strictly commentaries, are of great assistance to pastors in understanding and applying God's Word. The focus is upon pericopae rather than verse by verse exegesis. They are reasonably priced paperbacks—only a few have been published in hardback—and are highly recommended. They try to bridge the gap between homiletical commentaries, which often fail to pay close enough attention to the text, and scholarly works, which often seem more concerned with historical and critical issues than with the text's message. The series covers both testaments and is very close to completion; I believe we lack Joshua, Kings, Lamentations, and several Minor Prophets. The NT was completed in 2000 by Michael Green, *The Message of Matthew.* [PL]

Calvin   CALVIN'S COMMENTARIES. Baker regularly reprints the 22-vol. set which covers both OT and NT. It is a mid-19th century production of the Calvin Translation Society and is well worth the investment! He was "a superb exegete…[and] his insight into literary form and function is exceptional" (Johnson, *The First and Second Letters to Timothy*, p.38). The more you read Calvin, the more you'll appreciate his carefully nuanced comments and rich theological insights. Another fine point: he takes care not to allow his commentary to come between the text and the reader. His OT commentaries cover the Pentateuch, Joshua, Psalms, and Isaiah–Malachi. Banner of Truth has reprinted some OT commentaries (Genesis, Jeremiah/Lamentations, Daniel, and the Minor Prophets); they have not yet reprinted two of his best: Psalms and Isaiah. Please note that the lengthy process of retranslating his OT commentaries began under the title, "Rutherford House Translation," but the project seems stalled. Newer translations of all the NT commentaries have already been done under the editorial direction of David W. and Thomas F. Torrance (Eerdmans). This 13-vol. set gets my highest recommendation; do add it to your library. For a detailed examination of Calvin's commentary writing, see the two volumes by T.H.L. Parker, *Calvin's Old Testament Commentaries*, and *Calvin's New Testament Commentaries* (American editions published by WJK, 1993), as well as the diverse essays in Donald K. McKim (ed), *Calvin and the Bible* (CUP, 2006). The 22-vol. set can be purchased quite reasonably—I saw a price of $99.99 at CBD. You will find the entire set on the internet: <www.ccel.org/c/calvin/comment3/comm_index.htm>. [PSL]

CBC   CAMBRIDGE BIBLE COMMENTARY ON THE NEW ENGLISH BIBLE. ‡ (CUP). This popular-level series was produced in the 1960s and 70s. The NT was completed in 1967, and the OT section saw publication between 1971 and 79. They were well written examples of British, more moderate historical criticism during that period. I will infrequently note these volumes. They had few sales in North America, due in part to the little-used translation upon which it was based (NEB). See also NCBC. [LP]

CCSS CATHOLIC COMMENTARY ON SACRED SCRIPTURE. ‡ (BakerAcademic). A new series on the NT which, according to the publisher, "implements the theological principles taught by Vatican II for interpreting Scripture 'in accord with the same Spirit by which it was written'—that is, interpreting Scripture in its canonical context and in light of Catholic tradition and the analogy of faith (*Dei Verbum* 12)." It looks to be very much the product of mainstream American Catholicism, with the participation of leading critical scholars such as Daniel Harrington and Frank Matera. Regular references to the *Catechism of the Catholic Church* indicate that the project is as much about nurture as scholarship. Proposed to be a 17-vol. set. It seems to be written for clergy, yet accessible to the laity. [PL]

CGTC CAMBRIDGE GREEK TESTAMENT COMMENTARY. ‡ (CUP). Sadly, this series barely got off the ground in the late 1950s. Only two volumes were published, but both—C.F.D. Moule on Colossians-Philemon and Cranfield on Mark—are models of patient, careful, conservatively critical exegesis. Do be advised, Cambridge has set high prices on them ($50.00 for Cranfield in pb). [PS]

Concord CONCORDIA COMMENTARY SERIES: A THEOLOGICAL EXPOSITION OF SACRED SCRIPTURE. (Concordia). These large-scale expositions from a conservative Lutheran publishing house are "written to enable pastors and teachers of the Word to proclaim the Gospel with greater insight, clarity, and faithfulness to the divine intent of the biblical text." Along with a commitment to inerrancy, contributors generally reject the assumptions and methods of higher-criticism in favor of a grammatico-historical approach. All volumes contain valuable textual notes on the Hebrew and Greek, some very extensive. The theology is soundly Lutheran, occasionally with the taking up of cudgels against Calvinism and other traditions. Readers may discover that some volumes are not as rich, deep, and well-researched as their size might lead one to expect. That said, the reverent love for the Scriptures helps counterbalance the negatives. Over 20 volumes have appeared. [P]

ContC CONTINENTAL COMMENTARIES. ‡ (Fortress, previously Augsburg). Augsburg, the old Lutheran publishing house merged with Fortress Press (see Hermeneia below). The two publishers, first separately and now jointly, have undertaken the effort of getting as many as possible of the scholarly German commentaries translated. The later works by Hans Walter Wolff for BKAT, for example, have been translated for this series. ContC is intended to cover both OT and NT. With the release of Milgrom's *Leviticus* (2004), we learned that not all the volumes will be translations of European "Continental" works and that the series is possibly adopting a less technical orientation. The NT section has not seen a publication since 1993. [SP]

CorBC CORNERSTONE BIBLICAL COMMENTARY. (Tyndale House). After publishing the New Living Translation, the publisher commissioned a set of evangelical commentaries. The contributors are first-class, but the volumes are not in-depth. The aim of the series is to "provide pastors and laypeople with up-to-date evangelical scholarship on the Old and New Testaments. It's designed to equip pastors and Christian leaders with exegetical and theological knowledge to better understand and apply God's Word by presenting the message of each passage as well as an overview of other issues surrounding the text." [PL]

CrossC CROSSWAY CLASSIC COMMENTARIES. (Crossway Books). As the series title suggests, these are republications of vintage commentaries. Editors J.I. Packer and Alister McGrath have chosen works, from the time of the Reformation (Calvin) to the early 20th century (Griffith Thomas), which offer "practical exposition promoting godliness" (series' preface). I cannot argue with any of the selections thus far; they are superb. Examples would be Calvin on John's Gospel; Luther on Galatians; Hodge on Ephesians; Spurgeon on Psalms. Some of these classics are heavily edited for a popular readership (Lightfoot's commentary on the Greek text of Philippians), or drastically scaled down in size (Owen's seven volumes on Hebrews are distilled into one volume). The series covers mainly NT rather than OT books and is very reasonably priced in pb. [PL]

DRC DIGEST OF REFORMED COMMENT. (Banner of Truth). Geoffrey Wilson, a pastor in Huddersfield, England, "has undertaken the herculean labor of distilling the best of Puritan, Reformed and modern comment on the Pauline letters in a most attractive fashion, since these quotations are interwoven with his own observations on the text of Paul's writings from a pastoral viewpoint" (Martin). These will not be listed under each individual book, but you should realize they are out there and can be useful. The publisher has recently (2005) re-released the commentaries in two large volumes, covering *Romans to Ephesians* and then *Philippians to Hebrews and Revelation*. [PL]

DSB DAILY STUDY BIBLE. ‡ (Westminster John Knox Press). William Barclay's well known series on the NT hardly needs much introduction. He is excellent for pithy comment and homiletical helps. Many pastors have used the series to add sparkle to their sermons. But it has something of a bad reputation among conservatives because of its decidedly liberal, critical interpretation of the gospels. Take a look at a miracle passage to see my point. Barclay is better on the epistles, especially Hebrews. The careful student will note that in his frequent word studies he tends to over-interpret individual words and draw their significance from Classical Greek usage. The later, multi-author OT series was designed to be a companion set to Barclay's popular NT commentaries and has several evangelical contributions of note. The NT volumes, though of value, will not be listed under the individual books. [PL]

EB EXPOSITOR'S BIBLE. (Eerdmans – o/p). This old series (late 19th century) was long the mainstay of many pastors and had an interesting Victorian flavor to it. Some of the works still have real profit to them (e.g., Genesis, Leviticus, Joshua, Samuel, Psalms, Romans, 2 Corinthians). A few of the commentaries have been reprinted. Some are a bit critically oriented (e.g., Farrar on Kings). [PL]

EBC EXPOSITOR'S BIBLE COMMENTARY. (Zondervan). This series, edited by the late Frank E. Gaebelein, was perhaps meant to replace the old EB. There were some worthy contributions to this 12-vol. set. There were also some inadequate ones, and what made our choices difficult was that the worthwhile and the pedestrian could be bound up in the same volume. The commentators were all evangelicals, writing in the 1970s and 80s. Overall, it was quite helpful considering the space allotted each scholar, but the set now feels dated (especially vols. 6, 10–12). Theological stance varied from book to book, but tended to be Premillennial "where it counts." The best commentaries were on Numbers, Samuel, Job, Psalms, Matthew, Acts, 2 Corinthians, and Revelation. Zondervan brought out an abridgment of EBC in two volumes called, "The NIV Bible Commentary," but don't bother with it. Some of the best commentaries on the NT side have been published separately in pb:

Matthew (2 vols.), Luke, Acts, etc. The whole EBC set was out on CD for about $75 at discount booksellers.[1] A full-scale revision (EBCR) of this set is now being released; see below. [P]

EBCR EXPOSITOR'S BIBLE COMMENTARY, REVISED EDITION. (Zondervan). The old EBC (see above) badly needed an update because of the age of the set and its unevenness in terms of both quality and quantity of comment. Psalms had an excellent 900pp exposition dating from 1990, while 1 Corinthians was published in 1976 with an allotted 120pp. The EBCR (2005–) has commissioned new book treatments in certain cases and revisions of original EBC contributions in others. This is shaping up to be a very good set for pastors, and some contributions like Psalms will be valued highly by students too. Because brevity of treatment is a common drawback here, I wish the series had left out the biblical text so as to provide more comment. [P]

ECC EERDMANS CRITICAL COMMENTARY. ‡ (Eerdmans). This newer series offers exhaustive and technical commentaries on both testaments, but production is slow. The releases indicate that ECC may run down much the same track as The Anchor Bible. David Noel Freedman has been the general editor here—as he was for AB—and two of the volumes which have appeared thus far were, I believe, originally intended for AB: see Quinn/Wacker on Timothy, and Barth/Blanke on Philemon. The latter volume runs on for over 500pp (or 20pp per verse on average). Expect more fat, pricey volumes. [SP]

EEC EVANGELICAL EXEGETICAL COMMENTARY. (Logos). Planned for release in both print and electronic form, this just-conceived series will have a long gestation. One of the contracted authors, Rod Decker, reveals that the aim is to produce works "between BECNT and WBC" with regard to academic level. [?SP]

EKK EVANGELISCH–KATHOLISCHER KOMMENTAR. ‡ (Neukirchener). A prominent, large-scale German series with exacting exegesis and theological commentary. Only English translations of these volumes will be noted. See ContC and Herm in this section, Schweizer on Colossians, and Bovon's *Luke 1*. [S]

EPSC EP STUDY COMMENTARY. (Evangelical Press). The UK publisher has several commentary series (see WCS below), and this one is produced in hb. While one may be glad for the durable binding, it does make volumes rather expensive as popular-level expositions for pastors. EPSC is like the "Mentor" commentary (see below) with regard to reading-level and Reformed theological orientation, but EPSC sometimes has more study behind it (as shown in the citations of literature). See Duguid on Haggai-Malachi for a good example of the series. [PL]

FOR EVERYONE SERIES. [*M*], (WJK). These titles—a representative would be *Mark for Everyone* by N.T. Wright—share some of the same aims as DSB. The series is quickly developing to cover both testaments, enlisting mainly British scholars interested in theological exposition. Wright, John Goldingay, and Walter Brueggemann are among those contributing so far. Though I will not be noting these under Bible books, many Christians are talking about how certain volumes (especially Wright on the Gospels) are lively and abounding with devotional in-

---

1 A missionary friend, Rev. Doug Stelzig, gives the following counsel: "I have the CD. It is great if you have the books, but it contains no bibliographic info, does not list the authors of the introductory articles (vol. 1) or commentaries and is filled with typos in the scriptural and bibliographic references—2-3 per page of the book is not uncommon; the usual error being the ommission of hyphens from scanning, e.g. John 1:1-4 becomes John 1:14 on the CD-ROM. This drives me nuts and might be worth noting in your recommendations."

sights into the text. "This enterprise is probably the most exciting thing to have happened in Christian education in Britain for many years" (*ExpTim*). I find I like Wright on the gospels more than on the epistles. Some OT volumes have a more obvious critical/liberal orientation. [L]

FOTL   FORMS OF THE OLD TESTAMENT LITERATURE. ‡ (Eerdmans). A unique and specialized set offering form-critical analyses of OT books, focusing on matters of genre, setting, and structure. "[T]he entire series cannot quite decide whether it is a full-blown commentary or a form-critical survey" (Brueggemann, *JBL* 105.1 [1986]: 130). These studies are of interest to academics (specialists and advanced students), but it is the rare pastor who could profit much from them. Moderately critical. Great bibliographies! For a stimulating discussion of current developments in the form-critical field, see *The Changing Face of Form Criticism for the Twenty-First Century* (Eerdmans, 2003), which a guy named Evans reviews in *Old Testament Essays* 17.3 (2004). [S]

GNC   GOOD NEWS COMMENTARY. [*M*], (Harper & Row). In this popularly-styled series, competent scholars commented on the text of the Good News Bible/Today's English Version. Only a few volumes were published, because the public lost interest in the GNB after the NIV came out. See NIBC below. [P]

GS   GENEVA SERIES. (Banner of Truth). By and large, the publisher has made excellent choices in republishing these old Reformed works. When used alongside a good modern exegetical commentary, these volumes on both OT and NT books will aid the preacher very much. Banner is to be saluted for including Calvin's commentaries on Genesis, Jeremiah-Lamentations, Daniel, and the Minor Prophets in the series. [PLS]

Harper's HARPER'S NEW TESTAMENT COMMENTARY. ‡ (Harper & Row – o/p). See BNTC above.

Herm   HERMENEIA. ‡ (Fortress Press). "A very high level of technical scholarship is evidenced in this...series" (Childs). For specialists and advanced students. About 37 volumes of Bible commentaries have appeared so far in Hermeneia. Most of those which are available are standout critical exegetical works, and all will be discussed below. Generally, the older volumes are translations and offer "heavy doses of German theological discussion" (Horsley). For example, Zimmerli's and Wolff's exhaustive works come from the technical German series *Biblischer Kommentar Altes Testament*. The OT series is more valuable than the NT, perhaps because the NT editorial board has been dominated by radical *religionsgeschichtliche* (history of religions) types who made some strange assignments (e.g., publishing Haenchen on John and Bultmann on John's Epistles). The more recent NT volumes, like Achtemeier on 1 Peter, are much finer and more useful. Like OTL, the series has become more American with the passage of time. The series continues to showcase mainly historical-critical scholarship. Note the recent release of "Hermeneia on CD-ROM 2.0." [S]

HCOT   HISTORICAL COMMENTARY ON THE OLD TESTAMENT. ‡ (Peeters). It is good to see some well esteemed works from the Dutch series, *Commentar op het Oude Testament*, coming into English translation. The original Dutch series, which used to be fairly conservative under Aalders as editor, is of a very high caliber and thoroughly treats philological, historical and theological matters. The approach is mainly a restrained form of traditional historical criticism (continental European variety). It is now clear that not all the HCOT volumes will be translations of

Dutch commentaries, though that is how the series began. (See Houtman on Exodus, Beuken and Koole on Isaiah, Renkema on Lamentations, Vlaardingerbroek on Zephaniah, and Spronk on Nahum.) New commentaries in English are being commissioned. Note that at the beginning of its history HCOT was published by Kok. [SP]

HolNT   HOLMAN NEW TESTAMENT COMMENTARY. (Broadman & Holman). Begun in 1998 and completed in a mere three or four years, the series offers ready-made sermonic material. You are even provided with a closing prayer! The authors are mainly successful "senior pastors" of large conservative Baptist-type churches, though there are a few seminary faculty contributors, too. The editor and main author is Max Anders. There is very little "commentary" on the biblical text at all, which most will view as a serious shortcoming. But for pastors who have done their own in-depth study, these inexpensive hb volumes may spawn ideas for application. *I will not note these under individual Bible books.* OT volumes in the same mold are appearing as "Holman's Old Testament Commentary" (HolOT). [L]

I   INTERPRETATION. ‡ (Westminster John Knox Press). A moderately critical series which focuses more on theological exposition than on technical, critical issues, and is designed with the pastor in mind. One of the contributors, Gaventa, says that, rather than seek to replace scholarly historical critical works or common homiletical resources, Interpretation offers "commentary which presents the integrated result of historical and theological work with the biblical text." Some of the acclaimed commentaries in this series are on Genesis, Exodus, Deuteronomy, 1 & 2 Samuel, Job, Psalms, Lamentations, and 1 Corinthians—I find the OT section is stronger than the NT. The publisher is now releasing paperback editions. [P]

IB   INTERPRETER'S BIBLE. ‡ (Abingdon). This unique set from the 1950s covers the entire Bible with double treatments of each book: exegesis by a scholar and homiletical comments from a pastor. The series was eventually pronounced a failure by almost everybody. The rare helpful exegetical work will be mentioned below (e.g., Wright on Deuteronomy, Bright on Joshua, Muilenburg on Second Isaiah). The homiletical sections at the bottom of the page are usually insipid and can conflict with the exegesis at the top of the page. Abingdon's full-scale revision entitled, *The New Interpreter's Bible*, was completed in 2002. See NewIB. [P]

ICC   INTERNATIONAL CRITICAL COMMENTARY. ‡ (T. & T. Clark). Under revision. Most of the volumes in the series are quite dated by now. Much new linguistic, textual, historical and archaeological evidence has become available since the older volumes were published (1895–1951), and exegetical methods have drastically changed. Some of these commentaries, however, in their full handling of the technical questions remain helpful; they are valuable for little else. Among the best of the older vintage were Genesis, Numbers, Deuteronomy, Judges, Kings, Job, Ezekiel, Daniel, Luke, Romans, 1 Corinthians, Galatians, Revelation. The series has been undergoing a thorough revision under the direction of editors G.I. Davies and G.N. Stanton (†2009), with consultation of former editors J.A. Emerton and C.E.B. Cranfield. Only a few commentaries have appeared so far in the OT section (Isaiah 1–5, Isaiah 40–55, Jeremiah, Hosea). The NT replacement volumes on Romans, Matthew, Ephesians, 2 Corinthians, Pastoral Epistles, and Acts are magisterial! The series is still incomplete. The many who have put off buying these volumes because of expense—the Davies/Allison set on Matthew lists for $462 (hb)—will be glad to know they are now being published in pb as well, and at a huge savings too. [SP]

ITC   INTERNATIONAL THEOLOGICAL COMMENTARY. ‡ (Eerdmans). A series of expositions which seeks "diversity" of theological and cultural comment on the Old Testament. As one might expect, there is unevenness here. Some are thin and not very competent. Others are worth more than a second look: Brueggemann's 540pp on Jeremiah; Beeby's *Hosea*; Sakenfeld on Numbers; and Janzen on Genesis 12–50. Overall I am not impressed with ITC. Moderately critical, with many examining the "final form" of the text. It appears that ITC has gone o/p. [P]

IVPNT   IVP NEW TESTAMENT COMMENTARY. (IVP). This series began under the editorship of I. Howard Marshall in 1991 and was completed in 2009. The contributors are mainly professional scholars, with a few pastors like the late Ray Stedman and the PCA's George Stulac. While all the authors are evangelicals, some are appreciative of critical scholarship and may employ critical methods in a mild fashion. The series is practically oriented, like BST, but includes lots of good exegetical notes. I consider them a bit expensive in hb for their size and depth; better they had been released in pb. The best volumes are probably Bock on Luke; Whitacre on John; Larkin on Acts; Osborne on Romans; Belleville on 2 Corinthians; Fee on Philippians; Beale's Thessalonians; Towner on the Pastorals; Marshall on 1 Peter; and Michaels on Revelation. Now appearing in pb. [P]

JPS   JPS TORAH COMMENTARY. ‡ (Jewish Publication Society). These moderately critical commentaries on the Pentateuch are useful to scholars and students. They treat the Hebrew text, provide good ANE background information, incisive commentary from a Jewish perspective, and quotes from Rabbinic scholars down through the centuries. The contributors may express reservations about traditional source criticism. Milgrom on Numbers is especially deep and thorough (520pp). As an aside, it is a minor irritation learning to turn pages filled primarily with English text in the reverse direction. We have begun to see additional volumes of commentary on books outside the Pentateuch: "The JPS Bible Commentary." See Simon on Jonah, Berlin on Esther, Fox on Ecclesiastes. [SP]

KD   KEIL & DELITZSCH. (Eerdmans or Hendrickson). Years ago I considered this a wise purchase for several reasons: 1) KD is an evangelical set covering the entire Old Testament in ten fat volumes; 2) Both men were very able theologians and biblical scholars; 3) They offered a full treatment without being verbose; 4) They were remarkably affordable (about $100 through discount booksellers). Please note that their expositions are more helpful than their now dated philological comments—so you need not be put off by the Arabic you run across. These commentaries were first published 1861–75 in German. Keil did Genesis to Esther and Jeremiah to Malachi, while Franz Delitzsch covered Job to Isaiah. With all the recent works now available, I do not recommend this purchase as heartily as I once did. But make no mistake, "[t]hese commentaries remain even today veritable storehouses of learning and insight" (Rogerson). In my opinion the greatest work in the set was Delitzsch on the Psalms. [PS]

Lenski   LENSKI'S COMMENTARY ON THE NEW TESTAMENT. (Augsburg). Depending on the printing, this Lutheran commentary covers the NT in 12 or 20 volumes. Lenski is similar to NTC is some ways, but not as well done and much more dated (R.C.H. Lenski, 1864–1936). A truly conservative work both in its evangelical stance and its militant defense of orthodox Lutheran distinctives (especially over against Calvinists), Lenski doesn't compete well with the other works now available to us. This will not be listed under individual books but is worth consulting on occasion. The series is occasionally reprinted. [P]

Lange   LANGE'S COMMENTARY. (Scribners). This classic 19th century set (mainly 1870s) covered both testaments and was highly valued by preachers and scholars alike. It was well-rounded, with exegetical, theological and homiletical comment. The great historian and theologian, Philip Schaff, was editor of the ET. Contributors to this monumental effort were deeply learned, fairly conservative—especially by German standards—and drew from the whole history of interpretation. This series and KD introduced English readers to the best conservative continental scholarship. Originally published in 13 volumes, Lange's OT series was reprinted in 7 huge volumes by Zondervan in 1960. At least a portion of the OT and NT series was reprinted by Wipf & Stock in 2007. A couple of the works are definitely worth reprinting (e.g., Bähr on Kings, Schröder on Ezekiel). The theological expositions are obviously more valuable today than the philological comments. [PS]

       MASTERING THE NEW TESTAMENT. (Word/Nelson). See WCC: Word Communicator's Commentary below.

       MASTERING THE OLD TESTAMENT. (Word/Nelson). See WCC: Word Communicator's Commentary below.

Mentor   MENTOR COMMENTARY. (Christian Focus). Published out of Britain, these accessible commentaries by both British and American Reformed scholars aim to provide a fair measure of faithful exegesis and full theological exposition. John L. Mackay has contributed several of these hb volumes: Exodus, Jeremiah (2 vols), Lamentations. In the USA they have been difficult and quite expensive to obtain, which is a pity since a couple of these are very good for pastors (e.g., Pratt on Chronicles). See EPSC above for a similar series. [PL]

NBBC   NEW BEACON BIBLE COMMENTARY. (Beacon Hill). I was not acquainted with this series on both testaments until recently (2010) and have only seen one volume: Dean Fleming on Philippians. The series comes from the Wesleyan tradition, and is deliberate about presenting a well-rounded work for pastors. There are sections on literary and historical background ("Behind the Text"), exegesis ("In the Text"), and application ("From the Text"). Any references to the original languages are transliterated. There are no footnotes or endnotes. [P]

NAC   NEW AMERICAN COMMENTARY. (B&H). A more recently begun series on both testaments with conservative (mostly Southern Baptist) contributors, some excellent ones too: Daniel Block, Craig Blomberg, Robert Stein and Thomas Schreiner. These are full commentaries, some over 700pp, in a readable format. The set tends to be Dispensational "where it counts" (i.e., Ezekiel, Daniel). Conservatives will view NAC as a huge improvement over the old Broadman Bible Commentary set, both in terms of scholarship and theological stance. That being said, Gerald Hawthorne is on the mark to say that this series usually does not break new ground or add fresh insights into the meaning of the text; rather it helpfully gleans information from recent commentaries [*JETS* 3/96]. NAC typically draws on selected scholarly works without adding much to them. This is probably truer for the NT than for the OT section. The stated aim of NAC is to meet the needs of ministers, not graduate students. [P]

NCB   NEW CENTURY BIBLE. ‡ (Sheffield, previously Eerdmans). The volumes, which treat the RSV or NRSV, range from being mildly critical to moderately so, with most in the latter category. This exegetical series is rather undistinguished in the OT, better in the NT. Most of the entries were contributed by British critics, seem a bit stodgy, and offer little theological reflection. There are several excellent commentaries in this set which can be recommended. NCB was nearly complete and under revision before it finally petered out. In the USA Eerdmans dropped it. Sheffield briefly picked it up in the United Kingdom, shipping what had then become expensive pb volumes to the States. The latest works contracted for the series, e.g., Joyce on Ezekiel, are being published in the expensive T&T Clark "Library of Hebrew Bible/OT Studies." [PS]

NCBC   NEW CAMBRIDGE BIBLE COMMENTARY. ‡ (CUP). Building well upon the tradition of the accessible Cambridge Bible Commentary of the 1960s and 1970s, the NCBC looks to be fuller in exegesis and more useful to students (see the recommended reading sections). The series "is pitched at a higher academic level than the old CBC" (G.I. Davies). The first few commentaries released show that it is well-edited, well-informed, and less concerned with older historical critical (diachronic) questions than the old series. The blurb says, "Volumes utilize recent gains in rhetorical criticism, social scientific study of the Scriptures, narrative criticism, and other developing disciplines to exploit advances in biblical studies." The contributors are a diverse lot with a surprising number of Americans: liberal Protestants (Brueggemann, Douglas Knight), Catholics (Neyrey), Evangelicals (Bill Arnold), and Jewish scholars (Halpern and Fox). The NRSV text is printed in the volumes. [P]

NCCS   NEW COVENANT COMMENTARY SERIES. (Wipf & Stock). This forthcoming series intends to be both internationally and theologically diverse while remaining in the evangelical camp. For more information see <http://euangelizomai.blogspot. com/2008/05/new-commentary-series-on-new-testament.html>. [P?]

NewIB   NEW INTERPRETER'S BIBLE. ‡ (Abingdon). Quickly brought to completion, the NewIB is an entirely new, ecumenical, 12-vol. series on both testaments—sharing the aims but not the theological stance of the evangelical, 12-vol. EBC. The commentaries print the NIV and NRSV, provide a basic exegesis, and homiletical guidance for ministers. A wide (inclusive) net has been cast to enlist male and female contributors from different denominations. Even the evangelical Walter Kaiser is there. Other scholars include James D.G. Dunn, Walter Brueggemann, N.T. Wright, and Carol Newsom. Generally, the work is very competent, moderately critical, dependable rather than bold and creative. Hermeneutical approaches vary from book to book; most seek to provide a more literary and theological "reading" of the final form of the text, while some others employ more traditional historical critical methods. That "text-centered" emphasis is indicative of the sea-change in biblical studies over the past couple decades. All contributors are supposed to take the theology of the text seriously. The whole project is more successful than the old IB, but I'm not rushing out to buy the set. (Expense and my preference for fuller commentaries are primary reasons.) Perhaps the NewIB is most valuable for commentary on those parts of the canon which have been underserved by other scholarly series: Judges, Kings, Ezra-Nehemiah, Job, Proverbs, etc. I will note each individual commentary in this guide. [P]

NIBC   NEW INTERNATIONAL BIBLICAL COMMENTARY. [*M*], (Hendrickson). This pb series was initially an attempt to refurbish the Good News Commentary on the NT by re-editing those volumes to explain the NIV text instead of the GNB. Also, brand new commentaries on the NT were solicited. The publisher launched an OT section in 1995 with Provan's superb volume on Kings. OT volumes are now appearing regularly. Most contributors are strong evangelicals who are comfortable using critical methods, but a few are thorough-going critics (e.g., the master

Catholic exegete, Roland Murphy). Among the best in the series are Deuteronomy, Kings, Psalms, Isaiah, the Pastorals, Luke, Acts, Hebrews, and James. This series is one of the least expensive (about $10–12 per volume on sale) and is nearly complete. [P]

NICNT NEW INTERNATIONAL COMMENTARY ON THE NEW TESTAMENT. (Eerdmans). This evangelical series has been the mainstay of my own NT collection and hardly needs much introduction. NICNT gives readers a fairly comprehensive treatment of exegetical questions, but always with a focus on expounding the text's message. Technical discussion of the Greek text is relegated to the footnotes. "Greek clearly informs the exegesis, but the reader unfamiliar with the original language is not prevented from making good use of this commentary" (Aageson on Fee's *Thessalonians*). The quality of the set over the years owed much to its ongoing revision, also to the long-term editorial direction and several contributions of first F.F. Bruce and second Gordon Fee. I have recommended most volumes in the collection, which covers all the NT except 2 Peter/Jude. Our long wait for volumes on Matthew and the Pastorals has been rewarded with stellar works by France and Towner. The series' revision continues under the capable editorship of Gordon Fee, and has less and less of its old Reformed savor. Like its sister, NICOT, the series is also becoming slightly less conservative. A note to bibliophiles: Eerdmans' printings before 1985 had sewn bindings; since then the publisher has mainly used 'perfect bindings' (glued) which don't hold up so well. For another series rather similar to NICNT, see Pillar. Eerdmans and Logos are releasing the series with NICOT on CD-ROM. [PS]

NICOT NEW INTERNATIONAL COMMENTARY ON THE OLD TESTAMENT. (Eerdmans). Promises to continue providing pastor and teacher with a bevy of valuable exegetical tools. Twenty-three volumes have been published, and there are many more on the way. Most are highly recommended. Like NICNT this evangelical series has had a new editor for 15 years or so; the able (and less conservative) Robert Hubbard heads up the project after the death of R.K. Harrison (†1993). The most recent contributions to NICOT indicate a trend toward publishing more extensive commentaries which will better serve scholars' needs. The best example is Daniel Block's two volumes on Ezekiel, which total over 1700pp. This trend may help explain the slowed release of new works in the series (since 1998 only 5 volumes have been published: *Song of Songs, Proverbs 1–15, Proverbs 16–31, First Samuel,* and *Hosea*). Eerdmans and Logos are releasing the series with NICNT on CD-ROM. [PS]

NIGTC NEW INTERNATIONAL GREEK TESTAMENT COMMENTARY. [*M*], (Eerdmans). A prestigious technical series being edited by I. Howard Marshall and Donald Hagner (replacing Ward Gasque). This mildly critical set is marked by very thorough, careful exegesis of the Greek text, and full bibliographies. Like the ICC, the NIGTC generally contains less exposition and theological reflection than preachers want. Still, the studious pastor could put these volumes to excellent use; there isn't a single poor commentary in the whole set. Most of the authors (Marshall, Dunn, Bruce, Thiselton, Nolland, etc.) are in the more critically oriented wing of evangelicalism; Knight and Harris are exceptions. Word is out that some of the older volumes (e.g., Marshall on Luke) will be revised to extend their usefulness. [SP]

NIVAC NIV APPLICATION COMMENTARY. (Zondervan). User-friendly. My enthusiasm for this evangelical series has grown. The editors have done a good job enlisting both veterans and able younger scholars to contribute. The goal articulated for the series is to bridge the divide between the original context in which the biblical text spoke and the contemporary context in which the text still speaks. In the better volumes there is a good measure of interpretation before the writer moves on to consider practical application. That is a good and safe pattern. But what makes NIVAC unique and even more helpful is that, in between exegesis ("Original Meaning") and application ("Contemporary Significance"), the authors discuss the process of moving from the world of the text to our own. Often those "Bridging Contexts" sections offer astute counsel to preachers. Thus far, most, not all, volumes released have reached the goal. Among the most successful volumes are Walton on Genesis; Enns on Exodus; Jobes on Esther; Wilson on Psalms; Duguid on Ezekiel; Longman on Daniel; Moo on Romans; Hafemann on 2 Corinthians; Snodgrass on Ephesians; Garland on Mark and Colossians/Philemon; Guthrie on Hebrews; McKnight on 1 Peter; Moo on 2 Peter/Jude; and Burge's *Letters of John*. Compare this series with BST. Look for the volumes' annotated bibliographies of commentaries (a few don't have them). The NT section is complete, while the OT lacks volumes on Deuteronomy, Ezra/Nehemiah, Job, and Psalms 73–150. [PL]

NTC NEW TESTAMENT COMMENTARY. (Baker). Often simply called "Hendriksen," after William Hendriksen (1900–82) who began the project, the NTC was steadily and carefully brought to completion by Simon Kistemaker of RTS in Jackson, MS. The final volume, *Revelation*, appeared in 2001. Most students have a settled opinion about the worth of these volumes. Several criticisms could be leveled (particularly at Hendriksen's volumes): they tend to be verbose, to jump too quickly from the text to systematic theology concerns, may pack individual words with too much theological freight, and sometimes are not so good in filling out the broader historical context. But their good points outweigh their faults. These commentaries directly serve the preacher in their full expositional style. They are distinctively Reformed, conservative, and reasonably well-grounded in their scholarship. One reviewer sums things up this way: "what it lacks in theological profundity and ethical richness it makes up for with clarity and thoroughness" (Padgett). The publisher does not appear to be promoting this 12-vol. series as it once did. The complete set is a great deal at discounters for about $100. [P]

NTL NEW TESTAMENT LIBRARY. ‡ (Westminster John Knox Press). The publisher of OTL conceived a NT counterpart which includes mid-level exegetical commentaries, reprinted classics of NT scholarship (e.g., Martyn on John, Minear's *Images of the Church in the New Testament*), and other general NT reference works (theologies, hermeneutics, etc.). Two of the more recent commentary issues are superb: Johnson on Hebrews and Lieu on the John's Epistles. It does not appear that the planned commentaries will provide much discussion of such technical matters as textual criticism; instead they will serve preachers by focusing more on the literary features and theological message of the text. The volumes so far and the list of distinguished contributors indicate that the series will be consistently strong. [PS]

NTM NEW TESTAMENT MESSAGE. ‡ (Michael Glazier). These are critical expositions from Roman Catholic scholars. Usually not in-depth, they will occasionally be noted under individual books. [P]

OTL OLD TESTAMENT LIBRARY. ‡ (Westminster John Knox Press). This important series used to contain mainly German works in ET and was born out of the "Biblical Theology" movement of the 1950s. The volumes reflect varying critical approaches and most are aging. New volumes are being added at a quicker pace than 10 years ago, and the series is becoming more and more American. A good example of this trend is Childs' Isaiah commentary (2001) being added alongside the Kaiser/Westermann 3-vol. set (ET 1969–83). Many of the volumes are of real value if used with discernment. Conservatives would say they can be dangerous if used as one's sole resource. This series contains other OT tools besides commentaries. The publisher is releasing both newer and older OTL volumes in pb, but they are not cheaper. For example, Childs on Exodus in hb was earlier priced at $39.95, but the new pb lists for $59.95. More positively, readers are glad to note that the newer hb volumes have sturdy, sewn-down bindings. [PS]

OTM   OLD TESTAMENT MESSAGE. ‡ (Michael Glazier). See NTM above. [P]

PentC   PENTECOSTAL COMMENTARY. (Deo Publishing). There are several releases now, but I have not used any. [P?]

Paideia   PAIDEIA COMMENTARIES ON THE NEW TESTAMENT. ‡ (Baker). These volumes of exegetical commentaries aimed at students are just now beginning to appear. The make-up of the editorial board indicates that this will be a moderately critical series. (Some will not expect the "moderately critical" label on these Baker publications.) Talbert's volume, *Ephesians and Colossians* (2007), may be taken as a strong representative of Paideia, perhaps even as a model of these compact pb commentaries. Both Protestants and Catholics have been enlisted to contribute. [P]

Pillar   PILLAR NEW TESTAMENT COMMENTARY. (Eerdmans). The volumes available are strongly evangelical, well grounded in scholarship, insightful, and warmly recommended. The aim of Pillar is faithful exegesis moving toward biblical-theological reflection. I regard over half of the series as first choices for pastors: Carson on John, Peterson on Acts, O'Brien on Ephesians and Hebrews, Moo's two volumes on Colossians-Philemon and James, and Davids on 2 Peter-Jude. The depth, format, and conservative stance of these works is similar to NICNT. That is to say, they leave the technical discussion of the original Greek text in the footnotes and concentrate on exegesis and evangelical theological reflection, rarely dealing directly with application. Carson's editorial work helps keep the standards high. [PS]

THE PREACHER'S COMMENTARY. (Word/Nelson). See WCC: Word Communicator's Commentary below.

PTW   PREACHING THE WORD. (Crossway). This series of thoughtful expositions was birthed by R. Kent Hughes of College Church, Wheaton, who has written on most of the NT. Other contributors who share Hughes' warm-hearted Reformed theology are being enlisted. Philip Ryken has done Jeremiah-Lamentations and Exodus. Iain Duguid has produced a fine study of Numbers. I believe Sinclair Ferguson may be doing the Minor Prophets. See Hughes under Mark. Some of the volumes are exceedingly large. [PL]

Read   READINGS: A NEW BIBLICAL COMMENTARY. ‡ (Sheffield Academic Press, now Sheffield Phoenix). Begun in 1987 and taking off in the 1990s, "Readings" had aims similar to the "Berit Olam" series listed above. (I am not sure of the series' status: still active?) The editors and contributors meant to move beyond the older historical critical methods of research (source, form, redaction criticism) and to study the final form of the text using newer literary critical and socio-rhetorical approaches. Though "critical" in several respects, these newer approaches sometimes read the text with more sympathy and respectfulness. See my comments on Conrad's Zechariah commentary for further review of this series. "Readings" varies a great deal in length and depth of treatment: Miscall's *Isaiah* is 185pp, while the Meadowcroft *Haggai* volume is 259pp. What is confusing to some is the similarity of this series to another one published by Routledge: "OT Readings." [PS]

REC   REFORMED EXPOSITORY COMMENTARY. (P&R). This young series is similar to PTW and looks very promising as a help to preachers. REC has the following characteristics: homiletically oriented exposition, sticking close to the text; adherence to Reformed theology as outlined in the Westminster Confession and Catechisms; a redemptive historical approach to interpretation; and a concern to apply the text's message to heart and daily life. The tendency here is to produce lengthy, but not stodgy, expositions. I am enthusiastic about the series, because it is good for both mind and heart and because it encourages growth in grace. Wisdom and experience have often shown that graces are even more important than gifts in the ministry; a pastor's usefulness much depends upon character, spiritual insight, and factors such as confidence in the life-giving power of God's Word, devotion to Christ, a love for the people of God and the lost. Those working hard on this project include Phil Ryken, Dan Doriani, and Rick Phillips. [LP]

RNT   READING THE NEW TESTAMENT. ‡ (Smyth & Helwys). It remains to be seen how successful and useful this series will be. The only volume I've handled is *Reading Acts*, contributed by the series editor, Baylor's conservatively-critical Charles Talbert. The approach is not verse-by-verse, but section-by-section (e.g., Acts 11:19–12:25). It displays interest in literary, socio-historical, and theological questions. [PS]

RRA   RHETORIC OF RELIGIOUS ANTIQUITY. ‡? (Deo Publishing). This projected series is meant to provide "socio-rhetorical commentaries on the Bible and other ancient religious literature" (blurb on the Deo Publishing website: http://www.deo-publishing.com/rhetoricofreligiousantiquity.htm). One of two main editors, V.K. Robbins, is a liberal practitioner of rhetorical criticism (see his influential book, *Exploring the Texture of Texts*), but some contracted authors are more conservative. [?SP]

SacPag   SACRA PAGINA. ‡ (Liturgical Press). A critical series on the NT produced by Roman Catholics. Some volumes in SacPag are rigorous, large-scale studies, while others are less weighty. I must confess I've not used these as much. They should be of greater interest to the Reformed student than the Reformed pastor. Most interesting or influential are probably Donahue/Harrington on Mark; Luke Timothy Johnson on Luke and Acts; Moloney on John; Byrne on Romans; Collins on 1 Corinthians; Matera on Galatians: and Richards on Thessalonians. This now-completed series is being released in both pb and hb. [PS]

S&H   SMYTH & HELWYS BIBLE COMMENTARY. ‡ (Smyth & Helwys). An elegantly produced and moderately critical series of expositional commentaries on both testaments. If the WJK Interpretation series is a Ford, this is a Lexus or BMW. Yes, S&H is expensive (most list for $65), and discount booksellers like CBD are hardly discounting. The preacher will likely enjoy spending time with the visually stimulating volumes—they also include CDs—and will appreciate their theological approach (though not always the theology, which ranges from left-wing evangelical to liberal). There is an abundance of maps, art (from the ANE to Chagall), pictures of ancient artifacts, sidebars. Perhaps S&H aspires to redefine the commentary genre for our postmodern age (our "visual generation of believers"). A potential drawback is that some readers may find the illustrations distracting and intrusive at points. Two of the first volumes—Fretheim on Jeremiah and Brueggemann on Kings—set a high standard that is generally not being met by the other contributors. Note to bibliophiles: S&H volumes have good paper and sturdy, sewn-down bindings. Because of the price tag, it's hard to recommend any but the very best in the series. [P]

SRC SOCIO-RHETORICAL COMMENTARY. (Eerdmans). I am a little uncertain about the nature of this project, for Witherington has been publishing many such commentaries, not only with Eerdmans but with IVP and others. My best guess is that this series is composed of his Eerdmans releases, with a few other authors joining in. [PS]

T&I TEXT AND INTERPRETATION. ‡ (Eerdmans). A moderately critical series which was practical in its aim but not all that successful. The project died in the late 1980s. [P]

TCB THE CHURCH'S BIBLE. (Eerdmans). This commentary set, begun in 2004, has an intention similar to the "Ancient Christian Commentary on the Scriptures" (see ACCS above), but may be much more ambitious in the amount of comment. Compared with ACCS, TCB has longer quotations and adds medieval thinkers. The first volume, *Song of Songs*, has the subtitle, "Interpreted by Early Christian and Medieval Commentators," and is remarkably full at nearly 350pp. On a similar scale, how many volumes might be scheduled for Psalms? [SP]

THC TWO HORIZONS COMMENTARY. [*M*], (Eerdmans). This newer series seeks to blend and represent both biblical-exegetical and systematic-theological approaches to Scripture. For decades these have been viewed as divided and even in conflict. THC was introduced by a volume of essays entitled *Between Two Horizons: Spanning New Testament Studies & Systematic Theology* (Eerdmans, 2000). Originally I believed this would be merely a NT set, but OT volumes are commissioned as well. For excellent initial volumes, see Grogan on Psalms, Fowl on Philippians, and Green on 1 Peter. The approach is more paragraph-by-paragraph than verse-by-verse. Because the series has a disciplined focus upon theological interpretation, which is where so many other series are weak, it is more valuable to preachers than its middling size might indicate. For an earlier attempt to bridge the gap between biblical scholarship and theology, see the SPCK series "Biblical Foundations in Theology." [PS]

TNTC TYNDALE NEW TESTAMENT COMMENTARIES. (Eerdmans/IVP). This set covers the NT in 20 volumes and could be a good first set for beginners to purchase. More advanced students will consider it useful as a quick reference. It is evangelical and is marked by attention to both text and message, broad coverage, and brief, apposite comments. Matters of critical scholarship are usually not discussed. The series has long been under revision; I believe Kruse's volume on John's Gospel (2004) completes that process. [PL]

TOTC TYNDALE OLD TESTAMENT COMMENTARIES. (IVP). This thoroughly evangelical series is more even in quality than most, and D.J. Wiseman (†2010) deserves praise for his work as editor. "Pithy" is the best description for this set: brief, packed, often weighty exegetical comments rather than full exposition. The strongest volumes are written by Kidner, Wenham, Baldwin and Hess. It was completed with the publication in the 1990s of long-awaited works on Joshua and Isaiah. Some volumes are now over 40 years old and could use revising or replacing (e.g., Judges/Ruth; Ezekiel). TOTC is undergoing a thorough revision (see the new entry on Esther by Reid), first under Martin Selman (†2004) and then with David Firth as Series Editor. [PL]

TPI TRINITY PRESS INTERNATIONAL – NEW TESTAMENT COMMENTARY. ‡ (Trinity Press). The publisher took over the old Pelican series and commissioned new works, but not much happened. See WPC below. [PS]

TTT TEACH THE TEXT. (Baker—forthcoming). The series title may still be provisional. I heard about this from Hassell Bullock while in Cambridge. He is working on the Psalms for this series, which is edited by Bill Arnold. The structure of the commentary (on the NIV) has several parts: Big Idea, Key Themes, The Text and Its Meaning, Teaching the Text (textual notes), and Illustrating the Text (bridging the so-called two horizons). My guess is that the initial volumes are still a long way off.

UBS UNITED BIBLE SOCIETIES: HANDBOOK SERIES. (United Bible Societies). These handbooks are designed for Bible translators working around the world; the chief aim is lucidity in the receptor language. Some of these volumes can be quite useful to pastors who seek to understand the meaning of the original text and explain clearly the nuances of grammar and vocabulary to their congregations. Don't go looking for theology. UBS has some first-rate scholars working on this series, e.g., Paul Ellingworth on 1 Corinthians. Normally I will note these without comment. [PS]

WBC WORD BIBLICAL COMMENTARY. [*M*], (Nelson, previously Word). Valuable for its good textual work, new translations, and exegesis. At points one could wish that the contributors and editors placed a greater emphasis on theological reflection. This significant series is exciting and frustrating at the same time. One frustration is that insightful comment on a text can be distributed across 3 different sections. Some have expressed frustration that many contributors to this "evangelical" series are, in fact, "moderates." Be cautioned against buying on the basis of the evangelical label, because some, even by the most charitable estimate, do not fit into that category. (E.g., note the participation of the brilliant Roman Catholic critic, Roland Murphy, and the discussion in *ExpTim* 101.6 [1990]: 184). At the same time, I must say that there are a large number of strong contributions to the set which can be considered "top picks" and which you would do well to add to your library. The NT series is a little more successful than the OT. For the pastor some volumes are more accessible (Leviticus, Hebrews), and some less accessible (Ruth/Esther, Revelation). WBC is nearing completion and under revision. The 60 or so available volumes have been released in CD-ROM format. The newer printings by Nelson use much better quality paper and sturdy, sewn-down bindings. These commentaries are a boon to students of the original languages. [PS]

WCC WORD COMMUNICATOR'S COMMENTARY. (Nelson, previously Word). This easy-to-read homiletical series is a really mixed bag, both in regard to quality and theological stance (broadly evangelical and generally more conservative than WBC, its scholarly counterpart). This series was completed in the early 1990s and has some really good contributions (e.g., Allen on Chronicles, Stuart on Ezekiel) and some dogs (more in the NT). Usually you can ignore WCC. I will note the better volumes under individual books. The series was renamed and reissued in paperback under the titles, "Mastering the Old Testament" and "Mastering the New Testament." Then in the late 1990s I saw it again renamed as "The Preacher's

Commentary." Despite the name and cover changes, the contents remain the same. [PL]

WCS WELWYN COMMENTARY SERIES. (Evangelical Press). These easily read, edifying paperbacks provide fine expositions for the pastor or Sunday School teacher. The comments are perceptive and simple without being obvious. This British series now covers most Bible books. P&R is the North American distributor for this series, which tells you something about its theological orientation. I will not often comment on these. [PL]

WEC WYCLIFFE EXEGETICAL COMMENTARY. (Moody Press). A series begun in the late 1980s, WEC looked like it would be a success but was killed by the publisher. The NT portion of the project was taken over by Baker (see BECNT above). The few volumes published in WEC were solid and evangelical (e.g., Silva's Philippians volume). They provide a scholarly exegesis and exposition of the Hebrew or Greek text. The OT volumes in WEC went o/p but have lately been reprinted in pb by Biblical Studies Press (see Numbers and the Minor Prophets). [PS]

Wesley WESLEYAN BIBLE STUDY NEW TESTAMENT COMMENTARY. (Wesleyan Church). Though this 15-vol. set does not probe deeply, it is a useful guide for pastors seeking a reliably Wesleyan-Arminian interpretation of the Scriptures. There is also an Old Testament set. I will not note these commentaries below. [PL]

WestBC WESTMINSTER BIBLE COMPANION. ‡ (WJK). The Presbyterian publisher means this series to "assist laity in their study of the Bible as a guide to Christian faith and practice. Each volume explains the biblical book in its original historical context and explores its significance for faithful living today." The flavor of WestBC is somewhere between commentary and study guide, and the series resembles BST in several respects. These theological expositions are based on the NRSV and the better entries will serve the discerning pastor in sermon preparation. But because of their critical orientation, WestBC will not be broadly recommended to Bible study groups in evangelical churches. For disparate representatives of this newer series, see Peterson on Samuel and Brueggemann on Isaiah. [PL]

WPC WESTMINSTER PELICAN COMMENTARY. ‡ (Westminster). This series was taken over by SCM Press in Britain and Trinity Press in North America. See TPI above. WPC included some of the old "Penguin Commentaries." It was moderately to very critical, uneven, and rather undistinguished. I won't mention these under individual books, except J.P. Sweet on Revelation. [P]

ZEC ZONDERVAN EXEGETICAL COMMENTARY. (Zondervan). A forthcoming conservative series, edited by Clinton Arnold, which looks very promising. Only one volume has appeared, and it is excellent: Blomberg and Kamell on James (2008). ZEC aims to glean the best fruit from scholarly discussions, while remaining focused on close exegesis of the text. Probably the feature that sets the series apart is its "Translation in Graphic Layout," where it "presents a translation through a diagram that helps readers visualize the flow of thought within the text" (publisher's description). Readers also find an abundance of structural outlines. There is some attention given to biblical theological reflection and questions of contemporary relevance. We will wait to see how ZEC develops, but so far it appears well-conceived and executed as a well-rounded exegetical tool. [PS]

—∽∾—

OLD TESTAMENT COMMENTARIES

THE PENTATEUCH

★ Alexander, T. Desmond. *From Paradise to the Promised Land*, 2nd ed 2002. Helpful as a theologically sensitive content survey. There is a reasonably up-to-date evangelical assessment of the old Documentary Hypothesis and recent critiques (pp.7–94). The main value, however, is the tracing of Pentateuchal theological themes which will be developed in subsequent Scripture (OT and NT). For another, fuller content survey, see Hamilton. [*Them* Spr 04; *RelSRev* 1/05; *ExpTim* 11/04; *Evangel* Aut 07].

★ Alexander, T. Desmond, and David W. Baker (eds). *Dictionary of the Old Testament: Pentateuch*, 2002. Invaluable for students. [*Them* Sum 04; *EvQ* 4/05; *CurTM* 10/05; *Anvil* 21.1].

★ Wenham, Gordon J. *Exploring the Old Testament, Volume One: A Guide to the Pentateuch*, 2003. There is probably no better, more lucid and accessible introduction to the Pentateuch for the beginning student (207pp). More advanced students might skip this purchase. [*EvQ* 4/05; *JETS* 9/05; *RelSRev* 1/06; *CurTM* 6/05].

☆ Alter, Robert. ‡ *The Five Books of Moses: A Translation with Commentary*, 2004. See Genesis. [*JSOT-BL* 2005].

✓ Blenkinsopp, Joseph. ‡ *The Pentateuch: An Introduction to the First Five Books of the Bible* (ABRL) 1992. Added to this is *Treasures Old and New: Essays in the Theology of the Pentateuch*, 2007 [*BSac* 10/07; *JAOS* 126.4; *CJ* 10/06].

 Campbell, Antony, and Mark O'Brien. ‡ *Sources of the Pentateuch: Texts, Introductions, Annotations*, 1993. Following this is *Rethinking the Pentateuch: Prolegomena to the Theology of Ancient Israel*, 2005. Both authors pursue and promote (with some vigor) more traditional source criticism. By contrast, many conservatives (Wenham) and critics (Whybray) believe source criticism has had poor returns for a long time.

✓ Clines, David J.A. ‡ *The Theme of the Pentateuch*, 1978, 2nd ed 1996. A much cited study proposing partial fulfillment (and non-fulfillment) of the promises as the main theme.

 Dozeman, Thomas, and Konrad Schmid. ‡ *A Farewell to the Yahwist? The Composition of the Pentateuch in Recent European Interpretation*, 2006.

✓ Fretheim, Terence E. ‡ (IBT) 1996. An excellent introductory guide into the Pentateuch from a moderately critical perspective.

☆ Hamilton, Victor P. *Handbook on the Pentateuch*, 1982, 2nd ed 2005. A solid content survey.

☆ Kitchen, Kenneth A. *On the Reliability of the Old Testament*, 2003. A strong (the critics would say "strident") challenge to higher critical skepticism about the Bible's historical worth. There is a massive amount of detail and learning here, especially

ANE inscriptional and archeological evidence. Wenham [*Anvil* 23.2] says "anyone who reads it will be bowled over by the breadth and depth of Kitchen's encyclopaedic knowledge," and he expresses hope that this "work will preserve another generation of theological students from losing faith in Scripture." [*JSOT* 27.5; *BSac* 4/05; *CTJ* 11/04; *CBQ* 7/07; *JETS* 3/05; *Them* Sum 05; *DenvJ* 5/04 (Hess); *HebStud* 2005; *JAOS* 124.2 (harsh); *VT* 56.2; *ExpTim* 11/04; *RTR* 4/05; *Presb* Fall 06; *RB* 4/05; *BASOR* 8/05; *CJ* 1/06].

✓ Knight, Douglas. ‡ "The Pentateuch" (pp.263–96) in *The Hebrew Bible and Its Modern Interpreters*, edited by Douglas Knight and Gene Tucker, 1985.

✓ Knoppers, Gary N., and Bernard M. Levinson (eds). ‡ *The Pentateuch as Torah: New Models for Understanding Its Promulgation and Acceptance*, 2007. A collection of studies by the world's leading scholars, presented at an international SBL meeting, heavily revised, and reflecting the movement of scholarship toward a later dating of the Pentateuchal materials and their compilation. [*BBR* 19.2; *VT* 59.2; *JHebS* 2009].

✓ Lohfink, Norbert. ‡ *Theology of the Pentateuch: Themes of the Priestly Narrative and Deuteronomy*, ET 1994.

✓ Mann, Thomas W. ‡ *The Book of the Torah: The Narrative Integrity of the Pentateuch*, 1988.

Moberly, R.W.L. *The Old Testament of the Old Testament*, 2001. A fascinating narratological-canonical reading and new proposal for the crux in Exod 3 and the revelation of the divine name.

✓ Nicholson, E.W. ‡ *The Pentateuch in the Twentieth Century*, 1998. [*JBL* Sum 01].

✓ Noth, Martin. ‡ *A History of Pentateuchal Traditions*, 1948, ET 1972.

☆ Poythress, Vern S. *The Shadow of Christ in the Law of Moses*, 1991.

✓ Rad, Gerhard von. ‡ *The Problem of the Hexateuch and Other Essays*, 1938, ET 1966.

✓ Rendtorff, Rolf. ‡ *The Problem of the Process of Transmission in the Pentateuch*, 1977, ET 1990.

✓ Rofé, A. ‡ *Introduction to the Composition of the Pentateuch*, 1999. A modification of the classic Wellhausen position.

✓ Sailhamer, John. *The Meaning of the Pentateuch: Revelation, Composition and Interpretation*, 2009. Evangelical scholarship on the canonical form, building upon *The Pentateuch as Narrative*, 1992. [*JSOT-BL* 2010].

☆ Schnittjer, Gary. *The Torah Story*, 2006. An engaging introduction and survey for laity and beginning students.

✓ Ska, Jean-Louis. *Introduction to Reading the Pentateuch*, ET 2006. Carr perhaps overdoes it in saying, "This book is now the best starting point for an introduction to past and present study of the formation of the Pentateuch" [*RBL*].

✓ Sparks, Kent. (IBR bibliography) 2002. [*RelSRev* 7/03; *EvQ* 1/05; *BBR* 15.1; *TJ* Spr 05].

✓ Van Seters, John. ‡ *The Pentateuch: A Social-Science Commentary*, 1999. [*JBL* Fall 01]. Earlier skeptical volumes on the Pentateuch were: *Abraham in History and Tradition*, 1975; *Prologue to History: The Yahwist as Historian in Genesis*, 1992; and *The Life of Moses: The Yahwist as Historian in Exodus–Numbers*, 1994.

☆ Vogt, Peter T. *Interpreting the Pentateuch: An Exegetical Handbook* (Kregel) 2009. Packs much useful learning and counsel into a brief guide (214pp).

Watts, James W. (ed). ‡ *Persia and Torah: The Theory of Imperial Authorization of the Pentateuch* (2001). Reflects how scholarship is pushing the date of the Pentateuch later. And so now we get books that never would have been written 40 years ago: Richard Wright, *Linguistic Evidence for the Pre-exilic Date of the Yahwistic Source*, 2005.

☆ Wenham, Gordon J. "Pondering the Pentateuch: The Search for a New Paradigm" (pp.116–44) in *The Face of Old Testament Studies: A Survey of Contemporary Approaches*, edited by David W. Baker and Bill T. Arnold, 1999.

☆ Wenham, Gordon J. *Story as Torah: Reading Old Testament Narrative Ethically*, 2000. I have found no wiser guide to the complicated topic in the subtitle. The book, though focused mainly on Genesis, can inform one's reading of all OT narratives. [*Anvil* 19.1 (Moberly)]. Important volumes on OT Law and ethics include: John Barton's two books on *Understanding OT Ethics* (2003) and *Theory and Practice in OT Ethics* (2004); Frank Crüsemann, *The Torah: Theology and Social History of OT Law* (1996); Waldemar Janzen, *OT Ethics* (1994); Dale Patrick's *OT Law* (1985); and J.W. Watts, *Reading Law: The Rhetorical Shaping of the Pentateuch* (1999). From the evangelical camp we have *Toward OT Ethics* by Walter Kaiser (1983); Hetty Lalleman's *Celebrating the Law? Rethinking OT Ethics* (2004); and, most recommended, C.J.H. Wright, *Old Testament Ethics for the People of God* (2004) [*JSOT* 6/05].

✓ Whybray, R.N. ‡ *Introduction to the Pentateuch*, 1995. Also important in the discussion is Whybray's earlier book, *The Making of the Pentateuch: A Methodological Study*, 1987.

✓ Wolf, Herbert. *An Introduction to the Old Testament Pentateuch*, 1991.

✓ Wynn-Williams, D.J. ‡ *The State of the Pentateuch*, 1997.

GENESIS

★ **Calvin, John.** (GS) 1554. I believe it is one of Calvin's three or four best commentaries. To save money, please see my review of Calvin in the section above on "Commentary Series." In an edited version, this has been included in the Crossway Classic series (2001) [*JSOT* 27.5]. In 2009 Banner of Truth published *Calvin's Sermons on Genesis, Chapters 1–11*, ET by Rob Roy McGregor.

★ **Hamilton, Victor P.** (NICOT) 2 Vols., 1989–95. Solid, dependable scholarship which can be heartily recommended. Though Wenham is more incisive, the pastor will not go wrong purchasing this as an exegetical work. Gives good attention to the exegetical details of Genesis, especially philology, semantics, and syntax. Hamilton may perhaps be faulted for giving us a better view of the trees than the forest. This is a rigorously academic evangelical work, and I predict that a few pastors might prefer Mathews' more accessible and less expensive commentary. [*HebStud* 1992, 1997; *CBQ* 1/93, 7/97; *Them* 10/93, 10/96; *ExpTim* 3/96; *EvQ* 10/98; *JETS* 6/99; *JSS* Spr 98; *RTR* 8/98; *SwJT* Spr 98]. Students should also note his well-written survey entitled, *Handbook on the Pentateuch* (1982, 2nd ed 2005).

★ **Mathews, Kenneth.** (NAC) 2 Vols., 1996–2005. Evangelical reviewers have been pleased. This full (1450pp) commentary is not quite as in-depth academically as Hamilton or Wenham and is more accessible. Mathews gives a dependable, balanced interpretation that pastors will appreciate. This NAC may be slightly less valuable to the student than, say, Hamilton and Wenham among evangelical works; at the same time one should note the more current bibliography. Mathews is about the best in the series, and I admire his exegetical good sense. [*EvQ* 10/98; *Them* 1/97; *JETS* 6/99, 3/06, 3/09; *SwJT* Fall 97, Fall 05; *HebStud* 1997; *CBQ* 4/06; *BSac* 7/06].

★ Ross, Allen P. *Creation and Blessing*, 1988. This is a good book and has always had a spot on the purchase list. A different sort of commentary with many insights for the pastor. Like Aalders it is strong on theological exposition but less useful to students. The work is quite lengthy at 750pp and now released in pb. Ross once taught at Dallas Seminary, then at the (conservative) Trinity Episcopal School for Ministry in Pennsylvania. He now teaches at Beeson. See Ross's CorBC below. [*JETS* 6/90; *Ashland Th Journal* 22 (1990)].

★ **Waltke, Bruce, with Cathi Fredricks**. 2001. This stand-alone commentary is published by Zondervan. It is packed with much structural and rhetorical analysis, but pastors will value this most highly for its biblical theological reflection. At points, I could wish for deeper, more current research than Waltke/Fredricks provides (e.g., they follow Speiser's discredited reference to Hurrian practice in explaining 12:13). [*BSac* 1/04].

★ Walton, John H. (NIVAC) 2001. One of the best in the series. Pastors will love the guidance provided by Walton and by Ross. The author has also published a volume wrestling with ancient cosmology and the interpretation of the Creation account in our scientific age: *The Lord World of Genesis One* (2009) [*Them* 11/09; *RevExp* Spr 10]. His conclusions seem to me to overreach—he contends that Genesis 1 concerns the functions of the created order, not the creation of matter, the substance of the universe.

★ **Wenham, Gordon J.** (WBC) 2 Vols., 1987–94. My main exegetical reference, with about 900pp including the introductions. This is simply one of the best evangelical biblical commentaries available on any book, treating every facet of the book's interpretation. Some conservatives would consider him just a bit too conciliatory toward critical theories about multiple sources and Genesis 1–11 as "an inspired re-telling of ancient oriental traditions about the origins of the world" (p.liii), but I'm glad he faces those issues head-on. He uses some newer literary criticism to good effect (undercutting source-critical divisions) and makes helpful comments on the structure of different narratives (e.g., the Flood). The theology is sound. [*RTR* 5/88; *Them* 4/89; *TJ* Fall 88; *JETS* 6/97; *JSS* Spr 98; *VT* 38.2, 47.4; *BSac* 10/96; *HebStud* 1988; *CRBR* 1990].

✧ ✧ ✧ ✧ ✧ ✧

☆ Aalders, G.C. (BSC) 2 Vols., ET 1981. In early editions of this guide I recommended this thorough (610pp) and insightful exposition for purchase. Its strengths lie in biblical theological comment, which is precisely where so many other modern works are weak. Aalders presents a Reformed, covenantal perspective and is unquestionably orthodox. However, you will likely have difficulty obtaining this—it has been o/p for years. The Dutch original is probably the 1974 5th edition of the commentary. [*HebStud* 1983].

✓ **Alter, Robert.** ‡ 1996. Particularly valuable for its fine, fresh translation. This Jewish scholar is known for helping spark today's strong interest in re-reading Scripture from the literary angle. He rarely fails to supply fresh insights. Anyone who dips into this work will soon see how valuable and even entertaining it is. The same is true of other works of his; I get amused every time I recall his explanation of the ironies lodged in the story of Balaam and his ass (*Art of Biblical Narrative*, 1981). This volume on Genesis is taken up into his 2004 book, *The Five Books of Moses*. See under Pentateuch above.

☆ Arnold, Bill T. [*M*], (NCBC) 2008. The author is in the evangelical camp—this is not a typical commentary in this mainstream critical series—yet his work is praised highly by liberal scholars like W. Brueggemann. Arnold is also an editor of NCBC. Here he builds on his upper-level college textbook, *Encountering the Book of Genesis* (Baker, 1998) and produces an attractive, up-to-date, more exegetical work on Genesis. One of his intentions is to combine diachronic and synchronic interpretation. [*CBQ* 1/10; *JSOT-BL* 2010; *BBR* 20.2]. By the way, the *Encountering* book is one of the most inviting surveys I've seen, with its well-written, well-researched text, accompanied by teaching material (stated aims, study questions, etc.), many pictures and maps, brief discussion of authorship and scholarly methods of interpretation. *Encountering* would be useful to the pastor in planning an adult Sunday School class on Genesis. It was one of my textbooks when I taught a college course on Genesis [*RevExp* Sum 00].

☆ Atkinson, David. *Genesis 1–11* (BST) 1990. Good devotional exposition; well grounded in its scholarship. Many pastors will be drawn to the Atkinson and Baldwin set. [*Chm* 107.1 (1994)].

F Baker, David W. (Apollos). Baker serves as coeditor of this series.

☆ Baldwin, Joyce. *Genesis 12–50* (BST) 1986. The usual, solid work from this prolific evangelical scholar. This book is a bit better than Atkinson and is highly recommended for preachers. [*EvQ* 1/88].

☆ **Bandstra, Barry L.** *Genesis 1–11: A Handbook on the Hebrew Text* (BHHB) 2008. Quite full (629pp) and helpful as a tool for students reading the Hebrew narrative. Bandstra has critical sympathies, but, because of the nature of the work, there is little in the way of historical criticism to be found here. [*VT* 59.1].

☆ **Blocher, Henri.** [*M*], *In the Beginning*, ET 1984. An important monograph on the initial three chapters by a Reformed scholar (240pp). Covers a very broad range of issues in an incisive, capable manner. I used to include this among the recommended purchases for Genesis. Cf. Collins, Kelly, and Walton (2009). [*Evangel* Sum 85; *EvQ* 7/86; *Them* 5/85].

F Blum, Erhard. ‡ (HCOT).

Boice, James Montgomery. 3 Vols., 1982–87. Boice pastored historic Tenth Presbyterian in Philadelphia from 1968–2000. Many pastors will find this exposition homiletically suggestive, but it should be checked against a scholarly commentary. I have found that Boice's expositions are better on the NT, which makes sense since his ThD from Basel was in NT. Note: I think he misinterprets ch. 23. [*JETS* 3/87].

Brichto, Herbert Chanan. ‡ *The Names of God: Poetic Readings in Biblical Beginnings*, 1998. Contains insights into the narrative.

Briscoe, D. Stuart. (WCC) 1987. Definitely one of the better volumes in the series, but not researched very deeply—check his bibliography. (Like Boice he fails to see through all the courtesies and recognize the price gouging in ch. 23 and the irony of Abraham's victimization in the light of the land promise.)

✓ **Brodie, Thomas L.** ‡ *Genesis as Dialogue: A Literary, Historical and Theological Commentary*, 2001. This Oxford work is elegantly written, over 500pp long, and argues for unity and coherence in the book. Compare this literary reading with Alter, Waltke/Fredricks, and Cotter. [*CBQ* 10/04; *VT* 53.4; *BSac* 10/05; *JSOT* 99 (2002); *RelSRev* 10/02].

☆ **Brueggemann, Walter.** ‡ (I) 1982. Brueggemann's works can be serviceable for evangelicals because he treats the final form of the text ("canonical approach") and has great interest in theology. Very stimulating, for the author uses clear, powerful, provocative prose to unsettle Bible readers who might settle for safe, conventional (Western, pious, upper-middle class) interpretations. He wants to draw you into what he has termed "a dangerous conversation." Read with discernment; there's an agenda which is based in part on the influence of Gottwald's sociological approach. He also shows a postmodern discomfort with absolute truth claims. In early editions of this guide I made this a recommended purchase. [*TJ* Spr 83; *JBL* 104.1; *Interp* 7/83].

F Brueggemann, Walter. ‡ (Old Testament for Everyone) 2 Vols.

  Bush, George. 2 Vols., 1852. This set continues to be reprinted. Spurgeon blasts this scholar as about the most blatant plagiarizer he's ever met up with, and he calls this work a "wholesale plunder" of Andrew Fuller and George Lawson.

  Candlish, Robert S. 1869. Spurgeon's favorite—that's high praise! Strongly Reformed, theological, and lengthy. Can be quite profitable if the preacher perseveres in reading through some lengthy lectures.

✓ Carr, David M. ‡ *Reading the Fractures of Genesis*, 1996. Called a success in promoting a merger of "Historical and Literary Approaches" (the subtitle).

✓ **Cassuto, Umberto.** 2 Vols., ET 1964. This commentary covers chs. 1–11 (with much of the work through 13:4 also presented) and reflects careful scholarly work. Cassuto was a devout Jew who spent much of his life defending the integrity of the Pentateuch. Excellent on literary and philological details. Scholarly pastors would find great profit here.

F Clifford, Richard. ‡ (Herm). This is a reassignment—Bernhard W. Anderson had the contract earlier—and the volume will probably not appear for several years. Clifford is a Jesuit who has a major Proverbs commentary.

✓ **Coats, George W.** ‡ (FOTL) 1983. Only of use to students and academics interested in technical form-critical analysis. This is one of the better older volumes in the series. [*JBL* 105.1; *JETS* 9/84; *WTJ* Fall 84; *HebStud* 1986].

☆ **Collins, C. John.** *Genesis 1–4: A Linguistic, Literary, and Theological Commentary* (P&R) 2006. I only saw (and bought) this recently. My regret is that the treatment ends with ch. 4. The interests of Prof. Collins, as described in the commentary subtitle, are in line with those of much of the best contemporary scholarship. The review in *ZAW* 121.1 speaks of his "discourse-oriented literary approach" and the helpful distinction Collins draws between the text's worldview, "intended to be normative" (Collins, p.262) and the ancient cosmology reflected in the text, i.e. "a stationary earth with an orbiting sun." He is both keenly interested in, and well-qualified to address, the interface between scientific thought and Genesis. If one is particularly interested in chs. 1–4, this is an excellent commentary to pick up. [*BSac* 7/08; *JETS* 9/07].

✓ **Cotter, David W.** ‡ (BO) 2003. This Catholic priest serves as series editor. Both here and in Alter one finds literary insights. When Cotter reads Genesis, he sees "neither documents nor historical clues," but "story." [*Interp* 10/04; *HebStud* 2003; *JSOT* 28.5; *RelSRev* 4/04; *JETS* 3/05].

☆ Currid, John D. (EPSC) 2 Vols., 2003. See Exodus for an earlier, very similar two-vol. set, which offers an accessible and creative biblical-theological exposition. Preachers, especially the Reformed, will relish this in their study.

✓ Delitzsch, Franz. *A New Commentary on Genesis* (not KD) 2 Vols., ET 1888. Delitzsch was always brilliant and less conservative than Keil. This technical work is useful for studying the Hebrew. Later in life he began to be influenced by the Graf/Wellhausen theories of multiple sources, and this is reflected somewhat in these volumes (see vol. 1, p.53). But his conclusion regarding the compositional history remained moderately conservative: "a Mosaic Thorah is the basis of the Pentateuch" (p.10). This 5th edition in ET has been reprinted several times.

  Dods, Marcus. [*M*], (EB) 1893. A standard homiletical help for a bygone era.

  Driver, S.R. ‡ (Westminster Commentaries) 1904. Perhaps the clearest, most valuable presentation of the issues from the old liberal perspective. See Skinner also for turn-of-the-century scholarship.

☆ Duguid, Iain M. *Living in the Grip of Relentless Grace: The Gospel in the Lives of Isaac & Jacob*, 2002. Highly recommended for preachers.

✓ Fokkelman, J.P. ‡ *Narrative Art in Genesis*, 1975. This author also contributes "Genesis and Exodus" to *The Literary Guide to the Bible* (1987), edited by Robert Alter and Frank Kermode. See also Samuel below. The erudition here is accessible mainly to advanced students.

✓ **Fretheim, Terence.** ‡ (NewIB) 1994. Rewarding to consult for a mildly critical theological interpretation, but volumes in the New IB are so expensive that I predict many will be discouraged from purchasing them. This volume is more attractive than some others because it also contains Brueggemann on Exodus and Kaiser on Leviticus. Fretheim is more conservative than many other critical interpreters of Genesis; he refers to the early chapters as "story of the past," which, though it downplays historicity or "historicality," is better than the oft employed "mythology" or "legend" genre identification. Also, Fretheim, coming from the Lutheran tradition, has good theological perception—I would not be shy to call him one of the abler OT theologians in America. But he is not always to be followed, as in his work on "the suffering of God," which has been widely used by the open theists. [*PSB* 16.3 (1995); *CBQ* 4/96; *JETS* 9/96]. Students will want to look up Fretheim's theological introduction, *The Pentateuch*, in Abingdon's IBT (1996) [*RelSRev* 7/98].

Gibson, John C.L. ‡ (DSB) 2 Vols., 1981. The series editor gives a well-done liberal exposition, but the work is now showing its age. He spends too much time presenting the conclusions of 1960s and 1970s scholarship to his lay readership who pick up this series more for devotional reasons.

Gowan, Donald E. ‡ *From Eden to Babel: A Commentary on the Book of Genesis 1–11* (ITC) 1988. The author is a respected OT scholar at Pittsburgh Seminary (PCUSA). This work is brief (125pp), well written, but not as open to the text nor as theologically perceptive as Janzen's ITC on chs. 12–50. [*CBQ* 51.4; *ExpTim* 8/89].

☆ Greidanus, Sidney. *Preaching Christ from Genesis*, 2007. The author is learned in hermeneutics, biblical theology, and homiletics. He offers superb guidance on his topic, with special attention given to handling the narrative genre and understanding the structure of the book. These 500 pages are a good antidote to moralistic preaching. The skills learned in reading such a textbook can apply to a much larger body of OT literature. For a taste see "Detecting Plot Lines," *CTJ* 43.1 (2008): 64–77. [*RTR* 12/08; *CTJ* 11/08; *JSOT-BL* 2008; *Chm* Sum 09; *Anvil* 26.3–4].

✓ **Gunkel, Hermann.** ‡ 3rd Edition 1910, ET 1997. This is famous as the pioneering form-critical work on Genesis and the most influential work for scholars during the early 20th century. It was important that this finally got translated. [*ThTo* 1/98; *JSOT* 76; *CBQ* 10/98; *OTA* 2/00; *BSac* 4/98].

☆ **Hartley, John E.** (NIBC) 2000. I have warmly commended this Methodist scholar's other commentaries on Job and Leviticus. This work is valuable to pastors for several reasons. The scholarship is up-to-date and solidly evangelical. Also, the volume is both inexpensive and of manageable size (416pp). You could call it a best buy on Genesis. [*RTR*, 8/01; *Them*, Aut 01; Wenham does the review in *JSOT* 99 (2002); *Anvil* 19.1].

F **Hendel, Ronald S.** ‡ (AYB). A planned two-vol. set to replace Speiser. See his award-winning research on *The Text of Genesis 1–11: Textual Studies and Critical Edition* (Oxford, 1998) [*JBL* Sum 00]. The first AYB volume, covering chs. 1–11, had been projected to appear in late 2008, but there seems to be a major delay.

F Hiebert, Theodore. ‡ (AOTC).

☆ Hughes, R. Kent. (PTW) 2004. The expositor should consider this for purchase. [*JETS* 9/05].

✓ **Jacob, Benno.** ‡ *The First Book of the Bible: Genesis*, ET 1974. A 358-page abridgement of an extensive Jewish commentary published in German: *Das erste Buch der Tora*, 1934 (1055pp). Wenham once said this is "of great value." See too his Exodus commentary.

☆ Janzen, J. Gerald. ‡ *Abraham and All the Families of the Earth: A Commentary on the Book of Genesis 12–50* (ITC) 1993. Because the author focuses so much on drawing out the theology of the narratives, this book is very useful to the expositor. I consider it one of the best volumes in this series—"few…will match its depth of comment on Genesis 12–50" (W. Kaiser). For a taste, see his sparkling, "cut to the chase" discussion of R.W.L. Moberly, "supersession," and the proper relation among the Abrahamic, Mosaic and New Covenants (pp.6–12). Janzen taught Genesis to seminary classes for a couple decades, and it shows. This author has also written commentaries on Exodus and Job. I once included this among my purchase suggestions, but it is now harder to find a copy. [*JETS* 3/96].

✓ Keil, C.F. (KD) ET 1864. The whole set once was a recommended purchase. See under "Commentary Series."

Kelly, Douglas F. *Creation and Change: Genesis 1:1–2:4 in the Light of Changing Scientific Paradigms*, 1997. How do we read the biblical account of creation in our day, when evolutionary thought challenges many fundamental doctrines: God as Creator, sin and death (judgment), solidarity in our human nature, etc.? Kelly provides answers as a systematics professor at RTS Charlotte. Cf. Blocher. [*Chm* Spr 04].

☆ Kidner, Derek. (TOTC) 1967. Packs an amazing amount of information and theological insight for its brief format. Excellent, but accommodates an evolutionary viewpoint, which bothered American evangelicals more than the British. In early editions of this guide I recommended this for purchase; preachers find Kidner very suggestive for sermon preparation.

Lange, Johann Peter. (Lange) ET 1868. Certainly one of the best in this series (665pp). In his day Spurgeon judged it "in all respects beyond price" (p.51). Now dated of course.

Leupold, H.C. 2 Vols., 1942. A lengthy exposition by an evangelical Lutheran. Like Lenski on the NT, Leupold provides some good conservative exegesis, which often points to distinctives and concerns of Lutheran systematic theology. He has other commentaries on Psalms, Ecclesiastes, Isaiah, Daniel, and Zechariah.

Lawson, George. *Lectures on the History of Joseph*, 1989 reprint. This theological and devotional classic has been reprinted a couple times by Banner of Truth over the last 25 years.

Longacre, Robert. *Joseph, A Story of Divine Providence: A Text Theoretical and Textlinguistic Analysis of Genesis 37 and 39–48*, 2nd ed 2003.

☆ Longman, Tremper. *How to Read Genesis*, 2005. This follows his like-titled handbooks on Psalms and Proverbs and is well worth reading as a more popular orientation before digging deeper. [*CTJ* 4/08; *JETS* 9/06; *SwJT* Fall 04; *Anvil* 23.4].

☆ Louth, Andrew (ed). *Genesis 1–11* (ACCS) 2001.

Luther, Martin. "Lectures on Genesis," *Luther's Works*, Vols. 1–8, ET 1958–70.

Maher, M. ‡ (OTM) 1982.

McKeown, James. [*M*] (THC) 2008. I have not yet seen it, but this theological commentary was announced as 398pp and as focusing upon a triad of themes: descendents, blessing, and land. Some reviewers see the author, who teaches at Queens

University in Belfast, as both evangelically rooted and conciliatory toward more liberal positions. Alongside the many positive reviews, Hwang offers more criticism. [*CBQ* 4/09; *ThTo* 4/09 (Brueggemann); *JETS* 3/09 (Hwang); *JSOT-BL* 2009; *JTS* 4/10; *BTB* 5/10; *ExpTim* 7/09; *Interp* 4/10; *RTR* 12/09; *VT* 59.3].

Millard, Alan R., and Donald J. Wiseman (eds). *Essays on the Patriarchal Narrative*, 1980. An older conservative volume on the historical character of the narratives in Genesis 12–50. More theological is the volume edited by Hess, Satterthwaite, and Wenham: *He Swore an Oath: Biblical Themes from Genesis 12–50*, 2nd ed 1994.

Moberly, R.W.L. [*M*] *The Theology of the Book of Genesis*, 2009. From Cambridge's "Old Testament Theology" series. [*HBT* 32.1; *JETS* 9/10].

Morris, Henry M. *The Genesis Record*, 1976. This lengthy study published by Baker was especially concerned with scientific issues and was written for laypeople. Morris was one of the leaders of Scientific Creationism ("Young Earth" theorists). I can't recommend this as a commentary for the pastor. Some will argue that the restricted focus upon scientific and historical issues distracts the reader from the dominant theological interests of the narrator/text.

F   O'Connor, Kathleen M. ‡ (S&H).

F   Petersen, David L. ‡ (OTL). This is scheduled to replace von Rad.

Pink, Arthur. 1922. Cannot be recommended. Though his studies are reverent expositions, Pink is too easily distracted from the text before him and often goes overboard on typology. His earlier works (the "Gleanings" series published by Moody Press), such as this one on Genesis, tended to be Dispensational and not at all well-grounded in scholarship. He jumped to theological concerns and present day application before he had understood the text. One exception was his later (1956) work on Elijah, which, while not scholarly, is quite good.

✓   **Rad, Gerhard von.** ‡ (OTL) ET 1961, 3rd ed 1972. Building upon the form-critical work of Gunkel, von Rad has long been a standard critical commentary. Examines Genesis as part of a proposed "Hexateuch" (Genesis to Joshua). Even though the scholarly approach represented here has become obsolete, the commentary's highly theological discussion of the text retains value. [*ThTo* 20.1].

Reno, R.R. (Brazos) 2010. The author is series editor. I have not seen this yet.

Ross, Allen. (CorBC) 2008. This 550-page volume on Genesis and Exodus (see Oswalt) builds on the earlier Ross exposition, *Creation and Blessing*, but is much briefer.

☆   **Sailhamer, John H.** (EBCR) 2008. This sharp, mature, independently-minded scholar has taught at TEDS, Dallas Seminary, and more recently at Golden Gate Baptist Seminary. Here Sailhamer redoes Genesis after his successful effort in EBC. Do note, too, his theological/literary commentary on all five books of Moses, *The Pentateuch As Narrative*. In the EBCR series Genesis is bound with Exodus and Leviticus. [*JSOT-BL* 2010].

Sailhamer, John H. (EBC) 1990. This volume covers Genesis through Numbers. Preference must now be given to the EBCR volume above. [*Presb* Spr 91].

Sarna, Nahum M. ‡ *Understanding Genesis*. 1970. A Jewish work with archaeological data, ANE background, and interpretive issues presented in an interesting way. [*WTJ* 30.2].

✓   **Sarna, Nahum M**. ‡ (JPS) 1989. With its exegesis of the Hebrew, this is more technical and in-depth (414pp) than the previous work. The JPS series is valuable to scholars and students. But you probably won't know quite what to do with all the Rabbinics. [*ThTo* 46.3; *HebStud* 1992; *CRBR* 1990].

✓ Scullion, J.J. ‡ 1992. The literary concerns and method of interpretation here are more characteristic of critical scholarship 40 years ago. Still, it may be worth consulting for seminary papers.

✓ Sheridan, Mark (ed). *Genesis 12–50* (ACCS) 2002. See Louth above. [*Them* Spr 04; *JSOT-BL* 2007].

✓ **Skinner, John.** ‡ (ICC) 1910. Back in 1977 it could be said that "[f]or a full, technical handling of the issues Skinner…has not been surpassed in English." Westermann's commentary was not yet translated, nor was Wenham available when Childs wrote this. Skinner is now very dated, but as an academic I still consult him on rare occasion.

✓ **Speiser, E.A.** ‡ (AB) 1964. This was a Jewish work of impressive scholarship for its day, with discussion of the ANE background, some source-criticism and a more literal translation. Pastors will have little use for this dated commentary. Note that exposition and theology were not among the original aims of the series. See Hendel above.

Stigers, Harold G. 1976. A strong evangelical effort in its time, exegetical in its thrust. Now it is long o/p.

Thomas, W.H. Griffith. 1909. This rich, somewhat Dispensational, devotional commentary was first published in 3 vols. and has occasionally been reprinted.

Towner, W. Sidley. ‡ (WestBC) 2001. I have yet to use this nearly 300-page commentary, but the reputation of the author leads me to guess it serves as a leading popular-level exposition of Genesis for liberal pastors. Compare with the fuller works by Brueggemann, Fretheim, and the Gowan/Janzen set. [*Them* Sum 05; *Anvil* 19.3].

✓ Turner, Laurence A. ‡ (Read) 2000. I've not used Turner (230pp), who offers a narrative approach. [*JSOT* 94; *Anvil* 17.3].

✓ Vawter, Bruce. ‡ 1977. This critical interpretation by a Roman Catholic scholar was published by Doubleday and is a major work to be consulted, if one is doing exhaustive research with an interest in the results of older diachronic methods.

✓ **Westermann, Claus.** ‡ (ContC) 3 Vols., ET 1984–86. Authoritative…25 years ago. This mammoth, critical work delivers to us the most thorough exegetical treatment of Genesis, with over 1500pp of theologically charged commentary from the BKAT series (though I would have liked even more theology in such a huge set). Westermann's approach is mainly diachronic (especially source and form-critical) while making some use of synchronic methods. This scholar is one of the Pentateuchal interpreters tending toward a simpler source critical analysis, erasing "E" almost entirely. Students should note that his huge 256-page introduction to Genesis is also available in English translation (1992). Those with an academic bent might be inclined to take out a bank loan to buy this. Wenham [*BSB* 3/99] rightly speaks of how Westermann and other source critical treatments "in effect write commentaries on J's version of Genesis and P's version of Genesis rather than on the canonical Genesis" and usually "are better at describing elements within Genesis rather than the whole book." [*JBL* 6/72 and 6/77; *ThTo* 43.2; *HebStud* 1986; *CBQ* 49.3 (1987)].

Westermann, Claus. ‡ (T&I) ET 1987. This commentary, a translation from a Dutch series, makes his conclusions in the three-vol. ContC available to a larger audience. Popular and more practical in its aim. [*JETS* 6/90; *EvQ* 7/89; *CBQ* 51.4 (1989)].

☆ Young, E.J. *Studies in Genesis One*, 1964. A careful exegesis.

☆ Young, E.J. *Genesis Three*, 1966. Subtitled "A Devotional and Expository Study."

Youngblood, Ronald. 1991. This is a revision of his earlier two works on Genesis, and is definitely one of the better popularly-styled, evangelical expositions of Genesis. Good for a church library.

NOTES: (1) See C. S. Rodd's "Which Is the Best Commentary? II. Genesis," *ExpTim*, 3/86. (2) One of the best brief annotated bibliographies for Genesis is still R.W.L. Moberly, *Genesis 12–50* (Sheffield: JSOT, 1992), 102–07. (3) John Kselman, "The Book of Genesis: A Decade of Scholarly Research," *Interp* 45.4 (1991): 380–92.

EXODUS

★ **Childs, Brevard S.** ‡ (OTL) 1974. Very thorough and rewarding, this was for decades simply the best commentary on this portion of Scripture. "Unabashedly theological" in its purpose, Childs' work is what might be called "post-liberal" and a reaction against narrowly historical critical approaches. His "Canonical Approach" doesn't get mired in unraveling sources. He "subordinates the prehistory of the text to interpretation of its canonical form" (Danker). His concern to take into account the whole history of exegesis, ancient and modern, is laudable. Must be used with some discernment. Moderately critical. This used to be Longman's first choice. [*JBL* 95.2 (1976); *JETS* 9/75; *ThTo* 31.3].

★ **Currid, John D.** (EPSC) 2 Vols., 2000–02. The author has published a book on Egypt and articles on the Book of Exodus. Here he delivers a more conservative interpretation of Exodus in about 900pp. The work is both exegetical (not too detailed) and expositional—a lot like the notes you typically find in an excellent study Bible (one which occasionally moves to consider application or to develop a devotional thought). Currid is a beloved professor at RTS, and his love for the Scriptures shines through in these pages. See his companion set on Genesis in the same series, which also is strong on redemptive-historical aspects. The pastor especially will value this.

★ **Enns, Peter.** (NIVAC) 2000. A full treatment at 600pp. The author was until 2008 a professor of OT at Westminster Seminary in Philadelphia. He spent much time with Exodus in his Harvard doctoral research. Enns exhibits good sense in exegetical analysis, has a good eye for theological themes, and starts the reader down the path to discovering relevant applications. Though I value the volumes of Houtman, Cassuto, Sarna, Fretheim and Brueggemann highly, my present counsel to studious pastors is buy the trio of Childs, Stuart, and Enns together to start. If Childs is too critical or expensive for you, then substitute Motyer. (Note: Enns has a savvy annotated bibliography on pp.37–38 which lists Houtman, Sarna, and Fretheim as "musts.")

★ **Fretheim, Terence E.** ‡ (I) 1991. Fits well with series. An impressive theological exposition of Exodus, with an emphasis on a creation theology. "Not many commentaries make a good read—as opposed to a good reference—but this is certainly one of them" [*BSB* 3/99 (Wells)]. Having used Fretheim extensively myself, I have to include this among my recommendations, even though my "to buy list" is getting long. The pastor wanting a more conservative work should look at Cole, Kaiser, and Gispen (if you can find a copy). For additional comments on Fretheim, see under Genesis above. [*CRBR* 1992; *PSB* 14.1; *ThTo* 10/91; *Interp* 10/92; *CTJ* 4/95].

★ Motyer, J. Alec. (BST) 2005. I love this book as an inexpensive, suggestive biblical theological guide for expositional preachers. Another help for pastors, but several times as long, would be Ryken below. [*Chm* Aut 05; *JSOT-BL* 2006; *ExpTim* 2/06; *Anvil* 25.1].

★ **Stuart, Douglas.** (NAC) 2006. As with Motyer, many evangelicals were waiting for this. This is not the academic commentary that Stuart's *Hosea–Jonah* (WBC) is, and it does not have quite the interaction with scholarship that I had hoped for. The author seems to have aimed at producing a fresh, more independent interpretation. This volume, though valuable to students, is geared more for pastors. It is a very full (826pp), satisfying exegesis to set alongside Mathews' superb *Genesis* in NAC.

✧ ✧ ✧ ✧ ✧ ✧

F Alexander, T. Desmond. (Apollos). This may become the more technical evangelical exegesis of Exodus we have lacked for so long. I eagerly await this for yet another reason: Alexander pays close attention to biblical theology.

Ashby, Godfrey. [𝓜], (ITC) 1998. A slim, good theological interpretation with little attention given to historical and literary issues. I am especially interested in the book because Ashby ministered in South Africa (within the Anglican communion) and reads Exodus after seeing first-hand the gross injustices of Apartheid. One comes away from reading Ashby with the thought that Exodus is clearly a living book for the author. Desmond Tutu writes the foreword. [*CTJ* 11/98; *Interp* 1/99; *CBQ* 7/99; *HebStud* 1999].

F Behr, John. (Brazos). The author teaches at St. Vladimir's Orthodox seminary

✓ Bimson, John J. *Redating the Exodus and Conquest*, 1978, rev. 1981. Not a commentary, but a provocative monograph published by JSOT Press which argues for an early (15th century) date. Many conservatives seized on this as bolstering their conclusions. [*EvQ* 1/80; *JBL* 99.1 (1980); *VT* 31.1; *BAR* 13.6].

☆ **Bruckner, James K.** [𝓜], (NIBC) 2008. A readable, helpful, briefer evangelical commentary (348pp), Bruckner is also inexpensive and could be a best-buy for bargain hunters who want exegesis ($10 at CBD). The author teaches at North Park Seminary in Chicago and earlier contributed one of the better NIVAC volumes (see Jonah). He suggests a post-exilic date for the final redaction of Exodus. Bruckner's theology is fairly healthy and helpful, emphasizing that the liberation was more *for* than *from*, for service (verb עבד) to God rather than narrowly from political and economic servitude/oppression. Perhaps some will argue with me, saying this deserves a spot on the recommended list, especially at the price. [*JETS* 9/09; *CBQ* 1/09; *RBL*; *JSOT-BL* 2009; *JHebS* 2009].

✓ **Brueggemann, Walter.** ‡ (NewIB) 1994. Here are 300pp of stimulating theological exposition. Brueggemann is incapable of being dull. See my comments on his Genesis commentary above. [*PSB* 16.3 (1995); *CBQ* 4/96; *JETS* 9/96].

Burns, R.J. ‡ *Exodus, Leviticus, Numbers* (OTM) 1983.

Bush, George. *Notes on Exodus*, 1856. Written by an American scholar. Spurgeon does not believe he plagiarized here as on Genesis. This was reprinted in pb by Kregel not long ago.

☆ **Calvin, John.** *Harmony of the Pentateuch*, 1563. Though not a complete commentary on Exodus, it does cover most of the ground. This harmony is not considered among the Reformer's best, but it should not be forgotten. Reprinted by Baker. See my comments under Genesis.

F Carpenter, Eugene. (EEC). Originally this was scheduled for NICOT, and we looked for Carpenter to end the dearth of solid, large-scale, evangelical exegetical commentaries. Reports are that the commentary was completed several years ago, but will be included in a different series.

✓   **Cassuto, Umberto.** ET 1967. Probably this Jewish scholar's best piece of commentary work (500pp), but a bit hard to obtain. Old Westminster's E.J. Young had high praise for Cassuto's writings. See also my comments on his Genesis commentary. [*Biblica* 35 (1954); *JBL* 73 (1954)].

✓   Coats, George W. ‡ *Exodus 1–18* (FOTL) 1998. He also did Genesis for this series. Knierim will complete the book of Exodus, as poor health interrupted Coats' work. This work is technical, brief (178pp), and probably to be considered one of the weakest entries in the series. [*JSOT* 89 (2000); *Interp* 1/00; *CBQ* 1/00; *HebStud* 41; *RelSRev* 10/99; *JBL* Fall 01; *JSS* Spr 02].

     Coggins, Richard. ‡ (Epworth) 2000. [*Anvil* 17.4].

☆   Cole, R. Alan. (TOTC) 1973. This is an adequate, brief treatment from a conservative. The introduction contains a worthwhile summary of the theology of Exodus. For a long time Exodus was poorly served by evangelical commentaries, so Cole's work was more valuable than it might otherwise have been. In 1989 this was among my recommendations for purchase. [*EvQ* 4/74].

     Davies, G. Henton. ‡ (Torch Bible Commentaries) 1967. This work of 253pp was published by SCM Press and written for the general reader, though the J-E-P discussion does not interest the average church member. Childs calls Davies "disappointing," but I think it was well-written and, though brief, serviceable for its day.

F   Davies, G.I. ‡ (ICC–new series). The series never has had an Exodus volume, and Davies, who is now the OT editor, promises to deliver. Some early work is: "The Exegesis of the Divine Name in Exodus," in Robert P. Gordon (ed), *The God of Israel* (CUP, 2007). Here are my guesses: it will not appear anytime soon and will demonstrate his interests in biblical theology and source criticism.

     Davis, John D. *Moses and the Gods of Egypt*, 1971, rev. 1986. A conservative and popularly-styled work by a Grace Seminary professor. Looks at Exodus "in the light of recent archeological and historical studies" (p.9). Not of much help to students. There is also little help offered in wrestling with the theological message.

✓   **Dozeman, Thomas B. (ed).** ‡ (ECC) 2009. An approximately 780-page scholarly exegesis which builds upon his 1996 theological interpretation, *God at War: Power in the Exodus Tradition*, as well as the earlier *God on the Mountain: A Study of Redaction, Theology and Canon in Exodus 19–24* (1989). This well-researched volume will receive a warm welcome from critical scholars, especially those oriented toward diachronic literary criticism, but pastors of all types will probably just let the academics take account of it. Advanced students will make ready use of this, especially to understand how the work of certain Pentateuchal interpreters (e.g., Blum) is reshaping the discussion of genetic origins. [*JETS* 3/10; *JSOT-BL* 2010; *CBQ* 7/10].

     Dozeman, Thomas B. ‡ *Methods for Exodus*, 2010. Another volume in a developing CUP series, surveying the various hermeneutical approaches.

✓   **Driver, Samuel R.** ‡ (Cambridge Bible) 1911. The old standard critical work, widely used in lieu of an ICC volume on Exodus, is jam-packed and 443pp in length.

     Dunnam, Maxie D. (WCC) 1987. The author was President of Asbury Seminary and his sermonic commentary is quite full (nearly 400pp). This is not a throw-away, but I much prefer other expositional helps: Enns, Motyer, Ryken, J.G. Janzen, Currid.

☆   **Durham, John I.** ‡ (WBC) 1987. An extensive treatment that could have been more helpful had he followed through on his stated intent to treat the "final form" of the text. As it is, the commentary gets somewhat preoccupied with source, form, and tradition criticism—probably not what most pastors are looking for. On the plus side, Durham has more theology than some other volumes in WBC. Advanced students will take an interest in this volume. Most evangelical pastors will prefer Stuart and will keep waiting for Alexander and Carpenter. [*HebStud* 1988; *RTR* 5/88; *WTJ* Spr 88; *TJ* Spr. 87; *EvQ* 10/88; *Them* 1/90; *JETS* 9/89].

Ellison, H.L. (DSB) 1982. Theological, devotional exposition, but sketchy. More conservative than most other entries in DSB.

☆ Gispen, W.H. (BSC) ET 1982. This volume is helpful in much the same way as Aalders on Genesis, though the latter is richer theologically, in part because of its greater length. Pastors wanting another evangelical commentary, not a devotional-homiletical help like Ryken, could look to pick up the o/p Gispen secondhand.

✓ **Gowan, Donald E.** ‡ *Theology in Exodus: Biblical Theology in the Form of a Commentary*, 1994. Published by WJK, this is a rather different type of commentary from what pastors are used to. It is a hybrid of OT Theology and commentary. I judge the work a partial success. Gowan did make a contribution to my understanding of Exodus, especially with his lengthy discussion of the divine name. [*ExpTim* 11/95; *CBQ* 7/96; *JETS* 3/97; *JSOT* 75; *Interp* 7/96; *SwJT* Sum 98].

✓ **Greenberg, Moshe.** ‡ *Understanding Exodus*, 1969. Though not a lengthy study and now aging, Greenberg is still worth consulting—it is often cited. See, for example, Propp's recent commentary in AB. Greenberg's conservatively critical, Jewish stance is similar to Sarna's.

Hoffmeier, J.K. *Israel in Egypt*, 1996. Solidly conservative. See also his *Ancient Israel in Sinai* (Oxford, 2005).

✓ **Houtman, Cornelis.** ‡ (HCOT) 4 Vols., ET 1993–2002. Students should certainly consult Houtman, there being fewer in-depth, scholarly commentaries on Exodus. It is published in pb—initially by Kok and now by Peeters (www.peeters-leuven. be/)—and is difficult to obtain here in the USA. Were not so expensive (€160), I might urge that Houtman be considered for purchase by advanced students. Pastors with a scholarly bent and a sizable book allowance could profit from Houtman like they do from Westermann on Genesis or Zimmerli on Ezekiel. This work is about the best in its class of technical historical-critical commentary; it "provides the fullest modern treatment...of Exodus that is available in any language" (G.I. Davies). [*VT* 43 (1993) pp.115, 427–8; *VT* 48 (1998) p. 572; *VT*, 51.3; *Orientalis* 48 (1991) 885; *JSOT* 89 (2000); *BL* 1997; *CBQ* 4/01].

Humphreys, Colin. *The Miracles of Exodus*, 2003. Cannot be recommended. [*Them* Sum 04].

✓ Hyatt, James P. ‡ (NCB) 1971. I judge this volume (about 350pp) to be quite dated in approach and of little value today. Hyatt, Professor of OT at Vanderbilt University, published this just prior to his death.

✓ Jackson, Bernard S. ‡ *Wisdom-Laws: A Study of the* Mishpatim *of Exodus 21:1–22:16* (OUP) 2006. Being hailed as a breakthrough study, following many other technical publications on OT Law, such as his *Studies in the Semiotics of Biblical Law*, 2000. [*VT* 59.3; *JSOT-BL* 2007 (Davies)].

✓ Jacob, Benno. 1943, ET 1992. A remarkable, comprehensive (1100pp) study of the Hebrew text by a Jewish rabbi who escaped Hitler's Germany. Many first learned of this work through Childs' citations of it in the OTL volume. It is good to see it finally in English dress and published by KTAV. Though somewhat liberal in his general theological views, Jacob steadfastly rejected Wellhausen's approach to both source criticism and the evolution of OT religion. [*Book List* 1993; *JSOT* 79 (1998); *BSac* 10/93].

☆ Janzen, J. Gerald. ‡ (WestBC) 1997. A good theological exposition, but not as deep or thorough as Fretheim. The final six chapters are given only a glance. Could be put to excellent use in preparing a sermon. There is attention to exegetical points (and some brilliant insights along the way, e.g., at ch. 6) and to the flow of the book. This 275-page pb is well worth the money. Janzen is Harvard-trained, was ordained in the Anglican Church in Canada, and long taught OT at Christian Theological Seminary in Indianapolis (now retired). I'm glad to call him my friend. [*CBQ* 4/99; *Them* Aut 00; *Interp* 1/99; *JSOT Booklist* 1999].

☆ **Janzen, Waldemar.** (BCBC) 2000. Chooses to concentrate on the final form or canonical text, and does so even more than Childs. Though not always completely current with contemporary scholarship, Janzen is learned (Harvard PhD), devout in his Mennonite tradition, and concerned to apply Exodus in a pastoral way. I like this nearly 500-page book. [*CBQ* 1/02; *Them* Sum 03].

F   Johnstone, William. ‡ (S&H). See his past work listed under Chronicles. This has the potential to be one of the better theological expositions. Johnstone has long been on faculty at Aberdeen.

Kaiser, Walter C. (EBC) 1990. This is a solid work, but only about 200pp, much of which is consumed printing the NIV text. Once, in a review of some commentary, Don Carson suggested that the book did not make up in quality what it necessarily lost by brevity; you may have the same sentiment in using Kaiser. At one point evangelicals rated this exegesis highly—it was Stuart's favorite in 1990—especially because there was not a lot out there to choose from. Now look up Stuart, Currid, and Enns. See EBCR below.

☆ **Kaiser, Walter C.** (EBCR) 2008. These 225pp are only a slight improvement of EBC. Regrettably, there is not much updating here. [*JSOT-BL* 2010].

✓ Keil, C.F. (KD) ET 1864. Keil's work was once a real help, considering the paucity of good conservative commentaries on Exodus. Finally, pastors are getting a good stock of reference works.

F   Knierim, Rolf P. ‡ *Exodus 19–40; with an Introduction to Legal Genres* (FOTL). See Coats above.

Langston, Scott M. ‡ *Exodus through the Centuries* (Blackwell) 2006. Focuses on how Exodus has been interpreted and has influenced culture. Somewhat similar, and quite stimulating, is Göran Larsson, *Bound for Freedom: The Book of Exodus in Jewish and Christian Traditions* (1999).

✓ Lienhard, Joseph T. (ed). *Exodus, Leviticus, Numbers, Deuteronomy* (ACCS) 2001. [*RelSRev* 7/03; *JSOT-BL* 2007 (Davies)].

F   Longman, Tremper. (THC). Along the way, he has published *How to Read Exodus* (2009).

F   McBride, S. Dean. ‡ (Herm). At one point the publisher puzzled us by announcing the author as McBridge.

☆ Mackay, John L. (Mentor) 2001. This is a full (over 600pp), conservative exposition which the pastor could put to good use. "Mackay's theological comments are a strength of this commentary" (P. Barker). There is less in the way of footnotes and bibliography to assist the student working exegetically. [*Them* Spr 02].

McNeile, A.H. ‡ (Westminster) 1908, 3rd ed 1931. Best ignored now.

Meyer, F.B. *Devotional Commentary on Exodus*, n.d. At one point it was being kept in print by Kregel (1978). All of Meyer's works are warm-hearted. Close to 500pp and written in the early 20th century. For a study of the man, see Ian M. Randall, *Spirituality and Social Change: The Contribution of F.B. Meyer (1847–1929)*.

✓ **Meyers, Carol.** ‡ (NCBC) 2005. This elegantly and compactly written commentary can be recommended as a first stop for students seeking a mainstream critical interpretation of Exodus as "the commemoration of the past" and "a tribute to the imagination and creativity of those nameless people who…made the experiences of some the foundational stories of all" (pp.11–12). She sees the book of Exodus as presenting "the defining features of Israel's identity, as it took shape by the late biblical period" (p.xv), and as having little historical value. Though Meyers is known for expertise in archeology, she has a wide range of exegetical skills and provides a well-rounded commentary (except for those who want source criticism). [*CBQ* 4/07; *Interp* 7/07; *HebStud* 2006; *JSOT-BL* 2006; *JHebS*].

Moberley, R.W.L. ‡ *At the Mountain of God: Story and Theology in Exodus 32–34* (JSOTSup) 1983.

✓ Noth, Martin. ‡ (retired OTL) ET 1962. Noth was an extraordinarily influential critical scholar, but the old Noth/von Rad schema or synthesis has badly broken down. This narrowly historical-critical work was replaced by Childs and is no longer in print. There are other Noth commentaries on Leviticus and Numbers.

F Olson, Dennis. ‡ (AOTC).

Osborn, Noel D., and Howard A. Hatton. (UBS) 1999.

☆ Oswalt, John. (CorBC) 2008. This is part of a Genesis-Exodus volume and is excellent introductory reading.

Pink, Arthur. *Gleanings in Exodus*, 1962. See under Genesis. Available free on the internet at PBMinistries.

F Polak, Frank. ‡ (BO).

✓ **Propp, William H.C.** ‡ (AB) 2 Vols., 1999–2006. As we have come to expect from this series, Propp delivers an exceedingly full exegesis (1500pp). His commentary returns in some ways to a more traditional historical critical tack (lots of E, at the expense of J), but Propp is still a very important work. While there is some theological reflection here, that is not the focus. Propp is more interested in the sociological factors he believes gave rise to this literature (see p.39). As Davies notes [*JSOT* 89], Propp is independent-minded and, most importantly, is the first "to be able to deal fully with manuscript evidence from Qumran." He can be taken to task for his idiosyncratic translation, which is "extremely literal to the point of stiltedness" (Davies). While students will find these volumes valuable for lexical and grammatical studies, evangelical pastors won't find as much use for this work. Denver Seminary's list makes this a top pick. [*OTA* 2/00; *ExpTim* 5/00; *Interp* 1/01; *SwJT* Fall 00; *RelSRev* 10/00; *JR* 4/01; *CBQ* 1/01; *JBL* Win 01; *JSOT-BL* 2008].

Ramm, Bernard. *His Way Out*, 1974. Theological interpretation of Exodus. Short and helpful for the preacher, but o/p.

☆ Rosner, Brian S., and Paul R. Williamson (eds). *Exploring Exodus: Literary, Theological and Contemporary Approaches*, 2008. This is well described as "a survey in the use of the book of Exodus in contemporary theology, both practical and theoretical" (Fayette). [*ExpTim* 5/10 (Fayette)].

☆ Ryken, Philip G. (PTW) 2005. This is rich, thoughtful, God-centered preaching in a fat volume (cf. his Jeremiah volume in PTW). It is less attuned to OT scholarship than some other entries in the series such as Duguid on Numbers.

✓ **Sarna, Nahum.** ‡ (JPS) 1991. A 278-page entry in this elegantly produced Jewish series; I wish it were twice as long. Students can learn a great deal from this exegesis, and some will find themselves getting fascinated by the ins-and-outs of Rabbinic commentary. (On this point, Enns says Sarna "direct[s] the reader to elements of the text that Christian readers might otherwise pass over too quickly.") See his other JPS work on Genesis above. [*CBQ* 7/93]. Also note his insightful book, *Exploring Exodus* (1986, 1996), which takes up different interpretive issues than JPS [*CRBR* 1988].

Sprinkle, Joe M. *The "Book of the Covenant": A Literary Approach*, 1994.

F Strawn, Brent A. (NICOT). This would be in place of Carpenter. Strawn took his MDiv and PhD at Princeton Seminary and teaches at Candler-Emory.

Westbrook, Raymond, and Bruce Wells. ‡ *Everyday Law in Biblical Israel*, 2009. "The best and most up-to-date introduction available to the theory and practice of law in biblical times" (Patrick Miller). This brief volume (156pp) addresses texts throughout the OT with a special focus on the "*Mishpatim*" of Exodus.

White, John H. *Slavery to Servanthood*, 1987. A surprise. These 13 lessons published by Great Commission ("Adult Discipleship Series") are suggestive for either a Bible class or a sermon series. The subtitle is "Tracing the Exodus throughout Scripture." The author is a minister in the Reformed Presbyterian Church in North America ("Covenanters"). Pastors might consider this, if it is in print.

NOTE: C. S. Rodd's "Which Is the Best Commentary? Exodus," *ExpTim*, 9/87.

DECALOGUE

★ Calvin, John. *Institutes of the Christian Religion*, II.viii. Calvin's profound theological interpretation of the Law has had untold influence upon political, economic, cultural, and spiritual developments in the Western world. Some may be surprised by differences between Calvin and the Puritans on the application of the moral law (e.g., the 4th Commandment). By the way, the 1960 Battles translation of the *Institutes*, published by WJK, is the edition to possess. See Calvin's sermons and commentary below.

★ Douma, J. *The Ten Commandments: Manual for the Christian Life*, ET 1996. As is suggested in the subtitle, this fine Dutch work has a Reformed theological orientation. It is useful to both students and pastors. I have heard of its use as a textbook in seminary courses on ethics. Another rich ethics book, using the Ten Words to structure much of the discussion, is John Frame, *The Doctrine of the Christian Life*, 2008 [*Them* 7/09].

★ Hughes, R. Kent. *The Disciplines of Grace*, 1993. An excellent modern-day exposition by the pastor of the College Church in Wheaton, Illinois. For the preacher, this is well worth the money. See the series PTW. Compare with Ryken.

★ Miller, Patrick D. ‡ *The Ten Commandments* (I) 2009. An extremely valuable work, especially for students of OT theology and ethics. The author long taught an ethics course at Princeton Seminary based on his research on the Decalogue. Of special note are the length of this exposition (477pp including indexes) and the exploration of "the interplay and resonance of the Commandments with many other texts" (p.xi) in Scripture. Academically oriented pastors will receive much stimulation reading Miller. [*JSOT-BL* 2010; *JETS* 9/10].

★ Ryken, Philip G. *Written in Stone: The Ten Commandments and Today's Moral Crisis*, 2008. A lively, penetrating series of sermons with both theological depth and excellent application to the Church.

✓ Aaron, David H. ‡ *Etched in Stone: The Emergence of the Decalogue*, 2006. A quite critical interpretation, dating the Law late (Persian era), issued by T&T Clark. Regrettably, there is little discussion of the text itself. The scholarship is of a high order. [*RelSRev* 9/09; *JSOT-BL* 2007].

Barclay, William. ‡ *The Ten Commandments for Today*, 1973. Suggestive, and reprinted by WJK in 1998.

☆ Braaten, Carl E., and Christopher R. Seitz (eds). ‡ *I Am the Lord Your God: Christian Reflections on the Ten Commandments*, 2005. Though it is somewhat critically oriented, evangelicals would benefit greatly from reading this book. The authors are mainly theologians instead of biblical scholars. [*RTR* 8/08; *Them* 1/06; *ExpTim* 5/06; *SJT* 63.2].

✓ Brown, William P. (ed). ‡ *The Ten Commandments: The Reciprocity of Faithfulness*, 2004. This fascinating collection includes a few of the writings of Church Fathers and the Reformers, as well as essays from many contemporary OT scholars, theologians, and ethicists. [*CBQ* 10/05; *ExpTim* 2/06, 7/06; *CurTM* 8/06; *JSOT-BL* 2007].

☆ Calvin, John. *Sermons on the Ten Commandments*, ET 1980. The Farley translation published by Baker is reprinted every so often, but may now be o/p. [*WTJ* Spr 82]. Few people are aware of how massive an exposition Calvin published in his *Commentaries on the Last Four Books of Moses*; see vol. 1, pp.338–502; vol. 2, pp.5–472; and vol. 3, pp.5–201.

Clines, David J.A. ‡ "The Ten Commandments, Reading from Left to Right" (pp.26–45), in *Interested Parties: The Ideology of Writers and Readers of the Hebrew Bible* (JSOTSup), 1995. An influential denial of the Ten Words' revelatory character.

☆ Clowney, Edmund. *How Jesus Transforms the Ten Commandments*, 2007. A fresh, biblical-theological reading by the late President of Westminster Seminary in Philadelphia. Pastors and thoughtful Christians will relish this.

✓ Collins, R.F. ‡ "The Ten Commandments" in *ABD*, vol. 6.

Davidman, Joy. *Smoke on the Mountain*, 1953.

Freedman, David Noel. ‡ *The Nine Commandments*, 2000. A more popular 217-page study by one of America's most highly-esteemed Jewish Bible scholars. Conservatively critical.

✓ Harrelson, Walter. ‡ *The Ten Commandments and Human Rights*, 1980.

Heidelberg Catechism (1563), Questions 92–115. See also Ursinus' *Commentary on the Catechism* which has been reprinted by P&R.

Horton, Michael S. *The Law of Perfect Freedom*, 2nd ed 2004. Another good Reformed exposition.

Kuntz, Paul G. *The Ten Commandments in History: Mosaic Paradigms for a Well-Ordered Society*, 2004. Treats the Decalogue within the history of ideas.

Mohler, R. Albert. *Words from the Fire*, 2009. A Moody Press book, with a Reformed tone, strongly pressing the ethical claims of the Gospel.

Morgan, G. Campbell. *The Ten Commandments,* 1901.

✓ Nielson, E. ‡ *The Ten Commandments in New Perspective*, 1968.

Packer, J.I. *Keeping the Ten Commandments*, 2008.

Phillips, A. ‡ *Essays on Biblical Law*, 2002. His dissertation was published as *Ancient Israel's Criminal Law: A New Approach to the Decalogue*, 1970.

Rooker, Mark. *The Ten Commandments: Ethics for the Twenty-first Century*, 2010. I have yet to see this B&H publication. See Rooker's earlier work on Leviticus and Ezekiel.

✓ Segal, B.Z. (ed). ‡ *The Ten Commandments in History and Tradition*, ET 1990. These collected essays are worth looking up. The book is published by Magnes Press in Israel.

✓ Stamm, Johan Jakob, and Maurice E. Andrew. ‡ *The Ten Commandments in Recent Research*, 1967.

Wallace, R. S. *The Ten Commandments*, 1965. One could wish for a reprint.

☆ Watson, Thomas. *The Ten Commandments*, 1692. A classic Puritan exposition of the Decalogue (and the Westminster Assembly's Catechism on the Commandments,

WLC Questions 100–48) which is regularly reprinted by Banner of Truth. These same 200 pages are also found in the larger work, *A Body of Divinity*, also being kept in print by Banner. Watson's approximate dates were 1620–89.

Willimon, William, and Stanley Hauerwas. *The Truth About God: The Ten Commandments in Christian Life*, 1999. Engaging the debate in American religious circles, the Duke professors argue that the Decalogue does not present a set of "timeless ethical principles that are applicable to all." Rather, it guides the Church community toward holiness. Cf. Kuntz's argument.

NOTES: (1) Commentaries on the Book of Deuteronomy (ch. 5) will be quite useful—for example, in comparing the theology of the 4th Commandment in Exodus 20:11 with Deuteronomy 5:15. Weinfeld has nearly 100pp on the "Ten Words." (2) The evangelical debate over the role of the Law in the Christian life can be followed in Stanley Gundry (ed), *Five Views on Law and Gospel*, 1996, and Donald Alexander (ed), *Christian Spirituality: Five Views on Sanctification*, 1988.

LEVITICUS

★ **Gane, Roy.** *Leviticus, Numbers* (NIVAC) 2004. I have not had much opportunity to review this volume, but what I have read is well researched and helpful. Gane is an able scholar, interested in religious rituals, who has published an important study of the Israelite sacrificial system, especially the חטאת "purification offering" (*Cult and Character*, 2005) [*CBQ* 1/07; *BBR* 17.2; *JBL* Fall 06; *JAOS* 127.2; *JSOT-BL* 2007]. All the time he spent studying the Hebrew text of these two books under Professor Milgrom prepared him well to comment on them. More space in this volume is devoted to Leviticus than Numbers; similarly the commentary on Leviticus is the stronger. Gane teaches at Andrews University, a Seventh Day Adventist school. Both students and preachers will benefit from Gane.

★ **Hartley, John.** (WBC) 1992. A workmanlike exegesis of the Hebrew—superb complement to Wenham for the more studious. Has a full discussion of the text (nearly 500pp), and a judicious introduction (55pp), dealing with the revolutionary trends in Pentateuchal criticism. More conservative than most of the other WBC volumes on the Pentateuch. My first pick (but my academic bent may be coming to the fore at this point)! The average pastor would probably want to start with Rooker or Wenham. If you are more the advanced student type, want a rigorous technical commentary, have lots of money, and can speed-read, the best choice is doubtless Milgrom's AB set as a supplement to Hartley. Students should also look up Kiuchi. [*SwJT* Sum 94].

★ Mathews, Kenneth. *Leviticus: Holy God, Holy People* (PTW) 2009. This volume is near 300pp and should be of good help to the expositor. From what I've seen, this manageable homiletical treatment is the equal of Gane and Ross and replaces Tidballs's excellent commentary on my "buy list." See Mathews' two-vol. NAC on Genesis.

★ **Rooker, Mark F.** *Leviticus* (NAC) 2000. This is a fine piece of work, nearly as good as Wenham (who is better on ch. 16) and more up to date. Rooker would even be a good first purchase. This fellow did a Brandeis dissertation on Ezekiel's language and is fully convinced we Christians need to reconsider the theological significance of the OT priestly office. Note that there is a Dispensationalist orientation to the commentary. [*JETS* 3/02; *SwJT* Fall 01; *F&M* Fall 01].

★ Ross, Allen P. *Holiness to the Lord*. 2002. Much in the same mold as his exposition of Genesis, entitled *Creation and Blessing*. Ross is a fine preacher's help to set alongside Gane. Expositors who love Reformed theology and old books should also consider Bonar, while I regard Balentine as by far the best theological interpretation from the moderately critical side. [*CBQ* 7/03; *Them* Aut 04; *JETS* 6/03; *Interp* 4/03; *JSOT* 27.5].

★ **Wenham, Gordon J.** (NICOT) 1979. Excellent in every way! Especially helpful for its theological insight. Both Stuart and Longman have called this the best. Was certainly your first choice before Hartley and Rooker came along; compare them. I really like all three. [*JBL* 100.4 (1981); *EvQ* 1/81; *JETS* 12/80]. Many will find a subsequent Wenham article instructive: "The Theology of Unclean Food," *EvQ* 53 (1981): 6–15.

F Anderson, Gary. ‡ (Herm).

F Averbeck, Richard. (EEC).

F Baker, David W. (CorBC). To be bound with Numbers and Deuteronomy.

Bailey, Lloyd R. ‡ *Leviticus–Numbers* (S&H) 2005. There is some exegetical value here, if one is seeking to consult a non-technical, moderately critical commentary. Many will turn to Bailey more for ideas on how the message of these Bible texts can relate to today's world. I do not judge it to be one of the better volumes in the series or a good value for the money. [*Interp* 7/06].

✓ **Balentine, Samuel E.** ‡ (I) 2002. This author was chosen for his interest and expertise in scholarship on the "rituals of faith" and ancient Hebrew worship. See *The Torah's Vision of Worship*, 1999 [*Interp* 7/01; *JSS* Spr 02; *JR* 4/02]. Though not so lengthy (220pp), this theological exposition repays study. Younger evangelicals generally, with a growing aversion to anything that smacks of ritual or liturgy, should be prompted here to do more careful, balanced thinking about the relation of their faith to the forms of biblical worship. Balentine teaches at Baptist Theological Seminary in Richmond, Virginia. For a more conservative approach to OT ritual, see Gane. I pass along Jenson's recommendation that pastors consider Balentine, now (8/2010) his favorite exposition. [*ExpTim* 11/03; *JSOT* 28.5; *RelSRev* 4/04; *Interp* 1/05; *JHebS*].

☆ Beckwith, Roger T., and Martin J. Selman (eds). *Sacrifice in the Bible*, 1995. Superb conservative essays. For background reading on the rituals and theology of Leviticus, see especially the essays of Jenson and Wenham.

☆ Bellinger, William. [𝓜], *Leviticus, Numbers* (NIBC) 2001. The theology Bellinger draws from these Bible books is more conservative than his views on compositional history (final form in post-exilic times). The commentary is well-written by a mature, conservatively critical Baptist professor at Baylor. [*BBR* 14.1].

☆ Bonar Andrew A. (GS) 1846. A lovely devotional and theological exposition by one of the godliest ministers Scotland ever knew. Heavy on typology, but not irresponsible. Exegesis should be checked against Wenham, Rooker and Hartley. If you love Puritan-style commentaries, you will relish this.

Boyce, Richard N. ‡ *Leviticus and Numbers* (WestBC) 2008.

✓ **Budd, Philip J.** ‡ (NCB) 1996. This work takes a more traditional literary critical approach, employing source and form criticism to understand the text. Students will profit from consulting Budd, but the pastor will find a more reliable and theologically sensitive exegesis in Wenham and Hartley. This commentary replaces Snaith. For more comments on Budd, see Numbers below. [*BL* 1997; *ExpTim* 10/96; *Them* 1/97; *JETS* 12/99; *JBL* Spr 98; *JSS* Aut 98; *CBQ* 1/98; *BSac* 4/97; *HebStud* 1998; *RelSRev* 7/97].

Bush, George. 1857. See under Exodus.

☆ **Calvin, John.** *Harmony of the Pentateuch* (Calvin) 1563. See under Exodus.

☆ Currid, John D. (EPSC) 2004. See his other similar volumes on Genesis and Exodus, which are arguably more successful efforts than this one (398pp). This is still a very good book for pastors who want to recover for the pulpit this neglected portion of the OT. [*RTR* 8/06; *BSac* 1/07].

✓ Day, John (ed). ‡ *Temple and Worship in Biblical Israel*, 2007. Top-notch scholarship on the topic.

☆ Demarest, Gary W. (WCC) 1990. Written by an evangelical PCUSA minister, this exposition is better researched than many others in the OT series.

✓ Douglas, Mary. ‡ *Purity and Danger*, 1966. To this seminal study of the "Priestly conception of holiness" many more have been added. Douglas has also written *Implicit Meanings*, 1975; *Leviticus as Literature*, 1999 [*BSac* 10/03]; and *Jacob's Tears: The Priestly Work of Reconciliation*, 2004. Her interdisciplinary efforts [*JR* 4/09] have encouraged many others to study these matters, especially through an anthropological approach, and there has been an explosion of work on Leviticus in the last 30 years. Note that Douglas' work has sparked a fair amount of controversy.

✓ **Gerstenberger, Erhard S.** ‡ (OTL) 1993, ET 1996. A significant exegetical commentary, originally for the ATD series (Das Alte Testament Deutsch), to be consulted by students. Takes a standard critical line on most interpretive issues, dating the book in the post-exilic period. The author is a prominent form critic, best known for his work on Psalms. This volume replaces Noth in the series. [*CBQ* 10/94; *BL* 1994; *JETS* 12/99; *JSOT* 65, 79; *Interp* 10/99; *HebStud* 1999; *CRBR* 1995; *RelSRev* 1/98; *JR* 10/98].

✓ **Gorman, Frank.** ‡ (ITC) 1997. Not as critically oriented as some others in this series, this ITC is both well written and well researched. He has an interest in the approach of "ritual studies" and the idea of "enactment"; see his volume *The Ideology of Ritual: Space, Time and Status in the Priestly Theology* (1990). Though a slim work of about 150pp, this commentary is not so popularly-styled and does not cater to the needs and interests of church people and pastors quite like some other volumes in the series. [*CBQ* 4/99; *HebStud* 41; *Interp* 10/99; *CTJ* 4/99; *RelSRev* 1/99; *JSOT-BL* 1999].

✓ Haran, M. ‡ *Temples and Temple-Service in Ancient Israel*, 1978.

Harris, R. Laird. (EBC) 1990. Quite brief at only 150pp (including NIV text). By the way, Harris was the translator of Leviticus for the NIV. He passed away in April 2008. See Hess below for the replacement series.

☆ Harrison, R.K. (TOTC) 1980. Brief and no competition to Wenham, but has been helpful and handy (252pp). Do not discard. This used to be fourth down the priority list. [*RTR* 9/81; *JBL* 102.1 (1983); *EvQ* 7/82].

☆ **Hess, Richard.** (EBCR) 2008. This volume also covers Genesis (Sailhamer) and Exodus (Kaiser) and is a big improvement on the old EBC. From what I have seen in these 265pp, and on the basis of the author's past work, I judge that this may possibly be the best briefer evangelical exegesis of Leviticus now available. [*JSOT-BL* 2010]. See also the Hess volume on *Israelite Religions*, 2007 [*WTJ* Spr 09; *BSac* 1/09; *Interp* 7/09; *HBT* 30.2; *VT* 60.2; *BASOR* 2/09], regarded as the standard evangelical treatment of the topic.

F Hutton, Rodney R. ‡ (FOTL).

✓ Jenson Philip P. [*M*], *Graded Holiness: A Key to the Priestly Conception of the World*, 1992. A highly regarded, conservatively-critical study which can placed alongside the Douglas work. Jenson teaches at Ridley Hall, Cambridge and is writing a new edition of the "OT Guides" volume on Leviticus, replacing Grabbe (1993).

☆ **Kaiser, Walter.** (NewIB) 1994. It is something of a surprise to see an evangelical writing for the *New Interpreter's Bible*, but Abingdon Press, it seems, wanted to cast a wider net than with the old IB. Kaiser is better here than on Exodus. Because this NewIB volume also contains sterling theological commentaries on Genesis by Fretheim, and on Exodus by Brueggemann, you would not go wrong buying it (if you don't mind the more liberal theology). Kaiser's contribution, perhaps by design, is briefer (a bit over 200pp) than Fretheim (350pp) or Brueggemann (over 300pp). [*PSB* 16.3 (1995); *CBQ* 4/96; *JETS* 9/96].

✓ Keil, C.F. (KD) ET 1864. See under Genesis.

☆ Kellogg, S.H. (EB) 1891. Has been reprinted by Klock & Klock and by Kregel (1988). A good exposition which a pastor could put to good use if he has the funds and shelf space. The typological interpretation here is more restrained than Bonar's.

☆ **Kiuchi, Nobuyoshi.** (Apollos) 2007. This author has written *A Study of Ḥāṭā* and *Ḥāṭṭā't in Leviticus 4–5* (2003), a revision of *The Purification Offering in the Priestly Literature* (1987), which received good reviews. It needs to be mentioned, however, that Kiuchi's research on *ḥāṭā* (חטא) is revisionist; he argues the root term means "to hide oneself" and not "to sin" in the sense of transgressing a moral code. For a critique see Leigh M. Trevaskis, "On a Recent 'Existential' Translation of *ḥāṭā*," *VT* 59.2 (2009): 313–19. This commentary will stimulate discussion among scholars and reflection among academically-oriented pastors. Some of the exegesis here is insightful, but this volume should not replace Wenham and Hartley on the preacher's shelf. It seems less dependable exegetically and theologically— e.g., he speaks of the people at Sinai as "yet unredeemed" (p.28)—than is required to be on the "recommended" list. For some rather eccentric interpretation, see his exploration of the rationale for, and symbolism behind, the clean/unclean distinction (pp.207–10). Students must take account of Kiuchi's work which interacts with so much current scholarship. Kiuchi takes a strong stand in defending Mosaic authorship. [*JSOT-BL* 2008; *JETS* 3/08].

✓ **Kleinig, John W.** (Concord) 2003. This 610-page Lutheran commentary I have not had much opportunity to use. It is reputed to be a strong representative of the series, well-informed by scholarship (Kleinig earned a PhD at Cambridge) and strictly adhering to a Lutheran interpretation. See the valuable sections on "Fulfillment by Christ." [*CBQ* 4/07; *CJ* 7/05].

☆ Knight, G.A.F. ‡ (DSB) 1981. Very rewarding in places for theology, but hampered by format and space restrictions. Moderately critical. [*EvQ* 1/84; *JETS* 6/84].

✓ **Levine, Baruch.** ‡ (JPS) 1989. Covers this Bible book in 284pp. Scholars often read Levine and Milgrom side-by-side for both Leviticus and Numbers. OT specialists have a high regard for Levine because "in philology he is nonpareil" (Milgrom, p.2438). See Numbers below. [*JR* 1/95; *CRBR* 1991; *HebStud* 1994 (Wenham)].

✓ Lienhard, Joseph T. (ed). *Exodus, Leviticus, Numbers, Deuteronomy* (ACCS) 2001. See under Exodus.

☆ Longman, Tremper. *Immanuel in Our Place: Christ in Israel's Worship*, 2001. A huge help to the preacher with its redemptive-historical interpretations of OT religion and worship rituals; that theological approach to this Bible material is not well represented in the literature. [*Them* Aut 02; *JETS* 6/03; *F&M* Spr 03; *CJ* 7/05].

Mays, James L. ‡ (Layman's Bible Commentary) 1963. Brief and popular. This work used to be noted often in commentary surveys, but there are now many more valuable tools available.

✓ **Milgrom, Jacob.** ‡ (AB) 3 Vols., 1991–2001. Call this the leading critical work. Evidently the author set out write the most exhaustive and exhausting commentary on Leviticus ever published. The three volumes total over 2700pp, with indexes and bibliography included. This is a fairly technical work by one of the foremost Jewish Pentateuchal scholars. Though he does engage in diachronic source and redaction criticism (P_1, P_2, P_3, H, etc.), he is more interested in the final form of the text. This book would have been much shorter had he not purposed to provide a catalog of medieval Jewish comment. He is pulling some of OT scholarship in a rightward direction (e.g., his arguments for "P" being earlier). Students will certainly look this up, but very few pastors will purchase this monumental set, which was the crowning achievement of Milgrom's long career. Thankfully, the next entry makes his learning available to a wider audience, including busy pastors. Two caveats: do not follow him in his interpretations of 17:11 (see Emile Nicole's chapter in Hill/James, *The Glory of the Atonement*, 2004) or of the proscription of homosexual activity (see www.robgagnon.net/articles/homoMilgrom.pdf). Note also Milgrom's work on Numbers below. [*JSOT* 12/93; *JBL* Sum 93; *VT* 1/94; *Biblica* 74.2 (1993); *CBQ* 1/03; *JTS* 4/02; *Interp* 4/02; *BSac* 7/02; *JSOT* 99 (2002); *AsTJ*, Spr 03; *JR* 7/03; *CurTM* 12/02; *HebStud* 2004; *JHebS*; *RBL*].

✓ **Milgrom, Jacob.** ‡ (ContC) 2004. This distillation of the AB is a welcome addition to the literature. He covers Leviticus in 344pp. [*Chm* Aut 05; *JETS* 9/05; *JSOT-BL* 2005; *SwJT* Fall 04; *RelSRev* 1/06; *JHebS*; *BSac* 4/08; *ExpTim* 12/05; *Anvil* 22.4].

✓ Miller, Patrick D. ‡ *The Religion of Ancient Israel*, 2000. Though not a commentary, this volume is highly instructive and generally dependable for the student researching this key topic in Leviticus. For the evangelical student or preacher who puzzles over how to approach the latter half of Exodus and the book of Leviticus, this book will provide a store of information. See also Longman above. [*Them* Spr 02; *JTS* 4/02; *JETS* 6/03; *JBL* Spr 02; *Interp* 1/02; *ThTo* 7/01; *SwJT* Sum 02; *BBR* 13.1; *DenvJ* (Hess); *Anvil* 18.4]. Compare with the Hess and Zevit major works.

☆ **Noordtzij, A.** [𝓜], (BSC) ET 1982. There is some depth of insight to Noordtzij's commentaries (see Numbers as well). Though he confronts the school of Wellhausen, there are still remnants of critical thought here. (Can one trace the influence of J.P.E. Pedersen?) Overall, a fine work which you could add to your library, if you are fascinated by Leviticus and found this o/p volume in a secondhand shop.

✓ **Noth, Martin.** ‡ (retired OTL) ET 1965, rev. 1977. Thorough in its old-style literary critical discussion. He disassembles the text and treats the text exclusively from the historical angle. There is hardly any theology in this o/p volume. See under Exodus. Noth has been replaced in the series by Gerstenberger above.

Porter, J.R. ‡ (CBC) 1976.

Radnor, Ephraim. (Brazos) 2008. I have not had occasion to use this. [*JETS* 6/09; *CBQ* 4/09; *Them* 4/09; *RBL*; *JSOT-BL* 2009].

✓ Rendtorff, Rolf, and Robert Kugler (eds). ‡ *The Book of Leviticus: Composition and Reception*, 2003. [*JSOT* 28.5; *RelSRev* 1/06].

✓ Römer, Thomas (ed). ‡ *The Books of Leviticus and Numbers*, 2008. Another huge volume of essays from the Colloquium Biblicum Lovaniense. [*JSOT-BL* 2009; *JTS* 4/10; *ExpTim* 5/10; *ETL* 86.1; *JHebS* 2009].

✓ Sherwood, Stephen K. ‡ *Leviticus, Numbers, Deuteronomy* (BO) 2002. This is one of the less successful volumes in the series. Sherwood seeks to cover a huge amount of biblical material in about 300pp, and the results are, shall we say, sketchy. There is some data here for students to work with, but nothing of substance for the pastor. [*JETS* 6/03; *Interp* 4/03; *JSOT* 27.5; *RelSRev* 7/03].

F Sklar, Jay. (TOTC replacement). His published dissertation, *Sin, Impurity, Atonement: The Priestly Conceptions* (2005) [*CBQ* 10/07; *Them* 1/07; *TJ* Spr 07; *RelSRev* 1/07; *JETS* 9/08; *JSOT-BL* 2007], written under Gordon Wenham, leads us to expect a fine replacement volume. See Harrison above.

✓ Snaith, N.H. ‡ (retired NCB) 1967. Covers Numbers as well. Critical and tends to be more academic and technical in its approach to the text than other contributions to the series. Snaith had a well established reputation as a linguist, in part because of his several volumes of study notes on the Hebrew text published by Epworth.

☆ Tidball, Derek. (BST) 2005. With a fairly full contribution to the series (327pp), Tidball does well in delivering a readable exposition of the message of the book. He focuses on the topic of holy relationships, first of all between God and his people, and then secondly in human relationships among the Israelites. He also helps the preacher by exploring Christological and other NT connections. [*Chm* Aut 08; *JSOT-BL* 2006; *ExpTim* 1/07].

☆ Vasholz, Robert I. (Mentor) 2007. This exegetical and expositional work is 372pp., and I regret I have not seen it. One reviewer [*WTJ* Fall 09] commends the fine points of exegesis but wishes for a clearer view of the big picture and a more nuanced approach to typology. Vasholz writes that "an allegorical approach assumes that these laws were basically to teach spiritual lessons" (p.143), and in rejecting allegory he appears reluctant to draw out the lessons. As his former student I am certain Vasholz will be very useful to preachers.

✓ Vaux, Roland de. ‡ *Ancient Israel: Religious Institutions*, ET 1968. Not a commentary, but a valuable monograph on Israel's religious leadership and worship as prescribed in Leviticus.

F Watts, James W. ‡ (HCOT). Some preliminary work is published as *Ritual and Rhetoric in Leviticus*, 2007 [*ExpTim* 4/09; *VT* 59.2; *JSS* Spr 10; *VT* 59.2; *JSS* Aut 10].

✓ Willis, Timothy M. ‡ (AOTC) 2009. A compact (241pp), moderately critical exegesis with less attention to theological matters, Willis will be more useful to students than to pastors. Jenson terms it "now one of the best introductory commentaries." [*JETS* 12/09; *JSOT-BL* 2010 (Jenson)].

F Yoder, Perry. (BCBC).

✓ Zevit, Ziony. *The Religions of Ancient Israel: A Parallactic Approach*, 2001. Hess calls this tome "the most complete inventory of the relevant data on the history of ancient Israelite religion yet available" (*Israelite Religions*, 77). [*DenvJ* 1/02].

—⟋w⟍—

NUMBERS

★ **Ashley, Timothy R.** (NICOT) 1993. This huge commentary (650pp) from a professor at Acadia Divinity College, Nova Scotia, gives the Hebrew text almost as much attention as Harrison. Those wanting a more in-depth work than Wenham could make Ashley their first choice. Includes some excellent theological reflection on this Bible book. Compare with Cole's NAC and with Harrison, which are both more conservative. [*JR* 4/95; *SwJT* Spr 98; *BSac* 10/94].

★ **Cole, R. Dennis.** (NAC) 2000. The author teaches at New Orleans Baptist Seminary, where he also earned his doctorate. This is a full work (550pp), especially concerned with structural matters. Too many scholars in the past have considered Numbers to be a catchall with a disorganized conglomeration of material. While it is true that the "generic variety that characterizes Numbers surpasses that of any other book of the Bible" (Milgrom, p.xiii), there is an inner cohesiveness found by more recent commentators like Milgrom and Olson. Cole joins them in seeking to integrate the materials in Numbers. Cole has worked hard to produce this work and he gives copious citations of others' research. On the negative side, this author is less well versed in biblical theological interpretation (cf. Duguid, Sakenfeld), and more finely-tuned narrative criticism (à la Alter, Sternberg, Bar-Efrat, etc.). Cole's literary observations sometimes lack an interpretive/theological pay-off. Also, Cole's writing style can be awkward and lacking organization. (For examples I refer to p.36, which has section three begin with subsection eight [editor's goof?], and which also has several sentences which I re-read repeatedly without clear understanding.) Students will consult Cole for his more up-to-date bibliographies and comments on structure. Many pastors, too, will appreciate Cole, but I still prefer Ashley as a large-scale conservative commentary. Longman gives Cole the highest rating: five stars. [*JETS* 6/02; *RelSRev* 7/02]. See also Cole below.

★ Duguid, Iain M. (PTW) 2006. I have not found any better expositional guide than this. There is good scholarly exegesis (in the background), stimulating biblical theological reflection, and searching application for the people of God today. Those scouting for still more preaching helps should consider Philip (previously on my recommended list), Sakenfeld, Olson, Brown, Gane, and Keddie.

★ **Milgrom, Jacob.** ‡ (JPS) 1990. This is an extraordinary, learned Jewish commentary which mainly treats the "final form" of the text. Every student doing careful research on Numbers should consult this work (520pp), described by Wenham [*BSB* 12/96] as "much the most stimulating historical-critical commentary." Quite expensive. A pastor with the money and wish to build a first-class exegetical library will buy Milgrom or Levine (I much prefer JPS). If you're less the scholarly type, skip this purchase or replace it with either an exegetical work (Harrison, Allen) or a good exposition (Brown). See also my comments on Milgrom under Leviticus. [*CRBR* 1992; *CBQ* 1/93; *VT* 1/94; *HebStud* 1995].

★ **Wenham, Gordon J.** (TOTC) 1981. Wenham is easy to read, very insightful, and adds real luster to the series. In short compass you can't do any better. This used to be the hands-down first choice, not only because of its excellence but also because there was pretty much nothing else. Now we are swamped with worthy commentaries; this often neglected book is now one of the best served. The evangelical pastor still does well to start with Wenham, and not just because it's easier on the pocketbook either. Stuart's first pick. [*TJ* Fall 82]. Also, don't miss Wenham's "Old Testament Guides" volume, 1997 [*JSOT* 79; *CBQ* 7/99; *DenvJ*].

☆ **Allen, Ronald B.** (EBC) 1990. A well-known, respected scholar, Allen goes into much greater depth (350pp) than the others in this volume. His hard work shows. I would like to have included this work above as a recommended purchase. Cole builds upon Allen's work, which goes all the way back to a strong Dallas Seminary dissertation, *The Theology of the Balaam Oracles: A Pagan Diviner and the Word of God*, 1973.

F Allen, Ronald B. (EBCR). Do look for this.

Bailey, Lloyd R. ‡ *Leviticus–Numbers* (S&H) 2005. See Leviticus.

F Baker, David. (BCBC).

☆ Bellinger, William. ‡ *Leviticus, Numbers* (NIBC) 2001. See Leviticus.

Binns, L. Elliot. ‡ (Westminster) 1927.

Boyce, Richard N. *Leviticus and Numbers* (WestBC) 2008.

☆ Brown, Raymond. (BST) 2002. This stands alongside his exposition of Deuteronomy in the same series and will be of very good service to the evangelical preacher. [*Them* Sum 03; *JSOT* 27.5; *Evangel* Spr 03].

F   Brueggemann, Dale A. (CorBC).

✓   **Budd, Philip J.** ‡ (WBC) 1984. Well-written and of value to students with interests in diachronic criticism, the history of interpretation, and bibliography. The first of the recent spate of academic commentaries on Numbers providing an exacting exegesis of the Hebrew text. The others build on Budd's work. One could wish he didn't take such a skeptical view of Numbers as history. Hardly any theology. This tome is for scholars, is something of a missed opportunity, and is scheduled to be replaced by John Sailhamer (a considerably more conservative scholar). [*RTR* 9/85; *EvQ* 7/87; *JBL* 106.1 (1987); *JETS* 12/85; *HebStud* 1987].

☆   **Calvin, John.** *Harmony of the Pentateuch* (Calvin) 1563. See under Exodus.

F   Cole, R. Dennis. (EEC).

✓   **Davies, Eryl W.** ‡ (NCB) 1995. This is a sizable contribution (lxxiv + 378pp) to the series, but I am disappointed by its skepticism and its hermeneutical approach which is too narrowly concerned with historical critical issues. That said, Davies is better than many others that run down that diachronic track. He long taught at the University of Wales. [*ExpTim* 2/96; *Them* 10/96; *JETS* 6/98; *JSS* Aut 97; *JTS* 10/97; *JSOT* 74; *CBQ* 7/97; *RTR* 9/96; *BSac* 1/97; *HebStud* 1997; *RelSRev* 1/97].

    Douglas, Mary. ‡ *In the Wilderness: The Doctrine of Defilement in the Book of Numbers*, 1993. The author is best known for her decades-long anthropological research on Leviticus. [*BSac* 10/03].

✓   **Dozeman, Thomas B.** ‡ (NewIB) 1998. The author is a noted exegete and theologian, who has done fine critical work on the exodus and wilderness "traditions." E.g. *God at War: Power in the Exodus Tradition* (Oxford, 1996). See Dozeman under Exodus. [*ExpTim* 1/99].

F   Elwolde, John F. ‡ (HCOT). This are conflicting announcements; see Gosling.

    Erdman, Charles R. 1952. Once a notable exposition, because there were few on Numbers during his time. Erdman can be suggestive to the preacher.

☆   Gane, Roy. *Leviticus/Numbers* (NIVAC) 2004. Well worth buying, especially for pastors. See Leviticus.

F   Gosling, Frank A. ‡ (HCOT). See Elwolde above.

✓   **Gray, George B.** ‡ (ICC) 1903. This was long the standard reference work for scholars, particularly for its source critical discussion. It is still widely consulted, though none today considers it authoritative in technical matters.

☆   **Harrison, R.K.** (was WEC) 1990. With dependable work on the Hebrew text, this is one of the most valuable evangelical works on Numbers, written by the then general editor of NICOT. Readers will find it to be a well-rounded commentary treating grammatical, historical, and theological issues. One could wish that a bibliography had been appended to this worthy commentary of 452pp. This was reprinted by Baker in 1992 and more recently by Biblical Studies Press. [*EvQ* 7/94; *JETS* 5/95; *RTR* 9/95; *CTJ* 4/95; *CBQ* 7/94].

☆   Keddie, Gordon J. *According to Promise* (WCS) 1992.

✓   Keil, Carl F. (KD) ET 1864. Was long an important resource. See under Genesis.

✓   **Knierim, Rolf P., and George W. Coats.** ‡ (FOTL) 2005. The same pair are responsible for the latter half of Exodus in the series. This volume is mainly for advanced students interested in form criticism. [*RTR* 4/06; *CBQ* 10/05; *JTS* 10/07; *JETS* 3/06; *BSac* 7/06; *JSS* Spr 08; *JSOT-BL* 2006; *VT* 57.4; *RelSRev* 4/06; *RBL*].

✓   Lee, Won W. [𝕸], *Punishment and Forgiveness in Israel's Migratory Campaign*, 2003. An important discussion of the structure and cohesiveness of Numbers 10:11–36:13, applying the synchronic "conceptual analysis" method of Lee's Claremont doctoral supervisor, Rolf Knierim. [*WTJ* Fall 04; *JETS* 3/05; *JTS* 10/05; *Them* Win 05; *JBL* Win 04; *JSS* Spr 06; *JNES* 4/08].

✓ **Levine, Baruch**. ‡ (AB) 2 Vols., 1993–2000. A massive exegesis (about 1100pp), like so many recent AB volumes—former editor Freedman leading the way. This work from a Jewish, critical scholar is similar to Milgrom's above, though more in-depth and diachronic in its approach to the text, and providing more discussion of the ANE context. My strong preference is for Milgrom. See Levine on Leviticus. [*PSB* 15.2 (1994); *CBQ* 1/95; *JR* 1/95; *JSS* Spr 95; *ExpTim* 5/01; *JTS* 10/01; *JETS* 6/02; *VT* 53.1; *JSOT* 94 (2001); good trenchant reviews are *CBQ* 7/01 and *Interp* 10/01].

✓ Lienhard, Joseph T. (ed). *Exodus, Leviticus, Numbers, Deuteronomy* (ACCS) 2001. See under Exodus.

Maarsingh, B. ‡ (T&I) 1987.

F MacDonald, Nathan. (THC).

Mays, James L. ‡ (Layman's Bible Commentary) 1963. See Leviticus above.

✓ **Noordtzij, A.** (BSC) ET 1983. See Leviticus above. [*JETS* 6/84].

✓ **Noth, Martin**. ‡ (OTL) ET 1968. Thorough from his particular historical critical slant, but theologically sterile. Reprinted a few years ago in pb. See also his works on Exodus and Leviticus for OTL. [*JBL* 88.2 (1969)].

☆ **Olson, Dennis T.** ‡ (I) 1996. I imagine that Olson, Sakenfeld and Dozeman would be the expositions of Numbers recommended in mainline seminaries. There is much to be learned from Olson; his work here for the "Interpretation" series is no breezy homiletical treatment. He presents some of the fruit of his previous research contained in *The Death of the Old and the Birth of the New: The Framework of the Book of Numbers and the Pentateuch* (1985), a significant monograph on the book's structure. His well-founded conclusion is that the book's structural move-ment is tied more to the shift from first to second generation than to geography. I would argue that this fine commentary is of far greater use to students than most in the Interpretation series. This is my favorite theological interpretation from the more critical side. "It is written with insight, energy and conviction…the most use-ful for the preacher today," according to Wenham (*BSB* 12/96). [*JETS* 6/98; *BL* 1997; *CBQ* 10/97; *BSac* 10/97; *PSB* 17.3; *RelSRev* 1/97; *RBL*].

☆ Philip, James. (WCC) 1987. A successful effort by the famous evangelical minister of the Holyrood Abbey Church in Edinburgh, Scotland. Lucidly written and excellent for expositors.

Riggans, Walter. ‡ (DSB) 1983. Fuller than many others in the series at 252pp and well written. [*JBL* 104.4].

✓ **Römer, Thomas (ed).** *The Books of Leviticus and Numbers*, 2008. See Leviticus.

F Sailhamer, John. (WBC replacement). Budd wrote the initial WBC. Lately, Nelson is not showing a proposed release date. Watch for this.

☆ **Sakenfeld, Katherine Doob.** ‡ (ITC) 1995. What I have read here is superbly written and highly theological. The commentary is about 210pp long with indices. This OT professor at Princeton is not a conservative in her views of authorship and date, but she treats the final form of the text. This book is serviceable to the evangelical pastor. [BL 1997; *PSB* 17.2 (1996)].

✓ Sherwood, Stephen K. ‡ *Leviticus, Numbers, Deuteronomy* (BO) 2002. See under Leviticus.

✓ Snaith, N.H. ‡ (retired NCB) 1967. See under Leviticus. Now replaced by Davies.

Stubbs, David L. ‡? (Brazos) 2009. Announced as 272pp, but I have not seen it yet. The author teaches at Western Theological Seminary and is ordained in the PC(USA). [*JSOT-BL* 2010].

Sturdy, John. ‡ (CBC) 1976.

F   Weinfeld, Moshe. ‡ (Herm). I had expected he would finish the AB set on Deuteronomy before publishing on Numbers. This will certainly need to be reassigned after Weinfeld's recent death. See Deuteronomy.

DEUTERONOMY

★   **Craigie, Peter C.** (NICOT) 1976. For its time, this was a substantial and accurate exegesis from an exceptional Hebraist (see his translation). Craigie used to be the pastor's first pick for careful work with the English text and help in understanding the covenant treaty background of Deuteronomy. But we have long lacked a full-length evangelical treatment of the Hebrew, which McConville has now at last partially supplied. Note: Craigie can be a bit dry, so pastors have wanted an expositional work like C. Wright alongside. Years ago, Craigie was Stuart's and Longman's favorite. Scholarly pastors, who want to add an in-depth exegetical work alongside these suggested works, will likely pick Weinfeld or Tigay. [*EvQ* 10/77; *JBL* 6/78].

★   **McConville, J. Gordon.** (Apollos) 2002. This was an excellent assignment. See the author's dissertation, *Law and Theology in Deuteronomy* (1984) [*HebStud* 1988]—well worth reading by the way—for evidence of the author's long hard work on Deuteronomy. Perhaps on the negative side, the amount of time McConville has spent in research makes this a deep, cerebral, complicated commentary that the less studious will struggle with. For an exegetical reference, McConville is now my first pick. The commentary was discussed in a symposium, and the record of the scholarly give-and-take is found in *SJT* 56.4. Some conservative reviewers might call this [*M*], mediating. [*Them* Spr 04; *JETS* 6/03; *VT* 54.2; *JSOT* 27.5; *Chm* Win 04; *BSac* 4/04; *Evangel* Spr 03; *Anvil* 20.3].

★   **Miller, Patrick D.** ‡ (I) 1990. Miller is one of the most prominent American OT critics. To those sharing Miller's moderately critical views, this is probably the most valuable theological commentary on the book, rivaled only by Brueggemann and Clements. It is quite readable and covers Deuteronomy in 245pp. [*CBQ* 10/92; *ThTo* 10/91; *BL* 1997].

★   **Wright, Christopher J.H.** (NIBC) 1996. Wright is a leading evangelical scholar; specifically, he is one of the finest OT ethicists in the world. Well-trained at Cambridge, he here delivers a more popularly-styled, theologically-sensitive exposition. A distinctive contribution, according to McConville [*BSB* 6/99], is the commentary's "orientation to missiology, for which Deuteronomy is shown to have interesting and unexpected implications (relevant, incidentally, to the troublesome problem of the book's attitude to the non-Israelite peoples of Canaan)." You won't go wrong if you, as a pastor, make this your first purchase on Deuteronomy. (Disclosure: I may be biased in my assessment, for I count it among the highlights of my family's missions experience to have hosted him for dinner in our African home.) Wright also has a good commentary on Ezekiel. See Block below. [*JSOT* 79 (1998); *CBQ* 7/98; *Chm* 112.2 (1998); *RelSRev* 7/97].

F   Arnold, Bill T. (NICOT replacement). This is probably a very long way off.

Barker, Paul A. *The Triumph of Grace in Deuteronomy*, 2004. [*EuroJTh* 15.1].

Biddle, Mark E. ‡ (S&H) 2003. Over 500pp of clear, attractively presented, theological exposition from a moderately critical perspective. I do not regard this as one of the best books in the series.

F   Block, Daniel I. (NIVAC). Should be of good service to expositors. I expect this work to be quite large for the series and to be released in the near future. Will this be a top pick for pastors? Probably so.

F   Braulik, Georg, and Norbert Lohfink. ‡ (Herm). These brilliant critics have worked for decades on Deuteronomy, and specialists would love to see what they produce. Unfortunately, there's no word of this appearing anytime soon.

☆   Brown, Raymond. (BST) 1993. One of the more sermonic and devotional entries in the series, this volume is fairly full (350pp) and works diligently to apply the message to our day. The scholarship here is not profound. Brown was formerly principal of Spurgeon's College in London and writes as a pastor; he should not be confused with Raymond E. Brown, the distinguished Catholic NT critic. This Brown wrote the BST books on Numbers, Nehemiah, and Hebrews. [*Them* 5/95; *Evangel* Spr 95; *SBET* Aut 96].

☆   **Brueggemann, Walter.** ‡ (AOTC) 2001. See my review of his earlier commentaries on Genesis, Exodus, Samuel, etc. This volume has a bit more exegesis and a lesser amount of high-flying, creative, theological exposition and application than in his contributions to the WJK Interpretation series. [*CBQ* 1/03; *JETS* 12/03; *Interp* 7/02; *ExpTim* 1/03; *VT* 53.2; *JSOT* 99 (2002); *ThTo* 7/02; *RelSRev* 7/03; *Anvil* 19.2].

Cairns, Ian. ‡ (ITC) 1992. One of the better volumes in the series. Along with Miller, Brueggemann, and Clements, one of the best theological commentaries from the critical camp for pastors. [*HebStud* 1994].

☆   **Calvin, John.** *Harmony of the Pentateuch* (Calvin) 1563, ET 1852–55. Gives a great deal of space to the fifth book of Moses. By the way, I would counsel you not to dole out your money for the Banner of Truth reprint, *Sermons Upon Deuteronomie*. I agree with Childs that this 1584 edition is "virtually inaccessible" and really cannot be used as a tool because of its antiquated script and translation. Leave it for the bibliophile with lots of money to spend on an impressive looking library.

✓   **Christensen, Duane L.** *Deuteronomy 1:1–21:9* (WBC) 2001; *Deuteronomy 21:10–34:12* (WBC) 2002. The initial release, *Deuteronomy 1–11* (WBC) 1993, was not so well received, and so Christensen went back to work to expand and defend his approach. The actual amount of commentary in the older volume was less than expected from this series. The new set is much, much fuller (900pp). Christensen calls this Bible book a "didactic poem" (*Deut. 1–11*, p.lx) and is mainly occupied with structural and rhythmical analysis. Academic types will compare this set to other technical commentaries and find Christensen pursuing a different agenda. Pastors will find it slow-going as they plow through a lot of apparently arcane stuff, irrelevant for preaching. Students might be intrigued, however. Reviewers see the new set as an improvement but still question the basic interpretive approach. Take note of his Nahum commentary. [*JETS* 12/03, 5/05; *CBQ* 1/04; *Them* Spr 04; *Interp* 1/04; *JSOT* 27.5; *BBR* 14.2; *BSac* 10/03].

✓   Christensen, Duane L. (ed). ‡ *A Song of Power and the Power of Song: Essays on the Book of Deuteronomy*, 1993. This collection is a resource students should not miss. [*Them* 1/95].

✓   **Clements, Ronald E.** ‡ (NewIB) 1998. The author builds upon his 1969 study of the theological issues: *God's Chosen People*. This NewIB work is seeing a lot of use in mainline circles. [*ExpTim* 1/99]. Following close on its heels was a "Preacher's Commentary" published in 2001 by Epworth [*JSOT* 99; *Anvil* 19.2].

☆ Currid, John D. (EPSC) 2006. This follows his solid, readable commentaries on Genesis, Exodus, and Leviticus. Pastors will find Professor Currid a dependable guide in both exegesis and Reformed theological exposition. [*RTR* 4/09].

✓ **Driver, Samuel R.** ‡ (ICC) 1895. Helpful for minutiae, especially the Hebrew, but there is little interest in theology. This liberal classic was acclaimed as one of the best volumes in the old series and is still consulted often by scholars—"still an indispensable tool," says McConville [*BSB* 6/99].

F Gerbrandt, Gerald. (BCBC).

F Grisanti, Michael. (EBCR). This contribution replaces Kalland.

F Houtman, Cornelis. ‡ (HCOT). The same scholar wrote the four-vol. Exodus set in the HCOT series.

Kalland, Earle S. (EBC) 1992. This 230-page work has a practical, devotional tone and has been of use to pastors, but not to students. Found in the series' vol. 3, which covers Deuteronomy through Samuel. Buy the volume for Youngblood on Samuel, and you've got this. See Grisanti above.

✓ Keil, C.F. (KD) ET 1864. See under Genesis.

Kline, Meredith G. *Treaty of the Great King*, 1963. Years ago, this was a favorite of many evangelicals. Some might still consider it useful to have, but it is o/p [*WTJ* 26.2]. As the title indicates, this work argues for an early (2nd-millennium) covenant treaty structure. Kline has given us one of the better brief commentaries on Deuteronomy in the old one-volume *Wycliffe Bible Commentary*, which includes the substance of *Treaty*.

✓ Lienhard, Joseph T. (ed). *Exodus, Leviticus, Numbers, Deuteronomy* (ACCS) 2001. See under Exodus.

F Lundbom, Jack. ‡ (ECC).

Luther, Martin. "Lectures on Deuteronomy," *Luther's Works*, Vol. 9, ET 1960.

Mann, Thomas W. ‡ (WestBC) 1996. The author used to teach OT at Princeton Seminary. See my comments above on the series as a whole. [*Interp* 7/96; *BL* 1997; *CBQ* 7/97; *RelSRev* 1/97].

Maxwell, J.C. (WCC) 1987. Fuller than some others in the series at 350pp. Helpful overall.

✓ **Mayes, A.D.H.** ‡ (NCB) 1979. More substantial than NCB usually is (416pp), and a fairly good representative of this moderately critical British series. Students should consult this work, long praised in critical circles. [*JBL* 102.3 (1983); *TJ* Fall 80].

☆ **Merrill, Eugene H.** (NAC) 1994. Though not considered an incisive work which advances scholarly discussion, this is a very good and full commentary (477pp)— I could well include it above. Most pastors will gain from adding this dependably conservative work to their personal libraries. In a number of ways, Merrill provides an updating of Craigie and Thompson, the evangelical standbys from the 1970s. Furthermore, he develops the intriguing suggestion made years ago by Yehezkel Kaufmann that Deuteronomy's legislation is organized according to the Decalogue. [*EvQ* 10/96; *JETS* 9/96; *HebStud* 1995].

F Merrill, Eugene H. (CorBC). To be bound with Leviticus and Numbers.

F Merrill, Eugene H. (EEC).

Millar, J. Gary. *Now Choose Life: Theology and Ethics in Deuteronomy*, 1998. This reworked Oxford DPhil dissertation is conservative, fairly accessible, and well worth reading by evangelical preachers. [*JNES* 10/07].

✓ **Nelson, Richard D.** ‡ (OTL) 2002. This 400-page commentary replaces von Rad and sits alongside Nelson's recent Joshua work in the same WJK series. If McConville is the lauded conservative exegesis published lately, Nelson would be an authoritative, new, liberal exegesis. Ralph Klein says this "ranks first." For further comment on this scholar, see under Joshua. Students should certainly consult this mature critical work. [*JTS* 10/04; *CBQ* 1/04; *ExpTim* 11/03; *JSOT* 28.5; *RelSRev* 1/04; *BBR* 15.1; *JETS* 12/04; *CurTM* 4/05 (Klein); *JHebS*; *RBL*].

Payne, D.F. [*M*], (DSB) 1985. One of the more conservative and more useful volumes in the series.

✓ Polzin, Robert. ‡ *Moses and the Deuteronomist: A Literary Study of the Deuteronomic History: Part One. Deuteronomy, Joshua, Judges*, 1980. Of greater value for Joshua and Judges than for Deuteronomy.

✓ **Rad, Gerhard von.** ‡ (retired OTL) ET 1966. Still a standard, critical commentary, but it is quite brief and has become obsolete as an exegetical tool. He gives a lot of attention to the prehistory of the text (tradition history). The author's forte was biblical theology, and the theological discussion here is of more lasting value than the exegesis. "His recognition that Deuteronomy has the characteristics of preaching has endured," says McConville [*BSB* 6/99]. See also von Rad's theological essays in *Studies in Deuteronomy*, ET 1953. This commentary is now replaced by Nelson above. [*ThTo* 24.3].

F Richter, Sandy. (THC).

☆ **Ridderbos, Jan.** (BSC) ET 1984. Lots of good theology, but the author did better on Isaiah (same series). Many years ago I used to recommend this volume for purchase; it is now o/p. For those wanting multiple evangelical works, Thompson is a good alternate, though not as theological, and Merrill is more valuable.

✓ Sherwood, Stephen K. ‡ *Leviticus, Numbers, Deuteronomy* (BO) 2002. See under Leviticus.

✓ Smith, George Adam. ‡ (Cambridge Bible for Schools and Colleges) 1918. Still referenced in the literature. For a study of the enigmatic man—who was deeply affected by Moody's preaching and pushed German higher criticism in Britain—see Iain Campbell, *Fixing the Indemnity: The Life and Work of Sir George Adam Smith (1856–1942)*.

F Strawn, Brent. ‡? (NCBC).

☆ Thompson, J.A. (TOTC) 1974. Very helpful, in my view, and well worth the money. Like Craigie he finds a covenant treaty structure in the book. The drawback is the age of the volume. [*EvQ* 1/76; *JETS* 6/77; *JBL* 95.2].

F Tiffany, Frederick G. ‡ (FOTL).

✓ **Tigay, Jeffrey H**. ‡ (JPS) 1996. See my comments above on the whole series. Students should not miss this as they work with the Hebrew (548pp) for it is among the top scholarly commentaries on this Bible book. This Jewish scholar takes greater interest in source criticism than evangelicals will. Moshe Greenberg can be considered to have had a small hand in this publication, since he made available to Tigay his own notes on the whole book. [*JBL* Win 97].

✓ Vogt, Peter T. *Deuteronomic Theology and the Significance of Torah: A Reappraisal*, 2006. A valuable dissertation. "Certainly, widespread assumptions about how the book reflects a secularization and demythologization of earlier modes of thinking, acting, and seeing will require reevaluation in the light of Vogt's careful reading of the text of Deuteronomy" (Miller). [*EuroJTh* 18.2].

☆ **Weinfeld, Moshe**. ‡ *Deuteronomy 1–11* (AB) 1991. One of the world's most respected Jewish OT exegetes, Weinfeld was especially known for his critical work, *Deuteronomy and the Deuteronomic School*, published by Oxford's Clarendon Press (1972). This commentary is very full and scholarly—the first volume is 458pp long and has over 90pp on the Ten Commandments. Specialists in the OT field have been excited about this immensely learned work, and more academically-minded pastors would benefit from it if they make the purchase. "Indispensable for the serious student" (Clements). The publisher indicated that two more volumes would be coming, but Professor Weinfeld's death (April 2009) may mean the commentary will remain incomplete. [*JBL* Sum 93; *JSS* Spr 93, Spr 94; *HebStud* 1996].

Work, Telford. [*M*], (Brazos) 2009. The author earned his PhD at Duke and teaches theology at Westmont College. I have had little opportunity to use this theological commentary. For exegetical guidance, Work appears to draw mainly on Tigay, Alter, Nelson, and Brueggemann. He walks through the text using the topics of Faith, Hope, and Love (circumscribed allegory) to illumine the Plain meaning in stimulating ways. I have not used it enough to make up my mind about this and some other Brazos titles that seem to range into a kind of Christian midrash at points. [*JTI* Spr 10; *JETS* 6/10; *Interp* 4/10 (Nelson); *JSOT-BL* 2010].

✓ Wright, G.E. ‡ (IB) 1953. To be valued more than most commentaries in the old series because of the author's academic rigor and theological interests.

NOTE: Under the auspices of the University of Vienna, Braulik and Lohfink have placed on the internet a free interactive Analytical Bibliography for Deuteronomy (*AnaBiDeut*). The reach and size of the database are stunning: nearly 12,000 titles and 22.000 chapter/verse references to Bible passages. Besides the main German version, there is an English one as of 2010. See "What is AnaBiDeut?" at <www.univie.ac.at/anabideut>.

READING NARRATIVE & THE FORMER PROPHETS

NOTE: The terms "Former Prophets" and "Deuteronom(ist)ic History" both designate the sequence of four books in the Hebrew Bible: Joshua, Judges, Samuel, and Kings.

★ Alter, Robert. ‡ *The Art of Biblical Narrative*, 1981. This classic ought to be read in the library, if you don't purchase it. Alter can easily be found cheaply in secondhand bookstores. It represents the exciting "Bible as Literature" movement which took hold in the 1970s.

★ Arnold, Bill T., and H.G.M. Williamson (eds). *Dictionary of the Old Testament: Historical Books*, 2005. More valuable for academic than pastoral work. Indispensible for serious study of this portion of the Bible. Articles are contributed by conservatives and moderate critics. [*CTJ* 11/07; *CBQ* 1/07; *SBET* Spr 08; *BSac* 1/07].

★ Fokkelman, J.P. ‡ *Reading Biblical Narrative: An Introductory Guide*, ET 1999. Among the very best introductions available to students. See the ten guiding questions on pp.208–209. Compare with Walsh below. [*Them* Aut 00; *RelSRev* 1/01; *CBQ* 4/01; *BSac* 10/03; *VT* 54.1 and Moberly's cautions in *VT* 53.2].

★ Howard, David M. *An Introduction to the Old Testament Historical Books*, 1993. This fine conservative textbook can be compared with the briefer, more current Satterthwaite/McConville below. [*CTJ* 11/96].

★ Long, V. Phillips. *The Art of Biblical History*, 1994. A thought-provoking and trustworthy guide into the basic questions arising from this literature: what kind of literature is this? what were the narrators seeking to accomplish? how did they intend their books to be read? For more probing discussion of OT historiography and the challenge of skeptical "minimalists," see Day and Long/Wenham/Baker below, and then the Provan/Long/Longman volume, *A Biblical History of Israel* (2003).

★ Pratt, Richard L. *He Gave Us Stories: The Bible Student's Guide to Interpreting Old Testament Narratives*, 1990. Ryken and Pratt are valuable and accessible evangelical introductions to the topic, and they both help students read OT narrative theologically. Pratt has the more redemptive-historical perspective.

★ Satterthwaite, Philip E., and J. Gordon McConville. *Exploring the Old Testament, Vol. 2: A Guide to the Historical Books*, 2007. Start here for an introduction to Joshua through Esther. [*ExpTim* 11/08; *JETS* 9/08; *Anvil* 26.1].

✓ Amit, Yairah. ‡ *Reading Biblical Narrative: Literary Criticism and the Hebrew Bible*, 2001. [*Interp* 4/02; *JSS* Aut 03; *BSac* 10/03].

✓ Bar-Efrat, Shimon. ‡ *Narrative Art in the Bible*, 1989. Superb work by an Israeli scholar.

Barstad, Hans. ‡ *History and the Hebrew Bible*, 2008. Includes what Hugh Williamson has termed the "extremely influential monograph *The Myth of the Empty Land* (1996)." [*ExpTim* 11/09].

✓ Berlin, Adele. ‡ *Poetics and Interpretation of Biblical Narrative*, 1983.

✓ Brooks, P. ‡ *Reading for the Plot: Design and Intention in Narrative*, 1984.

✓ Campbell, Antony F., and Mark A. O'Brien. ‡ *Unfolding the Deuteronomistic History: Origins, Upgrades, Present Text*, 2000. [*BSac* 4/02].

✓ Campbell, Antony F. ‡ *Joshua to Chronicles: An Introduction*, 2004. [*CBQ* 10/05; *BBR* 17.2; *JETS* 3/06; *RelSRev* 7/05].

Cate, Robert L. *An Introduction to the Historical Books of the Old Testament*, 1994. Does not compare favorably with the Howard or Satterthwaite/McConville introductions.

✓ Childs, Brevard S. "Introduction to the Former Prophets," in *Introduction to the Old Testament as Scripture*, 1979. Having taught several courses on these books over the years, I assure you there is, in fact, a huge difference between regarding this literature as prophetic or as composing a Deuteronom(ist)ic History. Wrestle with Childs' 10pp on the topic (pp.229–38). See also Kaufmann under Joshua.

☆ Chisholm, Robert B. *Interpreting the Historical Books: An Exegetical Handbook*, 2006. [*JETS* 12/07; *JSS* Spr 08; *JSOT-BL* 2008].

✓ Culler, J. ‡ *Structuralist Poetics: Structuralism, Linguistics, and the Study of Literature*, 1975.

✓ Day, John (ed). ‡ *In Search of Pre-Exilic Israel*, 2004. Essays, some from Oxford dons, critiquing the revisionist/minimalist school.

✓ De Pury, A., T. Römer, and J.-D. Macchi (eds). ‡ *Israel Constructs Its History: Deuteronomistic Historiography in Recent Research*, 2000. [*Them* Aut 01; *BSac* 7/02].

✓ Frei, Hans W. ‡ *The Eclipse of Biblical Narrative*, 1974.

✓ Fretheim, Terence E. ‡ *Deuteronomic History*, 1983. From the IBT series.

Grabbe, Lester L. ‡ *What Do We Know and How Do We Know It?* 2007. The author is associated with the so-called revisionists/minimalists, and this book is useful to students for getting to know the lines of the debate over the history of Israel. Cf. Kitchen, who argues we know a lot more than Grabbe thinks. [*BASOR* 2/10 (Halpern, Dever); *Interp* 7/09; *TJ* Fall 09; *VT* 60.1 (Moberly); *JTS* 4/09 (Williamson)].

✓ Gunn, David M., and Danna N. Fewell. ‡ *Narrative in the Hebrew Bible*, 1993. For more advanced readers.

☆ Hamilton, Victor. *Handbook on the Historical Books*, 2001. This is a good content survey, just as valuable but in different ways as Howard above. Note that Hamilton seems more interested in the Former Prophets than in Chronicles, Ezra, Nehemiah, and Esther. Earlier he did a *Handbook on the Pentateuch*. [*RTR* 8/02; *Them* Sum 03; *TJ* Spr 03; *JSOT* 99; *BSac* 10/03].

✓   Halpern, Baruch. ‡ *The First Historians: The Hebrew Bible and History*, 1988. One of the better explorations of the redactional approach to the so-called Deuteronomistic History.

☆   Howard, David M., and Michael A. Grisanti (eds). *Giving the Sense: Understanding and Using Old Testament Historical Texts*, 2003. A large collection of essays by leading conservative scholars on the main questions and problems faced by interpreters and preachers. [*Them* Sum 05; *Chm* Win 05; *Anvil* 22.1].

☆   Kermode, Frank, and Robert Alter (eds). ‡ *The Literary Guide to the Bible*, 1987. This volume and Ryken below are good places to start understanding a literary approach and gain improved "reading competence." Kermode-Alter offers essays which introduce the Bible books. Available in pb. Often in secondhand shops.

☆   Kitchen, Kenneth A. *On the Reliability of the Old Testament*, 2003. See under Pentateuch.

✓   Knoppers, Gary N., and J. Gordon McConville (eds). *Reconsidering Israel and Judah: Recent Studies on the Deuteronomistic History*, 2000. [*JSS* Aut 02; *RelSRev* 1/02; *CurTM* 2/02].

✓   Kort, W. ‡ *Story, Text and Scripture: Literary Interests in Biblical Narrative*, 1988.

✓   Long, V.P., G.J. Wenham, and D.W. Baker (eds). *Windows into Old Testament History: Evidence, Argument, and the Crisis of "Biblical Israel,"* 2002. [*RTR* 12/02; *Them* Aut 03; *BSac* 10/03; *RelSRev* 10/03; *EvQ* 10/04]. For another, more archeologically based challenge to "minimalist" scholarship (Davies, Thompson, Lemche), see William G. Dever, *What Did the Biblical Writers Know and When Did They Know It?* (2001) [*JAOS* 122.3 (Rainey); *Anvil* 19.4 (G.I. Davies)].

✓   Long, Burke O. 1984. ‡ *1 Kings with an Introduction to Historical Literature* (FOTL) 1984.

☆   McConville, J. Gordon. *Grace in the End: A Study in Deuteronomic Theology*, 1993. [*SBET* Aut 94].

✓   McKenzie, Stephen L. ‡ *Introduction to the Historical Books: Strategies for Reading*, 2010. See his "Deuteronomistic History" in *ABD* (1992).

✓   Mayes, A.D.H. ‡ *The Story of Israel Between Settlement and Exile*, 1983.

✓   Millard, A.R., James K. Hoffmeier, and David W. Baker (eds). *Faith, Tradition, and History: Old Testament Historiography in Its Near Eastern Context*, 1994. Conservative discussion of the topic.

✓   Miscall, Peter D. ‡ "Introduction to Narrative Literature," *New Interpreter's Bible*, Vol. II, 1998.

✓   Nelson, Richard D. ‡ *The Historical Books, 1998*. This scholar and commentator earlier wrote an oft-cited book, *The Double Redaction of the Deuteronomistic History*, 1981.

✓   Noth, Martin. ‡ *The Deuteronomistic History*, ET 1981. The first half of his *Überlieferungsgeschichtliche Studien*, the 2nd edition of which appeared in 1967.

    Person, Raymond F. ‡ *The Deuteronomic School: History, Social Setting, and Literature*, 2002. [*Interp* 7/03; *ExpTim* 7/03; *JBL* Spr 03; *VT* 54.4; *BibInt* 12.4].

✓   Polzin, Robert. ‡ *Moses and the Deuteronomist*, 1980.

✓   Powell, M. A. ‡ *What Is Narrative Criticism?* 1990. Good for reading alongside is Satterthwaite, "Narrative Criticism: The Theological Implications of Narrative Techniques," *NIDOTTE*, Vol. 1:125–33.

    Provan, Iain W. *1 and 2 Kings* (NIBC) 1995. See the introduction. Another good initial read is Provan, "The Historical Books of the Old Testament" in *The Cambridge Companion to Biblical Interpretation*, 1998.

✓ Rad, Gerhard von. ‡ "The Deuteronomistic Theology of History in the Books of Kings," in *Studies in Deuteronomy*, ET 1953.

✓ Römer, Thomas. ‡ *The So-Called Deuteronomistic History: A Sociological, Historical and Literary Introduction*, 2007. [*HebStud* 2008; *VT* 58.4; *RelSRev* 9/09; *JSOT-BL* 2007].

☆ Ryken, Leland. *Words of Delight: A Literary Introduction to the Bible*, 1987, 2nd ed 1992. An evangelical standard.

✓ Simon, Uriel. ‡ *Reading Prophetic Narratives*, ET 1997. A brilliant narratological study of selected texts: 1 Sam 1–3; 1 Sam 28; 2 Sam 10–12; 1 Kings 13; 1 Kings 17–19; and 2 Kings 4. This Jewish scholar offers an exciting blend of literary and theological insights.

✓ Sternberg, Meir. ‡ *The Poetics of Biblical Narrative: Ideological Literature and the Drama of Reading*, 1985. Somewhat controversial as an introduction, but one of the three or four most important works on the topic.

✓ Walsh, Jerome T. ‡ *Style and Structure in Biblical Hebrew Narrative*, 2001. For students this is a fine introduction to OT narrators' conventions and stylistic devices. [*CBQ* 10/03; *ExpTim* 2/02; *HebStud* 2003]. Further, we have Walsh's *Old Testament Narrative: A Guide to Interpretation* (WJK, 2009).

✓ Watson, Duane F., and Alan J. Hauser. ‡ *Rhetorical Criticism of the Bible, A Comprehensive Bibliography with Notes on History and Method*, 1994. For advanced readers.

✓ Weinfeld, Moshe. ‡ *Deuteronomy and the Deuteronomic School*, 1972.

JOSHUA

★ **Hawk, L. Daniel.** [*M*], (BO) 2000. A 344-page work which gives diligent attention to the narrator's art and purposes. Hawk teaches at Ashland Seminary, and this would be one of the most conservative volumes in the series. Hawk builds upon his fine earlier study of different plots, their twists and turns, in Joshua: *Every Promise Fulfilled* (WJK, 1991) [*CRBR* 1993; *CBQ* 1/94; *HebStud* 1994]. This commentary will be of greater interest to students and scholarly pastors. [*CBQ* 4/02; *Them* Aut 01; *Interp* 7/02; *HebStud* 2002; *JSOT* 99; *F&M* Fall 01; *RelSRev* 1/02].

★ **Hess, Richard S.** (TOTC) 1996. A very fine addition to the Tyndale series. As one would expect, this work takes a thoroughly conservative approach. I was glad to see it because of its fairly current discussion of archeological, historical, and literary issues. Thankfully, this commentator on Joshua takes an interest in the theology of the book; many in the past have not. This balanced commentary is a great help to the preacher and the student. [*Chm* 111.3; *Them* 2/99; *JETS* 6/99; *BL* 1997; *RelSRev* 1/98].

★ **Howard, David M.** (NAC) 1998. The author did a creditable job in his *Introduction to the Old Testament Historical Books* (1993), and here he builds upon that earlier work. Evangelical pastors will be delighted with the help they get from Hess and Howard. I only wish Howard had given us more, for we lack a major, up-to-date, evangelical commentary to replace Woudstra. Holds to an early date, 15th century. [*HebStud* 01; *DenvJ*].

★ **Hubbard, Robert.** (NIVAC) 2009 I expected this to be among the best in this preacher's series, at least from the exegesis standpoint, judging from the quality of his past works. Surprisingly full at 652pp. For a very different sort of Hubbard commentary, see below. We need more pastoral/devotional works on Joshua; those scouting for such should strongly consider McConville/Williams and Ralph Davis below.

★ **Woudstra, Marten.** (NICOT) 1981. Though we could use more help with the Hebrew, we are well served by this commentary. There is some excellent discussion of theology and ethics in the introduction, but not as much as might be hoped for in the commentary proper. In 1990 Woudstra was Stuart's first choice. No other evangelical work prior to Hess and Howard came close to this. Becoming dated. [*TJ* Spr 83; *JETS* 9/82; *JBL* 102.2 (1983); *WTJ* Spr 82].

✧　✧　✧　✧　✧　✧

☆ Auld, A. Graeme. ‡ (DSB) 1984. Covers Joshua, Judges and Ruth and is quite suggestive in its exposition (290pp). Auld discounts these books historically and dates them late, but he is still one of the better volumes in the series and is profitable reading for one interested in the theology of the text. [*Them* 1/86; *EvQ* 10/86]. Students may note Auld's *Joshua Retold: Synoptic Perspectives*, 1998 [*JBL* Win 01; *DenvJ*], which prepares the way for the ICC (below).

F Auld, A. Grame. ‡ (ICC).

✓ Bimson, John. *Redating the Exodus and Conquest*, 1978, rev. 1981. See under Exodus.

☆ Blaikie, W.G. (EB) 1893. Has been reprinted by Klock & Klock and Solid Ground Christian Books (2005). This is an excellent exposition by a Free Church of Scotland luminary with many suggestive ideas for pastors. Years ago when few resources were available on Joshua, I used to make this a recommended purchase. It remains valuable, and I am glad to see it back in print.

☆ Boice, James M. *Joshua: We Will Serve the Lord*, 1989. About 200pp of sermons.

✓ **Boling, Robert G., and G. Ernest Wright.** ‡ (AB) 1982. Has strengths and weaknesses of the series as a whole. Much information on the historical backdrop. Wright contributed only the introduction, which is a pity since he had more sensitivity to matters theological. See Boling on Judges for more information. [*JBL* 103.3].

✓ Bright, John. ‡ (IB) 1953. Formerly it was valued highly because of the dearth of commentaries on Joshua. Bright was a leading OT historian, more conservative in his critical outlook (Albright school); he also had theological insight. See Coote below.

✓ **Butler, Trent.** [*M*], (WBC) 1983. Erudite. Gives greater attention to archaeological findings than does Woudstra. Some conservatives would say that the exegesis is misdirected, being framed by his argument for an exilic date. The late date tends to destroy any historical value given to the book—the distant past is ordinarily dim as well. Nevertheless, Butler has strengths in other areas and needs to be consulted by students. Scholarly pastors wanting to work with the Hebrew might be tempted to buy this, but do note the reports that a Butler 2nd edition is forthcoming. I expect it may be more conservative in approach, like his 2009 Word volume on Judges. [*RTR* 5/84; *EvQ* 10/85; *HebStud* 1985]. By the way, arguments for an earlier dating of the book of Joshua are well presented by Waltke in *ISBE, Revised* and in Howard above.

☆ **Calvin, John.** 1563. According to his friend Beza, this was Cavin's last commentary. The reader will notice that the work, due to physical weakness, is comparatively brief. Still, there is much excellent material here.

F Coleson, Joseph. (CorBC). Bound with Judges and Ruth.

Cooke, G.A. ‡ (Cambridge Bible for Schools and Colleges) 1918.

✓ Coote, Robert B. ‡ (NewIB) 1998. The old IB had a valuable commentary on Joshua by Bright, but the NewIB offers little help to either the student (on account of its brevity) or the pastor (on account of its negative, dismissive interpretation of these Scriptures). [*ExpTim* 1/99].

Creach, Jerome. ‡ (I) 2003. This is a surprisingly brief volume (130pp) for a 24-chapter Bible book which we preachers find a challenge. Not as successful an entry in the series. Creach gives us hardly more than a glance at chs. 13–22. [*CBQ* 10/04; *Interp* 10/04; *EuroJTh* 18.2].

F   Dallaire, Helene. (EBCR). Previously Michael Kelly was down to do this.

Davis, John. *Conquest and Crisis*. 1969. A popular, brief commentary by a conservative evangelical. Covers Joshua, Judges, and Ruth. Perhaps this was once helpful to the Sunday School teacher.

☆   Davis, D. Ralph. *No Falling Words*, 1988. Sermonic material from a former OT professor at RTS. Published by Baker. See under Judges for further comments applicable here. Preachers find this suggestive. I bought it myself. [*Chm* Sum 02].

Earl, Douglas S. ‡ *Reading Joshua as Christian Scripture*, 2010. A Durham dissertation which dispenses with historical categories and provides a close literary reading. The original function of the myth-narrative, he says, was to reshape the community identity (along Deuteronomic lines) by creating a "cultural memory." There is heavy use of Ricoeur and attention paid to the Church's interpretation of Joshua from the early Fathers to Calvin.

✓   Franke, John R. (ed). *Joshua, Judges, Ruth, 1–2 Samuel* (ACCS) 2005. [*JSOT-BL* 2008].

Garstang, John. *The Foundations of Biblical History, Joshua, Judges*, 1931. Many reprints. Pastors have long looked to this work for answers to their questions about the archaeology and geography relating to the books of Joshua and Judges. Garstang is now terribly out of date. Archeological findings from excavating Jericho (1930–36), written up in *The Story of Jericho* (rev ed 1948), were challenged by a subsequent dig (1952–58).

☆   **Goslinga, C. J.** (BSC) 1955, ET 1986. Also treats Judges and Ruth in a total 558pp. Theologically sensitive, Goslinga would be a worthy addition to the pastor's library, but it long ago went o/p.

✓   **Gray, John.** ‡ (NCB) 1967, rev. 1986. Covers Judges and Ruth as well. Though not one of the stronger volumes in NCB, this volume is constantly cited in the literature. Critical and skeptical for its time, Gray now sounds less critical as so much historical scholarship has become radicalized.

F   Greenspoon, Leonard. ‡ (JPS). The scholar wrote a Harvard dissertation on Joshua and is brilliant in working with the textual traditions and translation issues.

Hall, Sarah Lebhar. *Conquering Character: The Characterization of Joshua in Joshua 1–11* (LHB/OTS) 2010. A very fine Cambridge dissertation on a fascinating narratological topic.

Hamlin, E. John. ‡ (ITC) 1984. A theological interpretation which has received some attention in the journals. I find it to be of indifferent value. [*WTJ* Spr 88; *JETS* 9/84; *ExpTim* 8/84].

☆   **Harris, J.G.**, C. Brown, and M. Moore. *Joshua, Judges, Ruth* (NIBC) 2000. I have seen this work, but have not had opportunity to consult it at length. The treatments of Judges (160pp) and Ruth (80pp) are considerably fuller than the Joshua section (130pp). The publisher might well have devoted, instead, a whole volume to the Book of Joshua with its 24 chapters, especially since Harris does an admirable job on Joshua, given space constraints. The volume has received generally favorable reviews, with a warmer reception given to Judges than to Ruth. [*RTR* 8/01; *Them* Spr 02; *Interp* 1/02; *HebStud* 2002; *JSOT* 99 (2002); *SwJT* Fall 01; *Anvil* 19.3].

✓ **Harstad, Adolph L.** (Concord) 2004. This huge (906pp) undertaking is typical of the conservative Lutheran series of which it is a part. Harstad seeks to provide both exegetical guidance for seminarians and pastors studying the Hebrew text and theological (Christological) reflection. It is a reverent reading of Scripture but, on the negative side, is regarded by some as insufficiently rigorous for the academy. In light of the paucity of thorough evangelical expositions, this book is very welcome. [*EvQ* 10/07; *CBQ* 7/06; *JETS* 12/06; *JSOT-BL* 2006; *BSac* 4/08].

✓ Hess, Richard S., Gerald A. Klingbeil, and Paul J. Ray, Jr. (eds). *Critical Issues in Early Israelite History*, 2008. No doubt many will dismiss this volume as out-of-step with today's increasingly skeptical historiography, but the scholarship here is of a high-caliber, with eight essays relating to the Joshua narrative.

Hoppe, L. ‡ *Joshua, Judges* (OTM) 1982.

F Hubbard, Robert L., and Malcolm M. Clark. [*M?*], *Joshua, Judges* (FOTL). Perhaps there will be two volumes here instead of one. I expect Hubbard to be responsible for Joshua, and Clark for Judges. See Hubbard's NIVAC above.

☆ Huffman, John A. (WCC) 1986. Huffman makes one of the better contributions to the series. Will prompt the preacher to think theologically and practically about Joshua. The author is an evangelical PCUSA pastor.

Kaufmann, Yehezkel. *The Biblical Account of the Conquest of Canaan*, ET 1953, 2nd ed 1985. Kaufmann presents a conservative Jewish interpretation of the narrative and issues a bracing challenge to proponents of the DH theory.

✓ Keil, Carl F. (KD) ET 1865. Able exposition of the theological message.

F Knight, Douglas A. ‡ (NCBC). The author is an expert on tradition history.

F McCarter, P. Kyle. ‡ (Herm). This is expected to become a leading critical commentary for years to come.

☆ **McConville, J. Gordon, and Stephen Williams.** (THC) 2010. McConville provides able, though not detailed, exegesis (80pp), and Williams, a systematics professor, joins him in offering mature and helpful theological reflection (both systematics and biblical theology). Needing to examine the work more closely, I wonder if it might become a recommended purchase. Somewhat unique is the dialogue between the commentators, who share a Northern Irish Presbyterian heritage.

F McKenzie, Steven L. ‡ (S&H).

Madvig, Donald H. (EBC) 1992. Pedestrian. Quite brief at 130pp and has fewer exegetical notes than others in the series. Madvig is non-committal on dates for the Exodus and Conquest. See Kelly above.

F Matties, Gordon. (BCBC).

✓ Miller, J.M., and Gene M. Tucker. ‡ (CBC) 1974. Both scholars have a well established reputation in critical scholarship. Miller has made OT history his specialty. They are quite skeptical about the historical value of the book of Joshua.

✓ Mitchell, Gordon. ‡ *Together in the Land: A Reading of the Book of Joshua*, 1993. I am hoping works such as Mitchell and Hawk will encourage others to apply narrative criticism to Joshua. See Hall above.

✓ **Nelson, Richard D.** ‡ (OTL) 1997. Nelson has made the Deuteronomistic History his specialty and here provides us with a 310-page commentary in a prestigious series. The author is solidly in the liberal camp and, while paying close attention to historical questions, discounts Joshua's historical value. Replaces Soggin in the series. This is another volume for the scholarly pastor who is building a first-rate personal library, but note that Nelson does not help much with the Hebrew text. [*Them* 11/99; *JETS* 9/99; *JBL* Spr 99; *Interp* 10/98; *CBQ* 4/99; *HebStud* 1999; *ThTo* 1/99; *RelSRev* 7/98; *RBL*].

Pink, Arthur. *Gleanings in Joshua*, 1964. See under Genesis. This was one of his last series and is better than Genesis and Exodus.

F   Pitkanen, Pekka. (Apollos).

✓   **Polzin, Robert.** ‡ *Moses and the Deuteronomist: A Literary Study of the Deuteronomic History: Part One. Deuteronomy, Joshua, Judges*, 1980.

Pressler, Carolyn. ‡ *Joshua, Judges, and Ruth* (WestBC) 2002. [*ExpTim* 8/03; *JSOT* 27.5].

F   Rösel, Hartmut. ‡ (HCOT).

Schaeffer, Francis. *Joshua and the Flow of Biblical History*, 1975.

✓   **Soggin, J. Alberto.** ‡ (retired OTL) ET 1972. Mainly concerned with the archaeological, geographical, and historical problems of the text. Influenced by Noth's work on Joshua, Soggin comes to mainline critical conclusions. Use with discernment. Pastors should not expect to find any theological help in this volume, which, in any case, is now o/p and replaced by Nelson.

Stern, Philip D. *The Biblical Ḥerem: A Window on Israel's Religious Experience*, 1991.

Winther-Nielsen, Nicolai. *A Functional Discourse Grammar of Joshua*, 1995. Of course there is a lot of technical linguistics here, but for those who understand it Winther-Nielsen is useful indeed (353pp).

Younger, K. Lawson. *Ancient Conquest Accounts: A Study in Ancient Near Eastern and Biblical History Writing*, 1990.

NOTE: (1) Be sure to consult atlases and OT history volumes. Among the latter, many evangelical OT scholars now recommend *A Biblical History of Israel* by Provan-Long-Longman (WJK, 2003) and Merrill's *Kingdom of Priests* (Baker, 1987, 2nd ed 2008). (2) See "Joshua: An Annotated Bibliography," *SwJT* 41.1 (1998): 102–110. (3) Understandably, many people struggle with the slaughter in the book of Joshua. How do we read those narratives and make sense of them ethically, and what do they teach about the God of the Bible? The best quick help I can offer is to recommend Christopher J.H. Wright, "Appendix: What about the Canaanites?" in *Old Testament Ethics for the People of God* (IVP, 2004), 472–80, and the literature he cites there. A book edited by Stanley Gundry debates the best explanations: *Show Them No Mercy: Four Views of God and Canaanite Genocide* (Zondervan, 2003).

JUDGES

★   **Block, Daniel.** *Judges-Ruth* (NAC) 1999. The obvious first choice for the pastor's library. This extensive commentary (767pp) fills a huge hole as it provides a careful treatment of introductory matters, adequate and balanced exegesis, and good theological interpretation. After Block's appearance we still awaited a technical exegesis of the Hebrew original by a conservative, and Butler begins to meet our need. Looking over these recommendations, the student and more scholarly pastor should especially consider Butler, Block, and Schneider for purchase. Another pastor might prefer adding the superb BST and WCC expositions, and Davis, to Block. My counsel: mix and match these works as you please. Worth mentioning is that Block earlier wrote a comprehensive commentary on Ezekiel. [*JETS* 9/01; *BSac* 10/01].

★   **Butler, Trent.** (WBC) 2009. This scholar did one of the first commentaries in the whole series, on Joshua. Now this fat book (xcii + 538pp) comes a quarter century later and is more conservative in approach to such matters as dating (he suggests a compositional date in "the opening years of the divided monarchy" [lxxiv]). Butler no longer seems to follow a DH thesis. He offers a well-rounded commentary with textual criticism, philology and grammar, form and narrative/rhetorical criticism, historical study, and theological reflection (a bit anyway). Once again WBC has provided us with nearly exhaustive bibliographies. There is not much biblical theology, which makes me more eager for Webb. A criticism could be that he so catalogs others' arguments that some pages are composed of nearly ¾ quotation (e.g., pp.282, 325, 443); occasionally I am left without a clear idea of Butler's own conclusion. Students will relish the extensive research. [*Interp* 7/10].

★ Jackman, David. *Judges, Ruth* (WCC) 1991. The author, a well-known evangelical clergyman in the Church of England, does a very fine job here. Judged to be as valuable as Wilcock or Davis in the category of theological exposition (300pp on Judges). The pastor would be wise to purchase this (and consider the other two).

★ **Schneider, Tammi.** ‡ (BO) 2000. A well-researched, moderately detailed, and provocative literary reading of Judges which well complements other historical and theological commentaries. This is *not* to say Schneider takes no interest in the theology of the book. She does (from a Jewish perspective), and she makes astute comments on such issues as leadership and covenant faithfulness. I value her literary sensitivity, revealed particularly in her discussion of the women of Judges (commonly "foils" for male characters or male society). She has a contagious enthusiasm for the text in this 290-page commentary. I bought this and am learning much from it. More for the pastor with academic proclivities. [*Interp* 1/01; *RelSRev* 1/01; *OTA* 10/00; *CBQ* 10/02; *HebStud* 01; *JSOT* 94 (2001); *RelSRev* 1/01; *RBL*].

★ **Younger, K. Lawson.** *Judges/Ruth* (NIVAC) 2002. This commentary is more exegetical than the OT series as a whole and is, therefore, useful to students as well as pastors. Conversely, it is less helpful as a guide to applying the message of Judges to the present day. It may start expositors down the path of applying the Scriptures, but will not accompany them for very long a distance. The author is a much respected scholar at TEDS, who has expertise in the ancient Near Eastern background of the Bible and has jointly edited the important multi-volume series, *The Context of Scripture*. He agrees with Block who said the theme of Judges is "the Canaanization of Israelite society during the period of the settlement."

✧ ✧ ✧ ✧ ✧ ✧

✓ Amit, Yaira. ‡ *The Book of Judges: The Art of Editing*, 1998. A literary reading and redactional study published by Brill.

F Armerding, Carl E. (W̶B̶C̶). Was eagerly awaited, as we have needed an in-depth commentary on the Hebrew, and Armerding is an incisive and seasoned scholar. Regrettably, this will not appear. Butler delivered the WBC. There is a brief treatment of Judges by Armerding in *The International Bible Commentary*, 1979.

☆ **Auld, A. Graeme.** ‡ (DSB) 1984. See under Joshua. Auld has thought deeply about the Book of Judges and its relevance today. He teaches at the University of Edinburgh, is liberal in theology, and does well (within the confines of the series) in literary analysis.

Bal, Mieke. ‡ *Murder and Difference*, 1988; *Death and Dissymetry*, 1988. These two works are similar in their literary approach to texts in Judges and in their postmodern and feminist concerns. They are deeply learned and provocative, "focusing on characters rather than storyline, practices rather than events" (Groom [*BSB* 9/98]).

Barber, Cyril J. *Judges: A Narrative of God's Power*, 1990.

F Boda, Mark. (EBCR).

☆ **Boling, Robert G.** ‡ (AB) 1975. Lots of information and, like the AB volume on Joshua, reflects the more conservative historical approach of the Albright school.

The student or scholarly pastor wanting to do a thorough study of the Book of Judges (esp. the Hebrew) ought to use this work; the average pastor will not benefit so much. Boling has had prominence as the leading critical work mainly because there have been so few quality, in-depth works on Judges. I used to recommend this for purchase. Those who want another detailed commentary (besides Butler and Block) can use this as they wait on Webb, Mayes, and Sasson (Boling's replacement). [*JBL* 95.1 (1976)].

☆ **Brensinger, Terry L.** [*M*], (BCBC) 1999. His conservatively critical assumptions do not often intrude and mar his fine work of commenting theologically and practically on Judges. Though there is not a great deal of interaction with scholarship, the author does make good use of some literary treatments, e.g., Webb's. This volume could be put to good use by evangelical pastors. Has a bit over 200pp of actual commentary. At points I wonder if he moralizes the text in ways probably not intended by the narrator; an example would be interpreting Samson's character as the bad example not to be followed. While that's true, of course, is the Samson story in the Bible mainly to warn us all against hedonism and immoral sex? Brensinger does less to place the text in the course of redemptive history. Davis, Goslinga, and sometimes Wilcock do a better job in that respect. Still, I am very grateful to have this fine book available. [*CBQ* 4/01; *CTJ* 11/01].

✓ Brettler, Marc Zvi. ‡ *The Book of Judges*, 2002. A well-written introduction to reading the book in order to discover both its historical and its literary concerns. [*Interp* 1/03; *RelSRev* 1/03].

✓ **Burney, C. F.** ‡ 2nd ed 1920. Continues to be of real philological value. Burney had many of the same aims as Moore and continues to be consulted widely. For example, Lindars cites him 55 times. [*JBL* 90.2 (1971)].

Cassel, P. (Lange) ET 1872. Years ago some thought it quite good, in light of the scarcity of theological works on Judges. Moore asserted that it offered "ingeniously perverse exegesis" (p.l). Covers both Judges and Ruth. Spurgeon found the Joshua work by Fay in the same volume inferior.

F Chisholm, Robert B. (Kregel).

Cooke, G.A. ‡ *The Book of Judges, The Book of Ruth* (Cambridge Bible for Schools and Colleges) 1913.

Cundall, A.E., and Leon Morris. *Judges and Ruth* (TOTC) 1968. Cundall's work (about 200pp) was once a first choice only because there was little else to choose from. Cundall gives Judges a high credit rating historically. Morris' commentary on Ruth is quite full (100 pp), considering the series.

☆ Davis, D. Ralph. *Judges: Such a Great Salvation*, 1990. A homiletical commentary of good value. Maybe a bit too racy and clever to my liking at points, but I don't want to be dismissive. Davis is a good student of the Scriptures, and this book will help those it aims to: pastors and Sunday School teachers with the boldness to enter this forbidding territory. This author also has expositions of Joshua, Samuel and Kings, and all of them helpfully emphasize a redemptive historical approach. Preachers should consider buying these books. I myself purchased all of them.

Fausset, Andrew R. (GS) 1885. One of the more valuable old evangelical commentaries, reprinted in 1977 by James & Klock. Now Banner of Truth has added this to their Geneva Series; inclusion in GS can be rightly taken to indicate its expository and homiletical character. [*Evangel* Aut 01].

✓ Franke, John R. (ed). *Joshua, Judges, Ruth, 1–2 Samuel* (ACCS) 2005.

Garstang, John. 1931. See under Joshua.

☆ **Goslinga, C.J.** (BSC) 1966, ET 1986. See under Joshua. Now o/p. I used to recommend this for purchase for its theological worth, but that was back in 1989 when we had little from evangelicals besides Cundall's TOTC.

✓ **Gray, John.** ‡ (NCB) 1967, rev. 1986. See under Joshua.

✓ Groves, Alan. *New Geneva Study Bible*, 1995. My friend was also slated to write the Judges volume for THC, but he lost a brave fight with cancer. See McConville below.

Gunn, David M. ‡ (BBC) 2005. Evocative as it presents centuries of much-varied cultural and artistic responses (artwork, music) to the stories of Judges. [*EvQ* 10/07; *RBL* 10/05].

✓ Hamlin, E.J. ‡ (ITC) 1990. Strange in places, but ITC is meant to be a little exotic. This is certainly worth looking at. See Webb's judicious critique [*RTR* 5/91].

☆ Harris, J.G., **Cheryl Brown**, and M. Moore. *Joshua, Judges, Ruth* (NIBC) 2000. See Joshua above.

F Hubbard, Robert L., and Malcolm M. Clark. *Joshua, Judges* (FOTL).

F Hugenberger, Gordon. (Apollos). The author teaches at Gordon-Conwell Seminary.

Jeter, Joseph R. ‡ *Preaching Judges*, 2003. Should we attempt to preach on the dark, difficult material in Judges? Practically speaking, many of us preachers seem to believe we should not. Jeter makes a good case for opening up this book in the pulpit. This guide is an engaging read. Though there is often a liberal slant here, Jeter, a homiletics professor at Brite Divinity School, is fairly open to the text. He appears to eschew Christological interpretation in his homiletical strategy. [*Interp* 7/05; *CTJ* 4/10].

Jordan, James B. *Judges–God's War Against Humanism*, 1985. Though appreciating his concern to make this Bible book applicable to our context, I can't call this effort a success. Jordan can be insightful at times, but, more often than not, he seems to lack balance and good judgment in his exegesis, theological points and application. He needs some stricter controls in his hermeneutical method. The symbolism and allegorizing can be wild! He sometimes needs more guidance than he provides.

☆ Keddie, Gordon J. *Even in Darkness* (WCS on Judges and Ruth) 1985.

✓ Keil, Carl F. (KD) ET 1865.

✓ Klein, Lillian R. ‡ *The Triumph of Irony in the Book of Judges*, 1988. This literary study, like Webb's, may prove more useful to students than most of the commentaries available.

Lewis, Arthur. *Judges and Ruth*, 1979. Evangelical exposition published by Moody Press.

✓ **Lindars, Barnabas.** ‡ *Judges 1–5* (intended for ICC) 1995. This Catholic scholar long taught at Manchester and was an accomplished OT and NT exegete. Sadly, he died before he could complete this work, and the publisher has released it outside the ICC series. (In the 19th century another interpreter, Bachmann, also only got to ch. 5.) Here you'll find approximately 300pp of exceedingly careful and comprehensive textual analysis. Will be valued by serious researchers for decades to come. [*ExpTim* 12/95; *Them* 1/97; *JETS* 6/97; *CBQ* 7/97; *SJT* 52.2 (1999); *SwJT* Spr 98; *BSac* 4/96; *HebStud* 1997].

☆ **McCann, J. Clinton.** ‡ (I) 2002. A thoughtful, though brief (139pp) exposition from the critical camp which focuses upon the theology in the text and upon preaching concerns. The author is best known as a leading Psalms scholar. [*CBQ* 7/03; *ExpTim* 10/03; *JSOT* 28.5; *SwJT* Fall 03; *RelSRev* 10/03; *BSac* 10/05; *CurTM* 10/05; *JHebS*].

F McConville, J. Gordon, and Stephen Williams. (THC). This will follow their successful Joshua volume in the same series.

✓ **Matthews, Victor H.** [*M*], *Judges & Ruth* (NCBC) 2004. This was the first volume of the New Cambridge series, and I call it a success. Matthews is known for his strong interest in social scientific research. Among the scholars enlisted for NCBC, Matthews is one of the less critical. I confess to being nonplussed that he would cite a number of Block's articles and miss his large NAC commentary. Students should make use of Matthews' bibliographical guidance on pp. 18–36. [*CBQ* 1/05; *JETS* 6/05; *Interp* 1/06; *BSac* 10/06; *JSOT-BL* 2005].

F Mayes, A.D.H. ‡ (ICC–replacement). Mayes is to pick up the project after Lindars, but I do not expect him to incorporate Lindars' treatment of chs. 1–5. Note his 1985 work in JSOT's "OT Guides," one of the best in the series.

✓ **Moore, George F.** ‡ (ICC) 1908. Long the classic to consult for detailed textual work. While students must take account of Moore's brilliant research, pastors have little use for it and may be put off by the negatively critical spirit the author projects (often harsh with other scholars). See Burney.

F Nelson, Richard D. ‡ (ECC). A companion for his OTL commentaries on Deuteronomy and Joshua but in a different series.

✓ **Niditch, Susan.** ‡ (OTL) 2008. This replacement for Soggin is fairly brief for the series, with the commentary portion of the volume running to 211pp, including the biblical text. The appendix, "A Literal Translation of Judges" (pp.213–81), is a waste of space since it often has a stilted character and sometimes differs little from the translation already offered in the commentary section (cf. 14:1–4 in both). Niditch is well known for encouraging both a feminist and folklorist perspective in reading Bible tales. See her influential work, *Oral World and Written Word* (1996). This well-written OTL volume will be of interest to academics but few pastors. [*CBQ* 4/09; *ExpTim* 4/09; *RBL*; *JETS* 9/08; *CurTM* 2/09; *JSOT-BL* 2009; *BSac* 4/10 (Chisholm); *Interp* 4/09 (Meyers)].

✓ **O'Connell, Robert H.** ‡ *The Rhetoric of the Book of Judges*, 1996. This Cambridge dissertation "represents the most thorough literary analysis of the book of Judges available in English" (Block). You can compare this work with Webb. [*JETS* 3/99; *JTS* 4/98; *Biblica* 80.2 (1999); *CBQ* 7/98].

✓ **Olson, Dennis T.** ‡ (NewIB) 1998. One of the best available critical treatments of exegetical and expositional matters. The author previously did first-rate work on Numbers. [*ExpTim* 1/99].

✓ **Polzin, Robert.** ‡ *Moses and the Deuteronomist: A Literary Study of the Deuteronomic History: Part One. Deuteronomy, Joshua, Judges*, 1980. This presents a redaction-al approach which assumes that various unrelated tales have been woven together and interpreted by an editor, who has created a coherent whole.

Pressler, Carolyn. ‡ *Joshua, Judges, and Ruth* (WestBC) 2002.

Rogers, Richard. 1615 Original. This massive work, containing over 100 sermons by an English Puritan, has been reprinted by Banner of Truth in a "Facsimile Edition."

Ryan, Roger. ‡ (Read) 2007. Said to pursue competently a narrative critical approach and read the text with a good measure of sympathy (221pp). [*JSOT-BL* 2008; *VT* 60.2].

F Sanderson, Judith E. ‡ (S&H).

F Sasson, Jack. ‡ (AYB). This will replace Boling.

✓ **Soggin, J. Alberto.** ‡ (OTL) ET 1981, 2nd ed 1987. This remains an important older work from the standpoint of historical critical scholarship. Theological reflection is beyond his ken. I consider *Judges* a better work than Soggin's earlier *Joshua* in OTL. See Niditsch above for Soggin's replacement. [*HebStud* 1983; *JTS* 33 (1982)].

F Spronk, Klaus. ‡ (HCOT). See Nahum.

F Stone, Lawson. (CorBC). Bound with Joshua and Ruth.

✓ **Webb, Barry G.** *The Book of Judges: An Integrated Reading*, 1987. Pastors and Bible scholars have long been frustrated by the atomistic approach of verse by verse commentaries—too often the thread of the theological argument is lost and the literary structures of the book are obscured. Some feel the need for a more integrated, synthetic approach which goes beyond the older diachronic studies. The value of such a new approach is demonstrated here. This readable dissertation for Sheffield contains a sensitive literary analysis of the book as a complex whole and beautifully complements other works which focus on the historical and theological. Webb's study would be of immense help to any scholarly pastor preaching or teaching through Judges (even if you disagree with him over the centrality of the Jephthah narrative). His respect for the text makes this work palatable to the evangelical. Actually, Webb is an evangelical, but his dissertation hides that fact well at a number of points. Compare with O'Connell. Note the next entry. [*EvQ* 1/89; *RTR* 5/88; *Them* 10/88; more critical are the reviews in *HebStud* 1989, and *CRBR* 1990].

F Webb, Barry. (NICOT). This should be top-notch with regard to both exegesis and theological interpretation. For a foretaste see "The Wars of Judges as Christian Scripture," *RTR* 67.1 (2008): 18–28.

☆ Wilcock, Michael. (BST) 1993. A suggestive exposition for the preacher, rivaled by Jackman. Wilcock also did Chronicles and Revelation for this series. Some of the interpretations offered in this BST volume are a bit surprising and out of the ordinary. I am tempted to say "off-beat." [*Them* 10/94; *Evangel* Spr 95; *SBET* Sum 93 (Hess)].

Wolf, Herbert. (EBC) 1992. Rather brief (130pp), Wolf's work is mainly concerned with filling out the historical picture and capably does that. There is not much theology or literary interest; he didn't use Webb or other recent works—Wolf may have completed this commentary long before the publication date. See Boda for a replacement.

Wood, Leon. *Distressing Days of the Judges*, 1975. Fact-filled, but has no biblical theological reflection. This work is quite conservative, Dispensational. Many pastors may find this volume helpful, though I have come away disappointed the few times I have consulted Wood. It was influential in conservative circles many years ago, when there was nothing else but Cundall. Wood was reprinted a few years ago.

✓ Yee, Gale A. (ed). ‡ *Judges and Method: New Approaches in Biblical Studies*, 1995, 2nd ed 2007. [*JTS* 10/08; *BibInt* 17 (Schneider); *ExpTim* 10/09; *HBT* 30.2 (Butler)].

F Youngblood, Ronald. (EEC). I believe the author once had the NICOT contract.

NOTES: (1) One essay would be especially helpful for the preacher to look up: Daniel Block's "The Period of the Judges: Religious Disintegration under Tribal Rule," in the R.K. Harrison Festschrift, *Israel's Apostasy and Restoration* (Baker, 1988), pp.39–58. (2) See Raymond Bayley's "Which Is the Best Commentary? 14. Judges," *ExpTim* 2/92. (3) See, too, K.M. Craig, "Judges in Recent Research," *CBR* 1.2 (2003): 159–85.

RUTH

★ Atkinson, D. (BST) 1983. An excellent contribution to the series. Unfolds the many theological themes in this jewel of a book. Some might think it a bit expensive for its size (128pp). [*WTJ* Spr 84].

★ **Block, Daniel.** *Judges–Ruth* (NAC) 1999. This volume has been recommended above as a pastor's first choice for Judges. Block's commentary on Ruth will not disappoint, even though it is not quite as strong as the Judges portion. Block is useful to students for his interaction with Hubbard, Sasson, Bush, etc.

★ **Bush, Frederic.** [*M*], *Ruth, Esther* (WBC) 1996. This work treats the technical issues at even greater depth than Hubbard. The literary-critical approach he takes yields many new insights on the narrative art in Ruth. A superb scholarly work, though most evangelicals would want to date the Book of Ruth much, much earlier than the early post-exilic period. Among the contributions of the commentary is a thorough discussion and a new proposal for our understanding of *gō'ēl* (cf. Hubbard). This is for students and scholarly pastors. As noted above in the "Commentary Series" section of this guide, Bush is one of the more technical, less accessible volumes published in WBC. If you don't want this, you will already have another fine Ruth commentary by buying Younger on Judges. [*JETS* 3/99; *RTR* 9-12/97; *SwJT* Spr 00; *BSac* 10/98].

★ Duguid, Iain M. *Esther and Ruth* (REC) 2005. This volume on two challenging books for preachers is solidly based in exegesis, clearly expounds the theology of the text, and makes wise moves toward application. See his other books for preachers on Ezekiel and Haggai–Malachi.

★ **Hubbard, Robert L.** (NICOT) 1988. A very substantial, satisfying commentary (316pp) on this short book. Hubbard treats everything, and frankly, if you have this, you are well supplied on Ruth. When it appeared it was the best in the series by a long shot. This is Stuart's and Longman's first choice. The only drawback might be the age of the book for students needing bibliographical guidance. [*WTJ* Spr 91; *Them* 10/91; *HebStud* 1990; *Chm* 104.2; *ExpTim* 8/89].

★ Ulrich, Dean R. *From Famine to Fullness: The Gospel According to Ruth*, 2007. An excellent purchase for the preacher, Ulrich's work is readable, well-informed by OT scholarship (Westminster PhD), and displays both theological insight and a zeal to apply the text to daily life. In line with the subtitle, the exposition brings out gospel themes in a helpful way and provides guidance for a redemptive-historical approach—no barren moralism here.

☆ Auld, A. Graeme. ‡ (DSB) 1984. See under Joshua.

✓ **Campbell, Edward F.** ‡ (AB) 1975. A very good, thorough commentary, one of the best of the older contributions to AB in the OT section. Campbell reflects the more conservative (among critical scholars) historical approach of Albright. This doesn't compare with Hubbard, though, at this point in time. [*JBL* 9/77].

F Chisholm, Robert B. (Kregel).

De Waard, Jan, and Eugene A. Nida. *A Handbook on the Book of Ruth* (UBS) 1992.

F Driesbach, Jason. (CorBC). Bound with Joshua and Judges.

✓ **Farmer, Kathleen A. Robertson.** ‡ (NewIB) 1998. Well done. I am inclined to call it one of the best in the entire OT section of the series. [*ExpTim* 1/99].

✓ Fewell, Danna N., and David Gunn. ‡ *Compromising Redemption: Relating Characters in the Book of Ruth*, 1990. Another leading study which examines literary structure, characterization, and thematic development. I recommend skipping the dramatic retelling of the story (pp.23–66) to get to the "close reading" (pp.69–105). I note in passing an insightful, brief reading that is similar in approach: Phyllis Trible's chapter on Ruth in *God and the Rhetoric of Sexuality* (1992).

F Fowl, Stephen. (Brazos). See his earlier work on Philippians in THC.

✓ Franke, John R. (ed). *Joshua, Judges, Ruth, 1–2 Samuel* (ACCS) 2005.

☆ Goslinga, C.J. (BSC) 1966, ET 1986. See Joshua above.

✓ **Gow, Murray D.** *The Book of Ruth: Its Structure, Theme and Purpose*, 1992. A stimulating literary reading of the book from a conservative scholar. Gow suggests that the Book of Ruth is quite early—authored by the Prophet Nathan—and that it offers an apology for King David and his Moabite ancestry. [*SBET* Aut 93; *RTR* 5/97; *Them* 4/96; *BSac* 7/95].

✓ **Gray, John.** ‡ (NCB) 1967, rev. 1986. See Joshua above.

✓ Hals, Ronald M. ‡ *The Theology of the Book of Ruth*, 1969. [*JBL* 89.1 (1970)].

✓ Hamlin, E. John. ‡ *There Is a Future: Ruth* (ITC) 1996. [*VT* 47.2; *RTR* 9/96; *HebStud* 1997; *RelSRev* 1/97].

☆ Harris, J.G., C. Brown, and **M. Moore.** *Joshua, Judges, Ruth* (NIBC) 2000. See Joshua above.

F Hawk, L. Daniel. (Apollos). See his commentary on Joshua.

F **Holmstedt, Robert D.** *Ruth: A Handbook on the Hebrew Text*, 2010. There's much more here than one might expect (226pp).

  Huey, F.B. (EBC) 1992. A readable, informed, 40-page commentary which displays an interest in historical, literary and theological issues; however it is not all that penetrating. See Schwab for a replacement.

☆ Jackman, David. *Judges, Ruth* (WCC) 1991. See under Judges. Well done, but only half the size of Atkinson.

☆ Keddie, Gordon J. *Even in Darkness* (WCS on Judges and Ruth) 1985.

✓ Keil, Carl F. (KD) ET 1865.

✓ Knight, G. A. F. ‡ (Torch Bible Commentaries) 2nd ed 1966.

F Korpel, Marjo C.A. ‡ (HCOT). This scholar has already produced a ground-breaking study of *The Structure of the Book of Ruth*, 2001 [*RelSRev* 1/03].

✓ **LaCocque, André.** ‡ (ContC) ET 2004. This is a major exegetical and theological commentary, as befits the series, but one that also has several demerits. The author does not interact much with other scholars' views. There is a deep skepticism (the setting is "quite fictitious," p.18) and a controlling opinion that "the 'attitudes and actions' of Ruth's main characters 'make no sense' in any period prior to the postexilic" (Moore). Pastors will pass this by, but students doing advanced work on Ruth should not ignore this independent-minded exegesis. See also his work on Daniel. [*CBQ* 1/06; *JETS* 3/06; *Interp* 4/06; *BL* 2005; *RelSRev* 7/05; *JHebS*; *RBL*; *CurTM* 8/06].

  Lawson, George. *Expositions of Ruth and Esther*, 1805. A classic which is reprinted from time to time.

✓ **Linafelt, Tod,** and Timothy K. Beal. ‡ *Ruth, Esther* (BO) 1999. Fairly full, for the series, on the two books (approx. 100 + 135pp). Beal's work on Esther is cleverer and better, in my judgment, than Linafelt's, but both engage in what might be termed ideological manipulations of the text. Some of the newer literary criticism is tamer, more responsible text-oriented interpretation, but the reader-oriented, ideological approaches—predominant here—are often not seeking "determinate meaning" in the text at all. This volume is stimulating for students, but you won't learn as much about Ruth and Esther as you hope to. [*JSOT* 89 (2000); *OTA* 6/00; *Interp* 4/01; *CBQ* 1/01; *RelSRev* 10/02].

☆ Luter, A. Boyd, and Barry C. Davis. *God Behind the Seen*, 1996. A large volume on Ruth & Esther (350pp) published by Baker in the series, "Expositor's Guide to the Historical Books." This book provides some homiletical direction for the pastor, but perhaps is not as helpful as its size might indicate. [*JETS* 3/99; *BSac* 1/97].

  Matthews, Victor H. [*M*], *Judges & Ruth* (NCBC) 2004. See Judges above. The commentary section on Ruth is short (27pp), and the valuable portion of his treatment is perhaps the bibliographical guidance (pp.213–16).

  Morris, Leon. (TOTC) 1968. Bound with Cundall on Judges. Morris is edifying and, as a NT specialist, makes good NT connections. Pastors used to have little else but Morris and Keil in the evangelical category.

✓ Murphy, Roland E. ‡ *Job, Proverbs, Ruth, Canticles, Ecclesiastes, Esther* (FOTL) 1981. Murphy was, in my opinion, the foremost American scholar in the field of Wisdom Literature. This form-critical research of Ruth is for students and OT specialists, and it has a dated feel. [*WTJ*, Spr 84; *JETS* 9/82; *JBL* 103.3 (1984); *ThTo* 39.4].

✓ **Nielsen, Kirsten.** ‡ (OTL) 1997. The reviews all note her interest in intertextuality, and this book does succeed in prompting the thoughtful reader to explore possible interplay between the text/story of Ruth and other biblical texts. See especially her exploration of links to Genesis 38, though most scholars now want to distinguish more strictly the *gō'ēl* tradition from the levirate (e.g., Hubbard, 57). Of greater interest to students than to preachers. [*JBL* Sum 99; *JSOT* 79 (1998); *Biblica* 79.3 (1998); *Interp* 1/99; *CBQ* 4/98; *HebStud* 1998; *RBL*].

Pressler, Carolyn. ‡ *Joshua, Judges, and Ruth* (WestBC) 2002.

F Queen-Sutherland, Kandy. ‡ (S&H). This author also is scheduled to contribute the commentaries on Esther, Song of Songs, and Lamentations; I am unsure whether there will be one volume or several.

☆ Roop, Eugene F. [*M*], *Ruth, Jonah, Esther* (BCBC) 2002. One of the best in this Anabaptist series.

☆ **Sakenfeld, Katharine Doob**. ‡ *Ruth* (I) 1999. An attractive 90-page commentary, which fails even to mention Hubbard. She voices feminist concerns at some junctures. The theological exposition is reasonably well done and will help the preacher. However, I suspect the list price of $29.95 may discourage some from purchasing Sakenfeld. [*JSOT* 89 (2000); *OTA*, 6/00; *Interp*, 4/01; *VT*, 51.3; *JSOT* 94 (2001)].

✓ **Sasson, Jack M.** ‡ *Ruth: A New Translation with a Philological Commentary and a Formalist–Folklorist Interpretation*, 1989. This work published by Sheffield is of great interest to academics because it applies some of the newer literary critical methods (Vladimir Propp influenced) to uncover the narrative skill and artistry. Almost 300pp. Hubbard questions Sasson's philology at numerous points and finds him lacking in theological interest. An earlier form of this commentary was published under the same title by Johns Hopkins in 1979. His work on Jonah is better. [*JBL* 100.4 (1981); *JETS* 12/80].

F Schwab, George. (EBCR).

✓ Van Wolde, Ellen J. ‡ *Ruth and Naomi*, 1997. This scholar, here published by SCM, is known for her semiotic/structuralist approach to OT narrative and her feminist approach. [*Interp* 7/99].

Vance, D.R. *A Hebrew Reader for Ruth*, 2003. Useful and well-produced. [*VT* 54.4; *JAOS* 123.4].

☆ Webb, Barry G. *Five Festal Garments: Christian Reflections on the Song of Songs, Ruth, Lamentations, Ecclesiastes and Esther*, 2000. This 150-page book offers a biblical theological interpretation of the message of each of the five *Megilloth* (מגלות, scrolls). I have found it stimulating for both teaching and preaching purposes. It is recognized as all the more valuable by the fact that these Bible books are among the most difficult for preachers to handle. [*EvQ* 7/03; *VT* 51.4; *Chm* Aut 01].

Wilch, John R. (Concord) 2006. I have yet to use this large (418pp) Lutheran exposition and therefore cannot make any recommendation. [*JETS* 9/07; *BSac* 10/09; *JSOT-BL* 2007].

☆ Younger, K. Lawson. *Judges/Ruth* (NIVAC) 2002. See Judges above, where this is a recommended purchase.

SAMUEL

★ Arnold, Bill T. (NIVAC) 2003. Preachers value Arnold's large exposition (681pp), built upon good exegesis, especially for sermon preparation. Students of the Hebrew might replace this selection with either McCarter or the Klein-Anderson set.

★ **Bergen, Robert D**. (NAC) 1996. This commentary (512pp) was long recommended for purchase by the faculty of Denver Seminary, and upon taking a closer look at Bergen I made it a pick, too. (Cf. Gordon below.) The commentary is well-balanced and very readable, with good attention given to historical, literary, and theological issues. What distinguishes the work is Bergen's use of discourse analysis; he edited a book on the topic of *Biblical Hebrew and Discourse Linguistics* (Eisenbrauns, 1994). Bergen would not be a poor first purchase on Samuel.

★ **Brueggemann, Walter.** ‡ (I) 1990. About the best exposition one could hope for from the critical perspective (about 360pp). This is yet another work by this prolific scholar which really gets you thinking (see under Genesis). Use with discernment; there's a good bit with which the evangelical will disagree. Compare with Davis below, which some pastors will prefer. On 1 Samuel specifically, Woodhouse provides more in the way of pastoral exposition than anyone else. [*CRBR* 1991; *CBQ* 1/92; *ThTo* 4/91; *Interp* 7/92; *HebStud* 1993].

★ **Firth, David G.** (Apollos) 2009. Though still assessing this 614-page work, I am impressed by many of its features. It is well-rounded, current in scholarship, courageous to challenge the critical consensus at points (e.g., the DH), careful in its exegetical analysis, readable (less technical), sensitive to literary devices, and has a sharp eye for biblical theological themes. There is less textual analysis and it does not have a technical "feel." A special feature of Firth's commentary is his gathering many of Fokkelman's literary insights from that four-vol. enormous set which very few have time or competence to work through. The bibliography includes several 2007 works (but not Tsumura's NICOT). Only rarely will British parlance confuse his American readership (e.g., "kit-bearer"). One difference I have with Firth is his interpretation of the sex in 2 Sam. 11 as less about lust and more about "an assault on Uriah that ultimately requires his murder" (p.415). Firth continues, David "is not trying to cover his tracks but rather trying to create a legal pretence for Uriah's execution" (418). I aver that David *does* rather than "does not send for a woman because he sees her beauty" (417), and I think he subsequently attempts a cover-up. Believing that both students and pastors will benefit greatly from buying this book, I reckon it to be my first choice as an exegetical reference tool. The author also has a new commentary on Esther in BST.

★ **Gordon, Robert P.** [*M*], *1 & 2 Samuel: A Commentary*, 1986. Zondervan published this superb commentary which is conservatively critical. Students and pastors both have deep appreciation for this work, which employs some of the newer literary methods in ways which shed new light on the text. In recent years Gordon had become more difficult to obtain, and for that reason I moved this off the recommended purchase list (and Bergen on). It is widely available again and back on the list. Gordon is soon to retire as Regius Professor of Hebrew at Cambridge. [*Them* 1/88; *RTR* 1/88]. Not to be confused with the commentary is *I and II Samuel* (JSOT, 1984), a fine book of essays which helps the student grasp the issues being addressed by scholars working on this portion of Scripture [*EvQ* 10/86].

★ **Tsumura, David Toshio.** *The First Book of Samuel* (NICOT) 2007. This volume will prove to be more useful to students working closely with the Hebrew text—he usually defends the MT (p.xi)—than to pastors most interested in theological exposition, though there is some theology certainly. Tsumura is esteemed as a learned commentator on philological and grammatical/syntactical matters; he also does well with discourse analysis. The stance taken on introductory matters is solidly conservative. I tend to agree with Williamson who says this commentary "will probably be consulted more for its particular strengths than for general purposes." If you want a book for preachers instead, buy Davis or Woodhouse. [*BBR* 19.1 (2009); *CBQ* 1/08; *Interp* 10/08; *HebStud* 2008; *JSOT-BL* 2008; *ExpTim* 5/08; *VT* 58.3 (Williamson); *JETS* 3/08; *RBL*; *RelSRev* 9/09; *Anvil* 25.4].

★ **Youngblood, Ronald.** (EBC) 1992. A lengthy, well-rounded commentary (550pp) by one of the abler OT scholars in evangelicalism. Perhaps most useful for its literary reading (building on the works of Fokkelman, Eslinger, Gunn, Gordon, Miscall, etc.) and textual criticism. This reminds me of VanGemeren on Psalms and Carson on Matthew in that this work is fuller and more academic than its companions in the EBC volume (Vol. 3: Deut–Sam). My counsel has long been to make this your first choice because of its depth of treatment, but now I have reassessed the options. Buy Firth first and then Gordon for exegesis. Youngblood is scheduled to do the EBCR, and you could wait for that replacement. Students will also gravitate toward AB and WBC, and they might consult Fokkelman in the library.

Ackroyd, Peter R. ‡ (CBC) 2 Vols., 1977. Once a leading British critical scholar, Ackroyd did a capable job of explaining these books to a popular audience. Discounts the historical value of these Scriptures.

✓ **Alter, Robert.** ‡ *The David Story: A Translation with Commentary of 1 and 2 Samuel*, 1999. Pick this up to get a fresh literary reading of Samuel from a Jewish perspective. Alter has been a leading expert on ancient Hebrew narrative. He notes some of the insights found in modern Hebrew commentaries (e.g., Bar-Efrat and Garsiel). The translation is occasionally too literal but frequently brilliant; the commentary he offers is selective. Such selective engagement with the text is not such a bad thing. (One of the problems with the modern commentary genre is that scholars are required to say something about everything, whether or not they have anything to say.) See further comment on Alter's work under Genesis.

☆ **Anderson, A.A.** ‡ *2 Samuel* (WBC) 1989. A fine complement to Klein's work, though marred by many typos. Anderson is no conservative, but he is a very capable British exegete who uses a more restrained critical approach. Note to students: on text critical questions you will find Driver, Youngblood, McCarter and the 2-volume WBC set most helpful. [*WTJ* Fall 92; *JTS* 4/91; *EvQ* 7/91; *CBQ* 4/91; *RTR* 9/90; *Them* 10/92; *Chm* 104.3; *CRBR* 1991].

F Auld, A. Graeme. ‡ (OTL replacement). The author, at the forefront of what has been termed the "Edinburgh School," contests the priority of Samuel-Kings over Chronicles. (Both drew with adaptation from a common source, he says.) This commentary will spark debate. See his previous works: *Kings Without Privilege*, 1994, and *Samuel at the Threshold: Selected Works of Graeme Auld*, 2004 [*BSac* 4/08; *ExpTim* 10/05 (Williamson)].

☆ **Baldwin, Joyce G.** (TOTC) 1988. We went for so long without a good, conservative commentary on the books of Samuel. Then we quickly got several: Gordon, Baldwin, Youngblood, and Bergen. Baldwin's 300-page work is compact, very readable, and satisfying as more of a quick reference. Careful scholarship underlies her conclusions. The volume is helpful for theology too. [*EvQ* 1/91; *Them* 1/92; *Chm* 104.4 (1990)].

✓ **Birch, Bruce C.** ‡ (NewIB) 1998. Quite full at nearly 350pp. Birch knows this literature well, having written his dissertation on *The Rise of the Israelite Monarchy: The Growth and Development of 1 Samuel 7–15* (1976). He ignores almost all evangelical works on Samuel. [*ExpTim* 1/99].

Blaikie, W.G. (EB) 1888. Was reprinted in 1978 by Klock & Klock and most recently (2010) by Nabu Press. This two-vol. commentary is esteemed by all to be one of the best in the old Expositor's Bible. This will aid the preacher, but not the student so much. See Joshua also.

F Block, Daniel. (BCBC).

✓ **Bodner, Keith.** ‡ *1 Samuel: A Narrative Commentary*, 2008. Originally planned for the "Readings" series, this 340-page commentary has both a perceptive literary approach and great respect for the text. [*JSOT-BL* 2009].

☆ Calvin, John. *Sermons on 2 Samuel 1–13*, ET 1992. For the preacher, this large work repays study. Douglas Kelly, systematics professor at Reformed Seminary, Charlotte, is responsible for the translation, published by Banner of Truth. This is the first time in English for the sermons, delivered in French. [*RTR* 9/95; *SBET* Spr 95].

✓ **Campbell, Antony F.** ‡ (FOTL) 2 Vols., 2003–05. Campbell, a brilliant Jesuit, is known for being a revisionist on issues of form critical methodology. He is just as interested in the final form of the book of Samuel (the synchronic) as he is in the compositional history (the diachronic). This is only for advanced students and specialists. [*RTR* 4/04, 12/05; *BSac* 7/06; *JETS* 9/04; *Interp* 10/04, 4/08; *JSOT* 28.5; *VT* 54.4; *CBQ* 1/05, 1/06; *JTS* 4/06; *JSS* Spr 06; *JNES* 7/08, 1/09; *RBL*; *Presb* Spr 06; *JAOS* 124.1, 126.4; *ExpTim* 5/06].

☆ **Cartledge, Tony W.** ‡ (S&H) 2001. A very full (over 700pp), competent exposition. Very little of the OT scholarship, upon which he builds, is cited, and this makes the volume less useful to the student. Cartledge seems to take a more conservative approach; though he may not himself have full confidence in the historicity of the narrative, he interprets the theological "story" as we have it. The volume costs almost $70. [*Interp* 10/04; *JSOT* 99 (2002); *CurTM* 4/04].

Chafin, Kenneth L. (WCC) 1989. Not a poor entry, but not rich either. [*Chm* 104.4 (1990)].

Conroy, C. ‡ *1–2 Samuel, 1–2 Kings* (OTM) 1983.

☆ Davis, Dale Ralph. *1 Samuel—Looking on the Heart*; *2 Samuel—Out of Every Adversity* (Christian Focus), 2 Vols., 1988–99. See my comments on his Joshua and Judges books. These have been published in the U.K. by Christian Focus and total over 550pp. Some will prefer this set to Brueggemann; both authors offer quite lively and perceptive theological readings (one evangelical, the other not). [*TJ* Fall 96; *RTR* 9/96; *Anvil* 18.4 (Evans)].

✓ **Driver, Samuel R.** ‡ *Notes on the Hebrew Text and the Topography of the Books of Samuel*, 2nd ed 1913. One of the greatest works of textual criticism ever done—on a book that really needed it! This is not a commentary, but must be included on our list. Reprinted in 1984 (Alpha Publications, Winona Lake, IN). To review some of what we have learned since Driver, including the 4QSam discoveries, see Philippe Hugo, "Text History of the Books of Samuel: An Assessment of the Recent Research," in Hugo/Schenker (eds), *Archeology of the Books of Samuel* (Brill, 2010)—especially his fine bibliography.

Erdmann, Chr. Fr. David. (Lange) ET 1877. Well over 600 pages.

✓ **Evans, Mary J.** [*M*], (NIBC) 2000. Covers the vast material of 1 and 2 Samuel in 288pp, which seems too slight in the larger-print NIBC format. Power and political power-plays are major motifs or themes in her commentary; while interesting, her focus does not seem as beneficial to the preacher. It is certainly worth consulting, though not a technical, academic work for students. See also the expositional BST entry below. Evans has written an introduction to OT prophecy entitled, *Prophets of the Lord* (Paternoster, 1992). [*ExpTim* 2/01; *Interp* 7/01; *SwJT* Sum 01; *CBQ* 1/01; *RTR* 12/01; *JSOT* 94 (2001); *Chm* Spr 01; *Anvil* 19.3].

☆ Evans, Mary J. (BST) 2004. Perhaps one of the less helpful theological expositions in this series, yet there are many insights here. As with the NIBC above, Evans' literary interests and insight are up front. [*Chm* Spr 06; *Anvil* 21.4].

✓ **Fokkelman, Jan P.** ‡ *Narrative Art and Poetry in the Books of Samuel: A Full Interpretation Based on Stylistic and Structural Analyses*, 1981–93. Four volumes containing over 2000pp of painstaking literary research. Though not a full-orbed commentary, this set is valued very highly by advanced students and OT specialists with an interest in the art of OT narrative. Do not expect theological reflection. See also the poetry studies of this Leiden professor which focus on Job and Psalms (see below). [*JSS* Spr 99; *JSOT* 65; *CBQ* 1/94].

✓ Franke, John R. (ed). *Joshua, Judges, Ruth, 1–2 Samuel* (ACCS) 2005.

Gehrke, R.D. (Concordia Commentary) 1968. Evangelical and Lutheran.

✓ Gunn, David M. ‡ *The Fate of King Saul*, JSOTSup 14 (1980); *The Story of King David*, JSOTSup 6 (1978). There are reports of a forthcoming Blackwell Bible Commentary on Samuel.

✓ Halpern, Baruch. *David's Secret Demons: Messiah, Murderer, Traitor, King*, 2001. More of a historical/archeological study by a conservatively critical Jewish scholar. He mentions in passing a major work on the history of ancient Israel that he is writing for ABRL.

✓ **Hertzberg, Hans W.** ‡ (OTL) ET 1964. One of the better older volumes in the series. It gives attention to historical and literary details. Alert to theological motifs too. This classic of German scholarship was long o/p, but WJK has reprinted it in pb. This is now becoming rather dated.

F Hoffner, Harry. (EEC). The author is a world-leading Hittite scholar.

✓ **Jobling, David.** ‡ *1 Samuel* (BO) 1998. "If anything," Jobling is a provocateur. Here you'll find a lot of structuralism, Marxist analysis, and a variety of reading strategies. After using Jobling's very postmodern commentary, you will know better what you yourself think about the biblical text. As you disagree with his interpretations, you are forced to come up with reasons for disagreeing. Sometimes he has excellent insights, e.g., on the timing of Hannah's song: the dedication of the child. [*CBQ* 7/99; *RelSRev* 7/99; *JSOT-BL* 1999; *Interp* 4/01; *JBL* Sum 01; *RBL*].

☆ Keddie, Gordon J. *Dawn of a Kingdom* (WCS on 1 Samuel) 1988; *Triumph of the King* (WCS on 2 Samuel) 1990. These two are well done and will help the expositor.

✓ Keil, C.F. (KD) ET 1872.

F Kim, Jichan. ‡ *2 Samuel* (HCOT).

✓ Kirkpatrick, A.F. [*M*], (Cambridge Bible) 1881–88, rev. 1930. Still surprisingly useful, the "revised and reset" edition is 469pp. The same author has a fine Psalms volume.

☆ **Klein, Ralph.** ‡ *1 Samuel* (WBC) 1983, 2nd ed 2009. Klein isn't conservative, but his commentary is useful—he is one of the most accomplished OT text critics—and fairly complete. It serves us well in places as a corrective to McCarter. Intended for scholars and pastors who have kept up with the Hebrew. There is not much theology here to speak of, though Klein, a Lutheran scholar, has interests in that area. The revised edition was released in March 2009 and runs to 350pp. The difference is merely an additional chapter: "My Commentary on 1 Samuel after Twenty-five Years." [*RTR* 1/85; *WTJ* Fall 84; *EvQ* 4/87; *JBL* 104.4 (1985); *JSOT-BL* 2010].

Leithart, Peter J. *A Son to Me: An Exposition of 1 & 2 Samuel*, 2003. See Leithart under Kings. [*JETS* 3/05].

✓ Long, V. Phillips. (New Geneva Study Bible) 1995. This study Bible published by Thomas Nelson explains the New King James Version. Long, who did his Cambridge dissertation (published 1989 [*CRBR* 1991]) on the story of Saul's reign in 1 Samuel, offers his literary insights into these books. Don't miss his much-used 1994 work on *The Art of Biblical History* [*TJ* Fall 95; *VT* 47.1].

✓ **McCarter, P. Kyle.** ‡ (AB) 2 Vols., 1980–84. One of the fullest commentaries to date on Samuel (over 1000pp) and one of the leading scholarly works, in part because McCarter had access to the DSS (but see also Ulrich's Harvard monograph, *The Qumran Text of Samuel and Josephus*, 1978). McCarter's approach to textual criticism could, in my opinion, use more restraint and respect for the MT. Engages in traditio-historical analysis but has little interest in theology. The academically oriented pastor could put this set to good use, especially its detailed textual notes. Among OT scholars McCarter is considered to be more conservatively critical on questions of historicity. Also he is an expert in textual criticism. The Denver Seminary faculty continue to make this their top pick (alongside Tsumura). [*JBL* 101.3 (1982); *Biblica* 67.1 (1986)].

McKane, William. ‡ (Torch Bible Commentaries) 1963. Quite critical.

Mauchline, J. ‡ (NCB) 1971. One of the weakest entries in the series.

Miscall, P.D. ‡ *1 Samuel: A Literary Reading*, 1986. Only for students interested in the diverse approaches of the new literary criticism now being used in studies of OT narrative. [*HebStud* 1988; *CRBR* 1988].

F Morrison, Craig. ‡ *2 Samuel* (BO). Previously Stephen Pisano was listed as the contributor.

Murphy, Francesca Aran. *1 Samuel* (Brazos) 2010.

Omanson, Roger, and John Ellington. (UBS) 2 Vols., 2001. I have found occasion to consult this 1283-page set.

Payne, David F. [𝓜], (DSB) 1982. Conservative for the series, and insightful on more the devotional level.

☆ Peterson, Eugene H. (WestBC) 1999. Unlike many other contributions to the series, this work is not critically oriented and is almost entirely composed of devotional reflection and application. There is little historical background information provided, and there are few literary insights. In short, negatively, this is not valuable as a guide into the text. However, it is so pastoral and spiritually-minded that readers will relish it for "quiet times." I get the sense that Peterson has responsibly researched the text and knows it well, but in his writing he chooses to concentrate on devotional "pearls." Often I would be critical of this sort of approach, but I enjoyed reading in this book, especially after sweating it through a rigorous exegesis of the Hebrew text of Samuel. I predict that any preacher, by carefully reading this book, could learn about both feeding the sheep and preaching Christ out of the OT. Perhaps my recommendation is to consider using this as devotional material and not as commentary. [*ThTo* 7/00; *Interp* 1/01; *JSOT* 94 (2001)].

Pink, Arthur. *The Life of David*, 1958. Exceedingly lengthy exposition.

✓ **Polzin, Robert.** ‡ *Samuel and the Deuteronomist: A Literary Study of the Deuteronomic History, I Samuel*, 1989; *David and the Deuteronomist: A Literary Study of the Deuteronomic History, II Samuel*, 1993. Polzin is a challenging, provocative voice among those calling for literary readings of Scripture. Often it seems to me he reads against the grain of the text rather than with it. Still, this is important material these days in the scholarly discussion. Compare with Fokkelman. [*HebStud* 1993; *CRBR* 1990].

Robinson, Gnana. *Let Us Be Like the Nations: 1 & 2 Samuel* (ITC) 1993. This exposition, written by the principal of a seminary in India, interacts very little with the scholarly literature. Robinson does not bother to discuss critical issues; his focus is on the story line of these books and the contemporary relevance of the message. Of more interest to the preacher than to the student.

✓ Smith, Henry Preserved. ‡ (ICC) 1899.

Swindoll, Charles. *David: A Man of Passion and Destiny*, 1996. The review in *Christianity Today*, 6/16/97, is instructive reading and might save you both disappointment and a few shekels.

F Tsumura, David Toshio. *The Second Book of Samuel* (NICOT).

Van Seters, John. ‡ *The Biblical Saga of King David*, 2009. A major critical work issued by Eisenbrauns. See his many works on the Pentateuch and the DH. [*JSOT-BL* 2010].

F Vannoy, J. Robert. (CorBC). This will be bound with Kings. Vannoy served as Professor of OT at Biblical Seminary in Hatfield, PA and did an superb job on Samuel and Kings in the notes of the *NIV Study Bible* (1985), especially considering the prescribed length. He is a fine biblical theologian.

F Viberg, Ake. ‡ *1 Samuel* (HCOT).

☆ Woodhouse, John. *1 Samuel: Looking for a Leader* (PTW) 2008. This exposition (672pp), by the Principal of Moore Theological College in Sydney, builds upon solid OT scholarship (Woodhouse earned a PhD in OT at Manchester), is easy to read, and prompts the preacher to read 1 Samuel Christologically. The anointed leaders point to Christ in both their successes and failures, the latter giving the people of God a heightened sense of need for a perfectly righteous king. Pastors will want this book on their shelf, not only for its exposition of Samuel but also as a model for doing biblical theological interpretation of OT narrative (cf. Van't Veer on Kings).

F Youngblood, Ronald F. (EBCR).

NOTE: OT Histories are invaluable here. Likewise for Kings, Chronicles, and Ezra-Nehemiah. See the "Note" under Joshua.

KINGS

★ Dillard, Raymond B. *Faith in the Face of Apostasy: The Gospel According to Elijah and Elisha*, 1999. Published by P&R, this 170-page pb presents the thoughtful biblical-theological approach Dillard always did so well in the seminary classroom. He will lead you first to hear "the authentic voice of the OT" (my terms) and then teach you how to preach Christ out of the OT. I bought the book. Students working with the Hebrew might bypass this and Fretheim to purchase the two-vol. AB and/ or Sweeney. [*RTR* 12/00].

★ Fretheim, Terence. ‡ (WestBC) 1999. Fulfills the aims of the series. Though some may consider this volume a bit too short at 228pp to cover such a vast amount of material, Fretheim's theological and practical insights make this reasonably priced pb a very smart purchase for the preacher. Treats the final form of the text and could accurately be assessed as [*M*], or mildly critical. Fretheim is less critical and more in sympathy with the text than Nelson (see both on 2 Kings 4). [*JSOT* 89 (2000); *Interp* 4/00; *CBQ* 1/00; *RelSRev* 4/00].

★   **Hobbs, T.R.** [*M*], *2 Kings* (WBC) 1985. Until the mid-1990s it was difficult to suggest commentaries on Kings; so little had been written covering this fascinating portion of Scripture. Hobbs had begun to meet the need. This work is very thorough, reads narrative well, and provides a lot of help with the Hebrew text. This would be a worthy addition to your library, though it does not have all the elements I look for in an exegetical commentary. Hobbs' approach is less critical than DeVries'. I find little objectionable here. [*RTR* 5/87; *TJ* Fall 86; *CRBR* 1988]. See also the volume on *1, 2 Kings* by Hobbs (1989) in the Word Biblical Themes series.

★   **House, Paul.** (NAC) 1995. A solid, well-rounded effort in this newer series, House's commentary on Kings fills a void in the conservative pastor's library. It is valuable exegetically and theologically. After teaching at a variety of schools, including Taylor University, Southern Baptist Seminary, and Wheaton, he joined Beeson Divinity School. See Lamentations. [*VT* 7/96; *JETS* 12/97; *BL* 1997; *BSac* 1/96].

★   **Provan, Iain. W.** (NIBC) 1995. This commentary launched the series' OT section, and its theological exposition is profitable for pastors. The author's previous work on this literature—see *Hezekiah and the Book of Kings* (1988)—was somewhat critical and diachronic. This superb commentary takes a more synchronic and evangelical approach, with good attention paid to literary features. And this believing scholar, now teaching at Regent College in Vancouver, is "taking the heat" for his courageous stance; see *JBL*, Winter 95, pp.585–606 and 683–705. [*BL* 1997; *CBQ* 4/98; *RTR* 4/01]. Students can also look up his witty contribution of *1 & 2 Kings* (1997) to Sheffield's "OT Guides" series [*EvQ* 10/99; *JSOT* 79; *DenvJ*].

★   **Walsh, Jerome T.** ‡ *1 Kings* (BO) 1996. As the very first work in the series, this set a high standard. Walsh has some fresh and fascinating literary insights. (Among the remarkably few good commentaries on 1 Kings, fewer still show an interest in the narrative art of this Bible book.) Students and more scholarly pastors will enjoy this 400-page work which focuses on the final-form, but that is not to say this commentary is less accessible and is difficult reading. Even the educated layman could use this volume. Little here would be objectionable to an evangelical interpreter. [*JSOT* 79; *JETS* 6/99; *CBQ* 4/97; *JBL* Spr 98; *RBL*].

☆   Auld, A. Graeme. ‡ (DSB) 1986. In much the same mold as his commentary on Joshua–Ruth for the same series. More helpful to expositors than to students. Well-done from the critical angle.

✓   Bähr, Karl Chr. W. F. (Lange) ET 1872. This is one of the best in that old series. Includes not only exegesis but also a most suggestive homiletical section. This 570-page volume (minuscule print) is praised to high heaven by Spurgeon, and, in looking over the copy passed down to me from my grandfather, I have concluded it deserved the praise. Zondervan reprinted this back in 1960. Would that somebody would again reprint Bähr!

F   Beal, Lissa Wray. (Apollos).

F   Brubacher, Gordon. (BCBC).

Brueggemann, Walter. ‡ (Knox Preaching Guides) 2 Vols., 1982. More cursory, but suggestive at points. You can bypass this now that the S&H volume below has appeared.

☆   **Brueggemann, Walter.** ‡ (S&H) 2000. This author of many commentaries loves OT theology, is creative and imaginative—communicating well with postmoderns. Brueggemann's commentary is weighty (over 600pp) and expensive. See his other works under Genesis, Exodus, Samuel, Isaiah, and Jeremiah. This is well worth purchasing, but only if it is to be used a good bit ($65 list). [*Interp* 1/02; *JSOT* 99 (2002); *RelSRev* 10/01; *CurTM* 2/02].

✓ Burney, Charles F. ‡ *Notes on the Hebrew Text of the Books of Kings*, 1903. Good text critical work, now superseded by the ICC volume and others. This same scholar gave us the massive two-vol. study on the Hebrew text of Judges. Burney was reprinted by Cambridge in 1983.

F Cathcart, Kevin J. ‡ *2 Kings* (HCOT).

✓ **Cogan, Mordechai, and Hayim Tadmor.** ‡ *II Kings* (AB) 1988; *I Kings* (AB) 2001. This technical and critical work by two Israeli scholars espouses the now standard double Deuteronomistic redaction; the authors would be considered conservatively critical within the OT guild. The volume on 1 Kings, done by Cogan alone, contains the introduction. The AB set is valuable for specialists and should be considered for purchase by scholarly pastors—the Denver Seminary OT bibliography recommends House, Provan, and Cogan-Tadmor. The authors' expertise lies in the history of Mesopotamia in the 1ˢᵗ millennium BC, and they provide extensive documentation for their historical conclusions. There is a lack of theology. [*JBL* 108.4 (1989); *HebStud* 1990; *BSac* 1/04; *JHebS*].

✓ **Cohn, Robert L.** ‡ *2 Kings* (BO) 2000. I have only dipped into it. At 175pp it is not a full-scale commentary on 2 Kings, but what it sets out to do—see "BO" in the commentary series section—it does well. Note Walsh's much fuller BO work above. What theological reflection there is comes from a Jewish perspective. [*OTA* 10/00; *Interp* 7/01; *CBQ* 7/01; *HebStud* 2002; *JSOT* 94 (2001); *RelSRev* 1/01].

Conroy, C. ‡ *1–2 Samuel, 1–2 Kings* (OTM) 1983.

✓ Conti, Marco (ed). *1–2 Kings, 1–2 Chronicles, Ezra, Nehemiah, Esther* (ACCS) 2008.

☆ Davis, Dale Ralph. *The Wisdom and the Folly*, 2002; *The Power and the Fury*, 2005. The first volume, a readable 350-page exposition of 1 Kings, has been published and warmly received in the U.K. I have yet to see it in an American bookstore. (Believe it or not, I found and bought a copy in central Africa!) These two pb volumes would be wise purchases for expositors. See his other lively theological commentaries on Joshua, Judges, and Samuel. Preachers might want to move this set up to the starred category. [*Chm* Aut 02, Win 06].

✓ **De Vries, Simon.** ‡ *1 Kings* (WBC) 1985, 2ⁿᵈ edition 2003. Not as thorough or responsible in his work as Hobbs, and takes a dimmer view of the book's historical worth. DeVries' other works show he has more interest in theological issues than he manifests here; this volume is a rather dry well for the expositor. Still, it should be consulted for academic work on 1 Kings. I regret that the 2ⁿᵈ edition offers no revision of the original commentary; it only adds 16pp of "Supplemental Bibliography" and a five-page excursus attacking the radical "minimalists" in OT scholarship, who denigrate the Scriptures as a source for history. If you own 1985, don't bother with 2003. [*Biblica* 68.1 (1987); *RTR* 5/86; *JETS* 12/86; *HebStud* 1986].

☆ Dilday, Russell H. (WCC) 1987. Some reviewers have called this homiletical commentary strong, while others find it mediocre. I vote more with the former group. Though Dilday misses the riches that can be mined out with a redemptive-historical (biblical-theological) approach, he does well at giving relevant background information (e.g., 1 Kings 16:29–34). Quite full at over 500pp.

Ellul, Jacques. [𝓜], *The Politics of God and the Politics of Man*, ET 1972. Ellul is always brilliant and interesting. This is a bold exposition of extensive parts of 2 Kings. Theologically sensitive (with essentially a Barthian viewpoint), Christological, and conservatively critical. Well worth buying if you can find this choice book secondhand. [*JBL* 92.3 (1973)].

Farrar, Frederic W. [*M*], (EB) 1892–93. Has been reprinted, but may be difficult to obtain apart from the whole EB set. "A rich and vigorous exposition," says Childs. There are some critical, rationalistic conclusions (e.g., comments on 1 Kings 17:6).

F   Fowler, Don. (CorBC). Bound with Samuel.

✓   **Fritz, Volkmar.** ‡ (ContC) 1996–98, ET 2003. This 450-page, historically-oriented commentary is not having the best reception. The main complaints are a narrow interest in discerning compositional layers and a lack of interest in the theological message. The great strength of the author is archaeology. Though this work is far less technical than others in ContC, Fritz is not for pastors. Students will look in vain for discussion of text, philology, grammar, narrative features, and theology. [*CBQ* 10/04; *JSOT* 28.5; *JHebS*; *RBL*; *ExpTim* 6/06; *CTJ* 4/10].

F   Fyall, Robert. (Mentor).

✓   **Gray, John.** ‡ (retired OTL) 1963, rev. 1970. Provan once remarked that few commentaries on the historical books were helpful for preachers: "Too often historical issues have dominated leaving little room for narrative and theological concerns" [*BSB* 3/97]. Gray is a case in point. Though he presents a lot of information (802pp), he is dry as dust. Pastors could glean very little to help them in sermon presentation; Gray seems to have no interest in theology. This has been considered one of the most important academic commentaries, but it is rather dated at this point (and o/p). Students should still consult it for research papers, but not before Sweeney's important replacement volume for OTL. [*JBL* 93.3 (1974)].

✓   Hens-Piazza, Gina. ‡ (AOTC) 2006. The author is a proponent of both *The New Historicism* (2002), which is a distinctly postmodern method, and socio-rhetorical interpretation. Hens-Piazza's interests are mainly literary and theological, rather than historical. The Hebrew is hardly mentioned. Reviews are mixed, with Miscall regarding her work as uneven and somewhat lacking in critical rigor, and Nelson praising it as a competent, accessible exegesis. She engages the text with a hermeneutic of suspicion and at points will deconstruct the heroes of the story. [*CBQ* 7/07; *Interp* 7/07; *BL* 2008; *JETS* 3/09; *JHebS* 2009].

F   Hess, Richard. (NICOT). Previously David Howard was said to have the NICOT contract. We have always lacked a "heavyweight" evangelical commentary on Kings and I hope Hess will deliver one.

✓   **Jones, Gwilym H.** ‡ (NCB) 2 Vols., 1984. Critical, lengthy (650pp), and sometimes of help. Jones is definitely preferable to Gray, but still is too skeptical and narrowly concerned with historical-critical issues. When it appeared it was among the best critical works and advanced students considered this for purchase, but Jones now seems rather dated. [*JETS* 12/85; *ExpTim* 12/85].

✓   Keil, C.F. (KD) ET 1857. I used to be in the habit of looking up Keil first, before Provan and House came on the scene. He is at his best in the historical material, and "often surprises the reader with a profound theological insight" (Childs). In a sense we are still waiting for Keil's replacement. NAC, NIBC and TOTC are great to have, but the task remains for an evangelical to give us an extensive exegetical study on the Hebrew text of Kings—especially 1 Kings, since we have Hobbs' good work on 2 Kings.

✓   **Knoppers, Gary N.** [*M*], *Two Nations under God: The Deuteronomistic History of Solomon and the Dual Monarchies*, 1993–94. This two-vol. dissertation for Harvard contains some valuable commentary on the text of Kings. Knoppers' work has been appreciated by evangelicals because it shows more respect for the text as providing valuable historical evidence (unlike some current, radically skeptical scholarship by the likes of P.R. Davies and T.L. Thompson). He is conservatively critical and often writes good reviews in *CTJ*. [*JETS* 9/96; *JBL* Win 96; *JTS* 10/96; *Interp* 7/96; *CBQ* 1/96].

☆ Konkel, August H. (NIVAC) 2006. Appropriately, a larger volume (704pp) in the series. I have had less opportunity to review this, but I agree with my friend, John Glynn, who proofread the book for Zondervan and called it "a very solid effort, multifaceted in Hebrew, ANE, archeological, and theological coverage."

F Le Roux, Jurie. ‡ *1 Kings*. Vol. 2, 1 Kings 12–22 (HCOT). See Mulder below.

Leithart, Peter J. (Brazos) 2006. The author has a brilliant mind and moves text-by-text, sometimes in a more cursory manner, offering a theological exposition and many redemptive-historical insights. There is heavy (sometimes indefensible?) typology in service of Christological interpretation. (He writes more as a systematic theologian than as an OT scholar.) Though Leithart's connections with the Auburn Avenue (Federal Vision) theology will be off-putting to some, he has done some good (but uneven) work here. The book is more stimulating than it is a dependable guide through the text. [*JETS* 12/07; *Interp* 1/08; *JSOT-BL* 2007; *ThTo* 4/09; *ExpTim* 9/07; *RelSRev* 3/08; *JSOT-BL* 2007].

✓ Lemaire, André, and Baruch Halpern (eds). ‡ *The Book of Kings: Sources, Composition, Historiography and Reception*, 2010. An enormous (710-page) treasure of essays, nearly a dictionary, on the topics taken up in an introduction to this Bible book. Published by Brill.

Leuchter, Mark, and Klaus-Peter Adam (eds). ‡ *Soundings in Kings: Perspectives and Methods in Contemporary Scholarship*, 2010. A Fortress Press issue.

✓ **Long, Burke O.** ‡ (FOTL) 2 Vols., 1984–91. This is for advanced students interested in a form critical approach to Kings, but as a very welcome addition Long departs somewhat from the standard format of the series and offers more extensive commentary on the structure and literary art of the text. A good bit can be learned from this set. [*JBL* 9/86, Sum 93; *RTR* 5/93; *JETS* 3/96; *JR* 7/93].

✓ **Montgomery, James A., and H.S. Gehman.** ‡ (ICC) 1951. A classic. "A superb example of text critical scholarship" (Childs). Adequate historical treatment as well (for its time), but Montgomery had no real theological interest. This was the last of the old ICC volumes to see publication, and it is still frequently consulted.

✓ **Mulder, Martin J.** ‡ *1 Kings*. Vol. 1, 1 Kings 1–11 (HCOT) ET 1998. Over 600pp of minute exegesis. This set promises to be the most thorough, technical historical-critical investigation yet of 1 Kings, and as such it will be invaluable to students. All we have had on the Hebrew text of 1 Kings heretofore is WBC and ICC, with help from the AB. Mulder of Leiden is now deceased (†1994); Jurie le Roux of Pretoria (see above) will carry on the project. [*Biblica* 81.3 (2000); *RelSRev* 7/00].

✓ **Nelson, Richard.** ‡ (I) 1987. The author is well known for his work on the supposed double Deuteronomistic redaction of these books. Despite the attention he pays to the message and theology of the text (in line with the series' aims), he retains a strong interest in narrower literary and historical issues. This is a noteworthy commentary for preachers, especially because expositions of Kings are few. Compare with Fretheim and Brueggemann, who have more to say theologically.

✓ Omanson, Roger, and John Ellington. *A Handbook on 1–2 Kings* (UBS) 2 Vols., 2008. [*JSOT-BL* 2009].

F Oswalt, John N. (EEC).

✓ Patterson, Richard D., and Hermann J. Austel. (EBC) 1988. Somewhat useful for the average pastor, but many have found it not very penetrating as it tends merely to retell the biblical story with some accompanying historical sidelights. See the next entry. I hope it will be of much higher caliber.

F   Patterson, Richard D., and Hermann J. Austel. (EBCR).

☆   Pink, Arthur. *Elijah*, 1956. This is Pink's most profitable exposition: warmly commended. Banner of Truth has been keeping it in print for years. But be sure to check his exegesis. Note: Pink's other exposition of the Books of Kings, *Gleanings from Elisha*, is not so good.

☆   Rice, G. [*M*], *1 Kings: Nations under God* (ITC) 1990. One of the better volumes in the series for the preacher, packed with relevant information and theological reflection. Very little here could prove objectionable to an evangelical preacher. Praised by Longman.

     Robinson, J. ‡ (CBC) 2 Vols., 1972–76.

✓   **Seow, Choon-Leong.** ‡ (NewIB) 1999. Well-researched yet surprisingly brief. The brevity is especially noticeable when one considers that both the NIV and NRSV texts are printed out, leaving less room for interpretation. Some other NewIB commentaries are much fuller; for example, while Kings (118pp in *BHS*) has only 295pp of discussion, Ezekiel (95pp in *BHS*) was allocated 533pp. This Princeton Seminary scholar has a standout commentary on Ecclesiastes. His theology is liberal. [*ExpTim* 2/00; *CTJ* 11/01].

     Skinner, John. ‡ (Century Bible) 1904. By the author of Genesis in the ICC.

F   Spina, Frank Anthony. (THC).

✓   **Sweeney, Marvin A.** ‡ (OTL) 2007. This learned Jewish scholar should be consulted by all students for an up-to-date, historical critical commentary on Kings. An introduction of 44pp is followed by 424pp of compact, rigorous exegesis. Sweeney is especially interested in King Josiah's place in the Deuteronomistic History (a Josianic redaction, among four other strata); see *King Josiah of Judah* (Oxford, 2001) [*JAOS* 122.1]. This commentary replaces Gray's much fatter volume and, like its predecessor, really does not venture much into theological interpretation. With regard to historical approach, Sweeney views himself as charting a middle way between those who read the Bible as fiction and those who accept the Bible's historical claims more at face value. Alongside the diachronic interests Sweeney has displayed over many years, he also takes seriously the final form of the text (the synchronic). [*WTJ* Fall 08; *CBQ* 4/08; *JSOT-BL* 2008; *ExpTim* 4/09; *Them* 4/09; *VT* 58.4 (Williamson); *RBL*; *BBR* 20.1; *Interp* 10/09].

✓   Thiele, Edwin R. *The Mysterious Numbers of the Hebrew Kings*, 1951, rev. 1965 and 1983. The thesis is rather complex, but I think the regularly-reprinted Thiele has done a brilliant job of dealing with the difficult problem of chronology from the conservative angle, though scholars like to point out that problems still exist [*JBL* 3/79]. Many conservatives believe that a few adjustments with co-regencies—see McFall, "A Translation Guide to the Chronological Data in Kings and Chronicles," *BSac* 148.1 (1991): 3–45 [available free on the internet]—cause the problems to disappear. Cf. J. Finegan, *Handbook of Biblical Chronology* (Hendrickson, 1998), who accepts the Thiele/McFall synthesis. Another strong work on chronology, this one from the critical camp, is John Hayes and P. K. Hooker, *A New Chronology for the Kings of Israel and Judah and Its Implications for Biblical History and Literature*, (Westminster Press, 1988). Among more recent books on the subject, my preferred book is Gershon Galil, *The Chronology of the Kings of Israel and Judah* (Brill, 1996) [*JTS* 4/98; *VT* 49.4]. Other works addressing the matter are helpfully listed in Hobbs' *2 Kings* (p. xxxviii). A newer, more radical attempt to untangle the knots is M. Christine Tetley, *The Reconstructed Chronology of the Divided Kingdom*, 2005 [*VT* 57.4; *JNES* 7/08 (Klein); *AUSS* 45.2 (2007)].

Van Groningen, Gerard. *Evangelical Commentary on the Bible,* 1989. This is from Baker Books' one-vol. commentary.

✓ Vannoy, J. Robert. *NIV Study Bible* notes, 1985. See under Samuel. You will be surprised, if you look closely at the notes, how packed it is. The biblical theology here is a good complement to Wiseman's work.

☆ Van't Veer, M.B. *My God Is Yahweh*, ET 1980. What a delight to come across this outstanding 400-page exposition of Elijah's early ministry (1 Kings 16:34–19:21)! To say that this man was theologically perceptive is an understatement. I can scarcely find any finer biblical theology drawn from the historical literature of the OT. Go to school on this. Was published by Paideia/Premier; P.O. Box 1450; St. Catherines, Ontario, Canada L2R 7J8. Is probably long o/p; I used to have Van't Veer on the recommended purchase list. Compare with the Jewish work of Simon mentioned above under "Reading Narrative."

☆ Wallace R.S. *Readings in 1 Kings*, 1995; *Readings in 2 Kings*, 1997. These two volumes build upon his older rich exposition, *Elijah and Elisha*. [*SBET* Spr 98].

F Wilson, Robert McL. ‡ (Herm).

☆ **Wiseman, D.J.** (TOTC) 1993. This author is universally held in high esteem; he was chosen as editor of this series, which tells you something. Wiseman is especially noted for his historical studies of the ANE, Assyriology in particular. See, for example, his groundbreaking *Chronicles of the Chaldean Kings*, 1956. The commentary's strength is in providing much information on the historical background— Provan and House are much better on the message of Kings. Up until the 2001 edition of this guide, I recommended this TOTC for purchase. See Keil above. [*CTJ* 11/94; *EvQ* 4/95; *Evangel* Spr 95; *JSOT* 61; *SwJT* Sum 94; *SBET* Aut 96].

NOTE: Michael Avioz, "The Book of Kings in Recent Research (Part I)," *CBR* 4.1 (2005): 11–55; and *idem*, "The Book of Kings in Recent Research (Part II), *CBR* 5.1 (2006): 11–57.

—〰—

CHRONICLES

NOTE: American missionaries joke about the paralysis of indecision they experience when, previously deprived, they come home and face a million choices while walking into the supermarket. Evans is having that kind of experience here with Chronicles commentaries. Please mix and match according to your needs and interests. All these recommended works are worth having.

★ **Dillard, Ray.** *2 Chronicles* (WBC) 1987. We are now blessed to have many fine commentaries on Chronicles. Dillard's volume is excellent all-round. There is some very creative biblical theological interpretation which will enrich a pastor's study of this long neglected book—there is no lack of scholarly interest now. Though he was committed to inerrancy, Dillard did not skirt the hard exegetical issues in Chronicles and drew some conclusions which raised questions among fellow evangelicals. (He resigned from the Evangelical Theological Society about the time this volume came out.) His death in October 1993 was a terrible loss to Westminster Seminary, OT scholarship, and the Church. Longman's first pick. [*JBL* 108.3; *HebStud* 1989; *JTS* 4/89].

★ Hill, Andrew E. (NIVAC) 2003. Hill provides a well done mix of exegesis and guidance for application. The research is solid, and the volume is quite full for the series (700pp). Though this is a book for preachers, students can also benefit as they ask their questions, "What does a learned evangelical approach to Chronicles look like? What are its challenges and advantages?" [*JETS* 6/05; *CTJ* 4/10].

★ **Japhet, Sara.** [*M*], (OTL) 1993. Magnificent and very valuable, particularly to specialists and scholarly pastors. Japhet is "the doyenne of Chronicles studies" (Williamson), and this conservatively critical work is the largest commentary yet on 1–2 Chronicles (1104pp). A keen Jewish scholar, she has worked on the exegesis and theology of Chronicles for decades. It seems a pity not to have any indices at the end. The average pastor might well leave this off the "to buy" list. For a fine, more accessible substitute, you should consider McKenzie. See Blenkinsopp under Ezra-Nehemiah. [*WTJ* Spr 95; *Interp* 4/96; *CBQ* 10/95; *JR* 4/95; *JSS* Spr 95; *JSOT* 65; *BSac* 1/95; *HebStud* 1995]. Students will note her newly-republished study focusing on the Chronicler's distinctives: *The Ideology of the Book of Chronicles and Its Place in Biblical Thought*, 1989, 2009 [*RBL*; *JSOT-BL* 2010], which has been tremendously influential. Useful for both Chronicles and Ezra–Nehemiah studies is *From the Rivers of Babylon to the Highlands of Judah: Collected Studies on the Restoration Period*, 2006.

★ **Knoppers, Gary.** [*M*], *I Chronicles* (AB) 2 Vols., 2004. The conservatively critical author teaches at Penn State. This will be a replacement set on all of Chronicles—see Myers below—but only the first half of Chronicles is complete. This is the fullest, most probing commentary ever published on 1 Chronicles (1000pp). The textual criticism is exceedingly thorough and careful. Also see Knoppers under Kings. Very few pastors will have the money for this or the interest, but it is a superb work, worthy of inclusion among the recommended works. As a technical exegesis, not an exposition, this is nearly definitive—Klein is the only close competitor. [*JTS* 4/06; *Interp* 7/06; *JSS* Aut 07; *JSOT-BL* 2005; *Biblica* 87.4; *RelSRev* 4/07; *RBL*].

★ Pratt, Richard. (Mentor) 1998. This 512-page, mainly theological commentary is somewhat like Currid's on Exodus. I think Pratt may have gotten started on this book by contributing the Chronicles notes to the *New Geneva Study Bible* or *Reformation Study Bible*. I haven't used this commentary extensively, but commend it to pastors for their consideration. More expositional than exegetical. The author has done good work with OT narrative—*He Gave Us Stories* (1990)—and long taught at RTS in Orlando. Compare with Hill. Other fine expositional helps are Allen (WCC), McConville, Wilcock. [*Them* 6/00].

★ **Selman, Martin J.** (TOTC) 2 Vols., 1994. Well over 500pp of informed, conservative comment. The author was able to build upon the excellent WBC volumes on Chronicles. I would not quarrel with anyone recommending this as a first purchase for a pastor's library; the price is right. Selman is particularly interested in theology and is a good partner to Williamson's or Japhet's exegesis. [*Them* 10/95; *JETS* 6/97; *JSOT* 71; *BSac* 7/95; *Chm* 110.2].

★ **Williamson, H.G.M.** [*M*], (NCB) 1982. A treasure trove. According to Dillard years ago, this was the best commentary on all of Chronicles. Well-reasoned and conservatively critical in his conclusions, Williamson seems to disdain as unscholarly attempts at harmonization (Chronicles with Samuel–Kings). Sadly, this appears to have gone o/p in the U.S. Compare with McKenzie. For a companion volume to this NCB, see Williamson under Ezra–Nehemiah. [*Them* 9/85; *ExpTim* 6/83].

✧ ✧ ✧ ✧ ✧ ✧

✓ Ackroyd, P.R. ‡ (Torch Bible Commentary) 1973. A critical work of note because of the author's "important role in the general rehabilitation of the Chronicler" [*BSB* 12/00]. But Williamson adds, "the commentary itself is very brief, and seems to have been hurriedly written." Ackroyd's expertise lay in the exilic and post-exilic literature. See also his OTL volume, *Exile and Restoration* (1968), and his book of collected essays, *The Chronicler in His Age* (1991), which contains a lifetime of learning (397pp).

☆ Allen, Leslie C. [𝓜], (WCC) 1987. This is so good I would like to include it above. A tremendous amount of research lies behind this work: Allen's two-vol. PhD dissertation concerned the LXX of Chronicles. This is one of the best researched volumes in the series, alongside Hubbard on Proverbs; Ecclesiastes–Song of Songs. We have another more exegetical work from Allen's word-processor; see immediately below.

✓ **Allen, Leslie C.** [𝓜], (NewIB) 1999. See entry immediately above. This mature commentary is 360pp and reworks some of his earlier material. Those building a first-class library will buy this. [*ExpTim* 2/00; *CTJ* 11/01].

✓ Ben Zvi, Ehud. ‡ *History, Literature and Theology in the Book of Chronicles*, 2006.

F Boda, Mark. (CorBC). Bound with Ezra–Esther.

F Bodner, Keith. (NICOT).

☆ **Braun, Roddy.** [𝓜], *1 Chronicles* (WBC) 1986. Quite helpful, especially on the genealogies. Braun is more technical but not as interesting as NCB. He knows this literature well and brings out some fine theological points. Braun is a Lutheran scholar who employs some newer-style literary criticism. He doesn't handle the text with quite the same respect as Dillard. (I wish he did not regard chs. 23–27 as secondary.) Advanced students may want to buy this one, but do note the more critical review in *HebStud* 1987. I now consider both Knoppers and Klein to have far eclipsed this work, but those volumes are a lot more expensive, too. [*EvQ* 10/88; *RTR* 9/87; *CRBR* 1988].

✓ Coggins, R.J. ‡ (CBC) 1976. One of the best in the series. [*EvQ* 10/77].

✓ Conti, Marco (ed). *1–2 Kings, 1–2 Chronicles, Ezra, Nehemiah, Esther* (ACCS) 2008.

✓ Curtis, E.L. and A.A. Madsen. ‡ (ICC) 1910. This volume, from a time when Chronicles was widely ignored, is consulted on technical questions by those interested in history of interpretation. Quite liberal and skeptical.

✓ **De Vries, Simon J.** ‡ (FOTL) 1989. At 439pp, this is a full-scale work to be consulted by students with form critical interests. DeVries was once in the evangelical camp, but became more critical. [*WTJ* Fall 91; *JETS* 6/92; *Them* 4/91; *BSac* 1/92; *HebStud* 1990; *CRBR* 1991].

✓ **Dirksen, Peter B.** ‡ *1 Chronicles* (HCOT) 2003, ET 2005. This technical exegesis of the Hebrew text is of manageable size (356pp) and of great value to students. It does not compete favorably, however, with the newer scholarly commentaries by Knoppers and Klein, nor with the older Japhet. As with some other continental European series, the treatment of a passage is divided into several (too many) sections: Introduction; Translation; Essentials and Perspectives; Scholarly Exposition (I); Scholarly Exposition (II); e.g., see pp.93–98. I regret there are no indexes. Kalimi is scheduled to complete the set. [*BBR* 19.1; *VT* 57.3].

F Duke, Rodney. (Apollos).

✓ Graham, Patrick, Kenneth Hoglund, and Steven McKenzie (eds). ‡ *The Chronicler as Historian*, 1997. Here the leading critical scholars on Chronicles contribute influential articles to a Sheffield collection. [*EvQ* 7/02; *BibInt* 9.2]. And added to this volume are *The Chronicler as Author: Studies in Text and Texture*, 2002 [*CurTM* 12/02], and a 2003 Festschrift for Ralph Klein, edited by Graham, McKenzie and Knoppers, entitled *The Chronicler as Theologian* (JSNT Supplement Series, #371) [*HebStud* 2005; *VT* 57.1].

F   Hahn, Scott. (Brazos). An able OT scholar, once a conservative Presbyterian but now a Catholic apologist.

      Hicks, John Mark. (College Press NIV Commentary) 2001. A rather large (540-page) exposition which tends to concentrate on theological matters. [*RelSRev* 4/02].

F   Hoglund, Kenneth E. (S&H).

      Hooker, Paul K. ‡ (WestBC) 2001. Can be compared with Tuell's exposition of similar length for WJK's Interpretation series (see the *Them* review which finds Hooker both more exegetical and more liberal). This is well done and highly theological from the critical camp. Preachers can learn from this reasonably priced pb (about 300pp), but it is not as much homiletical help as some might expect from this series. [*Them* Spr 04; *CTJ* 11/03; *Interp* 4/04; *ExpTim* 2/03; *RelSRev* 4/02; see Williamson's review in *JSOT* 27.5].

✓   **Jarick, John.** ‡ (Read) 2 Vols., 2002–07. This is an important literary critical reading, one which is pursued without constant comparisons to Samuel-Kings. [*JSOT-BL* 2005, 2009; *RBL*; *JTS* 10/09; *ExpTim* 11/09 (Klein)].

✓   **Johnstone, William.** ‡ 2 Vols., 1997. Published by Sheffield, this commentary of over 700pp tends to spurn historical questions and take up theological ones. It is a fresh, sympathetic reading of the text without a lot of wrangles with others' views. On the downside, Williamson says the work is "sometimes idiosyncratic" [*BSB* 12/00]. Johnstone contends that Chronicles is "a highly integrated theological statement… concerned with the universal relationship between God and humanity, and the vocation of Israel within that relationship" (I.10). See also his 1998 work, *Chronicles and Exodus: An Analogy and Its Application*. [*JBL* Spr 00; *JSOT* 79 (1998); *ExpTim* 10/98; *CBQ* 4/99; *RelSRev* 10/98; *EvQ* 4/03].

F   Kalimi, Isaac. ‡ *2 Chronicles* (HCOT). I note Peeters' decision to divide Chronicles between two scholars. Kalimi has proved his mettle in such works as *The Reshaping of Ancient Israelite History in Chronicles*, 2005 [*JETS* 6/06; *TJ* Fall 08; *JBL* Win 05; *JSS* Aut 07; *JSOT-BL* 2006], which is a high-level, detailed discussion of the Chronicler's redaction-work, and *An Ancient Israelite Historian*, 2005 [*JSOT-BL* 2006], which is a volume of his collected essays.

✓   Keil, Carl F. (KD) ET 1872. Long ago, Childs wrote that Keil is "invaluable as a very learned and carefully argued commentary which defends a traditional orthodox Protestant position."

✓   **Klein, Ralph.** ‡ *1 Chronicles* (Herm) 2006. Magnificent! Klein has been well-connected with, and productive among, the leading Chronicles scholars. This well-rounded, highly technical exegesis may be the capstone of Klein's honored career—which began, by the way, with a Harvard dissertation on Chronicles. He has strong historical interests and is an accomplished text critic. There is more theology in this volume (562pp) than in many others in Hermeneia, and Klein pays special attention to the theme of divine retribution. He joins so many of the leading scholars in distinguishing the Chronicler and his perspective from Ezra-Nehemiah. Klein's volume on 2 Chronicles is forthcoming. See above this Lutheran scholar's past work on Samuel, which makes him an astute commentator on the Chronicler's redactional activity. [*JETS* 9/07; *SwJT* Fall 05; *Interp* 7/08; *VT* 59.1; *CurTM* 6/07; *ExpTim* 9/07; *JHebS*; *RBL*; *CBQ* 7/09; *JSOT-BL* 2007].

F   Knoppers, Gary. [*M*], *II Chronicles* (AYB). We should probably anticipate another two-vol. contribution to complement the set on *I Chronicles*.

F   Konkel, Gus. (BCBC). See under Kings.

☆   McConville, J.G. (DSB) 1984. Most stimulating for pastors despite severe space limitations. This is a great little commentary by an able British evangelical scholar. In some early editions of the guide I included this among my purchase recommendations. [*EvQ* 7/86].

☆ **McKenzie, Steven L.** ‡ (AOTC) 2004. An excellent, though expensive ($38), exegetical work in pb by one of the leaders in recent Chronicles scholarship. I consider it something like a new "Williamson," though slightly more critically oriented. All of Chronicles is covered in about 380pp. Recommended for both students and pastors who desire a careful exegesis in line with the generally-accepted conclusions of current critical scholarship. [*CBQ* 1/07; *JETS* 3/06; *Interp* 4/05; *JSOT-BL* 2005].

F Mariottini, Claude. (NIBC?).

F Mayhew, Eugene. (EEC).

✓ **Myers, J.M.** ‡ (AB) 2 Vols., 1965. Has a stress on archaeological finds. Myers was good on background, not so strong on interpretation and theology—in other words, he was more in line with AB's original aims. Today it is considered a dated, weaker entry in the series and is scheduled for full retirement. See Knoppers above.

Payne, J. Barton. (EBC) 1988. Takes a different, more conservative approach than Williamson. Though Payne was a very able scholar (making many contributions to evangelical OT scholarship prior to his mountain-climbing death in 1979), other, more up-to-date evangelical works would be better guides for the pastor. This commentary was obviously completed long before the publication date. See Williams below.

Person, Raymond F. ‡ *The Deuteronomic History and the Book of Chronicles: Scribal Works in an Oral World*, 2010. Drafting a proposal that seems to be in line with the "Edinburgh School" (see Auld under Samuel), Person dates the DH as well as Chronicles to the Persian period. He considers them competing historiographies which descended from a common source.

F Schniedewind, William M. ‡ (NCBC). I expect this to be a fine work.

☆ **Thompson, J.A.** (NAC) 1994. From the pen of a well known and productive Australian evangelical scholar, this volume is solid and fairly full (400pp). The exegesis is in line with the publisher's commitment to biblical inerrancy; it would not be inaccurate to refer to this as a newer Barton Payne. As usual with NAC, this is not as penetrating as some other commentaries. Thompson has written other works on Jeremiah and Deuteronomy. [*SwJT* Fall 96; *VT* 46.4; *JSOT* 76; *HebStud* 1997].

☆ Tuell, Steven S. ‡ (I) 2001. This 250-page exposition shows the author's concern to see Chronicles, as a less popular portion of the Bible, preached upon more often. The commentary is well written (see his treatment of 1 Chron 17) and theologically oriented. He reads Chronicles as being of one piece with Ezra–Nehemiah. Tuell wrote his dissertation and a recent commentary on Ezekiel. [*CBQ* 10/03; *Them* Spr 04; *Interp* 1/03; *ExpTim* 10/04; *HBT* 12/02; *JSOT* 99; *SwJT* Fall 04; *Anvil* 19.4].

☆ Wilcock, Michael. (BST) 1987. If you can afford a third homiletical commentary (after Pratt and Hill), this one might barely nose out McConville and Allen (WCC). Yet they, not Wilcock, are the OT scholars. All three are well worth the money. [*EvQ* 10/88; *RTR* 1/88; *Evangel* Win 88; *Chm*, 107.1 (1993)].

Wilkinson, Bruce. *The Prayer of Jabez*, 2000. Yes, I am jocular here. But if you want to read an interesting review from an OT scholar, see Richard Schultz, "Praying Jabez's Prayer" in *TJ* Spr 03.

F Williams, Tyler. (EBCR). Vol. 4 will cover Chronicles to Job.

F Wright, John W. ‡ (BO).

NOTES: (1) William Johnstone's "Which Is the Best Commentary? 11. The Chronicler's Work," *ExpTim* 10/90. (2) Rodney K. Duke, "Recent Research in Chronicles," *CBR* 8.1 (2009): 10–50. (3) Students wanting to compare Samuel–Kings with Chronicles should consult one of the harmonies authored by Crockett (1959); Newsome (Baker, 1986); or Endres–Millar–Burns (Liturgical, 1998). The last two are much to be preferred. I chose to buy Endres.

—ɯ—

EZRA - NEHEMIAH

★ **Breneman, Mervin.** *Ezra, Nehemiah, Esther* (NAC) 1993. This ably covers the books in 383pp and would be a good purchase for the pastor to make. It is less valuable to students. I am less enthusiastic about this volume than most I recommend. These Bible books are not so well served by recent evangelical commentators; perhaps I could even say, more underserved by both evangelicals and the critics than any other portion of Scripture. (Advanced students can go looking for foreign language works like Rudolph's great *Esra und Nehemia* [1949] and Schunck's *Nehemia* in BKAT.) Compare Breneman with Fensham, and see the reviews [*JETS* 9/96 (Baldwin–complimentary); *VT* 46.2 (Williamson–critical)].

★ **Kidner, Derek.** (TOTC) 1979. An excellent, brief commentary which "deserves high praise," according to Williamson [*BSB* 9/00]: "his verse-by-verse comments never fail to provide fruit for searching reflection." Kidner does not attribute these books to the Chronicler and takes a more conservative approach than Williamson. Perhaps no one can write a short OT commentary as well as Kidner. A replacement by Boda is now in the works. [*WTJ* Fall 80; *JBL* 100.4 (1981); *JETS* 3/82].

★ McConville, J.G. *Ezra, Nehemiah, Esther* (DSB) 1985. Though hindered a bit by the format, McConville has given us another fine devotional exposition. Excellent OT scholarship undergirds his commentary. See under Chronicles. [*Them*, 9/85].

★ **Williamson, H.G.M.** [𝓜], (WBC) 1985. Still *the* benchmark scholarly study and the pastor's first choice in an exegetical work, though this volume makes many concessions to the critical position. Following on his superb Chronicles commentary, this work furnished further proof that Williamson was one of the world's foremost scholars in the area of post-exilic history and literature. Now one has to say that the Regius Professor of Hebrew at Oxford is one of the world's foremost OT scholars, period (see his more recent work on Isaiah). This rigorous WBC is not for the slothful and is Longman's favorite academic commentary. Williamson subsequently wrote [*BSB* 9/00], "I have been gratified to learn that preachers too have found it useful, perhaps especially in the 'explanation' sections, where I in fact wrote up my own sermon notes." [*CRBR* 1988; *RTR* 9/86; *TJ* Spr 86; *Them* 10/87; *JETS* 3/87; *HebStud* 1986]. For a more accessible overview of Ezra-Nehemiah and the key interpretive issues, see Williamson's slim 1987 volume in the *JSOT* "OT Guides" series. For further historical research, see his gathered *Studies in Persian Period History and Historiography* (2004).

✧ ✧ ✧ ✧ ✧ ✧

✓ Ackroyd, P.R. ‡ (Torch Bible Commentary) 1973. Bound with Chronicles commentary. This is one of the more valuable critical works suitable for beginners.

☆ **Allen, Leslie, and Timothy Laniak.** [𝓜], *Ezra, Nehemiah, Esther* (NIBC) 2003. Allen, an expert on Chronicles, contributes the commentary on Ezra and Nehemiah. It is well-researched and well-written. And the price is right for those who are on a tight budget. Conservative evangelicals will find Allen somewhat critical and will prefer Laniak's approach in this joint effort. See Esther. [*CBQ* 10/04; *RTR* 12/04; *JETS* 12/04; *Interp* 4/05; *BSac* 10/05].

✓ Batten, L.W. ‡ (ICC) 1913. Has retained value, more so than some others in the old series.

F Becking, Bob E.J.H. ‡ *Ezra* (HCOT). See also Noort below. Previously Istvan Karasszon was listed here.

✓ **Blenkinsopp, Joseph.** ‡ (OTL) 1988. This full-length commentary is an important addition to the literature, though perhaps not as seasoned as some other commentaries listed here. Blenkinsopp takes issue with the growing scholarly consensus (Batten, and now Japhet, Williamson, Klein, Braun, Dillard, Schunck) that distinguishes the author(s) of Ezra-Nehemiah from the Chronicler. This question of whether or not Chronicles and Ezra–Nehemiah come from the same hand has continued to generate work, but the consensus strengthens by the year (see Boda/Redditt). He is the same Roman Catholic scholar has produced the three-vol. AB set on Isaiah. [*Biblica* 71.1 (1990); *JSS* Spr 90; *HebStud* 1990]. Blenkinsopp's current thinking is set out in *Judaism, the First Phase: The Place of Ezra and Nehemiah in the Origins of Judaism* (2009); his program continues to be predominantly historical-critical [*CBQ* 4/10; *RBL* 8/10].

F Boda, Mark. (TOTC replacement).

Boda, Mark J., and Paul L. Redditt (eds). ‡ *Unity and Disunity in Ezra-Nehemiah: Redaction, Rhetoric, and Reader*, 2008. Quite a large body of cutting-edge scholarship (384pp), and all of it holds that Chronicles and Ezra–Nehemiah are not two parts of an overall chronistic history.

☆ Boice, James M. *Nehemiah*, 1990. Another exposition from the late pastor of Tenth Presbyterian in Philadelphia (PCA). More useful than Swindoll for the expositor because he sticks more with the text. Well, to be honest, I like his theology better as well.

Brockington, Leonard H. ‡ (retired NCB) 1969. A weak entry now replaced by Clines.

☆ Brown, Raymond. *The Message of Nehemiah* (BST) 1998. Will serve the pastor much like Packer does. This author has contributed several other commentaries to this series: Numbers, Deuteronomy, Hebrews. [*JSOT-BL* 1999; *Them* 11/99; *Chm* 113.2 (1999)].

☆ **Clines, David J.A.** [𝓜], (NCB) 1984. Covers Ezra, Nehemiah, and Esther. Clines' work here is always erudite and careful; also he uses the newer literary criticism to good effect. This commentary is still one of the best available and very serviceable for the evangelical interpreter. Clines has become increasingly critical over the last 25 years and his newer work cannot possibly be classed as [𝓜]. See Clines under Esther and under Job. [*ExpTim* 12/85; *JETS* 12/85; *Them* 9/85].

✓ Coggins, R.J. ‡ (CBC) 1976. Not as good as on Chronicles, but still a strong effort. [*EvQ* 10/77].

✓ Conti, Marco (ed). *1–2 Kings, 1–2 Chronicles, Ezra, Nehemiah, Esther* (ACCS) 2008.

✓ **Davies, Gordon F.** ‡ (BO) 1999. The author uses discourse analysis and speech-act theory to produce some good insights for students. Excluding the printing of Bible passages, Davies offers about 100pp of commentary and reflects on sections of narrative (not verse by verse). On the negative side, the discussion can be rather selective and some texts are neglected. [*JSOT* 89; *RelSRev* 10/99; *CBQ* 10/00; *Interp* 4/01; *JETS* 9/01].

F Eskenazi, Tamara Cohn. ‡ (AYB). This is a replacement for Myers. Eskenazi has already published a very well received volume on these books: *In an Age of Prose: A Literary Approach to Ezra-Nehemiah* (Scholars Press, 1988) [*HebStud*, 1990 (Dillard); *CRBR*, 1990]. Many specialists expect this AYB to be a jewel.

✓ Eskenazi, T.C., and K.H. Richards (eds). ‡ *Second Temple Studies 2: Temple and Community in the Persian Period*, 1994. There are several other titles named *Second Temple Studies*, edited by P.R. Davies and John Halligan.

Evers, Stan K. *Doing a Great Work: Ezra and Nehemiah Simply Explained* (WCS) 1996. This devotional and expositional commentary runs to about 225pp and emphasizes God-centered faith, service and worship.

☆ **Fensham, F. Charles.** (NICOT) 1982. A good piece of work by a great Semitics scholar, which is not quite so demanding on the reader as Williamson, who incidentally has found this volume "uniformly disappointing" [*BSB* 9/00]. Fensham is less critical and easier for fledgling students and busy pastors. Like Blenkinsopp, Fensham attributes these books to the Chronicler. He provides a healthy amount of detail, particularly in the areas of historical-cultural backdrop and Hebrew/Aramaic, but I judge it to be less valuable as a well-rounded commentary in literary and theological analysis. The early editions of this guide recommended Fensham for purchase. [*JBL* 104.1 (1985); *JTS* 4/85; *HebStud* 1983].

F Fried, Lisbeth. ‡ (ECC).

☆ Fyall, Robert. *Ezra and Haggai* (BST) 2008. I have not used this, but the author has published a worthy book on Job in the series, "New Studies in Biblical Theology."

✓ Grabbe, Lester L. ‡ (OT Readings) 1998. A very critical, close reading of the text. Williamson [*BSB* 9/00] once suggested going here "for a radical shake-up." [*OTA* 2/00; *JSS* Spr 02; *Anvil* 17.3].

F Green, Douglas J. (NIVAC). Green, an Australian who teaches at Westminster in Philadelphia, will do the Church a service here. I look for some good biblical theology to be brought out.

F Harrington, Hannah. (NICOT replacement). Fensham will be retired by this commentary.

F Hoglund, Kenneth E. (S&H). Previous work includes *Achaemenid Imperial Administration in Syria-Palestine and the Missions of Ezra and Nehemiah*, 1992.

☆ **Holmgren, F.C.** ‡ (ITC) 1987. Better than some others in the series. The author is one of the General Editors for ITC, and his theological exposition can complement the more exegetical works of Kidner, Williamson, etc. I believe this went o/p some time ago. [*HebStud* 1988].

✓ Keil, Carl F. (KD) ET 1873.

✓ **Klein, Ralph W.** ‡ (NewIB) 1999. A little less than 200pp and well done. For pastors, many call this the best critical work combining exegesis and theological exposition. There is good material here for the student exegete as well. This contribution can be considered among the most useful in the OT section of the NewIB. Klein is currently working on Chronicles and wrote the WBC volume on *1 Samuel*. [*ExpTim* 2/00; *CTJ* 11/01].

F Klingbeil, Gerald. (Apollos).

Laney, J. Carl. 1982. Popularly styled and published by Moody Press.

Levering, Matthew. (Brazos) 2007. I have not used this. [*CBQ* 7/08; *JETS* 12/08; *JSOT-BL* 2008 (Williamson); *JTI* Spr 10; *HBT* 31 (Dearman)].

F Loken, Israel. (EEC).

✓ **Myers, J.M.** ‡ (AB) 1965. This has the same strengths and weaknesses as his Chronicles volumes and has been considered a standard historical critical commentary. It has sharply declined in value since the publication of Clines and Williamson.

F Noort, Edward. ‡ *Nehemiah* (HCOT).

✓ Noss, Philip A., and Kenneth Thomas. *A Handbook on Ezra and Nehemiah* (UBS) 2005. This large translation help (577pp) can be classed as more valuable than some other UBS Handbooks, considering the lack of resources available on Ezra-Nehemiah. [*JSOT-BL* 2006].

☆ Packer, J.I. *A Passion for Faithfulness: Wisdom from the Book of Nehemiah*, 1995. Pastors will find much here to spur them on to think theologically and devotionally. [*Them* 1/96].

F Rata, Tiberius. (Mentor).

F Richards, Kent. ‡ (FOTL).

Roberts, Mark D. (WCC) 1993. One of the fuller expositional commentaries. Covers Ezra through Esther.

✓ Ryle, H.E. (Cambridge Bible for Schools & Colleges) 1897. According to Williamson, this packed little volume (328pp) was the best of the older English-language commentaries for pointing out key interpretive issues. May still be useful to consult, if a student is doing fuller research.

F Smith, Gary V. (CorBC) 2010. Bound with Esther. See the author's other commentaries on Isaiah and Amos.

Steinmann, Andrew E. (Concord) 2010. It is remarkable that he has churned out such a quick succession of huge commentaries: the 628-page *Daniel* (2008) was followed by the 719-page *Proverbs* (2009). Now comes this *Ezra and Nehemiah* which is 675pp. I have not yet used Steinmann.

Swindoll, Charles R. *Hand Me Another Brick*, 1978. This aims to help the communicator. Weak in biblical theology, it can still be suggestive for sermon preparation. Compare with Boice, Evers, Packer, and Roberts.

F Talmon, Shemaryahu. ‡ (Herm).

☆ **Throntveit, Mark A.** ‡ (I) 1992. Seems thin compared, say, to Roberts' expositional help, but is better informed. This work is more probing and learned than might first appear. Gives good direction to the expositor who wants to understand the message of the text. This work, van Wijk-Bos, Holmgren, and Klein should now be the first recourse for those seeking a thoughtful critical and theological exposition. [*Interp* 1/94; *BSac* 7/93; *HebStud* 1993; *CRBR* 1993].

White, John. *Excellence in Leadership*, 1986. An IVP issue which sold well.

van Wijk-Bos, Johanna W.H. ‡ *Ezra, Nehemiah, and Esther* (WestBC) 1998. I find Throntveit to be a much better researched work, but van Wijk-Bos is regarded as offering good help to the more liberally oriented expositor. Evangelicals will struggle at points with her labeling as "prejudice," "sexism," and "intolerance" some of the key concerns of the text. [*JSOT* 84 (1999); *Interp* 10/99].

☆ **Yamauchi, Edwin.** (EBC) 1988. Strong work by an able Bible historian. He chaired the Biblical Studies department at Miami University in Ohio. Pastors have found this to be a useful volume on their shelves, especially since Smick's fine contribution on the Book of Job is bound in the same volume. The author has expertise in Persian era history; see *Persia and the Bible* (1990). He is less adept at theological reflection. The revised EBC contribution will supersede this.

F Yamauchi, Edwin. (EBCR). In Vol. 4, covering Chronicles to Job.

ESTHER

★ **Allen, Leslie, and Timothy Laniak.** *Ezra, Nehemiah, Esther* (NIBC) 2003. Laniak is responsible for the Esther commentary (100pp) and builds upon his 1998 Scholars Press issue, *Shame and Honor in the Book of Esther*. He teaches at Gordon-Conwell Seminary in Charlotte, NC. This book is a good buy in pb, probably the best buy on Esther (cf. Baldwin, Reid). Laniak is also an excellent guide into the theology of the book. I can commend Laniak's overall conclusion, "It is not so much the *presence* of God but the *hiddenness* of God in human events that the story articulates. To be hidden is to be present yet unseen" (p.185). I'm still pondering his suggestion that "being a Jew means being the presence of YHWH in the world. We look in vain to find his name in Esther because his identity is joined to that of his people" (187). See Ezra-Nehemiah.

★ **Bush, Frederic W.** [*M*], *Ruth, Esther* (WBC) 1996. Is primarily interested in the form, function and theology of the stories, not their historicity. For a discussion of the scroll and history, see the 2ⁿᵈ edition of the LaSor-Hubbard-Bush *Old Testament Survey* (1996). Pastors with a scholarly bent will use Bush in their study of the original text, and they will also definitely want access to Fox's technical exegesis and Berlin's sensitive literary reading for JPS. This is not one of the more readable or accessible commentaries in the WBC. [*JETS* 3/99; *RTR* 9–12/97; *SwJT* Spr 00; *BSac* 10/98].

★ Duguid, Iain M. *Esther and Ruth* (REC) 2005. A well-thought-out, suggestive homiletical approach. In the same series, he has also done a superb job on Daniel. Preachers will find Duguid and Firth brimming with ideas that can be developed in expository sermons.

★ Firth, David. (BST) 2010. A well-researched, perceptive exposition for pastors. Firth has preached through this book and taught it numerous times in academic settings, and readers quickly realize that the author understands how the parts of the book come together in presenting *The Message of Esther*. The low price helps make this a preacher's best buy. It is worth adding that students will find some shrewd academic points made in Firth's introduction. Firth has done ministry in his native Australia, missionary work in Africa (two theological colleges), and now lectures at Cliff College, Derbyshire, England. See also his major commentary on the books of Samuel.

★ **Jobes, Karen H.** (NIVAC) 1999. The pastor or teacher will find much help here. The author did her Westminster Seminary dissertation on the LXX of Esther and wants this often neglected Bible book to receive its due. Though the main thrust of this work is theology and application, there is a lot of exegetical worth here, too. Could be the pastor's first choice; compare with Baldwin. [*DenvJ*]. For a slight update on introductory matters from Jobes, see "Esther 1: Book of" in *DOTWPW* (2008).

Anderson, Bernhard W. ‡ (IB) 1954.

☆ **Baldwin, Joyce G.** (TOTC) 1984. This volume is typical of her always helpful, well-researched work. For obvious reasons you will appreciate her womanly perspective on this particular book. This used to be the pastor's first choice for an accessible exegesis, though McConville is better at showing Esther's relevance for today, and Jobes is more up-to-date and well rounded (exegesis and exposition). In 1990 Baldwin was Stuart's favorite on this book. See Reid for the new replacement volume. I was a bit sorry to move this off the recommended list in this guide's 9ᵗʰ edition. [*JETS* 12/85].

✓ **Bechtel, Carol.** ‡ (I) 2002. This well-written, more liberal exposition follows several of the leads offered in Berlin's commentary. The literary reading, with its focus upon such things as characterization, could help preachers and teachers who take up the Book of Esther. Theologically, Bechtel is less help than some other volumes on Esther and also other volumes in this WJK series of expositions. [*CBQ* 1/04; *Interp* 10/03; *JSOT* 27.5; *SwJT* Fall 03; *CJ* 7/05; *BSac* 7/04; *RBL*].

Beckett, Michael. *Gospel in Esther*, 2002. This more allegorical reading is not recommended. [*Chm* Aut 03].

✓ Berg, Sandra B. ‡ *The Book of Esther: Motifs, Themes, and Structure*, 1979. A significant, oft-cited work, pointing to the striking parallels with the Joseph narrative. [*JBL* 100.2 (1981)].

☆ **Berlin, Adele.** ‡ (JPS) 2001. This is a major addition to Esther scholarship, and maintains the high standard set in her Zephaniah AB commentary. But this work for JPS has a different focus, as she writes for an audience keenly interested in the history of Jewish interpretation. Her literary approach to Esther is partially laid out in a *JBL* article (Spr 2001). Berlin is mainly for students. She identifies the genre of the book as burlesque. While she helpfully highlights the many humorous and ironic twists in the story, she downplays any historical value of the text. [*JETS* 12/02; *Interp* 1/02; *VT* 53.4; *JSOT* 99; *RBL*].

☆ **Breneman, Mervin.** *Ezra, Nehemiah, Esther* (NAC) 1993. See under Ezra-Nehemiah.

Brockington, L.H. ‡ (NCB) 1969. See Ezra-Nehemiah above.

Carruthers, Jo. ‡ (Blackwell) 2008. A full and fascinating reception history. [*CBQ* 7/09; *RelSRev* 9/09; *Anvil* 26.2].

Cassel, Paulus. *An Explanatory Commentary on Esther*, ET 1888. Few know of this large-scale exposition (400pp) for it appeared too late to be noted in Spurgeon's catalogue. Cassel was a famous, conservative professor at the University of Berlin, and there is a historical orientation to this commentary.

☆ **Clines, David J.A.** [*M*], (NCB) 1984. See under Ezra-Nehemiah. Advanced students may wish to note his Sheffield monograph, *The Esther Scroll* (1984), which includes some brilliant comments on the author's/redactor's literary skill [*HebStud* 1988 (Fox)]. This is the same scholar who has produced the massive WBC set on Job. Sadly, Clines now repudiates his fairly conservative approach in this more traditionally styled NCB work; see "Esther and the Future of Commentary" in Greenspoon/Crawford below.

Coggins, R.J. and S.P. Re'emi. ‡ *Nahum, Obadiah, Esther* (ITC) 1985. Noted mainly because commentaries on these Bible books are fewer. This commentary employs the usual critical methods and examines the relationship between the People of God and several surrounding nations: Assyria, Edom and the Medo-Persian Empire.

✓ Conti, Marco (ed). *1–2 Kings, 1–2 Chronicles, Ezra, Nehemiah, Esther* (ACCS) 2008.

Craig, Kenneth. ‡ *Reading Esther: A Case for the Literary Carnivalesque*, 1995. Another such approach is Andre LaCocque, *Esther Regina: A Bakhtinian Reading*, 2008 [*BibInt* 18.3].

✓ Crawford, Sidnie White. ‡ (NewIB) 1999. About 120pp. [*ExpTim* 2/00; *CTJ* 11/01].

Crawford, Sidnie White, and Leonard J. Greenspoon (eds). ‡ *The Book of Esther in Modern Research*, 2003. [*Them* 5/08; *ExpTim* 6/05].

✓ **Day, Linda M.** ‡ (AOTC) 2005. As expected in the series, Day provides a compact exegesis, well-informed by critical scholarship. She writes well and with insight. Her strength is in the area of close literary reading of the narrative (especially characterization), while some reviews find Day weaker in research of the historical-cultural backdrop and textual issues. She displays a largely atheological, feminist approach to the message and ethics of the book—"Esther, the hiding Jew, is analogous to the closeted gay" (p.3), while Mordecai the childless bachelor "represents an ambiguous sexual identity" (p.61). This makes Day unsuitable for evangelical pastors, who might be tempted to query whether she has bought an import license. [*CBQ* 7/08; *JETS* 12/06; *Interp* 10/06; *JSOT-BL* 2006; *VT* 57.3; *JHebS*; *HBT* 29.2; *RBL*;

RelSRev 9/09 (Sweeney)]. See also her published dissertation, *Three Faces of a Queen: Characterization in the Books of Esther*, 1995.

Fountain, A. Kay. ‡ *Literary and Empirical Readings of the Books of Esther*, 2002. [*RBL* 11/03].

☆ **Fox, Michael V.** ‡ *Character and Ideology in the Book of Esther*, 1991, 2nd ed 2001. This highly-touted work must be consulted by students; it does contain a commentary section. A skeptical, critical position is taken on the issue of the book's historical value. Students will appreciate the 2nd edition's postscript, "A Decade of Esther Scholarship." See Fox's works on Proverbs, Qoheleth, and Song of Songs below. [*JSOT* 55; *Biblica* 75.1 (1994); *JR* 1/94; *RTR* 12/02; *JTS* 4/03; *VT* 53.1; *JSOT* 99 (2002); *JSS* Spr 04; *JETS* 12/02 (Jobes)].

F Fox, Michael V. ‡ (Herm). This will build upon his 1991 work. Because so much spade-work is done already, the Hermeneia volume could appear sooner, rather than later. The learned Semitist, Jonas Greenfield, who died in 1995, originally had the contract.

Gordis, Robert. ‡ *Megillat Esther: The Masoretic Hebrew Text with Introduction, New Translation and Commentary*, 1974. Judicious, conservatively critical Jewish scholarship. A large portion of this slim volume is taken up with the printing of a Purim Service. For a distillation of Gordis' insights, see his later articles: "Studies in the Esther Narrative," *JBL* 95 (1976): 43–58; "Religion, Wisdom and History in the Book of Esther—A New Solution to an Old Crux," *JBL* 100 (1981): 359–88. It is good to read him saying in *JBL* 95, "the author of Esther has an excellent familiarity with Persian law, custom, and languages in the Achaemenid period" (p.44).

✓ Greenspoon, Leonard, and Sidnie White Crawford (eds). ‡ *Esther*, 2003. These are collected essays of a high standard.

F Hubbard, Robert. (NICOT). In his work on Ruth, Hubbard set an extraordinarily high standard of scholarship for the series, of which he is now general editor. This could wind up being the pastor's first choice.

Huey, F.B. (EBC) 1988. See Phillips for the upcoming replacement.

Kahana, Hanna. *Esther: Juxtaposition of the Septuagint Translation with the Hebrew Text*, 2005. Though focused mainly on the LXX, this work pays close attention to the Hebrew text (moving word by word) to evaluate the ancient translator's methods and translational preferences. Kahana is 474pp and is published by Peeters. An enormous amount of time and work went into this, but note the caveats in Jobes' review [*JTS* 10/07].

✓ Keil, Carl F. (KD) ET 1873.

F Klingbeil, Gerald. (Apollos).

Knight, G.A.F. ‡ (Torch Bible Commentary) 1955. Also covers Song of Songs and Lamentations.

F Korpel, Marjo C.A. ‡ (HCOT). Previously Henk Jagersma was listed here.

Larkin, Katrina J.A. *Ruth and Esther*, 1995. This slim volume in the "OT Guides" series helpfully reviews the history of interpretation.

☆ **Levenson, Jon D.** ‡ (OTL) 1997. Alongside Bush, Berlin and Fox, this volume by a Jewish commentator is one of the finest scholarly commentaries to be published in English in decades. Levenson does not believe there is much, if any, history in the book; instead there is an "enormous amount of exaggeration and inaccuracy" (p.26). Those less interested in technical translation issues and more interested in a literary reading or theology might want OTL instead of WBC. As a plus, Levenson treats the Additions to Esther, which have been receiving much appreciative attention in scholarship lately. [*JBL* Spr 99; *JSOT* 79 (1998); *Biblica* 79.3 (1998); *CBQ* 7/98; *HebStud* 1998; *RelSRev* 10/97, 10/98; *RBL*].

✓ **Linafelt, Tod, and Timothy K. Beal.** ‡ *Ruth, Esther* (BO) 1999. See Linafelt's Ruth above, and note Beal's earlier ideologically-charged reading in *The Book of Hiding: Gender, Ethnicity, Annihilation, and Esther* (1997), the title of which uses the wordplay on Esther (אסתר) and "to hide" (סתר).

✓ Lubetski, Edith, and Meir Lubetski (eds). *The Book of Esther: A Classified Bibliography*, 2008. [*RBL* 8/10].

☆ Luter, A. Boyd, and Barry C. Davis. *God Behind the Seen*, 1996. See Ruth above.

☆ McConville, J. G. (DSB) 1985. See under Ezra-Nehemiah. This was Longman's first choice years ago.

✓ **Moore, Carey A**. ‡ (AB) 1971. This offered some philological aid, but, like most of the old AB contributions, was "theologically anemic" (Kiehl). Moore is now regarded as dated. The volume's approach is somewhat conservative within the critical ranks, arguing for an earlier date of composition. [*JBL* 6/77]. Subsequently, Moore did scholarship a favor by republishing many of the most influential German, French, and English journal articles (1895–1977) in *Studies in the Book of Esther* (Ktav, 1982).

✓ Murphy, Roland E. ‡ (FOTL) 1981. See under Ruth.

F O'Connor, Michael. ‡ (Herm). See Fox for the conflicting report.

Omanson, Roger L., and Philip A. Noss. *A Handbook on the Book of Esther: The Hebrew and Greek Texts* (UBS) 1997. As the subtitle makes clear, this volume also covers the deuterocanonical Additions (pp.263–356).

✓ **Paton, L.B.** ‡ (ICC) 1908. Some solid work with the MT, which has held up reasonably well over the years. Hardly valuable for much else besides philology and textual criticism. Highly skeptical: "it is doubtful whether even a historical kernel underlies its narrative" (p.75).

F Phillips, Elaine. (EBCR). In Vol. 4, covering Chronicles to Job.

Prime, Derek. *Esther Simply Explained*, 2001. A well-done, edifying exposition from a English pastor in the Reformed Baptist circle. [*Evangel* Spr 04].

F Queen-Sutherland, Kandy. ‡ (S&H). See under Ruth.

☆ **Reid, Debra.** (TOTC replacement) 2008. Though having a higher page-count (168pp), Reid is approximately the same length as the Baldwin work it replaces. (This is the first of the TOTC replacement volumes to be released.) I agree with those who find in Reid an inclination to read the story as fictitious. She offers less comment on historical questions and chooses to emphasize literary features. Her narratological discussion is very good, by the way. At the same time she generally avoids the genre question: "it is advisable not to put the text into a genre straitjacket, but to be alert to the plethora of possibilities" (p.34). I find Jobes and Firth much more satisfying and clear about genre. [*JETS* 9/09; *JSOT-BL* 2009; *EQ* 4/10].

Roberts, Mark D. (WCC) 1993. Covers Ezra through Esther.

Rodriguez, A.M. *Esther: A Theological Approach*, 1995.

Roop, Eugene F. [𝔐], *Ruth, Jonah, Esther* (BCBC) 2002. One of the best in this Anabaptist series.

F Smith, Gary V. (CorBC) 2010. See Ezra and Nehemiah.

Thomas, W. Ian. *If I Perish, I Perish: The Christian Life as Seen in Esther*, 1967. Many pastors of the last generation had Major Thomas on their shelf, but I recommend Firth, Jobes, Duguid, and Webb for guidance in reading Esther as Christian Scripture. There is heavy, pious allegorizing: wicked Haman going to the gallows typifies how "my old sinful nature was nailed to the cross with the Lord Jesus Christ—executed and buried" (p.109).

F   Tomasino, Anthony. (EEC).

van Wijk-Bos, Johanna W.H. ‡ *Ezra, Nehemiah, and Esther* (WestBC) 1998. See Ezra-Nehemiah above.

☆   Webb, Barry G. *Five Festal Garments: Christian Reflections on the Song of Songs, Ruth, Lamentations, Ecclesiastes and Esther*, 2000. The volume offers good help to the preacher (on books where help is very much needed), especially with its wise guidance into theological interpretation. See under Ruth.

F   Wells, Samuel. (Brazos). This is expected to be bound with Stephen Fowl on Ruth.

Yamauchi, Edwin M. *Persia and the Bible*, 1990. A much-used work by an evangelical historian.

NOTE: For a brief discussion of Esther and scholarly skepticism about the story's relation to history, see Provan/Long/Longman, *A Biblical History of Israel*, pp.294–97. On the same topic one can also consult *DOTWPW*.

POETRY & WISDOM LITERATURE

★   Estes, Daniel J. *Handbook on the Wisdom Books and Psalms*, 2005. A fine, fuller, dependable introduction and content survey from a veteran evangelical scholar. He now has a commentary out on the Song of Songs. [*CBQ* 7/07; *JETS* 6/07; *VT* 57.4; *RelSRev* 10/06 (Crenshaw); *BSac* 1/07; *JSOT-BL* 2007 (Dell)].

★   Fokkelman, J.P. ‡ *Reading Biblical Poetry*, 2001. An understanding of Hebrew poetry is crucial for interpreting every OT book in our English canon after Esther, except Daniel. There is scarcely any better introductory guide than this one for the pastor. Adele Berlin says, "Few books for the uninitiated reader capture as much sophisticated information in such an intelligible way." For his application of the approach, see Job and Psalms. Compare with the much slimmer Petersen/Richards. Berlin (1985) should be read on parallelism, and Watson can serve as a more advanced textbook. [*CBQ*, 10/03; *ThTo* 1/03; *BBR* 15.2; *RelSRev* 10/06; *DenvJ* 1/02].

★   Kidner, Derek. *The Wisdom of Proverbs, Job and Ecclesiastes*, 1985. [*Presb* Spr 87].

★   Longman, Tremper, and Peter Enns (eds). *Dictionary of the Old Testament: Wisdom, Poetry & Writings*, 2008. As with the companion IVP volumes on the Pentateuch and the Historical Books, this gem is especially for students. Do note it covers the Megilloth: Ruth, Song of Songs, Ecclesiastes, Lamentations, and Esther. [*EvQ* 4/09; *BBR* 20.1; *CBQ* 10/09].

☆   Alter, R. ‡ *The Art of Biblical Poetry*, 1985. One of the most influential books on Hebrew poetry, offering his own approach to interpreting ancient poetic technique and critiquing the work of Kugel and others. [*VT* 1/93].

✓   Berlin, Adele. ‡ *The Dynamics of Biblical Parallelism*, 1985, 2nd ed 2008. Still the best, most manageable introduction to the subject. Note that the basic text is unchanged in the 2nd edition, which is regrettable. [*ExpTim* 4/09; *JTS* 4/09 (Watson); *JHebS* 2009]. Beginners will enjoy Berlin's "Introduction to Hebrew Poetry" in Vol. 4 of the *NewIB*, 1996 [*DenvJ*], while advanced students researching parallelism will supplement *Dynamics* with Watson (see below); N.P. Lunn, *Word-Order Variation in Biblical Hebrew Poetry*, 2006 [*JTS* 4/08]; and (if German-readers) Andreas Wagner (ed), *Parallelismus Membrorum*, 2007.

Berry, D.K. *An Introduction to Wisdom and Poetry of the OT*, 1995. Has received mixed reviews. [*JETS* 12/99; *VT* 46.4; *CBQ* 10/96].

Blenkinsopp, Joseph. ‡ *Wisdom and Law in the Old Testament*, 1983, rev. 1995.

Böstrom, L. ‡ *The God of the Sages: The Portrayal of God in the Book of Proverbs*, 1990.

✓ Brown, William P. [*M*], *Character in Crisis: A Fresh Approach to the Wisdom Literature of the OT*, 1996. [*JETS* 12/99; *Interp* 10/97; *CBQ* 1/97; *RTR* 5/97; *HebStud* 1997; *PSB* 18.3 (1997)].

☆ Bullock, C. Hassell. *An Introduction to the Poetic Books of the Old Testament*, 1979, rev. 1988, 2007. A valuable evangelical treatment, strangely missed by Enns. Compare with Estes above.

✓ Clements, R.E. ‡ *Wisdom in Theology*, 1989. [*VT* 46.2; *JSOT* 62; *CBQ* 10/94; *CRBR* 1994].

✓ Clifford, Richard J. ‡ *The Wisdom Literature*, 1998. From the IBT series.

Clifford, Richard J. (ed). ‡ *Wisdom Literature in Mesopotamia and Israel*, 2007. [*DenvJ*].

Clines, David J.A. (ed). *The Poetical Books: A Sheffield Reader*, 1997. Essays selected from *JSOT*. Similar is David E. Orton (ed), *Poetry in the Hebrew Bible* (2000), which collects key *VT* articles.

☆ Crenshaw, James. ‡ *Old Testament Wisdom: An Introduction*, 1981, 1998, 3rd ed 2010. All consider this a most valuable work from the critical camp. [*JBL* 102.2 (1983); *Them* 2/00; *HebStud* 41; *SJT* 55.1].

✓ Cross, Frank Moore, & David Noel Freedman. ‡ *Studies in Ancient Yahwistic Poetry*, 1975.

✓ Day, J., R.P. Gordon, and H.G.M. Williamson (eds). ‡ *Wisdom in Ancient Israel: Essays in Honour of J.A. Emerton*, 1995. A superb collection.

Dell, Katharine. ‡ "Reviewing Recent Research on the Wisdom Literature," *ExpTim* 119.6 (2008): 261–69.

Enns, Peter. *Poetry & Wisdom* (IBR Bibliographies #3) 1997. Gives trusty help in researching wisdom literature generally and the books of Job–Song of Songs, plus Lamentations. [*RelSRev* 10/98].

Follis, Elaine (ed). ‡ *Directions in Biblical Hebrew Poetry*, 1987.

☆ Gammie, John G., Leo G. Perdue (eds). ‡ *The Sage in Israel and the Ancient Near East*, 1990. For its time, I can hardly think of a more judicious selection of articles (on the critical side) for the student of OT wisdom. [*VT* 46.3; *JSOT* 58]. Another, earlier collection was *Israelite Wisdom: Theological and Literary Essays*, 1978.

✓ Geller, S.A. ‡ *Parallelism in Early Biblical Poetry*, 1979.

☆ Goldsworthy, Graeme. *Gospel and Wisdom: Israel Wisdom Literature in the Christian Life*, 1987.

Golka, F.W. ‡ *The Leopard's Spots: Biblical and African Wisdom in Proverbs*, 1993. Pursues a fascinating track—comparing biblical and African proverbs—in his argument that the proverb "is chiefly indigenous, popular wisdom," not necessarily tied to wisdom schools or the royal court context. Others recently have drawn the same conclusion while arguing different points. [*VT* 45.4; *JSOT* 64].

Gordis, Robert. ‡ *The Word and the Book*, 1976. See also *Poets, Prophets, and Sages*, 1971.

✓ Hallo, William W., and K. Lawson Younger (eds). *Context of Scripture*, 3 Vols., 1997–2002. A replacement for the old standard collection of ANE literature edited by Pritchard, useful for comparative work on the ancient international wisdom movement. This topic generates a lot of work and is controversial. Cf. G.E. Bryce, *A Legacy of Wisdom: The Egyptian Contribution to the Wisdom of Israel* (1979), and

K.A. Kitchen, "Proverbs and Wisdom Books of the Ancient Near East," *TynBul* 28 (1977): 69–114; these discuss Amenemope.

☆ Kugel, J.L. ‡ *The Idea of Biblical Poetry*, 1981. Challenges the emphasis on parallelism and is one of the most discussed books on the topic in recent decades. [*JBL* 102.4 (1983)].

Lowth, Robert. *Lectures on the Sacred Poetry of the Hebrews*, ET 1815 (*De sacra poesi Hebraeorum praelectiones*, 1753). This was the groundbreaking work on the subject by an English bishop.

☆ Lucas, Ernest C. [*M*], *Exploring the Old Testament: A Guide to the Psalms & Wisdom Literature*, 2003. There are few better, more accessible guides into this diverse literature for the beginning student (200pp). [*RelSRev* 4/06; *Anvil* 21.2].

Morgan, Donn F. ‡ *Wisdom in the Old Testament Traditions*, 1981.

☆ Murphy, Roland E. ‡ *The Tree of Life: An Exploration of Biblical Wisdom Literature* (ABRL) 1990, 1996, 3rd ed 2002. In previous editions of this Guide I recommended this as a purchase, since Murphy is a world authority on this literature. [*JSS* Aut 98; *HebStud* 41; *CRBR* 1992; *RelSRev* 10/97; *VT* 54.4]. See also his *Wisdom Literature and Psalms* (1983) from the IBT series, and his FOTL volume listed under Ruth.

O'Connor, M.P. ‡ *Hebrew Verse Structure*, 1980.

☆ Perdue, Leo G. ‡ *Wisdom and Creation: The Theology of Wisdom Literature*, 1994. Though his treatment of "Lady Wisdom" is unsatisfactory (pp.84–94) and he maintains a strange distinction between the creation of the cosmos and the creation of humanity—never found in ANE cosmogonies, by the way—Perdue's work is superb to start you thinking about this topic, which is sometimes neglected in seminary courses. In several ways he develops Zimmerli's dictum, "Wisdom thinks resolutely within the framework of a theology of creation" (*SJT* 6/64). Perdue and von Rad are probably the two most suggestive volumes on the theology of these Bible books. [*Interp* 1/96; *ThTo* 1/96; *JETS* 12/96; *JBL* Spr 96; *CBQ* 4/96; *JR* 10/96].

✓ Perdue, Leo G. ‡ *Wisdom Literature: A Theological History*, 2007. The fruit of a lifetime of study on biblical wisdom, this is an in-depth survey textbook which includes Ben Sira and The Wisdom of Solomon and which further develops the ideas in *Wisdom and Creation* [*CBQ* 10/08; *Interp* 4/08; *JETS* 3/09; *BBR* 19.3; *ExpTim* 8/09; *HBT* 30.2; *VT* 59.3 (McConville); *Them* 11/09]. Perdue goes over similar ground in *The Sword and the Stylus: An Introduction to Wisdom in the Age of Empires*, 2008, but with more of a focus on the historical-social context and the international wisdom movement [*CBQ* 4/09; *JETS* 3/10; *JSOT-BL* 2009; *ExpTim* 10/09; *Interp* 4/10]. I come away from reading this author mightily impressed by his scholarship but wishing he were more impressed by differences between Israel's Scripture and the nations' wisdom.

☆ Petersen, David L., and Kent Harold Richards. ‡ *Interpreting Biblical Poetry* (Guides to Biblical Scholarship, OT Series) 1992. [*CRBR* 1994].

☆ Rad, Gerhard von. ‡ *Wisdom in Israel*, 1972. A classic indeed! Advanced students will look to purchase this.

F Schultz, Richard L. *Interpreting the Wisdom Literature: An Exegetical Handbook* (Kregel).

✓ Scott, R.B.Y. ‡ *The Way of Wisdom in the Old Testament*, 1971, rev. 1988. [*JBL* 92.3 (1973)].

☆ Sparks, Kenton L. *Ancient Texts for the Study of the Hebrew Bible: A Guide to the Background Literature*, 2005. See pp.56–83 for a good selection of introductory readings in wisdom texts; then move on to Hallo.

☆ Watson, W.G.E. *Classical Hebrew Poetry: A Guide to Its Techniques*, 1984. An excellent textbook, probably the best single volume for one who's already done some initial study. The strength of the work lies in its "catalogs (of literary-poetic techniques) for reference rather than treatments outlining any particular way of reading poetry" (Howard). Watson followed up with *Traditional Techniques in Classical Hebrew Verse*, published in 1994 by JSOT Press, which was partially an updating of his previous efforts.

✓ Weeks, Stuart. ‡ *Early Israelite Wisdom*, 1994. Revisionist scholarship, said to be one of the best introductions to the wisdom literature (Waltke). Check the caveats in the reviews. [*JETS* 6/97; *JBL* Spr 96; *JSS* Aut 95; *JSOT* 71].

✓ Westermann, Claus. ‡ *Roots of Wisdom: The Oldest Proverbs of Israel and Other Peoples*, 1995. [*Interp* 1/97; *HebStud*, 1996].

NOTES: (1) See the two-part review-essay by J. Kenneth Kuntz on "Biblical Hebrew Poetry in Recent Research," *CurBS* 6 (1998) and 7 (1999). (2) Also see articles on Hebrew Poetry in *ABD*; *New Interpreter's Dictionary of the Bible*; *International Standard Bible Encyclopedia, Revised*. Older works include *Zondervan Pictorial Encyclopedia of the Bible*; *Interpreter's Dictionary of the Bible*; and monographs by Gray (1915), and Robinson (1947). (3) There is a fantastic bibliography on Hebrew poetry at John Hobbins' site: www.ancienthebrewpoetry.typepad.com.

—w—

JOB

★ **Andersen, Francis I.** (TOTC) 1976. Wrestles very well with Job's difficult message. The few textual notes are quite valuable too; Andersen is a renowned linguist. This 300-page work has retained its value over the years. Andersen has multiple commentaries in the AB (Hosea, Amos, Micah, Habakkuk) which are not so theological. [*JBL* 3/78; *EvQ* 4/78].

★ Atkinson, David. (BST) 1992. Another successful effort by the author of the volumes on Genesis 1–11 and Ruth in this series. I only wish he had written more. Believing that these recommendations need a theological supplement or two, I have chosen to include Atkinson and Balentine. Preachers should also look at Calvin (and Derek Thomas' guide), Janzen, Jones, and Campbell Morgan. Magary may soon be another option. [*EvQ* 7/93; *Them* 1/94; *SBET* Aut 96].

★ **Balentine, Samuel E.** ‡ (S&H) 2006. One of the strongest, most substantive (750-page) entries in the series, written by the OT editor, this Job volume makes a contribution to scholarship. Reviewers have piled up superlatives. The value of the work is not in any treatment of historical-critical questions (which are generally avoided), but in its profound, sustained, and widely-ranging theological reflection (suffering, evil, creation, God's rule). "Yet for all the intellectual breadth and seriousness of these discussions, they are eminently accessible and deeply evocative for the pastoral tasks of preaching, teaching, and pastoral care" (Newsom). This is a purchase recommendation for those with a big book allowance who intend to spend a lot of time with Job. I like the less expensive Janzen just as much, among critical writers. [*CBQ* 4/08; *JETS* 6/08; *Interp* 1/08; *RBL*].

★ **Clines, David J.A.** ‡ *Job 1–20* (WBC) 1989; *Job 21–37* (WBC) 2006. This set is overwhelming in its erudition and painstaking work. Clines has had tremendous influence in OT scholarship as a proponent of the new literary criticism at the University of Sheffield (England), as editor of the periodical *JSOT*, and as editor of the huge *Dictionary of Classical Hebrew*. There has been a long wait for the commentary on Job 21–42. I'll be frank here. Clines' more recent work worried me and made me suspect that volumes 2/3 would be more ideologically left-wing—i.e., his reader-response deconstruction—and less useful. Specifically, I was bothered by his chapter in *The Book of Job* (Leuven University Press/Peeters, 1994), edited by Beuken; and by "Job's Fifth Friend: An Ethical Critique of the Book of Job," *BibInt* 12.3 (2004): 233–50. For scholarly types these volumes are magisterial, though sometimes pushing quirky interpretations (e.g., vegetarian reading) and doubtful reconstructions of the canonical text (especially chs. 26–27). The average pastor will never be able to put the wealth of material here to full use. Clines is Longman's favorite on Job. Those wanting completed and more accessible commentaries instead have the other superb works listed here. I expect volume three on Job 38–42 to include some 200pp of indexes and to appear soon. [*Biblica* 72.3 (1991); *JETS* 3/94 (Smick); *JTS* 4/91; *EvQ* 7/92; *CBQ* 4/92; *Interp* 4/91; *ExpTim* 6/90; *RTR* 9/90; *VT* 10/95; *CTJ* 4/92; *ExpTim* 5/09 (Hartley); *JSOT-BL* 2007].

★ **Habel, Norman C.** [𝓜], (OTL) 1985. "Mildly critical" (Kiehl). Habel was formerly at Concordia Seminary in St. Louis. He emphasizes theology in this large work. This is an astute, thorough commentary which argues for the unity of Job and treats the "final form" of the text (except at chs. 25–27). Like Gordis, this work is highly regarded by scholars, and a pastor wishing to build a first-class reference library will purchase this. Crenshaw has called Habel "the best commentary in English." The conservative Anglican scholar Motyer said that "it is hard to conceive that the book of Job can ever receive a richer or more satisfying treatment than Habel provides." This good book used to be hard to find, but I'm glad to report that WJK has now reprinted Habel in pb. Do not confuse this work with Habel's 1975 CBC. [*ExpTim* 12/85; *JETS* 3/87; *HebStud* 1987; *Chm* 102.1 (1988)].

★ **Hartley, John.** (NICOT) 1988. Reviewers have been pleased. It is a substantial (550pp) commentary which ably treats the literary features and theology of Job (see the Christological texts). Is well-informed on the whole range of scholarly opinion and provides a good bit of discussion on the many text critical issues (conservative attitude toward the MT). Argues that the affinity between the Book of Job and Isaiah 40–55 is best explained as Isaianic dependence on Job (and dates both early). The volume is workmanlike, probably the best evangelical work on Job. [*HebStud* 1991].

★ **Wilson, Gerald H.** (NIBC) 2007. Published posthumously after Wilson died suddenly in late 2005; how appropriate, then, are the author's closing words in this commentary! This is one of the largest volumes in the series (494pp), is well-grounded in scholarship, and useful to both pastors and students. Wilson made his mark as a cutting-edge Psalms scholar and was adept at handling poetry. The theology drawn out emphasizes the sovereignty of God; Wilson sees Job as realizing that his affliction "must fall within the divine purposes" (466). He takes the traditional view of ch. 28 as belonging to Job. I regret that "bombastic" is used as an adjective for the divine speeches in chs. 38–41. Because NIBC is priced so cheaply (list $16.95), this is *the* bargain purchase on Job. [*JETS* 12/07; *BSac* 1/08; *BTB* 2/08; *RBL*; *JSOT-BL* 2009 (Clines); *BBR* 19.3].

✧ ✧ ✧ ✧ ✧ ✧

☆ **Alden, Robert L.** (NAC) 1993. Though not written at the same level of scholarship as NICOT or especially WBC, this is a fine commentary (432pp). Alden's work is helpful and clear, but note that the reviews have been mixed. [*WTJ* Spr 95; *CBQ* 10/95; *SwJT* Spr 95; *JSOT* 63].

Ash, Christopher. *Out of the Storm: Grappling with God in the Book of Job*, 2004. A brief homiletical study published by InterVarsity Press. [panned by a liberal in *JSOT-BL* 2005].

Bergant, D. ‡ *Job, Ecclesiastes* (OTM) 1982.

Ball, C.J. ‡ 1922. A detailed philological commentary on the Hebrew (Oxford), which showcases the author's learning in comparative Semitics; from the beginning it was in the shadow of the great ICC.

F   Burrell, David. (Brazos).

☆   Calvin, John. *Sermons on Job*, ET 1952 (Nixon Translation). Last issued by Baker in 1979, I believe, and now o/p. If they ever are republished, consider buying them. There has also been a reprint of the 1584 Golding translation in a "Facsimile Edition" by Banner of Truth. These 16th century translations are not very accessible on account of language, Elizabethan spelling, and poor print quality. Note: the "Facsimile Edition" contains all the sermons, whereas the Nixon Edition has only a selection. See also Thomas below. [*EvQ* 7/53; *CTJ* 11/95; *SBET* Spr 94].

F   Coogan, Michael David. ‡ (Herm).

✓   Davidson, Andrew B. ‡ (Cambridge Bible) 1884, 1918. An old standby, still referenced and quoted in the scholarship.

✓   Delitzsch, Franz. (KD) ET 1866. While Keil was a stand-out commentator on the historical books, Delitzsch was unsurpassed in his day as a scholar on the poetical books.

✓   **Dhorme, Edouard**. ‡ 1926, ET 1967. A massive commentary, mainly of interest to academic types, with "exhaustive handling of the textual problems" (Childs). Though it has the reputation of a classic, its value has declined with all the recent developments in the study of philology and Hebrew poetry. As one reviewer has noted, Dhorme himself made huge contributions to those developments by helping to decipher Ugaritic, the comparative study of which has shown much light on the language and grammar of Job. Thereby he ironically contributed to the obsolescence of his previous work. Still, this brilliant commentary will continue to be consulted for its discussion of grammar and syntax. Reprinted by Nelson in 1984. [*JBL* 87.1].

✓   **Driver, Samuel R. and George B. Gray.** ‡ (ICC) 1921. A classic, which has retained value for philological work.

✓   **Fokkelman, J.P.** *Major Poems of the Hebrew Bible*, Vols. 1–4, 1998–2004. Following on his enormous project covering Hebrew narrative (see under Samuel), the author took up the structural analysis of Hebrew poetry; he examines more the surface structures revealed in *analyse structurelle* than the deeper structures of *analyse structurale* (semiotics). Vol. 1: Exodus 15, Deuteronomy 32, Job 3 [*CBQ* 4/99; *Biblica* 81.2]. Vol. 2: 85 Psalms and Job 4–14 [*CBQ* 7/01; *Biblica* 83.1]. Vol. 3: The Remaining 65 Psalms [*CBQ* 7/04; *Biblica* 86.4; *VT* 56.4]. Vol. 4: Job 15–42 [*CBQ* 1/06; *JSS* Spr 07; *Biblica* 88.2; *VT* 56.4; *RelSRev* 10/06]. This set is only for advanced students who have great patience with detail-work. There is no theological interest here.

F   Fox, Michael V. ‡ (OTL replacement).

Fyall, Robert S. *Now My Eyes Have Seen You: Images of Creation and Evil in the Book of Job*, 2002. An evangelical minister and university lecturer here revises his very perceptive and theological Edinburgh dissertation. Much profit in the monograph and surprisingly accessible to non-specialists. An early popular-level exposition was *How Does God Treat His Friends?* (1995).

F   Garrett, Duane A. (EEC).

Gibson, E.C.S. [*M*], (Westminster Commentaries) 1919. Still of some value.

Gibson, J.C.L. ‡ (DSB) 1985.

✓ **Good, Edwin M.** ‡ *In Turns of Tempest: A Reading of Job, with a Translation,* 1990. A literary study with an abundance of fresh insights, published by Stanford University Press. I regard this as one of the most valuable and erudite recent treatments of Job (496pp). But do be warned: Good is a proponent of "deconstructive indeterminacy"—there is no one right meaning to be determined, rather there are infinite meanings. [*HebStud* 1992; *CRBR* 1992].

✓ Gordis, Robert. ‡ *The Book of God and Man,* 1965. A study preliminary to the work immediately below. Gordis was once the leading Jewish authority on Job. Extremely learned.

✓ **Gordis, Robert.** ‡ *The Book of Job,* 1978. A detailed textual and philological commentary on the Hebrew text, published by Ktav. Good attention to history of exegesis. An enormous amount of work went into this tome and specialists fell in love with it. There is high demand for this Jewish work on the secondhand market. [*JBL* 12/79].

F Greenstein, Edward. ‡ (BO).

✓ **Ḥakham, Amos.** *The Bible: Job with the Jerusalem Commentary,* 1970, ET 2009. I only saw this 456-page work the day this book was sent to the publisher. If it has anywhere near the quality of his Psalms commentary, it is worth looking up. What I have seen in an hour or so impresses me as a fresh, skillful, conservative handling of the MT; what Ḥakham does not do is lay out all the exegetical options for difficult texts like 19:25–26. In line with some old Jewish traditions (*Baba Bathra* 15a), he takes the book of Job to be a fable (p.xv). This is translated out of the Hebrew series *Da'at Miqra* and beautifully printed on large (8½ x 10) pages. According to WorldCat the author also has commentaries on Exodus, Isaiah, and the Five Scrolls (Ruth, Song of Songs, Qohelet, Lamentations, and Esther). Those familiar with the rich medieval tradition of Jewish philological exegesis will recognize Ḥakham as one of its heirs.

F Hess, Richard. (HCOT). This could be a standout commentary, both as a conservative in a critical series and in terms of quality.

Holbert, John C. ‡ *Preaching Job,* 1999. A thoughtful, liberal Methodist approach, written by a professor of homiletics at SMU.

✓ **Janzen, J. Gerald.** ‡ (I) 1990. A great entry in the series and an intelligent, reflective companion while reading Job. Never dull, Janzen's is probably to be considered about the best, most thought-provoking exposition written for the expositor and coming from the (moderately) critical camp. You are guaranteed to find frequent fresh insights. For further comment on this theologically oriented exegete, see Genesis and Exodus. [*ThTo* 43.4]. I am glad to report that another Janzen book on Job has been released: *At the Scent of Water: The Ground of Hope in the Book of Job* (Eerdmans, 2009). I have not seen it. The author told me that it is meant to be accessible to pastors but also includes some technical discussion for students' benefit (152pp) [*RBL* 6/10; *JSOT-BL* 2010; *RevExp* Spr 10].

Jarick, John. ‡ (Read) 1998. [*ExpTim* 1/00].

Jones, Hywel R. (EPSC) 2007. A spiritually edifying exposition by a professor of practical theology at Westminster Seminary, California. Previously he had pastored in the UK and served as Editorial Director at Banner of Truth. The publisher describes Jones' focus as "reading the Old Testament book through the eyes of New Testament revelation." Preachers will enjoy this (304pp).

Konkel, August H., and Tremper Longman III. *Job, Ecclesiastes, Song of Songs* (CorBC) 2006. Job is well handled by Konkel in 250pp. The volume is a solid representative of the series.

Kissane, Edward J. [*M*], 1939.

F   Longman, Tremper. (BCOT).

F   Magary, Dennis R. (NIVAC). There are reports this may be released soon. Magary teaches at TEDS.

McKenna, David L. (WCC) 1986. Meant to be suggestive for the preacher. [*RTR* 9/87].

Morgan, G. Campbell. *The Answers of Jesus to Job*, 1950. Suggests a fascinating homiletical approach to this Bible book, focused on Job's agonizing questions, which pulls both testaments together. Job is often neglected in the pulpit, and this little book could prompt many pastors to attempt their very first series of expository messages on the book.

✓   Murphy, Roland E. ‡ (FOTL) 1981. See under Ruth. Also see next entry.

✓   Murphy, Roland E. ‡ *The Book of Job: A Short Reading*, 1999. "The primary merit of the book lies in its succinctness and consistency" (G.Y. Kwak). About 140pp. [*JSOT* 89 (2000); *RelSRev* 7/00; *Scripture Bulletin* 1/01; *CBQ* 10/00; *Interp* 7/01; *JETS* 9/01; *HebStud* 2001; *VT* 51.3].

F   Neff, Robert. (BCBC).

✓   **Newsom, Carol A.** ‡ (NewIB) 1996. Found in vol. 4 of the series. The author teaches at Candler School of Theology, Emory University, and is regarded as one of this country's leading OT scholars. Newsom uses literary theory (especially Bakhtin's "dialogism") adroitly and finds much irony in Job. Because this commentary is bound up with Berlin's fine, succinct "Introduction to Hebrew Poetry" and McCann's (at the time) cutting-edge commentary on Psalms, some pastors wanting to build a first-rate exegetical library will consider purchasing this. [*CurTM* 6/97]. There's more from Newsom in *The Book of Job: A Contest of Moral Imagination* (Oxford, 2003) [*CBQ* 10/04; *JTS* 4/04; *Interp* 4/04; *JSOT* 28.5; *ThTo* 4/04; *VT* 57.2; *JR* 4/04 (Levenson); *DenvJ*].

Perdue, Leo G., and W. Clark Gilpin (eds). *The Voice from the Whirlwind: Interpreting the Book of Job*, 1992.

✓   **Pope, Marvin H.** ‡ (AB) 1965, 3ʳᵈ ed 1973. Helpful translation and close attention to philological details. This work has a strong appeal to OT specialists for a number of reasons; among them is Pope's great learning in the area of comparative ANE literature. Pastors won't find much help here; it will seem a dry well. For another Pope work, see Song of Songs.

☆   **Reyburn, W. D.** (UBS) 1992. Used to be a phenomenal buy at $16; I have no idea what the price is today. Reyburn's Handbook is well-written and has 840pp of exegetical guidance for translators. There is not the theological reflection one would expect from traditional commentaries, but this volume is quite valuable for helping the expositor explain the meaning of Job's difficult Hebrew text. [*CBQ* 10/94].

Rodd, C.S. ‡ (Epworth) 1990.

✓   **Rowley, H.H.** ‡ (NCB) 1970. Some good exposition in brief compass from a moderately critical perspective. Rowley was one of the most learned and judicious OT scholars of the mid-20ᵗʰ century in Britain. His turns of phrase are sometimes remarkable; e.g., he speaks of how in ch. 4 Eliphaz's "theology has dried the springs of true sympathy" (p.50). [*EvQ* 4/72].

✓   Scheindlin, Raymond P. ‡ *The Book of Job: Translation, Introduction, and Notes*, 1998. "A fresh and bold translation" by a scholar "concerned to break through the confines of conventional interpretation" (Dell). [*JSOT* 84 (1999); *RelSRev* 7/00].

Selms, A. van. ‡ (T&I) ET 1985. It would have been better if Eerdmans had, instead, sought to translate this South African scholar's much fuller "Prediking van het Oude Testament" two-vol. set than the "Tekst en Toelichting" work, which I found too cursory (160pp). [*Biblica* 66.4 (1985); *HebStud* 1986].

F   Seow, Choon-Leong. ‡ (ECC).

✓   Simonetti, Manlio, and Marco Conti (eds). Job (ACCS) 2006. [*JSOT-BL* 2007].

Simundson, Daniel J. ‡ 1986. This Lutheran OT scholar writes with some experience in hospital chaplaincy. This specifically theological commentary argues that Job is about the meaning of suffering rather than theology (the freedom and justice of God). I posit it is better to believe that Job 1:22 suggests the justice of God as the central issue, though we fall into the trap of Job's comforters if we treat the issue theoretically as if "conducting a seminar on theodicy at the local university" (p.20). [*CRBR* 1988; *WTJ* Fall 87].

☆   **Smick, Elmer B.** (EBC) 1988. Smick worked on Job for many years and this has been one of the very best evangelical commentaries for pastors. The author, now with the Lord, was respected as a great Hebraist (Dropsie PhD) and as a teacher with long years of experience defending the faith. Stuart makes this work and Clines his first picks. It has been declining in value with all the new works being published on Job. See the next entry for an updating of a trusty commentary.

F   Smick, Elmer B., and Tremper Longman III. (EBCR).

Terrien, S.L. ‡ (IB – Introduction & Exegesis) 1954. Has some contribution to make and is still consulted, though scholars pay greater attention to his later commentary in French for "Commentaire de l'Ancien Testament" (1963, 2nd ed 2005). This same scholar has published a huge one-vol. commentary on Psalms.

Thomas, David. 1878. A lengthy exposition from the 19th century. Only helpful on theological themes. This was reprinted by Kregel back in 1982, but is now o/p.

☆   Thomas, Derek. *When the Storm Breaks* (WCS on Job) 1995. Pastors will receive wise theological guidance in this exposition, which is strongly recommended by Fyall [*BSB* 3/98]. Thomas is a Welsh preacher-professor with deep appreciation for Calvin's exposition of Job. See the published dissertation, *Calvin's Teaching on Job* (Mentor, 2004) [*BSac* 7/06].

Van der Lugt, Pieter. ‡ *Rhetorical Criticism & the Poetry of the Book of Job*, 1995. For those with the learning to delve into this, van der Lugt provides an astonishing amount of detail on the Hebrew text, verbal repetitions, perceived chiasms, strophic analysis, etc.

✓   Westermann, Claus. ‡ *The Structure of the Book of Job: A Form-Critical Analysis*, ET 1981. Not a commentary.

☆   Wharton, James A. ‡ (WestBC) 1999. This 200-page exposition may be compared with Gibson and Atkinson. This would not be an unwise purchase for pastors, though his critical perspective intrudes at points and impoverishes the theological discussion. See the careful review in *JSOT* 89 (2000). [*Interp* 1/01; *Them* 6/00; *PSB* 21.1 (2000); *Perspectives in Religious Studies* Sum 00; *CBQ* 10/00; *HBT* 6/01].

✓   **Whybray, Norman**. ‡ (Read) 1998. A prolific scholar on Israel's poetic literature, Whybray here presents a fine personal literary reading. [*JSOT* 84 (1999); *Biblica* 80.4 (1999); *CBQ* 4/00; *RelSRev* 4/00].

F   Wilson, Lindsay. (THC).

Wolfers, David. *Deep Things Out of Darkness*, 1995. A sizable Eerdmans volume which includes a new translation, essays, and a commentary. The author was a physician who gave up his practice to devote the last 20 years of his life to researching the book of Job. [*JSOT* 72; *BL* 1996; *CBQ* 1/97; *HebStud* 1997].

Zöckler, Otto. (Lange) ET 1872. About 400pp of exegetical, theological and practical comment.

✓ Zuck, Roy B. (ed). *Sitting with Job. Selected Studies on the Book of Job*, 1992. Zuck has done similar projects with Proverbs and Ecclesiastes, though with arguably indifferent results. There is unevenness in his choice of material, and the reader may wonder what criteria were used in the selection process. Still, he does provide the student and pastor with ready access to materials that may prove difficult to find. Many of the articles he has selected are well worth reading. [*VT*, 47.4; *JSOT* 64; *BSac*, 1/93].

✓ Zuckerman, Bruce. ‡ *Job the Silent: A Study in Historical Counterpoint*, 1998. [*JSOT* 84 (1999); *HebStud* 1992].

NOTES: (1) C. S. Rodd's "Which Is the Best Commentary? IV. Job," *ExpTim*, 9/86. (2) Carol A. Newsom, "Re-considering Job," *CBR* 5.2 (2007): 155–82.

PSALMS

★ **Allen, Leslie C.** [*M*], *Psalms 101–150* (WBC) 1983, rev. ed 2002. A good commentary which, nevertheless, left me somewhat dissatisfied—particularly in the area of theological exposition. But Allen is "very helpful in the area of structure of the Psalms he covers," says Longman. The student will find much more to appreciate than the pastor will. In the last few editions of the guide, despite some misgivings, I have recommended this for purchase, because it works with the Hebrew. I am glad to say the revised edition does more to highlight the NT use and interpretation of these psalms. Note that in recent years we have all become more sensitized to the problem of ignoring the canonical division into five books, and Allen includes introductions to Book IV (90–106) and Book V (107–50). Students will note serious problems with the final forms of certain Hebrew letters in the revised edition; for example, μ replaces ם. [*JTS* 4/04; *WTJ* Fall 84; *JTS* 10/90; *JBL* 104.4 (1985); *JETS* 9/84; *CBQ* 1/04; *Interp* 1/05].

★ **Calvin, John.** 1557. Yale professor Brevard Childs judged the Reformer's work here to be "one of his most magnificent achievements." Calvin is particularly useful to me because many of today's newer scholarly commentaries fail to deliver a satisfying theological exposition. Calvin's lectures were born out of his sermons, and it shows in his Christological interpretations. About 2500pp! Calvin scholarship has recently been enriched with Herman Selderhuis, *Calvin's Theology of the Psalms,* 2007 [*Presb* Fall 08; *ThTo* 7/09].

★ **Craigie, Peter C.** *Psalms 1–50* (WBC) 1983, 2nd ed 2004. A fine work, since 1983 regarded as one of the best OT commentaries from an evangelical. It is valuable not only for its superb introduction, solid exegesis and poetical analysis, but also for its evaluation of Dahood's bold translation (see below). Craigie ably sifts out some of the more appropriate suggestions. Like Allen, this WBC volume doesn't often relate the Psalms to the NT. There have been major developments in Psalms studies over the last 25 years, and Craigie's commentary is not valued quite so highly as it once was. Nelson tries to remedy this, with a measure of success, by providing a 2004 supplement (115pp) which reviews recent Psalm scholarship and updates the bibliographies. Pastors with the 1st edition need not replace it, as the commentary section remains unchanged. Students will certainly want the 2nd edition. [*WTJ* Fall 84; *RTR* 9/83; *TJ* Fall 91; *JBL* 104.2 (1985); *EvQ* 4/87; *HebStud* 1984; *ExpTim* 2/09].

★ **Mays, James L.** ‡ (I) 1994. Covers the whole Psalter in, and packs a great deal of insight into, one vol. You'll find he is rather sketchy on some "less attractive" Psalms. Mays is a veteran at writing commentaries, so this is a mature product. But it is also fresh, riding the crest of the recent wave of works which focus a bit less on categorizing individual psalms (à la Gunkel) and attempt more of what Howard calls a "holistic analysis of the entire Psalter." "Today…the prevailing interest in Psalms studies has to do with questions about the composition, editorial unity, and overall message of the Psalter as a *book* (i.e., as a literary and canonical entity that coheres with respect to structure and message) and with how individual psalms and collections fit together." (Not all have jumped on this wagon, however; cf. R.N. Whybray's *Reading the Psalms as a Book*, 1996.) Mays' commentary reflects what J.K. Kuntz calls "the abundant energy of contemporary Psalms scholarship." Along with Miller's and Brueggemann's volumes, the best in the OT series. [*Them* 1/96; *ExpTim* 12/94; *Interp* 4/96; *ThTo* 4/95; *PSB* 16.1 (1995); *JETS* 3/99; *CBQ* 1/96; *RelSRev* 1/98]. Also worth consulting are Mays' *The Lord Reigns: A Theological Handbook to the Psalms*, 1994 [*JBL* Fall 96; *Interp* 4/96], and *Preaching and Teaching the Psalms*, 2006 [*ExpTim* 3/07].

★ **Tate, Marvin E.** [𝓜], *Psalms 51–100* (WBC) 1990. More extensive (578pp) than the other two WBC volumes, more cutting-edge in its scholarly approach too, but perhaps not always as incisive in its exegesis. Has many of the strengths and weaknesses of the series as a whole. A strong point would be that Tate shares some of Mays' interests. Among all these recommended purchases, this is perhaps one of the last which the average pastor would purchase. [*JTS* 4/94; *JSOT* 62; *HebStud* 1993].

★ **VanGemeren, Willem A.** (EBCR) 2008. The 1991 EBC edition—still useful, by the way—had almost 900 closely-packed pages of commentary from a Reformed viewpoint. The revision is a slight update (see pp.34–37) but not an expansion; the larger font size accounts for the increased page count (1000pp). Some bibliographies are reduced (cf. pp.39–47, 573, and 880 in the old edition with the new bibliographies). Longman used to say that, if you can have only one work on Psalms, this is it. That advice still holds. Pastors will learn much from VanGemeren's biblical theological approach here. Unlike the old edition, VanGemeren makes up the whole EBCR Vol. V. [*JSOT-BL* 2010].

★ **Wilson, Gerald H.** *Psalms Volume 1* (NIVAC) 2002. Only the first volume, covering Psalms 1–72, was published prior to Wilson's unexpected death in November 2005. Even though this is not meant to be a high-powered scholarly work, there is good, well-informed exegesis here. And when you look at the size of the volume (1024pp) together with the scholar's reputation, you know it is a good value. The expositor will relish this. Wilson's Yale dissertation on *The Editing of the Hebrew Psalter* (1985) has had extraordinary influence in recent years—that is partly what I'm referring to in my comments on Mays' volume above (the interest in, and emphasis on, canonical placement). For a good review and critique of Wilson's overall work, see David C. Mitchell, "Lord, Remember David," *VT* 56.4 (2006): 526–48. [*EuroJTh* 16.2].

✧ ✧ ✧ ✧ ✧ ✧

Alden, Robert. *Psalms: Songs of Discipleship*, 3 Vols., 1975. A seminarian once told me this was a favorite of his. Alden was a competent evangelical scholar, but this work is more popular in style.

☆ Alexander, Joseph A. 1850. A classic commentary from one of Old Princeton's greatest scholars. Much of the material here is admittedly from the great German professor, Hengstenberg. [*WTJ* 18.1].

F   Allen, Ronald B. (EEC).

☆   **Alter, Robert.** 2007. This fresh translation goes a long way toward conveying the power and compactness of the Hebrew poetry. Alter is a forceful intellect and has for decades taught at Berkeley. The 500-page volume includes a brief, unusually insightful exegetical commentary from a Jewish perspective. This is a most helpful book for its rendering of the Hebrew (few emendations of the MT), for prompting readers to reflect on the nuances of the original, and for his discussion of literary features such as parallelism. [*WTJ* Fall 08; *JETS* 9/08; *JSOT-BL* 2010].

✓   **Anderson, A.A.** ‡ (NCB) 2 Vols., 1972. A sober-minded survey of previous scholarship and careful form-critical exegesis from a middle-of-the-road perspective. This was a suggested purchase in early editions of this guide, but now we have Goldingay, WBC, EBC/EBCR, and ContC complete.

✓   **Anderson, Berhard W.** ‡ *Out of the Depths: The Psalms Speak to Us Today*, 1974, 3ʳᵈ ed 2000. This has long been a standard handbook for reading the Psalms form-critically. [*OTA* 10/00; *JSOT* 94 (2001)].

F   Bellinger, William H. ‡ (S&H).

✓   Blaising, Craig A., and Carmen S. Hardin (eds). *Psalm 1–50* (ACCS) 2008.

☆   Boice, James Montgomery. 3 Vols., 1994–98. This set of sermonic expositions is published by Baker. Used alongside the best, up-to-date, exegetical commentaries, it will prove quite useful to preachers.

F   Botha, Phil J., and Gert T.M. Prinsloo. ‡ (HCOT). Previously Willem S. Prinsloo was also listed as the contributor of *Psalms 73–150*.

✓   **Bratcher, R.G., and W.D. Reyburn.** *A Handbook on Psalms* (UBS) 1991. Over 1200pp and well worth consulting. "An indispensable resource not only for translators but also for every student, commentator, and teacher of the Book of Psalms" (McCann). [*CRBR* 1993].

     Bridges, Charles. *Psalm 119* (Banner of Truth reprint) 1857. This devotional commentary has been used by several friends of mine in their "quiet times." I would counsel you to add this volume to your library (not as a necessary commentary, but as devotional literature). Has something of a Puritan flavor to it. See Proverbs.

     Briggs, C.A., and E.G. Briggs. ‡ (ICC) 2 Vols., 1907–09. Of little account today.

☆   Brown, William P. ‡ *Seeing the Psalms: A Theology of Metaphor*, 2003. This book can be strongly recommended to students exploring either the psalmists' powerful use of metaphors or the theology of the Psalter. More academically oriented pastors will find plenty of grist for the mill here. [*Them* Sum 04; *Interp* 7/03; *ExpTim* 11/03; *HBT* 12/03; *JSOT* 28.5; *BBR* 14.2; *VT* 54.4; *BibInt* 14.3; *SJT* 60.3; *Anvil* 20.4]. See also the next entry and Brown's 2010 Psalms volume in "Interpreting Biblical Texts."

F   Brown, William P. ‡ (OTL replacement). This should be superb.

☆   **Broyles, Craig C.** (NIBC) 1999. About 525pp and well-done for a one-vol. commentary. The author's 1989 JSOTSup volume, *The Conflict of Faith and Experience in the Psalms*, is a fine piece of work with good discussion of form-critical categories—he distinguishes psalms of plea and psalms of complaint. He is more interested in "the psalms' original use as liturgies" (p.8) and in treating them singly; he is less interested in connections between psalms and the structure of the whole Psalter (cf. Wilson, Mays). The reviews of this newer commentary have been laudatory. And since the NIBC volumes are priced reasonably, this would be a wise purchase, even a "best bargain" pb on Psalms. [*Interp* 10/00; *Crux* 6/00; *RTR* 8/00; *Them* Spr 01; *VT* 51.2 (2001); *JTS* 4/01; *CBQ* 10/01; *JETS* 9/01; *HebStud* 2001; *JSOT* 94 (2001); *RelSRev* 7/02; *Chm* Aut 01].

✓ **Brueggemann, Walter.** ‡ *Praying the Psalms*, 1982, 2ⁿᵈ ed 2007 [*VT* 58.4]; and *The Message of the Psalms: A Theological Commentary*, 1984. The most important of Brueggemann's journal articles relating to the Psalms have been gathered into one-vol. by Patrick Miller: *The Psalms and the Life of Faith*, 1995. He is a shrewd and veteran interpreter, and has made a huge contribution to critical scholarship on the Psalms with his "life of faith" approach. He famously recategorized the laments/complaints, thanksgiving psalms, and hymns as psalms of disorientation, reorientation, and orientation. See Brueggemann's other commentaries on Genesis, Exodus, and Samuel. As usual, his works are packed theologically.

F Brueggemann, Walter, and Patrick Miller. ‡ (NCBC). This is planned as a two-vol. set.

☆ Bullock, C. Hassell. *Encountering the Book of Psalms*, 2001. An excellent piece of work that a long-ago graduate of seminary could use as a refresher course. I'd say this is perhaps the best in the whole Baker series thus far, and I chose it as one of the primary textbooks in a 2010 course I taught. [*Them* Spr 04; *RTR* 8/02; *JETS* 6/03; *ExpTim* 12/02; *JSOT* 99 (2002); *SBET* Aut 02; *BSac* 4/03; *CJ* 1/05].

F Bullock, C. Hassell. (TTT). The author, now retired from Wheaton, told me to expect two vols.

F Bush, L. Russ. (N̶A̶C̶). It is reported that Bush will not publish a Psalms commentary in NAC; perhaps his work, if completed, may be published elsewhere. He passed away in January 2008.

✓ **Clifford, Richard J.** ‡ (AOTC) 2 Vols., 2002–03. Turn to this for a current, concise, critical exegesis of the Psalter. Clifford attempts one of the first rhetorical-critical readings of the entire Psalter (see also Schaefer below). What he aims to do, he does well. Students will discover that Clifford does not cite much Psalms scholarship. See Clifford under Proverbs. [*CBQ* 4/04; *JSOT* 28.5; *CBQ* 4/05; *JETS* 3/05, 6/05; *Interp* 1/05; *VT* 56.4; *RBL*].

✓ Cohen, A. ‡ *Psalms. Hebrew Text, English Translation and Commentary*, 1992.

F Cole, Robert. *Psalms 1–89* (NAC). This younger scholar has published a monograph on the shape of Book 3: Psalms 73–89.

F Cooper, A.M. ‡ (AYB). This will be a replacement for Dahood.

✓ Crenshaw, James. *The Psalms: An Introduction*, 2001. [*RTR* 12/01; *Them* S̶p̶r̶/Sum 02; *JETS* 6/03; *Interp* 4/02; *HebStud* 01; *TJ* Spr 04; *JSOT* 99 (2002); *SwJT* Fall 01; *RelSRev* 1/02].

Dahood, Mitchell. ‡ (AB) 3 Vols., 1965–70. A wholesale reinterpretation of the Psalter on the basis of Ugaritic studies. Idiosyncratic! You might be curious enough to consult Dahood in writing an exegetical paper, but it would be best to leave it to the scholars to debate his novel suggestions. The fact that Tremper Longman, a specialist in the area of ANE cognate languages, dismisses this work outright should make you extremely cautious. See Cooper above. [*JBL* 88.2 (1969) and 93.2 (1974)].

☆ Davidson, Robert. ‡ *The Vitality of Worship*, (meant for ITC) 1998. Called a superb theological work by McCann. I'd say that, for the pastor, it is perhaps the most valuable expositional-devotional work on the Psalms from a mainline church position (Church of Scotland, which Davidson has served as Moderator of the General Assembly). Published in pb by Eerdmans, this delightful book often mines the richest veins of Reformed comment, including Calvin. Because of a relative lack of interaction with more recent Psalms scholarship, students will not value this conservatively critical volume as highly. Others may class this as [*M*]. Students will pass this by. [*Interp* 4/99; *CBQ* 10/99; *RTR* 8/00; *HebStud* 1999; *ExpTim* 5/01; *JTS* 4/02; *VT* 51.3].

✓ **Delitzsch, Franz.** (KD) 1859–60, 2ⁿᵈ ed 1867, ET 1871. His three-vol. work is masterful, but not at all easy to wade through. I would argue that it is this commentary in the KD set (and in its subsequent German editions up to the 5th in 1894) which has had the greatest and longest-lasting impact on scholarship. Delitzsch continues to be cited constantly, and the German work was reprinted in 2005 [*JSOT-BL* 2007]. Students should make use of this, assured that they will be surprised at numerous turns by the freshness of the treatment. Such learning! The latest English edition I have found is the Eaton translation (Hodder & Stoughton, 1894) of the 4th German edition (1883). I am guessing that the common KD reprints have the translation of the German 2nd edition of 1867. See also Kirkpatrick below.

☆ Dickson, David. (GS) 1653–55. The Puritans wrote few substantial commentaries on OT books. The few they did write are mostly on the Psalms. Dickson's lovely commentary is representative of their best work. "The exegesis is warm, vigorous, bold and devotional and is highly recommended" (Childs). Students who have appreciated Dickson might also want to look up the commentaries of Owen, Sibbes, and Spurgeon.

Eaton, J.H. ‡ (Torch Bible Commentary) 1967. Was more valuable than one might think, looking at its size (317pp). One of the better and last published works in this mid-century series. A representative interpretation from the cultic and ritual camp; unfortunately he buys Mowinckel lock, stock, and barrel. See also Eaton's *Kingship and the Psalms* (2nd ed 1986) and the entry immediately below.

✓ **Eaton, John H.** [𝓜], *The Psalms: A Historical and Spiritual Commentary, with an Introduction and New Translation*, 2003. Students now take account of this fatter (536-page) commentary produced near the close of the author's long career as a Psalms expert, rather than the Torch series volume. He continues to read a great many of the Psalms as representing the voice of the king, in line with his thesis in *Kingship and the Psalms*, 1986. What has changed over the years is that Eaton pursues a more literary approach, which is in line with the dominant trend in Psalm studies. Grant says, "Readers…should be careful to make their way to the appendix at the back of the book as they study each psalm. It is there that we find some very helpful discussion of translation questions and the historical interpretation of the text. …This is a truly sympathetic commentary with a great grasp of the tone and spiritual purpose" of each psalm. [*CBQ* 4/05; *JTS* 4/05; *VT* 56.4; *ExpTim* 12/04; *Anvil* 21.4; *EuroJTh* 16.2 (Grant)]. A more devotional and popular reading is *Psalms for Life: Hearing and Praying the Book of Psalms*, 2006 [*RTR* 4/08; *JSOT-BL* 2008].

☆ Firth, David G., and Philip S. Johnston (eds). *Interpreting the Psalms*, 2005. This volume of collected essays is just right for introducing seminarians to developments in the field of Psalms scholarship. The British edition orders the editors as "Johnston and Firth." [*Chm* Spr 07; *CBQ* 4/07; *JSOT-BL* 2006; *VT* 57.4; *BSac* 1/07; *CJ* 4/07; *ExpTim* 7/06; *Evangel* Aut 07; *Anvil* 23.3].

✓ Flint, Peter, and Patrick Miller (eds). ‡ *The Book of Psalms: Composition and Reception*, 2005. This large Brill volume contains cutting edge scholarship. [*JTS* 4/06; *VT* 57.3; *CurTM* 8/06].

✓ **Fokkelman, J.P.** ‡ *Major Poems of the Hebrew Bible: At the Interface of Prosody and Structural Analysis*, Vol. 2, 2000; Vol. 3, 2003. Extremely detailed structural analysis (see under Job) with scarcely any theological points. [*CBQ* 7/01, 7/04; *JSOT* 28.5].

✓ Foster, Robert L., and David M. Howard (eds). *"My Words Are Lovely": Studies in the Rhetoric of the Psalms*, 2008. [*JSOT-BL* 2009; *JHebS* 2009].

☆ Futato, Mark D. (CorBC) 2009. This work is paired with George Schwab on Proverbs in a 669-page volume. The two commentaries are sound guides, accessible even to educated lay readers. Futato has published both a popular introduction to the Psalter, *Transformed by Praise* (2002), and a more technical "Exegetical Handbook" entitled *Interpreting the Psalms* (Kregel, 2007). The latter is a dependable tool for seminarians beginning to use Hebrew in exegesis and for pastors wanting something like a refresher course [*BTB* 2/08; *JETS* 9/08; *JSOT-BL* 2009; *HBT* 31.2].

F   Geller, Stephen. ‡ (Herm). This Jewish scholar used to teach at Dropsie and earlier did some of the very best work on parallelism in Hebrew poetry.

✓   **Gerstenberger, E.S.** ‡ *Psalms, Part 1: With an Introduction to Cultic Poetry* (FOTL) 1989; *Psalms, Part 2, and Lamentations* (FOTL) 2001. A big name in Psalms study—"perhaps the most disciplined and intentional form critic of the present generation of scholars of the Hebrew Bible" (W. Brueggemann)! Gerstenberger is only for advanced students. Along with Westermann and Kraus, Gerstenberger has urged some important revisions of Gunkel's form critical categories of psalms. This volume is of greater value on the Psalms than on Lamentations. [*Biblica* 71.3 (1990); *JETS* 6/92; *Interp* 1/91; *Them* 10/91; *HebStud* 1990; *Them* Spr 04; *BSac* 10/03; *JTS* 10/02; *JSS* Spr 03; *VT* 53.1; *JSOT* 99 (2002)].

Gillingham, Susan. *Psalms through the Centuries* (BBC) 2008–. Only the first volume of this "reception history" is out, but it is generating excitement among many, especially in Britain. Cf. Holladay below. [*ExpTim* 7/09; *Interp* 4/10 (McCann); *Anvil* 26.3–4 (Firth)].

Goldingay, John. *Songs in a Strange Land: Psalms 42–51* (was BST) 1977. See now his full commentary.

☆   **Goldingay, John.** [*M*], (BCOT) 3 Vols., 2006–08. This is the fullest exegesis and theological exposition of the Psalms (near 2200pp) to be published in a long time, but there is a caveat for pastors. Goldingay treats the Psalms mostly within their OT context, and so this commentary will be considered deficient by those wanting a more forthrightly Christian or NT-related interpretation. In this one respect this commentary is different from the others in the BCOT series. The best Christian reflection in these volumes, what there is, comes from quotes of Church Fathers and Reformers. Goldingay is less interested in the older diachronic methods (especially redaction history) and prefers to treat the final form of the Hebrew. He is also "not enamored" of the newer scholarly questions about the shape and shaping of the Psalter as a whole book; his focus is the individual psalm. His basic interpretive questions are form-critical: what categories of psalms do we perceive, and what was their use in the community of faith? The author is a critically oriented British evangelical who has published widely in the fields of Hebrew/Aramaic exegesis (see Isaiah and Daniel), hermeneutics, and biblical theology; for an assessment of his critical views in this commentary, see VanGemeren in *Them* 11/09. These nicely-bound volumes are accessible to pastors, many of whom will want to make this purchase (list $150, $90 on sale). [*CBQ* 10/08; *Interp* 10/07; *JSOT-BL* 2007, 2008, 2010; *VT* 59.1, 59.4; *ExpTim* 2/09; *JETS* 3/08, 12/09, 3/10; *RBL*; *JHebS* 2009 (McCann); *BSac* 7/08; *BBR* 19.2, 19.4].

✓   **Goulder, Michael D.** ‡ *Studies in the Psalter I–IV* (JSOTSup #20, 102, 233, 258) 4 Vols, 1982–1998. A huge project spanning many years. Goulder is a trenchant critical scholar who is unafraid to challenge consensus (with wit) where he believes it is necessary. There is both much detailed exegesis of individual psalms and a general interpretive scheme which places great weight on the psalms' order. This is a set for students to consult; it is of little account to pastors. [*EvQ* 1/01 and *JSS* Spr 01].

F   Grant, Jamie. *Psalms Volume 2: Psalms 73–150* (NIVAC). This will complete what Wilson so ably began.

☆   Grogan, Geoffrey W. (THC) 2008. A delightful, brief theological exposition with se-lect exegetical notes on the Hebrew. Gillingham is correct to say it suffers some-what on account of its brevity. I can think of few better introductory guides into the Psalter's theology than the 200-page section concluding this book, "Theological Horizons of Psalms." [*RTR* 12/08; *VT* 59.1; *JETS* 12/09; *JSOT-BL* 2009; *BTB* 2/10; *CBQ* 10/09; *ExpTim* 7/09 (Gillingham)].

✓   **Gunkel, Hermann.** ‡ *Introduction to the Psalms: The Genres of the Religious Lyric of Israel*, 1933, ET 1998. The classic of early form-critical scholarship on Psalms. Still influential. [*JETS* 12/99; *Interp* 7/99].

✓   **Ḥakham, Amos** (עמוס חכם). *The Bible: Psalms with the Jerusalem Commentary*, 3 Vols., 1979–81, ET 2003. This large-scale work (1400pp) is a translation from the Hebrew commentary *Da'at Miqra* (דעת מקרא) and deserves to be better known in scholarly circles. Prof. Barry Eichler of the University of Pennsylvania sums up its strengths: "articulate exposition of the Psalms, often reflecting the discerning in-sights of classical Jewish exegesis…lucid translation…with a serious philological commentary containing grammatical and textual notes." I would add that Ḥakham highlights many psalm parallels (a kind of *intra*textuality). The tone of the com-mentary is devout, conservative (Judaism), and highly theological—scarcely any-thing here might be termed higher-critical. If you sample this, you will use it again and again. See also Ḥakham under Job.

Harman, Allan M. (Mentor) 1998. I have not yet used this briefer (450pp) theological exposition from a conservative Reformed scholar.

✓   Holladay, William L. ‡ *The Psalms through Three Thousand Years: Prayerbook of a Cloud of Witnesses*, 1993. There is nothing like this for appreciating the history of Jewish and Christian use of the Psalms. Another resource is Attridge and Fassler (eds), *Psalms in Community: Jewish and Christian Textual, Liturgical, and Artistic Traditions* (SBL, 2003) [*JNES* 4/10].

✓   **Hossfeld, Frank-Lothar, and Erich Zenger.** ‡ *Psalms 2* (Herm) 2000, ET 2005. This initial volume in a three-vol. set covers Psalms 51–100. As one would expect from the Hermeneia series, Hossfeld and Zenger present a technical exegesis and take up questions related to the psalms' compositional/redactional history. The authors tend to attribute rather late dates to individual psalms. They are also interested in the overall message of the Psalter and the relation between the part, the individual psalm, and the whole. Advanced students will interact with their conclusions, but few pastors will pay the price for this expensive work. The German version of the commentary on Psalms 101–150 appeared in 2008. [*CTJ* 4/06; *Interp* 4/07; *JSOT-BL* 2006; *RelSRev* 1/07; *BSac* 4/08; *RBL*; *ExpTim* 7/06; *EuroJTh* 16.2, 18.2].

Hunter, Alastair G. ‡ (Read) 1999. Not a full commentary, but a stimulating attempt to coordinate older methods of interpretation with newer literary (often postmodern) approaches. [*ExpTim* 4/00; *Interp* 7/01]. See also *An Introduction to the Psalms* (T&T Clark, 2008) [*JSOT-BL* 2009].

F   Jacobson, Rolf A., Nancy deClaissé-Walford, and Beth LaNeel Tanner. (NICOT). Note that certain lists of forthcoming commentaries misspell an author's name "Jacobsen."

☆   **Kidner, Derek.** (TOTC) 2 Vols., 1973–75. Over the years I have often started with Kidner, especially for quick reference. He never fails me when I am looking for theological insights on the text. Kidner offers a discerning corrective for the cultic interpretations one finds in the older, more critical commentaries (e.g., Weiser, and sometimes Anderson). This is a favorite of Stuart and Longman. In most previous editions of my guide, Kidner was a recommended purchase. See Longman below. [*JETS* 3/75, 12/76].

✓ **Kirkpatrick, Alexander F.** [*M*], (Cambridge Bible for Schools and Colleges) 1892–1902. Reprinted long ago in Baker's Thornapple series and by Scripture Truth Book Company. Definitely one of the best in the OT section of the old Cambridge series. I have found great profit in this solidly-packed volume (100pp of introduction, 850pp of commentary), which follows the old conservative grammatico-historical approach we also see in Delitzsch. This commentary, though dated, retains value. Kirkpatrick's prose is elegant.

Kissane, Edward J. [*M*], 2 Vols., 1953–54. A famous pre-Vatican II Catholic work.

Knight, George A.F. [*M*], (DSB) 2 Vols., 1982. Over 700pp of fine theological exposition and devotional reflection. The author is one of the more conservatively critical OT scholars in Britain. Worth looking up.

✓ **Kraus, Hans-Joachim.** ‡ (ContC) 2 Vols., ET 1987–89. These volumes are translated out of the BKAT (1961–66; rev. 1978), together with the author's *Theology of the Psalms* (ET 1986) [*JBL* 101.2 (1982)]. They have been quite important and total about 1100pp. Scholars are presently wrestling with the "problem of how to evaluate justly the relative proportions of individual creativity and social convention in the process of poetic composition" (Gerstenberger). Kraus argues that they should be viewed more as private compositions, which is the more traditional view. He also refines the form-critical categories which have customarily been used in cataloging the Psalms. Indispensable for scholars, this has been one of my favorite technical commentaries. The more historical approach here, however, has become dated. [*TJ* Fall 91; *CBQ* 7/91; *Interp* 4/91; *ExpTim* 1/92; *ThTo* 46.2].

Lennox, Stephen J. *Psalms: A Bible Commentary in the Wesleyan Tradition*, 1999.

Leupold, H.C. 1959. TEDS's annotated bibliography once listed Leupold as "the best commentary on this book." I have not found it to be as penetrating as some other works, and it appeared before the recent explosion of research into ancient Hebrew poetry. Leupold would be helpful for gaining insight into conservative Lutheran theological interpretation.

Lewis, C.S. *Reflections on the Psalms*, 1958. An insightful little book and very quotable.

Limburg, James. ‡ (WestBC) 2000. The largest volume in the series thus far at 500pp (one of the best too), Limburg is useful to consult for a moderately critical exposition. The reviews have been warm. For preachers. [*ExpTim* 5/01; *CBQ* 10/01; *JETS* 3/02; *Interp* 1/02; *VT* 53.1; *JSOT* 94 (2001); *BBR* 12.1; *Them* Sum 05; *Anvil* 18.4 (Johnston)].

Lloyd-Jones, D. Martyn. *Faith on Trial*, 1965. A moving exposition of Psalm 73 by one of the greatest 20th century expositors. This work is spiritually refreshing and challenging. Do note that it is now published with his fine exposition of Habakkuk in the volume *Faith Tried and Triumphant*.

☆ Longman, Tremper III. *How to Read the Psalms*, 1988. A useful handbook for the student wanting to get acquainted with "the Hebrew Hymnal" and to learn to interpret it. Not a commentary, though it includes some insightful studies of a few psalms as models. Accomplishing similar goals but critically oriented is James Crenshaw's *The Psalms: An Introduction* (Eerdmans, 2001).

F Longman, Tremper. (TOTC replacement).

Luther, Martin. "First Lectures on the Psalms," Vols. 10–11 in *Luther's Works*, 1513–15, ET 1974–76; "Selected Psalms, I–III," Vols. 12–14 in *Luther's Works*, 1521–46,

ET 1955–58. Both as a monk and afterwards, Luther's daily life was suffused with meditation on the Psalms.

✓ **McCann, C. Clinton.** ‡ (NewIB) 1996. Found in vol. 4 of the series. The author teaches at Eden Seminary in St. Louis, has chaired the Psalms group in SBL, and is a proponent of the "new approach to the Psalms" (cf. *The Shape and Shaping of the Psalter*, edited by McCann [1993]). Students should make ready use of this commentary. [*DenvJ*]. See also McCann's *Theological Introduction to the Book of Psalms: The Psalms as Torah* (1993), which has been used as a textbook in some evangelical seminaries [*CRBR* 1995; *RelSRev* 1/98].

Maclaren, Alexander. (EB) 1893. Representing some of the best of 19th century exposition, this was reprinted by Klock & Klock.

✓ Miller, Patrick. ‡ *Interpreting the Psalms*, 1986. This has long been, and still remains, one of the best written and most widely used introductions to the Psalms. More recent and on a related topic is *They Cried to the Lord: The Form and Theology of Biblical Prayer*, 1994.

✓ **Mowinckel, Sigmund.** ‡ *The Psalms in Israel's Worship*, 2 Vols, ET 1962. A seminal introduction—not a commentary—which sought to understand the Psalms as the compositions of temple singers and musicians and as destined for cultic use. Placed great stress upon an annual festival, which celebrated the "enthronement of Yahweh." In the mid-20th century Mowinckel was the don of the many Scandinavian scholars studying the poetical books. Eerdmans has republished Mowinckel as one pb volume (2004). See also Eaton and Weiser. [*VT* 57.3; *ExpTim* 10/05].

Murphy, Roland E. ‡ *The Gift of the Psalms*, 2000. [*Interp* 4/02; *JSOT* 99 (2002)].

☆ **Perowne, J.J.S.** 1890. A masterful classic. Childs says, "Its strength lies in its close attention to the Hebrew text." He adds that "the writer has a good knowledge of the history of exegesis and a profound sense of the unity of the two Testaments," and "provides an excellent balance to the modern commentaries which seldom deal with the New Testament's use of the Psalter." Perowne has been reprinted in both hb and pb (Kregel, 1989), and is still worth consulting as a compendium of the best old commentary on the Psalms.

Plumer, W.S. (GS) 1867. A massive work (1211pp) that I've never had the opportunity to use. Spurgeon records that he did not find Plumer all that helpful.

☆ Robertson, O. Palmer. *Psalms in Congregational Celebration*, 1995. Model preaching on 25 of the Psalms by a pastor, seminary prof, and missionary.

F Ross, Allen. (Kregel).

✓ Sabourin, Leopold. ‡ 2 Vols, 1969. A moderate Roman Catholic work which emphasizes the private origin of this poetry (*contra* Mowinckel, Weiser, et al.). At one time it was valued by specialists for its bibliographies. [*JBL* 89.2 (1970)].

Sarna, Nahum. *Songs of the Heart: An Introduction to the Book of Psalms*, 1993. I found this book of sensitive Jewish readings of selective psalms stimulating.

✓ **Schaefer, Konrad.** ‡ (BO) 2001. This volume has 45pp of introduction plus 358pp of commentary; it is one of the best in the series. Schaefer's approach has been strongly influenced by the pioneering literary critic, Luis Alonso Schökel (well known for *A Manual of Hebrew Poetics*, 1988), and can be profitably used alongside the form-critical commentaries. [*Interp* 4/02; *ExpTim* 9/02; *HebStud* 2003; *JSOT* 99 (2002); *CBQ* 7/05].

F Shepherd, Jerry. *Psalms 90–150* (NAC).

F Sommer, Benjamin D. (ed), Adele Berlin, Mark Zvi Brettler, Alan Cooper, Avigdor Shinan, and Yair Zakovich. ‡ (JPS).

☆ Spurgeon, Charles H. *The Treasury of David*, 1870–85. Many reprints available. Spurgeon is rich theologically and serves as a compendium of hundreds of old classics, including the Puritans. Unhappily, the exposition is sometimes unrelated to the text, and it is verbose. This is for the preacher rather than the scholar and should only be used with ready reference to a couple good exegetical works like VanGemeren and the WBC set. This exposition has been edited down to two pb volumes for CrossC.

✓ **Terrien, Samuel L.** ‡ *The Psalms: Strophic Structure and Theological Commentary* (ECC) 2003. This was completed shortly before the venerable professor's death at age 91: "a monumental tribute to a great scholar of the past, but will hardly be monumental for the future" (Johnston). This nearly 1000-page tome is faulted for being dated in scholarship, and yet "erudition and elevated language grace the commentary throughout" (Ryan). The theology here has sparkle and imagination, focusing a good bit on the theme of divine presence/absence—this was expected and in line with his 1978 OT Theology, *The Elusive Presence*. Eerdmans has now released a pb reprint in two volumes. [*CBQ* 7/04; *RTR* 8/03; *JTS* 10/03; *ExpTim* 1/04; *JSOT* 28.5; *ThTo* 4/04; *Interp* 10/05; *BSac* 4/06; *HebStud* 2005; *VT* 55.2 (Johnston); *JNES* 7/07; *TJ* Fall 04 (VanGemeren); *Anvil* 21.4; *EuroJTh* 16.1].

☆ VanGemeren, Willem A. (EBC) 1991. See VanGemeren's EBCR above. The older EBC volume was always an excellent purchase because this Psalms commentary was bound with a strong work on Proverbs by Ross. If you own the 1991 edition, you do not need to spend extra money to buy EBCR.

Wallace, Howard N. ‡ (Read) 2009.

☆ Waltner, James. [𝓜], (BCBC) 2006. This fat pb (831pp) by a studious old Anabaptist pastor has devotional value, though there is also some critical orientation. He has obviously spent thousands of hours exegeting and meditating upon the psalms. Pastors will appreciate how Waltner draws attention to related Bible passages (intertexts). To get the flavor of the work, see his treatment of 67, the great missionary psalm. [*JETS* 12/08].

✓ **Weiser, Artur.** ‡ (OTL) ET 1962. Was one of the leading critical commentaries but is now aging rapidly. Develops many of Mowinckel's cultic themes relating to the hypothetical annual festival; this is Weiser's prime demerit. (Note to students: Weiser redefines the festival as centered on covenant rather than Yahweh's enthronement.) The commentary has its weaknesses, but on the plus side is concerned with theology, the idea of the covenant, and its place in the people's worship.

F Wenham, Gordon J. (Apollos).

✓ Wesselschmidt, Quentin F. (ed). *Psalms 51–150* (ACCS) 2007. [*JSOT-BL* 2009].

✓ **Westermann, Claus.** ‡ *The Living Psalms*, ET 1989. A famous form-critic here explains the book of Psalms theologically [*JR* 4/91]. See also *The Psalms: Structure, Content and Message*, ET 1980 [*JBL* 101.2 (1982)]; and *Praise and Lament in the Psalms*, ET 1981, which includes Westermann's widely influential *The Praise of God in the Psalms*, ET 1965. Along with Brueggemann who builds upon him, Westermann transformed the older form-critical approach to the Psalms and reinvigorated scholarship.

☆ Wilcock, Michael. (BST) 2 Vols., 2001. This set, by the author of several BST volumes (Judges, Chronicles, Luke, Revelation), can be recommended to pastors. [*JSOT* 99; *Chm* Spr 05; *Them* Sum 05; *Evangel* Sum 03; *Anvil* 19.3].

Williams, Donald M. (WCC) 2 Vols., 1986–89. One of the largest commentaries in the series (1034pp). This work takes the form of a running exposition, and unfortunately seems to lack the insight and synthesis of material one finds in the best WCC volumes—too little time spent with the text? The impression I get is of a very well-trained, but time-pressed expositor. On the plus side, Williams' comments are theologically sound and don't lead the reader astray. The two volumes have the usual anecdotal, practical thrust which one expects from the series, usually found more in the chapter introduction and conclusion. For a much more positive assessment of these volumes, see Longman's *OT Commentary Survey*. [*CBQ* 4/92; *Chm* 104.4 (1990)].

☆ Witvliet, John D. *The Biblical Psalms in Christian Worship: A Brief Introduction & Guide to Resources*, 2007. This fits a niche with its synthesis of biblical scholarship, history of worship, musicology, and liturgics (many practical suggestions for using Psalms in corporate worship). The best way to learn the Psalms is by using them! The author heads up the Calvin Institute of Christian Worship, but this 169-page handbook treats nearly all Christian traditions.

NOTES: (1) The imprecatory Psalms have long baffled most Christians. An old, influential study of this troubling literature is Chalmers Martin's "Imprecations in the Psalms," *Princeton Theological Review*, 1903, pp. 537–53. See also James Adams' *War Psalms of the Prince of Peace*, (P&R, 1991). From the critical side, there is Erich Zenger's *A God of Vengeance? Understanding the Psalms of Divine Wrath* (WJK, 1996), which is reviewed in *JSOT* 79 (1998). Two of the latest contributions to the discussion, reviewed in *EvQ* 4/07, are: John Day's *Crying for Justice* (IVP, 2005) [*JSOT-BL* 2007], and David Firth's *Surrendering Retribution in the Psalms* (Paternoster, 2005) [*CBQ* 1/07; *Them* 10/06; *ExpTim* 10/06]. (2) Some scholars are now more trusting of the superscriptions. See Bruce Waltke, "Superscripts, Postscripts, or Both," *JBL* 110 (1991): 583–96; and Dale Brueggemann, "Psalms 4: Titles," in *DOTWPW* (IVP, 2008), 613–21. (3) For a general review of developments in recent Psalms scholarship, see both Susan Gillingham, "Studies of the Psalms: Retrospect and Prospect," *ExpTim* 119.5 (2008): 209–16; and David Howard's chapter in Firth/Johnston above.

PROVERBS

★ **Fox, Michael.** ‡ (AB) 2 Vols., 2000–09. This brilliant set replaces Scott. Fox, a Jewish professor at the University of Wisconsin, has previously done first-rate work on Esther, Ecclesiastes, and Song of Songs. His past work on Proverbs has also been careful and cutting-edge; see "The Social Location of the Book of Proverbs" in *Texts, Temples, and Traditions: A Tribute to Menahem Haran*, (Eisenbrauns, 1996), 227–239. Now complete, this set takes honors as the leading, most comprehensive, critical commentary available. Note that the AB is not for the faint of heart: it is packed with technical philological and textual research, and it extends to 1200pp. With Dell I do not recommend following Fox in his developmental view of Israelite wisdom, "from pragmatic, to moral to the more theological figure of Wisdom." Only for advanced students and scholarly pastors. [*ExpTim* 5/01; *CBQ* 10/01; *JTS* 10/01; *JETS* 3/02; *Interp* 10/02; *BSac* 10/02; *VT* 53.2; *HBT* 6/02; *JSOT* 94 (2001); *CurTM* 10/04; the best are *BBR* 13.2 and *ExpTim* 9/10 (Dell)].

★ **Hubbard, David A.** (WCC) 1989. A lengthy study (487pp) by the late President of Fuller Seminary. The commentary handles a large portion of Proverbs in a topical format. There is more scholarship behind this book than just about any other in the series. "This volume (like the volume on Daniel) makes the whole series worthwhile!" says Motyer. More for pastors than students. [*JETS* 3/94; *BSac* 4/92; *Chm* 104.4 (1990)].

★ Koptak, Paul E. (NIVAC) 2003. The fullest preacher's commentary now available at over 700pp. Koptak is a professor at North Park Seminary in Chicago and is an insightful guide through Proverbs. This would be an excellent addition to the pastor's library. [*WTJ* Spr 06].

★ **Longman, Tremper.** (BCOT) 2006. Though this is a very good interpretation, I had expected something more in-depth and useful to students (in line with Hess on Song of Songs); I was slightly disappointed. Since then I have come to recognize that Longman is merely wearing his learning lightly. He knows Proverbs and Proverbs scholarship very well. His focus on the text's theological message and ethical instruction is just what pastors want. They will think this commentary is pitched at just the right level and is written for them. The 30 essays in the appendix, synthesizing the proverbs' teaching on various topics, are worth the price of the book. [*JETS* 3/08; *JSOT-BL* 2007 (Firth)]. If you buy this, you do not need to bother with Longman's *How to Read Proverbs* (2002) [*RelSRev* 7/03; *CTJ* 11/04], which is a well-written introduction and hermeneutical guide that can be compared with the earlier handbook, *How to Read the Psalms* (1988).

★ **Waltke, Bruce.** (NICOT) 2 Vols., 2004–05. This is a publishing event for which some of us waited nearly 20 years. All his past articles on Proverbs suggested that his commentary would be full, conservative (à la Kidner), and highly theological. Previously, we had to content ourselves with Waltke's "Theology of Proverbs" in *NIDOTT&E* and "Wisdom Literature" in Baker Books' *The Face of Old Testament Studies* (1999). This commentary outdistances all previous evangelical exegeses of Proverbs and is my first choice for pastors and students. Students will learn much from the introduction and bibliography here, which run to 170pp. As one would expect from an expert grammarian, the discussion of the Hebrew text is superb (and difficult reading for non-specialists). This is now the fullest, most well rounded English-language commentary ever published on Proverbs; it should not be regarded, however, as more scholarly than Fox. For a stimulating example of how Waltke sees the wisdom of Proverbs applying in our cultural context, see "Righteousness in Proverbs" in *WTJ* 70.2 (2008). [*RTR* 12/06; *WTJ* Spr 06; *CBQ* 4/08; *JTS* 4/06; *JETS* 9/05, 6/06; *Interp* 4/06; *BSac* 10/06; *JSOT-BL* 2005, 2006; *JAOS* 126.1 (harsh); *VT* 57.3; *RBL*; *JHebS*; *CurTM* 6/07].

Aitken, K.T. ‡ (DSB) 1986.

☆ Alden, Robert. 1983. The average reader will find this commentary helpful for its practical suggestions. Most pastors, I think, are looking for something more thorough. Still, it is recommended for your consideration; a few may prefer it to Bridges. [*WTJ* Spr 86; *JETS* 12/84].

Arnot, William. 1882. This well-known exposition was reprinted by Kregel.

☆ Atkinson, David. (BST) 1996. Well done, though sketchy in places. [*Them* 11/99; *VT* 47.3].

☆ Bridges, Charles. (GS) 1846. Good for the soul, this wise old classic will be of help to the pastor. Childs' gentle critique of "moralisms" is probably deserved. I used to include this among my recommended purchases, but I think now the more modern expositions of Koptak, Hubbard, Garrett, and Ross displace it. That is not to say it is not worth buying any longer; it is. Bridges has been edited for CrossC (2001). [*JSOT* 27.5].

✓ **Clifford, Richard J.** ‡ (OTL) 1999. This volume replaces McKane's erudite but flawed commentary. Clifford, a Jesuit critic, builds upon his 1995 monograph, *The Book of Proverbs and Our Search for Wisdom*. (By the way, I regard the monograph as a better piece of work than the commentary.) As an academic who regularly taught a course on Psalms & Wisdom, I bought this OTL volume, but I would not recommend it to pastors. This commentary has already been reviewed, somewhat negatively but fairly, in *JSOT*'s Booklist (6/00). The upshot of the review is that this book "offers few new solutions to the many problems in Proverbs" and, in interpretation, too often moves outside the context of Hebrew society and Scripture—he repeatedly reads Proverbs "in terms of Mesopotamian mythology." On the plus side, Clifford pays attention to rhetoric, asking "how did the instructions and maxims engage its audience?" (vi). [*JR* 4/00; *ExpTim* 5/00; *CBQ* 7/00; *Interp* 10/00; *PSB* 21.2 (2000); *OTA* 2/00; and *Biblica* 81.3 (2000) if you read French; a more positive review is in *JTS* 4/04].

✓ Davis, Ellen F. ‡ *Proverbs, Ecclesiastes, and the Song of Songs* (WestBC) 2000. The author wrote a superb dissertation on Ezekiel at Yale and now teaches at Duke Divinity School. This treatment is competent, theologically oriented, and quite full for the WestBC series at 272pp. Worth consulting as a fresh exposition. More conservatively critical. [*ExpTim* 5/01; *VT* 53.2; *JSOT* 94 (2001); *RelSRev* 10/01].

✓ **Delitzsch, Franz.** (KD) ET 1875. He is truly at his best in this material. Still worth consulting.

Dell, Katherine J. ‡ *The Book of Proverbs in Social and Theological Context* (Cambridge) 2006. [*JR* 7/08; *ExpTim* 4/07; *Them* 5/08; *CJ* 7/08; *Biblica* 90.3; *JSOT-BL* 2007].

Estes, Daniel. *Hear, My Son*, 1997. A brief but probing evangelical exposition of chs. 1–9, focusing especially upon themes related to "personal formation" and moral education.

✓ Farmer, K.A. [*M*], *Proverbs and Ecclesiastes* (ITC) 1991. Argues that these two books were companions, meant to be read together. Applies feminist concerns. [*CRBR* 1993].

F Fredericks, Daniel. (Apollos). He is at home in the Wisdom Literature, having already published a dissertation on Ecclesiastes. For a contradictory report on this assignment, see Overland.

☆ **Garrett, Duane A.** *Proverbs, Ecclesiastes, Song of Songs* (NAC) 1993. A thoughtful, clear 448-page work from a Baptist scholar teaching at Gordon-Conwell. This is mainly an exposition for pastors, but Garrett knows the direction scholarship is heading and uses some of the best of it: he interprets individual proverbs within larger literary units. This volume was valued more highly ten years ago because, relative to some other Bible books, there were fewer good commentaries on Proverbs. We have much more to choose from now. The Denver Seminary OT faculty used to recommend purchasing Garrett; I am guessing that not only the quality of the commentary but also Garrett's coverage of three Bible books may have played a part in their value judgment. [*VT* 7/96; *CBQ* 7/94; *BSac* 10/94; *HebStud* 1995].

Heim, Knut. *Like Grapes of Gold Set in Silver: An Interpretation of Proverbial Clusters in Proverbs 10:1–22:16*, 2001. Noteworthy for proposing meaningful arrangement of individual proverbs in clusters. [*DenvJ*].

Horne, Milton P. ‡ *Proverbs–Ecclesiastes* (S&H) 2003. This work seeks to build an exposition while drawing from the fine exegeses recently published in various major commentary series. He does not interact much with conservative scholarship. Like all the S&H volumes which are meant to be visually engaging, Horne's commentary is nicely presented (578pp). The author teaches at William Jewell College. [*CJ* 1/06].

F Johnston, Gordon. (Kregel).

✓ Jones, D.R. ‡ (Torch Bible Commentary) 1961.

F Joosten, Jan. ‡ (ICC).

☆ **Kidner, Derek.** (TOTC) 1964. Excellent introduction. Solid exegesis, though too brief in some places. Includes fine summary treatments of various words and topics covered in Proverbs. Was once Longman's and Stuart's first choice. See Hubbard and Ross for other conservative works on a par with Kidner.

Kitchen, John. (Mentor) 2006. Quite a large pastoral and devotional work (789pp). [*JETS* 12/08].

Lawson, George. 1821. A reverent exposition, reprinted by Kregel.

Lennox, Stephen J. *Proverbs: A Bible Commentary in the Wesleyan Tradition*, 1998.

F Loader, James A. ‡ (HCOT).

☆ Longman, Tremper. *How to Read Proverbs*, 1992. A well-written introduction and hermeneutical guide that can be compared with the earlier handbook, *How to Read the Psalms*, 1988. [*RelSRev* 7/03; *CTJ* 11/04].

F McCreesh, Thomas. ‡ (BO).

✓ **McKane, William.** ‡ (retired OTL) 1970. Very learned and critical. Helpful introduction, but "the exegesis is dominated by a larger theory respecting the development of Israel's wisdom," according to Childs. "McKane envisions a growth from an early non-theological stage of simple empirical observation to a subsequent growth of 'God language'. The effect of these rigid categories is to rob the proverbs of much of their theological vitality." Simply put, this is a scholar's commentary. Other works are of much greater value to the pastor, and more current in their scholarship as well. Now replaced by Clifford. [*JBL* 90.2 (1971)].

Miller, John W. (BCBC) 2004. Well accomplishes the aims of the series. This 351-page commentary treats much of the material in a topical rather than verse-by-verse manner. [*JETS* 3/06].

☆ **Murphy, Roland E.** ‡ (WBC) 1998. I like this work a lot, for a variety of reasons. See my comments on Murphy's WBC on Ecclesiastes. Please note that he subsequently wrote a more compact, popularly-styled commentary on Proverbs for NIBC (see below). This WBC volume has more to offer as the in-depth treatment. I used to regard this as the best completed exegetical work on Proverbs for the well-trained pastor, but Waltke and Fox clearly supersede it. Though this 375-page book remains quite useful to students and to pastors working with the Hebrew, those with a healthy book allowance will want Fox. [*CBQ* 7/00; *Interp* 10/00; *JBL* Fall 01; *RelSRev* 10/01; *Chm* Spr 01].

✓ Murphy, Roland E. ‡ (FOTL) 1981. This preceded the valuable WBC above. See under Ruth.

☆ Murphy, Roland E., and Elizabeth Huwiler. [*M*], *Proverbs, Ecclesiastes & Song of Songs* (NIBC) 1996. Murphy contributes the commentary on Proverbs in this volume, while Huwiler takes the shorter books. Both do a good job within the confines of the series, though I judge the treatments of Proverbs and the Song to be better than Ecclesiastes. The Proverbs section is rather brief. Murphy's WBC is the more recommended work, not NIBC, because it offers so much more, especially to the pastor using the Hebrew. [*JSOT* 89 (2000); *CBQ* 10/00; *Chm* Win 00; *RTR* 4/01; *Them* Spr 01; *EvQ* 10/01; *VT* 53.2; *JSOT* 94 (2001)].

✓ Oesterley, William O.E. ‡ (Westminster Commentaries) 1929. Though dated, Oesterley has retained some of its original value. Crenshaw, I discovered, agrees with this assessment: "Valuable insights give this commentary staying power." Fairly complete in its treatment.

F Ortlund, Ray. *Proverbs: Skill in Living* (PTW).

F   Overland, Paul. (Apollos). See Fredericks above for an earlier, contradictory report.

☆   **Perdue, Leo G.** ‡ (I) 2000. This is well-done indeed but is perhaps not what most pastors expect from this series. There is much less verse-by-verse commentary and more discussion of the book's development of topics/themes in their theological and social context (late date). Much attention is paid to larger literary units. At times he seems to be attempting, in essay style, to synthesize the diverse materials—almost like a fine lecture in written form. This is a critical work, which dates both the materials and their redaction to the Persian period. The origin and early dating of this wisdom within the book itself (Solomon, Hezekiah, etc.) is "the fiction of tradition" (p.64). In brief, this is a more scholarly, and less accessible, volume in the series. It is one of the least successful in the series at helping preachers move toward application. [*ExpTim* 5/01; *Them* Spr/Sum 02; *Interp* 1/02; *VT* 51.4; *HBT* 6/02; *JSOT* 94 (2001); *RelSRev* 10/01; *Anvil* 18.4].

✓   Reyburn, William D., and Euan McG. Fry. (UBS) 2000. This 700-page volume can aid students as well as translators. [*RelSRev* 10/01].

☆   **Ross, Allen P.** (EBCR) 2008. At approximately 250pp, Ross's commentary is nearly as valuable as some of the suggested purchases above. The scholarship is careful, and the preacher's needs and interests are kept in mind. The topical index appended to the introduction is among the better ones available to the student in English (pp.38–45). Proverbs is bound with solid commentaries on Ecclesiastes by Shepherd, Song of Songs by Schwab, and Isaiah by Grogan. See the author's other works under Genesis and Leviticus. [*JSOT-BL* 2010].

Ross, Allen P. (EBC) 1991. Still useful, though it has been replaced by the EBCR above. The old EBC volume covered Psalms to Song of Songs.

F   Schipper, Bernd. ‡ (Herm).

F   Schwab, George. (CorBC). The Psalms (Futato) and Proverbs commentaries will appear in one volume.

Scott, Robert B.Y. ‡ *Proverbs, Ecclesiastes* (retired AB) 1965. Years ago Scott was somewhat valuable for its translation and introduction. It contains little exposition and is too brief. See Fox above.

Steinmann, Andrew E. (Concord) 2009. I have yet to see this 719-page exegesis *cum* theological exposition. The author has served long years as a seminary professor and has large-scale Concordia works on Ezra-Nehemiah and Daniel.

✓   **Toy, Crawford H.** ‡ (ICC) 1904. This was long used as reference in dealing with the Hebrew and the history of interpretation, but only advanced students doing in-depth research should bother with it now. See Joosten.

F   Trier, Daniel. (Brazos).

☆   **Van Leeuwen, Raymond.** [𝓜], (NewIB) 1997. The editors gave him about 250pp, and he did very well within those constraints. This commentary is particularly valuable for its efforts to interpret individual proverbs within larger literary units. Students should not miss this commentary, probably the best briefer work on Proverbs. If the volume were not so expensive, and if I valued some of Van Leeuwen's companions (less useful treatments of Ecclesiastes, the Song, Wisdom of Solomon, Sirach), it would be easier to consider this for purchase.

✓   Weeks, Stuart. ‡ *Instruction and Imagery in Proverbs 1–9* (Oxford) 2007. Brilliant scholarship which unsettles some longstanding critical scholarship; specifically, he posits that the first nine chapters are "a single composition, with a more-or-less coherent viewpoint." [*JR* 10/08; *VT* 58.2; *Them* 9/08].

☆   **Whybray, R.N.** ‡ (NCB) 1994. A substantial volume of nearly 480pp (xxxiii + 446) which builds on his earlier commentary for the CBC (1972). Crenshaw once spoke of this NCB as "judicious, perhaps the most useful commentary in English." This scholar is a moderate British critic, and his work here is strong. Also note Whybray's several monographs: *The Book of Proverbs: A Survey of Modern Study* (1995), which is masterful [*JSS* Spr 00; *RelSRev* 1/98]; *The Composition of the Book of Proverbs* (1994); *Wealth and Poverty in the Book of Proverbs* (1990); and *Wisdom in Proverbs* (1965), which treats the concept of wisdom in Proverbs 1:1–9:45. Note: I recommended Whybray for purchase in the 1996 edition as a thorough exegetical supplement to the more expositional commentaries; thereafter I gave Murphy the spot. [*JETS* 12/97; *CBQ* 10/96; *RTR* 1/97; *JSS* Spr 99; *HebStud* 1997].

✓ Wright, J. Robert (ed). *Proverbs, Ecclesiastes, Song of Solomon* (ACCS) 2004. [*CTJ* 4/07; *JETS* 3/06; *JSOT-BL* 2007].

Yoder, Christine Roy. ‡ (AOTC) 2009. A good example of the series, with middle-of-the-road, concise scholarship on exegetical questions and little exposition. Yoder sees a lack of purposeful editorial arrangement in Proverbs and displays good interpretive skill. Call this a useful but not indispensable reference tool. [*ExpTim* 8/10; *JSOT-BL* 2010 (Weeks)].

Zöckler, Otto. (Lange) ET 1870. The volume covers Proverbs through Song of Solomon.

—— ⚋ ——

ECCLESIASTES

★ **Bartholomew, Craig G.** (BOTC) 2009. His dissertation which was published in 1998, *Reading Ecclesiastes: Old Testament Exegesis and Hermeneutical Theory* [*Chm* Aut 01; *Interp* 4/00], demonstrated that the author has an excellent grasp of scholarly developments and hermeneutics. It was a probing exploration of the philosophical underpinnings or presuppositions of contemporary OT scholarship, with particular reference to Ecclesiastes. Bartholomew is a South African who did his PhD in England and who now teaches in Canada. This new commentary (448pp) reveals his own exegetical skill and keen interest in biblical theology. He chooses to translate *hebel* (הבל) as "enigmatic," arguing against Seow's rendering of "vanity" and his interpretation that the word reflects Qoheleth's anthropology. Bartholomew says, "Rather than his anthropology, what is at stake in Qohelet's quest is his epistemology, how we come to know that we can trust the results of our explorations. Qohelet embarks on a quest for knowledge, and it is this exploration of the meaning of life that continually runs down into the conclusion: utterly *hebel*" (106). Though still evaluating and not convinced the quest is quite so philosophical—Qoheleth seeks satisfaction (1:8) and "to see what is good to do" (2:3)—I now make this my first pick as a scholarly exegesis. Students might note that critical scholars complain that Bartholomew tends to make Qoheleth too "orthodox." Compare with Seow, Murphy, Krüger, Gordis, and Fox. [*JETS* 6/10; *BSac* 7/10 (misleading); *HBT* 32.1; *JSOT-BL* 2010; *CBQ* 7/10; *RelSRev* 12/09 (Crenshaw)].

★ **Fredericks, Daniel C.**, and Daniel J. Estes. *Ecclesiastes & Song of Songs* (Apollos) 2010. Judging from the strength of Fredericks' dissertation on *Qoheleth's Language* (1988), which argued the case for an earlier dating of the book, I expected this commentary to be a very competent and conservative work. It is indeed excellent, and slightly more approachable than Bartholomew as a briefer work (approx. 250pp). Fredericks steers away from interpretations of *hebel* as "vanity, futile, meaningless, absurd, foul, false" because these "are inconsistent with the explicit content of Ecclesiastes, or are foreign to the OT's meanings" of the word. Instead, "by considering *hebel* to mean 'temporary', the reader will discover a book that speaks clearly to the effects of the Fall" (p.70). "The book's message is clearly about *transience*, not minimal purposefulness" (43). He helpfully cites James 4:14 as a NT parallel. I propose that pastors will find this to be one of the two or three most serviceable commentaries on Qoheleth, even though I balk at his view that "the book consoles rather than disturbs the realist" (45). There are reviews of his PhD work [*JTS* 4/90; *CBQ* 4/91; *JBL* Win 89; *HebStud* 1990]. His partner, Estes, does a capable job on Song of Songs; they are a well-matched pair.

★ **Hubbard, David A.** *Ecclesiastes-Song of Solomon* (WCC) 1993. Building on his insightful little book entitled, *Beyond Futility* (1976), Hubbard is stronger on "Koheleth" (238pp) than the Song (93pp). Excellent for the pastor! Both Hubbard and Kidner are also worth reading by the student for their discussion of the message of the book. Only the dating of Koheleth (4th or early 3rd century BC) would suggest the commentary is mildly critical ([*M*]).

★ **Kidner, Derek**. *A Time to Mourn and a Time to Dance* (BST) 1976. I am not satisfied with his thesis that the "Preacher" merely assumes the posture of the secularist—his dark mood and worldly perspective—for the sake of apologetics. Surely, instead, we are reading the record of Qoheleth's inner turmoil and debate. But this is still a great book for the preacher. Compare with Hubbard, Provan, Brown, and Ryken; these five expositions are tops for the pastor's study. [*EvQ* 1/77; *JETS* 3/78].

★ **Longman, Tremper.** (NICOT) 1998. This commentary, following the Dillard/Longman *Introduction* of 1994, is influential in conservative circles on the issue of authorship and genre. Longman speaks of Qoheleth as "framed wisdom autobiography" (p.17). I wrestle with some of the interpretive maneuvers in this fine NICOT volume. Though there is obviously an editorial voice ("frame-narrator") in chs. 1 and 12, does setting pious editor over against skeptical Qoheleth serve to answer the problems and resolve the tensions? Does not the epilogist affirm the wisdom of the Teacher (12:9)? One comes away from Longman wondering if anything positive, from the NT standpoint, can be said for the Teacher's message. Instead, the message must be challenged and wholly redirected at the conclusion of the book. "Here is the conclusion of the matter": there is nothing like Longman to sensitize the reader to the real tension between much of Qoheleth's seemingly "secular" advice and other biblical exhortations (self-denial, etc.). The pastor who uses this volume will be helped in preaching Christ, but this is not a definitive evangelical commentary like, say, Hubbard's on Ruth. Perhaps, owing to the diversity of opinions on this book, a definitive evangelical commentary can never be written on Ecclesiastes. For understanding the message of Ecclesiastes, I prefer Hubbard's lines of interpretation and am intrigued by Fredericks (who finds a bit too positive a message). [*JBL* Win 99; *JSOT* 79 (1998); *Interp* 1/99; *CBQ* 1/99; *SwJT* Fall 99; *BSac* 4/98; *HebStud* 1999; *RelSRev* 7/98; *VT* 54.2]. Longman's views are distilled in the CorBC volume below by Konkel/Longman.

★ **Provan, Iain.** *Ecclesiastes, Song of Songs* (NIVAC) 2001. The interpretation of Ecclesiastes is, in my opinion, more convincing and helpful than his treatment of the Song. In the latter he revives the so-called dramatic interpretation (also found in Delitzsch); specifically he opts for the three-character version, proposed long ago by Ewald and developed by S.R. Driver. This reading of the Song reminds me of "The Princess Bride," in which a lovely, simple girl is taken by royalty, but she pines for her one true love, a country boy. Provan has also written excellent commentaries on Kings and Lamentations. See Provan under Kings.

✓ **Barton, George A.** ‡ (ICC) 1908. The author treats the book as quite late. This may still be of some use to students researching philology, textual issues, and history of interpretation. Barton's own contribution to interpretation is unsatisfactory, as he opts to explain the tensions in the book by source criticism.

Bergant, D. ‡ *Job, Ecclesiastes* (OTM) 1982.

Berlejung, A., and P. van Hecke (eds). *The Language of Qohelet in Its Context: Essays in Honour of Prof A. Schoors on the Occasion of His Seventieth Birthday*, 2007. An enormous volume (742pp).

F Bollhagen, James G. (Concord).

☆ Bridges, Charles. (GS) 1860. Not Bridges' best effort, but still helpful to some all the same, especially for theology and pastoral reflection. See his more famous work on Proverbs.

☆ **Brown, William P.** ‡ (I) 2000. Though brief, this is a very good, informed, and balanced book to guide the expositor. I myself bought Brown for his theological interpretation. Brown dates the book earlier (*ca.* 300) than many critics. He interacts less with scholarship than some students would prefer. The author is a rising star in academia, who teaches at Union Seminary (VA) and has published several well-received books on Psalms and the Wisdom Literature. [*OTA* 10/00; *Them* Spr 01; *Interp* 7/01; *VT* 53.2; *JSOT* 94 (2001); *SwJT* Sum 02; *RelSRev* 1/01 (Crenshaw)].

Christianson, Eric S. *Ecclesiastes through the Centuries* (BBC) 2007. [*JSOT-BL* 2007].

✓ **Crenshaw, James L.** ‡ (OTL) 1987. Crenshaw is a leading critical authority on sapiential literature. He offers a 32-page intro and 138pp of commentary (no indexes). He compels you to think hard about the perplexing tensions in the message of the book, which he dates between 250 and 225, and champions the view that Qoheleth is best read as a bitter skeptic. Frankly, numbers had hoped for a more substantial and thorough commentary, especially in documented interaction with other scholarly views, and were disappointed. I admit I don't care for this commentary. Longman likes it a lot, however, which may explain why his NICOT follows this OTL in its deeply pessimistic reading of Qoheleth's worldview. [*TJ* Spr. 88; *HebStud* 1989]. You will find Crenshaw's views only slightly updated in the revised later editions of his textbook, *Old Testament Wisdom*.

Davidson, Robert. ‡ *Ecclesiastes and Song of Solomon* (DSB) 1986. This well researched devotional commentary is marred slightly by its critical approach.

✓ Davis, Ellen F. ‡ *Proverbs, Ecclesiastes, and the Song of Songs* (WestBC) 2000. See Proverbs above.

✓ Delitzsch, Franz. (KD) ET 1891. Full of insight.

F Dell, Katherine. ‡ (ECC).

✓ **Eaton, Michael A.** (TOTC) 1983. Adequate, but not one of the strongest commentaries in the series. Still, students should consult it. Eaton's is a voice to be counted in the debates on this book. Some conservative scholars have a higher opinion of this book than I do. For example, Hill and Walton call Eaton "the most helpful of the evangelical commentaries" in their *Survey of the Old Testament* (both 1991 and 2000 editions). Eaton reads the message of the book more positively. [*EvQ* 7/86; *WTJ* Fall 84].

✓ Ellul, Jacques. [𝓜], *Reason for Being: A Meditation on Ecclesiastes*, ET 1990. Focuses less on exegesis and more on the meaning and theology of the book. As with all Ellul's books, this examines the Scriptures' relevance today in a most incisive fashion. His essay style is a joy to read, but the message may afflict the comfortable/contented. See another of his works under Kings. [*RTR* 5/92].

F Enns, Peter. (THC).

✓ Farmer, K.A. [*M*], *Proverbs and Ecclesiastes* (ITC) 1991. See Proverbs above.

☆ **Fox, Michael V.** ‡ *A Time to Tear Down and a Time to Build Up: A Rereading of Ecclesiastes*, 1999. Published by Eerdmans, "Fox's rereading of Qoheleth is priceless" (Murphy). It's hard to overestimate the influence this seminal study will have in years to come. I accept his theory that the book is a narrative unity in which the voice of an anonymous frame-narrator quotes the words of the persona Qoheleth (though form-criticism is of less value for this Bible book). I am less convinced that "absurd" is the best rendering of *hebel*, or that we should read the book as if it were existentialist literature. Fox says he is impressed with the similarities between Qohelet and Camus (see pp.8–15), and I think that explains a lot about his approach. He here updates and expands his earlier *Qohelet and His Contradictions* (1989), which was an erudite, lengthy (almost 400pp) study published by JSOT Press. It also included a brief commentary [*JTS* 10/90; *CBQ* 4/91]. *A Time to Tear Down* is definitely worth consulting! Fox is a Jewish scholar and his work is a favorite of Longman. This, Seow, and Murphy are "must buys" for the scholarly pastor with money and keen interest in OT wisdom literature. [*JSOT* 89 (2000); *PSB* 21.3 (2000); *ExpTim* 12/00; *Interp* 7/00; *CBQ* 4/00; *Them* Aut 00; *JR* 7/00; *Biblica* 82.1; *RTR* 4/01; *EvQ* 10/01; *VT* 53.2].

✓ **Fox, Michael V.** ‡ (JPS) 2004. This work offers a more concise, more accessible commentary, and more discussion of traditional Jewish reflection on Qoheleth than the previous entry. [*JETS* 6/05; *Interp* 4/05; *JSOT-BL* 2006; *BSac* 7/07; *RBL*].

Fuerst, W.J. ‡ *The Books of Ruth, Esther, Ecclesiastes, The Song of Songs, Lamentations* (CBC) 1975.

F Garfinkel, Stephen. ‡ (BO).

☆ **Garrett, Duane A.** *Proverbs, Ecclesiastes, Song of Songs* (NAC) 1993. See Proverbs.

✓ Ginsburg, Christian David. *The Song of Songs and Coheleth*, 1857–61. The work of a somewhat critical, converted Jewish scholar which is well known for its treatment of the history of exegesis (pp.27–243 in the 1861 *Coheleth*). It is worth consulting the 1970 Ktav reprint. This scholar should be distinguished from the liberal H.L. Ginsberg, who authored *Supplementary Studies in Koheleth* (1952).

✓ **Gordis, Robert.** ‡ *Koheleth: The Man and His World*, 1951, 3rd ed 1968. Magnificent! One of the best exegetical commentaries on the book, rivaling Seow, Fox, and Murphy except that it is more dated. Gordis was a leading Jewish scholar of the last generation, known for careful and thorough textual work and profound learning in the Jewish exegetical tradition. Fairly conservative.

☆ Greidanus, Sidney. *Preaching Christ from Ecclesiastes: Foundations for Expository Sermons*, 2010. I have not yet reviewed this surprisingly full book on the topic (376pp). See his earlier helpful works on *Preaching Christ from the Old Testament* and *Preaching Christ from Genesis*. The author is professor emeritus of preaching at Calvin Seminary.

✓ **Hengstenberg, Ernst W.** 1860. Childs calls it his best—a full, vigorous commentary. This was reprinted by Sovereign Grace publishers in 1960. I know of no other reprints. Still worth consulting for papers, etc., if one is pursuing fuller research. Critical scholars have sometimes accused Hengstenberg of confusing apologetics and exegesis, but here that is not an issue.

Horne, Milton P. ‡ *Proverbs–Ecclesiastes* (S&H) 2003. See under Proverbs.

F Johnston, Gordon. (Kregel).

F Johnston, Gordon. (EEC).

✓ Jones, E. ‡ (Torch Bible Commentary) 1961.

Kaiser, Walter C. *Ecclesiastes: Total Life*, 1979. Well researched, practical exposition, but you may prefer Kidner's interpretation. The approach here raises questions in my mind. Every Bible student struggles with the severe tensions in Ecclesiastes between dark despair and hope, skepticism and faith. How can both attitudes or outlooks be contained in one integrated book? What do we do with the contradictions? I believe these true-to-life tensions need to be retained in our interpretation of this Bible book rather than resolved in some facile way. The liberals have tended to over-emphasize the forlorn, skeptical tone of the book, while some believers have overstressed the notes of hope and the positive exhortations. I am less than pleased with any commentary which attempts to ease these tensions. I find that Kaiser tends to relativize the pessimistic/skeptical portions and misses the pathos of the book.

☆ Keddie, Gordon. *Looking for the Good Life* (P&R) 1991. A popular level exposition from a devout Reformed Presbyterian minister.

Konkel, August H., and Tremper Longman III. *Job, Ecclesiastes, Song of Songs* (CorBC) 2006. Longman offers the commentary on the latter two Bible books, distilling his scholarship published earlier in NICOT.

✓ **Krüger, Thomas.** ‡ (Herm) ET 2004. Specialists and advanced students will take note of this technical exegesis, which includes 38pp of introduction, 180pp of commentary on the Hebrew, and the fullest available bibliography for Qoheleth studies (55pp). There is heavy interaction with German scholarship. Krüger says that reconstructing the history of the text's origin is the special focus of his work. He also devotes a lot of attention to structural issues and textual criticism. While this scholar finds rhetorically cohesive units in the book, Qoheleth as a whole is contradictory ("conveys no clear teaching") and reveals an internal debate. Within the book, he says, "the form of wisdom teaching…is adopted critically and ironically," and so we can draw "no direct conclusions regarding the social and institutional context in which and for which it was written" (p.12). Krüger attempts to teach us how much we don't know. Not for pastors. He varies his interpretation of *hebel* as meaning "futility" or "fleeting" in different places. Ralph Klein calls this "the best of the current commentaries on Ecclesiastes/Qoheleth." [*ExpTim* 2/06; *BSac* 4/08; *CurTM* 6/07 (Klein)].

Leupold, H.C. 1952. A thorough, old Lutheran commentary. See Genesis for more on this scholar.

Limburg, James. ‡ *Encountering Ecclesiastes: A Book for Our Time*, 2006. This thoughtful, brief, personal exposition, more along thematic lines, from a retired Lutheran OT scholar is published by Eerdmans. It is meant for preachers interested in Qoheleth's message. [*ExpTim* 10/07; *Chm* Aut 09].

✓ **Loader, J.A.** ‡ (T&I) ET 1986. This author's more important (and provocative) work was *Polar Structures in the Book of Qoheleth* (1979). This commentary is supposedly written for pastors and laypeople, but few such folk will find this work accessible. [*HebStud* 1987; *Chm* 101.1 (1987) (Kidner)].

✓ **Lohfink, Norbert.** ‡ (ContC) ET 2003. The effort expended both to translate the 1980 German commentary and to expand the work subsequently shows its importance. As compared with other recent commentaries, Lohfink tends to put more emphasis upon the positive message of the book—and this was before Whybray's interpretation. There is also more Christian reflection than we might have anticipated. Another contribution is said to be the structural analysis, which differs from the famous A.D.G. Wright structure which I like (see below). This volume is more accessible than some others in the same series; Lohfink states up front that he did not set out to write an academic commentary (vii). [*JTS* 4/04; *JSOT* 28.5; *Interp* 1/05; *CJ* 7/05; *JBL* Fall 04 (Van Leeuwen); *RBL*; *JHebS*].

Luther, Martin. ET 1972. His exposition is found in Vol. 15 of *Luther's Works*.

✓ Miller, Douglas B. (BCBC) 2010. Earlier he published *Symbol and Rhetoric in Ecclesiastes: The Place of Hebel in Qohelet's Work* (2002), which is instructive, even if his conclusion (bad/foul air) doesn't hold up [*JR* 1/05; *JNES* 7/07].

Moore, T.M. *Ecclesiastes: Ancient Wisdom When All Else Fails*, 2001. This IVP issue translates the Hebrew into a poetic form with which we in the West are more familiar: iambic pentameter.

✓ Murphy, Roland E. ‡ (FOTL) 1981. See under Ruth. Superseded in every way by Murphy's WBC.

☆ **Murphy, Roland E.** ‡ (WBC) 1992. Among the best studies of the Hebrew available from one of the world's greatest scholars on the Wisdom Literature; there is a lengthy introduction and 155pp of commentary. Murphy works hard to do justice to the tension between joyful preacher (3:11–13; 8:15) and the frustrated skeptic (2:10ff; 4:1ff). This is not nearly as in-depth as his Hermeneia commentary on Song of Songs. From Murphy's publication in 1992 up to my guide's 7th edition in 2005, this was a recommended purchase, but now Bartholomew takes its place. By the way, I regard Seow as equally valuable. [*RTR* 9/93; *Interp* 7/95; *BSac* 4/94].

Murphy, Roland E., and Elizabeth Huwiler. [𝓜], *Proverbs, Ecclesiastes & Song of Songs* (NIBC) 1996. See Proverbs above.

✓ **Ogden, Graham S.** ‡ (Read) 1987, 2007. An influential study published by Sheffield, not to be missed by students. He was among those, early on, who urged a more positive reading. Ogden is a favorite of Bartholomew. See also the large-scale handbook below. A few fellow scholars have told me this is their favorite book on Qoheleth. [*Biblica* 71.3 (1990); *CRBR* 1989; *RBL*].

✓ **Ogden, Graham S., and Lynell Zogbo.** (UBS) 1998. The *Handbook* runs to 471pp.

Olyott, Stuart J. *A Life Worth Living and a Lord Worth Loving* (WCS) 1983. Covers Ecclesiastes and the Song.

✓ Plumptre, Edward H. ‡ (Cambridge Bible) 1881. Childs' favorite (back in the 1970s) among commentaries in English. The author is notable in the history of interpretation for pressing arguments that Qoheleth betrays the influence of Greek thought.

Reynolds, Edward. 1998 reprint. This massive Puritan commentary can be found in the set of Reynolds' collected works, reprinted by Soli Deo Gloria. Compare with Bridges.

☆ Ryken, Philip G. *Ecclesiastes: Why Everything Matters* (PTW) 2010. I regret I have not yet seen this. The author is always brimming with ideas for exposition and application. See his big books on Exodus, Jeremiah, Luke, etc.

F Schoors, Anton. ‡ (HCOT).

✓ Schoors, A. (ed). ‡ *Qohelet in the Context of Wisdom*, 1998. From the 1997 Colloquium Biblicum Lovaniense, this large volume (526pp) contains cutting-edge scholarship for its time.

Scott, Robert B.Y. ‡ (retired AB) 1965. See Proverbs above. Seow is Scott's replacement.

☆ **Seow, Choon-Leong.** ‡ (AB) 1997. The reviewers have given this volume high praise. "[I]f readers and pastors can afford only one book on Ecclesiastes, I would suggest Seow" (Van Leeuwen). It might be helpful to some readers to know that the Denver Seminary OT faculty pick Seow and Bartholomew as their favorites. Seow dates the book to the Persian period—earlier than many other critical scholars—and seems disposed to take the view that the book is a substantial unity. There is a wealth of textual study, linguistic analysis, and theological interpretation in this commentary, which is aimed more at scholars, yet accessible and readable. He urges that we see Qoheleth as a wise realist. See my remarks on Fox above. [*JBL* Fall 99; *PSB* 20.2 (1999); *JSOT* 79 (1998); *Interp* 1/99; *JR* 10/98].

☆ Shepherd, Jerry. (EBCR) 2008. I have not had much opportunity to use this 110-page commentary, but what I have seen is well-studied and well-written. What a change from EBC! Shepherd's approach to the message of the book owes much to Longman: "Qohelet serves as a foil for the frame-narrator to get across his message of the danger of pessimistic, skeptical wisdom" (p.269). He admits that this stance raises serious questions as to whether we should even preach and teach out of Qoheleth's words. See J. Stafford Wright for the weaker EBC predecessor. [*JSOT-BL* 2010].

Shields, Martin A. *The End of Wisdom: A Reappraisal of the Historical and Canonical Function of Ecclesiastes*, 2006. This runs as far as possible with the negative reading of Qohelet (see Crenshaw and Longman). [*JSOT-BL* 2007].

✓ **Towner, W. Sidley.** ‡ (NewIB) 1997. This commentary is a little short of 100pp and does not compete seriously with heavyweight works like Longman, Murphy, Fox, Seow and others. This is a fallback for students. Qoheleth is dated around 250. Towner is best known for his commentary on Daniel.

F Treier, Daniel. (Brazos).

☆ Webb, Barry G. *Five Festal Garments: Christian Reflections on the Song of Songs, Ruth, Lamentations, Ecclesiastes and Esther*, 2000. See under Ruth.

F Weeks, Stuart. (ICC). I expect this to be excellent; see Weeks under Wisdom Literature and Proverbs above.

✓ Whitley, C.F. ‡ *Koheleth: His Language and Thought*, 1979. A detailed, technical treatment of the book.

✓ **Whybray, R.N.** ‡ (NCB) 1989. One of the more important critical commentaries, this parts company from the usual critical interpretations in that it emphasizes the positive, even "joyful" aspects in Ecclesiastes. He builds on his earlier article, "Qohelet: Preacher of Joy," *JSOT* 23 (1982): 87–92. (On the same topic, see Eunny P. Lee's *The Vitality of Enjoyment in Qohelet's Theological Rhetoric*, 2005.) Whybray's volume is quite useful, though I think he dulls the sharp pessimistic edge of this Bible book. [*CBQ* 7/91; *RTR* 9/90; *HebStud* 1990]. See also Whybray's Sheffield volume in the series OT Guides (1989).

Williams, A.L. ‡ (Cambridge Bible) 1922.

Wright, A.D.G. ‡ "Ecclesiastes," *New Jerome Bible Commentary*, 1990. Said by some to be an outstanding treatment in a one-vol. commentary. The author made a significant contribution to studies of this book with articles on the structure of the book. See "The Riddle of the Sphinx: The Structure of the Book of Qoheleth," *CBQ* 30 (1968): 313–34; and "The Riddle of the Sphinx Revisited," *CBQ* 42.1 (1980): 38–51.

Wright, C.H.H. 1883. Still consulted by scholars.

✓ Wright, J. Robert (ed). *Proverbs, Ecclesiastes, Song of Solomon* (ACCS) 2004. [*CTJ* 4/07].

Wright, J. Stafford. (EBC) 1991. Finds a prominent note of joy in Ecclesiastes. This 60-page commentary is thoughtful at points and includes a fair amount of application. However, it does not probe very deeply. It helps that, in the editing process, John Walton made a few apt additions to the introduction. Wright is non-committal on the issue of authorship. The other commentaries in this EBC volume are strong. See Shepherd.

✓ Zuck, Roy B. (ed). *Reflecting with Solomon: Selected Studies on the Book of Ecclesiastes*, 1994. A sizable (432pp) collection of book chapters and journal articles—some significant from an academic standpoint, some not at all—treating the text and message of Ecclesiastes. Contributors range all the way from critical scholars like Crenshaw, Fox, and Murphy to evangelical pastors like Warren Wiersbe. [*Them* 1/96].

—𝔴—

SONG OF SONGS

★ Fredericks, Daniel C., and **Daniel J. Estes**. *Ecclesiastes & Song of Songs* (Apollos) 2010. Prior to writing his commentary, Estes taught classes on the Song in his church and college for 25 years. This is a wise, mature work that can long serve as a dependable tool for pastors and teachers. There are no new, revolutionary interpretive schemes. He avoids reading the Song as an allegory of divine love. "Neither is it a drama or narrative tracing the actual experience of a specific couple. The extravagant descriptions, rather, seem to point in the direction of an idealization of love" (p.300), prompting "reflection on the nature of love itself" (Webb). Estes believes this biblical poetry, focused on erotic love, is a corrective to debased sexuality in the world of the ANE and today; he says "the numerous links to the wisdom literature suggests [*sic*] an additional didactic purpose as the Song endeavors to teach about the nature of intimacy" (300). Note that Estes permits himself "the minor literary license" of referring to the Beloved as by name: "Shulammith." This is the most conservative volume in the series thus far; for additional comment see Ecclesiastes. Note also Estes' solid *Handbook on the Wisdom Books and Psalms* (2005).

★ **Garrett, Duane,** and Paul House. *Song of Songs, Lamentations* (WBC) 2004. After Hubbard's death, the publisher announced that Duane Garrett and Paul House would complete the project. The result is a solid exegesis, more conservative than many other WBC volumes on the OT. Garrett does Song of Songs, building upon his earlier mid-level commentary for NAC. This volume will be appreciated by both students and pastors working with the Hebrew text. Other important technical commentaries are Murphy Keel, Fox, and Pope, with Hess, Longman, and Exum containing much important scholarship as well. Though a bit sad to remove Murphy's Hermeneia commentary from this list—it remains my favorite—I have replaced it with WBC for a complex of reasons. (i) Murphy lists for $49 and WBC is cheaper; (ii) Garrett is bound together with House, which is a top pick for Lamentations; (iii) Garrett interacts with Murphy and with more recent scholarship (the bibliography issue); and (iv) I know I have to be realistic about how many books and how much money pastors and students will spend on this Bible book. I regard a number of Garrett's conclusions, especially those along the psychological line, as being too speculative. Hess and Longman are more trustworthy, in my opinion. Can you tell I am more enthusiastic about House's work in this volume? [*JETS* 9/05; *Interp* 7/05; *ExpTim* 9/09; *JSOT-BL* 2007].

★ **Gledhill, Tom.** (BST) 1994. A very full exposition (254pp), including a study guide. He says he plows his own furrow (p.13) without a lot of interaction with other interpreters. I like his approach. Longman once gave this book his highest recommendation (5 stars). Compare with Provan. [*JETS* 12/96; *CTJ* 4/96].

★ **Hess, Richard S.** (BCOT) 2005. An excellent, accessible commentary which interacts a good bit with Longman (editor for this newer series), as well as with other important scholarship, and which contains good insights related to the ANE background (archeology, Semitics, comparative literature, cultural studies, etc.). This is wise and mature evangelical scholarship, and the book is very well written and engaging. Many pastors will prefer this to (the similarly learned) Longman. It is now the reference volume I reach for first. [*EvQ* 7/08; *CBQ* 7/07; *BBR* 18.2; *JETS* 12/05; *BSac* 7/06; *JSOT-BL* 2006; *VT* 58.4; *RBL*; *JHebS*].

★ **Longman, Tremper.** (NICOT) 2001. A well-rounded, satisfying reference work which treats questions regarding the original text; the structure, imagery and conventions of the Hebrew poetry; the possible social and cultural background; verse by verse exegesis; and theology, while making a few suggestions for contemporary application (see pp.58–70). The introduction is pleasingly full, especially on the history of interpretation (pp.20–47). This or Hess should be an evangelical pastor's first purchase for the Song. Realistically, most pastors would be content with either Hess or Longman on their shelf (or even just Schwab or Carr). There is probably some truth in Gledhill's assertion [*Them* Sum 03] that Longman gives us a better view of the trees than the forest [*RTR* 4/02; *JTS* 4/03; *Interp* 10/02; *VT* 53.1; *JSOT* 99; *CBQ* 4/04 (peevish); *SwJT* Spr 03; *F&M*, Fall 02; *ExpTim* 11/04]. For a distillation of Longman, see the CorBC volume below by Konkel/Longman.

☆ **Bergant, Dianne.** ‡ (BO) 2001. One of the best recent liberal commentaries, which emphasizes (in keeping with the series' aims) a literary approach. Compare with Exum's fuller work which has strengths in the same area. Beautifully written and "suggestive" in the best sense of the word. Since the most prominent voice in the Song is the maiden's, I believe that it helps to read a woman's interpretation. Bergant teaches at Catholic Theological Union, Chicago. [*Interp* 10/02; *JSOT* 28.5; *RBL*].

Bernard of Clairvaux. 1135–1153. A medieval allegorical approach. There are various translated editions of the 86 sermons.

✓ **Bloch, Ariel, and Chana Bloch.** ‡ 1995. A Random House hb (republished in 1998 by U. of California Press), noted by many especially for its translation and sensitivity to poetic conventions. This fine study includes about 90pp of commentary on the Hebrew text and should be taken into account by students. [*JSOT* 72; *JSS*, Spr 98; *JSOT-BL* 1999; *HebStud* 1996; *VT* 51.2 (2001); *RelSRev* 10/01].

F Bucher, Christina. (BCBC).

Burrowes, George. (GS) 1853. Allegorical approach. Compare with Durham in the same Reformed series.

☆ **Carr, G. Lloyd.** (TOTC) 1983. A full (for Tyndale—175pp) and informative commentary on this short book. Years ago this was the favorite evangelical work of Longman and Stuart. The average pastor probably doesn't feel the need for anything more than this. [*EvQ* 4/86].

✓ Davidson, Robert. ‡ (DSB) 1986. See Ecclesiastes.

✓ Davis, Ellen F. ‡ *Proverbs, Ecclesiastes, and the Song of Songs* (WestBC) 2000. See Proverbs above.

✓ Delitzsch, Franz. (KD) ET 1891. An important commentary in the history of interpretation, even if it is not convincing. Delitzsch put forward the idea that this song was a drama.

Dillow, S.J. *Solomon on Sex*, 1977. I would ignore this one. See Glickman below.

F Dobbs-Allsopp, Frederick W. ‡ (ECC).

Durham, James. (GS) 1668. Takes an allegorical approach; highly valued by Spurgeon. See Burrowes above.

✓ **Exum, J. Cheryl.** ‡ (OTL) 2005. This volume completes the OTL series' coverage of the OT canon, and is a brilliant reading by a leading literary critic. Though not extreme, her approach is more reader-centered. Exum has long had an interest in the Song; note her early article, "A Literary and Structural Analysis of the Song of Songs," *ZAW* 85 (1973): 47–79. Academics with an interest in OT poetry (and gender studies) will definitely want this volume, but pastors will prefer to work with Hess, Estes, and Longman. [*CBQ* 10/06; *JTS* 10/07; *JETS* 6/07; *Interp* 1/07; *Biblica* 89.3; *BibInt* 16.1; *BSac* 4/07; *JAOS* 126.4; *RBL*; *JNES* 4/10; *RevExp* Spr 08; *JSOT-BL* 2007].

✓ **Falk, Marcia.** ‡ *Love Lyrics from the Bible: A Translation and Literary Study of the Song of Songs*, 1982. A exceedingly fine poetic translation and some cogent arguments that that we cannot discover a dramatic structure or "plot" as such. This work, originally a dissertation for Stanford University, was updated in 1990 as *The Song of Songs: A New Translation and Interpretation*. The translation was published alone in pb in 1993. "It's always a thrill when (as rarely happens) the scholar's mind and the poet's soul come together" (A. Rich). Like the Song itself, Falk's is "a delightful book" (Moshe Greenberg).

F   Fishbane, Michael. ‡ (JPS).

✓ **Fox, Michael V.** ‡ *The Song of Songs and Ancient Egyptian Love Songs*, 1985. Murphy calls this "a superb accomplishment." Here is an in-depth study which includes a fresh translation and commentary. One drawback is that Fox insists, "as a matter of doctrine" (Hess, 139), that the lovers must be unmarried. Cf. Estes, 293–99. Fox establishes by his research into comparative ANE literature that love songs are a distinguishable genre, and that Song of Songs should be interpreted for what it is: a celebration of human sexual love. Scholars debate his conclusion that "the Song is a single poem composed, originally at least, by a single poet. The poet may have used earlier materials…" (p.220). [*Biblica* 68.1 (1987); *HebStud* 1985].

☆ Garrett, Duane A. *Proverbs, Ecclesiastes, Song of Songs* (NAC) 1993. See Proverbs. For the student, this competent commentary is now outstripped by the WBC, which I recommended above.

✓ Ginsburg, C.D. 1857–61. See Ecclesiastes above. He develops the drama interpretation of the Song.

☆ Glickman, S. Craig. *A Song for Lovers*, 1976. A much better, practically-minded commentary than Dillow. (Dillow is too practically-minded, if you know what I mean.)

✓ **Gordis, Robert.** ‡ *The Song of Songs and Lamentations*, 1954, rev. 1974. A very fine discussion of the technical data, but scholarship on the Song has come a long way in recent decades. Gordis was an astute critical scholar, specializing in the Poetical and Wisdom Literature. See his other works on Job and Ecclesiastes.

F   Griffiths, Paul. (Brazos).

✓ Hagedorn, Anselm C. (ed). ‡ *Perspectives on the Song of Songs: Comparative Approaches to a Biblical Text*, 2005. [*JSOT-BL* 2006; *JTS* 4/09].

☆ Hubbard, David A. *Ecclesiastes–Song of Solomon* (WCC) 1993. I have already recommended this volume for Ecclesiastes. Hubbard does a fine job on the Song too. There was to have been another more scholarly work on the Song (WBC), but Hubbard died suddenly, soon after retiring (†1996). See Garrett and House above.

✓ **Jenson, Robert W.** [*M*], (I) 2005. This commentary by a systematic theologian chooses to "read the Song as a solicitation of theological allegory" and argues that "the Song's canonical plain sense *rightly* takes human sexual love as an analogue of the love between the Lord and Israel" (p.13). For more on this scholar, see his work on Ezekiel. Cf. Knight below. [*JETS* 9/06; *Interp* 1/07; *HBT* 29.1; *JSOT-BL* 2007].

F   Johnston, Gordon. (Kregel).

✓ **Keel, Othmar.** ‡ (ContC) ET 1994. This commentary downplays the erotic a bit and is praised by some prominent scholars as about the very best technical interpretation available. At 272 packed pages, this work rivals Murphy and Pope in scholarship and detail. My preference for Murphy's volume over this one is slight. "For all its appeal to ANE carvings and imagery as parallels, this commentary is typically postmodern" (M. Elliott). [*ExpTim* 3/95; *JETS* 12/96; *JSOT* 68; *Them* 4/96].

Kinlaw, Dennis F. (EBC) 1991. A 44-page, readable exposition which some pastors will probably think sufficiently covers this Bible book for their library, if they bought the volume for VanGemeren's Psalms commentary—few preach on the Song anymore. See now Schwab's replacement work.

✓ **Knight, G.A.F.,** and F.W. Golka. ‡ *The Song of Songs and Jonah* (ITC) 1988. A fascinating surprise in the late 1980s! Knight revived the interpretation of the Song as referring to the love relationship between God and humanity. See also his 1955 Torch Bible Commentary which covers this book. By the way, pursuing basically the same line of interpretation are Jenson; the well-written OUP dissertation by Edmeé Kingsmill, *The Song of Songs and Eros of God*, 2009 [*JSOT-BL* 2010]; and Larry Lyke's *"I Will Espouse You Forever": The Song of Songs and the Theology of Love in the Hebrew Bible*, 2007 [*VT* 59.2]. I believe I have seen enough to call this a trend.

Konkel, August H., and Tremper Longman III. *Job, Ecclesiastes, Song of Songs* (CorBC) 2006. Longman offers the commentary on the latter two Bible books, distilling his scholarship published earlier in NICOT.

Luther, Martin. ET 1972. Found in the 15ᵗʰ volume of *Luther's Works*.

✓ **Mitchell, Christopher W.** (Concord) 2003. I had heard about it, but I had to see this exceedingly large work to believe it. Yes, it is 1300pp (without the bibliography)—could anyone fail to get lost in the detail of a book this fat? The Song is only 117 verses of poetry! The introduction alone is 543pp. According to reviewers, the quality of scholarship in this tome is higher than usual for the series. The textual notes, Christological interpretations, and recommendations for using the Song in Lutheran worship services are extensive. [*EvQ* 7/08; *CBQ* 7/06; *BSac* 1/07; *CJ* 10/06].

☆ **Murphy, Roland.** ‡ (Herm) 1990. Magisterial! Though few will spring for this volume at the bookstore, it is arguably the best technical commentary on this love poem. Keel, Fox, and Pope are close rivals, with rather different interests. Murphy is especially useful because he treats the "final form" of the text. It tickles me to think of a Catholic priest writing the best-rated modern commentary on Song of Songs. See also his 1981 FOTL commentary under Ruth. In early editions of this guide, Murphy was a recommended purchase. Almost all evangelical pastors, however, will be content to skip this and have some mix of NICOT, WBC, the Baker volume, BST, TOTC, and NIVAC. A memorial for this great scholar is written in *CBQ* 10/02. [*JBL* Fall 93; *JTS* 4/93; *CBQ* 10/92; *VT* 1/96; *Them* 10/94].

Murphy, Roland E., and Elizabeth Huwiler. [*M*], *Proverbs, Ecclesiastes & Song of Songs* (NIBC) 1996. See Proverbs above.

✓ Norris, Richard A., Jr. (ed). (TCB) 2004. The inaugural volume (347pp) in the series. [*CTJ* 4/07; *VT* 55.3; *BibInt* 13.4; *Pro Ecclesia* Win 09].

Ogden, Graham S., and Lynell Zogbo. (UBS) 1998.

Olyott, Stuart J. *A Life Worth Living and a Lord Worth Loving* (WCS) 1983.

✓ **Pope, Marvin H.** ‡ (AB) 1977. Excels in presenting philological detail. Longman celebrates this tome as "one of the best commentaries written on any book of the Bible." But then Longman goes on to say, "His overall approach to the book as connected with the love and death cults of the ancient world leaves much to be desired, but it is interesting." In brief, this is something of an eccentric commentary, one only an OT specialist could love. Few ministers have money for a work of this size (750pp) and type on a Bible book they almost never preach from. See Pope on Job. [*JBL* 3/79; *ExpTim* 12/78].

☆ Provan, Iain. *Ecclesiastes, Song of Songs* (NIVAC) 2001. See under Ecclesiastes.

F Queen-Sutherland, Kandy. (S&H). See under Ruth.

✓ Roberts, D. Phillip. *Let Me See Your Form: Seeking Poetic Structure in the Song of Songs*, 2007. A lengthy, lightly-revised 2001 dissertation for Westminster Seminary with meticulous exegesis of the Hebrew. Sadly, it is a posthumous publication (†2005).

☆ Schwab, George. (EBCR) 2008. This is a great improvement on Kinlaw's EBC. Schwab earned a PhD in OT at Westminster Seminary and is also a trained counselor. He teaches at Erskine Seminary. He earlier published *The Song of Songs' Cautionary Message Concerning Human Love* (2002), offering good guidance on a variety of questions including the marital status of the lovers in the early chapters. His work in EBCR is a little over 60pp and is well worth looking up. [*JSOT-BL* 2010].

Seerveld, C. *The Greatest Song*, 1967. A clear presentation of the three-player drama view.

✓ **Snaith, John G.** ‡ (NCB) 1993. A phrase by phrase exegesis of the Song by a Cambridge lecturer (140pp) which is quite useful to the student, but less so to the preacher. Snaith does not interact as much as he could with other scholars' views; he does not cite Keel. [*JTS* 4/94; *VT* 47.1; *JSOT* 64; *CRBR* 1995; *Criswell Th. Review*, Spr 94].

Stoop-van Paridon, P.W.T. *The Song of Songs: A Philological Analysis of the Hebrew Book* שִׁיר הַשִּׁירִים (Peeters) ET 2005. This massive Leiden dissertation (539pp) is only for the most patient specialists. [*Biblica* 89.4; *JSOT-BL* 2007 (Watson)].

F Watson, Wilfred G.E. ‡ (HCOT).

☆ Webb, Barry G. *Five Festal Garments: Christian Reflections on the Song of Songs, Ruth, Lamentations, Ecclesiastes and Esther*, 2000. Excellent reading for expositors and teachers, especially as a theological guide. See under Ruth.

✓ Weems, Renita J. ‡ (NewIB) 1997. This 70-page commentary by a Vanderbilt professor is learned. She obviously has an affinity for the "black-skinned" maiden with her poetic longings. (Perhaps we need a reminder here, however, that the "blackness…has nothing to do with race" [Fox, 101].) Weems causes the reader to reflect upon the possible literary purposes of the poet. She takes a feminist approach, as expected from the author of *Battered Love: Marriage, Sex, and Violence in the Hebrew Prophets*, 1995. I found myself frequently disagreeing with her conclusions or her perspective, especially where feminist resentments seem to rise to the surface (e.g., p.381).

Wesley, John. *Explanatory Notes on the Old Testament*, Volume 3, 1765. Allegory.

✓ Wright, J. Robert (ed). Proverbs, Ecclesiastes, Song of Solomon (ACCS) 2004. [*CTJ* 4/07].

NOTE: Students interested in the history of various interpretations would also do well to consult H.H. Rowley's "The Interpretation of the Song of Songs," *JTS*, 38 (1937). This article is revised and expanded in *The Servant of the Lord and Other Essays on the Old Testament* (Blackwell, 1965). See also the discussions of the history of interpretation in Pope's (140pp), Murphy's, Longman's, and Garrett's commentaries.

PROPHETS & PROPHETIC LITERATURE

★ Blenkinsopp, Joseph. ‡ *A History of Prophecy in Israel*, 1983, rev. 1996. Advanced students and academically oriented pastors can learn much from this more traditionally historical-critical introduction. (However, scholars today often choose to approach prophecy differently, researching the use of metaphor, innerbiblical interpretation, poetry in prophetic language, rhetoric, etc., in a more holistic, final-form approach [cf. Seitz].) Just as good as Blenkinsopp really, but briefer, are Sweeney and Petersen below. See also his Prophecy and Canon, 1977.

★ Chisholm, Robert B. *Handbook on the Prophets*, 2002. This is more content-survey than introduction; readers will find it to be mildly Dispensational, learned, and well written. [*Them* Sum 04; *CJ* 10/05; *RelSRev* 4/06; *DenvJ* 1/03].

★ McConville, Gordon. *Exploring the Old Testament, Volume 4: The Prophets*, 2002. As is true of Wenham's volume on the Pentateuch in this same series, I cannot think of a better initial guide into this portion of the Scriptures. It is a work of evangelical British scholarship and has a less conservative feel than many American evangelical books on the prophets. [*Them* Spr 04; *JETS* 9/04; *ExpTim* 7/03; *Anvil* 20.3].

★ Robertson, O. Palmer. *The Christ of the Prophets*, 2004. Superb as a conservative theological survey. [*TJ* Spr 06].

★ VanGemeren, Willem A. *Interpreting the Prophetic Word*, 1990. This volume pays good attention to theology in the prophets and is a reliable guide for pastors and students. [*Chm* 111.4 (1997)].

✓ Achtemeier, Paul J., and James Luther Mays (eds). ‡ *Interpreting the Prophets*, 1987.

✓ Ackroyd, Peter R. ‡ *Exile and Restoration*, 1968.

☆ Baker, David W. "Israelite Prophets and Prophecy" (pp.266–94) in *The Face of Old Testament Studies*, edited by D.W. Baker and Bill T. Arnold (1999). Exceptionally helpful for understanding currents in scholarship. More up-to-date is Lena-Sofia Tiemeyer, "Recent Currents in Research on the Prophetic Literature," *ExpTim* 119.4 (2008): 161–69.

Barton, John. ‡ *Oracles of God: Perceptions of Prophecy in Israel after the Exile*, 1986, 2007. See also Ehud ben Zvi (ed), "Rereading Oracles of God: Twenty Years After John Barton, *Oracles of God: Perceptions of Prophecy in Israel After the Exile* (London: Darton, Longman and Todd, 1986)," *JHebS* 7, Article 14 (on-line).

Brueggemann, Walter. ‡ *The Prophetic Imagination*, 1978.

☆ Bullock, C. Hassell. *An Introduction to the OT Prophetic Books*, 1986. Compares with G. Smith below as a fine conservative introduction. This now has a dated feel and has lost some of its value as a textbook. A 2007 "revised" edition was released, but it is a reformatting rather than a true revision—e.g., in the Ezekiel section there is a single reference to a work published since 1982.

✓ Carroll, Robert P. ‡ *When Prophecy Failed*, 1979. This very critical and influential study argues that so-called "prophecy" is ever failing, and the community's leaders, dealing with the "cognitive dissonance" thus produced, reshape the materials to interpret new contingencies and revitalize the people's hope.

✓ Childs, Brevard S. ‡ *Introduction to the Old Testament As Scripture*, 1979. The prophets section is shrewd.

✓ Clements, R.E. ‡ *Old Testament Prophecy: From Oracles to Canon*, 1996. Preachers will be glad to find an emphasis on theology here. [*JETS* 6/98; *JBL* Spr 98; *JSS* Spr 99; *CBQ* 4/97; *HebStud* 1997]. Earlier Clements wrote *Prophecy and Tradition*, 1975.

Conrad, Edgar. ‡ *Reading the Latter Prophets: Towards a New Canonical Criticism*, 2003.

Crenshaw, James. ‡ *Prophets, Sages & Poets*, 2006.

Davidson, A.B. ‡ *Old Testament Prophecy*, 1904. An old classic in the history of British scholarship, introducing some of the ideas of German criticism to the English-speaking world.

✓ Davies, Philip R., and David J. A. Clines (eds). ‡ *Among the Prophets*, 1993. Add to this Davies (ed), *The Prophets: A Sheffield Reader*, 1996, which includes valuable articles such as Hans Barstad's "No Prophets? Recent Developments in Biblical Prophetic Research," *JSOT* 57 (1993): 39–60.

✓ Day, John (ed). ‡ *Prophecy and the Prophets in Ancient Israel: Proceedings of the Oxford Old Testament Seminar,* 2010.

Emmerson, Grace (ed). ‡ *Prophets and Poets: A Companion to the Prophetic Books of the Old Testament*, 1997.

✓ Fishbane, Michael. ‡ *Biblical Interpretation in Ancient Israel*, 1985. Hugely important for arguing that the Old Testament is an exegetical work in its own right, often interpreting earlier Scriptures.

☆ Gordon, Robert P. (ed). ‡ *The Place Is Too Small for Us: The Israelite Prophets in Recent Scholarship*, 1995. A superb collection for the student to consult. [*Them* 1/97; *JETS* 3/99].

✓ Gowan, Donald E. ‡ *Theology of the Prophetic Books: The Death and Resurrection of Israel*, 1998. [*ThTo* 10/99; *CBQ* 10/99; *RelSRev* 7/99].

F Grisanti, Michael A. *Interpreting the Prophets: An Exegetical Handbook* (Kregel).

Habel, Norman. ‡ "The Form and Significance of the Call Narratives," *ZAW* 77 (1965): 297–323

Hayes, John H. ‡ "The History of Form-Critical Study of Prophecy," in *SBL 1973 Seminar Papers.*

Hengstenberg, Ernst. *Christology of the Old Testament and a Commentary on the Messianic Predictions*, ET 1836–39. See Van Groningen.

✓ Heschel, Abraham. ‡ *The Prophets*, 2 vols., 1962.

Hillers, Delbert. ‡ *Treaty Curses and the Old Testament Prophets*, 1964.

Hutton, Rodney. ‡ *Fortress Introduction to the Prophets*, 2004.

✓ Koch, Klaus. ‡ *The Prophets*, 2 Vols., ET 1983–84. [*JBL* 105.3 (1986)].

✓ Lindblom, J. ‡ *Prophecy in Ancient Israel*, ET 1962.

Matthews, Victor H. ‡ *Social World of the Hebrew Prophets*, 2001. [*Interp* 7/03; *ExpTim* 3/03; *VT* 54.2].

Mays, James Luther, and Paul J. Achtemeier (eds). ‡ *Interpreting the Prophets*, 1987.

Mowinckel, Sigmund. ‡ *Prophecy and Tradition*, ET 1946.

Muilenburg, J. ‡ "The 'Office' of the Prophet in Ancient Israel," *Israel's Prophetic Heritage*, 1965.

Newsome, James D. ‡ *The Hebrew Prophets*, 1984.

Nissinen, Marti, C.L. Seow, and Robert K. Ritner. ‡ *Prophets and Prophecy in the Ancient Near East*, 2003. [*DenvJ* 10/04; *RBL*].

Nielsen, K. ‡ *Yahweh as Prosecutor and Judge: An Investigation of the Prophetic Lawsuit*, 1978.

✓ Peckham, Brian. ‡ *History & Prophecy* (ABRL) 1993.

☆ Petersen, D.L. ‡ *The Prophetic Literature*, 2002. [*Interp* 4/03; *ExpTim* 3/03; *BSac* 10/04; *HBT* 12/03; *CJ* 1/07]. Petersen has done much work here; see his OTL volumes on Haggai–Malachi, and *Late Israelite Prophecy*, 1977.

✓ Rad, Gerhard von. ‡ *Old Testament Theology*, Vol. II, ET 1965; *The Message of the Prophets*, ET 1967.

Redditt, Paul. ‡ *Introduction to the Prophets*, 2008. One of the most up-to-date critical introductions. [*VT* 59.4 (Williamson); *ETL* 86.1; *RelSRev* 12/09; *Them* 4/10].

Robinson, T.H. ‡ *Prophecy and the Prophets in Ancient Israel*, 2ⁿᵈ ed 1953.

Rofé, Alexander. ‡ *Introduction to the Prophetic Literature*, 1997.

Rowley, H.H. ‡ *Studies in Old Testament Prophecy*, 1950.

✓ Sandy, D. Brent, and Daniel M. O'Hare. *Prophecy and Apocalyptic: An Annotated Bibliography* (IBR) 2007. Includes a selective bibliography for studies in each of the Major and Minor Prophets. See too the online supplement—an extra 1500 items—of this work at <www.ibr-bbr.org/IBR_Studies.aspx>. [*RelSRev* 9/08].

Sawyer, John F.A. ‡ *Prophecy and the Biblical Prophets*, rev. ed 1993.

☆ Seitz, Christopher R. ‡ *Prophecy and Hermeneutics: Toward a New Introduction to the Prophets*, 2007. Mainly focused upon Isaiah and "The Twelve," Seitz explores the newer canonical, holistic approaches, as opposed to the older historical critical scholarship which tended to fragment the text. [*EvQ* 7/08; *JETS* 6/08; *JTS* 10/08; *Interp* 7/08; *RelSRev* 12/08; *HBT* 31.2; *Them* 7/09].

Smith, W. Robertson. ‡ *The Prophets of Israel*, 1895.

☆ Smith, Gary V. *An Introduction to the Hebrew Prophets: The Prophets as Preachers*, 1994. [*VT* 47.1].

☆ Sweeney, Marvin A. ‡ *The Prophetic Literature*, 2006. From the widely used IBT series, this is among the best brief critical introductions to the subject [*CBQ* 7/06; *Interp* 4/07; *VT* 57.4; *ExpTim* 4/07; *CJ* 4/07; *JSOT-BL* 2007; *Anvil* 23.4]. Also recent is *Form and Intertextuality in Prophetic and Apocalyptic Literature*, 2005 [*JTS* 10/07].

☆ Van Groningen, Gerard. *Messianic Revelation in the Old Testament*, 1990.

✓ Westermann, Claus. ‡ *The Basic Forms of Prophetic Speech*, ET 1967; *Prophetic Oracles of Salvation in the OT*, ET 1991. Seminal form-critical work from a great German scholar.

✓ Wilson, Robert R. ‡ *Prophecy and Society in Ancient Israel*, 1980. Encouraged sociological research. For more on this, see Thomas W. Overholt, *Channels of Prophecy: The Social Dynamics of Prophetic Activity*, 1989.

Wilson, Robert R. ‡ "Current Issues in the Study of Old Testament Prophecy" (pp.38–47), in J. Kaltner and L. Stulman (eds), *Inspired Speech*, 2004.

☆ Young, Edward J. *My Servants the Prophets*, 1952. [*EvQ* 4/53]. This monograph retains value because Young clearly shows that there is wide cleavage between the critic and the believing scholar on the matter of prophecy. Young would agree with Calvin who wrote, "Let us, then, by prophets...understand, first of all, eminent interpreters of Scripture, and farther, persons who are endowed with no common wisdom and dexterity in taking a right view of the present necessity of the Church, that they may speak suitably to it, and in this way be, in a manner, ambassadors to communicate the divine will." The believing scholar teaches that the prophets were interpreters of the Law who were calling the people back to the covenant relationship Yahweh established first in choosing Abraham and then in redeeming his descendants out of Egypt (all recorded in Scripture). The written Law begat the prophets, not the other way around, as the critics have often taught.

Zimmerli, Walther. ‡ *The Law and the Prophets*, ET 1965.

NOTE: The literature on the prophets is so copious that this must be a very selective list of excellent and influential works.

—ɯ—

ISAIAH

★ Calvin, John. 1551. "One of the Reformer's best" (Childs). Previously, this 2000-page commentary was available only in the Baker set, but Crossway has now issued it in a much condensed CrossC pb edition (2000) [*JSOT* 94 (2001)].

★ **Childs, Brevard S.** ‡ (OTL) 2001. Actually released in late 2000. This is a major interpretation, one which picks up where Childs left off in his *Introduction to the Old Testament as Scripture*. He believes that "the crucial questions turn…on how one understands the process of the book's editorial shaping" (p.371). If only there were more focus on the final shape! Frankly, he spends more time discussing diachronic issues and pursuing his own particular redactional approach than I had expected. There is also less theology than I had hoped. I judge this work to be much less useful to evangelical pastors than Childs' Exodus volume. This commentary has been especially valuable to students for its fine bibliographies, its review of the history of interpretation, its exegetical findings, and for passing on to English-speakers the insights of some key European interpreters like Beuken, Steck, and Elliger. See the older Isaiah volumes in OTL by Kaiser and Westermann. Motyer [*Anvil* 19.3] expresses deep disappointment with this volume. [*CBQ* 1/02; *Them* Spr 02; *JETS* 12/02; *JBL* Sum 02; *Interp* 10/02; *ExpTim* 11/01; *BSac* 10/02; *Biblica* 83.4; *BibInt* 12.3; *JSOT* 99 (2002); *SwJT* Sum 02; *Chm* Win 01; *BBR* 14.2; *ThTo*, 4/02 (Williamson); *CurTM* 2/02 (Klein); *RBL*; *Evangel* Sum 02]. Much more discussion of the history of interpretation is offered in Childs' more recent Eerdmans release, *The Struggle to Understand Isaiah as Christian Scripture*, 2004 [*RTR* 4/05; *CBQ* 1/06; *JETS* 12/05; *Interp* 1/06; *JSOT-BL* 2005; *ExpTim* 1/07; *Anvil* 23.1 (Motyer); *EuroJTh* 18.1 (Firth)].

★ **Goldingay, John.** ‡ (NIBC) 2001. While I like the (often brilliant) theological reading of Isaiah here, I am concerned about how Goldingay's higher critical approach is pulling evangelical OT scholarship to the left, both in the Commonwealth and in America. He argues for four voices (or pens), for the theological unity of the prophecy (through redaction and inner-biblical interpretation), and for a post-exilic date of the final form. Goldingay teaches at Fuller Seminary. If you're a student choosing between Goldingay and Childs, pick the latter; students will mainly use Goldingay's more important scholarly work on chs. 40–55 (see below). The evangelical pastor who doesn't want the higher criticism should rely instead on Webb and Oswalt's NIVAC for guidance in exposition and biblical theological reflection. [*CBQ* 10/04; *Interp* 1/04; *HebStud* 2006].

★ **Motyer, J. Alec.** 1993. An excellent exegetical and expositional commentary in the mold of TOTC except more lengthy (544pp). In fact, this entry was originally intended for TOTC. This should be reckoned the best one-vol. evangelical work on Isaiah on the strength of its careful exegesis and astute theological comment. Motyer views the messianic hope as central to this prophecy. Your first choice, though the critics pan it for maintaining the authorial integrity of all 66 chapters. I have several notes to students. This volume is valuable for its structural analysis. It mainly puts forward the author's mature perspective and research and is not a repository of others' scholarship. That is not to say, however, it is an isolated piece of work. Also, note the misspelling "Wilderberger" (*passim*). IVP has now issued this commentary in pb. Motyer wrote the BST volumes on Amos, Philippians and James. See also his TOTC below. By the way, since I have repeatedly been asked about the pronunciation of the surname, I will assure you it is "Moh-teer." [*BSac* 1/96; *VT* 10/94; *CBQ* 7/95; *EvQ* 4/95; *Them* 1/95; *SwJT* Spr 95; *JETS* 12/96; *SBET* Spr 96].

★ **Oswalt, John.** (NICOT) 2 Vols., 1986–98. Stuart's first pick in 1990 (before Motyer). With capable scholarship (especially in the areas of text-criticism and grammatical analysis), Oswalt takes a decidedly and dependably conservative approach. The commentary is relatively up to date, though some might wish for an appendix discussing the vast amount of recent research into "Isaianic coherence." In the rich theology of the prophecy, Oswalt gives prominence to the contrast between the greatness of a holy God and the corruption of humanity, on the one hand, and, on the other, the "amazing paradox that if humanity will lay aside its pretensions to deity, the true God will raise us to fellowship with himself" (vol. 1, p.32). The matter of true service and servanthood repeatedly comes to the fore. See also Oswalt's NIVAC below, which distills the scholarship in NICOT and may be more useful to the busy expositor. [*Biblica* 69.2 (1988); *TJ* Spr 87; *WTJ* Fall 87; *JETS* 9/88, 12/99; *JSOT* 84 (1999); *Interp* 4/00; *SwJT* Spr 99; *RelSRev* 1/99; *CBQ* 1/02; *DenvJ*].

★ **Smith, Gary V.** (NAC) 2 Vols., 2007–09. This rivals Oswalt as a full (over 1400pp), highly competent, conservative exegesis; it beats Oswalt in the sense that Smith interacts with the last 20 years of scholarship. He has already published a good bit on the prophets and has a first-rate commentary on Amos. Will this set become the evangelical pastor's first choice? I am still evaluating, but the Denver Seminary faculty are making this a top pick. Take note that Smith pays especially close attention to chs. 40–66.

★ Webb, Barry. (BST) 1996. One of the highest compliments that can be paid to a book is that one wishes to have written it—or to have been able to have crafted such a fine book. Webb's is exactly the kind of approach that makes the OT come alive. It is (1) conservative and evangelical, viewing the text as God's authoritative revelation; (2) rich in theology (a biblical theological approach); (3) sensitive to the literary features of the Bible; and (4) engagingly written. Pastors can start off with Motyer, Oswalt, Smith, and Webb, then perhaps buy Childs, if they have a scholarly bent. [*Them* 10/97; *BL* 1997; *RelSRev* 7/98].

✧ ✧ ✧ ✧ ✧ ✧

☆ Alexander, J.A. *The Prophecies of Isaiah*, 1847. A standard resource for many generations, often reprinted. Mature theological reflection abounds in this volume by an old Princeton Seminary professor. [*EvQ* 4/54].

✓ Allis, O.T. *The Unity of Isaiah*, 1950. A valuable old defense of the orthodox position and an explanation of why this issue has been a watershed for biblical studies and theology. See Young below.

F Baer, David. *Isaiah 1–39* (NCBC).

✓ **Baltzer, Klaus.** ‡ *Deutero-Isaiah* (Herm) ET 2001. A translation of the 680-page German commentary on Isaiah 40–55 (KAT) published in 1999. Baltzer has been working on this for decades, and his commentary is proving controversial in critical circles. He supposes the prophecies are set in the form of a liturgical drama (in six scenes), are to be dated to the mid-5th century, and are drawing from the Pentateuch (among several intertexts). There is less textual criticism than we have come to expect in Hermeneia, and less theological reflection, too, than we find in other works like Zimmerli's Ezekiel. Of interest only to OT specialists and advanced students. See Roberts below. [*CBQ* 1/04; *JTS* 4/02; *JBL* Spr 04; *JETS* 6/03; *Interp* 7/03; *ExpTim* 8/01; *SJT* 56.1; *CurTM* 2/03; *RBL*; *JHebS*; *DenvJ* 1/03].

F Bartelt, Andrew, and Paul Raabe. *First Isaiah* (ECC). This will be a more conservative work in the series.

✓ **Beuken, Willem A.M.** ‡ *Isaiah II, Chapters 28–39* (HCOT) ET 2000. This volume contains hardly any introduction—relying instead on Leene?—and 420pp of detailed exegesis. It is valued highly for its intertextual interests. There will be another volume on chs. 13–27. Childs speaks of how his "illuminating articles and magisterial four-vol. commentary in Dutch on chs. 40–66 have opened the way to a new era in interpreting the book of Isaiah." See Leene and Koole below. Would that some publisher would undertake to put Beuken's volumes on Isaiah 40–66 into English translation! See *Biblica* 72.2 (1991). [*CBQ* 4/01; *JETS* 6/03; *VT* 51.4; *JSOT* 94 (2001)].

Beyer, Bryan E. *Encountering the Book of Isaiah*, 2007. A useful college-level handbook. [*CBQ* 7/08; *TJ* Fall 08; *ExpTim* 10/08 (Goldingay); *RelSRev* 3/08; *JETS* 9/08].

✓ **Blenkinsopp, Joseph.** ‡ *Isaiah 1–39* (AB) 2000; *Isaiah 40–55* (AB) 2002; *Isaiah 56–66* (AB) 2003. The author is a leading Catholic OT scholar, long at the University of Notre Dame. In the first volume, he takes a more conventional historical-critical approach, offering an excellent new translation (68pp), a well-written 39-page introduction, a 53-page bibliography, and 319pp of exegesis. The commentary is not as full as some other entries in the series, such as Lundbom's three volumes on Jeremiah, Greenberg on Ezekiel, or Andersen-Freedman on Micah. Blenkinsopp believes "that the book has undergone successive restructurings and rearrangements in the course of a long editorial history" (p.83), and these diachronic matters appear to be of greater interest to him than a reading of Isaiah as a rhetorical and structural unity. I grow weary of all the confident talk about "editorial addenda," their dating, and even the frame of mind or intention of the "scribes" responsible (e.g., ad locum 19:16–25). The second and third volumes capably carry forward Blenkinsopp's program. The completed set is for students, not pastors. [*JTS* 10/04; *CBQ* 7/01, 10/03, 7/04; *JETS* 12/02; *JBL* Spr, Fall 04; *CurTM* 12/02; *Interp* 7/02; *HebStud* 2003; *SwJT* Fall 01; *VT* 54.1, 54.4; *JSOT* #94, 27.5 and 28.5; *JSS* Aut 05, Spr 06; *BSac* 10/04, 1/06; Williamson has reviews in *JSS* Aut 02; *HebStud*, 2004; Beuken writes his in *Biblica* 83.2, 84.3, and 85.3; *SJT* 60.4 (Seitz); *RelSRev* 10/04 (Sweeney); *RBL*; *CurTM* 8/06].

☆ Brueggemann, Walter. ‡ (WestBC) 2 Vols., 1998. About 575pp of theological commentary aimed at the educated laity, but of real assistance to the pastor as well. Read with some discernment, for example at ch. 53. See also the author's commentaries on Genesis, Exodus, Samuel, and Jeremiah. Those stimulated by interaction with the critics may like the more liberal, provocative Brueggemann as much as Goldingay. [*Them* 11/99; *JSOT* 89 (2000); *Interp* 10/99; *HBT* 12/03].

✓ **Clements, Ronald E.** ‡ *Isaiah 1–39* (NCB) 1980. Has value as a reference tool for students. Prior to Childs, I judged the two-vol. NCB set and three-vol. OTL commentary to be close rivals for pride of place as the best completed critical exegesis of this prophecy. Both sets employ a form critical approach, with NCB being more restrained. [*WTJ* Fall 83; *ExpTim* 9/81; *EvQ* 4/82; *JBL* 102.1 (1983)].

✓ Conrad, Edward W. ‡ *Reading Isaiah*, 1991. Literary analysis which lends support (unintentionally) to other, even evangelical, readings of the prophecy as a coherent whole. [*BSac* 4/92; *HebStud* 1992].

✓ Delitzsch, Franz. (KD has the 2nd ed, 1869). "A monument of immense learning" (Childs). This work is justly famous. Conservatives regret that Delitzsch came to moderate his position on the unity of Isaiah in his 4th edition of this commentary (1889). All four editions were translated into English.

F Dempsey, Carol. ‡ *Isaiah 1–39* (BO). See Franke and Polan.

✓ Elliott, Mark W. (ed). *Isaiah 40–66* (ACCS) 2007. [*JSOT*-BL 2008].

F Emerton, John A. ‡ *Isaiah 28–39* (ICC–new series). The learned, aged author is professor emeritus at Cambridge and long served as general OT editor for the new series of the ICC. The strange allocation of chs. 28–39 derives from the fact that a much earlier volume by Gray (see below) covered chs. 1–27.

☆ Firth, David G., and H.G.M. Williamson. *Interpreting Isaiah: Issues and Approaches*, 2009. These 287pp are the product of the Tyndale Fellowship. See the similar Firth-edited volume on Psalms. [*ExpTim* 7/10].

F Franke, Chris. ‡ *Isaiah 40–55* (BO). Her published dissertation was *Isaiah 46, 46, and 48: A New Literary-Critical Reading* (Eisenbrauns, 1994). See Dempsey and Polan for other expected BO releases.

Friesen, Ivan D. ‡ (BCBC) 2009. Well-informed in his critical scholarship (Toronto PhD), the author writes for pastors, especially those sharing his Mennonite faith. Friesen sees the prophecy as cohesive because it is a "composite unity," and he then pursues a theological reading and issues of application.

✓ **Goldingay, John, and David Payne.** ‡ *Isaiah 40–55* (ICC–new series) 2 Vols., 2006. I heard this work was actually completed about six years before the set was finally published. Pastors with financial means will prefer the one-vol. commentary immediately below. This ICC is expensive and, with its sometimes severe focus on exegetical minutiae, is meant for scholars and reference libraries. With regard to critical orientation, the new ICC works on Isaiah by Goldingay/Payne and Williamson must be classed as more conservative. The difference, in my humble opinion, between this *Isaiah 40–55* and Williamson is that the later is twice as thorough and deep in textual analysis. Though "more conservative," Goldingay/ Payne do uphold the higher critical conclusion that Second Isaiah addresses the Israel of the Babylonian exile (ca. 540 BC). The exegesis is more focused on the final form (p.9) than we've come to expect from ICC. Because so much of the theological reflection was jettisoned—see the Literary-Theological Commentary below—this ICC seems dry and even truncated in one respect, as compared with some other series. Isn't the point of meticulously detailed exegesis to drive at the message of this highly theological literature? Yes, but ICC has always tended to leave that theological work to its readers. [*CBQ* 4/08; *Interp* 1/09; *JSOT-BL* 2008; *RelSRev* 10/07 (Sweeney); *RBL*; *BSac* 10/08; *JETS* 12/09; *HebStud* 2009].

☆ **Goldingay, John.** ‡ *The Message of Isaiah 40–55: A Literary-Theological Commentary*, 2005. This more accessible volume builds upon his ICC and presents Goldingay's theological conclusions, but without such a mass of technical scholarship on the exegetical fine-points like textual criticism. However, this is still a very full treatment (600pp) of these 16 chapters. Regrettably, this volume is rather expensive. See also the author's (happily inexpensive) NIBC work above on the whole prophecy. [*CBQ* 7/07; *RelSRev* 1/07; *CJ* Win 09; *ExpTim* 5/07; *RBL*; *BSac* 7/08; *Interp* 1/09; *JSOT-BL* 2007].

✓ **Gray, George B.** ‡ *Isaiah 1–27* (ICC) 1912. Years ago this offered students much help with philology, grammar, etc. In the history of scholarship, it is a pity that Gray's completed commentary on chs. 28–39 in this same series was never published. See Williamson below for a developing replacement set.

Grogan, Geoffrey W. (EBC) 1986. In vol. 6 which covers Isaiah through Ezekiel. See the next entry.

☆ Grogan, Geoffrey W. (EBCR) 2008. The author has updated and improved his earlier accessible commentary for a new generation of seminarians and ministers. It is a better update than some of the other EBC works received. This thoughtful exegesis and exposition runs to about 430pp and is a good, sound guide to Isaiah. [*JSOT-BL* 2010].

F Groves, J. Alan. *The Gospel According to Isaiah: God with Us* (P&R). Professor Groves is with the Lord, and I don't expect this to appear.

✓ **Hanson, Paul D.** ‡ *Isaiah 40–66* (I) 1995. This 272-page work, by an expert on the Apocalyptic genre, completes the Isaiah set which Seitz began. Hanson emphasizes "God's compassionate justice" as the central theme. The approach is broadly liberal and theological. [*JETS* 3/99; *CBQ* 1/97; *BSac* 4/97; *HebStud* 1997; *RelSRev* 1/97].

✓ Hayes, John H., and Stuart A. Irvine. ‡ *Isaiah: His Times and His Preaching*, 1987. This commentary on the so-called First Isaiah (chs. 1–39) has a critical orientation, but the authors go their own more conservative way when they attribute almost all the material in these chapters to Isaiah ben Amoz. "The major contribution of this work…is their focus on the historical backdrop of the latter half of the eighth century without which…Isaiah remains incomprehensible" (Vasholz). Because historical concerns dominate, this work feels somewhat dated with regard to approach. [*Presb* Spr 90; *JTS* 10/90; *CRBR* 1991; *ExpTim* 8/89].

F House, Paul R. (Mentor).

✓ **Kaiser, Otto.** ‡ *Isaiah 1–12* (OTL) ET 1972, rev. 1983; *Isaiah 13–39* (OTL) ET 1974. A prominent historical critical commentary translated out of the German. Note that this scholar became more radical since he began commenting on Isaiah, and he seems supremely confident about his redaction theories. Westermann completes this series. Compare with Clements and the much more thorough Wildberger. [*ExpTim* 6/83; *JBL* 94.3 (1975)].

✓ Kissane, Edward J. 1941–44. This Catholic scholar takes a more conservative approach.

✓ **Knight, G.A.F.** ‡ (ITC) 2 Vols., 1984–85. About 330pp of exegesis and exposition of chs. 40–66. Knight's is better than many other critics' interpretations of Isaiah. He takes a more conservative theological approach. Back in 1965 Knight published *Deutero-Isaiah*, a well received commentary in which he tried to reconstruct a 6th century milieu of chs. 40–55.

✓ **Koole, Jan L.** ‡ *Isaiah III*, Vol. 1, *Isaiah Chapters 40–48* (HCOT) ET 1997; *Isaiah III*, Vol. 2, *Isaiah Chapters 49–55* (HCOT) ET 1998; *Isaiah III*, Vol. 3, *Isaiah 56–66* (HCOT) ET 2001. Among the three volumes now available, there are about 1700pp of detailed commentary on these 27 chapters: a rich harvest of sober, meticulous, Dutch critical scholarship. Koole's more traditional historical critical approach can be contrasted with Beuken's. Students, don't be confused by the title, *Isaiah III*. Koole covers so-called Second and Third Isaiah. [*CBQ* 1/99, 7/99; *JBL* Spr 01; *RelSRev* 10/99, 7/00; *JSOT-BL* 1998, 1999; *JSOT* 27.5].

F Leene, Hendrik. ‡ *Isaiah I, Chapters 1–12* (HCOT).

Leupold, H.C. 2 Vols., 1968–71. There is some solid exposition here from a conservative Lutheran angle.

☆ Lloyd-Jones, D. Martyn. *The All Sufficient God*, 2005. Banner published these fine sermons on Isaiah 40.

Mackay, John L. *Isaiah* (EPSC) 2008–. Only the 864-page first volume (chs. 1–39) has appeared in this conservative Presbyterian exposition published in the UK. The author has many commentaries on OT books. [*SBET* Spr 09].

McKenna, David. (WCC) 2 Vols., 1994.

McKenzie, J.L. ‡ *Second Isaiah* (AB) 1968. Not so valuable. Covers all of chs. 40–66, not merely 40–55, despite the reader's expectations. McKenzie has been replaced in the series by Blenkinsopp. [*JBL* 88.1 (1969)].

✓ McKinion, Steven A. (ed). *Isaiah 1–39* (ACCS) 2004. [*JSOT-BL* 2008].

MacRae, Allan A. *The Gospel of Isaiah*, 1977. This is an exposition of Isaiah 40:1–56:8 by a conservative who left the Northern Presbyterians (old PCUSA) over liberalism and the reorganization of Princeton Seminary. This book focuses on

Isaiah

Christ, the true Servant of Yahweh and is perhaps worth a one-time read through. MacRae had the best of scholarly training, but this Moody publication is written on a popular level.

✓ Margalioth, Rachel. *The Indivisible Isaiah*, ET 1964. Professor Vasholz of Covenant Seminary has been enthusiastic about this apology for the orthodox position, which is translated from Modern Hebrew. Not a commentary. Her work anticipated much of the scholarly interest today in the coherence and (redactional) unity of Isaiah.

F Melugin, Roy F. ‡ *Isaiah 40–66* (FOTL). See Sweeney for the companion volume.

✓ **Miscall, Peter D.** ‡ (Read) 1993, 2ⁿᵈ ed 2006. Interprets the book as a whole, while ignoring the "seams" between the different Isaiahs which critical scholars allege. This book had a very friendly reception. [*CBQ* 7/94; *CRBR* 1995; *JSOT-BL* 2008]. Added to it is "Quinn-Miscall," *Reading Isaiah: Poetry and Vision*, 2002 [*Interp* 7/03; *VT* 54.3; *BibInt* 12.1; *Evangel* Spr 05].

☆ Motyer, J. Alec. (TOTC) 1999. Presents most of the author's conclusions from his 1993 commentary (not much of the more recent Isaiah scholarship is discussed). Having both volumes might be a waste of shelf space. No commentary I have ever seen rivals this Tyndale volume in terms of compactness. [*Chm* Spr 00; *Them* Spr 01; *EvQ* 7/04; *JETS* 9/01; *JSOT* 94 (2001)].

✓ Muilenburg, James. ‡ (IB—exegesis section) 1956. For his time, he brilliantly treats chs. 40–66. See Scott below.

✓ North, C.R. ‡ *Isaiah 40–55* (Torch Bible Commentary) 1952. Longman finds North's work valuable, especially on the "Servant Songs." Must be used with discretion. Also note his more technical work for OUP entitled, *The Second Isaiah* (1964).

☆ Ortlund, Raymond C. (PTW) 2005. This exposition of over 450pp reads like printed sermons; that might not sound exciting, but Ortlund is both an OT scholar and an engaging preacher (now at Immanuel Church in Nashville). He provides good guidance to today's expositors (48 sermons on the 66 chapters). What he does not provide is a lot of his undergirding exegesis. [*JETS* 3/07; *BSac* 1/07; *CJ* 4/07].

☆ Oswalt, John. (NIVAC) 2003. This single volume exposition, of course, builds upon his twenty-something years of research for the NICOT set. Pastors will take an interest in this, perhaps buying this NIVAC or Ortlund's PTW volume, but students will make use of Oswalt's older two volumes.

F Paul, Shalom. ‡ *Isaiah 40–66* (ECC). Paul is a very capable, conservatively critical Jewish scholar. A two-vol. Magnes Press commentary in Hebrew appeared in 2008 [*JSOT-BL* 2009; *VT* 59.2].

✓ Pieper, August. *Isaiah II: An Exposition of Isaiah 40–66*, ET 1979. The conservative Lutheran Pieper provides a careful exegesis based on thorough work with the MT, and theological exposition.

F Polan, Gregory J. ‡ *Isaiah 56–66* (BO). See Dempsey and Franke.

☆ Ridderbos, Jan. (BSC) ET 1984. Though shorter than many other commentaries on Isaiah, Ridderbos offers valuable theological commentary in a very readable translation. Now o/p. Before Motyer was published and Oswalt was completed, Longman counseled you to purchase this first. [*WTJ* Spr 88; *JETS* 3/87].

F Roberts, J.J.M. ‡ *First Isaiah* (Herm). See Baltzer above.

Sawyer, John F.A. ‡ (DSB) 2 Vols., 1984–86. Exposition based on critical assumptions [*EvQ* 10/86]. The more recent Sawyer publication is *The Fifth Gospel: Isaiah in the History of Christianity*, 1996, which studies the history of interpretation [*EvQ* 1/03].

F Schultz, Richard. (Apollos). Perhaps this will be a one-vol. conservative exegesis to rival Motyer's. Schultz is an exceptionally able evangelical scholar who did his Yale PhD on Isaiah.

✓ Scott, R.B.Y. ‡ (IB–exegesis section) 1956. Covers the first 39 chapters. Among older commentaries, this is prized by Childs. The exegesis of the "Book of Comfort," chs. 40–66, is ably done by Muilenburg. Thirty years ago this two-part Isaiah commentary in IB was an important reference, but most ignore it today.

✓ **Seitz, Christopher R.** ‡ *Isaiah 1–39* (I) 1993. Seitz has done important prior work on Isaiah. More conservatively critical. From the standpoint of interpreting the message of the prophecy, this series is much more interesting than OTL or NCB. Preachers have gravitated to the Interpretation series for coverage of Isaiah. See the next entry, and also Hanson above for the volume which completes the set. [*JBL* 114.3 (1995); *Interp* 7/95; *JR* 4/95; *JETS* 3/99; *JBL* Fall 95; *BSac* 4/96; *HebStud* 1995; *AsTJ* Fall 97].

✓ **Seitz, Christopher R.** ‡ *Isaiah 40–66* (NewIB) 2001. This completes the author's treatment of the prophecy, though in two different series. The approaches and depth of treatment in both are very similar. Seitz has an eagle-eye for theological themes. First Isaiah in the NewIB is covered by Tucker. [*CurTM* 2/03].

✓ Skinner, John. ‡ (Cambridge Bible) 2 Vols., 1910–15.

Smith, G.A. ‡ (EB) 1888.

✓ **Sweeney, Marvin A.** ‡ *Isaiah 1–39 with an Introduction to the Prophetic Literature* (FOTL) 1996. This author teaches at Claremont and is a trenchant critical scholar. This work will be cited in the literature for a long time to come. Students will consult this for bibliography, form-critical, redactional and structural analysis. The author does better than many others in the series at examining texts within the prophecy's structure as a whole—i.e., a bit more attention is paid to the "final form." [*BSac* 1/97; *JETS* 6/98; *JSS* Spr 98; *Biblica* 78.2 (1997); *BL* 1997; *CBQ* 4/98; *HebStud* 1999; *BibInt* 9.1].

☆ Thomas, Derek. *God Delivers: Isaiah Simply Explained* (WCS) 1991. A solid, spiritually helpful, Reformed exposition pitched at a level suitable for both laity and ministers. See also his books on Job. [*SBET* Aut 96].

✓ Tucker, Gene M. ‡ *Isaiah 1–39* (NewIB) 2001. Tucker is a leading form critic, and his 300-page interpretation is less valuable for theological reflection than Seitz's section on the last 27 chapters.

F Tull, Patricia K. ‡ (S&H). Her dissertation topic (under a previous name, Willey) was well-chosen: *Remember the Former Things: The Recollection of Previous Texts in Second Isaiah*, 1997.

✓ Van Ruiten, J., and M. Vervenne (eds). ‡ *Studies in the Book of Isaiah: Festschrift W.A.M. Beuken*, 1997.

✓ Vermeylen, J. (ed). ‡ *The Book of Isaiah*, 1989.

Vine, William E. 1953. Once F.F. Bruce commended Vine's work saying, "The author has concentrated on the moral and spiritual lessons of Isaiah, and presented them in a way which will prove very helpful for the general reader." Vine wrote expositions of both OT and NT books, and they have been reprinted.

Walker, Larry L., and Elmer A. Martens. *Isaiah, Jeremiah, Lamentations* (CorBC) 2005. I have not had opportunity to use this volume. Walker's work was originally scheduled for NAC.

✓ **Watts, John D.W.** ‡ (WBC) 2 Vols., 1985–87, rev. 2005. I'm not all that enthusiastic about these volumes. Watts presents Isaiah as a drama, and, while there is much learning in this commentary to appreciate, I find the scheme too farfetched and idiosyncratic to be of much help. Watts concludes that the Isaianic materials were gathered and reshaped quite late, about 435 BC (p.xli). As noted by one reviewer [*JSOT-BL* 2007 (Day)], among his oddest conclusions is "that the 'messianic' oracles in Isaiah 9 and 11 are to be regarded as the words of Isaiah's opponents." Twenty years ago this had some prominence as one of the few recent, complete technical commentaries on Isaiah. I am glad to report that the revision is a substantive one. [*HebStud* 1987, 1993; *RTR* 1/87; *ExpTim* 3/88 and 1/91; *JETS* 9/88 and 3/94; *Them* 10/89; *EvQ* 10/88; *Chm* 102.2 (1988); *CRBR* 1988, 1992].

✓ **Westermann, Claus.** ‡ *Isaiah 40–66* (OTL) 1969. Some theology buried in form critical analysis of the oracles. This is an important critical work which completes the series of volumes on Isaiah begun by Otto Kaiser. Scholars still make constant reference to Westermann. The more academically-oriented pastor and the student will make use of this rigorous exegesis. See Childs above. [*JBL* 88.3 (1969)].

✓ **Whybray, R. Norman.** ‡ *Isaiah 40–66* (NCB) 1975. [*EvQ* 10/76].

✓ **Wildberger, Hans.** ‡ *Isaiah 1–12* (ContC) ET 1991; *Isaiah 13–27* (ContC) ET 1997; *Isaiah 28–39* (ContC) ET 2002. A treasure trove for the specialist with lots of theology. From BKAT. Typical of almost all German scholarship, Wildberger views it as his exegetical task to delineate the earliest individual prophetic utterances by form-critical means and then trace the development of the book through its redactional layers. Wildberger is considerably more conservative than Kaiser and more confident that we can reconstruct the historical proclamation of Isaiah ben Amoz. It is instructive to note that the *JBL* reviewer, Blank, finds little to which an adherent of Judaism would object. Note also that volume three contains the introduction. [*JBL* 91.1, 94.2; *SwJT* Fall 93; *JSOT* 89; *JETS* 12/99; *BSac* 1/93; *RelSRev* 7/98; *JSS* Spr 02; *JSOT* 27.5; *RelSRev* 1/04; *Interp* 10/05; *RBL*].

Wilken, Robert Louis (ed). (TCB) 2007. Nearly 600pp of patristic and medieval commentary. Compare this with ACCS. [*Chm* Win 08; *RTR* 8/08; *JTS* 10/08; *ExpTim* 4/08; *VT* 58.3 (Williamson); *Pro Ecclesia* Win 09].

✓ **Williamson, H.G.M.** ‡ *Isaiah 1–5* (ICC–new series) 2006. I must pile up the superlatives, for this is the best technical OT commentary I have ever seen. Specialists expect this three-vol. commentary on chs. 1–27 to be a conservatively critical and invaluable reference work (particularly for diachronic and textual issues); it is already shaping up to be a magisterial technical exegesis [*JTS* 4/08; *VT* 60.1 (Millard); *Biblica* 91.2; *JSOT-BL* 2007]. The author is Regius Professor of Hebrew at Oxford with a background in evangelical circles in the UK. Based on comments made in his WBC commentary on Ezra-Nehemiah (pp.9–10, 133), I expected him to posit the usual threefold division of Isaiah. Clarendon published *The Book Called Isaiah* (1994) in which Williamson argues that the author(s) of chs. 40–66 consciously used First Isaiah as a model, and that there is a definite redactional unity [*JETS* 3/98; *JSS* Spr 96; *JTS* 10/96]. See also *Variations on a Theme: King, Messiah, and the Servant in the Book of Isaiah*, 1998 [*SJT* 53.4 (2000)].

Wolf, Herbert. *Interpreting Isaiah: The Suffering and Glory of the Messiah*, 1985. A conservative, popularly-styled commentary which focuses upon Messianic revelation. Probably written more for an educated lay readership. Wolf contributed the Judges commentary in EBC.

☆ **Young, E.J.** (formerly NICOT) 3 Vols., 1965–72. Still in print, this was a dependable commentary with an immense amount of learning for its time. There was much to appreciate in these volumes, but the set now feels older than it is and readers will feel they are plodding through the text. There is not as much theology as could be hoped for in such a massive work. [*EvQ* 7/73]. Students may find it profitable to consult Young's strong apologetic for the unity of the prophecy: *Who Wrote Isaiah?* (1958). For an older review of the history of Isaianic interpretation, see his *Studies in Isaiah* (1954).

Youngblood, Ronald. 2nd ed 1993. A thoughtful, popularly-styled exposition from Baker (174pp).

NOTES: (1) Richard J. Coggins' "Which Is the Best Commentary? 12. Isaiah," *ExpTim* 1/91. (2) See the four review-essays now gathered in Alan J. Hauser, *Recent Research on the Major Prophets* (Sheffield Phoenix, 2008); two of them are drawn from *Current in Research: Biblical Studies.* (3) The most valuable quick review of current scholarship is Williamson's leading chapter in Firth/Williamson above.

JEREMIAH

★ Calvin, John. (GS) 5 Vols., 1563. Astonishingly, 2,400 pages! Its theological treatment more than makes up for Thompson's inadequacy; they are good companions. An edited version (320pp) of both the Jeremiah and Lamentations commentaries is published in CrossC (2000) [*JSOT* 94 (2001)].

★ Dearman, J. Andrew. [*M*], *Jeremiah, Lamentations* (NIVAC) 2002. Dearman offers a nearly 500-page exposition which will aid pastors, but students will have less use for it. His past work has been somewhat critical. See also Lamentations, and his Hosea work. [*RTR* 1/96].

★ **Fretheim, Terence E.** ‡ (S&H) 2002. An expensive work ($65) of nearly 700pp with CD-ROM that focuses helpfully on theological exposition. If you balk at the price and want another (critical) theological treatment, buy Brueggemann. If you want a conservative substitute, buy Martens. Fretheim is a veteran writer of commentaries, having already done Genesis, Exodus, and Kings in other series. [*Interp* 4/04; *CBQ* 1/05; *CJ* 4/06].

★ **Huey, F.B.** *Jeremiah, Lamentations* (NAC) 1993. This is the first OT volume in the NAC series and runs to 512pp. It received fairly generous reviews [*CBQ* 7/95; *Them* 5/95]. Lawson Younger notes that "Huey's commentary on Jeremiah is stronger than his commentary on Lamentations." I am less enthusiastic about this recommendation than most, especially for students, because of depth of treatment and my sense that this work is already becoming dated. [*VT* 46.3; *HebStud* 1995].

★ **Lundbom, Jack R.** [*M*], (AB) 3 Vols., 1999–2004. This three-vol. set replaces Bright and follows the recent AB pattern of exhaustive, detailed exegesis. It is a magnificent achievement, with attention given not only to modern exegesis but also to the long history of interpretation. (Calvin is cited more than Carroll.) Lundbom—not to be confused with Swedish OT scholar Lindblom—must be consulted by students, but many pastors will find less use for it. Though well-written and accessible, the sheer detail (2207pp) will overwhelm many. The more scholarly pastor, however, will be delighted to own the set. The key contribution made by this commentary is its attention to textual criticism (usually supporting the MT) and rhetorical questions (vol 23A, pp.68–85)—the latter a lively topic in current scholarly discussion of the prophets. His critical approach to Jeremiah is not nearly as skeptical as some others' (e.g., Carroll), and he finds trustworthy biographical information. He emphasizes the unity, coherence, and literary artistry in the final form of the text, rejecting scholarly attempts to get "behind the text" and discover many layers or voices. Along with Hill on Malachi, this is one of the more conservative contributions to AB, but don't call it evangelical. See Holladay below. If you are not ready to handle this heavyweight—academically or financially—and you don't mind a mildly to moderately critical work, try Allen or Stulman (the more synchronic of the two). [*Interp* 7/01, 10/05; *CBQ* 4/01, 7/05, 7/06; *CurTM* 10/04; *JTS* 10/07; *JBL* Sum 05; *JSOT-BL* 2005; *VT* 56.2; *RelSRev* 1/05, 7/05; *RBL*; *ExpTim* 8/06].

★ **Thompson, J.A.** (NICOT) 1979. Most conservative pastors have used this as their first resource. Something of an evangelical standard, but too thin in its theological discussion. There are so many allusions to and even citations of Jeremiah in the NT which Thompson misses. There is an excellent introduction, which is now rather dated (130pp), and a fine treatment of historical data. In the past, both Longman and Stuart have said Thompson is the best conservative work. See Scalise below. [*TJ* Fall 81; *JBL* 101.4 (1982); *JETS* 9/81].

✧ ✧ ✧ ✧ ✧ ✧

☆ **Allen, Leslie C.** ‡ (OTL) 2008. I am happy to welcome this excellent addition to OTL, replacing a volume by Carroll which was both influential and rather out of sympathy with the text (in the sense of finding little coherence, little reliable historical information about Jeremiah, and regarding large portions of text as later redactions). Allen teaches at Fuller but is more critical than some might guess; he sometimes finds less material belonging to the prophet than, say, Holladay (Allen, 509–10). That said, he is also more conservative theologically than the usual OTL contributor. Though majoring on the final form, he is also more interested in literary development (diachrony) than a lot of younger OT scholars these days. Were there more theology here, it might have been a recommended purchase for students; this deficiency makes the book less useful for the pastor's study. As expected from Allen, he deals a good bit with textual issues (MT vs. LXX traditions). Strong points of this volume include its attention to the rhetorical structure and style of the prophecy and a learned, up-to-date handling of the main historical, linguistic, and form-critical questions. One also appreciates the discussion of "the purposeful trajectory of overriding grace that stretches over the book like a rainbow" (p.17). Allen is a veteran commentator, having written on Chronicles, Psalms, Ezekiel and a few Minor Prophets. [*JETS* 6/10; *Interp* 1/10; *JSOT-BL* 2010; *VT* 60.2; *Anvil* 26.3–4].

F Arnold, William. (Apollos).

✓ Boadt, Lawrence. ‡ (OTM) 2 Vols., 1982. Also treats Nahum, Habakkuk, and Zephaniah. This Catholic is highly respected for his work in the prophets and is a gracious, conservatively critical scholar.

☆ Bracke, John M. ‡ *Jeremiah 1–29* (WestBC) 2000; *Jeremiah 30–52 and Lamentations* (WestBC) 2000. I value this set especially for its treatment of Lamentations (60 out of 470pp). Bracke follows Brueggemann in three respects: (1) he teaches at Eden Seminary, where Brueggemann formerly was on faculty, (2) he has written here a fine theological exposition of Jeremiah, and (3) he takes more of a canonical approach. See Lamentations below. [*OTA* 10/00; *JSOT* 94 (2001)].

✓ **Bright, John.** ‡ (AB) 1965. Years ago this was an especially good treatment of the historical background, offering some theology and a few homiletical hints. Bright was one of the more conservative AB volumes and more in line with the series' original aims. A frustration for readers is that the author rearranged the text according to chronological sequence. This aged commentary is now replaced by Lundbom.

F Brown, Michael. (EBCR). This volume will contain Jeremiah to Ezekiel.

☆ **Brueggemann, Walter.** ‡ (ITC) 2 Vols., 1988–91, rev. 1998. A valuable theological work from a critical standpoint. Brueggemann focuses less on historical criticism and more on the message of the "final form" of the text (about 540pp). See his other commentaries on Genesis, Exodus, Samuel, and Isaiah. [*CRBR* 1993; *BL* 1990, 1993; *CBQ* 7/91; *RTR* 1/90 and 9/94; *BSac* 7/92; *HebStud* 1990, 1993]. This has been republished (with a very slight update) in a more convenient one-vol. format by Eerdmans:

A Commentary on Jeremiah: Exile and Homecoming (1998). Those preferring a more conservative or more homiletic exposition could purchase Ryken. [*JETS* 12/99; *ExpTim* 10/98; *CBQ* 4/00; *SwJT* Fall 98; *HebStud* 1999; *RBL*]. Yet two more Brueggemann works are his collected essays: *Like Fire in the Bones: Listening for the Prophetic Word in Jeremiah*, 2006 [*CBQ* 7/07; *JR* 7/08; *EuroJTh* 18.2], and his Cambridge volume on *The Theology of the Book of Jeremiah*, 2007 [*Interp* 7/08; *JR* 4/08; *CBQ* 7/08; *EuroJTh* 18.1].

✓ **Carroll, Robert P.** ‡ (retired OTL) 1986. A huge tome of almost 900pp. After such a long stretch of time when no scholarly commentaries appeared except NICOT, we rapidly received Carroll, Holladay, Jones, WBC, McKane, and three volumes of Lundbom! Carroll is quite critical, denigrating any approach which tries to make sense out of the book's historical aspects and to form a portrait of the man Jeremiah and his life. (In his view, that portrait is irretrievable because redactors have completely reworked the traditions for a subsequent generation.) He also applies some of the heavier ideological criticism in OT scholarship. Advanced students have to take account of Carroll as "the most influential [Jeremiah] interpreter of our generation" (Brueggemann [*CBR* 6/10]), but this is not for pastors. See Carroll under "Prophets & Prophetic Literature" above. This work had a better reception in the UK than in the USA, and Sheffield Phoenix reissued a two-vol. edition in 2006. For Carroll's later, changed views regarding Jeremiah, see his essays in Diamond/O'Connor/Stulman. Note the OTL replacement volume by Allen above. [*CBQ* 7/91; *TJ*, Fall 87; *JETS* 9/88; *Interp* 7/88 (Brueggemann); *JSOT* 45; *BibInt* 17 (2009)].

✓ **Clements, R.E.** ‡ (I) 1988. Rather brief on such a big, complex book—the longest book in the Bible. Pursues the aims of the series well enough. Clements is a much-respected, moderately critical British scholar, now retired after teaching at Cambridge and London. This book, Fretheim, Brueggemann, and Bracke would be considered the leading expositions from the critical camp. [*JETS* 6/92; *CBQ* 4/91; *CRBR* 1990].

✓ **Craigie, Peter C., Page H. Kelley, and Joel F. Drinkard, Jr.** [*M*], *Jeremiah 1–25* (WBC) 1991. This work was begun by Craigie, but had to be completed by the others when he died in a car accident (†1985). They are mainly responsible for the commentary, not Craigie. It covers the first 25 chapters in 375pp. The approach here includes careful textual criticism (using the DSS and expressing confidence in the MT), conservative form-criticism, and thorough research in the vast literature. The pastor wanting another careful exegetical commentary will find this less rigorous than either Lundbom or Holladay, but also less liberal (than Holladay) and less expensive. [*CBQ* 7/93; *VT* 46.2; *BSac* 7/93]. See Keown below.

Davidson, Robert. ‡ (DSB) 2 Vols., 1983–85. Covers Lamentations as well (in 45pp). Because this is a popularly-styled and devotional commentary, he does not go much into issues of criticism. More useful than many other liberal works on this book. From the critical angle you may prefer the fuller ITC or WestBC.

De Waard, Jan. *A Handbook on Jeremiah*, 2003. For textual criticism.

✓ Diamond, A.R.P., K.M. O'Connor, and L. Stulman (eds). ‡ *Troubling Jeremiah*, 1999. Cutting-edge scholarship at the time.

✓ Feinberg, Charles L. (EBC) 1986. Published separately in pb as well. Reformed folks should not despise this commentary because it is Dispensational. Feinberg was an able Hebraist. There is some profit in consulting this or having this on your shelf. [*JBL* 103.4 (1984)]. See Brown above for the EBCR replacement.

☆   Guest, John. (WCC) 1988. Covers Lamentations too. Old Testament specialists will not regard this volume as stellar Bible interpretation, but it is thoughtful and better than many others in the series.

F   Halpern, Baruch. ‡ (NCBC).

☆   Harrison, R.K. (TOTC) 1973. A good, older treatment which is even more valuable because it covers Lamentations as well. Pastors and students could add this to their library for its coverage, evangelical stance, and its dependable scholarship in brief compass (240pp). [*EvQ* 7/74].

☆   **Holladay, William.** ‡ (Herm) 2 Vols., 1986–89. Years ago, before Lundbom was complete, I regarded this two-vol. work as the best exegetical, historical-critical commentary available. Holladay has been among the foremost Jeremianic scholars in America. He uses a lot of form criticism, but takes a more conservative approach than Carroll or McKane. "In a magisterial effort, he sought to push to its furthest reach the direct and concrete connection between text and specific historical location" (Brueggemann). The scholarly pastor, who desires to build a first-class exegetical library, might save up to buy this technical and expensive set. Among reviews note especially Williamson's [*VT* 7/93] and Brueggemann's critiques [*Interp* 42 (1988)]. [*Biblica* 69.3 (1988); *SJT* 89.1, 93.1; *JETS* 9/88 and 9/92; *JSOT* 45 (1989); *JBL* 107.4 (1988); *CBQ* 10/91; *ExpTim* 6/90; *HebStud* 1991]. A brief, more accessible interpretation from Holladay is *Jeremiah: A Fresh Reading*, 1990.

✓   **Jones, Douglas Rawlinson.** ‡ (NCB) 1992. A work of 560pp, it seems to be fairly typical of the series: solid but unexciting phrase by phrase exegesis. Jones does not appear to have interacted as much with the other major works at the time. On the plus side, it is less focused on diachronic issues and treats the text with more respect than some other commentators. [*JBL* 113.2 (1994); *VT* 7/96].

F   Kaiser, Walter C. (EEC).

✓   Keil, Carl F. (KD) ET 1874.

✓   **Keown, Gerald L., Pamela J. Scalise, and Thomas G. Smothers.** [𝔐], *Jeremiah 26–52* (WBC) 1995. This volume completes the WBC set (see Craigie above). I note the publisher's strange decision to use six scholars on this prophecy, with not one of them contributing to both volumes. Deadlines! A bit uneven in quality and thoroughness, this set is still useful to students. [*SwJT* Fall 98; *RelSRev* 10/98].

☆   Kidner, Derek. *The Message of Jeremiah: Against Wind and Tide* (BST) 1987. A good help to preachers and anyone else who wants to understand this book. One only wishes the exposition were more in-depth—176pp on the longest book of the Bible is short indeed. [*Evangel* Sum 88].

✓   **King, Philip J.** *Jeremiah: An Archeological Companion*, 1993. This is an excellent book on its topic. [*Them* 1/95; *HebStud* 1995; *CRBR* 1990, 1995].

    Laetsch, Theodore. 1952. This reverent, Lutheran, expositional commentary directly serves the preacher, and 20 years ago I made this a recommended purchase. Communicates the painful message of this book; theology is Laetsch's main thrust. Covers Lamentations too (30 of 412pp). [*Interp* 7/53].

☆   **Longman, Tremper.** *Jeremiah, Lamentations* (NIBC) 2008. A handy (400-page), inexpensive, and accessible evangelical commentary with a healthy mix of both exegesis and exposition. Here Longman moves away from his area of specialization: wisdom literature. [*CBQ* 4/09 (Lundbom); *RelSRev* 3/08; *JETS* 3/09; *JSOT-BL* 2009; *RTR* 4/09; *RevExp* Sum 09].

✓   **McConville, J. Gordon.** *Judgment and Promise*, 1993. An excellent work which points to the important theological relationship between Deuteronomy and Jeremiah and discusses it from the conservative angle. Students, look this up! [*JSS* Aut 96; *CBQ* 10/94; *Them* 1/95; *SBET* Spr 94, Spr 97].

✓ **McKane, William P.** ‡ (ICC–new series) 2 Vols., 1986–96. Meticulous textual and philological work and very critical. As one would expect, McKane has modeled his commentary after the earlier ICC volumes. If anything, McKane has limited himself to philological and syntactical concerns even more than the old series. Personally, I often find it nigh-impenetrable. McKane continues to believe the old theory that prophecies of deliverance and restoration must be dated to the post-exilic period. Redaction-critical concerns dominate the discussion (note his idea of a "rolling corpus"), and there is little theological reflection. This is only for specialists, but students should try to consult it for in-depth exegetical work. [*Them* 4/88; *JETS* 9/88; *JBL* 107.1; *Interp* 7/88 (Brueggemann); *JSOT* 45; *EvQ* 7/99; *JSS* Aut 98; *JTS* 4/99 (Carroll); *BL* 1987, 1997; *HebStud* 1998; *RelSRev* 1/98].

Mackay, John L. (Mentor) 2 Vols., 2004. The theological approach of Mackay is conservative and Reformed. He provides a very full (over 1100pp), accessible exegesis and exposition for pastors. The aim is not so much to provide an academic commentary, though he is clearly a diligent, practiced student of God's word.

McKeating, Henry. ‡ (Epworth) 1999. For preachers. [*Anvil* 18.4 (McConville)].

☆ **Martens, Elmer A.** (BCBC) 1986. Valuable for its exposition. This work is written on the popular level (327pp), and deserves to be better known among preachers than it is. The same could be said for his fine OT Theology, *God's Design* (2nd ed 1994). Martens is extremely well read in the field and astute theologically. See also Walker below. [*WTJ* Spr 89; *JETS* 3/91].

✓ **Miller, Patrick D.** ‡ (NewIB) 2001. This is of special interest because Miller well knows Deuteronomy, the theological mate to Jeremiah. The commentary here is strong, but I wish that the longest book of the Bible had been allocated more than 370pp in the series—Ezekiel by comparison gets over 500pp. So much space is taken up by printing both the full NRSV and NIV text. Miller probes questions of contemporary application from the liberal angle.

Morgan, G. Campbell. *Studies in the Prophecy of Jeremiah*, 1931. A well known exposition from one of the 20th century's greatest preachers, reprinted in 1963 and 1982. I do not know whether this is in print.

Nägelsbach, C.W. (Lange) ET 1871. Covers both Jeremiah and Lamentations.

Newman, Barclay M., and Philip C. Stine. (UBS) 2004. This "Handbook" is 1052pp.

Nicholson, E.W. ‡ (CBC) 2 Vols., 1973–75. More important for scholars is his *Preaching to the Exiles: A Study of the Prose Tradition in the Book of Jeremiah* (1970), which sees the prophecy as being produced by Deuteronomic preachers who reworked Jeremianic traditions (the prose sections in particular) to address the post-exilic situation. A similar diachronic theory stands behind a couple other well-known commentaries: McKane and Clements.

O'Connor, Kathleen M. *The Confessions of Jeremiah: Their Interpretation and Role in Chapter 1–25*, 1988. Published about the same time was the similarly strong dissertation by A.R. Diamond, *The Confessions of Jeremiah in Context*, 1987.

F Oosterhoff, Ben J., and Erik Peels. ‡ (HCOT).

Orelli, H.C. von. 1887 (German original). This exposition, reprinted by Klock & Klock, is now digitalized by Google.

✓ Peake, A.S. ‡ (Century Bible) 1910–12. Perhaps still worth consulting.

☆ Ryken, Philip. *Jeremiah and Lamentations* (PTW) 2000. The first volume in an OT set complementing R. Kent Hughes' expositions on the NT, this is an excellent book to get one thinking homiletically. It is also a tome of approx. 800pp. Ryken has a DPhil from Oxford, is a gifted preacher, and pastored Tenth Presbyterian in Philadelphia. See also his more recent work on Exodus in the same series.

F   Scalise, Pamela J. (NICOT replacement).

✓   Skinner, John. ‡ *Prophecy and Religion*, 1922. A seminal work, long consulted by scholars. One could say with Davies [*BSB* 6/03] that Skinner "treats the book as the spiritual biography of Jeremiah." [*ExpTim* 9/78].

✓   Smith, G.A. ‡ 1929.

Stedman, Ray C. *Expository Studies in Jeremiah*, 1976. About 250pp of basic sermon material broken down into 14 studies.

☆   **Stulman, Louis.** ‡ (AOTC) 2005. The author did his doctoral work on the prose sermons in Jeremiah and here provides an accessible exegesis which is interested in finding literary structure (in what seems a disorganized book) and theological meaning. It is well-grounded in scholarship, though it wears its learning lightly, and explains the text instead of scholars' disagreements about Jeremiah. Stulman's focus is certainly upon the final-form of the text. Students should note his discussion of "macro-units" of text and their contribution to overall coherence in the book. Stulman is a more conservative critic (cf. Allen), and "mediating" [*M*] may be more accurate than "critical." [*CBQ* 1/06; *JETS* 3/06; *Interp* 1/06; *JSOT-BL* 2006; *BibInt* 15.1; *ExpTim* 2/06; *RBL*; *CJ* 1/07; *JHebS*; *HBT* 29.1 (Dearman)].

F   Vanhoozer, Kevin. (Brazos). To be one of the more conservative books in the series.

F   Viviano, Pauline A. ‡ *Jeremiah and Lamentations* (BO).

☆   Walker, Larry L., and Elmer A. Martens. *Isaiah, Jeremiah, Lamentations* (CorBC) 2005. I have not yet had opportunity to use this volume. Martens contributes the commentary on Jeremiah & Lamentations. Knowing his excellent, somewhat fuller BCBC from years ago (see Martens above), I expect the second half of this CorBC is very strong and worth buying.

F   Weiss, Richard D. ‡ (FOTL).

✓   Wenthe, Dean O. (ed). *Jeremiah, Lamentations* (ACCS) 2009.

NOTES: (1) C. S. Rodd's "Which Is the Best Commentary? VI. Jeremiah," ExpTim, 3/87. (2) Claire E. Carroll, "Another Dodecade: A Dialectic Model of the Decentred Universe of Jeremiah Studies 1996–2008," *CBR* 8.2 (2010): 162–82. (3) Robert Carroll has two reviews of Jeremiah studies in *CurBS* (vol. 4, pp.115–59, and vol. 8, pp.18–58), which are helpfully collected in Alan J. Hauser (ed), *Recent Research on the Major Prophets* (Sheffield: Sheffield Phoenix, 2008); Carroll's are supplemented by a sagacious review-essay by A.R.P. Diamond.

LAMENTATIONS

★   Calvin, John. (GS) 1563. A deeply moving set of lectures, as the Reformer reflects on both the pathos of the literature and its witness to the sufferings of God's people and ultimately to Christ who suffered for them. Quite lengthy (250pp).

★   Dearman, J. Andrew. [*M*], *Jeremiah/Lamentations* (NIVAC) 2002. One of the very best resources available to the pastor preaching on Lamentations. While students may be instructed by Dearman's engagement with other scholarly views and interpretations, the main help of this commentary is its suggestive guidance for proclamation. Dearman, a more conservative PCUSA minister, used to teach at Austin Seminary. See his Hosea work. [*CTJ* 4/04].

★   **Dobbs-Allsopp, F.W.** ‡ (I) 2002. Doubtless the best theological exposition from the critical camp for the preacher. But students are mistaken to think this slim volume is useful only for theological reflection. Dobbs-Allsopp has been publishing on Lamentations for about 20 years and, even as a relatively young man, is regarded as a world authority on this literature and the city-lament genre. The author would be classed as moderately critical. One caveat for evangelicals: his liberal theology, seemingly offended by the doctrines of God's wrath and judgment, leads him to some offensive conclusions about the portrait of God in this book. [*CTJ* 4/04; *CBQ* 4/03; *Interp* 1/03; *HBT* 12/02; *JSOT* 27.5; *BBR* 14.2; *BSac* 4/05; *SwJT* Fall 04; *RelSRev* 10/06].

★ Garrett, Duane, and **Paul House.** *Song of Songs, Lamentations* (WBC) 2004. See under Song of Songs. House contributes the commentary on Lamentations in this volume, and I class it as better than Garrett's work. (House seems more dependable as a guide toward exposition.) This is, without question, the most thorough and up-to-date evangelical commentary on this portion of Scripture. Students and pastors who work in the Hebrew will be glad to have it. Because there has been a veritable explosion of scholarship on Lamentations in recent years, the WBC's bibliographical help alone is worth the price of the book. The other key commentaries for students are: Berlin (from whom House draws much), Hillers, Renkema, Westermann, and Gordis. [*JETS* 9/05; *Interp* 7/05; *ExpTim* 9/09].

★ **Provan, Iain W.** [𝓜], (NCB) 1991. This 160-page work received good reviews. Provan has become more conservative since his doctorate days and now teaches at Regent College, Vancouver. Though trained thoroughly in a more diachronic approach, Provan is interested in synchronic literary readings. Many pastors will find the less expensive Provan more than adequate for their library. Regrettably, it has become difficult to obtain after Eerdmans dropped the series. If you cannot find a copy of Provan and love deep scholarship, consider buying Berlin, Bergant, Hillers, or Westermann. [*VT* 4/95; *JETS* 6/95; *BSac* 10/92].

★ Ryken, Philip. *Jeremiah and Lamentations* (PTW) 2000. See Jeremiah above.

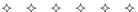

✓ **Albrektson, B.** ‡ *Studies in the Text and Theology of the Book of Lamentations*, 1963. This work moved the scholarly discussion farther along, especially with his critique of Gottwald and his counter-proposals regarding the theology of the book. Albrektson construes Lamentations as presenting a painful tension between two teachings: breaking covenant with God brings retribution (Deuteronomistic theology) and belief in God's promises of protection for Jerusalem (the Zion theology of the psalmists).

F Bailey, Wilma. ‡ (BCBC).

✓ **Bergant, Dianne.** ‡ (AOTC) 2003. This scholar, who teaches at Catholic Theological Union in Chicago, has written much on OT poetry. E.g. see her work on Song of Songs. If Provan proves difficult to find, and you want to save money, buy this 144-page book instead of Berlin. Bergant's writing is very clear, her exegesis is laudably careful, and she cares about the theology of the book. [*CBQ* 4/04; *JETS* 9/04; *Interp* 10/04; *JSOT* 28.5].

✓ **Berlin, Adele.** ‡ (OTL) 2002. This superb scholarly commentary on the Hebrew text pays attention to rhetorical and poetic features—more on metaphor and imagery than on parallelism, the building and declining acrostic patterns, and structure. Berlin aims to keep the forest, not just the trees, in view. Students must take account of her findings, but most pastors won't be able to make full use of the scholarship here (e.g., discussion of the genre "Jerusalem lament" here and in Psalms 74, 79, 102, 137, etc). Theologically, this Jewish author is keenly interested in the faith community's response to an evil catastrophe; her focus is more on the human side than on the divine and how this book's heart-cry is also divine revelation. In other words, she is less helpful in addressing the preacher's concern as to what God is saying in Lamentations. There is some feminist critique and less interest in historical criticism (e.g., form criticism), textual criticism, and philology. Berlin offers her own translation. The 135-page volume was expensive as a hb, but is now available in pb for $30. [*CTJ* 4/04; *CBQ* 10/03; *Interp* 10/03; *ExpTim* 8/03; *HBT* 12/02; *JSOT* 28.5; *BBR* 14.2; *BSac* 1/05; *CurTM* 10/05; *RBL*].

☆ Bracke, John M. ‡ *Jeremiah 30–52 and Lamentations* (WestBC) 2000. Gives serious attention to the book (60pp). This is to be considered, from a critical standpoint, one of the better theological expositions for pastors.

☆ Brooks, Richard. *Great is Your Faithfulness* (WCS) 1989. This Reformed exposition is quite full (160pp) for its series and has a lot of heart.

☆ Davidson, Robert. ‡ *Jeremiah, Volume 2, and Lamentations* (DSB) 1985. See under Jeremiah.

☆ Ellison, H.L. (EBC) 1986. A highly respected Jewish Christian scholar who for many years taught at London Bible College, Cambridge University, and Moorlands Bible College. Ellison was a "moderating" influence on evangelical OT scholarship years ago. His work here deserves praise and will aid the pastor.

F Ferris, Paul. (EBCR). I expect this should be quite good. See his dissertation on *The Genre of Communal Lament in the Bible and the Ancient Near East*, 1992.

✓ **Gerstenberger, E.S.** ‡ *Psalms, Part 2, and Lamentations* (FOTL) 2001. Advanced students may consult this form-critical treatment.

✓ **Gordis, Robert.** ‡ 1954, rev. 1974. See under Song of Songs. There is also an earlier two-part commentary on Lamentations in the *Jewish Quarterly Review*, 1967–68, and that was published in 1968 as a monograph. Then that work was thoroughly revised and expanded for the 1974 commentary. This is one of the most valuable older studies of Lamentations' Hebrew text.

✓ Gottwald, N.K. ‡ *Studies in the Book of Lamentations*, 1959, rev. 1962.

F Greenstein, Edward. ‡ (JPS).

Guest, John. (WCC) 1988. See under Jeremiah.

Habel, Norman C. [*M*], (Concordia Commentary) 1968. Safe to ignore; too brief to count.

☆ Harrison, R.K. (TOTC) 1973. See Jeremiah above.

☆ **Hillers, Delbert R.** ‡ (AB) 1972, rev. 1992. An excellent commentary with careful exegesis (fairly mild in its criticism), offering help with the Hebrew text, and some good theological insights. This AB almost doubled in size from the first edition. Hillers was long the best scholarly work on this book of the Bible in English—for German readers there has been incredible wealth: Kraus, Plöger, Rudolph, Weiser, Wiesmann, and Westermann. Years ago, Longman and Stuart agreed that Hillers' commentary had no serious rivals, but now we have a good number of excellent books. The student and the more academically-oriented pastor will best appreciate this work; the average pastor would have plenty with House, Provan, and Ryken.

F Hubbard, Robert. (NICOT).

☆ **Huey, F.B.** (NAC) 1993. See under Jeremiah. This volume is not as recommended for interpreting Lamentations.

F Joyce, Paul. ‡ (Blackwell).

Kaiser, Walter. *A Biblical Approach to Suffering: A Study of Lamentations*, 1982. Written with the pastor's needs in mind, but probably o/p now.

✓ Keil, Carl F. (KD) ET 1874.

✓ Knight, G.A.F. ‡ (Torch Bible Commentary) 1955.

Laetsch, Theodore. 1952. Bound together with the Jeremiah commentary. Written for pastors.

✓ Lee, Nancy C., and Carleen Mandolfo (eds). ‡ *Lamentations in Ancient and Contemporary Cultural Contexts*, 2008. This book of essays, not commentary, reveals the shape of up-to-date Lamentations scholarship, and is especially welcome because Lamentations has been a growth industry for the last 20 years. But there is more, as the volume includes lengthy discussions of the lament genre and its use in various contexts. [*RBL*; *JSOT-BL* 2009; *VT* 59.4; *ExpTim* 9/10].

✓ Linafelt, Tod. ‡ *Surviving Lamentations: Catastrophe, Lament and Protest in the Afterlife of a Biblical Book*, 2000. [*ThTo* 1/01; *Interp* 7/01; *CBQ* 1/01; *JBL* Win 01].

☆ **Longman, Tremper.** *Jeremiah, Lamentations* (NIBC) 2008. See under Jeremiah.

☆ Mackay, John L. (Mentor) 2008. This 240-page exposition was preceded by a two-vol. set on Jeremiah.

✓ Martin-Achard, R., and S. Paul Re'emi. ‡ *Amos and Lamentations* (ITC) 1984. Not particularly remarkable, but was once worth consulting because of the paucity of works.

✓ Middlemas, Jill. ‡ *The Troubles of Templeless Judah*, 2005. This Oxford imprint has nearly 60pp (pp.171–228) treating Lamentations and is worth consulting. [*VT* 57.1].

Nägelsbach, C.W. (Lange) ET 1871.

✓ **O'Connor, Kathleen M.** ‡ (NewIB) 2001. Added now to this is an applicatory exposition published by Orbis: *Lamentations and the Tears of the World*, 2002 [*BibInt* 13.2]. O'Connor is an able, learned scholar and an excellent writer.

F Parry, Robin A. (THC) 2010. Promised as a full theological commentary of 280pp with a Christological emphasis.

Peake, A.S. ‡ 1912. Bound with Jeremiah.

F Queen-Sutherland, Kandy. ‡ (S&H). See under Ruth.

✓ **Renkema, Johan.** ‡ (HCOT) ET 1998. Translated from the Dutch, this is a stunningly comprehensive work of 641pp. Makes compelling arguments for the unity of the book. Despite the series title, this is more a literary than an historical commentary. Renkema certainly makes "a strong contribution to the burgeoning scholarship on the Book of Lamentations" (*CBQ*). [*JSOT* 84; *Biblica* 81.2; *CBQ* 4/00; *OTA* 2/00; *JBL* Spr 01; *VT* 51.3].

✓ **Reyburn, William D.** (UBS) 1992. Well deserves to be consulted, though some of the lengthy discussion meant to help translators sift through appropriate terms in various target languages won't be relevant.

F Roberts, J.J.M. ‡ (Herm).

F Salters, Robert. ‡ (ICC). Preparing the way was an "OT Guides" volume on *Jonah and Lamentations* (1994).

F Viviano, Pauline A. ‡ *Jeremiah and Lamentations* (BO). Publication had been expected in 2009. The author is a Catholic teaching at Loyola University.

☆ Walker, Larry L., and Elmer A. Martens. *Isaiah, Jeremiah, Lamentations* (CorBC) 2005. See under Jeremiah.

☆ Webb, Barry G. *Five Festal Garments: Christian Reflections on the Song of Songs, Ruth, Lamentations, Ecclesiastes and Esther*, 2000. See under Ruth.

✓ Wenthe, Dean O. (ed). *Jeremiah, Lamentations* (ACCS) 2009.

✓ **Westermann, Claus.** ‡ *Lamentations: Issues and Interpretation*, 1990, ET 1994. Includes over 100pp of commentary. The author experienced suffering in WW II, and this prepared him to reflect profoundly on the place, meaning, and expression of suffering in the life of God's people. Perhaps the most outstanding and valuable section of Westermann is on the history of interpretation. This volume is called by one reviewer "a *sine qua non* of Lamentations study." It will long be useful to serious researchers. [*ExpTim* 3/95; *Them* 1/96; *JSS* Spr 96].

NOTE: C.W. Miller, "The Book of Lamentations in Recent Research," *CBR* 1.1 (2002): 9–29.

—⟐—

EZEKIEL

★ **Block, Daniel**. (NICOT) 2 Vols., 1997–98. Like Oswalt on Isaiah in the same series, this is a massive two-vol. work (over 1700pp). Block's commentary is painstakingly exegetical, includes some mild form criticism, rhetorical criticism, and is mainly concerned with the final form of the text (à la Greenberg). This is an outstanding work: comprehensive in scope, lucid, quick to discuss both biblical and extra-biblical parallels, structural patterns, grammar, and translation issues. The organization of the volumes is similar to BKAT or WBC, which some believe makes them easier to consult: after his 60-page introduction Block deals with each section of text in (a) translation; (b) nature and design; (c) verse by verse exegesis; and (d) theological implications. Though I would never want to be without my Zimmerli and Greenberg sets, this is the best pick for the studious evangelical pastor. The manuscript was given to Eerdmans in early 1994. *Personal disclosure: Block was the external examiner for my dissertation.* [*CBQ* 4/99, 10/99; *Biblica* 80.1; *Interp* 7/99; *JETS* 12/99; *WTJ* Spr 99; *SwJT* Fall 00, Sum 01; *BSac* 10/98, 7/99; *JSOT-BL* 1998, 1999; *JSOT* 78 (throw away); *RelSRev* 10/99].

★ **Duguid, Iain M.** (NIVAC) 1999. This 550-page exposition builds upon his doctoral research at Cambridge: *Ezekiel and the Leaders of Israel* (Brill, 1994). He used to teach at Westminster Seminary California and is now at Grove City College. I like this professor's biblical-theological approach which is sensitive to redemptive history themes. Though he was a young scholar when he wrote this volume, there is mature reflection, as seen in the lengthy "Authors Cited" index which includes Church Fathers and Puritans alongside today's OT scholars. This book rivals Stuart for a place on the pastor's shelf; Duguid knows the literature better and is more up-to-date. I warmly commend Duguid's work—buy it prior to Stuart and Wright—which is aimed at meeting the inadequacy he perceives in Block's and Greenberg's sets (see his review of Block in *WTJ* Spr 99). Students will find savvy exegesis here. By the way, people ask me how to pronounce his name; it is "Do-good."

★ Stuart, Douglas. (WCC) 1989. There is more substance to this volume than one normally finds in the series and it is a good theological guide. Stuart is one of the few full-time biblical scholars who has written for the WCC; he pastors a church besides being Professor of OT at Gordon-Conwell Seminary. This is an excellent commentary for pastors and teachers. I only wish he—and other commentators as well—had wrestled more with the constant refrain, "you/they shall know that I am Yahweh," which S.R. Driver once called "the keynote of Ezek.'s prophecies." (See Zimmerli below.)

★ Wright, Christopher J.H. (BST) 2001. This is a fine pb volume for preachers which could spark many sermons. Wright has long loved the book of Ezekiel and Ezekiel's theology (see his editor's column in *Them* 5/94), and it shows in his exposition here (368pp). As a BST work it contains a pleasing amount of exegesis; some others in the series do not. One quibble: I question his proposal that Ezekiel teaches the salvation of the nations, even while I love his passion for missions reflected in his best-known book, *The Mission of God* (2006), a most impressive piece of work.

[*JSOT* 99 (2002); *Chm* Win 02; *Them* Sum 05; *Anvil* 19.4, 20.4 (Renz)]. The other commentary from Wright's pen is the NIBC on Deuteronomy.

✧　✧　✧　✧　✧　✧

✓　Alexander, Ralph H. (EBC) 1986. Useful for its evangelical viewpoint. Has been praised, but it seems to lack depth, especially in light of publications since 1986. Premillennial in its interpretation of the latter chapters.

F　Alexander, Ralph H. (EBCR).

☆　**Allen, Leslie C.** [*M*], *Ezekiel 20–48* (WBC) 1990; *Ezekiel 1–19* (WBC) 1994. The initial volume picked up where Brownlee left off and did a competent job. This is quite valuable as a reference tool because of its strong scholarship and close working with the Hebrew. He states on pp.xix-xx that he carves out a niche for himself between practitioners of traditional historical critical methods, especially form-criticism (Zimmerli), and those using a synchronic approach on the final form of the text (Greenberg). Allen does not often relate Ezekiel's message to the NT. Consistent evangelicals will especially disagree with his treatment of the prophecy's (alleged) multiple layers of redaction material. Also, I personally have greater confidence in the MT over against the LXX than Allen. The most recent volume replaces Brownlee and completes a useful reference set. Prior to NICOT, when I recommended purchasing Zimmerli, I wrote, "the frugal may prefer Allen to Zimmerli (Allen's two volumes together cost about the same as one Hermeneia volume)." [*CRBR* 1996; *WTJ* Fall 91; *VT* 1/93; *CBQ* 10/92; *SwJT* Spr 96; *JTS* 4/96; *JSOT* 74; *OTA* 2/96; *BSac* 1/96; *HebStud* 1993].

Blackwood, Andrew W. *Ezekiel: Prophecy of Hope*, 1965; *The Other Son of Man: Ezekiel/Jesus*, 1966. The sermonic material in these books gives good direction to the preacher. Blackwood was the longtime conservative professor of homiletics at Princeton Seminary.

✓　**Blenkinsopp, Joseph.** ‡ (I) 1990. A good expositional commentary which fulfills the aims of the series. Blenkinsopp is an expert on OT prophecy—see his AB volumes on Isaiah. This volume is not as good as Stuart, though, in explaining the message of the book. One minus, relative to Stuart, is his critical approach (closer to Zimmerli than to Greenberg). Another main drawback would be Blenkinsopp's general failure to discuss views which differ from his own. [*CBQ* 1/93; *Interp* 1/92; *JETS* 6/95; *CTJ* 4/91; *HebStud* 1991; *CRBR* 1992].

Bowen, Nancy. ‡ (AOTC) 2010. Announced as 328pp. From the advance praise of Smith-Christopher, this seems to be an atypical contribution to the series: "Bowen in particularly interesting as she weaves contemporary culture, trauma studies, and even insights of traditional 'Spirituals' where Ezekiel was a favored subject." I have yet to see this.

Briscoe, D. Stuart. *All Things Weird and Wonderful*, 1977. A popular, somewhat Dispensational exposition.

✓　Brownlee, William H. ‡ *Ezekiel 1–19* (WBC) 1986. Called a memorial volume. This noted professor at Claremont died before the commentary could be completed. Some good scholarship at points, but in the main a disappointment. Brownlee would fall into the more critically oriented wing of evangelicalism, and I mark his work as critical (‡) because he argues against a Babylonian locale for the prophecies and because of all the supposed redaction. Actually, one could argue that he is more eccentric than liberal. This volume is basically a museum piece already; see Allen. [*RTR* 9/87; *WTJ* Fall 88; *Them* 4/90; *EvQ* 1/89; *HebStud* 1987].

☆　Calvin, John. 1564. Covers only the first 20 chapters and is less valuable for that reason. The lectures were halted by serious illness, and the preface for its first publication was written by Beza after Calvin's death. Much fine theology here. The second volume published in the new Rutherford House translation project covers Ezekiel 1–12 and is out in both hb and pb (ET 1994).

☆ Clements, Ronald E. ‡ (WestBC) 1996. A moderately critical treatment of the message of the prophet. Clements gives attention to expositional and theological concerns rather than textual issues. He seeks to understand Ezekiel by using traditio-historical research; the volume is less helpful to preachers, for the author has concentrated almost wholly on what Ezekiel *meant* and not on what it *means* today. Clements certainly knows this book well. He undertook the translation of Zimmerli's first vol. [*Them* 2/99; *Interp* 1/98; *CBQ* 10/97; *SwJT* Sum 98; *BSac* 4/98; *HBT* 6/97].

✓ Cook, Stephen L., and Corrine L. Patton (eds). ‡ *Ezekiel's Hierarchical World*, 2004. Collected essays from SBL symposia. [*JSS* Spr 08; *VT* 57.3].

✓ **Cooke, G.A.** ‡ (ICC) 1937. Fairly conservative as a commentator on Ezekiel in the 1930s; in some respects Cooke's approach anticipates developments in Ezekiel studies 25 years later. "Cooke stands out for his particularly careful work on the text" (Zimmerli). The student will find this ICC volume easier to use than many others in the series.

✓ **Cooper, Lamar E.** (NAC) 1994. Well written from a Dispensational perspective, but not a profound work (NAC usually does not aim to be). Useful for understanding the Dispensational approach to this book. The Reformed pastor will find Duguid, Stuart, and Craigie to be more helpful and sounder theological guides. There are both scathing reviews [*JSOT* 12/95; *VT* 46.2] and fairer, kinder ones [*HebStud* 1995 (Boadt)].

☆ Craigie, Peter C. (DSB) 1983. Lots here for the pastor. Good scholarship underlies this more devotional exposition. Provides more background information than most others in the series. Longman once suggested you start with this commentary. I used to recommend it as a purchase. [*JBL* 104.4 (1985)].

✓ **Darr, Katheryn Pfisterer.** ‡ (NewIB) 2001. A pleasingly full interpretation (over 530pp) which students should consult. Darr is more conservative (like Greenberg and Block) in the way she treats the text and questions of compositional history. I have few quarrels with her approach—only where a reader-oriented emphasis seems overdone. Count this as one of the top five commentaries on the book at present.

✓ Davidson, Andrew B. [*M*], (Cambridge Bible) 1916. In my opinion, A.B. Davidson's volumes were the best in this old series. They are always lucid and reflect thorough scholarship. This particular book is still consulted. Davidson was partly responsible for the infusion of continental higher criticism into British scholarship.

✓ Davis, Ellen F. ‡ *Swallowing the Scroll*, 1989. Not a commentary, but a revised Yale dissertation. Davis, together with Brevard Childs' *Introduction to the Old Testament as Scripture*, pointed Ezekiel scholarship in a new direction by critiquing Zimmerli's approach of form-criticism. She argues that "the very thing for which we lack evidence is the fundamental stratum of orally conceived preaching" (p.17), and that students of the prophecy should recognize that Ezekiel was composed as a literary work and must be interpreted as such.

☆ **Eichrodt, Walther.** ‡ (OTL) ET 1970. A highly respected critical work. The volume focuses on his forte, biblical theology. Valuable for that theological discussion. The commentary is marred somewhat by textual emendations in deference to the shorter LXX (see his introduction, p.12). [*JBL* 86.3 (1967)].

Fairbairn, Patrick. 1851. Reprinted by Klock & Klock in 1989 and by Wakeman Trust in 2000, this warm exposition has long been a useful tool for pastors. The approach is strongly theological with stresses on covenant and Amillennial eschatology. Fairbairn was a pastor and seminary professor in the (Presbyterian) Free Church of Scotland. Today, pastors will view recent commentaries as more valuable, but if you are the type who loves Banner's "Geneva Series," consider this for purchase.

Feinberg, Charles L. 1969. From the Dispensational camp. This is an exposition rather than an exegesis, written with the layman in mind. Better, from that same theological camp, is Cooper.

✓ **Greenberg, Moshe.** ‡ *Ezekiel 1–20* (AB) 1983; *Ezekiel 21–37* (AB) 1997. This scintillating commentary far extends our knowledge of the prophecy. An excellent resource for its philological work and its sensitive, patient literary reading of Ezekiel. (See his explanation of his "holistic interpretation" in *Ezekiel 1–20*, pp.18–27.) Greenberg teases out interesting links with other biblical texts. He has respect for the Hebrew text and takes a conservative approach toward text criticism. This commentary and Zimmerli's are the most influential right now in academic circles— two of the very best modern critical commentaries written on any OT book. (Block writes, "No scholar has had a greater influence on my understanding of and approach to the book than Professor Greenberg.") This work does not provide any Christian interpretation of this prophecy for Greenberg's faith is Judaism; that is not to say there is no theology here. The publisher tells us to expect one more volume to complete this set (see Milgrom below). That will give us three AB three-vol. sets on the Major Prophets. [*JBL* 105.1; *Interp* 38, pp 210–17; *JETS* 12/99; *WTJ* Spr 99; *JSOT* 79; *JR* 7/99].

☆ Greenhill, William. (GS) 1645–67, 1995 reprint. As is typical of Puritan works, Greenhill is very large (859pp), and provides good food for thought, if one is willing to plow through a lot of pages. I was pleasantly surprised by Greenhill because I expected him to expound points of systematic theology suggested by the text (the typical Puritan approach) and provide less exegesis and interpretive comment than he does. He generally sticks with the text. I like Greenhill better the more I use him. [*CTJ* 11/95; *RTR* 9/95].

✓ **Hals, R.M.** ‡ (FOTL) 1989. One of the best volumes in this form-critical series and especially useful to specialists, few others. [*CRBR* 1991; *HebStud* 1991; *JETS* 9/92; *VT* 7/93; *Them* 10/91].

✓ Hengstenberg, E.W. ET 1869. Still valuable. Many pastors in past generations have found this volume helpful, but today it is hard to find a copy (o/p). Hengstenberg and Keil were stalwart conservatives in German OT scholarship, fighting the incoming tide of what was termed "destructive criticism" during the mid-19th century.

✓ **Hummel, Horace D.** (Concord) 2 Vols, 2005–07. This is a massive conservative Lutheran treatment of Ezekiel by a longtime seminary professor. There is exegesis of the Hebrew, but the theological (quite Christological) exposition of the prophet's message is accessible to laypeople. The first vol. runs over 600pp, and the seocnd is nearly 900. See my comments above on the series as a whole. [*EvQ* 10/07; *BSac* 7/06; *JETS* 3/09].

☆ Jenson, Robert W. [*M*], (Brazos) 2009. About 350pp of theological reflections by a famous retired systematic theologian (Lutheran), who has become a more conservative voice in mainline circles over the last couple decades at St. Olaf College and then at the Center of Theological Inquiry in Princeton. He is issuing appeals for the Church to return to a sturdy Nicene faith. Pannenberg has spoken of Jenson as "one of the most original and knowledgeable theologians of our time." Thankfully, this commentary on Ezekiel is more closely tied to the text than some other entries in the Brazos series. It is stimulating, widely-ranging, brainy stuff, but students should expect minimal interaction with OT scholarship. [*JTI* Spr 10; *JSOT-BL* 2010].

☆ **Joyce, Paul.** ‡ (T&T Clark) 2007. Ezekiel scholars expected a strong entry, considering the promise shown in his dissertation, *Divine Initiative and Human Response in Ezekiel* (1989) [*CRBR* 1990], and the leadership he has given to the SBL Ezekiel study group. Originally this commentary was scheduled for release in NCB, but that series is now defunct. Joyce teaches at Oxford and has given us a stellar, compact (somewhat selective), theologically oriented exegesis in about 300pp. One no longer has to pay $140 for the Continuum hb; a pb edition has been released ($30 on sale). I am glad for this because Joyce deserves wide usage. [*JSOT-BL* 2008; *ExpTim* 7/08; *JHebS* 2008 (Sweeney); *RBL* 11/08 (Tuell); *JTS* 4/10; *BibInt* 18.2; *CBQ* 7/09; *HebStud* 2009; *JSS* Aut 09 (Allen)]. I am glad to pass on Joyce's commendation of Duguid and Wright as well suited for "preachers seeking encouragement and help in relating Ezekiel to the present day" [*BSB* 12/06].

✓ Keil, Carl F. (KD) ET 1882. I have found this commentary to be rich and full (860pp). Excellent treatment of theological issues and careful (now very dated) work with the language.

✓ Levenson, Jon D. ‡ *Theology of the Restoration of Ezekiel 40–48*, 1976. An important scholarly monograph, one with origins as a Harvard dissertation, with much to teach the student. Conservatively critical.

Lind, Millard. [𝓜], (BCBC) 1996. The author as well as the series comes out of the historic Anabaptist tradition, and the peace-movement affiliation is reflected in the exegesis and application. Lind detheologizes Gog and understands it as a reference, not to ungodly powers who fiercely oppose the people and purposes of God, but as a "metaphor for greedy, militaristic politics" (p.317). A proper reading of Ezekiel 38–39 then leads us to fight the Strategic Defense Initiative of the Republicans (321). That is all very interesting, but I count it one example among several in the book where Lind seems to father his own convictions onto the OT prophet and mutes "the authentic voice of the OT." [*OTA* 10/97; *RelSRev* 1/98].

✓ Lust, J. (ed). ‡ *Ezekiel and his Book*, 1986. A much-cited collection of essays.

F Mackay, John L. (Mentor).

F Mein, Andrew. ‡ (Blackwell). This younger scholar earned his DPhil at Oxford and teaches at Westcott House in Cambridge. He is a recognized Ezekiel scholar and co-edits the monograph series, LHB/OTS.

F Milgrom, Jacob. ‡ *Ezekiel 38–48* (AYB). Greenberg, contributor of the AB volumes on Ezekiel 1–37, had a long illness and passed away in May 2010. Years back, Milgrom was announced as authoring the final volume. I have heard reports that Milgrom did complete this work prior to his death in June 2010 and that he understands the temple of Ezekiel 40–48 to have been patterned, surprisingly enough, on Delphi. Did he have any notes from Greenberg on these last 11 chapters, incorporating them in something of a joint publication?

✓ **Odell, Margaret S.** ‡ (S&H) 2005. The author has been engaged in Ezekiel studies for over 20 years, including (often leading) participation in SBL's Ezekiel Seminar. She knows the scholarship, has thought deeply about Ezekiel and its relevance, and writes well. My trouble here is that Odell believes we must look outside the prophet's Jewish heritage (see p.4) to find the main influences or models influencing Ezekiel as a cohesive, primarily literary prophecy. For example, she goes to 7th century Assyrian building inscriptions, when I want to go to Exodus and Leviticus. Darr's more mainstream exposition, though without Odell's visually engaging illustrations, is both more theological and more valuable among critical interpretations. [*Interp* 4/07; *ThTo* 1/07; *RBL*; *CJ* 7/07].

✓ Odell, Margaret S., and John T. Strong (eds). ‡ *The Book of Ezekiel: Theological and Anthropological Perspectives*, 2000. This book of essays from SBL was followed by Cook/Patton above. [*VT* 55.2; *JAOS* 123.4].

F Patton, Corrine. ‡ *Ezekiel 25–48* (HCOT). See Herrie van Rooy below.

F Rooker, Mark F. (EEC). The author has both a dissertation and an expositional commentary (HolOT) on Ezekiel already published.

F Ruiz, Jean-Pierre. ‡ (BO).

Schröder, F.W.J. (Lange) ET 1873. This remarkable but forgotten work examines all aspects of the prophecy. It is conservative in approach with full exegesis and many homiletical hints. Forty years ago Charles Feinberg said that this is still "among the finest on Ezekiel." Wipf & Stock reprinted this in 2007.

Skinner, John. ‡ (EB) 1895.

✓ Stevenson, Kenneth, and Michael Glerup (eds). *Ezekiel, Daniel* (ACCS) 2008. Some of us find it regrettable that Ezekiel has far fewer pages in this volume than Daniel.

Taylor, John. (TOTC) 1969. A competent exposition by an Anglican bishop. Helpful for the beginner, but Ezekiel studies have come a long way since 1969. Quite readable; I read it all the way through.

☆ Thomas, Derek. God Strengthens: *Ezekiel Simply Explained* (WCS) 1991.

F Thompson, David L., and Eugene Carpenter. *Ezekiel, Daniel* (CorBC) 2010. Thompson is slated to do Ezekiel.

F Tiemeyer, Lena-Sofia. (Apollos).

Tooman, William A., and Michael A. Lyons (eds). ‡ *Transforming Visions: Transformations of Text, Tradition, and Theology in Ezekiel*, 2010.

☆ **Tuell, Steven S.** [𝓜], (NIBC) 2009. This volume of 368pp is written by a recognized Ezekiel scholar teaching at Pittsburgh Theological Seminary. In light of my reading of Tuell's past research, I would class this inexpensive and well-written exegesis as conservatively critical. [*JETS* 9/09; *Them* 4/10; *BTB* 8/10].

F Van Rooy, Herrie F. ‡ *Ezekiel 1–24* (HCOT). See Corrine Patton above.

✓ Vawter, Bruce, and Leslie J. Hoppe. ‡ (ITC) 1991. As a brief critical treatment with theological concerns, this has value. [*HebStud* 1993].

✓ Wevers, John W. ‡ (NCB) 1969. Gives a concise, useful treatment of the historical-critical issues confronting the interpreter 40 years ago, but the commentary is not very interesting and is hard of hearing when it comes to theology. Wevers was to have been replaced by Joyce.

☆ **Zimmerli, Walther.** ‡ (Herm) 2 Vols., ET 1979–82. "It is hard to believe that this exhaustive commentary will be superseded within the next few generations" (Childs). Relatively critical, this magisterial work reflects a lifetime of assiduous form-critical research. This commentary is not for everyone, but if you are very serious about studying the Hebrew text and understanding Ezekiel in depth, you ought to purchase these volumes. The cost is substantial, so I counsel you not to invest your money if you're not planning on investing some hard hours of study. But if you buy it, this commentary will more than repay study. Prior to the publication of Block's volumes, I recommended purchasing Zimmerli. [*JBL* 105.2; *ThTo* 37.1; *CBQ* 10/81; *Interp* 4/84; *HebStud* 1984]. Note: students may want to consult Zimmerli's important little book of essays entitled, *I Am Yahweh* (ET 1982), which includes an important study of the "recognition formula" (see note below for more on the topic).

NOTES: (1) See the three review-essays now gathered in Alan J. Hauser (ed), *Recent Research on the Major Prophets* (Sheffield Phoenix, 2008). They are: K. Pfisterer Darr, "Ezekiel among the Critics," *CurBS* 2 (1994): 9–24; Risa Levitt Kohn, "Ezekiel at the Turn of the Century," *CBR* 2.1 (2003): 9–31; and *idem*, "Ezekiel Update." (2) The keynote of Ezekiel is the recognition formula, "you/they shall know that I am Yahweh," which occurs over 70 times. Those interested in the topic may hunt for my 2006 dissertation: "An Inner-Biblical Interpretation and Intertextual Reading of Ezekiel's Recognition Formulae with the Book of Exodus." I hope to see it published by the end of 2011.

—⟋⟍—

DANIEL

★ **Baldwin, Joyce G.** (TOTC) 1978. First-rate when it appeared, but now it is showing its age in a few areas (e.g., the handling of apocalyptic). Fine introduction, responsible exegesis and solid theological comment. She packs a great deal of content into 210pp. The 75-page introduction alone is probably worth the price of the book. Years ago, this was Stuart's first pick among the conservative works. The critical commentator Redditt, even in 2008, called this "excellent." [*WTJ* Fall 79; *EvQ* 4/79; *JBL* 99.3 (1980); *JETS* 12/80].

★ Calvin, John. (GS) 1561. About 800pp of commentary from the great Reformer. Calvin's commentary on Daniel is being retranslated, and the first volume (covering chs. 1–6) was published in 1993 by Eerdmans ("Rutherford House Translation").

★ Duguid, Iain M. *Daniel* (REC) 2008. These are exemplary expositions by an excellent OT scholar, one who spends time in the pulpit; they prompt the preacher to interpret Daniel along redemptive-historical lines and to develop the connections between the testaments. Despite the series being termed a "commentary," this is a book of sermonic material. Students will look elsewhere. [*JETS* 3/09]. See Duguid on Ezekiel and Ruth/Esther.

★ Ferguson, Sinclair B. (WCC) 1988. Anyone who has read Ferguson's books will be interested in obtaining this. He has done pastoral work at St. George's Tron Parish Church in Glasgow and taught systematics at Westminster Seminary. Presently he pastors First Presbyterian (ARP) in Columbia, SC. Along with Stuart on Ezekiel, perhaps the best in the WCC series in providing theological guidance. Ferguson tries to be suggestive rather than exhaustive. There are helpful anecdotes, pastoral insight, great theology, and *sane* exposition (on a book that needs it). Compare with Wallace and Longman; all three are superb.

★ **Goldingay, John E.** ‡ (WBC) 1989. Though he stands painfully loose on matters of date, *Sitz im Leben*, and historicity (assumes a late date and doubts the inspiring stories are grounded in historical events), Goldingay has given us a valuable commentary for close work with the Hebrew and Aramaic. He engages in what may be termed "double tracking," often masterfully drawing out the theological message of the narrative (even from an evangelical perspective), while talking about folktales and legendary materials. He debases the coinage with which he trades. It all makes some conservatives nervous about the future of American/British evangelical scholarship. Though WBC as a series makes few concessions to our concerns as preachers and determinedly sticks to exegesis, this volume includes some very thoughtful application. Advanced students and scholarly pastors will definitely want this; compare with Collins, which is also considered indispensable for scholars. Goldingay is Longman's and Stuart's favorite technical commentary. [*Them* 1/92; *CRBR* 1990].

★ Longman, Tremper. (NIVAC) 1999. Like Ferguson, his former colleague at Westminster in Philadelphia, Longman is a great expositional and theological help. Of course they also share a Reformed orientation. Where they differ is in their areas of expertise: Longman is an OT scholar and Ferguson a systematic theologian who is nonetheless alert to redemptive historical themes. I would not want to pick between them. I assure you they both will inspire you to do a sermon series on Daniel. (Aside: It wouldn't hurt Longman to express a bit more confidence in his conservative views on the dating issue.)

★ **Lucas, Ernest C.** [*M*], (Apollos) 2002. With regard to both critical dating and main lines of interpretation, this well-researched volume can be likened to Goldingay. (Lucas believes "it is possible to make a reasoned, and reasonable, defence of a late sixth-century or early fifth-century date for the book," but doesn't.) Perhaps one might say it is like an updated, less technical Goldingay. Some conservatives were hoping this series would offer an updated, more technical Baldwin instead. Most pastors would be well content with the exegetical guidance offered in the trio of Baldwin, Longman, and Lucas; they would not feel a lack without Goldingay and Collins on their shelf. Students are likely to learn more from Goldingay than Lucas. [*Them* Sum 04; *JETS* 6/03; *Interp* 4/04; *JSOT* 27.5; *Chm* Sum 04; *EvQ* 1/05; *Evangel* Sum 04; *Anvil* 20.3].

✓ Anderson, Robert. *Daniel in the Critics Den*, 1902. An old apology for the traditional view of Daniel as 6th century prophecy. Don't confuse this work with Josh McDowell's popular book of the same title.

Anderson, Robert A. ‡ *Signs and Wonders* (ITC) 1984.

✓ Archer, Gleason L. (EBC) 1985. A Premillennial, but not Dispensational, commentary worth consulting. Archer gives a strong defense of the orthodox position on higher critical matters and delivers a solid exposition of Daniel. (The former is perhaps more valuable than the latter, and one can find many of those arguments in his OT introduction.) It might be said that theological interpretation is not his strong point, but he is usually on the mark. See Hill for the EBCR replacement. [*JBL* 3/87].

F Boadt, Lawrence E. ‡ (BO).

☆ Boice, James M. *An Expositional Commentary*, 1989.

✓ Buchanan, George Wesley. ‡ (Mellen Biblical Commentaries) 1999. I have yet to see this large (500+ pages) and expensive ($120) volume. It reportedly is especially concerned with intertextuality. [*OTA* 10/00; *JSOT* 94].

F Carpenter, Eugene, and David L. Thompson. *Ezekiel, Daniel* (CorBC) 2010. Carpenter is slated to do Daniel.

☆ Chapell, Bryan. *Standing Your Ground*, 1990. Like Boice, this series of sermons has served preachers well as a model for preaching Christ from this OT book. It has also been attractive because of its reasonable price.

✓ Charles, R.H. ‡ 1929. Charles is best known for editing the massive *Apocrypha and Pseudepigrapha of the Old Testament* and for his two-vol. commentary on Revelation in the ICC. Here he takes up an OT apocalyptic book. This work on Daniel was published by Oxford's Clarendon Press and is very technical.

✓ **Collins, John J.** ‡ *Daniel. With an Introduction to Apocalyptic Literature*, (FOTL) 1984. A slim but useful handbook which fulfills the aims of the series. The author builds on his earlier monograph, *The Apocalyptic Vision of the Book of Daniel* (1977). This commentary is superseded by the Hermeneia work below. [*EvQ* 4/87; *JBL* 106.2 (1987); *JETS* 12/85; *Evangel* Spr 86; *Them* 1/86].

✓ **Collins, John J.** ‡ (Herm) 1993. This comprehensive historical-critical commentary (528pp) follows on the heels of the above FOTL volume and is now the leader in its category. Though Montgomery will continue to be consulted for decades to come, Collins is probably now to be considered the most important reference volume for specialists doing philological work and detailed exegesis. Note, however, that he largely confines himself to the older historical and literary-critical methods, which is in keeping with the overall aims of the series (excluding Shalom Paul on Amos). Compare with the WBC volume by Goldingay, which has much more to say theologically. Pastors will much prefer WBC! [*Biblica* 77.4 (1996); *JSOT* 6/95; *CBQ* 10/95; *JTS* 4/95; *Interp* 1/96; *Them* 10/95; *JETS* 3/98; *JSS* Spr 99; *VT* 46.4; *SJT* 49.3 (1996); *JR* 7/96].

✓ Collins, John J., and Peter W. Flint (eds). ‡ *The Book of Daniel, Composition and Reception*, 2 Vols., 2001. This huge project forms part of a new series, "Formation and Interpretation of Old Testament Literature," published by Brill in the *VT* Supplement series. [*JTS* 4/03; *JBL*, Fall 02; *JSOT* 99 (2002); *RelSRev* 10/02; *BBR* 14.2].

Culver, R.D. *Daniel and the Latter Days*, 1954. Dated and strongly Dispensational. See Miller for the best current presentation of that more literalistic, prophetic approach to Daniel.

✓ Davies, Philip R. ‡ (OT Guides) 1985. Quick survey of critical scholarship and its conclusions done by a brilliant and quite critical Sheffield professor.

✓ Driver, Samuel R. ‡ (Cambridge Bible) 1900. This is a classic statement of the liberal position. The old Robert Anderson published his volume in response two years later (1902).

✓ **Fewell, Danna Nolan.** ‡ *Circle of Sovereignty*, 1988, 2nd ed 1991. Provides a "close reading" of chs. 1–6, using the new literary criticism. This work is often cited in the literature and deserves attention as one of the very few examples of narrative criticism in Daniel studies. The conclusion drawn, that the stories develop the theme of conflict between human and divine sovereignty (the Kingdom of God), is convincing and also helps readers integrate the stories with the visions. Conservatives will probably ignore the reader-response elements here. [*CRBR* 1991].

✓ **Gowan, Donald E.** ‡ (AOTC) 2001. Another accessible, mainline critical exegesis from this newer series. Those who are intimidated by Goldingay and Collins might turn here. Gowan's theological interpretation emphasizes the sovereign rule of God as the hope of the faithful in trying situations. Lucas knows Daniel scholarship better than Gowan and is a better, more conservative guide for exegesis and theology. [*CBQ* 7/03; *JETS* 6/03; *ExpTim* 3/03; *JSOT* 99 (2002); *ThTo* 7/02].

☆ Harman, Allan. (EPSC) 2007. A full (333pp), fresh, conservative interpretation which will aid preachers especially. Harman can teach the student too, but this does not contain the detailed and deep scholarship one finds in technical works. He places emphasis, rightly in my view, on the kingdom theology in the book. [*RTR* 4/08].

✓ **Hartman, L.F. and A.A. DiLella.** ‡ (AB) 1978. Though not one of the stronger volumes in AB, in places it contributes to the scholarly discussion. The authors are Roman Catholic critics who well present the critical arguments that the stories and visions of Daniel address the situation of the Maccabean revolt and its aftermath. [*JBL* 12/79].

Heaton, E. ‡ (Torch Bible Commentary) 1956.

Hebbard, Aaron B. ‡ *Reading Daniel as a Text in Theological Hermeneutics*, 2009. [*JETS* 6/10].

☆ Hill, Andrew. (EBCR) 2008. This is a fine piece of work (190pp) and an improvement upon Archer. While solidly conservative, the tone of Hill's commentary is less polemical than Archer on historical critical matters. As with the old EBC, a volume on Daniel to Malachi completes the OT section. Worth buying. [*JSOT-BL* 2010].

St. Jerome. *Jerome's Commentary on Daniel*, ET 1977. The translation was done by Archer.

✓ Keil, Carl F. (KD) ET 1872.

✓ **Lacocque, André.** ‡ ET 1979. John Knox Press thought this French work important enough to put into translation. Accessible to non-specialists, but includes critical notes on the Hebrew. Davies opines that the work can be "erratic, but often brilliant, especially on the literary qualities of Daniel" (p.9). Note: the author, long at Chicago Theological Seminary, prefers the spelling LaCocque. He followed up his quite critical commentary with a 1988 monograph, *Daniel in His Time*. [*EvQ* 4/79; *JBL* 100.2 (1981); *RTR* 1/80].

Lang, George H. *The Histories and Prophecies of Daniel*. 1950. This work expounds the book within a historic premillennial framework.

F Lapsley, Jacqueline. ‡ (OTL replacement). See Porteous below.

Lederach, Paul. [*M*], (BCBC) 1994. Wants to take a mediating position, that the stories are early but the book is 2ⁿᵈ century BC. Lederach is an educator rather than OT specialist. This is not designed for students.

Leupold, H.C. 1969. Another fairly thorough exposition from this old evangelical Lutheran scholar. [*WTJ* 13.1].

F Mastin, Brian. ‡ (ICC–new series).

✓ **Miller, Stephen R.** (NAC) 1994. Though I've not had occasion to make much use of this sizeable commentary, I know Miller is the work to consult to get the best Dispensationalism has to offer in interpreting Daniel. It is best described as a more moderate Dispensationalism—more cognizant of, and in tune with, developments in broader evangelicalism than that school used to be. The conclusions are "vintage dispensationalism" (Schibler), except for his interpretation of chs. 10–11. Much more valuable than Walvoord, both in terms of OT studies and theology. [*Them* 10/95; *CBQ* 1/97].

✓ **Montgomery, James A.** ‡ (ICC) 1927. This is definitely a classic with its full treatment of textual and philological matters, but with little theology. Prior to Goldingay and Collins' Hermeneia—to consider only works in English—Montgomery's technical commentary was *the* starting point in scholarly discussion. It still is *a* key starting point.

F Nelson, William. (NIBC). This may see publication this year.

Olyott, Stuart. *Dare to Stand Alone* (WCS) 1982. Provides expositional help to the preacher.

Pace, Sharon. ‡ (S&H) 2008. The author, who teaches at Marquette, aims to offer a theological exposition (350pp), building on the base of historical critical conclusions regarding compositional history. I judge that this volume will be of less use to students than many others in the series. Perhaps the volume is of limited use for (evangelical) pastors too, since the reflections on contemporary relevance ("Connections") tend not to focus on the text as God's word or as containing any gospel. E.g., see pp.183–92, where the story of Belshazzar's feast is a springboard to talk about inter-religious respect and dialogue. Is that what ch. 5 is about? [*JETS* 3/10; *Interp* 7/09 (Towner)].

✓ Péter-Contesse, René, and John Ellington. (UBS) 1994. One of the most recent issues in the series, full (352pp), and reasonably priced. [*CBQ* 7/95; *JSOT* 90 (1996)].

✓ **Porteous, Norman W.** ‡ (OTL) 1965, rev. 1979. "Often penetrates to the heart of the theological issue and sets the critical questions in a fresh light" (Childs). Granting this, I must note that Porteous interprets Daniel as 2nd century history rather than revelatory prophecy, constantly pointing to the clash between Hellenism and Judaism. Porteous is more expositional than exegetical, and builds on Montgomery. This work is becoming less and less important with the passage of time. Porteous is scheduled to be replaced by Lapsley.

F   Price, Randall. (EEC).

      Pusey, E.B. 1869. Reprinted a number of years ago by Klock & Klock. Famous for its strongly-worded defense of the integrity and historicity of the book.

✓   **Redditt, Paul L.** ‡ (NCB) 1999. This was the last OT volume to appear in this now defunct series; Redditt's work on Haggai to Malachi in 1995 was the next to last. This commentary is based on the NRSV and is of reasonable size for NCB's format: xxvi + 211pp. Students may want to refer to Redditt's bibliography; the exegesis seems unexciting and pedestrian. [*JSOT* 89 (2000); *ExpTim* 4/00; *RelSRev* 1/01; *CBQ* 10/00; *Them* Spr 01; *JTS* 4/01].

✓   Russell, D.S. ‡ (DSB) 1981. Russell has published important books and journal articles on apocalyptic literature, so this more lengthy work for the devotional DSB (244pp) interests us. Takes the standard critical line on date. There is further work in his *Daniel, An Active Volcano: Reflections on the Book of Daniel*, 1989.

      Seow, Choon-Leong. ‡ (WestBC) 2003. This same author produced the well-received AB volume on Qoheleth. Here Seow provides a liberal exposition, accessible even to a lay readership. [*CBQ* 7/04; *Interp* 10/03; *JSOT* 28.5; *HebStud* 2004; *JAOS* 124.4].

✓   Smith-Christopher, David L. ‡ (NewIB) 1996. Found in Vol. 7, which covers Daniel and the Minor Prophets. [*CurTM* 6/97]. Also to be noted is his volume, *A Biblical Theology of Exile*, 2002 [*VT* 54.4; *BibInt* 13.3], which is worthwhile for students of Lamentations and Ezekiel.

☆   **Steinmann, Andrew E.** (Concord) 2008. This conservative Lutheran series continues to build a tradition of issuing large-scale theological commentaries. The mold is an older-style grammatico-historical exegesis with much attention to philology, linguistics, etc. Steinmann is over 650pp and emphasizes both the historicity of the stories and a Christological approach to the book. The author is learned and clear, in writing for both students and pastors. Specialists will not judge this to be a new (and conservative) Montgomery. [*RBL* 6/10].

✓   Stevenson, Kenneth, and Michael Glerup (eds). *Ezekiel, Daniel* (ACCS) 2008. See under Ezekiel.

      Stortz, Rodney. (PTW) 2004. Born out of the sermons of an able Presbyterian pastor in St. Louis (PCA), this exposition had to be published posthumously.

F   Sumner, George. (Brazos).

✓   **Towner, W.S.** ‡ (I) 1984. Proportional to the length of the text, this entry is more in-depth than others in the series, but probably not one of the best. Theological, practical, with a liberal viewpoint. The author is explicit about his critical assumptions: there is no such thing as predictive prophecy. The "inspired writers" were "limited in the same way all other human beings are, namely, by an inability to foresee the future" (p.178). You might term this Porteous' replacement for the shelves of mainline pastors, though Towner does not have an equal measure of exegesis. Widely used and quoted. [*JBL* 105.2 (1986)].

      Veldkamp, Herman. *Dreams and Dictators*, ET 1978. A very perceptive theological commentary written in sermonic style by a minister in the Reformed Church in the Netherlands. The pastor with this on hand will be helped in preaching Christ from Daniel's prophecy, but Veldkamp is difficult to obtain.

☆ Wallace, R.S. (BST) 1979. Originally published under the title, *The Lord is King*. Evangelicals will find this worth consulting or buying for its excellent theological exposition, and because Wallace still maintains the early date on Daniel—which probably irked a few of his colleagues at Columbia Theological Seminary, where he taught Biblical Theology. I agree with Wallace that the Kingdom of God may be the main theme of the book. This is well worth the price; if you don't want Calvin's hefty tome, you might choose to get this one. [*EvQ* 4/80].

Walvoord, John F. *Daniel, The Key to Prophetic Revelation*, 1971. A strongly Dispensational commentary by the sometime president of Dallas Seminary. More oriented toward dogmatics than OT interpretation, this volume is not recommended. See Miller above.

F Wesselius, Jan-Wim. ‡ (HCOT). Previously Tibor Marjovszky was listed here.

✓ Wilson, Robert Dick. *Studies in the Book of Daniel*, 1917; *Studies in the Book of Daniel: Second Series*, 1938. These present a thorough apology for the orthodox position. From the pen of one of old Princeton's greatest OT scholars. Now quite dated.

✓ Wiseman, D.J. (ed). *Notes on Some Problems in the Book of Daniel*, 1965. Not a commentary but provides well-informed answers to some issues raised by the critics; the issues haven't changed as much as some think.

Wood, Leon J. 1973. A comprehensive commentary from the Dispensational camp, and prior to Miller the best presentation of that position by a long shot.

F Wooden, R. Glenn. (NICOT). Previously T.C. Mitchell was listed as having the contract.

✓ Woude, A.S. van der (ed). ‡ *The Book of Daniel, in the Light of New Findings*, 1993. At the time, cutting-edge essays from many of the world's leading scholars on Daniel.

☆ **Young, E.J.** (GS) 1949. Though it is now getting quite old, this is still a valuable exegetical work from an evangelical Amillennial perspective. Young and Baldwin have been viewed as a conservative corrective to critical works like Montgomery, Porteous, and Goldingay. One drawback is that Young, like the ICC work he builds upon, did not have access to the Qumran literature or to the important Babylonian Chronicles, published in 1956. [*EvQ* 10/49]. Over the years both Banner and Eerdmans have kept this commentary in print. See also Young's *Messianic Prophecies of Daniel*, 1954.

NOTE: David Valeta, "The Book of Daniel in Recent Research (Part 1)," *CBR* 6.3 (2008): 330–54.

—ɯ—

APOCALYPTIC LITERATURE

PRELIMINARY NOTES: For many years I recommended the purchase of Hanson, *The Dawn of Apocalyptic* (1979), which dealt primarily with the OT, and Leon Morris' *Apocalyptic* (1972), which was both a conservative counterbalance and more focused on the NT. Both works are now quite dated. I am forgoing any purchase recommendations, except to urge that OT students consider Collins, *The Apocalyptic Imagination* (1998). For general introductions covering OT and NT, one can look up Cook's *The Apocalyptic Literature* (2003) or the more popularly-written Carey (2005). It is truly regrettable that evangelicals have written no major introductions that can be recommended.

To get a quick initial grasp of both the OT genre and recent scholarly work, I would recommend a careful perusal of (1) Longman/Dillard, *An Introduction to the Old Testament*, pp.384–89; (2) Hanson's "Appendix: An Overview of Early Jewish and Christian Apocalypticism," pp.427–44 in *The Dawn of Apocalyptic* (1979); and (3) Oswalt's essay listed below. For a discussion of apocalyptic in the NT more up-to-date than Morris, see especially the Aune/Geddert/Evans article below and Scott M. Lewis, *What Are They Saying about New Testament Apocalyptic?* (2004). Lewis has an annotated bibliography (pp.108–15).

✓   Aune, D.E., T.J. Geddert, and C.A. Evans. "Apocalypticism" (pp.45–58), in *Dictionary of NT Background*, 2000.

✓   Aune, David E. *Apocalypticism, Prophecy, and Magic in Early Christianity: Collected Essays*, 2006 (Baker, 2008). Of "unquestionable utility for scholars of Revelation" (DiTommaso), but helpful well beyond that.

✓   Barr, James. ‡ "Jewish Apocalyptic in Recent Scholarly Study," *BJRL* 58 (1975): 9–35.

✓   Bauckham, Richard. *The Fate of the Dead: Studies on the Jewish and Christian Apocalypses*, 1998.

     Block, Daniel I. "Preaching Old Testament Apocalyptic to a New Testament Church," *CTJ* 41.1 (2006): 17–52. Normally I don't list articles, but this is a gem on the book of Daniel, with wise guidance for handling other texts. There are several other fine essays here in *CTJ* 41.1 on the theme of "Preaching Apocalyptic Texts." Monographs addressing the theme include Larry Paul Jones and Jerry L. Sumney, *Preaching Apocalyptic Texts* (1999); and Dorothy Jonaitis, *Unmasking Apocalyptic Texts: A Guide to Preaching and Teaching* (2005).

☆   Carey, Greg. ‡ *Ultimate Things: An Introduction to Jewish and Christian Apocalyptic Literature* (Chalice) 2005.

✓   Charlesworth, James H. (ed). *The Old Testament Pseudepigrapha. Vol. 1: Apocalyptic Literature and Testaments*, 1983. The standard reference for Jewish apocalyptic texts, superseding the 1913 R.H. Charles' set.

✓   Collins, John J. ‡ *The Apocalyptic Imagination: An Introduction to Jewish Apocalyptic Literature*, 2nd ed 1998. This is the premier scholarly introduction to Apocalyptic as "the Jewish Matrix of Christianity" (the original subtitle in 1984). The slight drawback for the student or pastor wanting a general introduction to the genre/literature is that Collins only deals with the NT in one concluding chapter (pp.256–79). Collins' own views feature strongly here, as one would expect. See too the 1984 FOTL volume on Daniel mentioned above.

✓   Collins, J.J., and J.H. Charlesworth (eds). ‡ *Mysteries and Revelations: Apocalyptic Studies since the Uppsala Convention*, 1991.

✓   Collins, John J., Bernard McGinn, and Stephen J. Stein (eds). ‡ *The Encyclopedia of Apocalypticism*, 3 Vols., 1998. The broadest available treatment of the genre, thought forms, and historical development (both ancient and modern) of the tradition. This massive work (1520pp) on ANE, Jewish, and Christian apocalyticism contains careful distinctions among, and definitions of, apocalypse (genre), apocalypticism (ideology), and apocalyptic eschatology. Authoritative as a survey of the whole history. Do note that the set is composed of long essays and is not in a typical encyclopedia format. Only Volume 1 deals directly with biblical materials. [*RelSRev* 7/00; *JR* 10/00; *WTJ* Fall 02].

☆   Cook, Steven L. ‡ *The Apocalyptic Literature*, 2003. This is a fine volume in the IBT series and well worth purchasing. Do note that his speciality is Old Testament.

[*JETS* 3/05]. Earlier Cook gave us *Prophecy and Apocalypticism: The Postexilic Social Setting* (1995). There, using a social-scientific method and focusing on Ezekiel 38–39, Zechariah 1–8, and Joel, Cook challenges the usual interpretation of apocalyptic as always originating among the alienated, powerless, and deprived.

✓   DiTommaso, Lorenzo. "Apocalypses and Apocalypticism in Antiquity (Part I)," *CBR* 5.2 (2007): 235–86. The second review-essay appeared in *CBR* 5.3 (2007): 367–432.

Frost, S.B. ‡ *Old Testament Apocalyptic*, 1952.

✓   Grabbe, L.L., and R.D. Haak (eds). ‡ *Knowing the End from the Beginning: The Prophetic, the Apocalyptic, and Their Relationship*, 2003.

☆   Hanson, Paul D. ‡ *The Dawn of Apocalyptic: The Historical and Sociological Roots of Jewish Apocalyptic Eschatology*, 1975, rev. 1979; and *Old Testament Apocalyptic*, 1987. The former is his major work (still in print), and the latter is a shorter, popular work in Abingdon's IBT series. Hanson and Collins have been leading American OT critics dealing with this genre. Hanson in particular is noted for stressing the relationship between Apocalyptic and Prophecy, whereas others like von Rad urge that Apocalyptic has little to do with Prophecy and should be linked instead with Wisdom traditions. See also his summary of past work on the topic in SBL's *The Hebrew Bible and Its Modern Interpreters* (1985), and in *ABD*. For a more accessible and up-to-date introduction, see Carey. [*JSOT* 14 (Carroll)].

✓   Hanson, Paul D. (ed). ‡ *Visionaries and Their Apocalypses*, 1983. A collection of key early essays in the field. Also quite valuable from the same era is J.J. Collins (ed), *Apocalypse: The Morphology of a Genre* (*Semeia* 14 [1979]), which built well upon Hanson's Dawn and is constantly cited.

✓   Hellholm, David (ed). *Apocalypticism in the Mediterranean World and the Near East*, 1983. A giant leap forward in the study of the genre for its time, this product of the 1979 International Colloquium on Apocalypticism (Uppsala) remains important today. See Collins and Charlesworth for a follow-up.

✓   Koch, Klaus. ‡ *The Rediscovery of Apocalyptic*, ET 1972.

Ladd, George E. "Why Not Prophetic-Apocalyptic?" *JBL* 76 (1957): 192–200. For study of the book of Revelation.

☆   Lewis, Scott M. ‡ *What Are They Saying about New Testament Apocalyptic?* 2004. A basic, concise discussion. [*CBQ* 10/04].

✓   Marcus, Joel, and Marion L. Soards (eds). ‡ *Apocalyptic and the New Testament*, 1989.

✓   Minear, Paul S. ‡ *New Testament Apocalyptic* (IBT) 1981.

☆   Morris, Leon. *Apocalyptic*, 1972. For pastors at least, this is still a fine brief introduction to the topic from the conservative standpoint. Because Morris' expertise is NT and this book is quite old, students of the OT would be wise to start elsewhere. [*EvQ* 1/75].

✓   Murphy, Frederick J. ‡ "Introduction to Apocalyptic Literature," (NewIB) Vol. 7, 1996.

✓   Reddish, Mitchell G. (ed). ‡ *Apocalyptic Literature: A Reader,* 1990. Those who want to move beyond this, see Charlesworth (ed), *The Old Testament Pseudepigrapha, Vol 1: Apocalyptic Literature and Testaments*, 1983. Another route is to use Online Critical Pseudepigrapha: <www.stfx.ca/academic/religious-studies/ocp/>.

✓   Rowland, Christopher. ‡ *The Open Heaven*, 1982. More useful for NT students.

✓   Rowley, H.H. ‡ *The Relevance of Apocalyptic*, rev. 1963.

✓   Russell, D.S. ‡ *The Method and Message of Jewish Apocalyptic: 200 B.C.–A.D. 100* (OTL) 1964. See also his later scholarly work, *Divine Disclosure: An Introduction* to *Jewish Apocalyptic* (1992). On a more basic level are *Apocalyptic: Ancient and Modern* (1978), and *Prophecy and the Apocalyptic Dream* (1994).

✓ Sacchi, Paolo. ‡ *Jewish Apocalyptic and Its History*, ET 1996.

☆ Sandy, D. Brent, and Daniel M. O'Hare. *Prophecy and Apocalyptic: An Annotated Bibliography*, 2007. See under Prophets. Students doing more extensive work in these areas may wish to make the purchase.

✓ Schmithals, W. ‡ *The Apocalyptic Movement: Introduction and Interpretation*, ET 1975.

Stone, Michael E. "Apocalyptic Literature" (pp.383–441), in Michael E. Stone (ed), *Jewish Writings of the Second Temple Period*, 1984.

F Taylor, Richard A. *Interpreting Apocalyptic Literature: An Exegetical Handbook* (Kregel).

✓ Watson, Duane F. (ed). *The Intertexture of Apocalyptic Discourse in the New Testament* (SBL) 2002.

✓ VanderKam, James C. *An Introduction to Early Judaism* (Eerdmans), 2001.

NOTE: For reviews of the *status quaestionis* in apocalyptic studies, see the very thorough DiTommaso above; Frederick J. Murphy, "Apocalypses and Apocalypticism: The State of the Question," *CurBS* 2 (1994): 147–79; and John N. Oswalt, "Recent Studies in Old Testament Apocalyptic," in *The Face of Old Testament Studies*, edited by David W. Baker and Bill T. Arnold, 369–90 (Baker, 1999).

THE TWELVE MINOR PROPHETS

★ Calvin, John. *Commentaries on the Twelve Minor Prophets* (GS) 5 Vols., 1559. A most helpful and full guide to theological exposition, which you can put to good use alongside the modern exegetical works. Extends to 500pp on Hosea, which gives one a sense for the fullness of the treatment. Both the GS and Baker editions have reprinted the 19ᵗʰ century translation. See Calvin under "Commentary Series."

★ **McComiskey, Thomas E. (ed).** *The Minor Prophets: An Exegetical and Expository Commentary*, 1992–98. This set from Baker was originally published in three vols. but has recently become available in a huge single volume (nearly 1500pp) at a much cheaper price. It is beautifully presented, a delight to use, and "should be a first resource to look at when asking what the Hebrew text of the minor prophets says" (Oswalt). Perhaps the most valuable book treatments are Hosea, Zechariah (McComiskey), Joel (Dillard), Micah (Waltke), and Nahum (Longman). The series includes the RSV and the scholar's own translation; then it treats the Hebrew in an exegesis section and concludes each pericope with a theological exposition. Contributors are listed below. My recommendation is to buy the single volume edition, but note that years have passed since this first appeared, and it is not necessarily the "first-stop" recourse it was. [*JSOT-BL* 1993, 1995, 1999; *EvQ* 1/94; *Them* 10/93; *VT* 47.1; *BSac* 10/94; *HebStud* 1994, 1997, 2000; *RelSRev* 7/99].

☆ Boice, James. 2 Vols., 1986. This expositional commentary has been a great help to pastors. I used Boice on Jonah and found him suggestive. It has been issued in both hb and pb. The scholarship could be updated at points; use with a thorough exegetical commentary. Premillennial. [*JETS* 9/91].

☆ Craigie, Peter C. (DSB) 2 Vols., 1985. In the main, this is an inspiring devotional commentary. My only disappointment was his reading of Jonah as a parable. One of the very best sets covering the Twelve. The Craigie and McConville commentaries are the best in the DSB Old Testament section. [*EvQ* 7/86].

Driver, S.R. ‡ (Century Bible) 2 Vols., 1906. This is still consulted by some.

Feinberg, Charles L. 1947–52. A capable work for the evangelical church long ago, these commentaries are still in print. Formerly published under the title *Major Messages on the Minor Prophets*.

F   Ferguson, Sinclair. (PTW). I plan to purchase this when it appears.

✓   Ferreiro, Alberto (ed). *The Twelve Prophets* (ACCS) 2003. [*BSac* 7/05; *JSOT-BL* 2007].

Gaebelein, Frank E. (ed). (EBC) Vol. 7, 1985. Though something of a mixed bag, this volume was worth owning, especially if you were just beginning to build your library. Contributors to this volume covering Daniel to Malachi included Armerding, Alden, and McComiskey; each contributor is listed below under the individual prophets. Note that most of the authors have Premillennial convictions. This commentary feels dated, is being heavily discounted, and has been replaced by a much improved EBCR. [*JETS* 3/87].

Hailey, Homer. 1972. Includes a paraphrase and brief exposition.

House, Paul R. *The Unity of the Twelve*, 1990. Helped to spur research with its thesis that the Minor Prophets are organized along the lines of thematic/theological progression, from sin to judgment to restoration.

Hutcheson, G. 1657. A reprinted Puritan work I've never seen.

✓   Keil, Carl F. (KD) ET 1871. The careful, conservative exegesis here—this volume is among Keil's best—has long been appreciated. Conservatives do not use this as much now, with the multiplicity of newer works.

Laetsch, Theodore. 1956. This devotional exposition shares the same qualities as his Jeremiah-Lamentations commentary. Twenty years ago, when resources were scarcer, I recommended that preachers buy this.

Lange's Commentary. ET 1874. The commentaries by Paul Kleinert on Obadiah through Zephaniah are especially deserving of mention.

Morgan, G. Campbell. *Voices of Twelve Hebrew Prophets*, n.d.; also *The Minor Prophets*, 1960. The former is a series of expositions, and the latter book prints the KJV together with outlines and brief analyses of the Twelve, their message, and the relevance of that message for today.

✓   Nogalski, James D., and Marvin A. Sweeney (eds). ‡ *Reading and Hearing the Book of the Twelve*, 2000. This presentation of scholarly discussions within SBL is important reading for more advanced students. As with the Psalms, scholarship is wanting to interpret the collection more as a cohesive and coherent whole, rather than as strictly independent and individual writings. [*CBQ* 1/03; *HebStud* 2002; *VT* 53.1; *JSS* Spr 04]. See Paul Redditt, "The Formation of the Book of the Twelve: A Review of Research," in *Society of Biblical Literature 2001 Seminar Papers* (pp.58–80). For a protest against this shift in scholarship, read Ehud Ben Zvi, "Twelve Prophetic Books or 'The Twelve': A Few Preliminary Considerations," in *Forming Prophetic Literature: Essays on Isaiah and the Twelve in Honor of John D. W. Watts* (1996), pp.125–56.

Orelli, Conrad von. 1893. Studies by an old moderately conservative German theologian. These have been reprinted.

Pusey, Edward B. 2 Vols., 1860. The same commentary is included in the classic set, "Barnes' Notes." You will find it a mature exposition with some attention given to the interpretations of churchmen down through the centuries. Not as strong as some of Pusey's other biblical studies.

✓   Redditt, Paul L., and Aaron Schart (eds). ‡ *Thematic Threads in the Book of the Twelve*, 2003. These collected SBL essays are a follow-up to Nogalski/Sweeney above. [*JBL* Fall 04; *RelSRev* 4/07; *CJ* 4/05; *JSOT-BL* 2007].

    Smith, George A. ‡ (EB) 1901. The liberal standard of a former generation of preachers. Today's evangelical pastor won't get much of anything out of it.

✓   **Sweeney, Marvin A.** ‡ *The Twelve Prophets* (BO) 2 Vols., 2000. About 750pp of careful, fresh literary analysis. Though Sweeney is one of the leading American scholars on OT prophecy, this set does not have the same research behind it that, say, McComiskey above has. It will be of special interest to students because Sweeney, more than most, explores the literary and theological links among the Twelve. Note that Sweeney has more in the way of diachronic interests than some others in the series, and his faith is Judaism. [*Scripture Bulletin* 1/01; *CBQ* 10/01; *ExpTim* 7/01; *HebStud* 2002; *VT* 53.1; *JSOT* 99 (2002); *RelSRev* 7/03].

NOTE: Added to the discussion of Nogalski/Sweeney above is Paul Redditt, "Recent Research on the Book of the Twelve as One Book," *CurBS* 9 (2001): 47–80.

HOSEA

★ **Dearman, J. Andrew.** [𝓜], (NICOT) 2010. With this single volume on Hosea, Dearman has provided the Church with the best evangelical exegesis now available. It is full (400pp), conversant with all the important scholarship, sensitive to literary features, extremely well informed about socio-historical and archeological background issues, and provides good (mildly critical) theological exposition. I am delighted with the astute discussion of the Hebrew text and the author's treatment of "Hosea's Theology" (pp.29–59). Other high-points are the discussion of Baalism in the 8th cent., early covenant theology in the writing prophets, and the controversial topics of sexual infidelity and metaphor in this prophetic book. My only unfulfilled wish was for the exegetical sections to draw more theological conclusions. Dearman is a PCUSA minister who wrote the NIVAC work on Jeremiah-Lamentations, and who now teaches at Fuller Seminary, Houston. This is the studious pastor's first-pick.

★   **Garrett, Duane.** *Hosea, Joel* (NAC) 1997. Surely one of the better OT commentaries in the series. It can't compete with AB, WBC and ICC in detail of scholarship, but it presents the fruits of much commentary work over the preceding 30 years. The more up-to-date bibliography is helpful for students. This is one of the more conservative works on this list and is a good choice for most pastors. I note that Garrett also did the NAC work on Proverbs, Ecclesiastes, and Song of Songs; this is a better piece of work.

★   Kidner, Derek. *Love to the Loveless* (BST) 1981. A boon for the preacher. Full of pastoral and theological insight into the message of the prophecy and backed up with competent scholarship. [*EvQ* 1/84].

★   **McComiskey, Thomas E.** 1992. See "McComiskey" under The Twelve Minor Prophets. This is already a suggested purchase.

★   Smith, Gary V. *Hosea/Amos/Micah* (NIVAC) 2001. Pastors will appreciate the guidance of this OT professor in learning how to apply the message of these three lengthier Minor Prophets. About 180pp are devoted to Hosea. Amos is treated to 215pp of commentary, and Micah to nearly 170pp. Do note that, while this is more of a homiletical commentary, Smith has a good measure of dependable exegesis as well.

★ **Stuart, Douglas.** *Hosea–Jonah* (WBC) 1987. First-rate, original work by the Gordon-Conwell professor and one of the best in the OT series. Some evangelicals find Stuart readier to emend the MT tradition than they are. Also, he does not always set forth opposing viewpoints (e.g., at Hosea 6:7). Yet there is so much good to say about this volume. Stuart is especially valuable because he views the prophetic office much as Calvin did: the prophets' foremost calling was to be interpreters of the Torah, demanding a loving loyalty and trust in the God of the covenant. Longman says this should be a top priority; I agree. There are unconfirmed reports of a forthcoming revision by Stuart. [*JETS* 9/92].

✧ ✧ ✧ ✧ ✧ ✧

☆ **Andersen, Francis I., and David Noel Freedman.** [𝓜], (AB) 1980. The most thorough work on this prophet (699pp) with nearly exhaustive textual analysis. There is an excellent conservative commentary by Andersen (he contributed the Job volume in TOTC). Freedman's syllable counting can be discounted. I fear, though, that pastors don't have the time to work through a tome like this or Macintosh's. Hubbard, McComiskey, and Garrett are excellent in shorter compass. [*JBL* 101.2 (1982); *ThTo* 38.1; *JSS* Aut 88].

✓ Achtemeier, Elizabeth. [𝓜], *Minor Prophets I* (NIBC) 1995. Covers Hosea through Micah. The author is conservatively critical and a respected scholar. Ten years previously, Achtemeier published a work on Nahum–Malachi in the WJK series "Interpretation," so this NIBC work marks her completion of the Twelve. [*Them* 10/97; *WTJ* Spr 99; *JSOT* 79 (1998); *Interp* 7/98; *Chm* 113.1 (1999); *RelSRev* 10/97; *RTR* 4/01].

☆ Barrett, Michael V.P. *Love Divine and Unfailing: The Gospel According to Hosea*, 2008. From the well-received "Gospel According to the Old Testament" series published by P&R.

✓ **Beeby, H.D.** ‡ (ITC) 1989. I like this conservatively critical interpretation better than any of the other works in this series, excepting the commentaries on Genesis 12–50 and Jeremiah. Some good theological reflection (189pp). The author was a missionary professor in Taiwan and had a role, with others like Lesslie Newbigin, in the "Gospel and our Culture" movement. [*CBQ* 10/91; *HebStud* 1991].

✓ **Ben-Zvi, Ehud.** ‡ *Hosea* (FOTL) 2005. This rigorous contribution to the series gives ample evidence that the whole form critical enterprise is reforming and has moved with the rest of scholarship toward synchronic readings (e.g., Ben-Zvi speaks of *Sitz im Buch*, not *Sitz im Leben*). This "is a significant work not only on the book of Hosea, but also on the theory of literary study of the Bible" (Hutton). [*RTR* 8/07; *CBQ* 10/06; *JETS* 6/07; *Interp* 4/07; *JSS* Aut 08; *JSOT-BL* 2006; *VT* 57.4; *ExpTim* 11/06; *JAOS* 126.4 (Hutton); *RBL*; *CJ* 7/07].

☆ Birch, Bruce C. [𝓜], *Hosea, Joel, Amos* (WestBC) 1997. For the series, this is a more evangelically oriented interpretation of these prophets. Birch's commentary especially focuses upon the social critique offered by these prophets. This is a well written book and it speaks to the heart of the human problem: the problem of the human heart. See for example his poignant comments on p.91. [*Them* 2/00; *JSOT* 79; *CBQ* 7/98; *RelSRev* 7/98].

Brown, Sydney L. ‡ (Westminster Commentaries) 1932.

✓ **Brueggemann, Walter.** ‡ *Tradition for Crisis*, 1968. Pays good attention to the book's so-called complexes of tradition (Patriarchs, Exodus, Sinai covenant, etc.) and to theological issues. This has been a seminal work over the years. [*JBL* 91.1 (1972)].

Burroughs, Jeremiah. *An Exposition of the Prophecy of Hosea*, 1643. One of the greatest Puritan OT commentaries (699pp), completed posthumously.

☆ Carroll R., M. Daniel. (EBCR) 2008. This Denver Seminary professor is incisive and does consistently high-quality, carefully researched work. I am very pleased with this contribution. One wishes for more than these 90pp, and there had been word of a much fuller exegesis coming down the pike (Apollos). [*JSOT-BL* 2010].

F Daniels, Dwight R. ‡ (HCOT). I have already been impressed with this American scholar's Hamburg dissertation: *Hosea and Salvation History: The Early Traditions of Israel in the Prophecy of Hosea* (de Gruyter, 1990). He is more conservatively critical in approach and perhaps should be marked [*M*].

✓ **Davies, G.I.** ‡ (NCB) 1992. A very thorough work (315pp) by a leading OT scholar (a professor in Cambridge), to be consulted by students. Many years of research went into this. Yes, chs. 1 and 3 can be difficult to bring together, but Davies strangely argues that Gomer the prostitute bore Hosea's children but was never his wife (p.108). Only this late in the decline of Western morals could the notion of Hosea as "john" be countenanced! [*SwJT* Spr 94; *VT* 46.3; *RTR* 1/97; *CRBR* 1994]. Davies also has a good volume in the "OT Guides" series (1993).

✓ Emmerson, G. ‡ *Hosea: A Northern Prophet in Southern Perspective*, 1984. A valuable monograph from JSOT Press, notable for its more cautious approach to the redaction issue. [*Them* 9/85].

F Grisanti, Michael. *Hosea–Micah* (EEC).

☆ Guenther, Allen R. *Hosea, Amos* (BCBC) 1998. A fine, devout treatment of these two more significant Minor Prophets. The commentary is geared for the pastor or studious lay reader, employs both diachronic and synchronic approaches, and has many insights. Quite full at over 400pp. [*CBQ* 4/00].

Harper, W.R. ‡ (retired ICC) 1905. Some technical information can be gleaned from the three older ICC volumes on the Minor Prophets, but it is usually buried pretty deep in a lot of outdated data. Other volumes (AB, Herm, OTL, WBC, new ICC, NICOT) will be more helpful in this regard. Macintosh replaces Harper in the series.

☆ **Hubbard, David A.** [*M*], (TOTC) 1989. Perhaps the most scholarly entry thus far in the series. Seems to have been allowed a good deal more space than other commentators. This is an in-depth, exegetical work which pays close attention to theology. Hubbard was certainly in the critically oriented wing of evangelical scholarship, and one of the strongest influences on evangelicalism as general editor for WBC and former President of Fuller Seminary—now with the Lord. A favorite of Longman.

✓ **King, Philip.** ‡ *Amos, Hosea and Micah: An Archeological Commentary*, 1988. Excellent. See Jeremiah also.

✓ Knight, G.A.F. ‡ (Torch Bible Commentary) 1960. Mildly critical and filled with insightful comments.

Landy, Francis. ‡ (Read) 1995.

Limburg, James. ‡ *Hosea–Micah* (I) 1988. A solid entry in the series, though somewhat brief in covering these six prophets (201pp). [*CRBR* 1990].

✓ **Macintosh, A.A.** ‡ (ICC–new series) 1997. This replaces Harper. "An important landmark in the study of Hosea" (Davies), with the philological strengths we normally associate with ICC. There is more focus upon the text and less on the text's alleged pre-history (esp. redaction-critical matters) than we find in McKane's Jeremiah set for ICC. Also distinctive for the series is the author's effort "to mediate the insights of the mediaeval Jewish writers" (R.P. Gordon) on this Prophet. Evangelicals will find his approach more conservative than most in the ICC—I'm almost inclined to mark it [*M*]. [*Chm* 113.4 (1999); *JETS* 9/99; *JSOT* 79 (1998); *CBQ* 7/98; *OTA* 10/97; *RelSRev* 7/98; *EvQ* 4/01; *VT* 51.1 (2001); *DenvJ*].

McKeating, H. ‡ *Amos, Hosea, Micah* (CBC) 1971. I am clueless as to how Longman could give this work four stars and Mays only three. McKeating covers these three important Minor Prophets in about 200pp, and is a good, interesting work from the critical perspective.

☆ **Mays, James L.** ‡ (OTL) 1969. One of the strongest volumes in OTL, one which I have valued highly. Many studious pastors might like to add Mays to their library. Seems to have been written with the pastor in mind, but this is not shallow stuff at all. He concentrates on Hosea's message. Stuart once said this is the best liberal volume on Hosea. Students must reckon with a flood of scholarship on this prophet since Mays was published. [*WTJ* 34.1].

☆ Morgan, G. Campbell. *Hosea: The Heart and Holiness of God*, 1934. A very helpful exposition by Lloyd-Jones' famous predecessor at Westminster Chapel in London. Penetrates to the core of Hosea's message. This has been repeatedly reprinted and sits on many a pastor's shelf.

F Nogalski, James D. ‡ (S&H).

Ogilvie, Lloyd J. *Hosea, Joel, Amos, Obadiah, Jonah* (WCC) 1992.

☆ Patterson, Richard. (CorBC) 2008. This 672-page book is the joint effort of Patterson and Andrew Hill, covering all 12 Minor Prophets in the *New Living Translation*. It is competent and handy. Not for students.

F Roberts, J.J.M. ‡ (NCBC).

✓ Simundson, Daniel. ‡ *Hosea, Joel, Amos, Obadiah, Jonah, Micah* (AOTC) 2005. This exegetical work is not as dense as many others in the series and is thought by some reviewers to be a weaker volume in AOTC. Others like Ralph Klein praise it (but they share critical and Lutheran commitments). I was not impressed. It is clearly written and accessible. [*CBQ* 4/06; *JETS* 9/06; *Interp* 1/06; *JSOT-BL* 2006; *CurTM* 6/05; *RBL*; *ExpTim* 4/06; *HBT* 29.2].

Vawter, Bruce. ‡ *Amos, Hosea, Micah* (OTM) 1981. The author is a respected critic, but other works, from both the liberal and conservative camps, are much more thorough.

Ward, James M. ‡ *Hosea: A Theological Commentary*, 1966. Critically oriented and widely used decades ago.

✓ **Wolff, Hans Walter.** ‡ (Herm) ET 1974. This exhaustive work became the standard critical work along with AB. Liberal and very technical. The advanced student will find a mine of information here, especially with regard to textual criticism, form-critical analysis, tradition-history research, and theological commentary. Wolff was assigned the monumental task of treating all 12 Minor Prophets for BKAT. Each of his works—Hosea; Joel–Amos; Obadiah–Jonah; Micah; Haggai—is a standout commentary. The "fledgling student" would do well to steer clear of Wolff until capable of handling these commentaries with some discernment and understanding of Wolff's methodology.

Wood, Leon J. (EBC) 1985. See Carroll R. for Wood's replacement.

✓ Yee, Gale A. ‡ (NewIB) 1996. Students might find reason to consult this commentary, which builds upon her earlier study, *Composition and Tradition in the Book of Hosea*, 1987.

NOTES: (1) Harry Mowvley's "Which Is the Best Commentary? XVI. Amos and Hosea," *ExpTim*, 9/92. (2) Brad Kelle, "Hosea 1–3 in Twentieth-Century Scholarship," *CBR* 7.2

(2009): 179–216; and "Hosea 4–15 in Twentieth-Century Scholarship," *CBR* 8.3 (2010): 314–75. (3) Also consult the list of works in the above section, "Twelve Minor Prophets."

JOEL

★ Baker, David W. *Joel, Obadiah, Malachi* (NIVAC) 2006. Considering the brevity of these three Bible books, this 352-page homiletical commentary seems pleasingly full. In relation to other volumes in the series as a whole, generally speaking I find it provides better exegetical guidance and fewer wise thoughts on application. [*Anvil* 24.4].

★ **Dillard, Raymond.** 1992. See McComiskey under "Twelve Minor Prophets." This has been my favorite on Joel. Dillard of Westminster Seminary was able to build on Stuart's and Allen's excellent work. It is an interesting study to compare Dillard and Stuart on the question of whether to take the locust invasion of ch. 1 as literal or metaphorical. Great theology here for the preacher. Students working on Joel will also make ready use of Allen, Barton, Coggins, Crenshaw, and Wolff.

★ **Garrett, Duane.** *Hosea, Joel* (NAC) 1997. See Hosea. The more current bibliography helps students. This is one of the fullest (over 400pp) and best in the OT series.

★ Robertson, O. Palmer. *Prophet of the Coming Day of the Lord* (WCS) 1995. Normally I do not recommend these popularly styled paperbacks, but the theological exposition here is rich. Students will look elsewhere. Pastors may supplement this with Robertson's theological introduction, *The Christ of the Prophets*, 2004.

★ **Stuart, Douglas.** (WBC) 1987. See Hosea above.

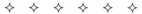

✓ Achtemeier, Elizabeth. [*M*], *Minor Prophets I* (NIBC) 1995. See Hosea above. This same scholar has also contributed the Joel commentary for the NewIB (1996).

☆ **Allen, Leslie C.** [*M*], *The Books of Joel, Obadiah, Jonah and Micah* (NICOT) 1976. A good commentary, but I'm bothered by some of his critical conclusions. Despite the volume's age, this is still one of the top evangelical works on Joel and "[o]ffers a very valuable survey of earlier scholarship" (Mason, 10). [*JBL* 3/78].

✓ **Barton, John.** ‡ *Joel and Obadiah* (OTL) 2001. One expects a highly competent commentary from this well-read Oxford scholar, and Barton delivers. The price (about $40) for this slim volume (170pp) will cause pastors to look elsewhere for reference works on these short prophets. Students will want to make ready use of this in the library. The exegesis is mainly pursued with older historical critical methods, and there is a good measure of theological reflection. [*CBQ* 10/02; *Them* Aut 02; *JTS* 4/03; *Interp* 10/02; *ExpTim* 1/03; *Biblica* 84.3; *VT* 54.2; *JSOT* 27.5; *RelSRev* 7/02; *Chm* Sum 05; *BSac* 4/03; *RBL*; *Anvil* 19.4].

F Ben-Zvi, Ehud, Gene M. Tucker, and J. William Whedbee. ‡ *Minor Prophets, Part 1* (FOTL). I believe this volume will cover Joel to Jonah. Ben-Zvi has already published separate volumes on Hosea and Micah.

✓ Bewer, J.A. ‡ (ICC) 1911.

☆ Birch, Bruce C. ‡ *Hosea, Joel, Amos* (WestBC) 1997. See Hosea.

Busenitz, Irvin Albert. *Joel and Obadiah* (Mentor) 2003. I have not used this commentary but it is said to be a clear, fairly full theological exposition at 288pp. The conservative author has taught for many years at Talbot and at The Master's Seminary. [*Chm* Spr 05; *RTR* 4/05].

✓ **Coggins, Richard J.** ‡ *Joel and Amos* (NCB) 2000. This marked the brief continuation of the series with a new British publisher (Sheffield). I have not seen this work in North America, but when I consulted it abroad I found it to be succinct (170pp), well reasoned, and helpful in discussing inner-biblical allusions and interpretation. Preachers are helped less is discerning the prophetic message in the text. [*ExpTim* 5/01; *CBQ* 10/01; *JSOT* 94 (2001); *RelSRev* 1/03; *Anvil* 18.3 (Renz)].

✓ **Crenshaw, James.** ‡ (AB) 1995. This volume is about 240pp long and adds luster to the series. Crenshaw is known as a trenchant critic, long at Vanderbilt and then at Duke. In my opinion this is now the most valuable liberal work on Joel. The scholarly pastor who intends to do some preaching on Joel's prophecy should definitely consider buying this. See Wolff below. [*JETS* 3/99; *BSac* 4/97].

✓ Driver, Samuel R. ‡ *Joel and Amos* (Cambridge Bible) 1897. Classic liberal work by one of the greatest British scholars around the turn of the century. There was a later revision (1915) with additions by H.C.O. Lanchester.

☆ **Finley, T.J.** *Joel, Amos, Obadiah* (WEC) 1990. This careful, balanced work is similar to Stuart's in that both are thoroughly evangelical, exegetical, and treat the Hebrew. This volume is worth buying, if you desire to build a first-class reference library. Moody allowed Finley to go o/p, but it has been reprinted by Biblical Studies Press. [*JETS* 9/93].

F Gordon, Robert P. [*M?*], (ICC–new series). This will be a treat indeed, covering Joel, Amos, and Obadiah, I believe. Gordon is Regius Professor of Hebrew at Cambridge and has more conservative sensibilities.

F Grisanti, Michael. *Hosea–Micah* (EEC).

F Hiebert, Ted. ‡ (Herm). To be added alongside Wolff; the publisher did the same thing with Shalom Paul on Amos.

☆ **Hubbard, David A.** [*M*], *Joel and Amos* (TOTC) 1989. Very useful and full treatment for the series (245pp). An excellent companion to the suggested works above. See also under Hosea. [*EvQ* 7/92; *Evangel* Win 89; *BSac* 10/92].

F Kwakkel, Gert. ‡ (HCOT). There was an earlier report of Willem Van der Meer having the contract.

✓ Limburg, James. ‡ *Hosea–Micah* (I) 1988. See under Hosea.

✓ Mason, Rex. ‡ *Zephaniah, Habakkuk, Joel* (OT Guides) 1994.

F Naylor, Peter. (Apollos).

F Nogalski, James D. ‡ (S&H).

Ogden, G.S., and R.R. Deutsch. ‡ *Joel and Malachi* (ITC) 1987.

Ogilvie, Lloyd J. *Hosea, Joel, Amos, Obadiah, Jonah* (WCC) 1992.

Patterson, Richard D. (EBC) 1985. Solid work from a well-respected evangelical, now a professor at Liberty University. See EBCR below.

☆ **Patterson, Richard D.** (EBCR) 2008. The earlier EBC received an update in these 37pp, and it is a worthwhile commentary for pastors. Students will look for more, however. [*JSOT-BL* 2010].

☆ Prior, David. *Joel, Micah, Habakkuk* (BST) 1998. Fairly full at over 250pp. I am not sure why these three prophets were grouped together for this exposition. Well done in the main, with many insights into the texts and their applicability in the world today. This can be recommended to all preachers. [*Chm* 113.4; *CTJ* 4/01].

F Roberts, J.J.M. ‡ (NCBC).

✓ Simundson, Daniel. ‡ *Hosea, Joel, Amos, Obadiah, Jonah, Micah* (AOTC) 2005. See under Hosea.

✓ Thompson, John A. "The Book of Joel, Exegesis" (IB) 1956. Said by Mason to be an "excellent commentary by one who studied the book in great depth over a long period" (p.10).

✓ **Wolff, Hans Walter.** ‡ *Joel and Amos* (Herm) ET 1977. Another exhaustive, rigorous critical resource from BKAT. See comments above under Hosea. Wolff's treatment of Joel is not quite as thorough as that of Amos, but, then again, a little less thoroughness in excavating redactional layers in Amos (six!) might actually have improved the commentary. For purposes of grasping up-to-date scholarship (especially in the North American context) the student will need to depend more upon Crenshaw's and Barton's bibliography. Wolff's theological interests are always close to the surface, and he argues for the unity of Joel.

NOTES: (1) Consult the list of works in the above section, The Twelve Minor Prophets. (2) See the review of recent research in Richard Coggins, "Joel," *CBR* 2.1 (2003): 85–103.

AMOS

★ Motyer, J.A. *The Day of the Lion* (BST) 1975. Typical of the series in general. Motyer contributed the Philippians and James volumes to BST and has always proved to be insightful in his expositions. [*EvQ* 10/75; *JETS* 12/75].

★ **Niehaus, Jeffery.** 1992. See McComiskey under Twelve Minor Prophets. This is already a suggested purchase. The author's strengths in the area of ANE studies well complement the other recommended works on this prophecy.

★ **Smith, Gary V.** 1989, rev. 1998. This thorough exegetical commentary was initially published by Zondervan. The author once taught at Bethel Seminary and Midwestern Baptist Seminary; now he is a professor at Union University. This is the best conservative work on Amos (fuller than Stuart and Niehaus) and should be your first choice, according to Stuart and Longman. I have seen a review of the 400-page "Mentor" commentary, which is a slight revision. Though these four selections for purchase are probably the most useful to the pastor, students will give prominence to the critical works by Paul, Andersen-Freedman, Wolff, Jeremias, and Mays—probably in that order. For pastoral reflection and application, Smith's new work for NIVAC, *Hosea/Amos/Micah*, is quite good but not stellar. The two Smith commentaries put me in a quandary: which to recommend? The earlier exegetical book has much more to teach, and the later NIVAC has more practical help for preachers moving from ancient text to application. [*CRBR* 1990; *Them* 2/00].

★ **Stuart, Douglas.** (WBC) 1987. See Hosea above.

✓ Achtemeier, Elizabeth. [*M*], *Minor Prophets I* (NIBC) 1995. See Hosea above.

✓ **Andersen, Francis I., and David Noel Freedman.** [*M*], (AB) 1989. Their superlative Hosea commentary was 650pp. This exhaustive work on a shorter prophecy is 1050pp! We would certainly have been better served by a rigorous pruning of material. I guess it is tough to edit your own work—Freedman was general editor for the series. This is among the best, most complete commentaries on Amos, but I won't recommend you purchase it unless you are an advanced student or scholarly pastor. (I am trying to be a realist; unless you are something of an OT specialist, you will be lost in all the detail.) This volume and those on Hosea and Micah are generally mild in their criticism, compared with most others in the AB. [*SJT* 93.2; *JBL* Fall 91; *Interp* 4/91; *CBQ* 7/91; *JNES* 4/95; *HebStud* 1991].

✓ Auld, A. Graeme. ‡ (OT Guides) 1986.

Beeley, Ray. 1970. This is a fine 120-page commentary by a godly English schoolmaster, published by Banner. Draws from Calvin, the Puritans and the older classics. Includes searching questions for applying the message. Probably o/p.

F   Ben-Zvi, Ehud, Gene M. Tucker, and J. William Whedbee. ‡ *Minor Prophets, Part 1* (FOTL). See under Joel.

☆   Birch, Bruce C. ‡ *Hosea, Joel, Amos* (WestBC) 1997. See Hosea.

F   Cardiff, Peter. (Apollos). There are conflicting reports. See Naylor below.

F   Carroll R., M. Daniel. (NICOT). This should be sterling. Will be a single volume on this prophet. Amos is receiving an exceptional amount of scholarly attention these days, and Carroll R. has contributed brilliantly to that scholarship: *Contexts for Amos* (1992); and *Amos, The Prophet and His Oracles* (WJK, 2002) [*CBQ* 7/03; *SwJT* Fall 04; *Interp* 4/04; *JSOT* 28.5; *JAOS* 123.3].

✓   **Coggins, Richard J.** ‡ *Joel and Amos* (NCB) 2000. See Joel above.

✓   Cripps, Richard S. ‡ 1955. An older commentary by a Cambridge don (first ed. was published in 1929).

F   Dijkstra, Meindert. ‡ (HCOT).

✓   Driver, Samuel R. ‡ *Joel and Amos* (Cambridge Bible) 1897. More valuable than Cripps and Harper, says Childs. See under Joel.

☆   **Finley, T.J.** Joel, *Amos, Obadiah* (WEC) 1990. See under Joel.

☆   **Garrett, Duane.** *Amos: A Handbook on the Hebrew Text* (BHHB) 2008. See under Commentary Series. The author here is a much-published, conservative Southern Baptist, and his work is full (304pp) and helpful to students, as well as to pastors wanting to stay in the Hebrew. [*RelSRev* 9/09; *JHebS* 2010; *CBQ* 4/10].

F   Gordon, Robert P. [*M*?], (ICC–new series). See under Joel.

✓   **Gowan, Donald E.** ‡ (NewIB) 1996.

F   Grisanti, Michael. *Hosea–Micah* (EEC).

☆   Guenther, Allen R. (BCBC) 1998. See under Hosea.

✓   **Hammershaimb, E.** ‡ ET 1970. Deals with technical matters, but is still fairly accessible. This has been one of the standard commentaries but has steadily lost value over the last 20 years or so with all the new publications now available. [*JBL* 91.2 (1972)].

✓   Harper, W.R. ‡ (ICC) 1905.

✓   **Hasel, Gerhard F.** *Understanding the Book of Amos*, 1991. Excellent analysis of the book. Hasel treats all the basic introductory questions and issues of interpretation. Published by Baker. The perfect guide for the student getting introduced to this prophecy, which has been receiving so much scholarly attention of late. [*BSac* 4/93; *CRBR* 1992]. Books of this kind are multiplying: see Auld and Carroll R. above and Watts below. I'll call Carroll R. the best of the lot.

✓   **Hayes, John H.** ‡ 1988. [*CRBR* 1990].

☆   Hill, Andrew. (CorBC) 2008. See under Hosea.

☆   **Hubbard, David A.** [*M*], *Joel and Amos* (TOTC) 1989. See under Joel.

✓   **Jeremias, Jörg.** ‡ (OTL) 1995, ET 1998. As is typical of much German OT scholarship, "Jeremias's leading concern is the history of the growth and composition of the book" (Tucker). That critical approach wearies many of us today. This is an important commentary for students to consult. [*JBL* Fall 97; *JTS* 10/96; *JSOT-BL* 1996; *Interp* 7/00; *CBQ* 7/97; *PSB* 21.1 (2000); *RelSRev* 10/98; *RBL*; *DenvJ*].

✓   Kapelrud, A.S. ‡ *Central Ideas in Amos*, 1961.

     Keddie, Gordon. *The Lord Is His Name* (WCS) 1986.

✓   **King, Philip.** ‡ *Amos, Hosea and Micah: An Archeological Commentary*, 1988.

     Lessing, R. Reed. (Concord) 2009. Said to be 691pp.

✓   Limburg, James. ‡ *Hosea-Micah* (I) 1988. See under Hosea.

     McComiskey, T.E. (EBC) 1985. When it was published, this was probably the leading conservative work.

☆ **McComiskey, Thomas E., and Tremper Longman III.** (EBCR) 2008. A solid work (see above) made better. These 70pp are valuable for both exegesis and theological exposition. [*JSOT-BL* 2010].

McKeating, H. ‡ (CBC) 1971. See under Hosea.

✓ Martin-Achard, R. ‡ (ITC) 1984. See under Lamentations. Hubbard uses Martin-Achard a good bit.

☆ **Mays, James L.** ‡ (OTL) 1969. Years ago the pastor looking for a supplement to Stuart and Smith would have been wise to pick up this commentary, but now Mays is getting dated and some newer works have greater appeal to the evangelical pastor. Mays is moderately critical in his approach and one of the most thoughtful liberal commentators on the OT I have read. See Jeremias above for a newer Amos volume in the OTL series. I do not know if the publisher, WJK, plans to retire this Mays volume. [*WTJ* 34.1].

F Möller, Karl. (THC). Preparing the way is his dissertation, *A Prophet in Debate: The Rhetoric of Persuasion in the Book of Amos*, 2003 [*BibInt* 12.4].

F Naylor, Peter. (Apollos). There are conflicting reports. See Cardiff above.

F Nogalski, James D. ‡ (S&H).

Ogilvie, Lloyd J. *Hosea, Joel, Amos, Obadiah, Jonah* (WCC) 1992.

☆ **Paul, Shalom.** ‡ (Herm) 1991. An impressive work (409pp) by a Jewish scholar, hailed by many as pointing in a new, more productive scholarly direction. This is not a replacement volume for Wolff, but a complementary study which takes a more holistic and more conservative approach to the text. Along with Andersen/Freedman and Wolff, this is a leading technical commentary. The pastor with the money and desire to build a first-class reference library will consider buying this. I bought Paul and find the commentary to be the most stimulating and satisfying technical work available on Amos for examining literary features, but I realize most pastors do not share my academic interests. There is little theology here. [*CBQ* 1/93; *JBL* Sum. 93; *Interp* 4/93; *VT* 4/95; *Them* 10/94; *JSOT* 57; *BSac* 10/92].

F Roberts, J.J.M. ‡ (NCBC).

✓ Simundson, Daniel. ‡ *Hosea, Joel, Amos, Obadiah, Jonah, Micah* (AOTC) 2005. See under Hosea.

☆ Smith, Gary V. *Hosea/Amos/Micah* (NIVAC) 2001. This volume has been recommended for purchase under Hosea. Many pastors will want NIVAC for Amos. See Smith's earlier Amos commentary listed above.

☆ Smith, Billy K., and Frank S. Page. *Amos, Obadiah, Jonah* (NAC) 1995. This work of over 300pp fulfills the aims of the series. The section on Amos is the best here; the Obadiah and Jonah sections are among the poorer contributions to NAC. [*JETS* 3/98; *VT* 47.1; *JSOT* 76; *SwJT* Spr 98; *HebStud* 1997].

✓ **Soggin, J. Alberto.** ‡ ET 1987. This critical commentary was published by Fortress Press and is worth consulting. [*Them* 1/89; *JBL* Sum 89].

Thorogood, Bernard. ‡ *A Guide to the Book of Amos*, 1971.

Vawter, Bruce. ‡ *Amos, Hosea, Micah* (OTM) 1981. See under Hosea.

Veldkamp, Herman. *The Farmer from Tekoa*, ET 1977. Rich sermonic material from a master preacher in the Dutch Reformed Church.

Waard, Jan de, and William Allen Smalley. (UBS) 1994.

Watts, John D.W. [*M*], *Vision and Prophecy in Amos*, 1958, 2nd ed 1997. [*DenvJ*].

✓ **Wolff, H.W.** ‡ (Herm) ET 1977. See Joel above. [*JBL* 90.4 (1971)].

NOTE: Consult the list of works in the above section, "The Twelve Minor Prophets."

—ɯ—

OBADIAH

★ Baker, David W. *Joel, Obadiah, Malachi* (NIVAC) 2006. See under Joel. This meets a real need, since we lack a good selection of strong expositions which offer guidance in applying Obadiah today.

★ **Niehaus, Jeffrey.** *The Minor Prophets: An Exegetical and Expository Commentary*, Vol. 2, Ed. by Thomas E. McComiskey, 1993. Already recommended for purchase; see the section above on the Twelve Minor Prophets. This second volume in the set seems every bit as strong as the first. On Obadiah specifically, Niehaus and Stuart are the best works, if we leave off Raabe. The number of good commentaries on this long-neglected prophet is nothing short of astonishing. Finding expositional help, however, has long been more difficult with Obadiah. At least now we have Baker. See also Brown, Busenitz, Calvin, Marbury, and Ogilvie.

★ **Raabe, Paul R.** (AB) 1996. This is a very substantial single volume on Obadiah (273pp). Few have the money to buy a book like this on such a short prophecy, but this is the best (because fullest). Raabe teaches at the conservative Concordia Theological Seminary in St. Louis. Andersen and Freedman originally had the contract. [*JBL* Fall 00; *JSOT* 79 (1998); *CBQ* 1/99; *RelSRev* 7/97; *RBL*].

★ **Stuart, Douglas.** (WBC) 1987. See Hosea above.

✓ **Achtemeier, Elizabeth.** [*M*], *Minor Prophets I* (NIBC) 1995. See Hosea above.

☆ **Allen, Leslie C.** [*M*], (NICOT) 1976. See Joel above.

Armerding, Carl E. (EBC) 1985. Brief but good scholarship (better than many others in EBC). Armerding taught alongside Bruce Waltke at Regent College in Vancouver. See the next entry.

☆ **Armerding, Carl E.** (EBCR) 2008. A lot of pastors would probably be content to have only these 27pp on this prophecy, which is so often ignored or regarded as unattractive. [*JSOT-BL* 2010].

☆ **Baker, David, T.D. Alexander, and Bruce Waltke.** *Obadiah, Jonah and Micah* (TOTC) 1988. This commentary is a 207-page gem, mainly because of Waltke's work on Micah and Alexander's 45-page, thoughtful introduction to Jonah (which defends the orthodox position). Baker's commentary on Obadiah is well reasoned, balanced and valuable—no "throw-away." Even if this is all you have on Obadiah, you may think you're still in good shape. [*JETS* 6/92]. Note Baker's more recent homiletical commentary above.

✓ Barton, John. ‡ *Joel and Obadiah* (OTL) 2001. See Joel above.

✓ **Ben Zvi, Ehud.** ‡ *A Historical-Critical Study of the Book of Obadiah*, 1996. See also his form-critical work on Hosea and Micah in FOTL. Students will consult this commentary for the rare exegetical paper on this Minor Prophet. Much attention paid here to the putative readers. [*CBQ* 7/98; *HebStud* 1999; *RelSRev* 7/97].

F Ben-Zvi, Ehud, Gene M. Tucker, and J. William Whedbee. ‡ *Minor Prophets, Part 1* (FOTL). See under Joel.

✓ Bewer, J.A. ‡ (ICC) 1911.

☆ Brown, William P. ‡ *Obadiah through Malachi* (WestBC) 1996. One of the few and most helpful pastoral expositions of Obadiah. Brown has also written a well-received exposition of Ecclesiastes. There are few remarks here to suggest higher criticism. [*JSOT* 79 (1998); *CBQ* 10/98; *RelSRev* 1/98; *Interp* 7/98].

Busenitz, Irvin Albert. *Joel and Obadiah* (Mentor) 2003. See under Joel.

Clark, David J., Norm Mundhenk, *et al. A Handbook on the Books of Obadiah, Jonah, and Micah* (UBS) 1993.

✓ **Coggins, R.J.** and S.P. Re'emi. ‡ *Nahum, Obadiah, Esther* (ITC) 1985. See under Esther. Mason once called Coggins' work on Nahum here "[t]he best of recent commentaries, emphasizing the function and cultic setting of such prophecy" (p.56). Obadiah is similarly well-done from the historical critical angle (38pp).

Eaton, J.H. ‡ *Obadiah, Nahum, Habakkuk, and Zephaniah* (Torch) 1961. At one time it was considered very useful because there were few commentators.

☆ **Finley, T.J.** *Joel, Amos, Obadiah* (WEC) 1990. See under Joel.

F Gordon, Robert P. [*M?*], (ICC–new series). See under Joel.

F Grisanti, Michael. *Hosea–Micah* (EEC).

✓ **Jenson, Philip Peter.** [*M*], *Obadiah, Jonah, Micah: A Theological Commentary*, 2008. Like Joyce's choice volume on Ezekiel, this book was to have been published in NCB, but that series is now defunct. It is a compact exegesis of 227pp with indices, aimed at explaining the theological message in its original context, with a few Christian reflections. The volume is divided as follows: Obadiah, pp.3–27; Jonah, 29–93; Micah, 95–189. Jenson is reluctant to say much about compositional history since it is so speculative; he prefers to take a canonical, synchronic approach. With regard to Jonah, he sees serious problems with reading it as a historical account and with discerning a fitting genre categorization. "Most recent commentators wisely leave the genre as general as possible" (p.34) and speak of "story." In coming to the exegetical treatment of the text, one finds Jenson astute, careful, and responsible. He has taught at the evangelical Trinity College, Bristol, and at Ridley Hall, Cambridge. For reasons of price ($140), this will regrettably have to be consulted only in the library. I trust it will soon appear in pb. [*CBQ* 10/09; *JSOT-BL* 2010; *VT* 60.2 (Williamson); *JHebS* 2009].

Kleinert, Paul. (Lange) ET 1874.

✓ Limburg, James. ‡ *Hosea–Micah* (I) 1988. See under Hosea.

Marbury, E. *Obadiah and Habakkuk*, 1649 (1865 edition reprinted). This Puritan work offers a lengthy Reformed exposition of these books. I have never used it, but you may wish to look it up. Warmly commended by Spurgeon.

✓ Mason, Rex. ‡ *Micah, Nahum, Obadiah* (OT Guides) 1991.

F Möller, Karl. (Apollos).

F Nogalski, James D. ‡ (S&H).

Ogilvie, Lloyd J. *Hosea, Joel, Amos, Obadiah, Jonah* (WCC) 1992.

✓ **Pagan, Samuel.** ‡ (NewIB) 1996.

Perowne, T.T. *Obadiah and Jonah* (Cambridge Bible for Schools and Colleges) 1889.

✓ **Renkema, John.** ‡ (HCOT) ET 2003. This well-done and large-scale (224-page) work is more focused upon historical critical concerns. Students will certainly consult this commentary, which is now a leading work. Compare with Raabe, who is more conservative. [*JSOT* 28.5; *VT* 57.2; *RelSRev* 10/04 (Sweeney)].

✓ Simundson, Daniel. ‡ *Hosea, Joel, Amos, Obadiah, Jonah, Micah* (AOTC) 2005. See under Hosea.

Smith, Billy K., and Frank S. Page. *Amos, Obadiah, Jonah* (NAC) 1995. See under Amos.

✓ **Thompson, John A.** "The Book of Obadiah, Exegesis" (IB) 1956. Few works in vol. 6 are worthwhile, but this one and Thomas' "Haggai" and "Zechariah 1–8" have been.

✓ **Watts, John D.W.** ‡ *Obadiah: A Critical, Exegetical Commentary*, 1969. Important since it was long the most in-depth commentary on this tiny book. "His cultic interpretation can be safely ignored" (Childs). Used to be reprinted every so often. If you are planning to do a lot of study in Obadiah, you will want to look this up.

Watts was usually spoken of as the authority to consult, at least prior to the publication of Raabe. [*JBL* 90.2 (1971)]. He also has a later commentary on this book in the CBC series (1975).

✓ **Wolff, H.W.** ‡ *Obadiah and Jonah*, (ContC) ET 1986. Another translation from the BKAT series, but this time the publisher for Wolff's work was Augsburg rather than Fortress Press. (Those two publishing houses have merged.) This volume meets the same standards established in the earlier Hermeneia commentaries. The student must consult Wolff on technical issues. Wolff's strengths were form criticism, tradition-history, and theological interpretation. See Hosea. [*JBL* 99.2 (1980); *CRBR* 1988].

NOTE: Consult the list of works in the above section, "The Twelve Minor Prophets."

JONAH

★ **Alexander, T.D.** (TOTC) 1988. See Baker (TOTC, not NIVAC) under Obadiah. Alexander has some excellent theological insights. He ably defends his conservative approach to the prophecy in this commentary. You might also consult "Jonah and Genre," *TynBul* 36 (1985) 35–59, a significant, wisely cautious article for conservatives to read. [*JETS* 6/92].

★ Bruckner, James K. *Jonah, Nahum, Habakkuk, Zephaniah* (NIVAC) 2004. Preachers especially will esteem this as an excellent addition to the series. Together with my friend, Dale Brueggemann [*CTJ* 4/08], I find his treatment of Jonah slightly inferior to the fine exposition of Nahum through Zephaniah. The particular weakness is a straining to rehabilitate Jonah as a good prophet. As I wrote earlier, one needs to remember that prophets, priests, and kings (2 Samuel 11 and 24) can point to Christ—the need for a perfect prophet, priest and king—in their failures as well as their successes. I note, however, that Longman finds the Jonah section "the most stimulating." Alongside this book and Ferguson, preachers should also consider Brown, Keddie, Martin, Nixon, and Robertson.

★ Ferguson, Sinclair. *Man Overboard*, 1982. Recently reprinted by Banner (2008), this theologically insightful study in sermonic form was originally from Tyndale House Publishers. I consider this to be model preaching. Ferguson has ministered both as a pastor (in his native Scotland and now in Columbia, SC) and as Professor of Systematics at Westminster Seminary (first in Philadelphia and then in Texas).

★ **Sasson, Jack M.** ‡ (AB) 1990. Along with Wolff, one of the leading scholarly commentaries in English. Sasson's approach is essentially synchronic, using the new literary criticism and focusing on the text's *being* rather than its *becoming*. Even fuller in its discussion than ContC or OTL. Specialists will consult this work often, and scholarly pastors will want to purchase it. [*JBL* Spr 92; *CBQ* 1/93; *Interp* 7/92; *JNES* 4/95; *AsTJ* Fall 92].

★ **Stuart, Douglas.** (WBC) 1987. See Hosea above. Evangelicals value this reverent defense of the miraculous in Jonah's prophecy, but there is far more substance to the work than just that. The exegesis is well-reasoned and insightful. Stuart's literary observations and theological guidance meet the needs of preachers. Stuart's favorite (kudos for humility?).

✓ Aalders, G. Charles. *The Problem of the Book of Jonah*, ET 1948. A short defense of the book as fitting the genre of history and as credible.

✓ Achtemeier, Elizabeth. [*M*], *Minor Prophets I* (NIBC) 1995. See Hosea above.

☆ **Allen, Leslie C.** [M], (NICOT) 1976. See Joel above and Micah below. The major deficiency here is the brevity of the commentary, a little over 30pp; by contrast Stuart spends 67pp. Allen reads Jonah as a non-historical parable, though it is certainly not an impossible "sea yarn"—see the note below. This has long been a leading evangelical commentary.

☆ **Baldwin-Caine, Joyce.** *The Minor Prophets: An Exegetical and Expository Commentary*, Vol. 2, Ed. by Thomas E. McComiskey, 1993. A solid work which rivals the other evangelical works now available, but this was perhaps not her finest hour—see her numerous volumes in the Tyndale series. This is not among my top picks for Jonah, but the whole set has been recommended for purchase.

F Ben-Zvi, Ehud, Gene M. Tucker, and J. William Whedbee. ‡ *Minor Prophets, Part 1* (FOTL). See under Joel.

✓ Bewer, J.A. ‡ (ICC) 1912.

☆ Brown, William P. ‡ *Obadiah–Malachi* (WestBC) 1996. Well done and conservatively critical. See Obadiah.

Cary, Phillip. (Brazos) 2008. I have not yet had a chance to explore this exposition by an Augustine scholar, said by reviewers to read Jonah as a humorous allegory. [*JETS* 6/09; *HBT* 31.2; *JSOT-BL* 2010; *RelSRev* 9/09; *CBQ* 4/10].

Clark, David J., Norm Mundhenk, et al. *A Handbook on the Books of Obadiah, Jonah, and Micah* (UBS) 1993.

Ellison, H.L. (EBC) 1985. Replaced by Walton.

✓ Ellul, Jacques. [M], *The Judgment of Jonah*, ET 1971. A stimulating and successful study which seeks to interpret the book's message Christologically; it is more of a reflection on Jonah than an exegesis or textual exposition. Though difficult to pinpoint on the theological spectrum, Ellul was essentially Barthian. Eerdmans has reprinted this.

☆ Estelle, Bryan D. *Salvation through Judgment and Mercy: The Gospel According to Jonah*, 2005. An attractive, well-studied, biblical theological reading (157pp) by a professor at Westminster Seminary California.

Fairbairn, Patrick. 1849. Another classic 19th century exposition besides Martin which would provide preachers with grist for the mill.

✓ Fretheim, T.E. ‡ *The Message of Jonah*, 1977. Warmly received in mainline circles as a theological exposition and literary analysis. It remains useful, if you make allowances for his critical stance. [*JBL* 9/79].

F Grisanti, Michael. *Hosea–Micah* (EEC).

✓ Hasel, Gerhard F. [M], *Jonah: Messenger of the Eleventh Hour*, 1976. A fine treatment of Jonah by an able biblical theologian.

✓ **Jenson, Philip Peter.** [M], *Obadiah, Jonah, Micah: A Theological Commentary*, 2008. See under Obadiah.

☆ Keddie, Gordon J. *Preacher on the Run* (WCS) 1986.

Kleinert, Paul. (Lange) ET 1874. Defends historicity of the account.

Knight, G.A.F., and F.W. Golka. ‡ *The Song of Songs and Jonah* (ITC) 1988.

F Kugel, James. ‡ (Herm). This will have some of the same strengths as Sasson's work, and I expect it to be of high quality as a technical research tool.

Legg, John. *When We Don't Understand: God's Ways with Jonah and Habakkuk* (WCS) 1986.

✓ **Lessing, R. Reed.** (Concord) 2007. A very large (451-page), reverent exegetical and theological treatment from an OT scholar at conservative Concordia Seminary. No doubt, he will be panned by critics for taking the fish story literally. He aims to help preachers and students in Christological interpretation and with proclamation. The usual Lutheran move from Law to Grace is common here. The complaint of some will be that, as he labors to explain elements of NT theology in Jonah, he seems to mute the "authentic voice of the OT." Students can also expect to find some penetrating exegetical insights, especially in the area of linguistic parallels (biblical intertexts). [*JETS* 12/08; *BSac* 10/09; *VT* 60.1; *CBQ* 7/10].

Limburg, James. ‡ *Hosea–Micah* (I) 1988. See under Hosea. For expositors.

✓ **Limburg, James.** ‡ (OTL) 1993. This is much more thorough and scholarly than his treatment of Jonah in the Interpretation series. Still, at 123pp it appears brief compared to, say, Sasson's work, which I also find more interesting. P.R. Davies writes with characteristic bite, "Rarely do I think a commentary might have been longer; here is an exception." Certainly classed as one of the most important commentaries from the critical camp. Some (e.g., Jenson [*BSB* 9/96]) have recommended Limburg highly. [*ThTo* 4/94; *Interp* 4/95; *JTS* 4/95; *VT* 10/95; *JSOT* 3/95; *Them* 10/95; *JETS* 3/96; *JSOT* 65; *HebStud* 1995, 1996].

Mackay, John L. *Jonah, Micah, Nahum, Habakkuk, Zephaniah* (Focus on the Bible) 2008. Lengthy exposition (420pp) from a Reformed perspective.

☆ Martin, Hugh. (GS) 1877. A classic theological exposition from the 19th century. Spurgeon rather overstated his case—even for his own day—when he wrote, "No one who has it will need any other." Still, it is very good, edifying, and worth buying. Twenty years ago I made this a purchase recommendation. (Frankly, it is one of my favorite older commentaries on either testament.) If you think Martin is verbose or you would like a more contemporary exposition, buy Estelle or Robertson.

F Möller, Karl. (Apollos).

☆ **Nixon, Rosemary A.** (BST) 2003. Though open to interpreting Jonah as allegory, Nixon is not insistent on that reading scheme. She is sharp in picking up literary features and offers a surprisingly full theological exposition (about 220pp on four short chapters). There is real learning here, and students can profitably consult Nixon. Evangelical pastors will find this BST homiletically rich and stimulating. [*JETS* 9/04; *JSOT* 28.5].

F Nogalski, James D. ‡ (S&H).

Ogilvie, Lloyd J. *Hosea, Joel, Amos, Obadiah, Jonah* (WCC) 1992.

☆ Patterson, Richard. (CorBC) 2008. See under Hosea.

Perowne, T.T. *Obadiah and Jonah* (Cambridge Bible for Schools and Colleges) 1889.

F Phillips, Richard D. *Jonah & Micah* (REC) 2010. I expect this will be quite useful as an example of rich, well-studied expository preaching. See the author's other volumes on Hebrews and Zechariah.

F Potgieter, Johannes H. ‡ (HCOT).

☆ Robertson, O. Palmer. *Jonah: A Study in Compassion*, 1990. An exposition from one of today's best OT biblical theologians in the Reformed camp. Published by Banner.

Roop, Eugene F. [*M*], *Ruth, Jonah, Esther* (BCBC) 2002. One of the finest in this Anabaptist series.

F Sherwood, Yvonne. ‡ (Blackwell).

✓ **Simon, Uriel.** [*M*], (JPS) ET 1999. This is the first JPS commentary outside the Pentateuch. "The author tries to combine the insights of the traditional Jewish commentators and modern biblical exegesis" [*JSOT* 89]. Though not of great length (xliii + 52pp), this book will set you back $35.00. Whew! A helpful commentary with much to offer in theological reflection (especially on the theme of God's compassion versus the prophet's demand for justice), grammatical analysis, and literary sensitivity. I find little in this work which could be termed higher critical, except the notion that the story is fictionalized. [*Interp* 10/00; *CBQ* 4/00; *RelSRev* 1/01; *DenvJ*].

✓ Simundson, Daniel. ‡ *Hosea, Joel, Amos, Obadiah, Jonah, Micah* (AOTC) 2005. See under Hosea.

Smith, Billy K., and Frank S. Page. *Amos, Obadiah, Jonah* (NAC) 1995. See under Amos.

✓ **Trible, Phyllis.** ‡ *Rhetorical Criticism: Context, Method, and the Book of Jonah*, 1995. One in the Fortress series, "Guides to Biblical Scholarship." She discusses the new rhetorical approaches and then applies the methods in interpreting Jonah. All in all, an excellent introduction to the newer synchronic approaches and a rich reading of Jonah—she wrote her 1963 dissertation on Jonah. [*CBQ* 7/96; *JBL* Win 95; *Interp* 1/97; *JR* 1/97]. Mention should also be made of her Jonah contribution to *NewIB*, 1996.

☆ **Tucker, W. Dennis.** *Jonah: A Handbook on the Hebrew Text* (BHHB) 2006. The first volume in the Baylor series (see under Commentary Series). Not a commentary in the traditional sense, this 120-page work will encourage students and pastors to make good progress in reading and understanding the Hebrew. [*VT* 58.1; *ExpTim* 9/08; *JETS* 3/08].

☆ **Walton, John H.** (EBCR) 2008. A fine replacement for Ellison. The quality here could make one wish for more than 38pp. The stance is conservative, saying that "the Israelite audience would have considered the narrative a reflection of reality" (p.463), and he will follow their lead. But this is not a "journalistic history." There is more straight exegesis here and less theological reflection. [JSOT-BL 2010].

✓ **Wolff, H.W.** ‡ (ContC) ET 1986. See Obadiah above.

NOTES: (1) Consult the list of works in the above section, The Twelve Minor Prophets. (2) In this modern age with its short attention-span, few OT books are as inviting as Jonah to the minister inclined to systematic book expositions. One article well worth reading prior to preaching on Jonah is John H. Stek's "The Message of the Book of Jonah," *CTJ* 4 (1969): 23–50. (3) See Kenneth Craig, "Jonah in Recent Research," *CurBS* 7 (1999): 97–118. (4) Critical scholars often speak of Jonah as a fictionalized story, perhaps in the genre of parable or allegory. Many church folk, too, consider it a "fish tale," and the expositor certainly must deal with the genré question before commencing a sermon series. With my own congregation I made the following points (in simpler language). First, it is a mistake to make the story's historicity and matters of piscine/cetacean anatomy our major concern. See the sage remarks of Ferguson (p.45) on this point. Second, while mere stories can teach truth (e.g., Jesus' parables), there are still reasons in the Jonah text for reading the account in a more straightforward fashion, not as a parable. "The incident is reported very matter-of-factly" (Brown, p.23). On the all-important genre question, see Alexander above. Third, there have been similar stupendous stories told of "fish swallows person." Some are obviously fiction while others seem quite within the realm of history (cf. Sasson, pp. 150–151; *Princeton Theological Review* 25 [1927] 630–642; but note also *ExpTim* 17 [1905/6]: 521, and *ExpTim* 18 [1906/7]: 239). Finally, our approach to Scripture ought to be "faith seeking understanding" (*fides quaerens intellectum* –Anselm). We begin our search with faith, not rationalism and positivism which *a priori* reject all supernatural claims. Instead of the world's "seeing is believing" skepticism, we stand on Jesus' principle that only by believing will we see—see the glory of God (John 11:40).

MICAH

★ **Allen, Leslie C.** [*M*], (NICOT) 1976. See Joel above. Allen gives proportionally more space and careful attention to Micah than to the other three Bible books covered: Jonah's four chapters get about 30pp, and Micah's seven chapters get 140pp of exegesis. Unfortunately, Allen treats portions of chs. 4 and 7 as non-Mican, which I consider unnecessary. So often a more fragmentary reading causes the interpreter to miss points in the book's unfolding theology. For one attempt to redress this limitation (though he denies single authorship), see David Hagstrom, *The Coherence of the Book of Micah: A Literary Analysis*, 1988. Allen is a good work to have, but I do not rave about it.

★ **Andersen, Francis I., and David Noel Freedman.** [*M*], (AB) 2000. Scholars waited a long time for this massive volume; the commentary was essentially completed in 1993. Along with Waltke, this volume is the most comprehensive commentary available on Micah, though lacking in the area of theological reflection. The co-authors are brilliant scholars who have a long history of collaboration in commenting upon the Minor Prophets—see Hosea and Amos above. Freedman was editor of the *ABD*. This 600-page work is definitely for the academically inclined; the average pastor will have difficulty digesting the vast material here without surrendering the time necessary for personal reflection and meditation. Students should make ready use of the 67-page bibliography! The scholarly approach in this AB volume is cautiously critical, patiently exegetical, detail-oriented, and more inclined to treat the final form of the text. Do note that Hillers and Wolff (ContC) below are both valuable in their own way—perhaps just as valuable for scholarship as Andersen/Freedman. Pastors not interested in buying this more expensive and technical volume should rely on Waltke and McComiskey/Longman for exegetical help. [*CBQ* 7/01; *JTS* 10/01; *JETS* 12/02; *JBL* Sum 02; *JSS* Spr 03; *BSac* 4/02; *VT* 53.2; *JSOT* 94 (2001); *RelSRev* 4/02; *BBR* 13.2; *TJ* Fall 04; *Interp* 1/05; *RBL*; *DenvJ* 1/02 (Carroll R)].

★ Kaiser, Walter. *Micah, Nahum, Habakkuk, Zephaniah, Haggai, Zechariah, Malachi* (WCC) 1993. If you are looking for a homiletical commentary on these books, you really cannot go wrong with this volume (nearly 500pp). It has pastoral insight and, as one of the few WCC volumes written by a professional OT scholar, is better researched than most. Among all these suggested purchases, the average preacher will prefer, and be more than satisfied with, having Waltke, Allen, and Smith on the shelf. Besides Kaiser and Smith listed here, Calvin, Prior, Craigie, and Boice (see "Twelve Minor Prophets" above) also offer good homiletical suggestions on Micah. Of note among critical expositions for pastors would be Brown and Limburg.

★ Smith, Gary V. *Hosea/Amos/Micah* (NIVAC) 2001. See Hosea above.

★ **Waltke, Bruce K.** *A Commentary on Micah*, 2007. Don't get confused. Waltke has three different works on Micah. First came the Tyndale Commentary (1988), superb but brief [*JETS* 6/92]. In 1993 he gave us a fuller exegesis with much more discussion of the Hebrew text; see the McComiskey-edited work below. Now we have the 2007 commentary, which is twice the length of the 1993 work and is the best evangelical exegesis (nearly definitive from the grammatico-historical angle). Students and more scholarly pastors should all start here, after first doing their own exegesis. Waltke is such a good Hebraist! [*CTJ* 4/08; *RTR* 12/07; *CBQ* 1/08; *BBR* 19.1 (2009); *JTS* 4/08; *Interp* 7/08; *JSOT-BL* 2008; *VT* 58.3; *RelSRev* 12/08; *JETS* 3/08].

✓ Achtemeier, Elizabeth. [*M*], *Minor Prophets I* (NIBC) 1995. See Hosea above.

Alfaro, Juan I. ‡ (ITC) 1989. Interesting majority-world (developing-world) perspective on Micah's issues of wealth and poverty. Many of us Americans do need our eyes opened to the fact that economic justice is a theological and spiritual concern. Somewhat brief (85pp). [*CBQ* 1/91; *HebStud* 1991].

☆ **Barker, Kenneth L.**, and Waylon Bailey. *Micah, Nahum, Habakkuk, Zephaniah* (NAC) 1999. A very competent Dispensational treatment by Barker. Bailey covers the three shorter books here. [*JETS* 9/00].

☆ Bentley, Michael. *Balancing the Books* (WCS on Micah and Nahum) 1994.

✓ **Ben Zvi, Ehud.** ‡ (FOTL) 2000. Here this erudite Jewish scholar, presently teaching at the University of Alberta, has written a dense 200-page form-critical treatment of Micah. It is a more critical interpretation than some other first-rate scholars have recently offered (e.g., Andersen and Freedman). As with almost all FOTL volumes, this work is solely of interest to academics. The author is well-known for advocating that form critical researchers consider "prophetic book" as a form. What is revisionist here is that, while older typical forms are discarded as useful categories, Ben Zvi's form critical approach treats every unit in Micah as a "prophetic reading." [*OTA* 10/00; *JTS* 4/01; *CBQ* 1/01; *JETS* 3/02; *JBL* Win 01; *HebStud* 2002; *VT* 51.4; *JSOT* 94; *RelSRev* 4/03].

☆ Brown, William P. ‡ *Obadiah–Malachi* (WestBC) 1996. See Obadiah.

☆ Calvin, John. *Sermons on Micah*, ET 1990. There was an initial translation published in hb that was terribly expensive; Blair Reynolds was the translator (Mellen, 1990). Now P&R has released an inexpensive 424-page pb translation done by Ben Farley: *Sermons on the Book of Micah*, 2003. This is different from the commentary and makes for fascinating reading.

Clark, David J., Norm Mundhenk, *et al. A Handbook on the Books of Obadiah, Jonah, and Micah* (UBS) 1993.

F De Moor, Johannes C. ‡ (HCOT).

F Grisanti, Michael. *Hosea–Micah* (EEC).

☆ Hill, Andrew. (CorBC) 2008. See under Hosea.

☆ **Hillers, D.R.** ‡ (Herm) 1984. Not as exhaustive (21pp of introduction and 70 packed pages of commentary) as Wolff's work and much more cautious in its critical approach (avoids redaction-critical analysis). A good, solid technical piece of work. Scholarly students and pastors (with money) wanting to do close work with the Hebrew text of Micah might be interested in obtaining this. Hillers was Stuart's first choice in 1990, but it is now becoming dated. [*TJ* Fall 84; *HebStud* 1985].

✓ Jacobs, Mignon R. *The Conceptual Coherence of the Book of Micah*, 2001. A reworked Claremont dissertation, completed under Knierim and employing the Doktorvater's "concept-critical method." The prophecy is coherent, she argues, mainly as the result of redactors' work, "contemporizing" even the oldest material.

✓ **Jenson, Philip Peter.** [𝕸], *Obadiah, Jonah, Micah: A Theological Commentary*, 2008. See under Obadiah.

✓ **King, Philip.** ‡ *Amos, Hosea and Micah: An Archeological Commentary*, 1988.

✓ Kleinert, Paul. (Lange) ET 1874.

✓ Limburg, James. ‡ *Hosea–Micah* (I) 1988. See under Hosea.

McComiskey, Thomas E. (EBC) 1985. Now superseded by the EBCR below.

☆ **McComiskey, Thomas E., and Tremper Longman III.** (EBCR) 2008. To be considered among the finest brief (60pp) evangelical treatments of this prophecy.

✓ **McKane, William.** ‡ 1998. Published by T&T Clark, this detailed critical commentary runs to 256pp. The prophecy suffers division into three parts at the hands of this scholar, who also did Jeremiah for ICC. Only chs. 1–3 are supposed to have come from the 8th century prophet. Few younger scholars today—outside Germany, I should say—have McKane's confidence that they can decide what the prophet could and could not have said (and therefore what must be ascribed to later redaction). This volume is for advanced students and scholars. [*JSOT-BL* 1999; *EvQ* 7/00; *JTS* 10/99; *CBQ* 10/99; *OTA* 6/99; *RelSRev* 7/99; *JSS* Spr 01; *VT* 51.3].

Mackay, John L. *Jonah, Micah, Nahum, Habakkuk, Zephaniah* (Focus on the Bible) 2008. See under Jonah.

McKeating, H. ‡ (CBC) 1971. See under Hosea.

✓ Mason, Rex. ‡ *Micah, Nahum, Obadiah* (OT Guides) 1991.

☆ **Mays, James L.** ‡ (OTL) 1976. One of the most suggestive critical commentaries available on this book. It is thorough, readable, and asks many of the right theological questions. His position is a bit more critical than Allen's, for he denies most of the book to Micah. Not as worthy as his OTL commentaries on Hosea and Amos. By the way, Mays later did exceptionally fine work on Psalms. [*JBL* 6/78].

F Möller, Karl. (Apollos).

F Nogalski, James D. ‡ (S&H).

F Ollenburger, Ben. (BCBC).

F Phillips, Richard D. *Jonah & Micah* (REC) 2010. See under Jonah.

☆ Prior, David. *Joel, Micah, Habakkuk* (BST) 1998. See Joel above.

✓ **Shaw, C.S.** ‡ *The Speeches of Micah: A Rhetorical-Historical Analysis*, 1993.

✓ **Simundson, Daniel J.** ‡ (NewIB) 1996. See also the next entry.

✓ Simundson, Daniel. ‡ *Hosea, Joel, Amos, Obadiah, Jonah, Micah* (AOTC) 2005. See under Hosea.

✓ Smith, J.H.P. ‡ (ICC) 1911.

✓ **Smith, Ralph L.** ‡ *Micah–Malachi* (WBC) 1984. Workmanlike, but not very stimulating. Not at all up to the standard of Stuart's work on the first five Minor Prophets and much more critical. I had hoped for more theological discussion. Overall it is a disappointment, though offering some help with the Hebrew. While students will consult Smith for papers, pastors should probably steer clear of this older WBC. In past editions I expressed my hope that Nelson would replace this volume. They are. See Stuart below. [*RTR* 1/86; *ExpTim* 6/85; *JBL* 105.3 (1986); *JETS* 6/85; *HebStud* 1984].

F Stuart, Douglas. *Micah–Malachi* (WBC replacement). I saw this announced for late 2009, but Nelson has often been terribly late on predictions for WBC. This is to replace Ralph Smith's work.

Vawter, Bruce. ‡ *Amos, Hosea, Micah* (OTM) 1981. See under Hosea.

☆ **Waltke, Bruce K.** *The Minor Prophets: An Exegetical and Expository Commentary*, Vol. 2, Ed. by Thomas E. McComiskey, 1993. Prior to the fuller 2007 work recommended above, I urged people to start here! This is still a very satisfying exegesis for pastors, who might even prefer this more condensed commentary (which is still quite full with 175 large pages).

✓ **Wolff, H.W.** ‡ (ContC) ET 1990. See under Hosea. Once again, as with the earlier BKAT volumes in translation, Wolff provides very valuable textual and exegetical notes, prior to probing theological reflection. No question, this continues to be a standard reference commentary. The demerits of the earlier Wolff volumes (Hosea; Joel and Amos) are present here too. [*SJT* 93.4; *Interp* 7/91].

✓ Wolff, H.W. ‡ *Micah the Prophet*, ET 1981. A different work than his entry in ContC, as is clear from the German title, best translated *Conversing with Micah*. This volume contains exposition and essays with some rich homiletical thoughts. Seems less critical in its approach than his other commentaries because he addresses a different audience: the Church rather than the academy. [*ExpTim* 1/82].

NOTES: (1) Consult the list of works in the above section, "The Twelve Minor Prophets." (2) See Sheri L. Klauda, "Micah: An Annotated Bibliography," *SwJT* 46.1 (2003): 48–56. (3) Mignon Jacobs, "Bridging the Times: Trends in Micah Studies since 1985," *CBR* 4.3 (2006): 293–329.

—⟶—

NAHUM

★ Bruckner, James K. *Jonah, Nahum, Habakkuk, Zephaniah* (NIVAC) 2004. See under Jonah. Other worthwhile pastoral commentaries are Boice, Calvin, Craigie, and Kaiser; more critical are Achtemeier and Brown.

★ **Longman, Tremper.** *The Minor Prophets: An Exegetical and Expository Commentary*, Vol. 2, Ed. by Thomas E. McComiskey, 1993. I believe I prefer Longman's exegesis to Patterson's more lengthy treatment. This is his first scholarly commentary, and it is well informed and presented. Because he has done so much research and reflection on the divine warrior theme, Longman was an excellent choice to cover this prophecy about Yahweh's vengeance against Assyria. Longman and Robertson are a perfectly matched pair.

★ **Patterson, Richard P.** *Nahum, Habakkuk and Zephaniah* (WEC) 1991. This provides the Hebrew exegetical helps for the student which aren't so plentiful in Robertson. Patterson is admired as a leading evangelical OT scholar, and he was one of the OT editors for this series (along with Ronald Youngblood). A full treatment at 416pp, this volume went o/p with Moody but has been reprinted by Biblical Studies Press. Longman and Robertson should take priority on your "to buy" list, especially if not working with the MT.

★ **Robertson, O. Palmer.** *Nahum, Habakkuk and Zephaniah* (NICOT) 1990. This quickly established itself as the standard conservative commentary on these books. Robertson excels at theological exposition, but does not include as much in the way of scholarly helps (philology, grammar, textual criticism, etc) as some might like—the relative neglect suffered by these books makes a detailed exegesis of the Hebrew text more valuable. This volume is among the very best for the preacher who wants to get at the message of the text. See Renz below. [*WTJ* Spr 92; *Them* 1/93; *Interp* 1/92; *CBQ* 7/92; *JETS* 6/95; *HebStud* 1994; *CRBR* 1992].

✦ ✦ ✦ ✦ ✦ ✦

☆ Achtemeier, Elizabeth. [*M*], (I) 1986. Covers Nahum through Malachi and is typical of the series. Good from a more conservatively critical perspective, even distinguished. You may think it suffers a bit on account of its brevity (200pp). As expected from this series, she focuses on the theological message. [*CRBR* 1988].

Armerding, Carl E. (EBC) 1985. See under Obadiah. Years ago I considered recommending this for purchase because it was one of the stronger evangelical exegeses. Now see EBCR.

☆ **Armerding, Carl E.** (EBCR) 2008. A good solid commentary made better with the revision. Twenty years ago we had hardly any in-depth exegetical commentaries on Nahum, but we have several excellent ones now. The competition makes this seem a bit lightweight, at least for students (47pp). The old EBC can be ignored.

☆ **Baker, David.** *Nahum, Habakkuk and Zephaniah* (TOTC) 1988. This is a thoughtful, well-researched volume of 120pp. It was the first pick in the 1989 edition of this guide. [*EvQ* 1/91; *JETS* 9/92].

☆ Barker, Kenneth L., and **Waylon Bailey**. *Micah, Nahum, Habakkuk, Zephaniah* (NAC) 1999. Bailey covers the three shorter books here, and some judge his work to be a better guide than Barker's Micah commentary in this same volume. This is very well done and of value to students as well as pastors. Some will argue that this deserves a place on the recommended purchase list. Praised by Longman.

☆ Bentley, Michael. *Balancing the Books* (WCS on Micah and Nahum) 1994.

Boadt, Lawrence. ‡ *Jeremiah 26–52, Habakkuk, Zephaniah, Nahum* (OTM) 1982.

✓ Bosman, Jan Petrus. ‡ *Social Identity in Nahum: A Theological-Ethical Enquiry*, 2008.

☆ Brown, William P. ‡ *Obadiah–Malachi* (WestBC) 1996. See Obadiah.

F Cathcart, Kevin J. ‡ (ICC–new series). Scholars anticipate good things here, as Cathcart's research on this Minor Prophet goes back to his much-cited *Nahum in the Light of Northwest Semitic* (1973). One wonders if this may be published together with Habakkuk and Zephaniah.

✓ **Christensen, Duane.** (AYB) 2009. Not for the faint-hearted! Peter Machinist of Harvard was once listed as under contract for this work, but Christensen now has delivered this extremely detailed, conservatively critical commentary (464pp). Pastors and seminarians won't invest in this ($65 list), but diligent doctoral students will, if focusing on Nahum. The obvious strengths here are exhaustiveness, poetic analysis (both larger structures and the fine points), interaction with previous interpreters, and bibliography (82pp). Very simply, nothing compares with this in scope. The problem is digging through all the—may I say idiosyncratic?—"logoprosodic analysis" of "the numerical and musical composition of the biblical text." Here are examples: "the balance in terms of mora count becomes $(24 + 16) \parallel (16 + 25) = 40 \parallel 41$ morae" (p.389). "The invariant five tones on the central axis (C G D A E) provide five pentatonic modal permutations" (p.37). Got that? Some bright students might be able to learn German and digest Rudolph's great commentary or Heinz-Josef Fabry's volume in Herders (2006) sooner than they could pick up on what the author is doing here. Christensen is obviously a genius, and you will discover he also has a large commentary on Deuteronomy. [*JETS* 9/10].

✓ Clark, David J., and Howard A. Hatton. (UBS) 1989. Covers Nahum to Zephaniah in 357pp. [*CRBR* 1992].

✓ **Coggins, R.J.** and S.P. Re'emi. ‡ *Nahum, Obadiah, Esther* (ITC) 1985. One of the best commentaries oriented more toward historical criticism (63pp). See under Esther and Obadiah. The problem that pastors may find in Coggins' work, both here and elsewhere, is that he tends to emphasize the great distance between the ancient text and modern day and what terribly hard work it is to find the text's relevance.

✓ Davidson, Andrew B. [*M*], (Cambridge Bible for Schools and Colleges) 1896. Also covers Habakkuk and Zephaniah. One of the more moderate old critical scholars from Britain.

Eaton, J.H. ‡ (Torch) 1961. See under Obadiah.

✓ **Floyd, Michael H.** ‡ *Minor Prophets, Part 2* (FOTL) 1999. Over 650pp of extremely detailed form-critical and structural analysis of the last six Minor Prophets. In keeping with recent developments in form critical research, Floyd shows interest in synchronic concerns, as well as diachronic. This has already become a standard reference commentary for scholars doing work on these books. [*JTS* 4/01; *Interp* 7/01; *CBQ* 4/02; *JSS* Spr 03; *HebStud* 2003; *VT* 51.4; *JSOT* 94 (2001); *RelSRev* 4/03; *JAOS* 122.1].

✓ Garcia-Treto, Francisco O. ‡ (NewIB) 1996.

Goldingay, John, and Pamela Scalise. *Minor Prophets II* (NIBC) 2009. Goldingay covers Nahum to Haggai, and his colleague at Fuller Seminary treats Zechariah and Malachi. I have not had opportunity to review this volume, but these authors are recognized and productive scholars on the left wing of evangelicalism. Expect clarity and critical acumen in a briefer exegesis.

☆ Kaiser, Walter. *Micah, Nahum, Habakkuk, Zephaniah, Haggai, Zechariah, Malachi* (WCC) 1993. See under Micah.

Kleinert, Paul. (Lange) ET 1874.

Mackay, John L. *Jonah, Micah, Nahum, Habakkuk, Zephaniah* (Focus on the Bible) 2008. See under Jonah.

☆ **Maier, Walter A.** 1959 (posthumous). This detailed commentary was written by a conservative Lutheran and had probably been the longest commentary on Nahum in any language at close to 400pp. Christensen now wins that prize, however. It is an aging (essentially late 1940s), technical and expositional work—still a good purchase for in-depth study. But it should be used with a more up-to-date commentary like Longman, especially on issues like textual criticism. This was Stuart's favorite back in 1990; I doubt it is now.

✓ Mason, Rex. ‡ *Micah, Nahum, Obadiah* (OT Guides) 1991.

F Nogalski, James D. ‡ (S&H).

✓ O'Brien, Julia. ‡ *Nahum, Habakkuk, Zephaniah, Haggai, Zechariah, Malachi* (AOTC) 2004. A brief (326-page) and competent exegesis which is sometimes regrettably out of sympathy with the theology of these prophets (e.g., pp.288–89). See her earlier commentary below. [*CBQ* 7/05; *Interp* 1/06; *JSOT-BL* 2005; *RBL*; *ExpTim* 10/05]. O'Brien's program for interpreting the prophets' theology is set out in *Challenging Prophetic Metaphor: Theology and Ideology in the Prophets* (2008) [*CBQ* 4/10].

✓ **O'Brien, Julia.** ‡ (Read) 2002. This is much more in-depth (162pp) than the AOTC commentary. She employs more postmodern synchronic analysis (intertextuality, etc.) in this work, which is of greater interest to students (especially those seeking a feminist reading) than to evangelical pastors. [*Them* Spr 04; *RelSRev* 1/04; *BBR* 16.1; *JSOT-BL* 2006, 2010; *JHebS*].

☆ Patterson, Richard. (CorBC) 2008. See under Hosea.

F Patterson, Richard. *Nahum–Malachi* (EEC).

F Renz, Thomas. (NICOT replacement). Though Robertson is still very serviceable for expositors of Nahum to Zephaniah, there is a replacement coming down the pike. Renz has a strong interest in prophetic rhetoric.

☆ **Roberts, J.J.M.** ‡ *Nahum, Habakkuk, Zephaniah* (OTL) 1991. This is now probably the leading critical interpretation of these three books (223pp). The author is retired from teaching OT at Princeton Seminary and is a proficient text critic, exegete, and theologian. "Roberts' commentary…is a jewel" (Hillers), and would not be an unwise purchase for the pastor who enjoys digging deep. I bought it and found it rich. The price in hb is much too high: $40. I counsel those making the purchase to look for the pb edition or buy secondhand. [*CBQ* 7/93; *JBL* Spr 93; *ThTo* 4/92; *JR* 10/94; *JETS* 6/95; *BSac* 1/93].

✓ Smith, J.M.P. ‡ (ICC) 1911.

✓ **Smith, Ralph L.** ‡ (WBC) 1984. See Micah above.

✓ **Spronk, Klaas**. ‡ (HCOT) ET 1997. A very full Dutch commentary for specialists and students: 144pp of introduction and exegesis. Spronk is keen to detail as far as possible the historical setting of the prophecy, which he dates earlier (660 BC) than many scholars. [*JSOT* 79 (1998); *RelSRev* 7/98; *JBL* Spr 01].

F Stuart, Douglas. *Micah–Malachi* (WBC replacement). See under Micah.

F Vanderhooft, David. ‡ (Herm).

NOTES: (1) Consult the list of works in the above section, The Twelve Minor Prophets. (2) Michael Weigl, "Current Research on the Book of Nahum: Exegetical Methodologies in Turmoil?" *CurBS* 9 (2001): 81–130.

HABAKKUK

★ **Andersen, Francis I.** [*M*], (AB) 2001. The advanced student and specialist have a treat here, but many pastors will find this 400-page volume a daunting challenge. There is help in the areas of philology, poetic analysis, structure, textual criticism, and translation. There are relatively few theological conclusions drawn. See the other Andersen/Freedman AB commentaries on Hosea, Amos, and Micah. If you are more academically oriented and plan to spend good time mining this prophecy to its depths, buy this. If your interests are less academic and technical, substitute Bailey or Baker. [*JTS* 10/02; *Interp* 7/02; *ExpTim* 6/02; *BSac* 10/02; *Biblica* 83.3; *JSOT* 99 (2000)].

★ Bruckner, James K. *Jonah, Nahum, Habakkuk, Zephaniah* (NIVAC) 2004. See under Jonah.

★ Lloyd-Jones, D. Martyn. *From Fear to Faith*, 1953. This is a very rich exposition from a Reformed perspective. Those who look to make this purchase will find that it has been republished with his exposition of Psalm 73 under the title, *Faith Tried and Triumphant* (IVP, 1987). [*EvQ* 7/54].

★ **Patterson, Richard.** (WEC) 1993. See under Nahum. Here he builds on his article, "The Psalm of Habakkuk," in *Grace Theological Journal* 8 (1987): 163–94. This commentary on Habakkuk may be the best researched in the volume and should be more widely available than it is.

★ **Robertson, O. Palmer.** (NICOT) 1990. See under Nahum. The more scholarly pastor would probably also want to consider purchasing Roberts below, in addition to these recommended works. See Renz below.

✧ ✧ ✧ ✧ ✧ ✧

Achtemeier, Elizabeth. [*M*], (I) 1986. See Nahum above.

Armerding, Carl E. (EBC) 1985. See under Obadiah. Back in 1990 this was Stuart's first choice. Armerding is so good it once vied for a place on the suggested purchase list above. See EBCR below.

☆ **Armerding, Carl E.** (EBCR) 2008. See EBC above. I am happy that the fine commentary now has extended life in the EBCR (44pp). On the negative side, there is less revision and update here. On the positive side, for students at least, there is fuller research and discussion of the Hebrew than in a lot of other EBCR contributions.

☆ Baker, D. (TOTC) 1988. See Nahum above.

☆ Barker, Kenneth L., and Waylon Bailey. *Micah, Nahum, Habakkuk, Zephaniah* (NAC) 1999. See Nahum above.

✓ **Boadt, Lawrence.** ‡ *Jeremiah 26–52, Habakkuk, Zephaniah, Nahum* (OTM) 1982. This is well done, by a highly-esteemed, conservatively critical Roman Catholic scholar.

☆ Brown, William P. ‡ *Obadiah–Malachi* (WestBC) 1996. See Obadiah.

☆ **Bruce, F.F.** *The Minor Prophets: An Exegetical and Expository Commentary*, Vol. 2, Ed. by Thomas E. McComiskey, 1993. Many students do not realize that Bruce, long the editor of the NICNT series, also commented on OT books in an able, sober way—see "The Legacy of F.F. Bruce" in *CT*, Nov. 5, 1999. This is not really one of my first picks on Habakkuk, but I have recommended the whole set above.

F   Cathcart, Kevin J. ‡ (ICC–new series). See under Nahum.

✓   Clark, David J., and Howard A. Hatton. (UBS) 1989. See Nahum above.

Davidson, A.B. [𝓜], (Cambridge Bible for Schools and Colleges) 1896. See Nahum above.

Eaton, J. H. ‡ (Torch) 1961. See under Obadiah.

✓   **Floyd, Michael H.** ‡ *Minor Prophets, Part 2* (FOTL) 1999. See Nahum above.

Goldingay, John, and Pamela Scalise. *Minor Prophets II* (NIBC) 2009. See under Nahum.

✓   Gowan, Donald E. ‡ *The Triumph of Faith in Habakkuk*, 1976. This useful theological study was published by John Knox Press.

✓   **Haak, Robert D.** ‡ (*VT* Supplement, #44) 1992. Haak's revised dissertation for the University of Chicago has received much attention. [*CBQ* 7/93; *JBL* Fall 93; *JTS* 4/93; *JSS* Aut 98; *VT* 46.3; *JSOT* 59; *BSac* 1/95; *HebStud* 1993].

F   Hartzfeld, David. (Apollos).

✓   **Hiebert, Theodore.** ‡ (NewIB) 1996.

F   Idestrom, Rebecca G.S. (Pentecostal Commentary).

☆   Kaiser, Walter. *Micah, Nahum, Habakkuk, Zephaniah, Haggai, Zechariah, Malachi* (WCC) 1993. See under Micah.

Kleinert, Paul. (Lange) ET 1874.

Legg, John. *When We Don't Understand: God's Ways with Jonah and Habakkuk* (WCS) 1986.

Mackay, John L. *Jonah, Micah, Nahum, Habakkuk, Zephaniah* (Focus on the Bible) 2008. See under Jonah.

Marbury, E. *Obadiah and Habakkuk*, 1650 Original. See under Obadiah.

✓   Mason, Rex. ‡ *Zephaniah, Habakkuk, Joel* (OT Guides) 1994.

F   Nogalski, James D. ‡ (S&H).

✓   O'Brien, Julia. ‡ *Nahum, Habakkuk, Zephaniah, Haggai, Zechariah, Malachi* (AOTC) 2004. See under Nahum.

☆   Patterson, Richard. (CorBC) 2008. See under Hosea.

F   Patterson, Richard. *Nahum–Malachi* (EEC).

F   Prinsloo, Gert T.M. ‡ (HCOT).

☆   Prior, David. *Joel, Micah, Habakkuk* (BST) 1998. See Joel above.

F   Renz, Thomas. (NICOT replacement). This should be a strong contribution. See under Nahum.

☆   **Roberts, J.J.M.** ‡ *Nahum, Habakkuk, Zephaniah*, (OTL) 1991. See under Nahum.

✓   **Smith, Ralph L.** ‡ (WBC) 1984. See Micah above.

F   Stuart, Douglas. *Micah–Malachi* (WBC replacement). See under Micah.

✓   Szeles, Maria E. ‡ *Habakkuk, Zephaniah* (ITC) 1987. [*JETS* 3/91; *Evangel* Spr 90; *HebStud* 1989].

F   Vanderhooft, David. ‡ (Herm). I saw this report but am not fully convinced it is accurate.

✓   Ward, W.H. ‡ (ICC) 1911.

☆   Wiersbe, Warren W. *From Worry to Worship*, 1983. This popular exposition rivals Lloyd-Jones. Wiersbe is easier reading, but Lloyd-Jones is more penetrating and forceful.

NOTES: (1) Consult the list of works in the above section, The Twelve Minor Prophets. (2) Oskar Dangl, "Habakkuk in Recent Research," *CurBS* 9 (2001): 131–68.

—ɯ—

ZEPHANIAH

★ **Berlin, Adele.** ‡ (AB) 1994. One of the three most complete scholarly commentaries available on this Bible book (too much of an expense to recommend to pastors for purchase?). The Jewish author is a shrewd exegete, shows good respect for the text and treats the final form. She has gained quite a reputation for her analysis of rhetorical devices, particularly parallelism, in the Hebrew Bible. The AB's literary sensitivity and "close reading" is the perfect complement to Robertson's theological exposition. Students will also gravitate toward Sweeney, Vlaardingerbroek, and Roberts. Pastors who would prefer an evangelical commentary should replace this recommendation with Bailey. [*SwJT* Spr 96; *JETS* 9/98; *Interp* 10/96; *CBQ* 1/97].

★ Bruckner, James K. *Jonah, Nahum, Habakkuk, Zephaniah* (NIVAC) 2004. See under Jonah. Other expository helps for the pastor's study, of which there are fewer on this prophecy, would be Calvin, Craigie, Boice, and Mackay. More critical but well-done are Achtemeier and Brown.

★ **Motyer, J.** Alec. *The Minor Prophets: An Exegetical and Expository Commentary*, Vol. 3, Ed. by Thomas E. McComiskey, 1998. I have already recommended this set for purchase above. Motyer is a veteran at writing commentaries, and I would argue he has done his best work on the prophetic literature. This is excellent. [*BSac* 1/99].

★ **Patterson, Richard.** (WEC) 1993. See under Nahum.

★ **Robertson, O. Palmer.** (NICOT) 1990. See under Nahum. His 95-page treatment of Zephaniah is especially fine.

Achtemeier, Elizabeth. [*M*], (I) 1986. See Nahum above.

☆ **Baker, D.** (TOTC) 1988. See Nahum above. Was Stuart's favorite in 1990.

☆ Barker, Kenneth L., and **Waylon Bailey**. *Micah, Nahum, Habakkuk, Zephaniah* (NAC) 1999. See Nahum above. With over 120 quality pages on this brief prophecy, the well-read Bailey deserves wide use by both students and pastors.

✓ **Bennett, Robert A.** ‡ (NewIB) 1996.

✓ **Ben Zvi, E.** ‡ *A Historical-Critical Study of the Book of Zephaniah*, 1991. Contains a lengthy commentary, which reveals the author's overriding form-critical concerns, and a vast section of exegetical and thematic notes. Published by de Gruyter. [*JSOT* 58].

Boadt, Lawrence. ‡ *Jeremiah 26–52, Habakkuk, Zephaniah, Nahum* (OTM) 1982.

☆ Brown, William P. ‡ *Obadiah–Malachi* (WestBC) 1996. See Obadiah.

F Cathcart, Kevin J. ‡ (ICC–new series). See under Nahum.

✓ Clark, David J., and Howard A. Hatton. (UBS) 1989. See Nahum above.

✓ Davidson, A.B. [*M*], (Cambridge Bible for Schools and Colleges) 1896. See Nahum above.

Eaton, J.H. ‡ (Torch) 1961. See under Obadiah.

✓ **Floyd, Michael H.** ‡ *Minor Prophets, Part 2* (FOTL) 1999. See Nahum above.

Goldingay, John, and Pamela Scalise. *Minor Prophets II* (NIBC) 2009. See under Nahum.

✓ **House, Paul R.** *Zephaniah: A Prophetic Drama*, 1988. This dissertation for Southern Baptist Theological Seminary includes a brief commentary. This evangelical author also has capable works on 1 & 2 Kings and Lamentations, and a full-length OT Theology. [*JBL* Fall 00; *CBQ* 7/90; *Interp* 10/90; *Chm* 103.4 (1989)].

F Idestrom, Rebecca G.S. (Pentecostal Commentary).

☆ Kaiser, Walter. (WCC) 1993. See under Micah.

✓ Kapelrud, A. ‡ *The Message of the Prophet Zephaniah*, 1975.

✓ Kleinert, Paul. (Lange) ET 1874.

F Luter, Boyd. (Apollos).

Mackay, John L. *Jonah, Micah, Nahum, Habakkuk, Zephaniah* (Focus on the Bible) 2008. See under Jonah.

✓ Mason, Rex. ‡ *Zephaniah, Habakkuk, Joel* (OT Guides) 1994.

F Nogalski, James D. ‡ (S&H).

✓ O'Brien, Julia. ‡ *Nahum, Habakkuk, Zephaniah, Haggai, Zechariah, Malachi* (AOTC) 2004. See under Nahum.

☆ Patterson, Richard. (CorBC) 2008. See under Hosea.

F Patterson, Richard. *Nahum–Malachi* (EEC).

F Renz, Thomas. (NICOT replacement). See under Nahum.

☆ **Roberts, J.J.M.** ‡ *Nahum, Habakkuk, Zephaniah* (OTL) 1991. See under Nahum.

✓ Smith, J.H.P. ‡ (ICC) 1911.

✓ **Smith, Ralph L.** ‡ (WBC) 1984. See Micah above.

F Stuart, Douglas. *Micah–Malachi* (WBC replacement). See under Micah.

✓ **Sweeney, Marvin A.** ‡ (Herm) 2003. The author teaches at Claremont. This is an exceedingly thorough and rigorous text-critical and (newer style) form-critical analysis, the conclusions of which can be compared with Floyd and Ben Zvi above. More conservative readers will like his arguments for an earlier, pre-exilic dating of the prophecy (with little secondary material). For a more diachronic approach, this is now the authoritative commentary to consult (but cf. Vlaardingerbroek). Berlin's more literary reading complements this nicely. [*JTS* 10/04; *CBQ* 10/04; *JSOT* 28.5; *JETS* 12/04; *Interp* 10/05; *VT* 57.1; *JNES* 7/08; *CurTM* 6/05; *RBL*; *JHebS* (Watts)].

✓ Szeles, Maria E. ‡ *Habakkuk, Zephaniah* (ITC) 1987. [*JETS* 3/91; *HebStud* 1989].

✓ **Vlaardingerbroek, Johannes.** ‡ (HCOT) ET 1999. This 222-page translation from the Dutch is called "a splendid tool" by Mason [*JSOT* 89 (2000)]. The thorough exegesis provided here will be consulted by students of the prophets for decades to come. Vlaardingerbroek rivals Berlin's work in quality and depth, though the exegetical method has a different focus (more historical critical), and he is not as practiced a literary critic as she. [*RelSRev* 4/00].

Walker, Larry. (EBC) 1985. You can ignore this in favor of the EBCR below.

☆ **Walker, Larry.** (EBCR) 2008. I have not used this 45-page commentary much but am glad there is a revised and updated work. Walker's EBC was not considered one of the best in the old volume, but he is a capable scholar and has done a thorough rewrite here, with many notes on the Hebrew. Worth having.

NOTES: (1) Consult the list of works in the above section, The Twelve Minor Prophets. (2) For a review-essay on scholarship, appearing prior to his commentary, see Marvin A. Sweeney, "Zephaniah: A Paradigm for the study of the Prophetic Books," *CurBS* 7 (1999): 119–45.

HAGGAI

★ **Boda, Mark J.** *Haggai, Zechariah* (NIVAC) 2004. This is a well researched expositional commentary by a Westminster Seminary graduate who did doctoral work on Zechariah; Boda now teaches at McMaster University and is considered a leading scholar on this literature. He gives Haggai about 100pp and Zechariah about 400pp. He is not as courageous as I wish he were on the higher critical issue of a divided Zechariah. Both exegetically and theologically, this work is satisfying; a little less satisfying is his guidance in application. For additional help in discerning the contemporary relevance of these books, one could look up the BST volumes, or from the more critical side, Achtemeier and Brown. [*CTJ* 4/08]. Students will gladly use another Boda work: *Haggai and Zechariah Research: A Bibliographic Survey*, 2003 [*JSOT-BL* 2005; *RelSRev* 1/05; *VT* 55.3; *ExpTim* 11/04].

★ **Motyer, J. Alec.** *The Minor Prophets: An Exegetical and Expository Commentary*, Vol. 3, Ed. by Thomas E. McComiskey, 1998. I have already recommended this set for purchase above. This is almost as valuable as Verhoef and is a little briefer. Motyer instinctively drives to the heart of a passage and its theological message. He takes a strongly conservative stance on critical issues. See Zephaniah.

★ **Taylor, Richard A., and E. Ray Clendenen.** *Haggai, Malachi* (NAC) 2004. This volume is so thoroughly researched and well-done that one may call it a good replacement for Verhoef's conservative exegesis. Both Taylor's "Haggai" and Clendenen's slightly less technical "Malachi" are competent and full (496pp total). There are differences in hermeneutical approach between these two. While Taylor pursues a traditional grammatico-historical exegesis, long taught at his own Dallas Seminary, Clendenen practices discourse-analysis. Boda and Motyer provide more biblical theological reflection than Taylor. Yes, there is a Dispensational orientation here, but it is not so noticeable. [*CBQ* 7/05; *JETS* 9/05; *BSac* 7/06; *SwJT* Fall 04].

★ **Verhoef, Pieter A.** *Haggai, Malachi* (NICOT) 1987. This fine commentary, from a professor emeritus at Stellenbosch, is an important addition to our literature on these Bible books. One only wishes he had had opportunity to interact with Petersen's 1984 commentary. Written at a higher scholarly level than most of the other older NICOT volumes, Verhoef's work (Motyer's above, too) complements Baldwin well. The advanced student and scholarly pastor will also be interested in Meyers, Petersen, and Wolff. Verhoef is to be replaced; see Jacobs below. [*WTJ* Spr 89; *JETS* 12/88; *Them* 4/88; *ExpTim* 3/88; *HebStud* 1987].

✓ Achtemeier, Elizabeth. [𝓜], (I) 1986. See Nahum above.

Alden, Robert L. (EBC) 1985. Fine work from a well known evangelical scholar who taught at Denver Seminary and who is now with the Lord. He also covers Malachi in this volume. See Merrill's EBCR below.

☆ **Baldwin, Joyce G.** *Haggai, Zechariah, Malachi* (TOTC) 1972. This excellent work used to be the first choice of the pastor. The series could now use something more updated after Meyers, Peterson, Verhoef and Wolff.

Barnes, W.E. ‡ *Haggai, Zechariah, Malachi* (Cambridge Bible) 1917.

☆ Bentley, Michael. *Building for God's Glory* (WCS on Haggai and Zechariah) 1989.

✓ Boda, Mark, and Michael Floyd (eds). *Tradition in Transition: Haggai and Zechariah 1–8 in the Trajectory of Hebrew Theology*, 2008. [*CBQ* 1/10; *JSOT-BL* 2010].

☆ Brown, William P. ‡ *Obadiah–Malachi* (WestBC) 1996. See Obadiah.

✓ **Clark, David J., and Howard A. Hatton.** *A Handbook on Haggai, Zechariah, and Malachi* (UBS) 2002. [*CBQ* 10/04].

F Coggins, Richard. ‡ (Blackwell). I anticipate a volume on Haggai–Malachi. Worth noting, too, is his brief "OT Guides" volume on *Haggai, Zechariah, Malachi* (1987).

✓ Driver, Samuel R. ‡ (Century Bible) 1906. See Nahum above.

☆ Duguid, Iain M. *Haggai, Zechariah, Malachi* (EPSC) 2010. I am in a quandary because I want to recommend that pastors purchase this rich, succinct theological exposition (255pp). It is built on exegetical decisions (as far as I have checked) with which I agree all the way down the line. The problem is that, with a larger font and clearly written on a popular level, the book doesn't have enough substance to list for $29.50, even in hb. Why not offer us this really good book in pb for $19.95? Unless they look closely, students are likely to miss the fact that Duguid offers his own (fine) translation of the Hebrew. See the author's other works on Ezekiel, Ruth & Esther, and Daniel.

✓ **Floyd, Michael H.** ‡ *Minor Prophets, Part 2* (FOTL) 1999. See Nahum above.

☆ Fyall, Robert. *The Message of Ezra and Haggai* (BST) 2008. See Ezra.

Goldingay, John, and Pamela Scalise. *Minor Prophets II* (NIBC) 2009. See under Nahum.

F Gordon, Robert P. [*M?*], (ICC–new series).

F Hanson, Paul D. ‡ (Herm).

☆ Hill, Andrew. (CorBC) 2008. See under Hosea.

F Jacobs, Mignon. *Haggai, Malachi* (NICOT replacement).

✓ Jones, D.R. ‡ *Haggai, Zechariah, Malachi* (Torch Bible Commentary) 1962. A brief, critical work of value years ago.

☆ Kaiser, Walter. (WCC) 1993. See under Micah.

✓ **Kessler, John.** *The Book of Haggai: Prophecy and Society in Early Persian Yehud*, 2002. A very large, expert, and more conservative study of Haggai's Prophecy, taken as a reproclamation of past traditions or Scriptures. This volume contains much of the material one would expect in a commentary. [*JSOT* 27.5; *VT* 54.4].

F Koopmans, William Th. ‡ (HCOT).

F Luter, Boyd. (Apollos).

☆ Mackay, John L. *Haggai, Zechariah, Malachi: God's Restored People*, 1994. Published by Christian Focus, this was until recently (see Duguid) about the best popular-level exposition from the Reformed side. I find it especially useful for Zechariah.

✓ **March, W. Eugene.** ‡ (NewIB) 1996.

✓ Mason, R.A. ‡ (CBC) 1977. Covers through Malachi. Mason has been a leading scholar on Zechariah since his groundbreaking dissertation, "The Use of Earlier Biblical Material in Zechariah 9–14: A Study in Inner Biblical Exegesis" (London, 1973), which has recently seen publication (see Boda/Floyd under Zechariah).

✓ **Meadowcroft, Tim.** *Haggai* (Read) 2006. This exceedingly full exegesis (259pp) has much to offer: historical-critical investigation (form, redaction, and reception history); a literary reading; discourse analysis; and theology. There are also forays into speech-act theory and contemporary application. Needless to say, there is a good mix of hermeneutics to try to meld. Discourse analysis features most prominently. He treats the prophecy as a unity. Meadowcroft teaches at Bible College of New Zealand. [*CBQ* 4/09; *JSOT-BL* 2008; *RelSRev* 12/09].

☆ **Merrill, Eugene H.** *Haggai, Zechariah, Malachi* (intended for WEC?) 1994. This careful work can certainly be appreciated by all evangelicals; Dispensationalists interpreting Zechariah will find it to be especially serviceable. Because it is thorough and includes some Hebrew exegesis, and because there are few conservative scholarly works on these books, preachers and students do well to consult Merrill, even buy it. It went o/p with Moody but has recently been reprinted by Biblical Studies Press. [*BSac* 7/96].

☆ Merrill, Eugene H. (EBCR) 2008. This replaces Alden's contribution to the old EBC and is a fine summary of his earlier dependable work (22pp).

☆ **Meyers, Carol L. and Eric M. Meyers.** ‡ *Haggai, Zechariah 1–8* (AB) 1988. This volume, which was very well received by the scholarly world, is moderately critical, helpful for philological details, and especially valuable for historical background. The Meyers couple, on the faculty of Duke University, provide an excellent commentary on Haggai, and the Zechariah treatment is even fuller and more detailed—perhaps more critical, too. Compare this volume with Petersen. The serious drawback, from the pastor's perspective at least, is that Meyers/Meyers and Petersen both have little to say theologically. [*JBL* 107.3, p.523 (1988); *JBL* Fall 95].

Mitchell, H.G. ‡ (ICC) 1912.

☆ Moore, Thomas V. *Haggai, Zechariah, Malachi* (GS) 1856. This is a warm, Reformed exposition from the 19th century, but not one of the best in the series. Still in print. For pastors, not students.

F Nogalski, James D. ‡ (S&H).

✓ O'Brien, Julia. ‡ *Nahum, Habakkuk, Zephaniah, Haggai, Zechariah, Malachi* (AOTC) 2004. See under Nahum.

F Patterson, Richard. Nahum–Malachi (EEC).

Perowne, T.T. *Haggai and Zechariah* (Cambridge Bible) 1888, 2nd ed 1901. Fairly conservative work by a leading scholar of that day that was replaced by Barnes.

☆ **Petersen, David L.** ‡ *Haggai, Zechariah 1–8* (OTL) 1984. Moderately critical, this commentary has many fine points. It repays close study, but read with discernment. Not dissimilar in its approach and conclusions to the Meyers' volumes. The commentaries for OTL, AB and ContC are the leading critical works available in English. See Zechariah below. [*JBL* 105.4 (1986)].

✓ **Redditt, Paul L.** ‡ *Haggai, Zechariah, Malachi* (NCB) 1995. This commentary covers these Bible books phrase-by-phrase in about 220pp. Redditt is professor emeritus at Georgetown College, Kentucky, and he strongly prefers the diachronic approach to the newer literary critical methods. Worth consulting for exegesis, but I doubt you will find it stimulating. [*CBQ* 7/96; *JETS* 6/97; *JSS* Spr 97; *VT* 47.1; *RTR* 1/97; *HebStud* 1997; *CRBR* 1996; *RBL*].

F Shelley, Patricia. (BCBC).

✓ **Smith, Ralph L.** ‡ (WBC) 1984. See Micah above.

F Stuart, Douglas. *Micah–Malachi* (WBC replacement). See under Micah.

✓ **Stuhlmueller, C.** ‡ *Haggai and Zechariah* (ITC) 1988. Along with Brueggemann's Jeremiah, one of the best in the series, even though it is somewhat brief (165pp). [*Evangel* Win 89].

✓ Thomas, D.Winton. "The Book of Haggai – Exegesis" (IB) 1956. Because the author was an excellent philologist, this is still worthwhile.

✓ **Tollington, Janet.** ‡ *Tradition and Innovation in Haggai and Zechariah 1–8* (JSOTSup) 1993. An Oxford dissertation.

✓ **Wolff, H.W.** ‡ (ContC) ET 1988. Certainly a leading critical exegesis for students to consult. As one might expect from this scholar, Wolff pays close attention to what he perceives as a complicated compositional history with three "growth-rings" (p.18). He pursues a form-critical and tradition history approach with theological goals. See his other volumes under Hosea, Obadiah-Jonah, and Micah.

NOTES: (1) Consult the list of works in the above section, The Twelve Minor Prophets. (2) Mark Boda, "Majoring on the Minors: Recent Research on Haggai and Zechariah," *CBR* 2.1 (2003): 33–68.

—◆◆◆—

ZECHARIAH

★ Baldwin, Joyce G. (TOTC) 1972. See Haggai above. Back in 1999 Wolters said, "For the preacher, the best current scholarly commentary in English is probably the little jewel by…Baldwin" [*BSB* 9/99], despite her "rather debatable overall literary structure" for the whole book of Zechariah. While we long had Verhoef's erudite work on Haggai and Malachi to complement Baldwin, we sadly lacked an in-depth, evangelical work on Zechariah. Merrill's work came along and was some help, but we especially looked forward to McComiskey and Stuart. In addition to consulting McComiskey—my present first choice—and Klein, students needing help with technical matters should look up the critics, especially Meyers/Meyers and Petersen, and the conservative Merrill. Baldwin was Stuart's first choice in 1990. Look for Stuart and Wolters to become the evangelical's likely first picks. But also keep in mind that Boda is a leader in evangelical scholarship on Zechariah, and his NICOT should be top-notch.

★ **Boda, Mark J.** *Haggai, Zechariah* (NIVAC) 2004. See Haggai above.

★ **Klein, George L.** *Zechariah* (NAC) 2008. This exegesis of nearly 450pp is more extensive and contains more substantive research than most other volumes in the series. The treatment of the Hebrew is careful and workmanlike. The theological approach is that of moderate or "progressive" Dispensationalism. Citing some of Blaising's work, Klein argues that "it remains preferable to view biblical references to 'Israel' as applying to national Israel, not the Church" (p.67). Reformed students of biblical prophecy will prefer Boda, Webb, and McComiskey at such points of interpretation where Klein marks a hard distinction between the OT and the NT people of God. Leaving aside eschatology, this is a useful companion in walking through the text. [*RelSRev* 9/09].

★ **McComiskey, Thomas E.** *The Minor Prophets: An Exegetical and Expository Commentary*, Vol. 3, Ed. by McComiskey, 1998. Up to the same standard of excellence found in the Hosea contribution. This whole set has been recommended for purchase above. This is a very dependable exegesis with solid theology, but evangelical OT scholars are looking forward to Stuart and Wolters. If, right now, you want another careful, conservative commentary alongside McComiskey and Klein, look for Merrill.

★ Webb, Barry G. (BST) 2003. This exposition, which is careful and creative in its exegesis and biblical theological reflection, is excellent for evangelical pastors. Webb also produced the fine volume on Isaiah in the same series. [*JSOT* 28.5].

Achtemeier, Elizabeth. [𝓜], (I) 1986. See Nahum above.

Barker, Kenneth L. (EBC) 1985. Ignore this and use the revision in EBCR.

☆ **Barker, Kenneth L.** (EBCR) 2008. This commentary is Dispensationally oriented, but still valuable to others who do not take that doctrinal stance. Barker is well-trained in Semitics (Dropsie PhD) and highly respected in evangelical circles, notably for his work as General Editor of the *NIV Study Bible*. Note: Barker produced the helpful notes on this book for the *NIV Study Bible* (1985, rev. 2002). His work here is about 90pp.

✓ Barnes, W.E. ‡ *Haggai, Zechariah, Malachi* (Cambridge Bible) 1917.

Baron, David. 3rd ed 1919. A substantial exposition, regularly reprinted by various publishers. Baron was a converted Jew and was strongly Premillennial.

☆ Bentley, Michael. *Building for God's Glory* (WCS on Haggai & Zechariah) 1989. For the expositor.

F Boda, Mark. (NICOT). See also his NIVAC above. On the strength of his many articles and the leadership he provides contemporary Zechariah scholarship (see the two volumes below), this should be superb. Earlier Douglas Stuart was said to have the contract.

✓ Boda, Mark J., and Michael H. Floyd (eds). *Bringing Out the Treasure: Inner Biblical Allusion in Zechariah 9–14* (JSOTSup) 2003. This volume includes the publication of Mason's groundbreaking dissertation, noted above under Haggai. [*RelSRev* 10/04].

✓ Boda, Mark, and Michael Floyd (eds). *Tradition in Transition: Haggai and Zechariah 1–8 in the Trajectory of Hebrew Theology*, 2008.

☆ Brown, William P. ‡ *Obadiah–Malachi* (WestBC) 1996. See Obadiah.

✓ **Clark, David J., and Howard A. Hatton.** *A Handbook on Haggai, Zechariah, and Malachi* (UBS) 2002. [*CBQ* 10/04].

F Coggins, Richard. ‡ (Blackwell). I anticipate a volume on Haggai–Malachi.

✓ **Conrad, Edgar W.** ‡ *Zechariah* (Read) 1999. At points Conrad is for me like a breath of fresh air. Reading Zechariah as a whole, instead of as a divided book, makes fresh insights possible. I am not saying he thinks the book is totally cohesive, however. Conrad uses literary methods like intertextuality in mainly unobjectionable ways. Some evangelical scholars will applaud Conrad's methods and conclusions; all can learn from them. About 220pp. [*JSOT* 89 (2000); *CBQ* 7/00; *Interp* 1/00; *OTA* 2/00; *RelSRev* 1/00].

Curtis, Byron G. *Up the Steep and Stony Road: The Book of Zechariah in Social Location Trajectory Analysis*, 2006. A Westminster Seminary dissertation defending both the unity of the prophecy and authorship by the historical Zechariah. I confess I am not clear on his hermeneutical method. [*CBQ* 1/08].

☆ Duguid, Iain M. *Haggai, Zechariah, Malachi* (EPSC) 2010. See under Haggai.

Feinberg, Charles L. *God Remembers*, 4th ed 1979. Dispensationalists always gravitate toward the apocalyptic literature (Daniel, Zechariah, and Revelation). This commentary is valuable to those sharing their perspective, but the Reformed interpreter will not be able to agree with this scholar's approach. Eschatology is the thrust here: Feinberg is militantly Dispensational, strictly separating God's program for Jews and Gentiles. He does, however, helpfully include many Rabbinic quotes from Kimchi and others. Barker, Merrill, and Klein are more moderate from a similar theological stance.

✓ **Floyd, Michael H.** ‡ *Minor Prophets, Part 2* (FOTL) 1999. See Nahum above.

Goldingay, John, and Pamela Scalise. *Minor Prophets II* (NIBC) 2009. See under Nahum. Scalise treats the last two prophets, Zechariah and Malachi, in this volume.

F Gordon, Robert P. [*M?*], (ICC–new series).

F Hanson, Paul D. ‡ (Herm).

☆ Hill, Andrew. (CorBC) 2008. See under Hosea.

✓ Jones, D.R. ‡ *Haggai, Zechariah, Malachi* (Torch Bible Commentary) 1962.

☆ Kaiser, Walter. *Micah, Nahum, Habakkuk, Zephaniah, Haggai, Zechariah, Malachi* (WCC) 1993. See under Micah. This is a suggestive, full (135-page) exposition of this prophet; the approach is Premillennial.

☆ Kline, Meredith G. *Glory in Our Midst: A Biblical-Theological Reading of Zechariah's Night Visions*, 2001. This is a full, vigorous theological exposition (300pp) published by Wipf & Stock. I regret that I have little opportunity to use this. He is so creative that readers often find him both stimulating and mystifying (how did he come up with that?).

Leupold, H.C. 1956. A somewhat dated, fairly thorough commentary, offering a traditional, conservative Lutheran interpretation (Amillennial perspective).

F Luter, Boyd. (Apollos).

☆ Mackay, John L. *Haggai, Zechariah, Malachi: God's Restored People*, 1994. See under Haggai.

✓ Mason, R.A. ‡ (CBC) 1977. See under Haggai.

☆ **Merrill, Eugene H**. *Haggai, Zechariah, Malachi* (intended for WEC?) 1994. See under Haggai. This has a Dispensational orientation; Merrill is among the best, most judicious OT scholars in that camp. This volume treats the Hebrew and is of greater value than Barker or Feinberg from that perspective. Many pastors would want to purchase this one; I did.

☆ **Meyers, Carol L. and Eric M. Meyers.** ‡ (AB) 2 Vols., 1987–93. See Haggai above. The second volume is astonishingly full; *Zechariah 9–14* runs to 552pp! They do not hold to the unity of Zechariah, but do take a more conservative approach to the text than many critics. There is an immense amount of learning in this set. Among critical commentaries on Zechariah, this is the first I reach for, if I'm not time-pressed. One caveat, though: pastors interested in theology will find that both the AB and OTL sets tend to read the book more as political document—answering scholars' questions about the socio-political context—and may disappoint in their theological discussion. This deficiency, I predict, will seem glaring when Boda's NICOT is published. [*JBL* 114.3 (1995)].

Mitchell, H.G. ‡ (ICC) 1912.

☆ Moore, Thomas V. (GS) 1856. See Haggai above.

F Nogalski, James D. ‡ (S&H).

✓ O'Brien, Julia. ‡ *Nahum, Habakkuk, Zephaniah, Haggai, Zechariah, Malachi* (AOTC) 2004. See under Nahum.

✓ **Ollenberger, Ben C.** [𝓜], (NewIB) 1996.

F Patterson, Richard. *Nahum–Malachi* (EEC).

Perowne, T.T. *Haggai and Zechariah* (Cambridge Bible) 1888, 2nd ed 1901. Fairly conservative work by a leading scholar of that day that was replaced by Barnes.

☆ **Petersen, David L**. ‡ *Haggai, Zechariah 1–8* (OTL) 1984; *Zechariah 9–14 and Malachi* (OTL) 1995. See Haggai above. He does not hold to the unity of Zechariah. The pastor wanting to build a first-rate exegetical library might wish to purchase the OTL set for its careful form-critical treatment and as a handier guide than AB. The Meyers' AB set is fuller, and marginally more useful for certain kinds of work with the text. [*Interp* 1/97; *CBQ* 7/96; *JTS* 10/96; *JETS* 6/97; *JSS* Spr 97; *JTS* 10/96; *JSOT* 76; *SwJT*, Sum 98; *BSac* 4/96].

☆ Phillips, Richard D. (REC) 2007. A well-done example of faithful, Christ-centered expository preaching. There is a lot of material here (351pp). See REC in the Commentary Series section, and note also Phillips' other REC contribution which is on Hebrews. [*JETS* 9/08].

✓ **Redditt, Paul L.** ‡ *Haggai, Zechariah, Malachi* (NCB) 1995. See Haggai above.

F Shelley, Patricia. (BCBC).

✓ **Smith, Ralph L.** ‡ (WBC) 1984. See Micah above. Believes Zechariah 9–14 to be a later gloss.

F Stuart, Douglas. *Micah–Malachi* (WBC replacement). See under Micah. Stuart had earlier been slated to do the NICOT volume on Zechariah, but that research will go into WBC.

✓ **Stuhlmueller, C.** ‡ *Haggai and Zechariah* (ITC) 1988.

✓ Thomas, D.Winton. "The Book of Zechariah 1–8, Exegesis" (IB) 1956. Because the author was an excellent philologist, this is still worthwhile.

Unger, Merrill. 1963. A Dispensational exposition, based on the Hebrew.

F Wolters, Al. (HCOT). This should be excellent. For a stimulating foretaste, try his "Confessional Criticism and the Night Visions of Zechariah" in *Renewing Biblical Interpretation, Scripture and Hermeneutics*, Volume 1, edited by Craig Bartholomew, et al (2000).

✓ Wright, C.H.H. *Zechariah and His Prophecies*, 1879. A fascinating volume for the student of Zechariah. These were the Bampton Lectures of 1878 and go into great depth (about 600pp). This is a true classic in the history of interpretation and for generations was a favorite among conservatives. I believe this was last reprinted by Klock & Klock in 1980.

NOTES: (1) Consult the list of works in the above section, "The Twelve Minor Prophets." (2) See Michael Floyd's "Zechariah and Changing Views of Second Temple Judaism in Recent Commentaries," *RelSRev* 25.3 (1999): 257–263. (3) Mark Boda, "Majoring on the Minors: Recent Research on Haggai and Zechariah," *CBR* 2.1 (2003): 33–68.

MALACHI

★ Baker, David W. *Joel, Obadiah, Malachi* (NIVAC) 2006. This meets a real need, since we lack a good selection of strong expositions which offer guidance in applying Malachi today. I missed not having any discussion of tithing, which inevitably comes up as a discussion topic in the churches. See under Joel.

★ **Hill, Andrew.** (AB) 1998. A full-length, satisfying commentary from an evangelical perspective—not really expected in AB, which is now more "ecumenical" than we thought. (Hill came to the attention of AB's editor, David Noel Freedman through doctoral studies at Michigan.) The best commentary on the book (because fullest), though compare with Stuart and Verhoef. There is more theological reflection here than in some other AB volumes. Advanced students interested in the finer points of philology and grammar may be disappointed by Hill's discussion in places; see Jack Collins' review in *TJ* Fall 00. [*JSOT-BL* 1999; *EvQ* 4/00; *JBL* Win 99; *JTS* 10/99; *Biblica* 81.1 (2000); *Interp* 4/99; *AsTJ* Fall 99; *JR* 10/99; *RBL*; *DenvJ*].

★ **Stuart, Douglas.** *The Minor Prophets: An Exegetical and Expository Commentary*, Vol. 3, Ed. by Thomas E. McComiskey, 1998. This set is already recommended for purchase above.

★ Taylor, Richard A., and E. Ray Clendenen. *Haggai, Malachi* (NAC) 2004. See under Haggai.

★ **Verhoef, Pieter A.** (NICOT) 1987. See Haggai above. Though this volume is beginning to have a somewhat dated feel, the rigorous exegesis and theological reflection keep this on the recommended list. In my opinion, he does not get the crux at 2:16 right.

Achtemeier, Elizabeth. [𝓜], (I) 1986. See Nahum above.

☆ Alden, Robert L. (EBC) 1985. See under Haggai.

☆ **Baldwin, Joyce G.** (TOTC) 1972. See Haggai above.

✓ Barnes, W.E. ‡ *Haggai, Zechariah, Malachi* (Cambridge Bible) 1917.

☆ Benton, John. *Losing Touch with the Living God* (WCS) 1985.

☆ Brown, William P. ‡ *Obadiah–Malachi* (WestBC) 1996. See Obadiah.

✓ **Clark, David J., and Howard A. Hatton**. *A Handbook on Haggai, Zechariah, and Malachi* (UBS) 2002. [*CBQ* 10/04].

F Coggins, Richard. ‡ (Blackwell). I anticipate a volume on Haggai–Malachi.

☆ Duguid, Iain M. *Haggai, Zechariah, Malachi* (EPSC) 2010. See under Haggai. It is worth noting that Duguid handles the difficult divorce text very well and succinctly.

✓ **Floyd, Michael H.** ‡ *Minor Prophets, Part 2* (FOTL) 1999. See Nahum above.

✓   **Glazier-McDonald**, Beth. ‡ *Malachi: The Divine Messenger*, 1987. This is a very important technical commentary published by Scholars Press which students should certainly consult. [*JBL* Spr 89].

    Goldingay, John, and Pamela Scalise. *Minor Prophets II* (NIBC) 2009. See under Nahum. Scalise treats the last two prophets, Zechariah and Malachi, in this volume.

F   Gordon, Robert P. [*M?*], (ICC–new series).

F   Hanson, Paul D. ‡ (Herm).

☆   Hill, Andrew. (CorBC) 2008. This slightly updates and popularizes the in-depth commentary in his AB work. See under Hosea.

✓   Hugenberger, Gordon P. *Marriage as a Covenant*, 1994. Not a commentary. This is a sterling dissertation, published first by Brill and then by Baker. Hugenberger focuses upon the Malachi 2 text but treats other Scriptures as well. This work is of interest to ethicists as well as OT exegetes. [*JBL* Sum 95; *VT* 46.3].

F   Jacobs, Mignon. *Haggai, Malachi* (NICOT replacement).

☆   Kaiser, Walter C. *Malachi: God's Unchanging Love*, 1984. With a fine analysis of the MT, the exposition is full, readable and well-researched. Kaiser is concerned to discuss the theological issues and their contemporary relevance. The author gave us a surprising bonus in his volume; Appendix B is entitled "The Usefulness of Biblical Commentaries for Preaching and Bible Study." I consider this paperback more useful than Kaiser's WCC work on Malachi listed below. The student prefers to work with this commentary since it deals some with the Hebrew. Preachers who are pressed for time will be tempted to opt for the Communicator's Commentary. This was Stuart's favorite in 1990. In early editions of this guide I recommended this book for purchase, but I believe it is o/p. [*JETS* 6/85].

☆   **Kaiser, Walter.** *Micah, Nahum, Habakkuk, Zephaniah, Haggai, Zechariah, Malachi* (WCC) 1993. See Micah.

✓   Jones, D.R. ‡ *Haggai, Zechariah, Malachi* (Torch Bible Commentary) 1962.

☆   Mackay, John L. *Haggai, Zechariah, Malachi: God's Restored People*, 1994. See under Haggai.

✓   Mason, R.A. ‡ (CBC) 1977.

☆   Merrill, Eugene H. *Haggai, Zechariah, Malachi* (intended for WEC?) 1994. See Haggai and Zechariah above.

☆   **Merrill, Eugene H.** (EBCR) 2008. There are few brief evangelical commentaries to compete with this (27pp). Students should use the fuller work of 1994.

    Moore, Thomas V. (GS) 1856. See Haggai above.

☆   Morgan, G. Campbell. *Malachi's Message for Today*, 1972 reprint. This book of messages, by one of the 20th century's greatest Bible expositors, was formerly titled *Wherein Have We Robbed God?* It remains very suggestive and well worth buying, if you can find it secondhand. See Hosea above.

F   Nogalski, James D. ‡ (S&H).

✓   O'Brien, Julia. ‡ *Nahum, Habakkuk, Zephaniah, Haggai, Zechariah, Malachi* (AOTC) 2004. See under Nahum.

    Ogden, G.S., and R.R. Deutsch. ‡ *Joel and Malachi* (ITC) 1987.

F   Patterson, Richard. *Nahum–Malachi* (EEC).

☆   **Petersen, David L.** ‡ (OTL) 1995. See Zechariah above.

✓   **Redditt, Paul L.** ‡ *Haggai, Zechariah, Malachi* (NCB) 1995. See Haggai above.

✓   Schuller, Eileen M. ‡ (NewIB) 1996.

F   Shelley, Patricia. (BCBC).

✓   Smith, J.H.P. ‡ (ICC) 1912.

✓   **Smith, Ralph L.** ‡ (WBC) 1984. See Micah above.

F   Snyman, S.D. ‡ (HCOT). Previously, Van Leeuwen was listed here.
F   Stuart, Douglas. *Micah–Malachi* (WBC replacement). See under Micah.
F   Van der Woude, A.S. ‡ (Herm). The author is one of the great South African scholars.
F   Wright, N.T. (BST).
NOTE: (1) Consult the list of works in the above section, "The Twelve Minor Prophets." (2) I recommend looking up David Jones' article, "Malachi on Divorce," *Presb* 15.1 (1989): 16–22. His defense of the superior Septuagintal reading—once properly understood—is right on target, and one needs to note it. He takes issue with a number of scholars over their exegesis of 2:16. Jones' further research on the LXX is reflected in an article published in the Winter 1990 issue of *JBL*. Another fine article is Markus Zehnder, "A Fresh Look at Malachi II 13–16," *VT* 53.2 (2003): 224–59. Among the commentaries, Clendenen has an especially full (14pp) and carefully thought-through exegesis of 2:15b–16.

New Testament Commentaries

★ Beale, G.K., and D.A. Carson (eds). *Commentary on the New Testament Use of the Old Testament*, 2007. Since the Church has always held to the principle that "Scripture interprets Scripture," and since the relationship between the testaments is key for understanding each, works such as this (going all the way back to the old *Treasury of Scripture Knowledge*) will prove spiritually and academically useful to a high degree. [*CBQ* 1/09; *RelSRev* 9/08; *JETS* 6/09; *BBR* 19.2; *JSNT-BL* 2009; *NovT* 52.2; *EuroJTh* 18.2].

★ *Calvin's New Testament Commentaries.* David W. Torrance and Thomas F. Torrance (eds), ET 1958–72. In 12 vols. and published by Eerdmans. These translations are competent, and Calvin's theological comments have carried great weight for centuries. The Reformer covers all the NT books except the last four (2 John through Revelation). This set of the Calvin's commentaries is to be preferred to the (still serviceable) Baker reprint of the 19th century edition by the Calvin Translation Society. [see *EvQ* 7/98].

★ Zerwick, Max, and Mary Grosvenor. *A Grammatical Analysis of the Greek New Testament*, 5th rev. ed. 1996. This covers the entire NT with meticulous accuracy. Every seminary student could profit immensely from this analysis. [*EvQ* 1/75; *JETS* 12/80]. Similar in scope and aim is the *Rodgers-Rodgers New Linguistic and Exegetical Key to the Greek New Testament* (Zondervan, 1998).

★ Metzger, Bruce. *A Textual Commentary on the Greek New Testament*, Corrected ed 1975; 2nd ed 1994. [*JBL* 92.4 (1973)]. Another, less in-depth UBS option is Roger L. Omanson, *A Textual Guide to the Greek New Testament*, 2006 [*NovT* 50.3; *ExpTim* 11/07].

—⁂—

JESUS & GOSPELS RESEARCH

★ Blomberg, Craig L. *Jesus and the Gospels: An Introduction and Survey*, 1997, 2nd ed 2009. I have not found a better accessible evangelical content-survey. The companion is *From Pentecost to Patmos*, 2006.

★ Green, Joel B., Scot McKnight, and I. Howard Marshall (eds). *Dictionary of Jesus and the Gospels*, 1992. This IVP publication is a standard evangelical reference work, though some of the contributors are leading critical scholars: Dale Allison, Frederick Danker, Edgar McKnight, and John Painter. Several of the articles are starting to show their age.

★ Wenham, David, and Steve Walton. *Exploring the NT: A Guide to the Gospels & Acts*, 2001. All six vols. in this IVP series are well worth purchasing. [*Anvil* 19.3].

✧   ✧   ✧   ✧   ✧   ✧

✓ Aland, Kurt (ed). *Synopsis Quattuor Evangeliorum*, 15th ed 1996; *Synopsis of the Four Gospels*, 10th ed 1993.

✓ Allison, Dale C. ‡ *Jesus of Nazareth: Millenarian Prophet*, 1998. See also the clever-ly-titled *The Historical Christ and the Theological Jesus*, 2009 [*Them* 11/09; *JTS* 4/10; *JETS* 6/10; *CBQ* 7/10; *DenvJ* 3/09 (Blomberg); *JSNT-BL* 2010].

Bailey, Kenneth E. *Jesus through Middle Eastern Eyes: Cultural Studies in the Gospels*, 2008. See also his research listed under Parables below. [*EQ* 7/09].

Barnett, Paul. *Finding the Historical Christ*, 2009. [*JSNT-BL* 2010].

✓ Barton, Stephen C. (ed). ‡ *The Cambridge Companion to the Gospels*, 2006. [*EuroJTh* 18.1].

✓ Bauckham, Richard. *Jesus and the Eyewitnesses: The Gospels as Eyewitness Testimony*, 2006. The thesis of this conservative work is having a strong impact in broader scholarship and is also under attack by skeptics. Do see Bauckham under John's Gospel. [*Biblica* 90.1; *JSNT* 31.2 (a review discussion); *NovT* 52.1; *JSHJ* 6.2 (review discussion); *EuroJTh* 16.2].

☆ Beilby, James K., and Paul Rhodes Eddy (eds). *The Historical Jesus: Five Views*, 2009. Getting Crossan, L.T. Johnson, Dunn, and Bock together in one book was a good idea and quite a feat. [*RevExp* Spr 10].

✓ Black, David Alan, and David R. Beck (eds). *Rethinking the Synoptic Problem*, 2001.

☆ Blomberg, Craig L. *The Historical Reliability of the Gospels*, 1987, rev. 2007. [*JSNT-BL* 2009]. See his companion vol. defending the reliability of John's Gospel (2001).

☆ Bock, Darrell L. *Jesus according to Scripture*, 2002; Studying the Historical Jesus, 2002. The first of these is a massive study (650pp) of the witness of the four Gospels to Jesus [*JSHJ* 1.2], while the second is a student "Guide to Sources and Methods."

✓ Bock, Darrell L., and G. J. Herrick. *Jesus in Context: Background Readings for Gospel Study*, 2005.

✓ Bockmuehl, Markus. *This Jesus: Martyr, Lord, Messiah*, 1994. Later he would edit *The Cambridge Companion to Jesus*, 2001 [*Anvil* 20.2].

✓ Bockmuehl, Markus, and Donald Hagner (eds). [ℳ], *The Written Gospel*, 2005. A fine *Festschrift* from the world's leading scholars for Graham Stanton. [*Anvil* 24.1 (France); *Evangel* Spr 07 (Wenham); *Anvil* 24.1 (France)].

✓ Bultmann, Rudolph. ‡ *The History of the Synoptic Tradition*, rev. 1963.

☆ Burridge, Richard A. [ℳ], *Four Gospels, One Jesus? A Symbolic Reading*, 1994, rev. 2005. Note too the earlier, widely-cited dissertation, *What Are the Gospels? A Comparison with Graeco-Roman Biography*, 1992, 2nd ed 2004.

✓ Charlesworth, James H. (ed). ‡ *Jesus and Archeology*, 2006. [*JSHJ* 8.2 (2010)].

✓ Chilton, Bruce, and Craig A. Evans (eds). *Studying the Historical Jesus*, 1994; and *Authenticating the Words of Jesus*, 1999. Both vols. are from Brill.

Crossan, John Dominic. ‡ *The Historical Jesus*, 1991. Highly critical and tendentious piece [*Interp* 7/93; *CBQ* 7/93], followed by *Jesus: A Revolutionary Biography*, 1994.

Dawes, Gregory W. (ed). ‡ *The Historical Jesus Quest: Landmarks in the Search for the Jesus of History*, 1999. Useful for surveying past work. [*JSHJ* 1.2].

Dungan, David Laird. ‡ *The Synoptic Problem: The Canon, the Text, the Composition, and the Interpretation of the Gospels*, 1999.

✓ Dunn, James D.G. [ℳ], *Jesus Remembered*, 2003. Yet again, Dunn has offered an enormous and lucid study for students. Blomberg writes, "While not replacing Wright in boldness of hypothesis and scope of coverage nor Meier in painstak-ing analysis of minute detail, Dunn's work deserves to take its place with that of Wright and Meier as one of the three most significant, comprehensive historical Jesus studies of our generation." [*JSHJ* 3.1; *Anvil* 22.3; *DenvJ* 1/03 (Blomberg)].

Dunn, James D.G., and Scot McKnight (eds). *The Historical Jesus in Recent Research*, 2005. Influential essays in the field over a 150-year period, collected in Eisenbrauns' "Sources for Biblical and Theological Study" series. [*JSHJ* 5.1].

Eddy, P.R., and Gregory A. Boyd. *The Jesus Legend: A Case for the Historical Reliability of the Synoptic Jesus Tradition*, 2007.

Edwards, James R. *The Hebrew Gospel and the Development of the Synoptic Tradition*, 2009. The claims made are drawing controversy. [*ExpTim* 6/10].

✓ Evans, Craig A. (ed). *Encyclopedia of the Historical Jesus*, 2008. Also titled *The Routledge Encyclopedia of the Historical Jesus*. Earlier he edited a four-vol. set, *The Historical Jesus* (2004). Evans has been productive, authoring the cleverly-titled Clarendon issue, *The Historical Christ and the Jesus of Faith* (1996); a book against the skeptics: *Fabricating Jesus* (IVP, 2006) [*JSNT-BL* 2009]; and the IBR Bibliography, *Jesus*, 1992.

✓ Evans, Craig A., and James A. Sanders (eds). *The Gospels and the Scriptures of Israel*, 1994. On the same fascinating topic, see Willard Swartley, *Israel's Scripture Traditions and the Synoptic Traditions* (1994), and Christopher M. Tuckett (ed), *The Scriptures in the Gospels* (1997).

✓ Gaventa, Beverly Roberts, and Richard B. Hays (eds). ‡ *Seeking the Identity of Jesus: A Pilgrimage*, 2008. First-rate essays illustrating the resistance of mildly and moderately critical scholars to today's hypercritical reconstructions of the historical Jesus. [*JSNT* 32.3 (a review discussion); *JSNT-BL* 2009; *Them* 7/09].

✓ Hengel, Martin. [*M*], *The Four Gospels and the One Gospel of Jesus Christ*, 2000. Reflects a lifetime of study by one of the leading (conservatively critical) German NT professors. Worth noting is that Hengel is fully on-board with the idea that the Gospels were not produced for single communities but were general ("catholic") tracts; cf. Bauckham (ed), *The Gospels for All Christians*, 1998. [*Anvil* 19.1].

☆ Hurtado, Larry W. *Lord Jesus Christ: Devotion to Jesus in Earliest Christianity*, 2003. Lucid, impressive, and influential scholarship, drawing together NT research, early Christian history, and theology (Christology). [*JSHJ* 3.1]. Added to this is *How on Earth Did Jesus Become God?* (2005) [*JSHJ* 5.2].

☆ Keener, Craig S. *The Historical Jesus of the Gospels*, 2009. A large (831-page) and learned treatment of the biblical material and scholarship today. [*Them* 4/10].

Kelber, Werner. ‡ *The Oral and the Written Gospel*, 1983. The challenges to, and refinement of, the thesis continue in Thatcher (ed), *Jesus, the Voice and the Text: Beyond* The Oral and the Written Gospel, 2008 [*JSNT-BL* 2010].

✓ Kingsbury, Jack D. (ed). ‡ *Gospel Interpretation: Narrative-Critical and Social-Scientific Approaches*, 1997.

✓ Koester, Helmut. ‡ *Ancient Christian Gospels: Their History and Development*, 1990.

McKnight, Scot. *Jesus and His Death: Historiography, the Historical Jesus, and Atonement Theory*, 2005. [*JSHJ* 5.1].

✓ McKnight, Scot, and Matthew C. Williams. *The Synoptic Gospels: An Annotated Bibliography*, 2000. From the IBR Bibliographies project, published by Baker. Badly needing an update is McKnight's useful *Interpreting the Synoptic Gospels* (1987), published by Baker.

McKnight, Scot, and Joseph B. Modica (eds). *Who Do My Opponents Say that I Am? An Investigation of the Accusations against the Historical Jesus*, 2008. Evangelical essays approaching the issue of Jesus' identity from a different angle. [*JETS* 6/09; *JSNT-BL* 2009 (Head); *EuroJTh* 18.2].

✓ Meier, John P. ‡ *A Marginal Jew* (ABRL) 4 Vols., 1991–2009. Probably the fullest, most detailed study ever produced in the field (3050pp). [*CBQ* 7/10; *BTB* 8/10; *JETS* 9/10].

 Meyer, Ben F. ‡ *The Aims of Jesus*, 1979. Though dated now, many still count it as seminal.

✓ Perkins, Pheme. ‡ *Introduction to the Synoptic Gospels*, 2007. [*JSNT-BL* 2009; *Anvil* 26.3–4].

✓ Powell, Mark Allan. ‡ *Jesus as a Figure in History: How Modern Historians View the Man from Galilee*, 1998.

✓ Riches, John. ‡ *The World of Jesus: First-Century Judaism in Crisis*, 1990. A Cambridge issue. For a well-written evangelical treatment, consult James Jeffers, *The Graeco-Roman World of the New Testament Era* (IVP, 1999).

✓ Riches, J., W.R. Telford, and C.M. Tuckett, with an Introduction by S. McKnight. ‡ *The Synoptic Gospels*, 2001. Collected vols. from Sheffield's "New Testament Guides."

✓ Robinson, James M., et al (eds). ‡ *The Critical Edition of Q* (Herm) 2000.

✓ Sanders, E.P. ‡ *Jesus and Judaism*, 1985. Followed by *The Historical Figure of Jesus*, 1993.

✓ Stanton, Graham N. ‡ *The Gospels and Jesus*, 1989, 2ⁿᵈ ed 2002. An Oxford publication and certainly among the best moderately critical introductions to the subject. See also his essays in *Jesus and Gospel*, 2004.

✓ Stegemann, W., B.J. Malina, and G. Theissen (eds). ‡ *The Social Setting of Jesus and the Gospels*, 2002. [*JSHJ* 2.1].

☆ Stein, Robert H. *Studying the Synoptic Gospels: Origin and Interpretation*, 2001. This mature evangelical book focuses on the Synoptic Problem and the older diachronic methods. It is a revised and expanded second edition of *The Synoptic Problem: An Introduction*, 1987. Also valuable is his *Jesus the Messiah: A Survey of the Life of Christ*, 1996, which has been widely used in Bible colleges and seminaries.

☆ Strauss, M.L. *Four Portraits, One Jesus: An Introduction to Jesus and the Gospels*, 2007. One of the best, most inviting evangelical introductions. [*JSNT-BL* 2009].

✓ Theissen, Gerd, and Dagmar Winter. ‡ *The Quest for the Plausible Jesus: The Question of Criteria*, ET 2002. Theissen is a leading European scholar in historical-Jesus study. [*JBL* Aut 99; *JTS* 49.2; *JSHJ* 1.2]. On the same specific topic is Porter, *The Criteria for Authenticity in Historical-Jesus Research*, 2000.

✓ Twelftree, Graham H. *Jesus the Miracle Worker: A Historical & Theological Study*, 1999.

 Witherington, Ben. *The Jesus Quest: The Third Search for the Jew of Nazareth*, 1995, 2ⁿᵈ ed 1997.

✓ Wright, N.T. [𝓜], *Jesus and the Victory of God*, 1996; *The Resurrection of the Son of God*, 2003. Two vols. (#2 and #3) from the author's series, "Christian Origins and the Question of God." A tour de force which seeks to understand, through research mainly on the Synoptics, "how Jesus' whole life, not just his death on the cross in isolation, was somehow 'gospel'" (*JVG*, xiv). The series is an apology for rigorous historical study of what he believes to be the most important religious question of all. For *The Resurrection of the Son of God* [*Evangel* Sum 04 (Turner); *DenvJ* 1/03 (Blomberg)], the review discussion in *JSHJ* 3.2 (2005) is well worth looking up, including as it does Wright, Allison, Habermas, Goulder, Hurtado, and Evans.

—ᘒ—

MATTHEW

★ **Carson, Donald.** (EBC) 1984. Even after the appearance of Blomberg and France, this may still be the most generally useful commentary on Matthew for the pastor. The adjective that comes quickly to mind for this work is "sure-footed." Carson was allowed a great deal more space than other contributors to the series, and he used it well. Almost 600 pages and uses mild redaction criticism (in an acceptable, defensible way). "He has done his homework with great care, and regularly launches into very thorough explanations of particular exegetical, historical or theological points" [*BSB* 9/04]. Zondervan has also published this commentary in two softcover vols. and separate from EBC's Mark and Luke. I am eager to see Carson's revision (EBCR) give extended life to this commentary; the expected release date is late 2010. [*JETS* 6/85; *TJ* Spr 85]. Pastors will also note Carson's homiletical expositions of the Sermon on the Mount (see below) and Matthew 8–10 entitled, *When Jesus Confronts the World* (1987). These expositions are essentially sermonic, but of a much, much higher caliber intellectually than the typical sermon.

★ **Davies, W.D. and Dale Allison.** ‡ (ICC–new series) 3 Vols., 1988–97. With painstaking work on the Greek text, the authors come to mainstream critical conclusions. These fat vols. must be consulted, but have been way too expensive for most pastors. (They list for \$468 in hb, but since 2004 are available in less pricey pb. With deals like CBD's offer of \$97 per set, I can recommend this for purchase, but only to advanced students and the most diligent and scholarly of pastors.) Specialists value this magisterial and encyclopedic work as about the finest exegetical tool available (2400pp). Compare with Luz, which along with the ICC is an authoritative reference set. Replaces Allen in the series. [*JTS* 4/92; *JBL* Sum. 91; *CBQ* 10/91; *Interp* 7/91; *ExpTim* 2/93; *ThTo* 47.1; *EvQ* 10/98; *NovT* 41.2; *CTJ* 11/91, 4/94; *Biblica* 78.4; *SJT* 54.1; *DenvJ*]. There is also a 2004 abridgement by Allison [*JTS* 10/07; *JSNT-BL* 2006; *RelSRev* 10/06]. Instead of Davies/Allison, the average pastor will choose another commentary such as Blomberg, or an exposition such as Doriani's REC and Green's BST.

★ **France, Richard T.** (NICNT) 2007. Those who anticipate forthcoming commentaries have had a long wait for NICNT on Matthew. The late Robert Guelich, Blaine Charette, and Scot McKnight in succession had contracts with Eerdmans. France has delivered, building upon his careful TNTC (see below). This could be considered a top pick for the evangelical pastor—but be aware of some of the exegetically and theologically controversial positions noted by Agan [*Presb* Spr 09]. France is one of the most respected evangelical NT scholars in the world, "a Matthean scholar par excellence" (Hagner), and he set out to "locate the individual parts of the gospel within the overall narrative flow of the whole" (xviii). One caution: you may not want to follow him in his argument that the "coming of the Son of Man" in 24:29–31 is not the Parousia. [*JTS* 10/08; *CJ* Win 09; *JSNT-BL* 2008; *ExpTim* 2/08; *RelSRev* 12/08; *JETS* 12/08 (Turner); *BSac* 10/08; *Anvil* 25.3].

★ **Hagner, Donald.** [*M*], (WBC) 2 Vols., 1993–95. This fine, redaction-critical work has been called "certainly one of the best available" [BSB 9/04]. Just a quick look at vol. One's 75pp of introduction and 400pp of comment on chs. 1–13 shows this exegetical study to be quite thorough, and the second vol. is even better. Unlike many other massive works, Hagner is interesting throughout and does not get lost plowing through the technical issues; he gives a great deal of attention to Matthew's distinctive message. The pastor working in the Greek should find these vols. most helpful. Hagner, who has long taught at Fuller Seminary, asks many of the right theological questions. Many pastors have probably bought this set in lieu of the formerly expensive ICC vols.—Hagner's two vols. together cost half the price of a single ICC hb. [*Them* 10/96; *JETS* 3/99; *JBL* Sum 96; *JTS* 4/96 & 4/01; *TJ* Spr 98; *CTJ* 11/00; *RTR* 1/97; *RelSRev* 10/97].

★ **Keener, Craig S.** 1999, (SRC) rev. 2009. The first edition was a massive one-vol. commentary (721 + 300pp of bibliography and indexes), of real usefulness to both pastor and student. Keener chose to focus especially upon "the social-historical contexts of Matthew and his traditions on the one hand, and pericope-by-pericope suggestions concerning the nature of Matthew's exhortations to his Christian audience on the other" (p.1). The new edition is a revision and slight expansion of the earlier work; I have not examined the 2009 edition closely. This book complements Hagner and Carson very well. Do not confuse this large pb with Keener's much briefer 1997 "IVP New Testament Commentary" work, which preachers will find much more accessible. [*ThTo* 1/00; *Interp* 10/00; *Them* Aut 00; *Presb* Spr 00; *Scripture Bulletin* 7/00; *Biblica* 82.1; *SwJT* Spr 01; *EvQ* 1/04; *JETS* 9/01; *TJ* Spr 02; *RelSRev* 4/01; *DenvJ*].

★ **Nolland, John.** [*M*], (NIGTC) 2005. As expected, Nolland has largely followed the research methods used in his three-vol. WBC work on Luke and produced a redaction-critical exegesis which is exceedingly thorough (nearly 1300pp + 200pp of bibliography). One difference is the more contemporary "feel" of *Matthew*, as Nolland gives greater attention to narrative criticism. I regard this as a better work for pastors than the earlier commentary because it is a little more focused on the text as we have it and spends much less time on the ins-and-outs of scholarly discussion. Contrariwise, some students might want more interaction with other exegetes. This is clearly one of the best commentaries on the Greek text, more accessible than Davies/Allison. The bibliographies are nearly exhaustive. Nolland wants to date Matthew prior to AD 70, yet thinks it "most unlikely" that the apostle Matthew authored the gospel. [*JTS* 10/07; *JETS* 9/06; *JSNT-BL* 2007; *RB* 1/08; *NovT* 48.4; *RelSRev* 10/06; *BSac* 7/07; *ExpTim* 7/06].

★ Wilkins, Michael J. (NIVAC) 2004. This is the largest volume so far in the series (over 1000pp) and builds upon a strong exegetical foundation. Wilkins develops the theme of discipleship, upon which he has written a monograph. The author completed his PhD at Fuller Seminary, has done pastoral ministry at a Presbyterian church, and now teaches at Talbot Seminary. As a preacher's companion alongside the more exegetical works, Wilkins has a much fuller discussion (e.g., see the Beatitudes) than most preacher's commentaries, but Green may be just as good a value for the money. Both are worth buying. [*JETS* 6/05].

✧ ✧ ✧ ✧ ✧ ✧

Alexander, J.A. 1861. Still being reprinted from time to time, this is a fairly well-known classic by an amazing Princeton Seminary polymath, who served alternately as professor of OT, Church History, and NT. This commentary was interrupted at ch. 16 by Alexander's last illness; the remainder of the gospel (chs. 17–28) was covered by his previously prepared chapter summaries.

Allen, W.C. ‡ (retired ICC) 3rd ed 1922. Scholars are divided over the value of this contribution to ICC. Carson rates it low, while Danker rates it more highly. Considering Carson's past work with Matthew, I place more weight on his judgment.

✓ Allison, Dale C. ‡ *Studies in Matthew: Interpretation Past and Present*, 2005. Collected essays from the main author of the Davies/Allison International Critical Commentary set. [*JETS* 12/06; *JBL* Win 06; *JSNT-BL* 2007]. Another, most stimulating read for students is *The New Moses: A Matthean Typology*, 1993.

Argyle, A.W. ‡ (CBC) 1963.

✓ Aune, David E. (ed). ‡ *The Gospel of Matthew in Current Study*, 2001. [*WTJ* Fall 03; *RTR* 12/02; *SwJT* Sum 02; *RelSRev* 1/02; *BBR* 13.1; *Anvil* 21.2]. A little more dated on the same topic is David Bauer and Mark Allan Powell (eds), *Treasures Old and New: Recent Contributions to Matthean Studies*, 1996.

Balch, David L. (ed). ‡ *Social History of the Matthean Community*, 1991. Approaching the same topic is Anthony Saldarini, *Matthew's Christian-Jewish Community*, 1994.

F Bauer, David. (RRA).

✓ Beare, Francis. ‡ 1981. Though a technical, lengthy commentary and widely consulted at one time, this is not regarded as of great value at this point. The scholarly approach seemed rather dated even when it appeared in print. [*JBL* 103.1 (1984)].

F Beaton, Rick. ‡ (BNTC).

F Black, C. Clifton. ‡ (NTL).

☆ **Blomberg, Craig.** (NAC) 1992. This work contains great insight, just as one would expect in light of his previous research on the gospels (e.g., *The Historical Reliability of the Gospels*) and parables (see that section below). This commentary is 460pp long and does not directly treat the original Greek text, though one senses that all the research is there to back up his conclusions. Along with Stein's *Luke*, Pohill's *Acts*, and Schreiner on Peter & Jude, this is the best in the NT series thus far. As valuable to the pastor as any of the above recommended commentaries on Matthew and well worth buying. The more I've used this, the more I have come to appreciate it. Comparing Keener with Blomberg, the former has more information and an impressive bibliography, while the latter is a wiser, more mature guide in exposition, with a minimum of distractions. Blomberg is also half the price. [*Them* 10/94; *CTJ* 11/94; *CBQ* 1/94; *CRBR* 1994].

☆ Boice, James Montgomery. 2 Vols., 2001. Not yet reviewed. See under John's Gospel.

✓ Boring, Eugene. ‡ (NewIB) 1995. The author also has a major commentary published on Mark's Gospel and on Revelation. [*JETS* 3/99].

Bornkamm, Gunter, Gerhard Barth and Heinz Held. ‡ *Tradition and Interpretation in Matthew*, ET 1963. This work is significant for launching redaction criticism on this gospel.

Broadus, J.A. 1886. An old standby of preachers which can still be consulted with profit. Its strengths lie more in the area of exposition and homiletical hints than exegesis.

☆ **Brown, Raymond E.** ‡ *The Birth of the Messiah*, 1977, rev. 1993. A notable, exceedingly full, and moderately critical commentary on the birth and infancy narratives in Matthew and Luke. Brown was a Catholic priest who long taught at Union Seminary in New York. This will be appreciated by the scholarly pastor who reads quickly. [*JBL* 9/79; *EvQ* 4/80].

✓ **Brown, Raymond E.** ‡ *The Death of the Messiah*, 2 Vols., 1994. This astonishingly learned historical and theological commentary on the passion narratives is over 1500pp long—much too long to recommend to the pastor, despite its value. [*Interp* 4/96; *PSB* 16.3 (1995); *JBL* Sum 96; *Chm* 108.4 (1994); *HBT* 12/96].

☆ **Bruner, Frederick D.** [*M*], *The Christbook (Matthew 1–12)*, 1987; *The Churchbook (Matthew 13–28)*, 1990. These books are subtitled, "A Historical/Theological Commentary." The set was revised and expanded (2004), interacting with the massive amount of NT scholarship published over the last 20 years (Davies-Allison, Luz, etc.) and with influential theologians. These massive vols. (1400pp total) are stimulating, mildly critical, and they underline many preaching themes in the Matthew's Gospel. Bruner is a mainline Presbyterian, best known for his valuable doctoral work in systematics, *A Theology of the Holy Spirit* (1970); this background helps explain why he is so theologically attentive. [*EvQ* 10/88; *RTR* 1/88 and 5/92; *JETS* 3/91; *Anvil* 22.3; *EvQ* 4/05; *Them* 4/06; *JSNT-BL* 2005; *SwJT* Fall 04; *ExpTim* 5/05; *CurTM* 12/07; *BSB* 9/04].

✓ **Buchanan, George Wesley.** ‡ (Mellen Biblical Commentary) 2 Vols., 1996. The set costs only $239.90. I haven't seen this, but I believe it is among the first works in a unique series of intertextual studies. See also Revelation. [*RelSRev* 1/98].

F   Chamblin, Knox. (Mentor) 2 Vols., 2010.

Dickson, David. (GS) 1647. Banner has thankfully reset this Puritan classic in modern typeface. Retains value as a theological exposition, but this vol. is not as worthwhile as his Psalms work. [*EvQ* 4/84].

☆ Doriani, Daniel. (REC) 2 Vols., 2008. Exemplary preaching which is the fruit of long academic study—he taught a course on this gospel for many years at Covenant Seminary—and which nurtures the Church with the life-giving word. Doriani models how to expound the Scriptures from the redemptive-historical angle.

F   Evans, Craig A. [*M*], (NCBC).

Fenton, J. ‡ (WPC) 1977. Critically oriented and uneven.

Filson, Floyd V. ‡ (BNTC) 1971. Disappointing, considering Filson's gifts.

☆ France, Richard T. (TNTC) 1985. Replaced Tasker's contribution. This is an excellent work, supplemented by his monograph, *Matthew: Evangelist and Teacher* (1989) [*JETS* 9/92]. Years ago France's TNTC edged out Morris (but not Blomberg) as a pick for Greek-less readers, especially if conserving funds. I was delighted with this fuller Tyndale entry (416pp), and am now even happier with the NICNT above, though the interpretation of ch. 24 is still off the mark. Note: the TNTC replacement vols. (France, Marshall, Wright, Moo, Grudem, Kruse), as a rule, are quite good.

✓ Gardner, Richard B. (BCBC) 1991. Receives a laudatory review in *CRBR* 1992.

✓ Garland, David E. *Reading Matthew: a Literary and Theological Commentary*, 1993. Well done indeed. This same evangelical scholar has written the NIVAC vols. on Mark and Colossians-Philemon, the *2 Corinthians* vol. in NAC, and *1 Corinthians* in BECNT. [*JETS* 9/97; *CBQ* 10/94; *CRBR* 1994; *RelSRev* 4/97].

✓ Gibbs, Jeffrey A. *Matthew 1:1–11:1* (Concord) 2006. This is the beginnings of a massive and conservative Lutheran exposition; the first vol. runs to 547pp. I have not had opportunity to use it, but reviewers say Gibbs follows the lead of Kingsbury in his narrative approach and finds a tripart structure: 1:1–4:16; 4:17–16:20; 16:21–28:20. [*JSNT-BL* 2008; *JETS* 3/08; *BSac* 4/09]. A second vol. on *Matthew 11:12–20:34* is expected to appear in 2010.

F   Graham, David J. (THC).

Green, H. Benedict. ‡ 1975. This Oxford vol. packs a lot of background information into small compass. At one time this was worth consulting, if one were doing more thorough research, but can now be safely ignored.

☆ Green, Michael. (BST) 2001. Almost 350 pages, this entry is an excellent companion to the more exegetical works I recommended above. Should this be added to your own list? Students may hold off, but many pastors will want to buy Green as a homiletical aid. The author builds upon his earlier *Matthew for Today* (1988); see below. He also taught a course on Matthew when he was a professor at Regent College. Preachers on the lookout for additional expository helps might consider the two-vol. sets of sermons by Doriani and Boice, the commentary by Bruner, and the old vintage Ryle.

Green, Michael. *Matthew for Today*, 1988. This 300-page exposition published by Word Books is thoughtful and seeks to interpret the book for today's reader. It is both theological and practical in its aim. I guess this is o/p and, in any case, is superseded by the BST entry above.

✓ **Gundry, Robert.** [*M*], *Matthew: A Commentary on His Literary and Theological Art*, 1982, rev. 1994. A brilliant, erratic commentary coming out of the evangelical ranks—was originally being written for EBC, believe it or not. One of the most heavily redaction-critical works ever written on Matthew, interpreting many elements of Matthew's "story" as Midrash. It's hard to assess the author's true critical stance for he has argued that he continues to believe in the full inspiration and authority of Scripture. [*WTJ* Fall 83; *JBL* 103.3; *EvQ* 7/83; *JETS* 3/83, 3/84; *TJ* Spr 82 (Carson)]. The 744-page revision is renamed, *Matthew: A Commentary on His Handbook for a Mixed Church Under Persecution*, and attempts to answer the many criticisms leveled at Gundry's method. (E.g. "Where are the methodological controls?") As a plus, Gundry prompts us to consider Matthew's distinctiveness as a gospel, which is a matter of vital interest to every preacher.

✓ **Gurtner, Daniel M., and John Nolland (eds).** *Built upon the Rock: Studies in the Gospel of Matthew*, 2008. From the Tyndale Fellowship NT Study Group, this is some of the best current evangelical scholarship. [*JSNT-BL* 2009].

Hare, Douglas R.A. ‡ (I) 1993. I have not used this work (320pp), but it was called splendid by one reviewer. His Mark commentary in WestBC is highly theological and well done, too. [*CBQ* 7/94; *CRBR* 1994; *HBT* 6/94].

✓ **Harrington, Daniel J.** ‡ (SacPag) 1991. This Jesuit author is also the editor for this Catholic NT series being published by Liturgical. Of greater interest to the student than the preacher. Evaluating the series as a whole, I judge the SacPag vols. on the Gospels as most valuable; that being said, the Matthew contribution is the weakest of the four. [*CBQ* 7/93; *Interp* 10/93; *EvQ* 1/95; *Biblica* 75.1 (1994); *CRBR* 1993].

Hatina, Thomas R. (ed). *Biblical Interpretation in Early Christian Gospels. II. The Gospel of Matthew*, 2008. For two companion vols., see Hatina under Mark and Luke. [*JSNT-BL* 2010].

Hauerwas, Stanley. ‡ (Brazos) 2006. This exposition by a famous American churchman/theologian will prompt preachers to think hard about the meaning of Matthew today. Reviewers are less sanguine about the quality of exegesis underlying the sometimes insightful exposition; see p.18 for a hint of his personal struggle to launch into the rough waters of commentary-writing and for his scheme to "retell" Matthew's story. Here is a provocative quote, reflecting on ch. 4: "Give the devil his due. He understands, as is seldom acknowledged particularly in our day, that politics is about worship and sacrifice." [*CBQ* 7/08; *JETS* 6/08; *JSNT-BL* 2008].

Hendriksen, William. (NTC) 1976. Has been valuable for preachers, especially those in the Reformed camp. He probes a number of Matthew's theological emphases such as the kingdom of God. Very long (over 1000pp) and sometimes prolix, this is one of his better commentaries.

✓ **Hill, David.** ‡ (NCB) 1972. A moderately critical commentary which in the past has been quite useful for students, less so for pastors. Years ago Hill was Ralph Martin's first pick. With the passage of time, this commentary has much declined in value and is nowhere near the top of anyone's list. [*EvQ* 1/73].

☆ Keener, Craig S. (IVPNT) 1997. See Keener above.

✓ Kingsbury, Jack D. ‡ *Matthew: Structure, Christology, Kingdom, 1975; Matthew as Story*, 2nd ed 1988. These redaction and narrative-critical works have had great influence in the discussion of Matthew's theology. Some of his conclusions are distilled in his brief Proclamation Commentary (Fortress, rev. 1981), but there may be a major work on the horizon: next entry. [*RTR* 1/77; *JBL* 6/77; *EvQ* 4/77].

F   Kingsbury, Jack D. ‡ (ECC). Originally he was to publish the commentary in Hermeneia, but that will not happen; see Luz below. According to reports, the work slated for Hermeneia will come out in ECC instead.

Long, Thomas G. ‡ (WestBC) 1997. [*Interp* 10/98; *PSB* 19.2 (1998); *RelSRev* 10/98].

F   Lowery, Dave. (EEC).

✓   **Luz, Ulrich.** ‡ *Matthew 1–7* (ContC) ET 1989. I recommend that this vol. be passed over in preference for the reformatted and retranslated Hermeneia vol. below [*ExpTim* 10/07]. This ContC vol., translated by Wilhelm Linss, is from the 1985 edition, while the 2007 translation by Crouch comes from a later, revised German edition. [*JBL* Fall 92; *Interp* 7/91; *ExpTim* 2/93; *CTJ* 4/94]. See also Luz's 1995 Cambridge work, *The Theology of the Gospel of Matthew* [*Interp* 7/97; *JR* 4/97; *HBT* 12/96].

✓   **Luz, Ulrich.** ‡ *Matthew 8–20* (Herm) 1997, ET 2001; *Matthew 21–28* (Herm) 1997–2002, ET 2005; *Matthew 1–7* (Herm) 2002, ET 2007. A brilliant technical work translated out of the German EKK series, this commentary is a little more accessible than ICC—for example, there is not a lot of textual criticism—and more concerned with interpreting Matthew's theology. Luz, a professor at Bern, is certainly worth consulting, particularly for the attention he pays to what German-speakers call *Wirkungsgeschichte* (more 'reception history' than 'history of interpretation'). The four vols. in German (1997–2002) become three in Hermeneia. Note that this is a distinctive contribution to this Fortress series, one that is far more useful to preachers than the other vols. on the Gospels. See Luz above for an earlier translation of the Matthew 1–7 commentary. [*CBQ* 1/02, 1/07; *JBL* Win 02; *Interp* 1/03, 4/09; *HBT* 6/02; *SwJT* Spr 02; *JR* 7/02; *RelSRev* 1/02; *CurTM* 12/03; *JETS* 6/08; *JSNT-BL* 2007, 2008; *ThTo* 4/08; *RelSRev* 10/06; *BSac* 4/07; *NovT* 52.3]. Students can also look up his *Studies in Matthew*, ET 2005 [*EvQ* 10/07; *RTR* 12/07; *JTS* 10/06; *JETS* 6/06; *Them* 5/07; *JBL* Win 06; *JSNT-BL* 2006; *RelSRev* 4/07, 9/08; *BTB* Win 07].

MacArthur, John. 4 Vols., 1985–89. These Matthew vols. were among the first published in this ambitious project to cover the whole NT. About 27 vols. are now out. I have to say I'm not real impressed with these expositions. There is some fine sermonic material in them, and I'm glad there out there for lay preachers and Sunday School teachers, but I would not consider them the most dependable tools for seminary-trained pastors. Only to be used after one's own exegesis. Of a similar genré (practical exposition) but more like commentaries are the Kent Hughes vols. in "Preaching the Word" series. [*JETS* 3/87].

✓   McNeile, A.H. ‡ 1915. On the Greek text, and still useful for that reason—more so than Allen's old ICC.

✓   Malina, Bruce J., and Richard L. Rohrbaugh. ‡ *Social-Science Commentary on the Synoptic Gospels*, 1992.

Mann, C.S., and William Albright. ‡ (AB) 1971. This AB vol. has a huge introduction, but spotty and disappointing exegesis. Defends the Griesbach Hypothesis (i.e., rejects the scholarly consensus of Markan priority and Matthew's dependence on the second gospel). This hypothesis, which goes back to the Early Church and held sway until it went into eclipse in the early 1800s, was essentially revived by W.R. Farmer's *The Synoptic Problem* (1964) [*EvQ* 10/77]. See also Farmer's vol., *The Gospel of Jesus*. For a thoroughgoing critique of that thesis, consult C.M. Tuckett's *The Revival of the Griesbach Hypothesis* (Cambridge, 1983). Attacking both the Griesbach Hypothesis and Q is Mark Goodacre, *The Case against Q* (Trinity Press, 2002) [*NovT* 46.4; *ExpTim* 12/05]. A lively evangelical roundtable discussion of the various synoptic theories is Black/Beck (eds), *Rethinking the Synoptic Problem* (Baker, 2001) [*NovT* 49.2].

Meier, John P. ‡ (NTM) 1979. A critical Catholic commentary by a man who has taken a lead role in Gospel scholarship since the 1980s. His influence continues today. His controversial four-vol. set, *A Marginal Jew: Rethinking the Historical Jesus*, doesn't please evangelicals. Meier has contributed to the spate of recent critical books, which amounts to a "Third Quest" to reconstruct the Jesus of history. This movement, while not as radical as the "'New Quest' Renewed" exemplified in the works of Mack and Crossan, alleges there is less continuity between the historical Jesus and the Christ of faith. See next entry. [*JBL* 101.2 (1982)].

F   Meier, John P. ‡ (AYB). Proposed as a two-vol. set to replace Mann-Albright. See previous entry.

☆   **Morris, Leon.** (Pillar) 1992. This joins his earlier commentaries on John and Romans; all are useful works for the expositor. This work on Matthew is not scintillating and doesn't break new ground, but it is solid, basic and dependable. Like Hendriksen, its size and thoroughness is a major strength. Compare with Blomberg's more incisive and up-to-date work. [*Interp* 1/94; *EvQ* 1/95; *RTR* 1/94; *CRBR* 1994].

Mounce, Robert A. (NIBC) 1985. Highly regarded by some as a basic work for introducing this gospel to beginning students. Mounce has written other fine commentaries, especially the NICNT on Revelation.

Mullins, Michael. *The Gospel of Matthew*, 2007. A large work (661pp) I have never seen, published in Dublin. [*ExpTim* 7/09].

✓   Newman, B.M., and P.C. Stine. (UBS) 1988. A translator's handbook which is over 900pp long.

F   Olmstead, Wesley. (BHGNT).

F   Osborne, Grant. (ZEC).

✓   **Overman, J. Andrew.** ‡ *Church and Community in Crisis: The Gospel According to Matthew*, 1996. A fine 400-page work from the "New Testament in Context" series. The author is particularly interested in "the social world of the Matthean Community," the subtitle of his earlier 1990 Fortress vol. on this Gospel. This work in pb is more important than its size might first indicate.

Patte, Daniel. ‡ 1987. Subtitled, "A Structural Commentary on Matthew's Faith." This is a specifically "structural" commentary that doesn't attempt to answer all the questions taken up in a full-orbed critical commentary. Those who are curious about this hermeneutical approach—part of what is called the New Literary Criticism—should consult Patte's *What Is Structural Exegesis?* Truth be told, structuralism's star was fading even when this was published. [*JBL* 107.4 (1988); *CRBR* 1990].

Pennington, Jonathan T. *Heaven and Earth in the Gospel of Matthew*, 2007. Originally published by Brill and now carried by Baker, the work argues that "kingdom of heaven" is not an insignificant variant on "kingdom of God." The reviews have been laudatory. [*BBR* 19.4].

✓   Plummer, Alfred. 1915. Has been reprinted many times but, like Allen and McNeile, is dated.

✓   Powell, Mark Allan. ‡ *Chasing the Eastern Star: Adventures in Biblical Reader-Response Criticism*, 2001. After explaining his take on this controversial method, Powell applies it to the story of the Magi. As several reviews have stated, the author is engaging and witty. [*Evangel* Sum 03; *Anvil* 19.3].

✓ Powell, Mark Allan (ed). ‡ *Methods for Matthew*, 2009. The publisher (CUP) describes this as "a primer on six exegetical approaches that have proved to be especially useful and popular." Leading scholars contribute. [*BBR* 20.2].

✓ Riches, J., and D.C. Sim (eds). ‡ *The Gospel of Matthew in Its Roman Imperial Context*, 2005.

☆ Ridderbos, Herman. (BSC) 1952–54, ET 1987. Quite helpful theologically and in a readable format [*JETS* 3/91 (Carson)]. My former professor, Karl Cooper, once told me that Ridderbos's *The Coming of the Kingdom* (P&R, 1962) is even more helpful and stimulating for work in Matthew's Gospel. He was right, and that study has been kept in print until recent years.

☆ Ryle, J.C. (CrossC) 1993.

✓ **Schnackenburg, Rudolf.** ‡ 1985–87, ET 2002. This commentary, heavy on redaction criticism, is written by a leading German Catholic scholar and can be consulted by students who want a more historically oriented and theological work from a Catholic and critical perspective. This vol. on Matthew is published by Eerdmans in pb (329pp). Schnackenburg is better known for his works on John's Gospel, Ephesians, and John's Epistles. Not one of his stronger efforts. [*EvQ* 7/04; *RTR* 12/03; *JETS* 12/03; *Interp* 7/03; *ExpTim* 10/04; *CurTM* 12/03].

✓ Schweizer, Eduard. ‡ ET 1975. His three vols. on the Synoptics make ready use of redaction criticism and are designed for pastors. Often has good insights into the text. Much better on Mark and Luke than on Matthew. Carson notes that "in this vol. Schweizer devotes almost all his space to non-Markan material in Matthew, making the work almost useless to those who do not have the other commentary." [*RTR* 1/77; *EvQ* 7/76].

✓ **Senior, Donald.** ‡ (ANTC) 1998. Though too often failing to interact with other scholarly positions—see the skimpy bibliography—Senior's work is probably now to be regarded as the best compact exegetical commentary on this Gospel from the critical side. The author, a recognized expert on Matthew, teaches at Catholic Theological Union in Chicago, has written *What Are They Saying About Matthew?* (2nd ed 1996), and has also contributed the Matthew vol. to the IBT series (1997). [*CBQ* 1/00; *ThTo* 7/98; *RelSRev* 7/99].

✓ Sim, David C. ‡ *The Gospel of Matthew and Christian Judaism*, 1998.

✓ Simonetti, Manlio (ed). (ACCS) 2 Vols., 2001–02. [*JETS* 9/03; *RelSRev* 10/02; *BBR* 13.1].

  Smith, Robert. ‡ (Augsburg Commentary on the NT) 1988.

  Spurgeon, Charles. *The Gospel of the Kingdom*, 1893. Reprinted from time to time.

  Sri, Edward, and Curtis Mitch. ‡ (CCSS) 2010.

✓ Stanton, Graham. ‡ *A Gospel for a New People*, 1992. A very stimulating read for the student and one of my favorite books on Matthew. See also Stanton's selection of key essays in the field: *Interpretation of Matthew* (1983, 2nd ed 1995).

✓ Stendahl, Krister. ‡ *The School of St. Matthew and Its Use of the Old Testament*, 2nd ed 1968. One of the first of a growing number of studies attempting to trace the alleged influence of the believing communities surrounding the apostles on the shaping of the gospels. [*JBL* 89.2 (1970)]. Compare with J. Louis Martyn's *History and Theology in the Fourth Gospel* (1968) and R.E. Brown's work on the Johannine literature, *The Community of the Beloved Disciple* (1979).

✓ Stonehouse, Ned B. *The Witness of Matthew and Mark to Christ*, 1944. To appreciate the significance of this work and its companion, *The Witness of Luke to Christ*, see Silva's two articles on "Ned B. Stonehouse and Redaction Criticism" in *WTJ* 40. Both of Stonehouse's works are now combined in one vol.: *The Witness of the*

Synoptic Gospels to Christ (1979). You'll find the author to be both a superb exegete and a pioneer.

Talbert, Charles H. ‡ (Paideia) 2010. I have yet to see this (384pp).

Tasker, R.V.G. (retired TNTC) 1961. Though now replaced, Tasker has some value as a quick reference.

☆ **Turner, David L.** (BECNT) 2008. A competent conservative exegesis by a professor at Grand Rapids Theological Seminary, who has been publishing on Matthew for a long time. Turner associates himself with the "progressive Dispensationalist" camp along with such people as Bock. He reads the Gospel as coming from a "Christian-Jewish" perspective, "as the voice of 'Jews for Jesus' as it were" (p.3). Interestingly, he did doctoral studies at Hebrew Union College as well as Grace Seminary. A strength of the commentary is his focus upon the narrative, its features and flow. He eschews a redactional approach which might read "Matthew as an adaptation of Mark" (p.3). [*ExpTim* 5/09; *RelSRev* 12/08; *Them* 9/08; *JETS* 9/09; *JSNT-BL* 2009].

Turner, David L., *The Gospel of Matthew*, and Darrell L. Bock, *The Gospel of Mark* (CorBC) 2005. Highly competent conservative scholarship, more from a moderate Dispensational perspective. [*JETS* 12/07].

F Willitts, Joel. (NCCS). The author teaches at North Park University in Chicago and has recently published his Cambridge dissertation, *Matthew's Messianic Shepherd-King*, 2007 [*JETS* 3/09; *EuroJTh* 18.1].

✓ Witherington, Ben. [𝓜], (S&H) 2006. This commentary of slightly over 500pp, by perhaps the most prolific NT scholar today, would be cause for more preachers' celebration, were it not so poorly edited and proofread, if proofread at all [*DenvJ* 11/06]. Though not a work of profound scholarship, it is the product of careful study and is a help to those preparing sermons. His writing and some of the accompanying artwork/illustration (e.g., p.518) provoke reflection. As with his work on John's gospel, he attempts a "sapiential reading," wanting to interpret Matthew as owing much to ancient Israel's wisdom tradition. The thesis is less than convincing, in my opinion. [*Interp* 1/08; *RelSRev* 12/08].

NOTES: (1) Please remember the recommendation of Calvin's Commentaries. (2) See, too, Richard France, "Matthew's Gospel in Recent Study," *Them*, 1/89; John Ziesler's "Which Is the Best Commentary? I. Matthew," *ExpTim*, 12/85; David C. Sim, "The Synoptic Gospels," *ExpTim*, 4/08. (3) In order to use many of these gospel commentaries you must learn something about Redaction Criticism. A quick way is to study through Don Carson's 24-page pamphlet, "Redaction Criticism: The Nature of an Interpretive Tool," (Christianity Today Institute, 1985) or the relevant section in *An Introduction to the New Testament* (2005) by Carson and Moo.

SERMON ON THE MOUNT

★ Ferguson, Sinclair B. *Kingdom Living in a Fallen World*, 1986. Excellent, edifying study now being published by Banner of Truth under the title, *The Sermon on the Mount*. Ferguson's is one of the very best devotional works on the Sermon, and has served well, I know, as a guide for Bible studies. [*RTR* 9/88; *SBET* Spr 90].

★ **Guelich, Robert A.** [𝓜], 1982. This immensely learned, mildly critical book has a wealth of information and, though aging, is still regarded as a standard historical critical commentary on this portion of Scripture. Compare to the other heavyweight academic studies by Allison, Betz, and Davies. This was reprinted by W

Publishing Group, and that pb edition, as of May 2009, is available for about $17. [*JBL* 103.3 (1984); *TJ* Fall 83 (Wenham)].

★ Lloyd-Jones, D. Martyn. 1959–60. This lengthy, reverent exposition deserves a place on every pastor's shelf! This collection of sermons will never lose its value to the preacher. Has been reprinted many, many times.

★ Stott, John R.W. (BST) 1978. Formerly titled *Christian Counter-Culture*, this is "a very crisp, clear and brief analysis" of the Sermon on the Mount, "standing alongside Lloyd-Jones" (George Knight). [*ExpTim* 5/78; *EvQ* 7/78; *JETS* 6/80].

✧ ✧ ✧ ✧ ✧ ✧

✓ **Allison, Dale C., Jr.** ‡ 1999. Building upon the three-vol. ICC on Matthew, "this book is to be commended to students and general readers alike" (Ruth Edwards). [*ExpTim* 1/00; *RelSRev* 1/01].

Augsburger, Myron. *The Expanded Life*, 1972. A popularly-styled exposition.

Barclay, William. ‡ *And Jesus Said*, 1970.

✓ **Betz, Hans Dieter.** ‡ (Herm) 1995. A huge (768-page) commentary on both Matthew 5–7 and Luke 6 which should be consulted. No previous exegetical work on the Sermon on the Mount has ever run to this length. This detailed, technical commentary, which emphasizes parallel texts and issues of rhetorical criticism, is mainly for specialists. It is the rare expositor who could put this tome to good use. Rather critical in its orientation. See also his *Essays on the Sermon on the Mount*, 1985. [*ThTo* 10/96; *JETS* 6/99; *JBL* Spr 98; *Interp* 7/97; *CBQ* 4/97; *SwJT* Sum 96; *PSB* 17.3 (1996); *JR* 1/98].

Boice, James M. 1972. A sermonic exposition of value, from early in his pastoral ministry.

☆ Bonhoeffer, Dietrich. [*M*], *The Cost of Discipleship*, ET 1959. Includes some arresting exposition of sections of the Sermon on the Mount. He argues that only the believing truly repent, and only the repentant truly believe. Bonhoeffer's personal history is well-known. Connected with the Neo-Orthodox "Confessing Church" during the Third Reich, he was imprisoned at Buchenwald for opposing Hitler, and finally martyred by the S.S. at Flossenburg concentration camp.

☆ Calvin, John. *Sermons on the Beatitudes*, 1560, ET 2006. A brief (114-page) but precious book. [*Presb* Fall 07; *RTR* 8/09].

☆ Carson, Donald. 1978. Superb exposition with exegetical depth to it. This was reprinted in 1999 by Global Christian Publishers, combined in an inexpensive pb vol. with Carson's exposition of Matthew 8–10, *When Jesus Confronts the World*. I expect this will retain value over the years. A good purchase for pastors.

Chambers, Oswald. *Studies in the Sermon on the Mount*, reprint 1960.

✓ **Davies, W.D.** ‡ *The Setting of the Sermon on the Mount*, 1964. A scholarly study of great importance, though Guelich and Betz are now the premier studies.

Greenman, Jeffrey, Timothy Larsen, and Stephen Spencer. *The Sermon on the Mount Through the Centuries*, 2007. [*RelSRev* 3/08].

Hendriksen, William. 1934.

☆ Hughes, R. Kent. (PTW) 2001. Another really thoughtful evangelical exposition to compete with Stott, Lloyd-Jones, Ferguson, etc. [*BSac* 1/03].

Hunter, A.M. [*M*], *A Pattern for Life*, 1965. Any who have used Hunter's works are grateful for his clear style and insights. He was a very careful, mildly critical NT professor at Aberdeen.

✓ Jeremias, Joachim. ‡ ET 1961.

✓ Kissinger, W.S. ‡ *The Sermon on the Mount: A History of Interpretation and Bibliography*, 1975.

Luther, Martin. "The Sermon on the Mount (Sermons)," *Luther's Works*, Vol. 21, ET 1956.

✓ Patte, Daniel. ‡ *The Challenge of Discipleship: A Critical Study of the Sermon on the Mount as Scripture*, 1999. [*Interp* 4/01].

✓ **Strecker, Georg.** ‡ ET 1988. This exegetical commentary published by Abingdon is "heavily Germanic and theological" [*ExpTim* 3/90]; it should be consulted by students who want to get a historical-critical reading.

Talbert, Charles H. *Reading the Sermon on the Mount*, 2004 (Baker, 2006). [*JSNT-BL* 2005, 2007; *BSac* 1/08].

✓ Vaught, Carl G. [*M*], 1987, rev. 2001. Subtitled *A Theological Interpretation*, and now published by Baylor. [*CRBR* 1989].

NOTE: Four fine books specifically on the Lord's Prayer are: Thomas Watson's Puritan exposition; Helmut Thielicke's sermons, *Our Heavenly Father*; the 1992 supplementary issue of the *PSB* on the Lord's Prayer ("1991 Frederick Neumann Symposium"); and Kenneth Stevenson's historical study, *The Lord's Prayer: A Text in Tradition* (2004).

MARK

★ **Edwards, James.** (Pillar) 2002. This commentary is clearly written, good and solid, offering a satisfying exegetical treatment and theological discussion. Reviewers have been very pleased with this 552-page vol., which pays attention both to matters of historical background and to narrative analysis (for more of the latter, see SacPag, BCBC, Witherington, and Moloney). The greatest strength here may be his attention to extra-biblical Jewish literature. Compare Edwards with Lane. Stein and France now take pride of place as the leading, recent evangelical exegeses, but they deal directly with the Greek, and some preachers may find Edwards less threatening. [*CTJ* 4/04; *Them* Aut 03; *Interp* 1/03; *JETS* 6/03 (Stein); *SwJT* Spr 03; *RelSRev* 7/03; *EvQ* 10/04; *BBR* 13.2; *RTR* 8/08; *Anvil* 20.1].

★ **France, Richard T.** (NIGTC) 2002. I find I now turn first to France and Stein (in that order), after I have done my own exegesis. This is a mature and excellent piece of work on the Greek text. Many, however, will refuse to follow him in his interpretation of "the coming of the Son of Man" texts. For the student and academically oriented pastor, the (slightly more) critically oriented Guelich and Evans set is just as valuable as NIGTC. [*CTJ* 4/04; *Them* Sum 03; *JTS* 10/03; *JETS* 6/03; *Interp* 1/03; *TJ* Fall 03; *RelSRev* 7/02; *BBR* 13.2; *RTR* 8/06; *CurTM* 12/05; *Anvil* 22.2].

★ Garland, David. (NIVAC) 1996. The author also contributed the Colossians-Philemon commentary in this series. Though English is good, this is fuller (630pp) and of greater help to the expositor. Less informed by NT scholarship but also very useful are Hughes and English below. Garland knows the gospels; see his earlier work on Matthew as well.

★ **Stein, Robert H.** (BECNT) 2008. Cause for rejoicing! Like France, Stein offers us brilliant technical exegesis which is also quite readable. For decades Stein has been a leading American evangelical scholar on the Synoptics, and I opine that he has given us some of his best work, near the close of his career, here in this full commentary (864pp). He gives considerable space to a discussion of the original ending or lack of one. See also his NAC work on Luke; both tend to pursue redaction critical questions instead of literary/narratological ones. Having a literary reading (e.g., Moloney or Witherington) and an incisive critical interpretation (e.g.,

Hooker or Marcus) alongside Stein makes for a well-rounded discussion. [*JETS* 12/09; *ExpTim* 10/09; *CBQ* 7/10; *BBR* 20.2; *JSNT-BL* 2010].

★ **Witherington, Ben.** *The Gospel of Mark: A Socio-Rhetorical Commentary* (SRC) 2001. Mark has been the subject of an increasing number of literary studies, which are chiefly concerned with the nature of the text, its rhetoric, settings, plot, and characterization. This nearly 500-page work is a good representative of a conservative literary approach, to be contrasted with liberal Robbins below. For further review see SRC under "Commentary Series" and the comments under 1 Corinthians. Witherington and Eerdmans appear to be developing an essentially one-man series (see deSilva on Hebrews for an exception). [*CTJ* 4/04; *CBQ* 4/02; *Them* Spr 03; *JETS* 9/02; *Interp* 7/02; *ExpTim* 8/01; *TJ* Spr 02; *SwJT* Fall 02; *RelSRev* 10/01; *BBR* 13.2; *Anvil* 19.4].

✧ ✧ ✧ ✧ ✧ ✧

Alexander, J. A. (GS) 1858. Even though dated, it is still useful as a theological exposition. Alexander has other commentaries on Isaiah, Matthew, and Acts.

✓ **Anderson, Hugh.** ‡ (NCB) 1976. Critical and sometimes frustrating in its skeptical approach, but has been a noted commentary. Has a full introduction. I bought it 20 years ago on Ralph Martin's recommendation and used to turn to this work when I wanted a scholarly, critical perspective. Like Hill on Matthew, this does not have prominence among commentaries as it once did.

✓ Anderson, Janice Capel, and Stephen D. Moore (eds). ‡ *Mark & Method: New Approaches in Biblical Studies*, 1992, 2nd ed 2008. This touted book should not be missed by students working on Mark or even the Synoptics generally, if they seek an understanding of the shape of Gospels-study today. [*BibInt* 18.3; *RelSRev* 9/09; *JSNT-BL* 2010].

Barbieri, Louis. (Moody Gospel Commentary) 1995. A fuller, popular-level commentary in pb.

F Barbour, R.S. ‡ (ICC–new series). This will replace Gould, but see also Dunn below.

✓ **Beasley-Murray, George R.** [𝑀], *Jesus and the Last Days: A Commentary on Mark 13*, rev. 1993. The original was published back in 1957. The revised edition published by Hendrickson is 600pp long, and gives a thorough treatment of Jesus' eschatological teaching.

F Beavis, Mary Ann. (Paideia).

F Black, C. Clifton. ‡ (ANTC).

✓ **Boring, M. Eugene.** ‡ (NTL) 2006. Considered to be in the top rank of mid-level critical commentaries on Mark. Not only is Boring's work quite full (482pp), it is also a model of compressed historical scholarship. The reader gets a great deal of information for the time invested. I have to class it as one of the better contributions to the NTL series. Boring pays attention to literary or narrative features but asserts that "the substantive content of Mark's narrative is theological" (p.24). There is properly a focus on Christ, since "[t]he Gospel of Mark is narrative Christology" (p.8). The translation offered is forceful and fresh. Boring holds that the evangelist drew from oral traditions, not being an eyewitness. Here "the approach is still heavily indebted to form-critical insights" (Foster). At points I find myself in strong disagreement with Boring, as when he opines that "for Mark, 'Son of David' is a misunderstanding of Jesus' true identity" (p.305). [*Interp* 10/08; *JSNT-BL* 2008; *RelSRev* 4/07; *ExpTim* 12/07; *CurTM* 12/08].

F Botha, P.J.J. (RRA).

Bratcher, R.G., and E.A. Nida. (UBS) 1961. One of the oldest in the series.

☆ Brooks, James A. (NAC) 1991. Some reviewers find it not as full, insightful or well-informed as the other NAC vols. on the Gospels. Clifton Black sees Brooks as surprisingly open to higher criticism. I have not made enough use of it to justify a personal opinion. Carson ranks this highly. [*EvQ* 1/94; *ThTo* 10/93; *CRBR* 1994].

☆ Cole, R. Alan. (TNTC) rev. 1989. Though not one of the best entries in the series, it is serviceable and thoughtful. The newer edition was more of a revision than many others in the series. [*RTR* 5/91].

✓ **Collins, Adela Yarbro.** ‡ (Herm) 2007. A publishing event! NT specialists were eagerly anticipating this technical, historical-critical exegesis for many years. It is quite critical in orientation (Bultmann is a favorite citation) and builds on earlier research published in *The Beginning of the Gospel: Probings of Mark in Context*, 1992, as well as an abundance of journal articles. Collins believes Mark has a long, complicated compositional history and can be termed "an eschatological counterpart of an older biblical genre, the foundational sacred history." In many places she shows that she shares her husband's (OT scholar John J. Collins) keen interest in apocalyptic. Portions of Mark receive very detailed exegesis, while others do not (e.g., four pages on Mark 1:35–45). Students must take account of this 800-page reference work, especially the massive number of literary parallels from the ancient world she adduces to help interpret this gospel. This and Marcus would be the leading liberal technical commentaries now. [*NovT* 51.2; *RelSRev* 3/08; *JETS* 3/09; *JSNT-BL* 2009; *Interp* 1/09 (Boring)].

☆ **Cranfield, C.E.B.** [𝓜], (CGTC) 1959. A clear, balanced, sensible commentary which you will consult often once you've sampled it. Mildly critical with incisive exegesis. Cranfield's method does not seem to have been influenced much by Marxsen's redaction critical approach (See p.478). For work on the Greek text, scholarly pastors keep this handy. It is a shame that Cambridge prices it at $50 (pb). Still in print. Through six editions of this guide I recommended Cranfield for purchase, but its place was given to France.

✓ **Culpepper, R. Alan.** ‡ (S&H) 2007. One of the best in the NT section of this series. The author is especially known for his expertise in narrative criticism, and in particular his research on the narratives in John. I have found this commentary (622pp) to be uncommonly insightful, yielding many insights that a preacher can bring into sermons. E.g., for 20 years I have found it remarkable that after cleansing the leper, who previously had been ostracized from the community, Jesus is put in the position of having to "stay outside in lonely places" due to the healed man's disobedience (1:45). Culpepper picks up on such narrative features and reflects on them theologically. [*RelSRev* 3/08; *Interp* 4/09].

F Decker, Rodney J. (BHGNT).

F Decker, Rodney J. (EEC).

✓ **Donahue, John, and Daniel Harrington.** ‡ (SacPag) 2002. This large scale (488pp), Catholic work interprets the Gospel of Mark through research into intertextuality and intratextuality, besides other more tried methods like redaction criticism and narrative criticism. There is great learning here as two veteran scholars have teamed up (Donahue is primarily responsible for 1–8 and 14; Harrington does the rest). [*CBQ* 1/03; *JETS* 6/03; *Interp* 1/03; *RelSRev* 10/02].

F Dunn, James D.G. ‡ (ICC–new series). This report conflicts with the older announcement of Barbour above.

☆ English, Donald. (BST) 1992. This work is a boon for the expositor. Very well written, with many theological and pastoral insights. [*Chm* 109.2 (1995)].

☆ **Evans, Craig.** [𝓜], *Mark 8:27–16:20* (WBC) 2001. This completes the work which Guelich so ably began (see Guelich below). Evans did the vol. on Luke for NIBC and is a first-rate scholar. It is very full (nearly 100pp of introduction and 500pp of commentary), and the theological approach seems to be similar to Gundry's. As we have come to expect of WBC, the bibliographies are very well prepared. Unfortunately, there are more than a few editorial problems—e.g., on p.131 the Hebrew for "Jericho" is misspelled in one place and in another "Jerusalem" is mistakenly written for "Jericho." Strangely, too, the hb cover to my copy is upside down. I value Evans more highly than Guelich, and not only because of more current bibliographies. The publisher has announced that Evans will write a new WBC vol. on 1:1–8:26. Students and scholarly pastors won't want to be without Evans in working with the Greek. [*CTJ* 11/02; *NovT* 44.4].

☆ **Geddert, Timothy.** (BCBC) 2001. An excellent, more literary commentary, which is one of the very best in the NT section of the series. The Anabaptist author has done previous work (Aberdeen PhD) on the Olivet Discourse in Mark. There is much to be enthusiastic about here. [*JETS* 9/02; *RelSRev* 10/01].

Gould, E.P. ‡ (ICC) 1896. Can be safely ignored.

☆ **Guelich, Robert A.** [*M*], *Mark 1–8:26* (WBC) 1989. This standard scholarly commentary needs to be consulted. Draws heavily from German scholarship on this gospel (Gnilka, Pesch, etc.) and is interested in tradition history. Sadly, Guelich died (†1991) in the prime of his career before finishing Mark for the series. Evans has completed the two-vol. set, and these vols. are highly recommended for advanced students. Guelich is the same scholar who produced the exceptional study of the Sermon on the Mount. This vol. is due to be replaced; see Craig Evans above. [*CRBR* 1992; *EvQ* 4/92; *CBQ* 10/91; *Them* 10/91].

☆ **Gundry, Robert.** *Mark: A Commentary on His Apology for the Cross*, 1993. An exhaustive and penetrating study of this gospel (1069pp in small print!). The subtitle gives his perspective on Mark's purpose. Many will be intimidated by the price tag and the sheer size and detail of this work. It is more of a purchase priority, if you are an advanced student or scholarly pastor. Gundry's friend, Moisés Silva, calls it "an enormous treasure of information." Douglas Moo says the provocative commentary "enhances this scholar's reputation as an original and independent thinker." Released in a two-vol. pb in 2004. [*JBL* 113.4; *CBQ* 4/95; *Them* 10/94; *CTJ* 4/95; *ExpTim* 1/95; *EvQ* 1/97; *SJT* 50.1; *Chm* 111.4].

☆ Hare, Douglas R.A. ‡ (WestBC) 1996. Has received complimentary reviews as a "thoroughly theological commentary" (Dale Allison). The author, Professor of NT Emeritus at the Pittsburgh Theological Seminary (Presbyterian), also wrote the Matthew vol. for the Interpretation series. [*Interp* 1/98; *HBT* 12/98].

✓ Hatina, Thomas R. (ed). *Biblical Interpretation in Early Christian Gospels. I. The Gospel of Mark*, 2006. For two companion vols., see Hatina under Matthew and Luke.

Healy, Mary. ‡ (CCSS) 2008. The initial vol. in the series. [*CBQ* 7/10].

☆ Hendriksen, William. (NTC) 1975. Not as prolix nor as good as Matthew in the series. The pastor could put his theological exposition to good use, though the advanced student will be looking for a more rigorous work. [*RTR* 1/76].

Hiebert, D.E. rev. 1979. An evangelical commentary of some size organized around the servant theme.

☆ **Hooker, Morna.** ‡ (BNTC) 1992. This replacement work for Johnson is a big improvement. Hooker's work has 411pp of phrase-by-phrase exposition and is easily accessible to non-specialists. This is also a significant commentary for students to consult. Hooker's stature among NT scholars and the low price of this vol. make it among the "best buys" for students. An excellent commentary which is moderately critical. [*EvQ* 7/93; *ExpTim* 2/93; *RTR* 9/92 and 1/94; *JBL* Spr 94; *JTS* 4/94; *Them* 10/94].

☆ Hughes, R. Kent. (PTW) 2 Vols., 1989. This series of commentaries has been praised highly as thoughtful and especially good for communicators. Carson speaks of it as one of the best in the genre of sermonic commentary. The series, which includes good theology, much illustrative material, and application, now covers Mark (2 vols.), Luke (2 vols.), John, Acts, Romans, Ephesians, Colossians, Pastoral Epistles, Hebrews (2 vols.) and James; vols. in the OT section are also appearing regularly. Hughes is pastor of the College Church in Wheaton, IL. The commentary on Mark is 480 pages total. See Garland above. [*JETS* 12/92].

Hunter, A.M. [*M*], (Torch Bible Commentary) 1967. Good, but sketchy compared with the recent exegetical commentaries on Mark.

☆ **Hurtado, Larry W.** [*M*], (NIBC) 1989. A 320-page work certainly worth consulting. Hurtado is a respected scholar, who lectures at the University of Edinburgh.

✓ **Iersel, Bas M.F. van.** ‡ *Mark: A Reader-Response Commentary*, ET 1998. [*CBQ* 7/00; *Biblica* 81.2 (2000); *JBL* Win 00; *JTS* 4/01; *RelSRev* 10/01]. Previously there was the more accessible *Reading Mark*, ET 1986 [*Biblica* 70.4 (1989)].

Johnson, Sherman E. ‡ (retired BNTC) 1960. Never particularly helpful. See Hooker above.

F Joynes, Christine. ‡ (Blackwell).

✓ Juel, Donald H. ‡ (IBT) 1999. A serviceable introduction to Markan studies by a Princeton Seminary professor.

Kernaghan, Ron. (IVPNT) 2007. The author is a PCUSA minister connected to Fuller Seminary. I have not had opportunity to use this. [*JSNT-BL* 2008].

☆ **Lane, William.** (NICNT) 1974. This was long considered the most valuable work for the evangelical pastor; now Edwards' Pillar commentary challenges its place, to say nothing of the newer, fuller works like France, Gundry and the WBC. Employs a mild form of redaction criticism (see p.7) in a responsible way. Lane has a standout commentary on Hebrews. For students' sake I have removed this from the purchase list, but pastors should still seriously consider it. [*WTJ* Spr 77; *RTR* 9/74; *JBL* 94.3 (1975); *EvQ* 1/75].

F Lührmann, Dieter. ‡ (ContC) 1987, ET ? From the "Handbuch zum Neuen Testament" series. Will it appear?

F McDermott, John Michael. (Brazos).

✓ Malina, Bruce J., and Richard L. Rohrbaugh. ‡ *Social-Science Commentary on the Synoptic Gospels*, 1992.

✓ **Mann, C.S.** ‡ (AB) 1986. This massive critical commentary argues the Griesbach Hypothesis. See Albright under Matthew, but note that this vol. is better and should be consulted by students. Those who consult Mann will find that the introduction is massive and the exegesis usually a bit disappointing. Mann has been replaced; see Marcus below. [*ThTo* 44.2].

✓ **Marcus, Joel.** ‡ *Mark 1–8* (AB) 2000; *Mark 9–16* (AYB) 2009. This two-vol. set replaces the Mann vol. The first vol. has a 65-page introduction, 49pp of bibliography, and approximately 400pp of mainly historical-critical exegesis, while the second is well over 600pp. This work can be compared to Guelich's, though more liberal and skeptical. What I have read of Marcus is pleasingly full, but I have not always trusted his exegetical judgment (e.g., at 1:43). He carefully notes some of the surprising ironies in Mark and the development of Isaianic themes (e.g., God's "way" of holy-war to liberate the people of God). As mentioned above, Marcus and Collins are the leading liberal technical commentaries on this Gospel. [*JTS* 4/02; *Interp* 1/02; *ExpTim* 8/01; *NovT* 44.3; *BBR* 13.2, 20.2; *RBL* 6/10; *HBT* 32.1; *CBQ* 4/10 (Moloney); *JETS* 9/10 (Stein)]. Marcus has made a special study of *The Mystery of the Kingdom* *of God* (1986) and Christological exegesis of the OT in Mark (*The Way of the Lord*, 1992 [*TJ* Spr 94; *CTJ* 4/95]).

Martin, Ralph P. [*M*], *Mark: Evangelist and Theologian*, 1973. Not a commentary, but one of the helpful introductions to the four evangelists published by Zondervan. Not as good as Marshall on Luke or France on Matthew. [*JBL* 94.1 (1975)].

✓ Marxsen, Willi. ‡ *Mark the Evangelist*, 1956, ET 1969. The ground-breaking redactional study on Mark and quite critical. To investigate more recent redaction criticism on this Gospel, see *The Disciples According to Mark* (1989) by C.C. Black.

☆ **Moloney, Francis J.** ‡ 2002. This mid-level commentary published by Hendrickson (outside any series) lucidly presents a moderately critical Roman Catholic interpretation. It pursues both literary and theological concerns and can be compared to Donahue/Harrington above. He seeks and finds narrative coherence. Quite a number of leading NT scholars have highly praised this commentary: "the finest one-volume commentary in English on Mark that I know" (Black). The author is better known for his extensive work on John. [*JTS* 10/04; *CBQ* 1/04; *RTR* 12/03; *JETS* 9/04; *ExpTim* 1/04; *RelSRev* 1/03; *Biblica* 85.4; *Interp* 10/05; *JSNT-BL* 2005; *CurTM* 10/05]. See the added introductory study of Mark (2004): *Mark: Storyteller, Interpreter, Evangelist* [*NovT* 48.4; *ExpTim* 3/07].

F Moritz, Thorsten. (THC).

Moule, C.F.D. ‡ (CBC) 1965. Insightful and brief.

Myers, Ched. ‡ *Binding the Strong Man: A Political Reading of Mark's Story of Jesus*, 1988. This large-scale (500-page) Orbis publication applies both literary criticism and a (leftwing) political hermeneutic. I note it because it won a book award and has been praised outlandishly—"most important commentary...since Barth's Romans."

Nineham, Dennis E. ‡ (Pelican) 1963. Destructively critical, as expected from a contributor to *The Myth of God Incarnate*. Though cited by some, it can be ignored, unless you are especially interested in form criticism.

✓ Oden, Thomas C., and Christopher Hall (eds). (ACCS) 1998. [*RelSRev* 7/99; *EvQ* 7/02; *NovT* 42.4].

✓ **Perkins, Pheme.** ‡ (NewIB) 1995. The author is a professor at Boston College and has written many books in the NT field. See, for example, her commentary on Ephesians. This work on Mark fits well into this much-used series for pastors. [*JETS* 3/99]. Her further research on the Gospels is now published as *Introduction to the Synoptic Gospels*, 2007 [*ExpTim* 11/08].

✓ Plummer, Alfred. [*M*], 1914. A dated but helpful commentary on the Greek text.

F Powery, Emerson Byron. (PC).

Rawlison, A.E.J. ‡ (Westminster) 1949. Can be ignored, despite Childs' comment.

✓ Rhodes, D., and D. Michie. ‡ *Mark As Story*, 1982, 2nd ed 1999. Riches says this interpretation "has been influential among a growing circle...in the States who wish to see the abandonment in biblical study of historical in favour of literary modes of investigation" (*A Century of NT Study*, 165).

✓ **Robbins, Vernon.** ‡ *Jesus the Teacher: A Socio-Rhetorical Interpretation of Mark*, 1992. Robbins teaches at Emory and has for some time been encouraging an integrated model of biblical interpretation, emphasizing synchronic methodologies. His book, *Exploring the Texture of Texts* (1996), has been seminal for many. Quite critical. Compare with the evangelical Witherington above.

☆ Ryle, J.C. (CrossC) 1993.

✓ **Schweizer, Eduard.** ‡ ET 1970. Much better on Mark than on Matthew. If you do some sifting, Schweizer is well worth reading. This vol. was written essentially for pastors, and readers with a sharp eye will find many theological insights and homiletical hints.

F   Strauss, Mark. (ZEC).

✓   **Swete, H.B.** [*M*], 1895, 3rd ed 1927. Something of a classic, at least for its thoroughness in explaining the Greek text. Now eclipsed by more recent commentaries.

F   Tan, Kim Huat. (NCCS). The author teaches at Trinity Theological College in Singapore.

✓   **Taylor, Vincent.** ‡ 1952, 2nd ed 1966. Admirable as a full-scale, painstaking work on the Greek. One of the standard critical commentaries which contributed the first thoroughgoing form-critical analysis of Mark. Taylor's vol. is less valuable for its theology. This has long been used alongside Cranfield.

✓   Telford, W.R. ‡ *The Theology of the Gospel of Mark*, 1999. Prior to this work for Cambridge [*EvQ* 7/01], he edited *The Interpretation of Mark* (1985).

       Thurston, Bonnie. ‡ *Preaching Mark*, 2002. [*Interp* 1/03; *SwJT* Spr 03].

F   Watts, Rikk E. (NICNT replacement). The author teaches at Regent College in Vancouver. Expect this to give prominence to the theme of his book, *Isaiah's New Exodus and Mark*, 1997.

       Wessel, Walter W. (EBC) 1984. Bound with Carson's work on Matthew in vol. 8 of the series. I consider it well-done, but I usually turn to fuller works and ignore this. See EBCR below. [*TJ* Spr 85].

F   Wessel, Walter W., and Mark L. Strauss. (EBCR).

       Williamson, Lamar. ‡ (I) 1983. I have never used it enough to form an opinion. Others assess it as a useful preacher's commentary.

NOTES: (1) See Hurtado's article on "The Gospel of Mark in Recent Study" in *Them* 1/89; and (2) John Ziesler's "Which Is the Best Commentary? VII. Mark," *ExpTim* 6/87.

LUKE

NOTE: I find the selection of recommended commentaries on Luke difficult, especially taking into consideration the different interests and needs of students and pastors. Because the choices are not so clear, I am restricting my list to four. Students who begin with Bock's BECNT, Stein, and Green's NICNT will look to make additional selections from among Fitzmyer, Marshall, Nolland, and Johnson. Busy pastors who give in to the temptation to bypass the massive BECNT in favor of NIVAC—which is not recommended, to begin with—should look to add a couple other exegetical helps like Liefeld-Pao, Johnson, or Craig Evans.

★   **Bock, Darrell.** (BECNT) 2 Vols., 1994–96. Baker Books is correct in describing the first vol. (nearly 1000pp) as "the most extensive, up-to-date, and consistently evangelical commentary on the first portion of Luke." In comparing Bock with the other recent exegetical works on the Greek text (i.e., Fitzmyer, Marshall, and Nolland), you will find this set to be the more easily accessible (less technical), more conservative and theological. I predict that most evangelical pastors would want this instead of Fitzmyer, so I removed the latter from my list of recommendations. Bock is professor of NT studies at Dallas Theological Seminary and is one of the leaders in the "Progressive Dispensationalist" movement. Stein's expertise in redaction criticism and Green's more refined literary investigations well complement Bock's grammatico-historical approach. See the other three Bock works below. [*Presb* Fall 95; *RTR* 1/96; *JETS* 9/98 (Blomberg); *JBL* Spr 98; *WTJ* Spr 96; *TJ* Fall 96; *SwJT* Fall 97; *AsTJ*, Fall 98; *RelSRev* 1/98].

★ Bock, Darrell. (NIVAC) 1996. "Darrell Bock has turned Lukan commentary into a growth industry" (C.R. Matthews). *Yes, three different commentary series in a three-year span!* BECNT gives you full exegesis, theological reflection, and some hints for appropriate application. IVPNT makes Bock's exegetical conclusions more accessible to a general audience and begins the move from text to sermon. NIVAC moves more quickly from original message to significance today (homiletical musings). I would not say this NIVAC is one of the four best works on Luke, but, for the preacher at least, it balances my other three recommendations. Students will probably pass this by and go hunting for another rigorously exegetical work. Preachers should also consider Calvin, Hughes, Ryken, Ryle, and Wilcock for help in applying the text to heart and life.

★ **Green, Joel B.** [𝓜], (NICNT) 1997. This replacement for Geldenhuys' 60 year old work is now a top pick (but not to be used by itself). Though so much work had lately been done on Luke, Green brought a fresh, more literary approach, which can be compared with L.T. Johnson's. (I use Johnson just as much as Green.) He is less interested in historical questions. Evangelical pastors may find that this vol. has a less conservative feel than others in NICNT. [*EvQ* 7/99; *Them* 5/99; *JTS* 10/99; *Biblica* 79.4; *CBQ* 1/99; *Chm* 113.2; *RelSRev* 10/98; *Presb* Spr 00]. See Green's well written vol. on Luke in the Cambridge NT Theology series (1995) [*Them* 10/97; *Interp* 7/97; *JR* 1/97; *CRBR* 1996; *CBQ* 1/97]. He also edited the Cambridge issue, *Methods for Luke* (2010) [*RBL* 8/10].

★ **Stein, Robert A.** (NAC) 1992. This is the heftiest (642pp) and one of the most thoughtful commentaries in the series. "Written with a pastor's heart," says Steve Walton [*BSB* 12/97]. Stein is an experienced, very sharp exegete (see his BECNT on Mark). Among the many features here to appreciate is "a regular summing up of Luke's distinctive redactional emphases in each passage" (Blomberg). Note that Stein uses the terminology "composition criticism," instead of "redaction." This work proves to be a good counterbalance to Green. [*ThTo* 10/93; *EvQ* 7/94; *JETS* 6/96; *CRBR* 1994].

✧ ✧ ✧ ✧ ✧ ✧

F Alexander, Loveday. ‡ *Luke Acts* (BNTC) 2010? The publisher's blurb indicates this is a commentary on the 2 vols., Luke-Acts, but then seems to describe the 456pp as focused on the book of Acts.

Arndt, W.F. 1956. A conservative Lutheran work designed for the pastor.

✓ Bartholomew, Craig G., Joel B. Green, Anthony Thiselton (eds). *Reading Luke: Interpretation, Reflection, Formation*, 2005. Essays published in Zondervan's "Scripture and Hermeneutics Series." [*JETS* 9/06; *Evangel* Aut 07].

F Bauckham, Richard. [𝓜], (ICC–new series). This may be a long way off, since Bauckham still seems mainly focused upon John's Gospel.

Bentley, Michael. *Saving a Fallen World* (WCS) 1992.

☆ Bock, Darrell. (IVPNT) 1994. A fine, well-informed commentary of about 400pp which the pastor can put to good use, being more manageable than the huge BECNT set. He aims to make the conclusions of his exegetical work in BECNT above available to a broader audience, but I do not think he gave us his best work here. [*Presb* Fall 95].

Borgman, Paul C. *The Way According to Luke: Hearing the Whole Story of Luke-Acts*, 2006.

✓ **Bovon, François.** ‡ *Luke 1* (Herm) ET 2002. A truly great commentary! This vol. covering 1:1–9:50 introduces what will be a three-vol. set of technical exegesis and probing theological interpretation. Only for advanced students. This 1989–2009 work for the EKK is coming into ET because of its influence in European scholarship. I expect two more vols. will follow—Bovon has not divided the Lukan material in Hermeneia as he has in the four-vol. German commentary (2048pp)—and that this set will be widely used in its well-presented English dress. Complaints are now arising from scholars about the slowness of the translation project. The announcement is for *Luke 2* to cover 9:51–19:27 and for *Luke 3* to provide exegesis of 19:28–24:53. [*Interp* 7/03; *ExpTim* 1/03; *CurTM* 4/05]. Likely the most valuable critical introduction to Luke and Lukan scholarship is Bovon's 681-page *Luke the Theologian: Fifty-five Years of Research* (1950–2005), 2nd rev. ed 2006 [*ExpTim* 2/07], while the fullest survey is Seán P. Kealy, *The Interpretation of the Gospel of Luke*, 2 vols., 2005 (1251pp).

F   Brown, Jeannine. (NCCS). The author teaches at Bethel Seminary in St. Paul, MN.

☆   **Brown, R.E.** ‡ *The Birth of the Messiah*, 1977, rev. 1993. See under Matthew.

Browning, W.R.F. ‡ (Torch Bible Commentary) 1982. Somewhat similar to Caird below: too brief to compete with the major works, but insightful nonetheless.

Caird, G.B. ‡ (Pelican) 1963. One of the better commentaries in the series. Caird was always incisive.

F   Carroll, John T. ‡ (NTL).

Craddock, Fred B. ‡ (I) 1990. Mainly for the communicator and very well done. [*Interp* 1/92; *ThTo* 48.2; *CRBR* 1992; *AsTJ* Fall 92].

Creed, J.M. ‡ 1930. Highly critical and dated. Though still cited in the literature, Creed can be safely ignored.

✓   **Culpepper, R. Alan.** ‡ (NewIB) 1995. This Baylor professor is well known for his literary critical work on John's Gospel (see below). His commentary on Luke will be of more use to the student than the pastor, though he seeks to assist preachers. [*JETS* 3/99].

☆   **Danker, Frederick.** ‡ *Jesus and the New Age*, 1972, rev. 1988. No, this is not a "New Age" book, but a stimulating commentary. It is easy to understand why this 432-page work is a favorite of I.H. Marshall. Danker's immense learning in the classics is put to good use, and there are many insights a preacher would find suggestive for sermon preparation. This is Danker of the BAGD/BDAG lexicon. [*CRBR* 1990].

F   Edwards, James. (Pillar). Ignore earlier reports of Peter Head doing this.

☆   **Ellis, E.E.** [*M*], (NCB) 2nd ed 1974. Still valuable, especially for understanding passages as a whole and their historical backdrop. An appealing evangelical work which is mildly critical and astute. Advanced students will also note his monograph, *Eschatology in Luke* (1972). Marshall really likes Ellis's lengthy introduction.

☆   **Evans, Craig A.** [*M*], (NIBC) 1990. Over 400pp. This is worthwhile to consult and perhaps purchase. Don't confuse with C.F. Evans, the very liberal scholar who has published a substantial work on Luke for TPI. A pastor friend, John Turner, once said in his commentary review that "Evans has stimulated a number of sermon ideas for me." Note also Evans' work on Mark for WBC.

✓   Evans, C.F. ‡ (TPI) 1990. This is the sort of work you would want to consult to get the radical, "Jesus Seminar" type of interpretation of this gospel. This is a large (933pp), significant work from the far left. The SCM 2nd edition (2008) is really just a reprint. [*JTS* 4/91; *CBQ* 7/92; *JSNT-BL* 2010].

☆   **Fitzmyer, Joseph A.** ‡ (AB) 2 Vols., 1981–85. Even Marshall humbly called this work the best on Luke. Over the years I have encouraged advanced students especially to consider buying this moderately critical, Roman Catholic commentary. Fitzmyer is one of the leading authorities on Aramaic and on the Semitic background of the NT. Many pastors find this set too skeptical as a commentary on the Greek text and are glad to have Bock's BECNT instead. Compare with Marshall and Nolland below.

Making choices among commentary sets is hard. [*Interp* 7/83; *SJT* 42.2; *JBL* 9/87; *EvQ* 10/83, 1/88; *ExpTim* 6/83]. See also Fitzmyer's follow-up study, *Luke the Theologian* (1989) [*JTS* 10/90; *JBL* Win 91; *EvQ* 4/91; *CBQ* 10/91]. Finally, note that Fitzmyer has multiple commentaries in AB: Acts, Romans, 1 Corinthians, Philemon.

F   Garland, David. (ZEC).

Geldenhuys, J. Norval. (retired NICNT) 1951. This was the first contribution to the series. This vol. once served preachers well; they appreciated the spiritually edifying exposition. E.g., his theological comments (pp.479–87) on Luke's account of the Triumphal Entry are among the more fruitful I have found for the preacher. Also, at 670pp it was a full commentary that covered many of the questions raised by the average Bible student. Similar to NTC in its Reformed orientation.

Godet, Frederic. 1887–89, ET 1893. Pastors over the generations have relied on Godet's insightful theological commentaries, which were reprinted by Kregel some 30 years ago. A great pastor-scholar with Arminian theology, Godet withdrew from the state church in Switzerland in protest against liberalism. He helped found a new seminary where he served as a professor in exegesis. He is not as good here as on John's Gospel. See the old review of Godet's gifts as a commentator in B.B. Warfield's *Selected Shorter Writings* (I: 432–36).

Gooding, David. 1987. A useful study guide with application for our time. I would classify Gooding's work as exposition focused on redaction critical concerns. Evangelical. [*Evangel* Win 88; *EvQ* 7/89].

✓   **Goulder, Michael D.** ‡ *Luke: A New Paradigm*, 2 Vols., 1989. A painstaking study (824pp) offering a new critical approach to this gospel which argues for dependence upon Mark and Matthew. The alleged sayings-source Q is dispensed with. Gives close attention to material unique to Luke and challenges traditional source criticism and redaction criticism. Includes a technical commentary of 600pp which applies his "new paradigm." [*WTJ* Fall 91; *JTS* 4/92; *JBL* Spr 91]. The Goulder thesis is now being pushed by his student, Mark Goodacre, in such vols. as *The Case Against Q* (2002) and Goodacre/Perrin (eds), *Questioning Q* (2004) [*BTB* Spr 06].

F   Gray, Timothy. ‡ (CCSS).

✓   Hatina, Thomas R. (ed). *Biblical Interpretation in Early Christian Gospels. III. The Gospel of Luke*, 2010. For two companion vols., see Hatina under Matthew and Mark.

F   Head, Peter M. (~~Pillar~~). Head, a Cambridge lecturer and an expert on ancient manuscripts and textual criticism of the Gospels, no longer has the contract. He told me he still plans a major Luke commentary. See Edwards.

☆   Hendriksen, William. (NTC) 1978. This was his lengthiest commentary at 1122pp, and was probably his most homiletically styled work too. [*RTR* 5/80].

☆   Hughes, R. Kent. (PTW) 2 Vols., 1998.

F   Jeffrey, David Lyle. (Brazos).

☆   **Johnson, Luke Timothy.** ‡ (SacPag) 1991. Delivers an interesting, sensitive, literary reading of this Gospel (466pp). Advanced students can learn a lot here, especially because Johnson has some respect for the text, involving a commitment to the Christian Faith. There is less of a hermeneutic of suspicion here. To be more accurate, there is suspicion of any attempt, either hyper-critical (Jesus Seminar) or supposedly uncritical (evangelicals), to discover the "historical Jesus." See his controversial book, *The Real Jesus: The Misguided Quest for the Historical Jesus and the Truth of the Traditional Gospels* (1996), and the high-level discussion of it in *BBR* 7 (1997). It was a wise choice for the series' editors to allow Johnson to contribute the vol. on Acts as well. Johnson wrote his dissertation on Luke-Acts.

Carson makes this SacPag work a top pick. [*JBL* 113.2; *Interp* 10/93; *Biblica* 74.2 (1993); *CBQ* 1/93]. In another series (AB), Johnson writes on James and Timothy.

✓ **Just, Arthur A.** (Concord) 2 Vols., 1996–97. A large-scale (1066-page) commentary with real exegetical value and theological exposition in a confessional Lutheran mold. The author is well-educated (Yale and Durham, beyond his Concordia Seminary training), and his aim clearly is to assist the preacher who is reading through the Greek text to compose a sermon. The intended audience is certainly studious pastors.

✓ Just, Arthur A. (ed). (ACCS) 2003. [*RelSRev* 4/04].

Leaney, A.R.C. ‡ (BNTC) 1958.

F Levine, Amy-Jill, and Ben Witherington III. (NCBC).

Liefeld, Walter L. (EBC) 1984. When it came out, it was regarded as a very good work, despite the brevity of the entry. Bound with both Carson's "Matthew" and Wessel's "Mark." Now see EBCR. [*TJ* Spr 85].

☆ **Liefeld, Walter L., and David W. Pao.** (EBCR) 2007. The older work has been improved in this collaborative effort of 320pp. It is competent, insightful, and well-written throughout.

Lieu, Judith. ‡ (Epworth Commentaries) 1997.

✓ Malina, Bruce J., and Richard L. Rohrbaugh. ‡ *Social-Science Commentary on the Synoptic Gospels*, 1992.

☆ **Marshall, I. Howard.** [*M*], (NIGTC) 1978. This is still one of the four or five most important scholarly commentaries on Luke. This work is more conservative than Fitzmyer—cf. their approaches to redaction and historical questions—and was Silva's first pick years ago. Many pastors will prefer Marshall's evangelical approach to Fitzmyer's assiduous criticism. Unfortunately, the format of this huge commentary (about 900pp) is somewhat self-defeating. It is laborious to use Marshall because, in Carson's words, it is so "densely-packed," with notes incorporated into the text of the commentary. But diligence on the part of the student does pay off. The advanced student working on Luke will want Marshall and Fitzmyer, in addition to Bock. Rather than write a new introduction for this vol., Marshall refers the reader to his excellent work, *Luke: Historian and Theologian* (1970, rev. 1979, Enlarged ed 1989). Though I haven't included this monograph among the above recommendations, it would be smart to obtain a copy for your studies in Luke and Acts. [*WTJ* Spr 80; *RTR* 1/79; *EvQ* 10/79]. There are unconfirmed reports that Marshall will do a 2nd edition of his NIGTC.

Morgan, G. Campbell. 1931. I do not intend to list all of Campbell Morgan's thoughtful expositions, but pastors should be reminded that they are available and useful. He was Lloyd-Jones' famous predecessor at Westminster Chapel in London.

☆ Morris, Leon. (TNTC) 1974, rev. 1988. Helpful and handy, Morris is definitely one of the more insightful works in the series. The financially-strapped preacher could start here. The revision is minor. [*EvQ* 1/75].

✓ **Nolland, John.** [*M*], (WBC) 3 Vols., 1989–93. One would have thought there was little to say after Marshall and Fitzmyer got done, but Nolland has written a fine, heavily redaction-critical commentary that goes on and on for 1300pp. After sampling it, one comes to the conclusion that this is more of an academic commentary, i.e., Nolland seems to spend proportionally more time interacting with the literature on Luke than bringing out the meaning of the evangelist himself. In other words, those working on the graduate or post-graduate level will find these three vols. more useful than the expositor preparing for Sunday. This set has received mixed reviews. One of the best is *CRBR* 1995. [*WTJ* Fall 91; *JTS* 4/91, 10/95; *EvQ* 1/93, 4/96; *CBQ* 4/92; *RTR* 1/91; *Them* 1/92 and 5/95; *BSac* 7/93].

F   Parsons, Mikeal C. (Paideia). See also *Luke: Storyteller, Interpreter, Evangelist*, 2007 [*BBR* 19.1; *RelSRev* 12/08].

F   Parsons, Mikeal C., and Martin Culy. (BHGNT).

Pate, C. Marvin. (Moody Gospel Commentary) 1995. A fuller, popular-level commentary in pb.

F   Porter, Stanley. (EEC).

✓   **Plummer, Alfred.** (ICC) 5th ed 1922. The standard of its day and still useful for work in the Greek. Silva calls it "first-rate." This commentary was about the most conservative work ever published in ICC. Should now be used in conjunction with AB, NIGTC, BECNT, and WBC.

Reicke, Bo. ‡ *The Gospel of Luke*, 1964.

Reilling, R., and J.L. Swellengrebel. (UBS) 1971. A translator's handbook of nearly 800pp.

Ringe, Sharon H. ‡ (WestBC) 1996. A feminist treatment by one of the editors of *The Women's Bible Commentary*. [*Interp* 1/98; *CBQ* 4/97].

F   Robbins, Vernon K. ‡ (RRA).

☆   Ryken, Philip. (REC) 2 Vols., 2009. Excellent sermonic material indeed. Were it not, then 1300pp would seem awfully excessive. Ryken has followed the grand tradition of Boice, his predecessor at famous Tenth Presbyterian. See other large-scale Ryken expositions of Exodus, Jeremiah, Galatians, 1 Timothy, etc.

☆   Ryle, J.C. (CrossC) 1997.

F   Schertz, Mary. (BCBC).

✓   Schweizer, Eduard. ‡ ET 1984. See under Mark.

✓   Spencer, F. Scott. ‡ *The Gospel of Luke and Acts of the Apostles*, 2008. This entry in Abingdon's IBT series gives less attention to Acts. [*JSNT-BL* 2009; *Interp* 7/10].

✓   Stonehouse, Ned B. *The Witness of the Synoptic Gospels to Christ*, 1979 reprint. See under Matthew.

F   Strauss, Mark. (THC).

✓   **Talbert, Charles H.** ‡ *Reading Luke: A Literary and Theological Commentary on the Third Gospel*, 1982. Provocative and packed commentary by a leading American Lukan scholar. The evangelical pastor found this useful years ago, but it is a little less valuable today. See also Talbert's fine work on Acts. [*JBL* 104.2 (1985)].

✓   **Tannehill, Robert.** ‡ *The Narrative Unity of Luke-Acts, A Literary Interpretation*, 2 Vols, 1990–91. An exciting study that provides a synchronic, literary reading of the "final form" of the Lukan corpus. There are many insights in this Fortress set. See the next entry. [*Biblica* 69.1 (1988); *CRBR* 1988 (more critical)].

✓   **Tannehill, Robert C.** ‡ (ANTC) 1996. This 378-page entry updates some of his past work and makes his conclusions available in a fairly inexpensive pb format. [*Interp* 7/98; *RelSRev* 1/98].

✓   **Tiede, David L.** ‡ (Augsburg NT Commentary) 1988. This full Lutheran work (457pp) is praised by Danker, who knows this Gospel well. [*CRBR* 1991].

Vinson, Richard B. ‡ (S&H) 2008. Substantial research underlies this, one of the largest vols. in the series (760pp). Vinson is open to "suspicious readings" of Luke and makes it a goal of his interpretation "to offer readings that support the full participation of women in ministry" (p.19). Application parts of this exposition sometimes have an oddly-loaded, unpracticed feel to them (e.g., commending the example of elaborate, expensive preparations for death after a palm-reading, p.473). Vinson teaches at Salem College in North Carolina. [*Interp* 4/10].

☆ Wilcock, Michael. (BST) 1979. Formerly titled, *The Saviour of the World*. Directly serves the expositor as it explains pericopae (not a verse by verse commentary). NOTES: (1) See Marshall's article, "The Present State of Lucan Studies," in *Them*, 1/89; and (2) C.S. Rodd, "Two Commentaries on Luke," *ExpTim* 9/90.

JOHN

★ **Barrett, C.K.** ‡ 2nd ed 1978. Moloney terms this "precise but rich." The Germans translated this for inclusion in their most prestigious NT series, MeyerK (1990). I call this indispensable for the student and scholarly pastor doing exegesis of the Greek text. Yes, you must have a handle on the Greek to make good use of this. Amazingly thorough, compressed and well-reasoned from the critical angle (638pp), with some fine theological points: "the Father is God sending and commanding, the Son is God sent and obedient" (p.468). The commentary really has not changed much since it was first published in 1955. Some would say that Barrett's argument has been partially vitiated because of a shift in scholarly opinion toward identifying a Palestinian milieu for the Fourth Gospel (see Martyn below). This commentary is complemented by his *Essays on John* (1982). Barrett is Carson's and Silva's favorite critical work and first pick. Compare with Brown's more expensive set, which some say has more for the pastor. Evangelicals may want the *caveat emptor* that Barrett believes the Fourth Gospel is theologically creative in presenting Jesus traditions which have little historical value. Any who wish to stick with conservative exegetical works are urged to buy Morris, Kruse or Blomberg instead. [*EvQ* 4/79; *JBL* 99.4 (1980)].

★ Burge, Gary. (NIVAC) 2000. A sizable (600-page) homiletical commentary which builds upon a solid foundation of NT scholarship (see Burge below). Burge did his PhD at Aberdeen and teaches at Wheaton College. This vol. ventures some bold, thought-provoking application and well complements these other exegetical commentaries. Other smart purchases for preachers would be Hughes, Boice, Milne, and Morris's *Reflections*. [*CTJ* 11/01].

★ **Carson, Donald.** (Pillar) 1991. This is, without a doubt, the evangelical pastor's first choice. This vol. was originally intended as Tasker's replacement in TNTC, and I'm very glad it proved much too lengthy. Dr. James Boice—who, incidentally, did his dissertation on John's Gospel and took six years preaching through John— called this 700-page work "the most exciting, helpful, and sound commentary on the Gospel of John in decades." I used it extensively during a 15-month series and believe Boice's comments are right on target. The strengths of his earlier Matthew commentary are mirrored here. [*WTJ* Fall 92 (Silva); *CBQ* 7/92; *RTR* 5/92; *EvQ* 1/95; *JETS* 6/95; *CRBR* 1992]. Pastors might also note Carson's exposition of chs. 14–17, *The Farewell Discourse and Final Prayer of Jesus* (1981).

★ **Keener, Craig.** 2 Vols., 2003. Published by Hendrickson, this exceedingly full evangelical interpretation displaced Morris on my list of suggestions. But perhaps Keener is too full for the pastor (1600pp). As with his huge one-vol. commentary on Matthew, this work is long on historical, cultural and ancient literary background. (He adduces far too many supposed parallels, in my opinion.) Those who want a more manageable evangelical commentary in one vol. can repair to Morris (still fat), Blomberg, or the new TNTC by Kruse. Students willing to work through the astonishing amount of detail will find this set a masterful guide into John's Gospel, where, Augustine famously said, a child may safely wade and an elephant can swim. The size and weight here suggest more of the elephant. [*CBQ* 10/04; *ExpTim* 8/04; *SwJT* Fall 05; *RTR* 12/08; *JTS* 10/05; *Interp* 7/06; *BSac* 1/09; *EuroJTh* 15.2].

★ **Köstenberger, Andreas J.** (BECNT) 2004. This welcome addition to the company of fat John commentaries has not superseded Carson, but is a good complement to it. Both are full (about 700pp), yet manageable and concise for busy pastors. BECNT reviews and culls the best recent Johannine scholarship and thereby supplements Carson; this will please NT students but cause some pastors to want to speed-read. Also, the theological discussion is sound and satisfying. Students will be glad for both the Greek exegesis and the bibliographical help they receive here. One criticism is that the work is not strong in narrative criticism. My counsel to the average pastor would be to buy Carson and Köstenberger (in that order) and then an expositional work like Burge. The more scholarly can then add some combination of Barrett, WBC, Keener, Ridderbos, Smith, Morris, Blomberg, Moloney, and perhaps Brown or Schnackenburg—but do start with Keener and Barrett. See below Köstenberger's earlier *Encountering John* and, far more impressively, *A Theology of John's Gospel and Letters*. [*CBQ* 1/06; *BBR* 16.2; *JETS* 9/05; *BSac* 4/06; *SwJT* Fall 05; *Them* 10/05; *JSNT-BL* 2006; *SBET* Aut 06; *RelSRev* 1/06; *ExpTim* 5/06; *EuroJTh* 15.2].

★ **Ridderbos, Herman.** *The Gospel of John: A Theological Commentary*, ET 1997. You ought to consider this for purchase, as extensive as it is, and as masterful a theologian as Ridderbos is. Though rich and profound, this work is not always lucid in ET and is not easy for beginners. Some pastors might prefer Morris. [*Them* 5/99; *JETS* 9/99; *WTJ* Fall 97; *TJ* Spr 98; *Interp* 7/98; *CBQ* 1/99; *RTR* 8/98].

F   Anderson, Paul. ‡ (S&H).

✓   Anderson, Paul N., Felix Just, and Tom Thatcher (eds). *John, Jesus, and History*. Vol. 1: *Critical Appraisals of Critical Views*, 2007. [*JSNT-BL* 2009; *JSHJ* 7.1].

✓   Ashton, John. ‡ *Understanding the Fourth Gospel*, 1993, 2nd ed 2007. Published by Oxford Press (624pp in 1993). [*JBL* Spr 93; *JTS* 10/92; *ExpTim* 10/91, 11/07]. Added to this is *The Interpretation of John* (2nd ed 1997), edited by Ashton, which is a valuable collection of critical essays by various scholars [*RelSRev* 7/00].

F   Attridge, Harold. ‡ (Herm). Some initial work is published in *Essays on John and Hebrews* (2010).

F   Bauckham, Richard. [*M*], (NIGTC). At one time Smalley supposedly had the contract. Bauckham could make a very important contribution to scholarship here, especially as he argues further the thesis proposed in Bauckham (ed), *The Gospels for All Christians: Rethinking the Gospel Audiences* (1998), which takes aim at the widely held idea of a conflicted Johannine Community. The thesis, that the gospels are general tracts "for all Christians," is applied to all four. He builds brilliantly on it in *The Testimony of the Beloved Disciple* (2007) [*JETS* 9/08; *CTJ* 11/09; *EQ* 7/09; *DenvJ* 12/07; *JSHJ* 8.2 (2010)], though I disagree with him identifying the author as John the Elder, not John, son of Zebedee. Cf. Martyn and Klink below. For Bauckham's rejection of a source and form-critical approach to the gospels, see *Jesus and the Eyewitnesses: The Gospels as Eyewitness Testimony*, 2006 [*BBR* 19.1; *JTS* 4/08; *TJ* Spr 08; *JSNT* 12/08; *Them* 5/08 (Wenham)].

F   Bauckham, Richard. [*M*], (THC).

✓   Bauckham, Richard, and Carl Mosser (eds). *The Gospel of John and Christian Theology*, 2008. [*CBQ* 4/09; *ExpTim* 4/09; *TJ* Spr 09; *Chm* Sum 09; *Them* 4/10; *JSNT-BL* 2009; *RelSRev* 12/09].

✓   **Beasley-Murray, George R.** [*M*], (WBC) 1987, 2nd ed 1999. This work is highly respected as an erudite, closely-packed commentary. I was somewhat disappointed by its critical stance on a number of issues. Barrett and Brown are better coming from the critical perspective, and Carson is more dependable and insightful from a consistently evangelical viewpoint. This commentary, says Silva, is exceeding rich on the last half of the Gospel. The 2ⁿᵈ edition contains the same commentary and a much lengthened introduction and bibliography. Students should note that the addendum gives an especially fine account of major developments in studies on John's Gospel from the late 1970s to late 90s. [*JTS* 40.1; *JBL* Winter 89; *WTJ* Fall 88; *JBL* 108.4 (1989); *RTR* 1/88; *Chm* 104.1 (1990)]. Students of John should also note the follow-up work by Beasley-Murray entitled, *Gospel of Life: Theology in the Fourth Gospel*, 1991.

Bernard, J.H. ‡ (ICC) 2 Vols., 1928. See McHugh below for what was the start of a replacement.

☆ **Blomberg, Craig.** *The Historical Reliability of John's Gospel*, 2002. Not only does the Denver Seminary professor address the scholarly wrangle mentioned in the book title, he also has a commentary in these pages. This is a good piece of work by a leading evangelical that can be recommended to both students and pastors. [*Them* Aut 02; *JETS* 6/03].

☆ Boice, James Montgomery. 1975–79. A huge vol. of exposition—really printed sermons (his series on John's Gospel began in 1971). Boice here builds on his doctoral dissertation at Basel. This would be useful to the preacher looking for a guide in preaching through John (hopefully more quickly). For further review of Boice's work, see Genesis. The more recent multi-vol. sets which he wrote (e.g., Psalms, Matthew) are better, more mature preaching.

☆ **Borchert, Gerald L.** (NAC) 2 Vols., 1996–2002. The set has received generally favorable reviews and has good research behind it, but I do not place Borchert in the top rank of evangelical commentators. Of special interest to some is the author's proposal regarding an alternative structuring of the Fourth Gospel. He sees ch. 1 as introductory. What follows are three sections he terms "cycles": the Cana Cycle (2:1–4:54); the Festival Cycle (5:1–11:57); and the Farewell Cycle (13:1–17:26). The pivot in the middle is ch. 12, while the passion and resurrection narratives form the Gospel's conclusion. Students could make use of Borchert. [*Them* Sum 04; *JETS* 9/04].

F Brant, Jo-Ann A. (Paideia).

✓ **Brodie, Thomas L.** ‡ 1993. This Oxford Press work is subtitled, "A Literary and Theological Commentary" (625pp), and urges readers to consider the evidence for literary unity and coherence. Compare this with another Catholic literary interpretation: Moloney. [*JTS* 4/95; *JETS* 3/96; *JBL* Sum 95].

☆ **Brown, R.E.** ‡ (AB) 2 Vols., 1966–70. Rich and incisive exegesis with a treasure trove of notes. This commentary, by one of the most prominent Catholic NT scholars of the 20ᵗʰ century, is quite a work to set one thinking, especially since there's a good bit to disagree with (e.g., the sacramental emphases). Brown's work is also significant because he was one of the first to recognize the importance of the Qumran discoveries for Johannine studies and to emphasize a Palestinian setting. Among critical works I find Brown marginally more useful than Barrett, but Brown is not worth $40 more than Barrett, which is what one pays through the discount booksellers. The scholarly student or pastor with means might try to obtain both. Brown's work on a revision of the commentary was cut short by his death in 1998. [*JBL* 90.3 (1971)]. The new introduction with updated notes was edited by Francis Moloney, filling almost 400pp, and was published by Random House in 2003 [*JTS*

4/05; *ThTo* 7/04 (Moody Smith)]. Additionally, see Brown's AB commentary on John's Epistles.

☆ Bruce, F.F. 1984. It is hard to beat this 400-page commentary in terms of value for your money. Most of the recommended works above will set you back about $25 or more, but Bruce in pb is only about $10. A solid, sober, careful grammatico-historical interpretation of John. Recommended. Please note that Eerdmans now has a one-vol. 600-page hb with this commentary and Bruce's work on John's Epistles, and I once saw it, too, selling for $10 at CBD. [*Them* 1/85; *EvQ* 4/86; *ThTo* 41.4].

✓ **Bultmann, Rudolf.** ‡ ET 1971. Called by many Bultmann's greatest work, this commentary is radically critical, proposes a complex source theory, and is stimulating (because it compels the reader to interact). It once had towering stature, but John studies have moved sharply away from his thesis that the Fourth Gospel addresses a Gnostic viewpoint and should be interpreted against a Hellenistic, non-Christian background of Mandaeism (see comments on Barrett above). Bultmann is only for advanced students.

✓ Burge, Gary. *The Anointed Community: The Holy Spirit in the Johannine Tradition*, 1987. Not a commentary, but a dissertation on the doctrine of the Holy Spirit in this literature. Such a work as this was needed "since pneumatology plays a fundamental role in the very fabric of the Fourth Gospel" (Silva). [*WTJ* Spr 88; *JBL* 108.1 (1989)]. Also helpful is Burge's book entitled, *Interpreting the Gospel of John* (1992), with a commentary guide as an appendix. See Burge's NIVAC vols. on both John's Gospel (above) and John's Epistles.

☆ Calvin, John. (CrossC) 1994.

✓ Carter, Warren. [*M*], *John: Storyteller, Interpreter, Evangelist*, 2006. This is one of the better introductions to John and Johannine scholarship. [*JSNT-BL* 2008; *ExpTim* 2/08; *BTB* Spr 08].

✓ **Culpepper, R. Alan.** ‡ *Anatomy of the Fourth Gospel: A Study in Literary Design*, 1983. A significant book not only for Johannine studies but also for the NT discipline as a whole. Culpepper applies the new literary criticism to John's Gospel. Though his conclusions are not compatible with a high view of Scripture, advanced students should acquaint themselves with the work. For something of an update and a survey of scholarship, consult *The Gospel and Letters of John* (IBT) 1998; he gives the Letters little attention (mainly pp.251–83). See also Moloney's works and Thatcher/Moore for further stimulating, fruitful research into John as narrative. [*TJ* Fall 83].

✓ Dodd, C.H. ‡ *The Interpretation of the Fourth Gospel*, 1953. A seminal study of the ideas behind and in this gospel. Stresses a Hellenistic background, which I don't find so plausible. He later published *Historical Tradition in the Fourth Gospel* (1963).

Dods, Marcus. [*M*], (EB, and Expositor's Greek Testament) 1886 and 1897. These are still somewhat useful. Dods imbibed some old-style liberalism.

Edwards, Mark. ‡ (BBC) 2004. [*EuroJTh* 15.2].

Ellis, Peter F. [*M*], *The Genius of John: A Compositional-critical Commentary on the Fourth Gospel*, 1984. This Catholic scholar comes to some surprisingly conservative conclusions about the composition of John and its literary unity.

✓ Elowsky, Joel C. (ed). (ACCS) 2 Vols., 2006–07.

☆ Godet, Frederic. ET 1886. This is a true classic from which the pastor can benefit, containing 1100pp of masterful exposition and theological exegesis. You can ignore the discourses on the religious issues of his day. "The thoughtful reader will always discern practical applications if he or she ponders Godet's remarks" (Carson).

Along with his commentaries on Luke, Romans, and 1 Corinthians, this has often been reprinted.

✓ **Haenchen, Ernst.** ‡ (Herm) 2 Vols., ET 1984. This expensive, very critical work has been called a major disappointment by almost everyone except the neo-Bultmannians. Completed posthumously by a student of Haenchen. Dated and sketchy at points. You'd best ignore it, unless you are doing the fullest research at an advanced level.

F Harris, Hall. (EEC).

F Heever, G. van den. (RRA).

☆ Hendriksen, William. (NTC) 1953. This commentary is not so prolix as some later ones, but it is also more dated. Sturdy, Reformed, and needs to be checked against an up-to-date work like Carson's. More useful to the preacher than to the student.

✓ **Hoskyns, Edwyn, and F.N. Davey.** ‡ 1940, 2ⁿᵈ ed 1957. A very rich theological commentary with something of a Barthian slant. In fact, Hoskyns interrupted his work on John's Gospel to translate Barth's *Der Römerbrief*, after he had experienced a kind of "conversion" from a liberal religion of experience to a religion of revelation. Unlike much English biblical scholarship from the 1920s and 30s, this work retains value down to today. For an account of the author's life work, see John M. Court, "Edwyn Clement Hoskyns (9ᵗʰ August 1884 – 28ᵗʰ June 1937)," *ExpTim* 118.7 (2007): 331–36. [*WTJ* Fall 40].

☆ Hughes, R. Kent. (PTW) 1999. A good choice for the preacher, if used in conjunction with a solid exegetical work. Approximately 500pp. See Mark above.

✓ Hunter, A.M. [𝓜], (CBC) 1965. Insightful in brief compass.

☆ Hutcheson, George. (GS) 1657. A great Puritan exposition. Spurgeon wrote that it was "[e]xcellent; beyond all praise…a full-stored treasury of sound theology, holy thought, and marrowy doctrine." Recommended for lovers of the Puritans.

F Kanagaraj, Jey. (NCCS). The author teaches at Hindustan Bible Institute and College in India.

Keddie, Gordon J. (EPSC) 2 Vols., 2001. [*Evangel* Spr 05].

✓ Klink, Edward W. *The Sheep of the Fold: The Audience and Origin of the Gospel of John*, 2007. Called a "splendid" dissertation [*Biblica* 90.1 (Kysar)], written under Bauckham at St. Andrews. It presents a trenchant critique of the long-standing consensus about John being written for a single Christian community. [*BBR* 19.2 (Carson)].

✓ Koester, Craig R. ‡ *Symbolism in the Fourth Gospel: Meaning, Mystery, Community*, 2ⁿᵈ ed 2003; *The Word of Life: A Theology of John's Gospel*, 2008 [*JETS* 3/10; *Interp* 10/09; *JSNT-BL* 2010].

Köstenberger, Andreas J. *Encountering John*, 1999. Part of a the Baker series of college-level textbooks, this preceded his large BECNT commentary listed above. Excellent. [*JSNT* 12/00; *CTJ* 11/00; *JETS* 9/01].

✓ Köstenberger, Andreas J. *A Theology of John's Gospel and Letters*, 2009. I have hardly used it yet, but it runs to 652pp, and one cannot help but be impressed with all he has published over the decade (1999–2009). The vol. is the first installment in an 8-vol. series, Biblical Theology of the NT (BTNT), edited by Köstenberger. [*Them* 7/10 (Kruse)].

☆ **Kruse, Colin G.** (TNTC) 2004. This handy 395-page exegesis replaces Tasker and completes the revision of the Tyndale NT series. Kruse knows the Johannine literature well—he produced the Pillar commentary on the Epistles—and does a fine job here. He chooses not to follow the scholarship that reads the Gospel as addressed to a particular Johannine community. This is what I would give to the thoughtful lay leader who is studying John's Gospel and who has questions which require well-founded and succinct answers. This can also serve the pastor well as a quick reference, unlike Keener. I believe this was published in 2003 in the UK, but 2004 in the USA. Worth buying. [*DenvJ* 8/04; *CBQ* 4/07; *ExpTim* 11/04; *Anvil* 21.4 (Smalley)].

✓ Kysar, Robert. ‡ *The Fourth Evangelist and His Gospel*, 1975. A survey of issues in the interpretation of John which is similar to Smalley's but more critical in outlook. See also his Augsburg Commentary (1986). The seminary student doing literature review will certainly consult *Voyages with John* (2005) and weigh his critique of some of Martyn's work.

Laney, J. Carl. (Moody Gospel Commentary) 1992. A popular-level pb (407pp).

✓ Lierman, John (ed). *Challenging Perspectives on the Gospel of John*, 2006. These essays from the Tyndale Fellowship explore new and different paths, often challenging dominant theories in higher criticism. [*BBR* 19.1; *JETS* 9/08; *EuroJTh* 17.1].

Lightfoot, R.H. ‡ 1969. A scholarly commentary published by Oxford.

✓ **Lincoln, Andrew T.** ‡ (BNTC) 2005. In the longest contribution to the series so far (584pp), Lincoln provides a fresh, lucid, mainly theological commentary on the Fourth Gospel. I found insights on nearly every page. When interpreting the passion narratives, he runs down the track he earlier set out in *Truth on Trial: The Lawsuit Motif in John's Gospel* (2000) [*BBR* 16.2; *JTS* 4/07]. This is an important moderately critical work for students to consult. He knows the scholarship and can summarize it well, but there is less interaction with differing views. As with so many other critical interpreters, Lincoln has little use for John as providing a historically grounded, reliable portrait of Jesus. [*CTJ* 4/07; *BBR* 17.2; *JTS* 10/07; *JETS* 12/06; *JSNT* 3/07; *JSNT-BL* 2007; *DenvJ* 1/06 (Blomberg-favorable); *ExpTim* 3/06].

✓ **Lindars, Barnabas.** ‡ (NCB) 1972. A highly praised commentary from a late, prominent Roman Catholic scholar who long taught at Manchester University. Be sure to consult this, even though there have been many developments in Johannine studies since. Moderately critical. [*EvQ* 4/73; *JBL* 95.4 (1976)].

Lüthi, Walter. ‡ 1942, ET 1960. Expositions by a once famous German Catholic preacher.

✓ **McHugh, John.** ‡ *John 1–4* (ICC–new series) 2008. This might have joined the ranks of Brown, Schnackenburg, Lindars, and Moloney as an immensely learned Roman Catholic commentary on John's Gospel. McHugh was due to replace the old Bernard work. The sad news is that the author died after making just a start, and Stanton (in the closing months of his own life) put it into publishable form. Foster calls it "a fragmentary work with no great coherence. Readers are only left with a sense of what might have been." Students doing full research on the early chapters will certainly make use of it. [*ExpTim* 7/09; *NovT* 52.3; *JSNT-BL* 2010].

✓ **Malina, Bruce J., and Richard L. Rohrbaugh.** ‡ *A Social-Science Commentary on the Gospel of John*, 1998. [*JBL* Sum 00; *CBQ* 4/00; *RelSRev* 4/99].

F Marshall, Bruce. (Brazos).

F Marshall, I. Howard. (ZEC).

F Martin, Francis, and William M. Wright IV. ‡ (CCSS).

✓ Martyn, J. Louis. ‡ *History and Theology in the Fourth Gospel*, 1968; 3rd ed (NTL) 2003. This study revolutionized John studies years ago and was further developed by others like Raymond Brown. But the notion that John's Gospel throughout reflects the history and conflicts of a mainly Jewish, Johannine Community—and is therefore more narrowly focused than a general Christian tract—is now being challenged by Bauckham, Carson, and others. [*ThTo* 10/03].

Michaels, J. Ramsey. (NIBC) 1989. This updates the 1984 entry in GNC to explain the NIV. At 400pp it is a probing exposition, but Bruce is a bit better. I look forward to the next entry.

Michaels, J. Ramsey. [*M?*], (NICNT replacement) 2010. Eerdmans has announced this as 1152pp with a late September release date. The author taught years ago at Gordon-Conwell and then was long at Missouri State. See also his WBC on 1 Peter. Regrettably I have not seen it yet.

☆ Milne, Bruce. (BST) 1993. A full 320pp of exposition on John's message. The theology drawn from John is well founded. Includes as an appendix a study guide which could be put to good use in a Bible study format.

✓ **Moloney, Francis J.** ‡ (SacPag) 1998. Highly theological from the Roman Catholic perspective, but also attentive to literary and rhetorical features of the text. Moloney attempts to aid preachers in calling their congregations to the response of faith. I call it a real success. The SacPag vol. of nearly 600 pages follows on the heels of a three-vol. set which focused more on "reader" and "narrator" (that term is preferred over "evangelist"). Those titles are *Belief in the Word: Reading John 1–4* (1993); *Signs and Shadows: Reading John 5–12* (1996); and *Glory Not Dishonor: Reading John 13–21* (1998). Those three vols. total about 700pp. [*Biblica* 80.4 (1999); *Interp* 1/99; *CBQ* 7/99; *RelSRev* 7/00]. There is also a follow-up vol. of essays entitled, *The Gospel of John: Text and Context*, 2005 [*JTS* 10/07; *JSNT-BL* 2006].

☆ **Morris, Leon.** (NICNT) 1971, rev. 1995. NICNT has long been the standard among evangelical works, and prior to my 7th edition I always recommended its purchase. However, I prefer Carson's approach to Morris's "strictly earthly-historical view of Jesus' ministry" (Carson's phrase). Still, the evangelical pastor is very much helped by Morris. [*EvQ* 1/73; *JBL* 91.3 (1972); *RelSRev* 4/99]. Honestly, the Sunday School teacher and expositor will find nearly as much help—help of a different kind—in *Reflections on the Gospel of John*, 4 Vols. (1986–89), now published by Hendrickson in one hb vol. (760pp). Students should note Morris's suggestive work on the theology of this gospel: *Jesus Is the Christ* (1989). Eerdmans plans to replace the Morris NICNT with Michaels (see above).

☆ Mounce, Robert. (EBCR) 2007. The author expressly writes for pastors in these 300pp. Students will see, even in the three-page introduction, that this is not written for them. Mounce is well-informed, insightful, and clear.

✓ Newman, B.H., and E.A. Nida. (UBS) 1980.

✓ Neyrey, Jerome H. ‡ (NCBC) 2007. This commentary by a Roman Catholic at Notre Dame is one place to go for a critically oriented, up-to-date, social science perspective. Students will appreciate his bibliographical guidance (pp.28–36), and may look up his complementing essays in *The Gospel of John in Cultural and Historical Perspective*. [*CBQ* 7/08; *JSNT-BL* 2008; *ExpTim* 3/08 (Keener); *RBL* 7/10; *HBT* 29.2; *Anvil* 25.3; *ExpTim* 9/10].

Ngewa, Samuel. 2003. A good-sized and helpful commentary, published by Evangelical Pub. House in Nairobi, and written by a professor at Nairobi Evangelical Graduate School of Theology.

✓ **O'Day, Gail.** ‡ (NewIB) 1995. The author teaches at Emory, and her commentary is bound up with Culpepper's work on Luke. I have not examined her work closely enough. [*JETS* 3/99]. Note that she has also co-authored a more accessible exposition with Susan E. Hylen in WestBC (2006) [*Interp* 1/08].

F Painter, John. ‡ (SRC). Earlier he wrote *The Quest for Messiah: The History, Literature, and Theology of the Johannine Community*, 2nd ed 1993. Compare Brown.

Peterson, Robert. *Getting to Know John's Gospel*, 1989. This is not a commentary, but a 135-page study guide on John which takes "a fresh look at its main ideas." Broken down into 13 chapters, this book would work quite well as a quarter-long Sunday School study. I'm guessing it fits a niche few other publications do.

F   Phillips, Richard D. (REC).

Pink, Arthur. 1945. If you are looking for a fat vol. of exposition, buy Boice.

Plummer. Alfred. 1882. Reprinted around 1985, but among the older English commentaries, Westcott's two are more useful.

Sanders, J.N., and B.A. Mastin. ‡ (BNTC) 1968. Never very good to begin with and now replaced by Lincoln.

✓   **Schnackenburg, R.** ‡ 3 Vols., ET 1968–82. This is surely one of the most valuable scholarly commentaries available and one of the best examples of the moderately critical scholarship coming out of the Catholic Church—a monument to it, really. Moody Smith says "Schnackenburg is for the European scene what Raymond Brown has been for the American." Just a note: Schnackenburg has, like Brown (compare his commentaries on the Gospel and the Epistles), become more critical with the passage of time. The third vol. does not compare favorably with the first. There is also a fourth vol. with essays to consult, but only if you read German (*IV: Ergänzende Auslegungen und Exkurse*, 1984). The author has other standout commentaries in ET on Ephesians and John's Epistles.

✓   Segovia, Fernando (ed). ‡ *"What Is John?" Readers and Readings of the Fourth Gospel*, 1996. A collection of 14 essays which deal primarily with the newer hermeneutical approaches and with important theological issues in John under discussion today. Also useful for students, especially in researching some of the older historical scholarly questions, is *The Johannine Writings*, edited by S.A. Porter and C.A. Evans (Sheffield, 1995). [*RelSRev* 1/99, 4/99].

Sloyan, Gerard. ‡ (I) 1988. Not of much account.

✓   Smalley, S.S. *John: Evangelist and Interpreter*, 1978, 2nd ed 1998. [*EvQ* 10/78; *JETS* 6/80]. Smalley also did the WBC vol. on the Johannine Epistles and is right at home in the Johannine literature. He takes a more critical view on issues such as authorship. He was supposedly doing the NIGTC, but see Bauckham above.

✓   **Smith, D. Moody, Jr.** ‡ (ANTC) 1999. This 400-page commentary, by a man C.K. Barrett calls "one of the highest authorities on St. John's Gospel," is not to be missed. Though not extensively footnoted and not evidencing much interaction with other scholars' work (especially in the area of narrative criticism), there is deep scholarship undergirding his clearly argued conclusions. [*CBQ* 1/04; *Them* Aut 01; *Interp* 4/04; *RelSRev* 10/02; *JTS* 10/01 (more critical)]. For a fine, critical, theological introduction to John's Gospel, see Smith's 1995 vol. in Cambridge's "NT Theology" series [*Interp* 1/97; *CRBR* 1996 (Carson)]. Yet more Smith works on this gospel are *John among the Gospels: The Relationship in Twentieth-Century Scholarship*, 2nd ed 2001 [*JTS* 10/03; *JBL* Sum 04; *RelSRev* 7/03]; and *The Fourth Gospel in Four Dimensions: Judaism and Jesus, the Gospels and Scripture* (2008) [*CBQ* 7/10].

✓   Stibbe, Mark W.G. ‡ (Read) 1993. [*CBQ* 10/94].

F   Swartley, Willard. (BCBC).

✓   Talbert, Charles H. ‡ *Reading John: A Literary and Theological Commentary on the Fourth Gospel and the Johannine Epistles*, 1992. This study complements his work on Luke. [*CRBR* 1994].

Tasker, R.V.G. (retired TNTC) 1960. Actually retains more value than some think. Packs a great deal of straightforward comment into 230pp. Still good for quick reference or to lend to a Sunday School teacher. See Kruse for the revised TNTC.

Tenney, Merrill C. *John: The Gospel of Belief*, 1948. This popularly-styled exposition, which was later joined by Tenney's weak EBC commentary of 1981, can now be honorably retired.

✓ Thatcher, Tom, and Stephen D. Moore, eds. ‡ *Anatomies of Narrative Criticism: The Past, Present, and Futures of the Fourth Gospel as Literature*, 2008. Compare this critical work with Culpepper above. [*JETS* 12/09; *JSNT-BL* 2010]. Also for students is Thatcher (ed), *What We Have Heard from the Beginning: The Past, Present, and Future of Johannine Studies* (Baylor, 2007) [*BBR* 19.3].

F Thompson, Marianne Meye. [*M*], (NTL). This should be well-done and conservative relative to the series. Earlier she wrote *The God of the Gospel of John*, 2001 [*Anvil* 19.4 (Smalley)].

F Wahlde, Urban C. von. ‡ (ECC). This is promised as a nearly 1000-page commentary in a three-vol. project. Look for *Vol. 1: Introduction, Analysis, and Reference* (768pp) and *Vol. 3: The Three Johannine Letters* (448pp).

Watt, Jan van der. ‡ *An Introduction to the Johannine Gospel and Letters*, 2007. [*JSNT-BL* 2009].

✓ Westcott, B.F. 1889, 1908. There are two different commentaries being reprinted: the earlier work treats the English text, and the later one exegetes the Greek. Both are classics still used by thousands of pastors.

Whitacre, Rodney. (IVPNT) 1999. I have not used it, but both Carson and Smalley commend it. [*CTJ* 11/00; *Anvil* 17.3 (Smalley)].

✓ **Witherington, Ben.** *John's Wisdom: A Commentary on the Fourth Gospel*, 1995. This amazingly prolific scholar has also published numerous other NT commentaries and a full-scale work on *Paul's Narrative Thought World*, 1994. All these books are worth consulting, but they needed better editing and proofreading. In this distinctive commentary, close attention is paid to various themes, especially "wisdom." I must say the author has not convinced me that wisdom is a strong motif in the fourth Gospel (my concordance shows that σοφια and σοφος are not even found in John). This vol. has numerous insights, though it is not one of Witherington's more successful efforts. See 1 Corinthians. [*EvQ* 1/98; *JETS* 3/99; *Interp* 7/97; *CBQ* 10/97].

Yarbrough, Robert. (Everyman's Bible Commentary) 1991. A popularly-styled, well researched commentary that has more substance to it than the other vols. in the series. Covers the Gospel and offers an annotated bibliography of the various commentaries in 216pp.

NOTE: See Don Carson's articles, "Selected Recent Studies of the Fourth Gospel," in *Them* 14.2., and "Recent Literature on the Fourth Gospel: Some Reflections," in *Them* 9.1. Other articles to help students understand where Johannine scholarship has come from are: S.S. Smalley, "Keeping up with Recent Studies; XII. St. John's Gospel," *ExpTim* 1/86; D. Moody Smith, "The Contribution of J. Louis Martyn to the Understanding of the Gospel of John," in *The Conversation Continues* (Nashville: Abingdon, 1990); Klaus Scholtissek, "Johannine Studies: A Survey of Recent Research with Special Regard to German Contributions," (part I) *CurBS* 6 (1998): 227–59, and (part II) *CurBS* 9 (2001): 277–305; and Paul N. Anderson, "Beyond the Shade of the Oak Tree: The Recent Growth of Johannine Studies," *ExpTim* 119.8 (2008): 365–73.

—ᴍ—

THE PARABLES OF JESUS

★ Blomberg, Craig. *Interpreting the Parables*, 1990. This superb contribution, I have argued for 20 years, should be required reading in a seminary's Gospels course.

For so long we had needed a solid, scholarly introduction to the parables from an evangelical standpoint. This is it. See Boucher below. [*Biblica* 72.4; *JETS* 6/92; *EvQ* 7/92; *Chm* 104.4]. Also excellent is Blomberg's *Preaching the Parables*, 2004 [*CTJ* 4/05; *Them* Win 05; *TJ* Spr 05; *Interp* 7/06].

★ Snodgrass, Klyne R. [*M*], *Stories with Intent: A Comprehensive Guide to the Parables of Jesus*, 2008. Snodgrass intended this tome (864pp) to be "a resource book for the parables," i.e., what the seminary professor with expertise in parables wanted to put in the hands of students. It is an up-to-date treatment from a evangelical fully abreast of critical scholarship—his earlier surveys of the field of research were "Modern Approaches to the Parables," in *The Face of New Testament Studies* (2004) and "From Allegorizing to Allegorizing" in Longenecker (ed), *The Challenge of Jesus' Parables* (2000). Especially appreciated by this student of the OT is the author's effort to place Jesus' parabolic teaching in the context of the Jewish prophetic tradition. Though seminarians will prefer Wenham and Blomberg (in that order) as introductory reading, this vol. is now the main reference text and replaces Hultgren as a recommended purchase. It is not too early to term this a "landmark study." [*ThTo* 1/09; *ExpTim* 5/08; *TJ* Spr 09; *RelSRev* 9/08; *Them* 9/08 (Wenham); *JETS* 6/09; *JTS* 4/09; *JSNT-BL* 2009; *BBR* 19.4 (Blomberg); *EQ* 7/09; *Interp* 4/09 (Hultgren); *RTR* 4/09; *RevExp* Fall 09].

★ Wenham, David. 1989. This vol., part of IVP's "The Jesus Library," is the best popular introduction to the parables on the market. This is a superb work by one of the editors of the *Gospel Perspectives* vols. [*EvQ* 4/91].

☆ Bailey, Kenneth E. *Poet & Peasant and Through Peasant Eyes*, 1976, 1980, Combined ed 1983. Argues capably that the parables can only be fully understood when studied in their cultural context. Our occidental canons of interpretation can be misleading. [*WTJ* Fall 78, Spr 81; *JETS* 3/82; *JBL* 96.4 (1977) and 102.2 (1983)].

✓ Boucher, Madeleine. ‡ *The Mysterious Parable: A Literary Study*, 1977. A much needed critique of the customary distinction—argued by Jülicher (1886–99), Jeremias, and Dodd—between parable (one point) and allegory (many points). Blomberg also presses this critique in a measured way. [*JBL* 12/78].

Bruce, A.B. *The Parabolic Teaching of Christ*, 1908. Still of some value, especially for those interested in the history of interpretation. Pastors should only use Bruce in conjunction with more recent works.

✓ Buttrick, David. ‡ *Speaking Parables: A Homiletic Guide*, 2000. This is no froth! Buttrick is a most thoughtful and skilled homiletician, and his guide will stimulate readers to approach the parables in fresh ways which capture the frequent surprises found in Jesus' stories.

Capon, Robert. ‡ *Kingdom, Grace, Judgment*, 2001. Bold exposition.

✓ Dodd, C.H. ‡ *The Parables of the Kingdom*, 1935. A classic in the field.

✓ Gowler, David B. ‡ *What Are They Saying about the Parables?* 2000. A good introduction to where parable research has been and where it may be headed. [*Interp* 7/01].

☆ Hultgren, Arland J. ‡ 2000. Considered by many a *tour de force*, published by Eerdmans. Within the 500pp he both introduces and comments upon the parables. There is good balance and judgment in his discussions. While he warns against a return to an allegorical method of interpretation, he also notes that parable and allegory were not sharply differentiated in Jesus' world. In the NT parables there are allegorical elements to which the reader should be alert. Hultgren provides a digest of much of the best recent work on parables and should be classed as conservatively critical. In the 6th and 7th eds. of this guide I recommended Hultgren for

✓ Hunter, A.M. [𝓜], *Interpreting the Parables*, 1960. A lucid, helpful introduction, but rather brief. See also his later work, *The Parables Then and Now*, 1971.

☆ Jeremias, Joachim. ‡ *The Parables of Jesus*, ET 1963. This has been the classic treatment of the genre. All modern discussion of the parables has had to begin with Dodd and Jeremias. Here you will find both strong criticism of allegorizing and a strong interest in possible reconstructions of the original parables (after they were corrupted or reworked by the early Church).

purchase, but I've given his place to Snodgrass. [*ExpTim* 5/01; *SwJT* Sum 01; *CBQ* 4/01; *EvQ* 7/03; *CTJ* 11/01; *JETS* 12/01; *TJ* Fall 02; *HBT* 6/02; *RelSRev* 1/02; *WTJ* Fall 01 (Poythress, more critical)].

✓ Johnston, Robert M., and Harvey K. McArthur. *They Also Taught in Parables*, 1990. A significant work published by Zondervan.

☆ Jones, Peter R. *Studying the Parables of Jesus*, 1999. Another good evangelical introduction.

✓ Kissinger, Warren S. ‡ *The Parables of Jesus: A History of Interpretation and Bibliography*, 1979. Those who are interested in an updated bibliography should see Hultgren and Snodgrass above, and also Blomberg's "The Parables of Jesus: Current Trends and Needs in Research," in *Studying the Historical Jesus: Evaluations of the State of Current Research* (Brill, 1994). [*JBL* 101.1 (1982)].

☆ Kistemaker, Simon J. 1980, rev. 2002. This is a worthwhile reference book for pastors which explains each parable in the Synoptics. A good expositional tool, which has been revised to become even better. The theology is solidly Reformed. [*WTJ* Spr 81; *RTR* 1/82; *JETS* 3/82].

Linnemann, E. ‡ ET 1966. A bright German scholar's treatment of the parables. It is of interest to note that this former student of Bultmann completely renounced her critical works—including this one—and converted to evangelicalism.

✓ Longenecker, Richard (ed). *The Challenge of Jesus' Parables*, 2000. [*EvQ* 4/02; *RTR* 8/02; *Them* Aut 02; *DenvJ*; *Anvil* 19.3].

✓ Marshall, I. Howard. *Eschatology and the Parables*, 1963.

✓ Michaels, J. Ramsey. *Servant and Son: Jesus in Parable and Gospel*, 1981.

✓ Perrin, Norman. ‡ *Jesus and the Language of the Kingdom*, 1976. Includes a survey of parable research since Jeremias together with his own critical views. Can be updated by checking the articles and vols. referenced with Kissinger above. You could also see *The NT and Its Modern Interpreters*, and Scott.

Schottroff, Luise. ‡ ET 2006. [*JSHJ* 5.2].

✓ Scott, Bernard Brandon. ‡ *Hear Then the Parable: A Commentary on the Parables of Jesus*, 1989. A 427-page work published by Fortress Press. Prior to Hultgren's appearance this was the fullest critical commentary on the parables, Scott's work exemplifies the highly skeptical work being done today, for example, in the "Jesus Seminar." E.g., he pays a lot of attention to the Gospel of Thomas. [*SJT* 93.2; *JBL* Win 91; *CBQ* 4/92; *Interp* 7/91].

✓ Shillington, V. George (ed). ‡ *Jesus and His Parables*, 1997.

✓ Sider, John W. *Interpreting the Parables*, 1995. [*JETS* 6/98].

☆ Stein, Robert H. *An Introduction to the Parables of Jesus*, 1981. An excellent conservative work. [*EvQ* 1/84; *WTJ* Spr 82; *JETS* 9/82].

Via, Dan O. ‡ 1967.

Westermann, Claus and Golka. ‡ *The Parables of Jesus in the Light of the OT*, 1990.

✓ Young, Brad H. ‡ *Jesus and His Jewish Parables: Rediscovering the Roots of Jesus' Teaching*, 1989 [*EvQ* 4/91]; *The Parables: Jewish Tradition and Christian Interpretation*, 1998. He studied under Flusser in Jerusalem.

—w—

ACTS

★ **Barrett, C.K.** ‡ (ICC–new series) 2 Vols., 1994–98. What excitement this entry generated! Most NT scholars expected this to be the crowning achievement of his long career, and it is. Takes a different view of Luke's historical accuracy than reverent evangelical scholarship, but it is less objectionable than the corrosive skepticism in Haenchen and Conzelmann, whom Barrett continually quotes in German. (And you have Latin citations from Bengel, St. Jerome, etc.) This two-vol. hb set is one of the most valuable and most detailed exegeses of the Greek text of Acts ever published in any language (1272pp)…and the most expensive. I used to say that scholarly pastors, and only scholarly ones, will want to take out a bank loan to buy this. Thankfully, ICC vols. are now being released in a less pricey pb binding. (CBD once offered the pb set on sale for $50. Now that is a deal! And it means Barrett can be recommended as a purchase [only to the most scholarly], whereas it previously could not be.) Unfortunately, as Kern writes, "because of its impenetrability to many, it may join that body of literature which is more often cited than read." As Walton notes, the weaknesses of the set are in the areas of narrative and theology: probably a big let-down for pastors. If you are a student ambitious to do a PhD in NT, you'll want this as a reference work. Be assured that Barrett will serve as a standard reference for decades to come. [*JETS* 3/98, 6/01; *NovT* 42.2; *RTR* 12/99; *RelSRev* 7/99; *Anvil* 18.3 (Walton)]. An abridgment in pb came out in 2002 [*Them* Aut 03; *RelSRev* 10/03]. The 95% of pastors who skip this, wanting something approaching homiletical questions, should especially look at Larkin, Fernando, Dennis Johnson, Hughes, and Green. If you are more interested in a narrative approach to exegesis, buy either L.T. Johnson or Witherington.

★ **Bock, Darrell.** (BECNT) 2007. This follows the two-vol. set on Luke's Gospel in the same series. Perhaps Bock will fill the role that Bruce's two works once did for evangelical pastors and students, in that Bock also has strong historical interests and takes a more conventional grammatico-historical approach to exegesis. I am not convinced that Bock quite lives up to the standards set in his Luke, which was over twice as lengthy. This is still a very valuable tool for students and pastors. I am already finding Bock and Peterson to be a well matched pair, with the latter providing more theology. One small complaint: more text criticism in a commentary on the Greek text would have been helpful. Ready yourself for evangelical exegesis of the Greek to become even richer and more sophisticated with Walton and Porter. [*JSNT-BL* 2008; *ExpTim* 1/09; *JETS* 12/08; *CBQ* 10/09 (Pervo, severe); *ExpTim* 11/09; *Interp* 7/09; *Anvil* 26.2; *EuroJTh* 18.1].

★ **Marshall, I. Howard.** (TNTC) 1980. Given a warm welcome when it first appeared, Marshall is excellent in almost every way—a little less conservative, though, than some would prefer. This is Marshall's expert sequel to his detailed commentary on Luke's Gospel. There is good balance between treating the history and theology of the text (see Bruce below) [*RTR* 5/81]. For an updated introduction to Acts and Acts scholarship, see Marshall's superb 1992 contribution to the "New Testament Guides" series, published by JSOT Press [*CRBR* 1993].

★ **Peterson, David G.** (Pillar) 2009. Certainly to be ranked as one of the best commentaries for the pastor seeking a robustly theological exposition, well-grounded in careful exegesis. The whole book is solid and balanced, and I make it my first pick. No important aspect of interpretation is given short shrift: textual criticism, philology and grammar, literary analysis, history, theology. The author teaches at Moore Theological College, the vibrant seminary of the Anglican diocese of Sydney, which has a strongly conservative and Reformed orientation. Previously he had been Principal of Oak Hill Theological College in London. At 790pp this is the fullest vol. in the series thus far; extensive interaction with many of the leading works on Luke-Acts dictated its large size (see the author index). But there were important works missed, such as Fitzmyer; for a critical review on this point, see Foster. Like Dennis Johnson, Peterson approaches Acts along redemptive historical lines. See also Marshall/Peterson below. [*Them* 11/09; *BBR* 20.1; *ExpTim* 6/10; *CBQ* 7/10; *DenvJ* 1/10; *JSNT-BL* 2010 (Foster)].

★ Stott, John R.W. *The Spirit, the Church and the World* (BST in hb) 1990. Certainly what you would expect from Stott: an excellent, clear, theological and pastoral exposition. This 400-page work is as valuable as any book can be to the preacher. [*CTJ* 4/91, 11/94; *Chm* 104.3 (1990)].

☆ Alexander, J.A. (GS) Third ed 1875. A lengthy, reverent exposition from one of old Princeton's greatest scholars; it needs to be supplemented by more recent scholarly commentaries.

F Alexander, Loveday. ‡ *Acts* (BNTC). The publisher's blurb wrongly indicated this would be a commentary on the two vols., Luke-Acts. I do not know if the announcement of the work as 456pp is also in error. The author is a classicist who has become an authority on Acts, and British academics tell me to expect a "cracker" (excellent/exciting piece of work). See her collected essays, *Acts in its Ancient Literary Context*, 2005 [*JETS* 6/07; *Interp* 1/09; *JR* 1/07; *RelSRev* 3/08; *BBR* 20.2; *EuroJTh* 18.1]. She is particularly interested in genre and makes a substantial contribution to scholarship in that area, arguing that Acts does not fit neatly the category of historiography, yet seems a factual account.

Arrington, French L. 1988. This is subtitled *A Pentecostal Commentary*.

☆ Boice, James Montgomery. *Acts: An Expositional Commentary*, 1997. About 450pp of fine, mature preaching.

☆ **Bruce, F.F.** *The Acts of the Apostles*, 1951/1952, rev. 3rd ed 1990. Vintage, judicious exegesis. Treats the Greek text and will assist the careful exegete—it is less help with exposition. Most preachers will prefer the NICNT entry below. I used to select this vol. on the Greek text for purchase instead, because the introduction is much fuller and better, and because the other suggested works I listed were so strong on exposition, but did not help as much with the original—textual criticism is important on Acts. (Note: the UBS *Textual Commentary on the Greek NT* by Bruce Metzger is also a big help.) The availability of Barrett's magisterial set in pb, the arrival of Bock, and the promise of Walton and Porter mean that Bruce on the Greek is not so valuable now. Reprinted by Wipf & Stock in 2000, but a bit hard to find. [*Evangel* Sum 92; *EvQ* 7/94].

☆ **Bruce, F.F.** (NICNT) 1954, rev. 1988. One could have wished in the revised edition for more attention to theology and the missionary aspect of the book, and Bruce admits this weakness (p.xvii). It is not enough to encourage readers to make up what is lacking by reading Marshall's *Luke: Historian and Theologian* (1970, rev. 1989). As a historical commentary, however, Bruce's NICNT is still among the best, most useful for the pastor. Having both commentaries—the scholarly vol. on the Greek text (see above) and the more expositional NICNT—is not a bad idea at all. Years ago the pastor looking for a single vol. to cover Acts might have preferred Longenecker or Marshall (as the more balanced works) to Bruce's NICNT. Do note that this work will eventually be replaced by Green's more literary commentary. Peterson has now displaced this on my list of purchase recommendations. [*EvQ* 7/90; *JTS* 4/90].

☆ Calvin, John. (CrossC) 1995. The commentary has been carefully distilled down.

☆ Calvin, John. *Sermons on the Acts of the Apostles: Chapters 1–7*, ET 2008. Banner of Truth has published several fat vols. of Calvin's sermons on different Bible books. See Samuel, Galatians and Ephesians. These nearly 700pp contain 44 sermons plus a fine introduction to Calvin the preacher. [*RTR* 8/09].

Chance, J. Bradley. ‡ (S&H) 2007. I have not yet used this book. [*Interp* 4/09].

F Cho, Youngmo. (NCCS). The author teaches at Asia Life University in South Korea.

✓ **Conzelmann, Hans.** ‡ (Herm) 1963, ET 1987. Along with Haenchen this has been a standard critical commentary. Takes a very skeptical view of the historical worth of the Book of Acts. German and English scholarship tend to go their separate ways on this point, though I have kept hoping works like Martin Hengel's *Acts and the History of Earliest Christianity* (ET 1979) might dampen German radicalism. Conzelmann is no longer as important a scholarly reference as it was when first published in ET. [*Them* 10/88]. See Pervo below.

✓ **Culy, Martin M., Mikeal C. Parsons.** *Acts: A Handbook on the Greek Text*, 2003. I have not used this book, but it has been recommended by some as a careful, thorough (579pp) guide to lexical, grammatical, and textual analysis of the book of Acts. Published by Baylor University Press. For a Parsons commentary on the English text, see below. [*EvQ* 10/07; *JSNT* 12/05; *RelSRev* 1/05; *ExpTim* 9/06].

✓ **Dunn, James D.G.** [*M*], (Narrative Commentaries) 1996. Originally published in the UK by Epworth, this well-written commentary (354pp) is published here by Trinity Press International. Gaventa has noted that, despite the series title, Dunn has less interest in matters literary and narratological. As one might expect from Dunn, there is a good measure of theology. Sadly, there are no indexes. If you keep in mind his own approach to Paul, this is a serviceable commentary for the pastor [*RelSRev* 10/98], but Dunn has not given us his best work here. For students the more important vol. to take account of, regarding Dunn's study of Acts and understanding of the early history of the Church (Easter to AD 70), is the enormous and engaging *Beginning from Jerusalem*, 2009 [*JETS* 3/10; *RTR* 4/10; *TJ* Spr 10; *Them* 4/10 (Barnett); *DenvJ* 1/10; *Interp* 7/10; *JSNT-BL* 2010].

F Evans, Craig A. (EEC).

Faw, Chalmer E. (BCBC) 1993.

☆ Fernando, Ajith. (NIVAC) 1998. This is a very well done exposition from a Sri Lankan church leader and can be compared with Stott. A number of preachers have spoken to me about the help Fernando has given them. There is a lot of heart and conviction here, but a little less in the way of careful, nuanced scholarship.

☆ **Fitzmyer, Joseph A.** ‡ (AB) 1998. This is a fitting companion to his commentary on Luke's Gospel—though not as thorough—and replaces the Munck vol. in AB. This big (824-page), moderately critical Catholic commentary is not quite as technical or full as Barrett, but is nearly as valuable. In reviewing AB and Barrett's ICC, one may also say, "Their discussion of issues of theological importance…is not as extensive as one might hope for" (*NT Abstracts*). That is a serious demerit from the pastor's perspective. Students can consult this more classically styled commentary for historical investigation, textual issues, and form-criticism. But for up-to-date literary/rhetorical analysis, see L.T. Johnson, Spencer, and Witherington. Fitzmyer has fairly traditional views on authorship and tentatively assigns an "intermediate date" of 80–85. I am glad to have such quality works as Barrett's and Fitzmyer's large-scale, technical commentaries on the Greek text of this, the largest book in the NT, which unfortunately has more than its share of text critical problems. [*Interp* 7/99; *CBQ* 7/00; *JBL* Spr 00; *NovT* 42.2; *Biblica* 76.3 (1995); *ThTo* 7/99; *SJT* 57.1 (Walton)].

✓ Foakes-Jackson, F.J., and Kirsopp Lake (eds). ‡ *The Beginnings of Christianity,* Part I: The Acts of the Apostles, 1920–33. "The monumental classic," according to Carson. Vols. 4 and 5 still see use today, the former being a commentary on Acts and the latter a vol. of additional notes and essays.

Gasque, W. Ward. *History of the Criticism of the Acts of the Apostles*, 1975. This excellent book is still valuable for advanced students working on a *Forschungsbericht*. For many years Gasque was under contract to write the NIGTC, in collaboration with the late Colin Hemer, who had considerable historical expertise.

✓ **Gaventa, Beverly.** ‡ (ANTC) 2003. There is nothing better than this and Barrett's abridgment for getting a concise critical exegesis of an Acts text. In more liberal Reformed circles, say at Princeton Seminary, this would probably be a recommended first stop for pastors, before they move on to expositional commentaries. She aimed to produce a dependable tool for ministry. One criticism here might be that Gaventa gives less attention to the historical-cultural context. She concentrates on Acts as the unfolding story of God's plan and actions in and through the Church. [*CBQ* 7/04; *ExpTim* 8/04; *RelSRev* 4/04; *EvQ* 1/07; *JETS* 3/05; *Interp* 7/05; *JSNT-BL* 2005].

F Green, Joel. (NICNT replacement). This will follow his work on Luke in this same series.

☆ Green, Michael. *Thirty Years that Changed the World: The Book of Acts for Today*, 2004. Excellent for pastors!

Hackett, Horatio B. 1851. This old 325-page commentary from a moderately Calvinistic perspective was reprinted by Kregel in 1992. Alexander is better.

✓ **Haenchen, Ernst.** ‡ ET 1971. A translation from the MeyerK series, Haenchen's has long been one of the most influential commentaries in the contemporary discussion of Acts. It is very demanding on the reader, highly theological, and radically critical in the neo-Bultmannian sense. This vol. disparages Luke as historian in order to focus upon the theological import of the story. Advanced students should wrestle with it, while evangelical pastors will choose to leave it alone. Becoming rather dated at this point. [*EvQ* 1/72, 4/78].

Hanson, R.P.C. ‡ (New Clarendon) 1967.

Harrison, E.F. *The Expanding Church*, 1976. A simply written but insightful exposition.

Hemer, Colin. *The Book of Acts in the Setting of Hellenistic History* (Eisenbrauns, 1989). An excellent piece of scholarship which challenged German skepticism regarding the reliability of Acts. How tragic that in 1987 this man with such promise died so suddenly (in his friend D.A. Carson's arms)!

F Holladay, Carl R. ‡ (NTL).

☆ Hughes, R. Kent. (PTW) 1996. About 350 pages. See under Mark.

✓ Jervell, J. ‡ *The Theology of the Acts of the Apostles* (Cambridge) 1996. This influential German scholar has stirred up much discussion with his proposal that Acts should be read as having a strongly Jewish character. (Note: He wrote a 1998 commentary replacing Haenchen in MeyerK.)

☆ Johnson, Dennis. *The Message of Acts in the History of Redemption*, 1997. Valuable because, though we have several redemptive-historical treatments of the Gospels and Paul's letters (e.g., Ridderbos), there's nothing quite like this on Acts. Johnson teaches at Westminster Seminary California and has also written on Revelation. This accessible work will be suggestive for pastors, but students will learn much, too. Published by P&R, the commentary is a corrective for those who are tempted to believe the Early Church's experience is the norm for today, too: Apostles, resurrections, prophetic revelations on a par with Scripture, etc. A smart purchase!

☆ **Johnson, Luke Timothy.** ‡ (SacPag) 1992. This is a continuation of Johnson's previous efforts in explaining Luke's Gospel. See Johnson under Luke. This commentary on Acts has been well received and is more oriented toward contemporary literary theory than others in this series. The scholarly pastor will be interested in purchasing this. I consider Johnson among the best critical commentaries on Acts over the last 20 years and the most interesting. Johnson can be innovative and independent-minded. On the negative side, he does not interact with much evangelical scholarship besides Bruce; there is not a single citation of Marshall or Longenecker. From a more conservative angle, Walton's WBC will offer an exacting literary reading of Acts. [*CBQ* 7/94; *CRBR* 1994].

Keddie, Gordon J. *You Are My Witnesses* (WCS) 1993.

✓ **Kee, Howard Clark.** ‡ *To Every Nation Under Heaven* (NT in Context) 1997. A well-written, accessible commentary by one of the leading NT scholars in the country. Superb on background. [*Interp* 1/99; *CBQ* 4/99].

F Keener, Craig. The report is that this will be published by Eerdmans and, like his massive commentaries on Matthew and John, will not be part of a series.

☆ Kistemaker, Simon J. (NTC) 1990. A massive tome of 1010pp. No disappointment here; I think this is one of the most valuable vols. in the series. Many preachers will gravitate toward this solidly Reformed work. You might take note of Longenecker's caveats, however. [*WTJ* Fall 93; *CTJ* 11/92].

Krodel, G.A. ‡ (Augsburg Commentary) 1986. Though a learned, full and accessible commentary, it takes a rather skeptical approach, which makes it less useful to evangelicals. [*JETS* 9/89; *CRBR* 1988].

F Kurz, William S. ‡ (CCSS).

☆ **Larkin, William.** (IVPNT) 1995. Having heard Larkin lecture, I know this vol. will be helpful to preachers who wish to understand the missionary outreach of the Early Church and the message of Acts. Appropriately this is one of the largest vols. in the series at over 400pp. The nice balance between exegesis and theological exposition here makes this a good first purchase for pastors. Great insight. [*RelSRev* 4/97].

☆ Lloyd-Jones, D. Martyn. *Authentic Christianity: Studies in the Book of Acts*, 2000–. So far I have seen six vols. published on Acts 1–8. [*RTR* 4/07].

Longenecker, Richard. (EBC) 1981. Along with Carson's Matthew, the very best in the series on the NT. Has 370 packed pages of sagacious exegesis and exposition. Once bound with Tenney's not so useful work on John's Gospel, Longenecker since 1995 was also published in pb separate from John and was in the running with Marshall to be the "best buy" on Acts for the pastor. The student will find it a bit dated. Longenecker lost value with the appearance of the recent heavyweight commentaries by Barrett and Fitzmyer, and with the publication of evangelical exegeses by Bock, Peterson, Larkin, Polhill, Kistemaker, Williams, and Witherington. I am, therefore, glad to see the EBCR. [*EvQ* 7/83; *JETS* 6/81].

☆ **Longenecker, Richard.** (EBCR) 2007. A welcome revision of 437pp, though I wish the update were more thorough and that we were given more citations of the recent literature (e.g., in the introduction). Some of the revisions are excisions of his discussion of contemporary relevance; cf. p.339 (1981) and p.816 (2007).

Lüdemann, G. ‡ *Early Christianity According to the Traditions in Acts*, ET 1989. The research is in line with recent German scholarship and mainly treats older literary questions about the alleged growth of apostolic traditions.

MacArthur, John. 2 Vols., 1994–96. See Matthew for a review of the series.

✓ Malina, Bruce J., and John J. Pilch. *Social Science Commentary on the Book of Acts*, 2008. I admit to being baffled. Malina/Pilch strangely view the early Christian mission as producing a *Heidenrein* ("heathen"-free) community where all have become "Judean" (Jewish). [*CBQ* 1/09; *JSNT-BL* 2010].

✓ Marshall, I. Howard, and David Peterson (eds). *Witness to the Gospel: The Theology of Acts*, 1993. Not a commentary, but collected essays meant to complement the Eerdmans multi-vol. series, "The Book of Acts in Its First-Century Setting." A very important book! [*Interp* 4/00; *RTR* 8/99; *RelSRev* 4/99; *Scripture Bulletin* 1/99].

✓ Martin, Francis (ed). (ACCS) 2006. [*JSNT-BL* 2007; *EuroJTh* 18.1].

Munck, Johannes. ‡ (retired AB) 1967. Brief and disappointing in light of his past works. Munck was a more conservative voice among continental critics. See Fitzmyer above.

Neil, William. ‡ (NCB) 1973, rev. 1981. Good but undistinguished.

Newman, B.M., and E.A. Nida. (UBS) 1972.

Parsons, Mikeal C. ‡ (Paideia) 2008. The approach here is mainly narrative criticism (rhetorical and compositional strategies are in focus). The few historical judgments he makes tend to be in line with Pervo (with whom he coauthored the 1993 book *Rethinking the Unity of Luke and Acts*). E.g., Parsons believes Acts dates to the first two decades of the 2nd century, ca. AD 110, perhaps some 20 years after the Gospel. [*CBQ* 7/09; *ExpTim* 11/09; *RelSRev* 9/09; *JSNT-BL* 2010].

Pelikan, Jaroslav. ‡ (Brazos) 2006. This is the inaugural vol. in Brazos, and I'm not sure what it means for the future of the series. On the one hand, Pelikan, a preeminent church historian, is an amazingly learned guide for readers interested to "place Acts in theological conversation with centuries of Christian creeds and other rules of faith" (Weaver). On the other, the commentary is "as much topic-driven as text-driven" and is deficient as an exegetical help. Some may wish to turn to this after all the exegesis is done. [*CTJ* 11/06; *CBQ* 4/08; *JETS* 12/06; *JSNT-BL* 2007; *ExpTim* 12/07].

F Penner, T. (RRA).

✓ **Pervo, Richard I.** ‡ (Herm) 2009. This rigorous 800-page technical commentary (100pp of bibliography and indexes) is added to the series alongside Conzelmann. Pervo has proposed that Acts fits into the genré of historical novel (*Profit with Delight: the Literary Genre of the Acts of the Apostles*, 1987) and dates to ca. 110–120 (*Dating Acts*, 2006 [*CBQ* 10/07]). While students will make use of this expensive reference work in libraries, few pastors will invest their time and money here. The author presents "a wealth of insights into the literary context of Acts. Techniques of rhetoric, narration and characterization are emphasized" (Elliott). What quickly comes across to a conservative reader is that "Pervo is extremely sceptical about the historical worth of Acts" (Edwards). [*JETS* 6/09 (Keener); *ExpTim* 9/09; *NovT* 52.3 (Elliott); *BBR* 20.2 (Schnabel); *JSNT-BL* 2010 (Edwards)]. Any wanting a summary of his interpretation may look up *The Mystery of Acts: Unravelling Its Story*, 2008 [*CBQ* 10/09].

Phillips, Thomas E. (ed). ‡ *Contemporary Studies in Acts*, 2009. This vol. was produced by the SBL Acts section. [*JSNT-BL* 2010].

☆ **Polhill, John B.** (NAC) 1992. A full and informed exposition (550pp), written on a level easily understood by the educated layman. Competes with Blomberg on

Matthew and Stein on Luke as the best in the NT series thus far. Well worth buying. This is also a commentary for students; Fitzmyer surprisingly quotes it more than Pesch, Roloff, or Bruce. [*EvQ* 1/94; *ThTo* 10/93; *CRBR* 1994; *Biblica* 75.4].

F Porter, Stanley E. (NIGTC). The author is a world-recognized Greek grammarian, who helped develop and refine "verbal aspect theory." In preparation for the commentary, he has many journal articles and *The Paul of Acts: Essays in Literary Criticism, Rhetoric and Theology*, 1999 [*JSNT* 76].

✓ Rackham, R.B. (Westminster) 1901, 5th ed 1910. This commentary is "written from a 'high' Episcopalian viewpoint" (Martin), has verve, and discusses the message of the text from a number of angles. Because Rackham shows an interest in matters ecclesial, I count this a useful work for evangelical preachers today—too many of whom have a lack of serious interest in ecclesiology. Look for it in the secondhand bookstores; I have seen it in quite a few. [*JETS* 6/79].

F Schnabel, Eckhard J. (ZEC). What adds interest here is the author's extraordinary research already published in two books, *Early Christian Mission*, and now *Paul the Missionary: Realities, Strategies, and Methods*.

✓ **Spencer, F. Scott.** ‡ (Read) 1997, 2nd ed 2004. This sparkling, fresh, literary interpretation is a more significant contribution than its size might indicate. For students. Spencer previously did excellent work on the character of Philip in the Acts narrative. The 2nd edition, with the body of the commentary left unchanged, was published by Hendrickson. [*Interp* 4/99, 7/05; *CBQ* 4/99; *CTJ* 11/07; *EvQ* 10/07; *Chm* Aut 06; *RTR* 12/05; *RelSRev* 1/06]. See under Luke for his IBT vol. on Luke–Acts.

✓ **Talbert, Charles.** ‡ *Reading Acts* (RNT) 1997, rev. 2005. Like Spencer from the same year, Talbert focuses upon literary features as pointers to theology.

✓ Tannehill, Robert. ‡ *The Narrative Unity of Luke-Acts, A Literary Interpretation*, 2 Vols., 1990–91. See under Luke. [*CBQ* 4/92].

F Thomas, Derek W.H. (REC).
Walaskay, Paul W. ‡ (WestBC) 1998. [*RelSRev* 7/99; *Interp* 7/02].

☆ **Wall, Robert W**. (NewIB) 2002. This would be one of the more conservative contributions to the NewIB project in the NT section. Wall is an able scholar and is known for his interest in final-form exegetical methods, such as Canonical Criticism. He was able to build upon the mountain of recent research in AB, ICC, SacPag, etc. See Wall's other commentaries on Colossians, James, and Revelation.

☆ **Walton, Steve.** (WBC) 2 Vols., 2012–? Ignore the announcements for 2008, then 2009, etc. The author told me he hopes the first vol. will appear in 2012. Earlier, Scott Bartchy and then Joel Green were said to have the contract. I expect this commentary and Porter's, alongside Peterson and Bock, to set a new standard for evangelical exegesis of Acts. Note that Walton's and Green's interests in narrative criticism are similar. I look forward to Walton's exegesis of the Greek text and anticipate that his Reformed theological interpretation will be a big plus, too.

F Weatherley, J. (THC). There is a conflicting that Bauckham has the contract.

✓ **Williams, C.S.C.** ‡ (BNTC) 1957, rev. 1969. A once useful but now dated work, with the more moderate historical perspective of the British critics. The pastor with Bruce, Longenecker or Marshall wouldn't have much use for it, but students could consult it for papers.

☆ **Williams, David John.** (NIBC) 1990. Quite full at 493pp, worth consulting, and reasonably priced. Williams' work was given a warm review by Colin Hemer [*JETS* 3/87], when it appeared in GNC.

Willimon, William. ‡ (I) 1988. Rather skimpy compared with other works on Acts. Good for the communicator from a mildly critical angle, but not a major interpretive work.

✓ Winter, Bruce W., *et al. The Book of Acts in Its First Century Setting*, 1993–. This multi-vol. series from Eerdmans is of the highest scholarly caliber, is mildly critical in approach, and of great use, even indispensable, to the serious student. Five vols. are out, and we await one more: *The Book of Acts in Its Theological Setting.* See also the Marshall-Peterson vol. below. [*EvQ* 7/97; *JETS* 12/96, 9/97, 6/99; *CTJ* 11/96; *CBQ* 4/97, 10/97, 4/99; *Presb* Spr 96; *JSNT* 71].

☆ **Witherington, Ben.** 1997. Another of this prolific evangelical's "socio-rhetorical" commentaries. Carson thinks the author did some of his best work here. See my comments under 1 Corinthians. I used to include this among the purchases because his approach is quite different from my other suggestions and yields some key insights (a goodly number of which have now been picked up by Peterson). By the way, Johnson and Spencer also provide fine works with literary/rhetorical savvy. Expect the forthcoming NICNT by Green and WBC by Walton also to focus on narrative and the social context. Note: This nearly 900-page commentary is very comprehensive, exploring more side roads than you'll probably care to. If you love to read and have found Witherington's works stimulating, then do move this up to the top-pick category. [*JBL* Sum 99; *Biblica* 81.1 (2000); *Interp* 4/99; *CBQ* 4/99; *AsTJ* Fall 98 (Marshall)].

Wright, Tom (N.T.). *Acts for Everyone*, 2 Vols., 2008. A sparkling exposition of 480pp. [*ExpTim* 4/09; *JSNT-BL* 2009].

NOTES: (1) See I.H. Marshall's "The Present State of Lucan Studies," in *Them* 1/89 and "Recent Commentaries on the Acts of the Apostles" by Ward Gasque in *Them* 10/88. (2) John Ziesler's "Which Is the Best Commentary? V. Acts of the Apostles," *ExpTim*, 12/86. (3) Students are helped by two review-essays. One by Patrick Spencer considers a specific recent scholarly controversy, "The Unity of Luke-Acts," *CBR* 5.3 (2007): 341–66. The other is a more comprehensive review: Todd Penner, "Madness in the Method? The Acts of the Apostles in Current Study," *CBR* 2.2 (2004): 223–93. (4) Saving the briefest (and best?) for last, I urge students to read I. Howard Marshall, "Acts in Current Study," *ExpTim* 115.2 (2003): 49–52.

PAULINE STUDIES

★ Bruce, F.F. *Paul: Apostle of the Heart Set Free*, 1977. Has a well deserved reputation as a rich, trustworthy overview of Paul as a man, his travels, and his theology. Bruce wrote commentaries on just about every epistle of Paul, so this book is well informed, to put it mildly. Note: some Reformed interpreters (e.g., George Knight) disagree with a certain Antinomianism they detect in Bruce's review of Paul's theology. For a more recent book accomplishing many of Bruce's same aims, see Polhill below. We are still waiting, really, for Bruce's replacement. [*RTR* 5/78; *EvQ* 10/78; *ThTo* 35.3].

★ Gaffin, Richard B. *Resurrection and Redemption: A Study in Paul's Soteriology*, 2nd ed. 1987. Formerly titled, *The Centrality of the Resurrection* (1978). I cannot think of any more valuable 125pp of text on Paul's theology. The student or pastor who digests this will gain an exciting new perspective on Paul's theology and a new appreciation for the truth that, in union with Christ, His resurrection is ours. This study can radically change the way you preach from Paul's letters. [*JETS* 12/80].

Similarly useful is Gaffin's *By Faith, Not by Sight: Paul and the Order of Salvation* (Paternoster, 2006), which discusses theology's *ordo salutis* and the doctrine of union with Christ, seen as the dominant, organizing truth in Paul's soteriology.

★ Hawthorne, G., R.P. Martin and D. Reid (eds). *Dictionary of Paul and His Letters*, 1993. [*JETS* 12/96; *Them* 1/95].

★ Ridderbos, Herman. *Paul: An Outline of His Theology*, ET 1975. Though the translation makes for tough going in places, this work has a treasure of insights into Pauline doctrine. His emphasis on *historia salutis* (history of salvation), which Gaffin picks up, was one of my most fascinating discoveries in seminary. Although he overstates his case at points (e.g., making Union with Christ almost always redemptive-historical and hardly ever mystical), Ridderbos is a needed corrective for those of us who were trained to think primarily in terms of *ordo salutis* (the order or method by which Christ's saving work is applied to us), which is our heritage from the Puritans. Do wrestle with this profound work, reprinted in pb. [*EvQ* 1/78; *ExpTim* 2/78; *JSNT* 71].

★ Schreiner, Thomas R. *Paul, Apostle of God's Glory in Christ*, 2001. This evangelical Pauline theology reveals that Carson helped change Schreiner's mind on justification since the publication of *Romans* in BECNT. Well worth buying as an introductory study. Those outside the Reformed tradition do not value this exposition of Paul's theology as highly. [*Them* Aut 02; *JETS* 12/02; *Chm* Aut 02; *RelSRev* 4/07; *DenvJ*].

★ Seifrid, Mark. *Christ Our Righteousness: Paul's Theology of Justification*, 2000. This IVP issue on a controversial topic is highly recommended to students for purchase, building as it does on his earlier, expensive (Brill), high-level discussion in *Justification by Faith*, 1992. [*Chm* Spr 01].

★ Thielman, Frank. *Paul and the Law: A Contextual Approach*, 1994. [*BSac* 4/96; *TJ* Spr 95]. I doubt anyone in evangelicalism knows this topic better than Thielman, with his Duke dissertation, *From Plight to Solution: A Jewish Framework for Understanding Paul's View of the Law in Galatians and Romans*, (Brill, 1989), reviewed in *NovT* 35.2. His accessible study of the NT use of νομος was published as *The Law and the New Testament*, 1999 [*ExpTim* 6/00]. Other notable evangelical discussions of this hot topic are Kruse, Schreiner, Westerholm, and especially Carson-O'Brien-Seifrid.

Barclay, John M.G., and Simon J. Gathercole (eds). ‡ *Divine and Human Agency in Paul and His Cultural Environment*, 2008. [*JSNT-BL* 2009; *ExpTim* 11/09].

✓ Barrett, C.K. ‡ *Essays on Paul*, 1982. [*EvQ* 1/84]. More recent are: *Paul: An Introduction to His Thought*, 1994 [*JETS* 12/96; *CTJ* 4/96], and *On Paul: Essays on His Life, Work and Influence in the Early Church*, 2003 [*JSNT-BL* 2005].

Bassler, Jouette. ‡ *Navigating Paul: An Introduction to Key Theological Concepts*, 2007. This book by a well-regarded Pauline scholar would have been so much better, had she interacted with conservative scholarship on topics such as Union with Christ.

✓ Becker, Jürgen. ‡ *Paul, Apostle to the Gentiles*, ET 1993. [*ExpTim* 1/94; *Interp* 4/95].

✓ Beker, J. Christiaan. ‡ *Paul the Apostle: The Triumph of God in Life and Thought*, 1980. Very influential in its stress on apocalyptic elements in Paul. [*JBL* 101.3 (1982)]. See also his shorter, more recent books: *Paul's Apocalyptic Gospel* (1982); *The Triumph of God: The Essence of Paul's Thought* (1990); and *Heirs of Paul: Paul's Legacy in the New Testament and in the Church Today* (1991) which mainly deals with the so-called Deutero-Pauline Corpus.

Bird, Michael F. *The Saving Righteousness of God: Studies on Paul, Justification and the New Perspective*, 2006. The author "attempts to reclaim much of Reformed theology in the face of the challenge of the New Perspective" (Foster), viewing those two as compatible to a degree. He seeks a *via media*. [*ExpTim* 1/08; *RelSRev* 9/08; *JETS* 3/09; *EuroJTh* 17.1]. See also his winsome, brief (192-page) *Introducing Paul* (IVP, 2008) [*JETS* 6/10].

Bornkamm, Gunter. ‡ *Paul*, ET 1971. Highly critical biography. [*JBL* 90.4 (1971)].

Campbell, Douglas A. ‡ *The Deliverance of God: An Apocalyptic Rereading of Justification in Paul*, 2009. Pushes a more radical revisionism of Pauline interpretation than the New Perspective. He wants to dispose entirely of a legal framework for understanding justification. This of course requires some gymnastics, and one move—among many in these 1248pp—is to propose that Rom 1:18–32 is actually the argument of a false teacher which Paul subsequently destroys. [*JSNT-BL* 2010; *JETS* 3/10 (Moo); *Them* 7/10 (Seifrid); *EC* 5/10 (Watson)].

Capes, D.B. *Old Testament Yahweh Texts in Paul's Christology*, 1992.

✓ Carson, D.A., Peter O'Brien, and Mark Seifrid (eds). *Justification and Variegated Nomism*, 2 Vols., 2001–04. Both conservatives and critical scholars cooperate here to produce an incredibly deep and valuable resource for weighing the strengths and weaknesses of E.P. Sanders' interpretation of 1st-century Palestinian Judaism as "covenantal nomism," as well as other brands of the New Perspective. I call this the most important response. [*Them* Spr 03, 1/06; *JETS* 3/03; *ExpTim* 6/02; *CBQ* 1/03, 10/05; *TJ* Spr 04 (Dunn), Fall 05; *BBR* 19.1 (2009, Beale); *JETS* 12/05; *TJ* Spr 08 (Beale); *BibInt* 13.1; *DenvJ* 1/02 (Blomberg)].

✓ Childs, Brevard S. *The Church's Guide for Reading Paul: The Canonical Shaping of the Pauline Corpus*, 2008. This work furnishes NT scholars with a fresh, outsider's perspective on their Pauline interpretation and with further evidence (as Childs' last book) of the author's extraordinary learning even outside his speciality. [*BTB* 40.1 (negative); *RelSRev* 36.2; *HBT* 31.2 (positive); *Anvil* 26.3–4 (Briggs); *Them* 11/09].

Conybeare, W.J., and J.S. Howson. *The Life and Epistles of St. Paul*, 1892. A two-vol. work that continues to be reprinted but deserves retirement.

✓ Cousar, Charles B. ‡ *The Letters of Paul*, 1996. From the Abingdon IBT series. Another fine critical introduction, more centered on theology, is J.A. Ziesler's *Pauline Christianity*, rev. ed (OUP, 1990).

✓ Das, A. Andrew. ‡ *Paul, the Law, and the Covenant*, 2001. [*Them* Sum 03; *SwJT* Fall 03; *RTR* 4/04 (O'Brien); *TJ* Fall 04 (Hafemann)]. Added to this is *Paul and the Jews*, 2003 [*RTR* 4/05; *Them* Sum 05; *Chm* Sum 06].

✓ Davies, W.D. ‡ *Paul and Rabbinic Judaism*, 1948, 1955, 1980. This work did much to spark today's interest in Paul's debt to, and later conflict with, his Rabbinic heritage. See also his *Jewish and Pauline Studies* (1984).

Donaldson, Terence. *Paul and the Gentiles: Remapping the Apostle's Convictional World*, 1997. Particularly helpful for tracing the development of the New Perspective from Stendahl's essay, "The Apostle Paul and the Introspective Conscience of the West," to Dunn and beyond.

✓ Dunn, James D.G. ‡ *The Theology of Paul the Apostle*, 1998. A *magnum opus* (737pp + indexes), which offers "a fresh, comprehensive treatment of the apostle's theology" (Weima). In its "freshness," however, Dunn's *Theology* reinterprets or denies many evangelical doctrines found in Paul: original sin, substitutionary atonement, etc. See my comments under Romans and Galatians. Dunn emphasizes Paul's Jewish background in making sense of his life and theology. The advanced student should consider buying this influential work. [*JETS* 6/01; *SJT* 53.3 (2000); *JTS* 4/99;

ThTo 10/99; *TJ* Spr 99; *CTJ* 11/99; *Interp* 1/99; *CBQ* 1/99; *RTR* 4/99; *AsTJ* Fall 99; *RelSRev* 4/99; *Scripture Bulletin* 1/99; *JSNT* 71; *EvQ* 4/02]. On the specific topic of the New Perspective, see the convenient collection of Dunn's work (1983–2004) in *The New Perspective on Paul: Collected Essays*, 2005, rev. 2008 [*Them* 4/06; *WTJ* Spr 09; *JSNT-BL* 2006; *RelSRev* 12/08; *JETS* 3/09; *EuroJTh* 15.2]. Despite his revisionism, Dunn still believes "Justification by faith alone needs to be reasserted as strongly as ever it was by Paul or by Augustine or by Luther" (p.87).

✓ Dunn, James D.G. (ed). ‡ *Paul and the Mosaic Law*, 1996, ET 2001. A collection of papers read at the 1994 Durham–Tübingen Research Symposium on Earliest Christianity and Judaism. The contributors are all stellar NT scholars like Hengel, Longenecker, Stanton, Wright, Hays, and Räisänen. [*RelSRev* 1/98, 1/03; *Them* Aut 01].

✓ Dunn, James D.G. (ed). ‡ *The Cambridge Companion to St. Paul*, 2003. For a quick introduction to current critical scholarship on Paul, I would turn here [*EvQ* 7/05; *Anvil* 22.1; *DenvJ* 1/04], to Hooker, *Paul: A Short Introduction* (2003) [*Evangel* Sum 04 (Marshall); *Anvil* 20.4], or to Thiselton, *The Living Paul* (2009) [*DenvJ* 4/10; *ExpTim* 9/10].

✓ Ellis, E.E. Paul's *Use of the Old Testament*, 1957. A work of lasting significance. See also his *Pauline Theology: Ministry and Society* (1989) [*WTJ* Fall 91; *CRBR* 1991].

✓ Fee, Gordon. *God's Empowering Presence: The Holy Spirit in the Letters of Paul*, 1994. A great book. This prolific Pauline scholar has produced a massive study (960pp) on a somewhat neglected topic. There is a definite, but moderate, Pentecostal slant to this theological work, but in saying that I do not mean to take away from its value. Some of Fee's views (e.g., Spirit-baptism at conversion), if adopted more broadly within his own tradition, could help heal some of the alienation between Pentecostals/Charismatics and other evangelicals. The more general conclusions of the book are very helpful and biblical, because drawn through careful exegesis. [*CBQ* 10/95; *RTR* 9/95; *JETS* 9/97; *JBL* Spr 97; *Interp* 7/97; *Chm* 111.1 (1997)].

☆ Fee, Gordon. *Pauline Christology: An Exegetical-Theological Study*, 2007. It is little short of thrilling to see a high Christology developed in a book-by-book study of this quality and thoroughness. That being said, many of us will strongly disagree with his contention that Paul does not use θεός to refer to Christ; cf. Murray Harris' exegesis of Rom 9:5 and Titus 2:13 in *Jesus as God* (1992). On other key points, he rejects a "wisdom Christology" and unfortunately misrepresents complementarian arguments regarding the Son's eternal functional subordination (better "submission," according to Letham). [*RTR* 12/08; *BBR* 19.1; *CBQ* 10/07; *JETS* 6/08; *TJ* Fall 08; *Interp* 1/09 (Martin); *WTJ* Spr 09; *ExpTim* 4/08; *RelSRev* 9/08; *JSNT-BL* 2009; *SBET* Spr 09].

✓ Fitzmyer, Joseph A. ‡ *Paul and His Theology*, 2nd ed 1989. Goes hand in hand with his commentary on Romans. [*JETS* 6/92; *EvQ* 7/89].

✓ Francis, Fred O., and J. Paul Sampley. ‡ *Pauline Parallels*, 2nd ed 1984. This vol. is meant to aid students in recognizing the repetition of themes and images in the Pauline corpus. (No Pastorals here.) See Wilson below.

✓ Furnish, Victor Paul. ‡ *Theology and Ethics in Paul*, 1968, (NTL) 2009. A standard work on the issue of Pauline ethics. More recent from Furnish is *The Moral Teaching of Paul: Selected Issues* (1979, 3rd ed 2009) [*JSNT-BL* 2010; *ExpTim* 9/10]. On the same subject, see also *Understanding Paul's Ethics*, edited by Brian Rosner (1995); *Theology and Ethics in Paul and His Interpreters: Essays in Honor of Victor Paul Furnish*, edited by E.H. Lovering and J.L. Sumney (1996); and Nijay Gupta, "The Theo-Logic of Paul's Ethics in Recent Research," *CBR* 7.3 (2009): 336–61. Recommended for NT ethics more generally are Richard Hays' widely-read vol., *The Moral Vision of the NT* (1996), and Richard Burridge on *Imitating*

Jesus: An Inclusive Approach to NT Ethics (2007) [*JSNT-BL* 2009; *SJT* 63.3 (a review discussion); *SBET* Spr 09].

F   Furnish, Victor Paul. ‡ *Pauline Theology* (NTL).

✓   Gorman, Michael J. ‡ *Apostle of the Crucified Lord*, 2004. A full (600-page), accessible, well done study of Paul, focused mainly on theology, published by Eerdmans. Call this a conservatively critical, content-oriented survey. [*Them* Aut 04; *Interp* 7/04; *CTJ* 11/04; *RTR* 4/05; *JSNT-BL* 2005; *SJT* 59.4; *Evangel* Spr 05 (Marshall); *Anvil* 21.3; *DenvJ* 6/04]. Also by Gorman is *Cruciformity: Paul's Narrative Spirituality of the Cross*, 2001.

Harink, Douglas. [𝓜], *Paul among the Postliberals*, 2003. Much discussed.

✓   Hays, Richard B. ‡ *Echoes of Scripture in the Letters of Paul*, 1989. One of my favorite intertextual studies on any portion of Scripture. The follow-up book, *The Conversion of the Imagination: Paul as an Interpreter of Israel's Scripture* (2005), is also very stimulating [*RTR* 12/05; *JETS* 3/07; *Them* 4/06; *JSNT-BL* 2006; *NovT* 49.3; *Evangel* Spr 07].

✓   Hengel, Martin, and Roland Deines. ‡ *The Pre-Christian Paul*, ET 1991. More conservatively critical. Later comes Hengel and Schwemer, *Paul between Damascus and Antioch* (1997).

✓   Hooker, M.D., and S.G. Wilson (eds). ‡ *Paul and Paulinism*, 1982. This *Festschrift* for C. K. Barrett has a wealth of essays.

✓   Horsley, Richard A. (ed). ‡ *Paul and Empire: Religion and Power in Roman Empirial Society*, 1997; *Paul and Politics: Ekklesia, Israel, Imperium, Interpretation: Essays in Honor of Krister Stendahl*, 2000. Helpful for understanding the newer political readings of Paul

Hunter, A.M. [𝓜], *Paul and His Predecessors*, 1961. Also worth noting is Hunter's *The Gospel According to St. Paul*, 1967.

✓   Käsemann, E. ‡ *Perspectives on Paul*, ET 1971. Advanced students will find this brilliant, most provocative; the author builds on Schweitzer and launched what Harink calls the "Apocalyptic Perspective" on Paul, that Beker, Martyn, and Hays (to some degree) develop.

✓   Kim, Seyoon. *The Origin of Paul's Gospel*, 1981, 2ⁿᵈ ed 2002. To characterize this work as a mere restatement or reworking of Machen would be unfair. Though pursuing the same questions and coming to much the same conclusions, this work stands in its own right as an immensely learned and valuable monograph. The best book on the subject. [*EvQ*, 7/82; *JBL*, 103.1 (1984)]. Kim critically addresses the Sanders and Dunn theses in *Paul and the New Perspective*, 2001 [*JTS* 4/04 (Dunn); *RTR* 12/02; *Them* Sum 03; *CTJ* 4/03; *JETS* 3/03; *JBL* Spr 03; *Interp* 4/03; *ExpTim* 8/03; *EvQ* 7/05; *BibInt* 13.1; *DenvJ* 1/02; *Anvil* 20.3].

☆   Kruse, Colin G. *Paul, The Law, and Justification*, 1997. [*JETS* 9/99; *RTR* 8/98].

✓   Longenecker, Bruce W. (ed). *Narrative Dynamics in Paul: A Critical Assessment*, 2002. An important and high-level discussion, no matter what you think about the value of examining narrative aspects of Paul's thought. Superb! [*ExpTim* 10/04; *Evangel* Spr 05].

✓   Longenecker, R.N. *Paul, Apostle of Liberty*, 1976. This prolific scholar at McMaster in Ontario has other works on Paul, including his collected *Studies in Paul: Exegetical and Theological*, 2004 [*ExpTim* 12/06; *BSac* 1/09]. Another fine vol. of essays edited by Longenecker is *The Road from Damascus: The Impact of Paul's Conversion on His Life, Thought and Ministry*, 1997 [*DenvJ*].

Machen, J. Gresham. *The Origin of Paul's Religion*, 1921. Conservative classic.

McRay, John. *Paul: His Life and Teaching*, 2003. [*Them* Aut 04; *JETS* 9/04; *CTJ* 11/04; *RelSRev* 1/05; *DenvJ* (negative)].

✓ Malina, Bruce J., and Jerome H. Neyrey. ‡ *Portraits of Paul*, 1996. [*JETS* 6/99].

✓ Malina, Bruce J., and John J. Pilch. ‡ *Social-Science Commentary on the Letters of Paul*, 2006. [*Interp* 10/06; *SwJT* Fall 05; *JSNT-BL* 2007; *BTB* Sum 07; *Them* 5/08].

☆ Marshall, I. Howard, Stephen Travis, and Ian Paul. *Exploring the NT, Vol 2: The Letters and Revelation*, 2002. An attractive survey from Britain with much learning behind it. [*Evangel* Sum 04].

✓ Martin, Ralph P. [*M*], *Reconciliation: A Study of Paul's Theology*, 1981.

✓ Martyn, J. Louis. ‡ *Theological Issues in the Letters of Paul*, 1997. [*JTS* 4/99; *RelSRev* 4/00; *ThTo* 1/99; *CBQ* 10/98]. See also his recent work on Galatians.

✓ Meeks, W.A. ‡ *The First Urban Christians, The Social World of the Apostle Paul*, 1983.

✓ Moyise, Steve. [*M*], *Paul and Scripture: Studying the NT Use of the OT*, 2010. An expert in the burgeoning field gives valuable help to students (160pp), taking them much further than one might expect from an introduction. I find it helpful to read Moyise and the more conservative Beale alongside each other. See also Porter/Stanley below.

✓ Munck, J. ‡ *Paul and the Salvation of Mankind*, ET 1959.

✓ Murphy-O'Connor, Jerome. ‡ *Paul: A Critical Life*, 1996. [*HBT* 6/98; *RelSRev* 7/97; *JR* 1/98].

✓ Neyrey, J.H. ‡ *Paul in Other Words*, 1990.

O'Brien, Peter T. *Gospel and Mission in the Writings of Paul*, 1995.

✓ *Pauline Theology*, 4 Vols., 1991–97. Fortress Press has published a vast SBL survey of the topic, moving through the epistles one after another, to understand the contribution of each book.

☆ Polhill, J.B. *Paul and His Letters*, 1999. A fine, fairly comprehensive evangelical textbook using a historical approach to reviewing Paul's life, labors, and letters. More up-to-date than Bruce and worth buying. [*DenvJ*].

✓ Porter, Stanley E. (ed). *The Pauline Canon*, 2004. This is from the Brill "Pauline Studies" series [*EuroJTh* 17.1], which now includes several more Porter-edited vols.: *Paul and His Opponents*, 2005; *Paul and His Theology*, 2006 [*EuroJTh* 18.2]; *Paul's World*, 2008 [*JSNT-BL* 2009; *ExpTim* 6/09]; and *Paul: Jew, Greek, and Roman*, 2008 [*BTB* 8/10; *JSNT-BL* 2010]. Also worth noting is Porter's substantial book on *Paul in Acts*, 1999, 2001 [*RTR* 12/03; *SwJT* Fall 03; *Interp* 4/03].

✓ Porter, S.E., and S.A. Adams (eds). *Paul the Letter Writer*, 2010. Also from Brill's "Pauline Studies" series.

Porter, S.E., and C.D. Stanley (eds). ‡ *As It Is Written: Studying Paul's Use of Scripture*, 2008. [*NovT* 52.2; *SBET* Spr 10; *JSNT-BL* 2010].

✓ Räisänen, H. ‡ *Paul and the Law*, ET 1983. Contends strongly that Paul is inconsistent. [*JTS* 4/90; *TJ* Spr 84].

Ramsay, W.M. *St. Paul the Traveller and the Roman Citizen*, 1896, 1920.

Richards, E. Randolph. *Paul and First Century Letter Writing*, 2004.

Ridderbos, Herman. *Paul and Jesus*, ET 1957.

✓ Riesner, Rainer. *Paul's Early Period: Chronology, Mission Strategy, Theology*, 1998. A conservatively critical work from a Tübingen scholar (colleague of Hengel and Stuhlmacher), manifesting confidence in both the reliability of Acts and the agreement of the Acts narratives with data derived from Paul's letters.

✓ Roetzel, Calvin. ‡ *The Letters of Paul*, 5th ed 2009. A fine, critically oriented seminary textbook. Added to this is *Paul: The Man and the Myth* (1998) [*JR* 7/01].

✓   Sampley, J. Paul (ed). ‡ *Paul in the Greco-Roman World: A Handbook*, 2003. "Exceedingly useful," says Proctor of Cambridge, especially for study of the intellectual culture of Paul's day. [*Anvil* 22.4].

✓   Sampley, J. Paul, and Peter Lampe (eds). *Paul and Rhetoric*, 2010. Quickly laying out the issues under debate is Michael F. Bird, "Reassessing a Rhetorical Approach to Paul's Letters," *ExpTim* 119.8 (2008): 374–79.

✓   Sanders, E.P. ‡ *Paul and Palestinian Judaism*, 1977. One of the two or three most important books on Paul in the last 40 years. Most basically, Sanders' contention is that scholarship has long mischaracterized 1st-century Palestinian Judaism as legalistic, without a theology of grace. By restudying the writings of Judaism, we are corrected to see there twin emphases on election by grace into the covenant and on law-keeping (covenantal nomism) for "staying in" covenant with God and in the covenant community. Sanders then interprets Paul against this backdrop, challenging the traditional understanding of Paul as opposing himself to "salvation by works." This book is critiqued by Gundry [*Biblica* 66.1] and others [*WTJ* Spr 82; *TJ* Spr 84; *JBL* 92.2, 104.3; *ThTo* 35.1]. Sanders followed up this seminal vol. with *Paul, the Law, and the Jewish People* (1983) and *Paul* (1991), the latter reviewed by Wright [*JTS* 10/92]. Cf. Dunn's "New Perspective," which accepts Sanders' reading of Judaism but (mildly) critiques and revises Sanders' reading of Paul.

☆   Schnabel, Eckhard J. *Paul the Missionary: Realities, Strategies, and Methods*, 2008. This is, at least partially, a distillation of his two-vol. *Early Christian Mission*. How can anyone arrive at a fair, well-balanced understanding of this missionary and his thought without studying his mission work? [*JETS* 9/09; *Them* 7/10].

✓   Schnelle, Udo. ‡ *Apostle Paul: His Life and Theology*, 2003, ET 2005. A comprehensive and critically-oriented (despite the Baker imprint) reference work from a famous professor at the University of Halle, Germany. He does not consider Ephesians, Colossians, 2 Thessalonians, or the Pastorals to be Pauline. He tends to delve more into the Hellenistic context of Paul's ministry and teaching. [*JETS* 9/06; *JSNT-BL* 2007; *RelSRev* 3/08].

☆   Schreiner, Thomas R. *The Law and Its Fulfillment: A Pauline Theology of Law*, 1993. Well done and comparable to Thielman above. [*TJ* Fall 94].

✓   Seifrid, Mark, and Randall Tan. *The Pauline Writings* (IBR Bibliographies), 2002. Students will be glad for this surprisingly full bibliography (nearly 250pp). [*SBET* Spr 03; *RelSRev* 4/03; *BBR* 14.2; *EvQ* 1/05].

☆   Stewart, J.S. *A Man in Christ: The Vital Elements of St. Paul's Religion*, 1935. Places great emphasis on Paul's phrase "in Christ" and the idea of mystical union with Christ. These emphases—strong in Calvin's interpretation of Paul too—are, in my opinion, the organizing key to Paul's soteriology: we are known, chosen, redeemed, and marked with the Holy Spirit only "in Christ" (Eph 1). This work can often be picked up secondhand.

    Stirewalt, M. Luther. ‡ *Paul: The Letter Writer*, 2003. [*JBL* Fall 04; *Interp* 7/04; *CBQ* 4/06; *Evangel* Sum 04 (Marshall)].

✓   Stuhlmacher, Peter. [𝓜], *Revisiting Paul's Doctrine of Justification*, 2001. A vigorous Lutheran protest against the New Perspective. The author is an outstanding German NT scholar. [*JETS* 12/02; *TJ* Spr 03].

✓   Terrell, Patricia Elyse. *Paul's Parallels: An Echoes Synopsis*, 2009. Similarly helpful is Walter T. Wilson's *Pauline Parallels: A Comprehensive Guide*, 2009, and the older Francis/Sampley vol. above.

☆   Vos, Geerhardus. *The Pauline Eschatology*, 1952. A classic by old Princeton's great biblical theologian which retains remarkable freshness. Amillennial. I have heard it said that the brilliant (secularist) Robert Kraft of the University of Pennsylvania believes Vos "got" Paul on the issue of imputation and justification better than anyone.

✓ Watson, Francis. [*M*], *Paul and the Hermeneutics of Faith*, 2004. A book of profound theology focused on Paul's own hermeneutic. We certainly have not thought enough about Paul as interpreter, as a consummate reader of Scripture. And when Martyn says it is "a stunning book," I take notice. [*CBQ* 7/06; *JTS* 10/05; *JETS* 3/06; *JBL* Fall 06; *Interp* 1/07; *JR* 1/07; see the discussions in *JSNT* 3/06 and in *SJT* 59.4].

✓ Watson, Francis. [*M*], *Paul, Judaism, and the Gentiles: Beyond the New Perspective*, rev. ed 2007. [*JSNT-BL* 2008; *JTS* 4/10; *Interp* 4/09; *Presb* Spr 10; *Anvil* 26.3–4].

✓ Wenham, David. *Paul: Follower of Jesus or Founder of Christianity?* 1995. [*Presb* Fall 95; *TJ* Fall 95; *JBL* Win 96; *HBT* 12/95].

✓ Westerholm, Stephen. *Perspectives Old and New on Paul: The "Lutheran" Paul and His Critics*, 2004. This updates and expands his earlier, well-received monograph, *Israel's Law and the Church's Faith: Paul and His Recent Interpreters*, 1988. That was perhaps the best and most judicious of the early studies of Paul's theology of the Law and the upheaval in the NT discipline over the topic. Of course, scholarship has travelled some distance since 1988, and now Westerholm has made his excellent contribution more current. [*Them* Aut 04; *Interp* 10/04; *TJ* Fall 04; *EvQ* 7/05; *RTR* 4/05; *JETS* 3/05; *JSNT-BL* 2005; *SJT* 60.4; *ExpTim* 1/07; *CurTM* 10/05; *Anvil* 21.4]. For a Westerholm introduction see *Understanding Paul*, 2004 [*Evangel* Spr 07 (Oakes)].

✓ Wilson, Walter T. *Pauline Parallels: A Comprehensive Guide*, 2009. [*JSNT-BL* 2010].

F Winter, Bruce W. *The Pauline Corpus Against Its Environment*.

✓ Witherington, Ben. *Paul's Narrative Thought World*, 1994. This work has been praised by a number of scholars, but see Spencer's review. [*JETS* 12/96; *CBQ* 1/96; *HBT* 6/95; *SBET* Spr 97]. The 1994 work was followed by *The Paul Quest: The Renewed Search for the Jew of Tarsus*, 1998 [*Scripture Bulletin* 7/99; *Chm* Spr 05; *DenvJ*].

✓ Wright, N.T. [*M*], *The Climax of the Covenant: Christ and the Law in Pauline Theology*, 1991. Published by Fortress, these essays are well worth reading, even if you don't agree with him. For a great example of the exegetical value of this work, see his discussion of Phil 2 on pp.56–98. Wright has been a "heavy-hitter" among left-wing evangelical scholars. Many are concerned because here and elsewhere he seems to recast the whole doctrine of justification in ecclesiological terms: it's about who counts as belonging to the people of God. Justification is not about soteriology, how the individual gets saved. Hearing Wright deny penal substitution and imputation, his critics have jumped to defend the Reformation stress on justification as involving imputed righteousness. [*JTS* 10/93; *ThTo* 1/94; *JETS* 12/96]. For an updated exposition of his brand of the New Perspective, see his commentary on Romans and his *Paul: Fresh Perspectives*, 2005 [*JSNT-BL* 2006; *RelSRev* 9/08], titled *Paul: In Fresh Perspective* on this side of the Atlantic. His answer to his critics—in particular Piper's *The Future of Justification*, 2007 [*Chm* Win 09; *EQ* 7/09]—can be read in *Justification: God's Plan and Paul's Vision*, 2009 [*EQ* 7/10; *ExpTim* 3/10; *DenvJ* 5/09; *JSNT-BL* 2010]. I tend to agree with Vanhoozer who suggests, echoing F.D. Maurice, that Wright is often right in what he affirms and wrong in what he denies. (On this point see the Wheaton Conference report of William B. Evans at <Reformation21.org>.) A recent exegetical defense of penal substitution is I. Howard Marshall's *Aspects of the Atonement*, 2008.

✓ Yates, John W. *The Spirit and Creation in Paul*, 2008. This strong Cambridge dissertation published by Mohr Siebeck suggests that "Paul's so-called 'soteriological pneumatology' is perhaps better understood within a wider framework of creation pneumatology." Yates was once Stott's research assistant. [*JETS* 12/09; *RBL* 6/10; *ExpTim* 4/10; *JSNT-BL* 2010].

☆ Zetterholm, Magnus. ‡ *Approaches to Paul: A Student's Guide to Recent Scholarship*, 2009. [*JETS* 9/10].

—ᄴ—

ROMANS

★ **Cranfield, C.E.B.** [𝓜], (ICC–new series) 2 Vols., 1975–79. Magisterial! Indispensable for close exegesis. Though you may not agree with some of his conclusions (e.g., on 5:12ff. and ch. 9), he does lay out carefully all the options. Having read the whole thing through, I think it is among the very best exegetical commentaries on any NT book. There is an abridged version of this commentary in pb (1988), but it does not give you an exegesis of the Greek. Its purpose is to make Cranfield's conclusions available to a wider segment of Bible students. Students should note that Cranfield wrote prior to the controversy over the E.P. Sanders thesis and Dunn's further development of it. Only later was Cranfield able to respond (urging rejection of Dunn's view); see "'The Works of the Law' in the Epistle to the Romans," *JSNT* 43 (1991): 89–101, reprinted in the superb collection, *On Romans: And Other New Testament Essays* (T&T Clark, 1998). [*RTR* 1/80; *TJ* Spr 80; *JETS* 12/86; *ThTo* 37.1].

★ **Moo, Douglas.** (NICNT replacement) 1996. Your first choice. A large work (1000pp) which shows shrewd exegetical judgment and understands the theology of the epistle. It is everything I expected when Eerdmans announced that Moo's WEC commentary—noted below—would be reworked for the NICNT series. His conclusions are pretty much in line with classic Reformed theology (a neo-Lutheran tinge here and there?), except his interpretation of ch. 7. I value Moo and Schreiner both for interacting with the Sanders thesis and Dunn's "New Perspective." See Moo's NIVAC below, which is also a wise purchase—having both NICNT and NIVAC is not a waste of money or shelf-space. [*Them* 6/00; *JETS* 12/98; *Biblica* 78.3 (1997); *CBQ* 4/98; *RTR* 9/97; *BSac* 4/98; *JTS* 10/98].

★ **Murray, John.** (retired NICNT) 1959–65. A superb theological commentary which shows good exegetical judgment. Murray was Professor of Systematics at Westminster Seminary. This commentary is especially helpful to the expositor because it is so very focused on Paul's flow of thought and message (Schreiner is also strong in this area). Murray did not interact as much with the (old) secondary literature and, therefore, was never valued highly by NT specialists—not valued as highly by those outside the Reformed tradition either. Years ago Silva counseled that Murray and Cranfield be your first purchases on Romans; I hazard the guess that today he might say Moo, Cranfield, and Murray (in that order). Murray's work has been replaced by Moo, but Eerdmans is keeping Murray in print, though not with the NICNT cover.

★ **Schreiner, Thomas R.** (BECNT) 1998. This evangelical's lengthy journal article and monograph, responding to E.P. Sanders' views on "works righteousness," piqued my interest in this work. See "Paul and Perfect Obedience to the Law," *WTJ* 47 (1985) 245–278, and *The Law and Its Fulfillment* (Baker, 1993). The approach is solidly, but not stolidly, Calvinistic. I consulted this fat (but manageable) vol. when I was called upon to teach a college course on Romans and found it trusty. Though Schreiner is perhaps not as incisive as Moo, I sometimes agreed with him over against Moo (e.g., the place of the law in the Christian's life). See Schreiner's two books under "Pauline Studies." His theology is Baptist and broadly Reformed. [*Them* 11/99; *Biblica* 81.3 (2000); *Interp* 7/99; *CTJ* 4/01; *DenvJ*].

★ Stott, John. (BST) 1994. This contribution to the series is excellent and can be found in both hb and pb. Stott's conclusions are usually in line with conservative, Reformed thought (see the cruxes at 5:12ff.; chs. 7, 9 and 11); at the same time, there is a freshness about his exposition which makes it attractive. Thorough and clear at 400pp, with more exegesis than expected in BST. Choose this over Bruce or Mounce. [*Them* 2/98; *JETS* 3/98; *Chm* 109.3 (1995)].

Achtemeier, Paul. ‡ (I) 1986. A fine, moderately liberal exposition, but this is not Achtemeier at his best. [*JBL* 106.4 (1987); *JETS* 3/87].

Barnhouse, D.G. 4 Vols., 1952–63. This set shows how vigorous an expositor he was at Tenth Presbyterian in Philadelphia. Dispensationally-oriented, helpful to the preacher. His exegetical judgment is sometimes a bit off-beat. I would, instead, choose the vols. by Boice (his successor at Tenth) or Lloyd-Jones.

✓ **Barrett, C.K.** ‡ (BNTC) 1957, 2nd ed 1991. Perhaps not so successful as his commentaries on the Corinthian letters but still a model of clarity and "remarkably interesting" (Martin). Certain theological inadequacies and errors are pointed out in John Murray's review of the work [*Collected Writings*, Vol. 4: 306ff.]. One of the worst is his statement that "Christ took precisely the same fallen nature that we ourselves have" (p.156 [1957], p.147 [1991])—he here, and in other places too, shows the influence of Barth. Students should be reminded of Barrett's notable survey entitled, *Reading through Romans* (1963).

Barth, Karl. ‡ 1919, 6th ed 1929, ET 1933. Truly a turning point in the history of theology! As an exposition of Paul's thought, Barth's *Römerbrief* has definite deficiencies; as a theological treatise in its own right, it changed the theological world. Note also his later *Shorter Commentary on Romans* (ET 1959).

Bartlett, David L. ‡ (WestBC) 1996. [*Interp* 7/97; *CBQ* 4/97].

✓ **Black, Matthew.** ‡ (NCB) 1973, rev. 1989. Has some value in the category of brief commentary, but Bruce is more perceptive and conservative. Black was a learned and mature scholar, but his work had a rather dated feel even when it appeared. [*RTR* 9/90; *JETS* 9/94 (kinder)].

F Blum, Edwin A. (EEC).

☆ Boice, James M. 4 Vols., 1992–95. Each of these vols. runs about 500pp. This is great preaching from an evangelical leader who long pastored historic Tenth Presbyterian in Philadelphia. [*CTJ* 11/94].

✓ Bray, Gerald (ed). (ACCS) 1998. "A wonderful gateway to the world of patristic thinking relating to this foundational biblical text." This is not a mere culling of materials in the 19th century Schaff set of the Church Fathers or the Catholic University of America Press's *Fathers of the Church* series, for Bray presents in English for the first time extensive citations of Origen's commentary on Romans. One of the very best contributions to the series. [*Them* 11/99; *NovT* 42.4; *RelSRev* 4/00; *SwJT* Sum 01; *EvQ* 7/02].

Briscoe, D. Stuart. (WCC) 1982. As with the Genesis vol., this is a thoughtful exposition but not especially well researched.

Brown, John. 1857. A Calvinistic commentary reprinted in 1981 (Baker) and 2003 (Wipf & Stock) which offers a deep theological exposition. Its flavor is reflected in a favorite quote found on pp.38–39: "…what to Him who paid the ransom is justice, may be grace, pure grace, to him for whom it is paid." See also Brown's works on Hebrews and 1 Peter.

☆ Bruce, F.F. (TNTC) 1963, rev. 1985. An insightful, handy commentary. See Stott above.

✓ **Byrne, Brendon.** ‡ (SacPag) 1996. "Dense brevity" (Lambrecht). One of the stronger, more widely used of current American Roman Catholic works on Romans. If you're comparing, Fitzmyer is the more careful and skilled exegete, while Byrne is more immediately helpful for proclamation concerns. Byrne uses rhetorical analysis on the letter. [*JBL* Spr 99; *Biblica* 78.2 (1997); *RelSRev* 1/98].

✓ **Calvin, John.** 1540, ET 1960. You haven't forgotten this series I hope. See the note at the head of the NT section of this guide. Calvin is at his very best here—amazingly, his first commentary. His "patient exegesis is a model of critical and theological thoroughness" (Barrett). "A library without Calvin's Romans and the magnificent English edition of Luther's commentary is sadly impoverished" (Childs).

F Campbell, W.S. (RRA).

Denney, James. (EGT) 1900. Contains some insights on the Greek text and some probing theology, too.

Dodd, C.H. ‡ (Moffatt series) 1932. Representative of the older liberal tradition, this work is famous for its cavalier dismissal of what Paul says about the wrath of God toward sinners.

✓ Donfried, Karl P. (ed). ‡ *The Romans Debate*, 1977, rev. 1991. Called "a standard sourcebook" [*JTS* 10/93], this heralded a new approach to Romans more as a situational letter than as a theological treatise. [*CTJ* 4/94; *RTR* 1/96].

✓ **Dunn, James D.G.** [*M*], (WBC) 2 Vols., 1988. The quick succession of NT professors at Durham who have commented on Romans is remarkable: Barrett, Cranfield, and then Dunn. This huge scholarly commentary rivals Cranfield's ICC vols. and is the most important interpretation of Romans along the lines of the New Perspective. He mastered a tremendous amount of literature to produce this work. However, I am much more impressed by Cranfield's mature exegetical judgment and would recommend the ICC over the WBC without hesitation (compare them on 9:5, for example). Dunn was once much more conservative and evangelically-minded. Though unable now to locate the quote, I recall that Dunn once said Barrett is a better theological guide to Romans than Murray; that tells you something. For more comment on this scholar's views, see Dunn under Pauline Studies and under Galatians. [*JTS* 4/91; *CBQ* 7/91; *Interp* 1/91; *RTR* 9/90].

Edwards, James R. (NIBC) 1992. A 395-page commentary which is superbly written but, I think, misconstrues Paul somewhat on law and grace. [*EvQ* 4/91; *CTJ* 4/95; *CRBR* 1993].

Esler, Philip F. *Conflict and Identity in Romans: The Social Setting of Paul's Letter,* 2004. [*ThTo* 7/05; *JR* 7/06; *BibInt* 14.4].

F Fiddes, Paul. ‡ (Blackwell).

✓ **Fitzmyer, Joseph.** ‡ (AB) 1993. About 800pp of first-rate critical commentary. The author is a Jesuit priest who also produced the exceptional works on Luke, Acts, and Philemon for the AB series. In this Romans commentary we Protestants are pleasantly surprised to find Fitzmyer agreeing with our interpretation at more than a few points. However, this is not my choice for a theological guide. Recommended only for advanced students; it is not so useful for pastors. [*PSB* 15.3; *Interp* 10/95; *CBQ* 7/95; *JBL* Win 95; *NovT* 37.2].

✓ Gathercole, Simon J. *Where Is Boasting? Early Jewish Soteriology and Paul's Response in Romans 1–5*, 2002. An important new critique of the New Perspective, which was written as a dissertation under Dunn. More than a few have been surprised. This rising star has now gone to Cambridge. [*JBL* Fall 04; *Interp* 7/04; *ExpTim*

8/03; *JSNT* 12/03; *JR* 7/04; *EvQ* 1/05; *WTJ* Fall 05; *BibInt* 13.1; *SJT* 62.1; *TJ* Fall 04 (Moo); *DenvJ* 1/02 (Blomberg); *Anvil* 20.4].

F Gaventa, Beverly Roberts. ‡ (NTL).

✓ Godet, Frederic. 1883. Quite perceptive as an Arminian theological exposition and worth consulting for the history of exegesis—Godet is very frequently cited in Moo's NICNT. This commentary and a huge vol. on John's Gospel are Godet's best known, but see the works on Luke and 1 Corinthians as well.

Greathouse, William M., and George Lyons. (New Beacon Bible Commentary) 2 Vols., 2008. A 570-page work "in the Wesleyan Tradition."

✓ Haacker, Klaus. ‡ *The Theology of Paul's Letter to the Romans* (Cambridge NT Theology) 2003. [*ExpTim* 9/04].

F Hahn, Scott. ‡ (CCSS).

☆ Haldane, Robert. (GS) 1874. Any familiar with Haldane's experiences in Geneva will take an interest in this reprint by Banner and by Kregel. After having been o/p, it is now back in print. An exposition full of heart.

Harrison, Everett F. (EBC) 1976. This was an adequate exposition in its time, but now in the company of so many giants it is less significant.

☆ Harrison, Everett F., and Donald A. Hagner. (EBCR) 2008. They have done much to help preachers with what is provided here in 217pp. The theological orientation is broadly and winsomely Reformed (e.g., 9:6–13). Just to note, Hagner does not buy into the New Perspective and, as one might expect, he made great improvements to the old EBC.

✓ Hay, Daniel M., and E. Elizabeth Johnson (eds). ‡ *Pauline Theology*, Vol. 3, *Romans*, 1995.

Hendriksen, William. (NTC) 1980–81. Not one of the better vols. in the series, though I'm sure many students and pastors have found it helpful. His last commentary, *Romans* lacks some of the vigor of earlier works. [*WTJ* Fall 82; *EvQ* 10/90].

☆ Hodge, Charles. (GS) 1864. Long ago eclipsed as the best Reformed study by Murray. Still, it is valuable as a theological exposition and for help in understanding the flow and connection of Paul's thought (which is important for Romans). Those without a background in Church History will not know that Hodge was one of the greats among American systematic theologians during the 19th century. He taught at Princeton Seminary his entire life and wrote excellent works on Paul's letters to the Romans, Corinthians, and Ephesians. Besides the GS reprint (1972), see also the edited Crossway Classic edition below.

☆ Hodge, Charles. (CrossC) 1994.

☆ Hughes, R. Kent. (PTW) 1991. See under Mark. This Romans exposition is 352pp.

Hunter, A.M. [*M*], (Torch) 1955. An exposition by a former professor at the University of Aberdeen, noted as having one of Scotland's more conservative divinity faculties.

✓ **Jewett, Robert.** ‡ (Herm) 2007. A formidable tome of over 1100pp by a leading American NT scholar, long at Garrett-Evangelical Seminary in Chicago. This is the fullest exegesis to appear in the last couple decades and contains copious foot-notes. Jewett approaches the text with a wide array of critical tools, with special place given to socio-rhetorical interpretation. His general thesis is cogent enough and sharply focused: "Paul writes to gain support for a mission to the barbarians in Spain, which requires that the gospel of impartial, divine righteousness revealed in Christ be clarified to rid it of prejudicial elements that are currently dividing the congregations in Rome." He interacts a good bit with Dunn's WBC, following his lead at a few points but also criticizing the New Perspective without engaging deeply in the controversy. What he shares with the New Perspective, I think, is a tendency "to let the ecclesiological dimension of Paul's gospel—setting Gentile believers on a par with Jews in the people of God—trump Paul's soteriological aim" (Rainbow). While one cannot help being impressed with the learning here, I agree with Moo [*JETS* 12/07] when he classes this work as less distinguished as a theological commentary; such an assessment makes sense since Jewett does not view the letter as a theological treatise. Schreiner contends, rightly in my view, that Jewett places too much weight on both his rhetorical approach and the specifics of his reconstruction of the historical context. Cf. Donfried. [*Interp* 4/08; *JSNT* 9/08 (a review discussion); *NovT* 50.3; *ExpTim* 10/07; *RelSRev* 9/08; *BSac* 1/09; *BBR* 19.3 (Schreiner); *Anvil* 26.3–4; *EC* 5/10 (Reasoner)].

✓ **Johnson, Luke Timothy.** ‡ *Reading Romans: A Literary and Theological Commentary*, 1997. [*RelSRev* 4/03].

✓ **Käsemann, Ernst.** ‡ ET 1980. This vigorous, individualistic commentary builds on a Lutheran base and makes for a very strenuous intellectual workout. Not necessarily dependable as a guide through Paul's thought, Käsemann's provocative exposition is, like Barth's, a theological treatise in its own right. This has been one of the five or six most influential commentaries on Romans (in English) from the academic point of view. He detects the influence of apocalyptic, stressing that δικαιοσυνη θεου is God's inbreaking and saving power. [*EvQ* 4/82; *JETS* 9/81; *Them* 7.3].

Kaylor, R. David. ‡ *Paul's Covenant Community: Jew and Gentile in Romans*, 1988.

✓ **Keck, Leander.** ‡ (ANTC) 2005. Highly successful as a learned, to-the-point, critical exegesis by a famous Pauline scholar. Keck is Winkley Professor of Biblical Theology Emeritus at Yale Divinity School. In a disciplined way, the author sticks to explicating Paul's line of thought/argument (e.g., ch. 9). One senses throughout that a lifetime of wrestling with Paul lies behind this work of compressed scholarship (400pp). His sympathy with the text might lead some to classify Keck as mildly critical. I bought this. [*JETS* 6/06; *JSNT-BL* 2006; *ExpTim* 2/07; *EuroJTh* 15.2].

Keener, Craig. (NCCS) 2009. The author teaches at Palmer Seminary in Philadelphia and is a co-editor for the series. I have yet to see this 272-page book, but suspect (on the basis of his reputation) it is dense, sensitive to rhetoric, and informed by his deep learning in 1ˢᵗ-century literature. [*JETS* 6/10].

Knox, John. ‡ (IB) 1954.

F Kruse, Colin. (Pillar). This will replace Morris.

Lampe, Peter. ‡ *From Paul to Valentinus: The Christians in the City of Rome of the First Three Centuries*, 2000.

Leenhardt, F.J. ‡ ET 1961. This is more of a pastor's commentary, written by a German Catholic.

✓ Lightfoot, J.B. 1904. See under 1 & 2 Thessalonians.

☆ Lloyd-Jones, D. Martyn. 14 Vols., 1970–2003. These vols. of exposition have been published by Zondervan and/or Banner of Truth. They cover chs. 1–14, but don't expect any more vols., so as to complete the epistle. Health problems brought a sudden end both to Lloyd-Jones' exposition at that point (14:17) and to his pastorate at Westminster Chapel in London. Most Reformed pastors know the virtues and worth of these powerfully compelling sermons. The set comes highly recommended by Moo.

F Longenecker, Richard. (NIGTC). This is expected to be an important contribution.

☆ Luther, Martin. 1515–16. There are many eds. and several translations available. I would suggest buying either the "Library of Christian Classics" edition in paperback

(Westminster Press, 1961) or the hardback edition in the series *Luther's Works* (Concordia). There is a contagious excitement in these lectures because Luther had recently "discovered" the gospel. It is a wonderful experience to read these pages and grasp the liberty of Christ's gospel along with Luther. It was Luther's preface to this commentary which God used to convert John Wesley.

MacArthur, John. 2 Vols., 1991–94. See Matthew for a review of the series.

F   Marshall, I. Howard, and Stephen N. Williams. [*M?*] (THC).

Matera, Frank J. ‡ (Paideia) 2010.

✓   **Moo, Douglas.** *Romans 1–8* (WEC) 1991. A huge entry (almost 600pp) which was quite valuable. When the WEC series died, Moo undertook to reformat his work and complete it for the NICNT series. See Moo above. This WEC vol. is now difficult to find. [*Them* 10/92; *CTJ* 4/92].

☆   Moo, Douglas J. (NIVAC) 2000. Great for pastors, but should not replace Moo's NICNT on your "to buy" list. The same can be said for his recent college textbook, *Encountering the Book of Romans*, 2002 [*Them* Sum 04; *RelSRev* 1/04; *RTR* 8/03; *Anvil* 20.4]. At one time Moisés Silva was listed for this commentary.

☆   **Morris, Leon.** (Pillar) 1988. Twenty years ago I said this deserves a place on your shelf, but now we have Moo and Schreiner. As a conservative Anglican clergyman, Morris held firmly to the moderately Calvinistic "Articles of Religion." This dependable work of 578pp is similar to Murray's great work, but more up-to-date and cognizant of developments in the NT field. This commentary would have been much more valuable to students, however, if the author had dealt more with the Sanders and Dunn theses. Morris's shortcoming made me all the more eager to see Moo's work. Morris is now more of interest to pastors than to students. Kruse will replace this vol. [*EvQ* 7/90; *JBL* Win 89; *RTR* 1/92; *Evangel* Sum 90].

✓   Moule, H.C.G. (Cambridge Bible for Schools and Colleges) 1879. A perceptive work exegeting the Greek text. There is also a devotional exposition in the old EB (1894) which would be useful for sermon preparation. The latter was reprinted by CLC in 1975 and, more recently, has been reissued in Crossway's "Classic Commentary" series. Reissue does not always indicate value, but here it does.

✓   Mounce, Robert H. (NAC) 1995. His commentary on Revelation proved him to be a fine scholar, but this commentary is not so much aimed at students as at pastors. [*Them* 1/97; *JETS* 3/98; *TJ* Spr 97].

Newell, William R. 1938. Very strongly Dispensational with a somewhat practical focus. Remains in print.

Newman, B.M., and E.A. Nida. (UBS) 1973.

✓   **Nygren, Anders.** ‡ ET 1952. A highly respected theological commentary from a Lutheran scholar. Thin on the last eight chapters. Still in print.

Olyott, Stuart J. *The Gospel as It Really Is* (WCS) 1979.

☆   **Osborne, Grant.** (IVPNT) 2004. This commentary of over 400pp was contributed by the series editor. It is exactly the right book, if one wants a compact, evangelical, Arminian exegesis. I regard it as fairer than Witherington in dealing with the Arminian-Calvinist controversy. Surprisingly, it is less helpful than some other vols. in the series for addressing contemporary relevance concerns. [*JETS* 3/05; *Them* 4/06; *RelSRev* 1/07; *Anvil* 22.2].

☆   Piper, John. *The Justification of God*, 1983, rev. 1992. The subtitle is "An Exegetical and Theological Study of Romans 9:1–23." This solid, in-depth commentary by a Baptist minister is a good addition to a pastor's library. Piper ably argues that Paul is concerned with the election and reprobation of individuals. Originally the work was a Munich dissertation. [*WTJ* Spr 84; *RTR* 1/84; *EvQ* 1/88; *JETS* 12/83].

F Porter, Stanley. (BHGNT).

Reasoner, Mark. *Romans in Full Circle: A History of Interpretation*, 2005. [*ExpTim* 6/09]. This follows a fine CUP monograph on *The Strong and the Weak: Romans 14.1–15.13 in Context*, 1999.

✓ **Sanday, W., and A.C. Headlam.** [𝓜], (retired ICC) 1895; 5th ed 1902. "Should in no way be disregarded" (Martin). One of the very best from the old series. Even if the advanced student has purchased Cranfield, it still would not be unwise to pick up Sanday & Headlam secondhand.

✓ Schlatter, Adolf. 1935, 1952, ET 1995. A welcome translation of a most thoughtful older German commentary, which emphasizes the righteousness of God as the unifying theme of this epistle. God's "righteousness establishes a relationship in which justice is effective." As David Kuck has noted, Schlatter's emphasis here anticipates Käsemann's reading of Paul in some respects. [*Them* 2/99; *JETS* 3/98; *RTR* 1/97; *SwJT* Sum 96; *HBT* 6/98]. In my personal study of Romans the righteousness of God works well as an integrating theme. That righteousness is declared in the gospel (1:16–17); contradistinguished by sin or human unrighteousness (1:18–3:20); imputed in justification (3:21–5:21); imparted in sanctification (6:1–8:39); defended as sinners challenge God's purposes in election (9–11); and practiced in all of life (12–16).

✓ Schnelle, Udo (ed). ‡ *The Letter to the Romans*, 2009. A huge vol. of 44 papers delivered at the Colloquium Biblicum Lovaniense. [*ExpTim* 8/10].

Shedd, William G.T. 1879. Continues to be reprinted every so often. Shedd was another of the great 19th century systematic theologians who commented on Romans. This work is interesting and important in the history of exegesis because Shedd took a "realistic" view of imputation in 5:12ff. (compare with Hodge's and Murray's "representative" or "federal" view).

✓ Soderlund, Sven, and N.T. Wright (eds). *Romans and the People of God*, 1999. [*EvQ* 4/02].

Stott, John R.W. *Men Made New*, 1966. This exposition of Romans 5–8 is succinct and masterful. It used to be reprinted from time to time. It must now be o/p since the BST vol. is available.

✓ **Stuhlmacher, Peter.** [𝓜], ET 1994. This major, but compact work by the brilliant Tübingen professor has been published in pb by WJK. Definitely to be consulted. Stuhlmacher has for some time been one of the most conservative university professors of NT in Germany. [*JETS* 12/96; *Interp* 10/96; *HBT* 12/95].

✓ **Talbert, Charles.** ‡ (S&H) 2002. Talbert is a highly respected Baptist theologian and Baylor professor, and here he contributes an attractively presented, accessible exposition of Paul's letter, which focuses largely on rhetorical features and following Paul's sustained argument. Talbert is rather uncomfortable with Reformed theology. This vol. seems expensive at over $50 for 340pp of introduction and commentary. [*JETS* 9/04; *Interp* 7/04; *DenvJ* 1/03 (Blomberg, sagacious)].

F Thielman, Frank. (ZEC). I expect this to be an expert, dependable guide through the epistle.

Thomas, W.H. Griffith. *Romans: A Devotional Commentary*, 3 Vols., n.d. Since 1946, this edifying book has often been reprinted by Eerdmans in a one-vol. pb. It may originally have appeared in 1912.

Tobin, Thomas H. ‡ *Paul's Rhetoric in Its Contexts: The Argument of Romans*, 2004. [*EuroJTh* 15.1 (Bird)].

Toews, John E. (BCBC) 2004.

☆   **Witherington, Ben** (with Darlene Hyatt). (SRC) 2004. This marks the continuation of Witherington's series and, alongside Osborne's new work for IVPNT, is the best recent evangelical Arminian commentary on Romans. There is more theology in this vol. than in some of his other works, and necessarily so. For a review of this essentially one-man series, see my comments under 1 Corinthians. Besides exegesis and rhetorical analysis, there is also exposition and application, occasionally with almost militant Arminianism—he is displeased at Augustinian/Reformed dominance among Romans commentators. Some will be put off by a feminism that both bemoans "the lack of genuine dialogue" between camps and (breathlessly?) condemns the "blatantly sexist statements" of Southern Baptists and complementarians in general (p.403). Students can learn from Witherington's discussion of the interrelation of the parts of the letter; his outline of Romans is oriented toward rhetorical aspects instead of theology. [*Interp* 7/04; *DenvJ* 1/04; *RTR* 12/08; *JETS* 6/05; *SwJT* Spr 05; *Them* 4/06; *JSNT-BL* 2005; *SBET* Spr 05; *RelSRev* 1/06; *BTB* Sum 06; *ExpTim* 1/05; *Anvil* 22.2].

☆   **Wright, N. Thomas.** [𝓜], (NewIB) 2002. This is not just good, it's really good. Certainly one of my favorite commentaries, though I disagree with him at many points (see Wright under Pauline Studies above). Wright is extraordinarily influential these days in the debate over Paul's theology and over NT theology more generally. Here we have a most engaging exposition of nearly 400pp, one which finds the righteousness/justice of God to be the central theme. Comparing the two leading Romans commentaries which propound the New Perspective, I find Wright more attractive than Dunn. [*WTJ* Fall 03].

F   Yeago, David. (Brazos).

✓   **Ziesler, John.** ‡ (TPI) 1989. This builds on his scholarly monograph for CUP, *The Meaning of Righteousness in Paul* (1972). Ziesler is a major work which shows the influence of E.P. Sanders and should be consulted; he is extraordinarily well-read. [*CBQ* 4/92; *Them* 1/92; *ExpTim* 3/90].

NOTES: (1) There are many other valuable works on Romans, but I have to stop somewhere. (2) James C. Miller, "The Romans Debate: 1991–2001," *CurBS* 9 (2001): 306–49.

—ɯ—

1 CORINTHIANS

★   Blomberg, Craig L. (NIVAC) 1994. A thoughtful and suggestive work, providing helpful exegesis and guidance for the expositor, but Blomberg is not necessarily to be followed each time he wades into the deep water of controversy. This is not the commentary to use as a shortcut past one's own exegesis directly to application—and Blomberg would not want you to do such a thing anyway. Well worth the preacher's money. [*JETS* 3/98]. Good expositional helps are fewer for this book, and alongside Blomberg one could add Hays, Kistemaker, and Prior.

★   **Fee, Gordon.** [𝓜], (NICNT) 1987. This has easily been the best mid-level commentary on this book of the Bible in English—Carson's and Silva's first choice, at least until Garland. It is so thorough and learned that one must have it. However, you may not wish to follow him at every point. His exposition of chs. 12–14 is clearly informed by his Pentecostal convictions, and he has strong feminist leanings (e.g., excising 14:34–36 completely out of the text without any 'external evidence' to back his decision!). Yet he can be openly critical of his Pentecostal heritage, as when he agrees that Paul in 12:13 teaches the Spirit-baptism of every convert. See my comments on Carson below. Fee is expected to revise this commentary as part of the ongoing updating of the series. [*WTJ* Fall 89; *JBL* 108.1 (1989); *EvQ* 10/88; *JETS* 9/89; *NovT* 31.2]. Now compare with Ciampa and Rosner.

★ **Garland, David E.** (BECNT) 2003. The author previously completed a major, mid-level commentary on 2 Corinthians, and this work is stronger for that earlier research into the Corinthian correspondence. Garland is a much published Baptist evangelical, and his work here is thorough and praiseworthy. Pastors should note that, in line with the series title, this is more a work of exegesis than theological exposition, though there is a good measure of theology and even hints at application. Much more accessible as a commentary on the Greek text than Thiselton. [*CBQ* 1/05; *JETS* 3/05; *Interp* 7/05; *JSNT* 6/05; *RelSRev* 1/05; *ExpTim* 9/05].

★ **Thiselton, Anthony C.** [*M*], (NIGTC) 2000. This 1400-page exegesis leaves no stones unturned. Thiselton is without doubt one of the world's leading NT scholars and is noted especially for expertise in both biblical and philosophical hermeneutics. Magnificent! Many pastors will find a tome like this too intimidating. (Fee is big enough already.) But those who love to dig deep will find their efforts repaid in full by Thiselton. Often the reader will appreciate the author's patient, meticulous, circumspect exegesis—in the best British classical tradition. Thiselton will be welcomed by students of 1 Corinthians because, outside of foreign language works, we have not seen a major commentary on the Greek text for decades. Now we have NIGTC, BECNT, and AYB. Also to be noted, this is the most thorough and useful application yet of speech-act theory to any biblical text. [*RTR* 12/01; *Them* ~~Spr~~/Sum 02; *JTS* 4/02; *JBL* Spr 02; *Interp* 1/02; *ExpTim* 8/01; *NovT* 44.2; *HBT* 6/02; *AsTJ* Spr 03; *JSNT* 6/04; *SwJT* Fall 01; *RelSRev* 7/02; *EvQ* 1/05; *JR* 7/02 (Furnish); *Evangel* Spr 02].

★ Thiselton, Anthony C. *1 Corinthians: A Shorter Exegetical & Pastoral Commentary*, 2006. More than a mere digest of his NIGTC, Thiselton has written a fresh exposition which reveals that the epistle has continued to be on his mind and heart. Preachers who find the earlier comprehensive work too daunting will appreciate this briefer work (300pp); the bonus is that the author includes sections offering wise pastoral reflection on the text's contemporary application. But students can learn here too! Don't miss his discussion (and acceptance) of Winter's new interpretation of 12:3 (pp.193–95). [*RTR* 4/08; *CBQ* 10/07; *JTS* 4/08; *JSNT-BL* 2008; *ExpTim* 7/07; *Anvil* 25.2].

Adams, Edward, and David Horrell (eds). ‡ *Christianity at Corinth: The Quest for the Pauline Church*, 2004. [*DenvJ* 3/05].

Baker, William. (CorBC) 2008. This vol. also includes Ralph Martin's commentary on 2 Corinthians.

☆ **Barrett, C.K.** ‡ (BNTC) 1968. This was the first choice on most bibliographies prior to Fee's appearance in 1987, and it is easy to see why. As V.P. Furnish once said, even when Barrett is not fully persuasive he is instructive (*II Corinthians*, p.ix). I recommended this vol. for purchase in the first six eds. of this guide. But newer, better works are now available for both pastors and students, and Barrett has been well mined by today's scholarship.

✓ Barth, Karl. [*M*], *The Resurrection of the Dead*, ET 1933. Mainly a theological exposition of ch. 15. There is some real power here. I have hope that he did indeed believe in a physical resurrection. (T.F. Torrance relates that, when he urged Barth to leave more room for an incarnational theology, Barth gently reminded him that the incarnation was in fact given its due weight in his theology, that he upheld the doctrine of a *leibliche Auferstehung*, or <u>bodily</u> resurrection.)

F Bonnington, Mark. (THC).

✓   Bray, Gerald (ed). *1–2 Corinthians* (ACCS) 1999. [*SwJT* Fall 00; *RelSRev* 4/00; *EvQ* 7/02].

F   Brown, Alexandra R. ‡ (NTL).

☆   **Bruce, F.F.** *1 and 2 Corinthians* (NCB) 1971. Though quite brief—256pp on both epistles—this commentary is valuable. He packs an immense amount of information into the format and has sound exegetical judgment. Really, the only serious difference I have with Bruce is over the interpretation of κεφαλη at 11:3. I believe "head" in context clearly means "authority over" and not "source." Also supportive of this understanding is (1) Paul's usage of the word in Eph. 1:22 and Col. 2:10; (2) the analogy of the husband's headship to Christ's at Eph. 5:23; and (3) the articles of Fitzmyer and Grudem regarding the word's extracanonical use—e.g., Grudem's articles in *Recovering Biblical Manhood and Womanhood* (1991) and *JETS* 3/01.

      Burke, Trevor J., and J. Keith Elliott (eds). *Paul and the Corinthians: Studies on a Community in Conflict*, 2003. This *Festschrift* for Margaret Thrall is published by Brill and includes a wealth of essays on both epistles. [*NovT* 47.2].

☆   **Carson, D.A.** *Showing the Spirit: A Theological Exposition of 1 Corinthians 12–14*, 1987. Years ago I used to say that, if (as a pastor) I could have only two books on 1 Corinthians, I might choose Fee and this 200-page commentary to counterbalance him on several points. Just the 10 pages on 14:33b–36 alone are worth the price of the book to me. The exegesis is detailed and slightly technical where it most needs to be. Because this book is becoming more difficult to obtain—usually not stocked by bookstores—I'm no longer recommending its purchase. This was reprinted in pb by Baker in 1996. See as well Carson's book, *The Cross and Christian Ministry: Studies in 1 Corinthians* (1993). [*RTR* 1/90; *Them* 1/90; *EvQ* 4/89; *SBET* Spr 90].

F   **Ciampa, Roy E., and Brian S. Rosner.** (Pillar) 2010. Eerdmans has announced an 11/15/2010 release with a total of 960pp. I expect that a strength of this commentary, in line with Ciampa's past work on *The Presence and Function of Scripture in Galatians 1 and 2* (1998), will be research into Paul's interpretation of OT texts. Ciampa has taught at Gordon-Conwell since 1998, and Rosner is a professor at Moore Theological College in Sydney. I suspect that this may possibly become a first-choice for pastors and students seeking a rigorous, yet accessible exegetical tool which has much to say theologically. Both authors, Ciampa (Aberdeen) and Rosner (Cambridge), are superbly trained.

F   Clarke, Andrew. (WBC). Ignore the earlier reports that Judith Gundry-Volf or Linda Belleville were to deliver this commentary. Clarke, at Aberdeen, has the contract and the release date now is supposedly 2013.

✓   **Collins, Raymond F.** ‡ (SacPag) 1999. A probing commentary from the Catholic tradition. Students benefit from consulting this full work (almost 700pp), which is so well done that it could be regarded as a "Gordon Fee from the critical side." [*CBQ* 7/00; *Biblica* 82.1; *SwJT* Fall 00; *Scripture Bulletin* 1/01; *RB* 4/01; *Them* ~~Spr~~/Sum 02].

✓   **Conzelmann, Hans.** ‡ (Herm) ET 1975. A highly critical and technical work which was long regarded by many scholars as the standard exegetical commentary on this letter. While Conzelmann will always be consulted by NT specialists, newer works like Fee, Thiselton, and Fitzmyer are displacing it. [*JBL* 89.1; *Them* 1 (1976): 56].

      Dever, Mark. *Twelve Challenges Churches Face*, 2008. A quickly moving and engaging exposition of the letter.

✓   Dunn, James D.G. (NT Guides) 1995. An excellent critical introduction to the main exegetical and theological issues faced by scholarship. Because of the influence of the author in Pauline studies, the guide should be consulted by students.

✓   Ellingworth, Paul, and H.A. Hatton. (UBS) 1985.

F   Ellis, E.E. (ICC–new series). This contribution will be evangelical and more conservative.

    Findlay, G.G. (Expositor's Greek Testament) 1901. Can be kept in reserve. For other Findlay works, see Thessalonians and John's Epistles.

✓   **Fitzmyer, Joseph A.** ‡ (AYB) 2008. This very full new work (660pp) is now among a scholar's first choices for a technical commentary reference. The philology, syntactical analysis, and bibliographies are a boon to students. Slightly on the downside, this is a more independent work in that he limits his interaction with other major commentaries like Thiselton and Schrage. He was trying to keep the vol. of manageable size. See the author's other AB vols. on Luke, Acts, Romans, and Philemon, all of them methodologically consonant with his recent work, *The Interpretation of Scripture: In Defense of the Historical-Critical Method* (2008). [*RBL* (Thiselton); *ThTo* 7/09; *JETS* 12/09; *Them* 7/09; *ExpTim* 11/09; *Interp* 7/09 (Witherington); *Them* 7/09; *EuroJTh* 18.2].

✓   Furnish, Victor Paul. ‡ 1999. From the Cambridge NT Theology series.

F   Gardner, Paul. (ZEC).

☆   Godet, Frederic. 1886–87. A mine of exposition to which preachers have turned again and again. Still useful because of its length and insight, but Godet is now difficult to obtain.

    Gromacki, R.G. *Called to Be Saints*, 1977. A popularly-styled, evangelical exposition.

    Grosheide, F.W. (retired NICNT) 1953. One of the first in the series but now replaced by Fee and o/p. Never considered the strongest effort. Few view Grosheide as still worth consulting. Those looking for a solidly Reformed exposition should purchase NTC or Hodge.

    Harrisville, Roy A. ‡ (Augsburg NT Commentary) 1987. [*CRBR* 1989].

☆   **Hays, Richard B.** ‡ (I) 1997. This commentary is so good and lively, from a less critical angle, that it is a top choice in mainline circles. The evangelical pastor, though probably wanting to tone down the apocalyptic emphasis, could put this to good use, with its sociological and literary analysis, its ethical discussion, and its theology. Hays is always an interesting read. [*TJ* Spr 00; *Interp* 1/99; *CBQ* 7/99].

✓   Héring, Jean. ‡ ET 1962. A significant older French work in translation. Advanced students may wish to consult his provocative exegesis, though this work does not have its former influence or prominence.

☆   Hodge, Charles. *I and II Corinthians* (GS) 1857–59. Though some may have considered this a quirky choice, I used to include these two vols. on the recommended list. The two commentaries are bound together in the GS hb edition (1974), and published separately in the 1993 Eerdmans pb eds. I have come to appreciate their theological worth for pastors (e.g., on ch. 15). And one does need a theological commentary on this letter. But compare Kistemaker below. There is an edited version of this commentary in pb noted below.

☆   Hodge, Charles. (CrossC) 1995. [*SBET* Spr 97].

✓   **Horsley, Richard A.** ‡ (ANTC) 1998. A fresh exegesis which runs down a particular track, one (thankfully) not taken by most interpreters. Horsley reconstructs the church situation. He believes that those "primarily addressed in 1 Corinthians... focused on their personal relationship with heavenly *Sophia* (Wisdom). ...As revealed apparently by the wisdom teacher Jesus and his apostle Apollos, *Sophia* provided her devotees with true spiritual knowledge of the divine and immortality of the soul" (p.37). Because of its individuality (quirkiness), this work won't be used as much as some other ANTC. Not for pastors. [*CBQ* 1/00; *RelSRev* 4/00; *SwJT* Sum 01].

F   House, H. Wayne. (EEC).

☆   Johnson, Alan F. (IVPNT) 2004. The author is a veteran NT scholar, providing a competent exegesis with brief consideration of contemporary relevance questions. [*JETS* 3/06; *Them* 4/06; *JSNT-BL* 2005; *RelSRev* 7/06].

✓   Keener, Craig. [*M*], *1–2 Corinthians* (NCBC) 2005. At less than 250pp for both books, Keener seems a bit thin. That being said, Keener is well-informed and interprets the letters from a socio-rhetorical angle. As usual for Keener, he is strong on details but a little less successful at the "macro-level." Students will benefit from looking up his "Suggested Reading" sections: pp.11–19 and 152–55; do note, however, that the suggestions are weighted toward critical works, ignoring some valuable conservative monographs and articles. [*CBQ* 10/06; *JTS* 4/07; *JETS* 9/06; *JSNT-BL* 2006; *RB* 4/07; *RelSRev* 4/07; *BSac* 1/07; *ExpTim* 8/06; *Anvil* 23.2]. There is now a report that Keener will produce another commentary on this epistle. No series is listed for this, and it may be another huge, stand-alone scholarly work like his commentaries on Matthew (Eerdmans) and John (Hendrickson).

☆   Kistemaker, Simon J. (NTC) 1993. Well worth owning (590pp) as a sure-footed theological guide, even if it is not the most original, scintillating commentary. Kistemaker's works tend to be fairly even in quality. NTC is especially of value to preachers, and the Reformed theology here is a big plus! Kistemaker is much better on the Greek text than Hodge too, if you are comparing them. See my comments on Carson above. [*CTJ* 11/95; *RTR* 9/96].

Kovacs, Judith L. (ed). *1 Corinthians: Interpreted by Early Christian Commentators*, 2005. I find the Bray edited vol. above easier to use and slightly more useful. Kovacs is much fuller in quotation length, however, thus providing more of a sense of literary context for the selections. [*Chm* Aut 06; *JTS* 10/07; *JSNT-BL* 2006; *RB* 4/07; *RelSRev* 3/08; *Pro Ecclesia* Win 09].

✓   Lightfoot, J.B. 1904. See under 1 & 2 Thessalonians.

Lockwood, Gregory J. (Concord) 2000. I have yet to see this 648-page book.

MacArthur, John. 1984. See Matthew for a review of the series.

Mare, W. Harold. (EBC) 1976.

Mitchell, M.M. *Paul and the Rhetoric of Reconciliation: An Exegetical Investigation of Language and Composition of 1 Corinthians*, 1991.

✓   Moffatt, James. ‡ (Moffatt) 1943. This older standard reference work, long ago superseded, is still cited. Quite critical, with rigorous historical inquiry.

F   Montague, George T. [*M?*], (CCSS).

☆   Morris, Leon. (TNTC) 1958, rev. 1988. Morris insightfully reads the text and is recommended as a small, handy guide through the book.

✓   Murphy-O'Connor, Jerome. ‡ *St. Paul's Corinth: Texts and Archeology*, 3rd ed 2002. From the trenchant NT Professor at the École Biblique in Jerusalem, who has expertise in archeology among several research fields. The spirit of criticism in this book and in its companion on Ephesus (see below) is rather negative.

Nash, R. Scott. ‡ (S&H) 2010. I have yet to see this.

Naylor, Peter. (EPSC) 2004.

F   Nighswander, Dan. (BCBC).

F   Okland, Jorunn. (Blackwell).

F   Omanson, Roger. (BHGNT).

Orr, W.F., and J.A. Walther. ‡ (retired AB) 1976. Of some worth perhaps for its introduction, but the exegesis is too spotty to be dependable. One of the less valuable commentaries in the series, now replaced by Fitzmyer.

Parry, R. St. John. [*M*], (Cambridge Greek Testament for Schools and Colleges) 1926, 1937. Remains a useful tool for the student working through the original.

F   Perkins, Pheme. ‡ (Paideia).

☆   Prior, David. (BST) 1985. Successfully pursues the aims of the series. This same author has also written on the Minor Prophets for the BST series. [*JETS* 3/87; *Chm* 101.4 (1987)].

✓   **Robertson, A., and A. Plummer.** [*M*], (ICC) 2nd ed 1914. A magnificent piece of work which is still of real value today. (Some seminary professors, e.g., George Knight, used to recommend its purchase as recently as the late 1980s.) This classic pays close attention to technical matters.

✓   Ruef, J.S. ‡ 1978. A critical commentary published by Westminster Press. Perhaps worth consulting.

✓   Sampley, J. Paul. ‡ (NewIB) 2002. This scholar has already contributed the commentary on 2 Corinthians. This interpretation of 1 Corinthians is approximately 230pp and seems to emphasize community living and ethical matters. But there can also be a tendency to skirt today's politicized topics like homosexuality (e.g., 6:9–11) where the Apostle takes them up.

Smedes, Lewis B. *Love Within Limits*, 1978. Chapter 13 is the springboard for reflection in this famous book.

☆   Soards, Marion L. [*M*], (NIBC) 1999. Nearly 400pp of conservatively critical commentary. The author is a professor at Louisville Presbyterian Theological Seminary. [*RTR* 4/01; *EvQ* 1/02; *Chm* Sum 04].

Stanley, Arthur P. *The Epistles of Paul to the Corinthians*, 1882. This classic was reprinted in years gone by, but most will be indifferent to it, considering the other resources available.

☆   Stott, John R.W. *Calling Christian Leaders*, 2002. This is a 150-page exposition of Chs. 1–4 that can be recommended to preachers. [*Chm* Aut 02].

✓   **Talbert, C.H.** ‡ *Reading Corinthians: A Literary and Theological Commentary on 1 & 2 Corinthians*, 1987.

F   Taylor, Mark. (NAC). Ignore earlier reports of George Guthrie contributing.

Thrall, Margaret. ‡ *The First and Second Letters of Paul to the Corinthians* (CBC) 1965. She has followed this up with a far more weighty commentary on 2 Corinthians in the ICC. This book is conservatively critical.

☆   Verbrugge, Verlyn. (EBCR) 2008. For preachers rather than students. This commentary of a little over 170pp is clear and simple without being simplistic. His exegetical decisions are consistently the right ones, in my opinion (e.g., rejecting the ploy of excising 14:34–36).

F   Wanamaker, C. (RRA).

F   Wannenwetsch, C. (Brazos).

F   Winter, Bruce. (NCCS). The author was long Warden of Tyndale House in Cambridge and has now returned to his native Australia. He is currently associated with Queensland Theological College. No one questions Winter's profound learning in Pauline studies and the Corinthian correspondence in particular. See his *Philo and Paul among the Sophists* (1997), and *After Paul Left Corinth* (2000).

☆   **Witherington, Ben.** *Conflict and Community in Corinth: A Socio-Rhetorical Commentary on 1 & 2 Corinthians*, 1995. Asks different, literary questions and provides a fresh reading. This isn't just another commentary. Specifically, Witherington pursues the "wholesale application of classical rhetorical categories" (Bill Salier) to the Corinthian correspondence and all the rest of the NT writings. His many works complement other, more traditionally-styled commentaries. I like

Witherington's insights, but, as has been pointed out numerous times in reviews, he seems to be overpublished or publishing too rapidly. This is betrayed in the poor proof-reading some of his books have been receiving, especially the earlier ones. See his other vols. on Mark, John, Acts, Romans, Galatians, and Philippians. In fact, he has now published on the whole New Testament canon. [*Them* 10/97; *JETS* 3/98; *TJ* Spr 96; *Biblica* 77.3 (1996); *Interp* 1/97; *CBQ* 1/97].

Wright, N.T. *Paul for Everyone: 1 Corinthians*, 2003. [*Chm* Win 05].

NOTE: See John Ziesler's article surveying commentaries on 1 Corinthians in *ExpTim*, 6/86.

—m—

2 CORINTHIANS

★ **Barnett, Paul.** (NICNT) 1997. "Now the evangelical commentary of choice on II Corinthians," said E.E. Ellis, prior to the publication of NIGTC. And it is still the best mid-level commentary available to pastors. Barnett follows Hughes in giving a strong defense of the unity of the letter, unlike Thrall and Martin who find a compilation of three letters, and Barrett, Bruce, and Furnish who find two. There is also an up-to-date, judicious discussion of introductory matters—a very important thing for a commentary on 2 Corinthians. Readers find much good theology here from an evangelical Anglican bishop in Australia. See BST below. [*RTR* 8/98; *SwJT* Spr 98; *CBQ* 10/98; *Biblica* 79.1; *EvQ* 7/99; *JTS* 10/99; *Chm* 113.1; more critical are *Them* 5/99 and *WTJ* Spr 01].

★ **Garland, David E.** (NAC) 1999. This approximately 550-page work reaps a rich harvest from other recent commentaries, including the 1997 Barnett NICNT. And Garland himself is a veteran interpreter with a half dozen major books to his credit. Though I continue to make NICNT my first pick among commentaries on the English text, this vol. deserves serious consideration as a priority purchase for evangelical pastors, particularly those whose Greek is rusty and who are intimidated by the size or price of NIGTC. [*Them* Sum 03; *JETS* 9/01].

★ Hafemann, Scott J. (NIVAC) 2000. One of the largest and best researched vols. in the series—see his twin monographs: *Suffering and the Spirit on 2 Cor. 2:14–3:3* (1986), and *Paul, Moses, and the History of Israel: The Letter/Spirit Contrast and the Argument from Scripture in 2 Corinthians 3* (1995, 2005) [*EuroJTh* 16.2]. Another, more exegetical commentary was supposedly coming down the pike (BECNT), but that will not happen. In any case one is glad to have this full (over 500pp) work. It is of value to students as well as pastors. Those looking for more pastoral/devotional expositions should consider Carson, Belleville, Hughes, and the old work by Denney.

★ **Harris, Murray J.** (NIGTC) 2005. A welcome publishing event! This is what students of the NT have been waiting for. One could describe this as a fitting complement to Thiselton's definitive NIGTC commentary on Paul's first letter to the Corinthians. Harris builds on his EBC work (see below), but this technical vol. far, far outstrips the earlier commentary. It offers a thoroughly satisfying exegesis and more theology than the series often has. There is meticulous discussion of grammatical matters. The one drawback is the list price of $75. Think of this conservative work as an investment which will repay study for decades to come. While students may now turn to Harris first, they will also be wise to consult Furnish, Thrall, Martin,

Belleville, Lambrecht, and Barrett. [*CBQ* 10/05; *Interp* 7/06; *BBR* 16.1, 16.2; *JTS* 4/07; *BSac* 4/06; *JETS* 3/06; *TJ* Spr 06; *JSNT-BL* 2006; *NovT* 50.2; *ExpTim* 12/06; *Presb* Spr 07].

✓ Baker, William R. (College Press NIV Commentary) 1999. Blomberg calls this 470-page work "probably the best vol. in the series thus far." [*Them* Aut 00; *JETS* 9/01].

☆ Barnett, Paul. (BST) 1988. This series is consistently thoughtful and stimulating for the preacher. No doubt, Stott the editor had a lot to do with keeping the standards high. Barnett is a leading example of the strongly Reformed Anglicans associated with Moore College in Sydney. See the NICNT entry above. [*JETS* 12/91].

☆ **Barrett, C.K.** ‡ (BNTC) 1973. Much in the mold of the commentary on the first epistle, though for some reason I value the earlier one more. Carson continued to make this his first pick even in 1993. Preachers will appreciate how the commentary is often theologically charged and eloquent (see 8:9 and his reference to "the absolute naked poverty of crucifixion"). I used to include this among my recommended purchases, and this compact exegesis is still a smart buy, especially if you agree with the ancient Greek saying that "a big book is a big evil." [*JBL* 94.3 (1975)].

☆ **Belleville, Linda.** (IVPNT) 1996. Careful, succinct exegesis is paired here with some fine theological reflection and pastoral application. Argues well for the unity of the letter. If all the vols. in the series were like this one, Fee on Philippians, and Marshall on 1 Peter, I would say buy the whole set. [*Chm* 112.2 (1998)].

Bernard, J.H. (Expositor's Greek Testament) 1903. Keep in reserve.

✓ Best, Ernest. ‡ (I) 1987. Perhaps the author put less effort into this book than he did into other projects.

✓ **Betz, Hans Dieter.** ‡ *2 Corinthians 8 & 9: A Commentary on Two Administrative Letters of the Apostle Paul* (Herm) ET 1985. Applies rhetorical criticism just to these two chapters. Students should certainly use their discernment here. Betz wrote on Galatians in the same distinguished technical series. [*JBL* 106.4 (1987)].

✓ Bray, Gerald (ed). *1–2 Corinthians* (ACCS) 1999. See 1 Corinthians.

☆ **Bruce, F.F.** (NCB) 1971. See under 1 Corinthians.

Bultmann, Rudolf. ‡ 1976, ET 1985. As any student familiar with this radical German critic might predict, he really disassembles the text. From the MeyerK series. You should ignore this.

✓ Burke, Trevor, and J.K. Elliott (eds). *Paul and the Corinthians: Studies on a Community in Conflict*, 2003. A *Festschrift* vol. for Dr. Thrall.

☆ Carson, D.A. *From Triumphalism to Maturity*, 1984 = *A Model of Christian Maturity*, 2007. Preaching the last four chapters can be extraordinarily difficult because of the change in Paul's mood from chs. 9 to 10. This exposition can really help the pastor, but one should get the above recommended exegetical works first. This used to be on my "to buy" list in previous eds. I am glad that it remains in print. Please note the change in book title. [*Evangel* Spr 88; *EvQ* 4/87; *JETS* 9/85; *BSac* 1/08].

F Collins, Raymond J. ‡ (Paideia).

✓ **Danker, Frederick.** [*M*], 1989. A commentary with lots to offer. Danker takes particular interest in the "sociology of benefaction" as a key to unlocking the main message of the epistle. Reads the letter as a unity—though chs. 10–13 are said to be written somewhat later. His broad learning is much in evidence. This work is published by Augsburg-Fortress. [*JTS* 4/91; *CRBR* 1991].

Denney, James. (EB) 1894. Ralph Martin gives this work a glowing recommendation and calls it "remarkably fresh and apropos on many issues." Denney is probably the best of the old homiletical commentaries.

F   deSilva, David. (NCCS). The author is a Methodist NT scholar at Ashland Seminary with several successful commentaries behind him. His socio-rhetorical approach is similar to Witherington's.

      Filson, Floyd V. ‡ (IB) 1953.

✓   **Furnish, Victor Paul.** ‡ (AB) 1984. A thorough introduction, the fullest of bibliographies (now dated), and well-reasoned exegesis from the critical perspective. This is still among the best scholarly commentaries available, though I suspect it may be too full (600pp) for some pastors. I would commend this moderately critical work especially to advanced students who will relish the scholarship—but compare with Harris, Martin and Thrall. He somewhat tentatively concludes that 6:14–7:1 comes from another hand. The pastor searching for another exegetical work, and who thinks Furnish too full, should consider Belleville's 350-page IVPNT or the more critical Roetzel in ANTC. [*WTJ* Fall 87; *ExpTim* 6/85; *JBL* 106.2; *EvQ* 7/87; *JETS* 9/85; *ThTo* 42.4].

F   Georgi, D. ‡ (Herm). But see also Betz.

F   Gooder, Paula. ‡ (Blackwell).

F   Graebe, Peter. (PentC).

F   Guthrie, George. (BECNT). Previously the publisher listed Scott Hafemann for this series.

      Harris, Murray J. (EBC) 1976. This is an excellent, packed commentary on the epistle. Years ago I would have liked to recommend it for purchase except for its brevity. Since the other commentaries in this vol. were not on the recommended list, I was reluctant to counsel purchasing the entire vol. in order to obtain this 100-page commentary. Thankfully, anticipation of NIGTC (above) made this decision easier. With the publication of other fine evangelical works, Harris's EBC declined in value. See EBCR below.

☆   Harris, Murray J. (EBCR) 2008. This distills down to 130pp his hugely detailed exegesis in NIGTC. Valuable indeed! Oliver Wendell Holmes Sr. reputedly said, "I would not give a fig for the simplicity this side of complexity but I would give my right arm for the simplicity on the other side of complexity."

✓   Hay, David M. (ed). ‡ *Pauline Theology, Vol. 2: 1 and 2 Corinthians*, 1993.

✓   Héring, Jean. ‡ ET 1967. A significant work, previously cited often in the literature on 2 Corinthians.

☆   Hodge, Charles. (GS) 1857–59. See under 1 Corinthians. Note, too, the Crossway Classic edition below.

☆   Hodge, Charles. (CrossC) 1995. [*SBET* Spr 97].

☆   **Hughes, Philip.** (retired NICNT) 1962. A dependable work which has been especially valued for its theological insights into this very personal and emotional letter (see the rich commentary on chs. 3–6). Hughes also stands out for drawing insights from the Church Fathers. The student should note that 2 Corinthians has received a lot of attention, long overdue, in the last 50 years, and Hughes *really* needs to be brought up to date. Therefore, use with Harris's NIGTC and Barnett's NICNT. In previous eds. of this guide Hughes was one of the top choices, and some pastors will still want this on their purchase list.

☆   Hughes, R. Kent. (PTW) 2006. [*BSac* 7/06].

✓   Keener, Craig. [*M*], 1–2 Corinthians (NCBC) 2005. See under 1 Corinthians.

☆   Kistemaker, Simon J. (NTC) 1997.

☆   Kruse, Colin. (TNTC) 1987. A good, solid commentary, but with Harris, Furnish, Martin, Bruce, Barnett, Barrett, and Hughes on my shelf, I find Kruse doesn't add to my study. It's excellent for the money. I used to call it the best brief commentary by far before Belleville and Scott came along. [*RTR* 5/88; *Evangel* Sum 89].

✓ **Lambrecht, Jan.** ‡ (SacPag) 1999. Not as full (250pp) as many others in this series and does not appear to interact as much with scholarship. Appearances can be deceiving. Lambrecht is a brilliant scholar and an expert on this so-difficult section of the Pauline corpus. Though he has not given us his very best work, he provides a valuable exegesis and theological interpretation from the critical angle. By the way, it is a more conservatively critical approach that he takes, upholding the unity and integrity of the epistle. Students should not miss this. [*Interp* 1/00; *SwJT* Fall 00; *CBQ* 10/00; *ExpTim* 8/08].

✓ Long, Fredrick J. *Ancient Rhetoric and Paul's Apology: The Compositional Unity of 2 Corinthians*, (Cambridge) 2004.

✓ McCant, Jerry W. ‡ (Read) 1999. [*JETS* 9/01; *Interp* 10/02; *RelSRev* 4/01].

☆ **Martin, Ralph P.** [*M*], (WBC) 1986, rev. 2010. This important scholarly work came out about the same time as Furnish, and it competed with that AB vol. One has to be grateful to the energetic "R.P.M." (once his secret nickname among suffering students at Fuller) for all his painstaking work; this commentary by the NT editor for WBC is a success. There is complete bibliographical control. To my mind, though, Furnish had a little more to offer in the way of well-considered exegesis. Their critical stances were very similar, as were their conclusions. Martin's theology is more conservative, and, as Hafemann once noted, he "provides the standard reference work for the history of interpretation." Harris's NIGTC now supersedes both WBC and AB as a guide through the exegetical options. Martin is expected to publish a revised edition of his WBC in Fall 2010, and I expect it to become the leading bibliographical help for students. [*WTJ* Fall 87; *SJT* 42.3; *RTR* 5/87; *JBL* 107.3 (1988)].

Martin, Ralph P. [*M*], (CorBC) 2008. This commentary is paired with William Baker on 1 Corinthians and offers a scaled-down version of his big WBC above.

✓ **Matera, Frank J.** ‡ (NTL) 2003. This is a new leading, mid-level, critical commentary which argues for the unity of the letter. Students should certainly consult this, especially for its discussion of rhetorical questions. There are some similarities of approach between Matera and Lambrecht, both lauded Catholic scholars. [*CBQ* 10/04; *Interp* 7/04; *ExpTim* 4/04; *RelSRev* 4/04; *JETS* 3/05; *RB* 10/05; *CurTM* 8/05].

Minor, Mitzi L. ‡ (S&H) 2010. I have yet to see a copy.

✓ Murphy-O'Connor, J. ‡ 1991. From the Cambridge NT Theology series.

✓ Murphy-O'Connor, Jerome. ‡ *St. Paul's Corinth: Texts and Archeology*, 3rd ed 2002. See under 1 Corinthians.

Naylor, Peter. (EPSC) 2 Vols., 2002. [*Evangel* Spr 05].

✓ Omanson, R.L., and J. Ellington. (UBS) 1994. [*JETS* 9/97].

F Oropeza, B.J. (RRA).

✓ **Plummer, Alfred.** [*M*], (retired ICC) 1915. A success in its day and still consulted by students and scholars, but this is not the classic that the ICC was on 1 Corinthians. In any case it has now been replaced by Thrall.

✓ Roetzel, Calvin. ‡ (ANTC) 2007. This compact exegetical reference by a noted American Pauline scholar strangely does not list Barnett, Harris, or Martin in its bibliography. How did that happen? Roetzel follows the five-letter hypothesis and organizes his commentary in a confusing way. [*JSNT-BL* 2009].

Sampley, J. Paul. ‡ (NewIB) 2000. [*Sewanee Theological Review*, Easter 01].

☆ Scott, James M. (NIBC) 1998. A fine piece of work of middling length (267pp), which competes with Kruse to be the "best bargain" in pb for the student. Scott is current with his NT scholarship, but is courageous to buck the critical consensus and argue for the unity of the letter.

F Seifrid, Mark A. (Pillar). This should be very good.

☆ Shillington, V. George. (BCBC) 1998. Certainly one of the best in the NT series. The author, who teaches at a Canadian college, did his PhD on Paul under E.P. Sanders at McMaster University. He writes with good scholarship in vigorous prose. Deep, yet accessible to laypeople.

Stanley, Arthur P. *The Epistles of Paul to the Corinthians*, 1882. See under 1 Corinthians.

Stegman, Thomas D. ‡ (CCSS) 2009. [*RBL* 8/10 (Collins)].

✓ **Talbert, C.H.** ‡ *Reading Corinthians: A Literary and Theological Commentary on 1 & 2 Corinthians*, 1987.

Tasker, R.V.G. (TNTC) 1958. Though now replaced by Kruse, Tasker remains insightful in short compass.

✓ **Thrall, Margaret E.** ‡ (ICC–new series) 2 Vols., 1994–2000. This valuable commentary is the result of over 35 years' work on 2 Corinthians, building on her more popularly-styled CBC (1965) and upon Furnish and Martin, too. Her work replaces Plummer and could be considered for purchase by advanced students and academically inclined pastors who have the money for, and interest in, building a first-rate personal library. She is judicious, though not unafraid to challenge consensus and go her separate way. The first vol. of 500pp includes an introduction and exegesis of chs. 1–7. The second vol. adds another 400pp of commentary along with helpful excurses and two concluding essays. Though not without a few demerits, this set presents a most exacting exegesis of the Greek text, carefully laying out the grammatical options. She holds that 2 Corinthians is a compilation of three letters. [*Biblica* 77.2; *ExpTim* 1/95; *JTS* 10/96, 4/02; *SwJT* Spr 95; *JBL* Fall 96; *JETS* 9/97; *Them* Spr 03; *ExpTim* 8/01; *NovT* 44.2; *JSNT* 9/01; *JR* 1/03; *EvQ* 10/04; *SJT* 58.3; *Anvil* 18.4 (Barclay)]. N.B.: I have been criticized a bit for labeling Thrall as critical. Let me be more precise. She is conservatively critical and has some ties to the broader evangelical movement in the UK—e.g., writing reviews for *EvQ*. I hope the designation ‡ is not off-putting. These vols. can be quite useful to conservative interpreters (mainly specialists), if they are willing to plow through some very dense, difficult material. "Even the knowledgeable exegete will find Thrall's work slow going," says Belleville.

F Towner, Philip. (THC).

Wan, Sze-kar. ‡ *Power in Weakness* (NT in Context) 2000. [*Interp* 10/02].

F Wannenwetsch, Bernd. (Brazos).

☆ **Witherington, Ben.** *Conflict and Community in Corinth: A Socio-rhetorical Commentary on 1 & 2 Corinthians*, 1995. See under 1 Corinthians above.

Wright, N.T. *Paul for Everyone: 2 Corinthians*, 2003. [*Chm* Win 05].

Young, Frances, and David Ford. *Meaning and Truth in 2 Corinthians*, 1987.

GALATIANS

★ **Bruce, F.F.** (NIGTC) 1982. Everything you would expect from this late scholar: excellent exegetical judgment, full historical background, a proficient handling of the Greek, complete bibliographical control, etc. This is such a good exegetical commentary that most well-trained pastors should add it to their library at some point. Not as much expositional help however. In the 7th edition I took Bruce off the recommended list, but that was a mistake. I use Bruce as much as Longenecker. [*WTJ* Fall 83; *RTR* 5/83; *JETS* 9/82; *JBL* 104.2 (1985)].

★ **Fung, R.Y.K.** (NICNT) 1988. A lucid mid-level commentary which builds on Bruce (Fung trained under him at Manchester) and is of greater help expositionally than the excellent NIGTC. This work is a laudable effort, but is beginning to show its age. I'm not sure of the reason for so many references to Kittel's TDNT. Students need to be made aware of James Barr's well-founded criticisms of that famous (and useful) dictionary, and cautioned against a naive use of the word study method. Barr's proposition needs to ring in our ears: theological thinking is done mainly in the phrase and in the sentence, not in the word. Fung is scheduled for replacement by deSilva. We really could use a newer evangelical, mid-level work that is well-balanced; I am looking for those by Carson, Schreiner, and Moo. [*WTJ* Fall 89; *JETS* 6/90; *JTS* 10/90; *EvQ* 7/90].

★ **Longenecker, Richard N.** [𝓜], (WBC) 1990. Superb introduction (119pp), taking the "South Galatian" view. At points, I am convinced, he should have treated the Scriptures with more respect, as when he speaks of the inspired Apostle unfairly caricaturing his opponents' teaching and activity (p.lxxxix)—are we supposed to sympathize with the opponents? All that aside, this is about the best I know of in the category of commentary on the Greek (323pp). As the most recent full exegesis by an evangelical, it builds on all the great studies of the past and interacts some with Dunn. Galatians is probably better served with commentaries on the Greek text than any other NT book. There is an *embarras de richesse* ("embarrassment of riches") here: Lightfoot, Burton, Bruce, Betz, Longenecker, and Martyn. That said, there is a pressing need for a newer, thorough evangelical exegesis which engages the New Perspective. One criticism has been that Longenecker "tries too often to combine the older and newer approaches in a synthesis of contradictory interpretations" [*BSB* 12/96]. See also Longenecker's *The Triumph of Abraham's God* (1998). [*WTJ* Spr 93; *JTS* 10/92; *EvQ* 7/93; *JBL* Win. 93; *CBQ* 10/92; *Them* 4/92; *JETS* 9/95; *CTJ* 11/92; *AsTJ* Spr 92].

★ Luther, Martin. 1519 and 1535. These two commentaries are available in the American Edition of *Luther's Works* (Vols. 26 and 27, Concordia Publishing House). One of the two is also available, I know, in a 19th century translation which is still being reprinted. Kregel has lately released the commentary in a "Modern-English Edition." And in 1998 the work was edited and published in the "Crossway Classic Commentary" series; that pb edition is certainly the cheapest. "It is Luther's Commentary on Galatians which has stimulated generations of readers to sense the power of Paul" (Childs). Actually, it isn't the power of Paul or the vigor of Luther; it is the emancipating power *of Christ* which comes through in these commentaries. You really must read Luther on Galatians. Paul's gospel of free grace will come alive for you in a new way as you read the great Saxon Reformer. Lightfoot gives this apt note of praise for this theological classic: "The value of Luther's work stands apart from and in some respects higher than its merits as a commentary" (p.ix).

★ Ryken, Philip. (REC) 2005. Model theological and practical exposition. While students pass this by, pastors will enjoy edifying food for the soul. Happy and healthy is the church that is fed like this.

★ Stott, John R.W. *Only One Way: The Message of Galatians* (BST) 1968. This vol. really is a must for the expositor. Stott's ability to grasp the theology of the text, his practicality, and his ability to communicate make this an ideal tool for sermon work, an ideal handbook for Bible studies, and devotional guide. For expositional help, pastors also look to George, Calvin, Ryken, and McKnight.

Arichea, D.C., and E.A. Nida. (UBS) 1976.

✓ Barclay, John M.G. ‡ *Obeying the Truth: Paul's Ethics in Galatians*, 1988.

✓ Barrett, C.K. ‡ *Freedom and Obligation*, 1985. A rigorous and penetrating study of Paul's argument. [*JBL* 106.4 (1987); *ThTo* 44.2].

Betz, Hans Dieter. ‡ (Herm) 1979. A significant work which has stimulated others to utilize classical rhetorical analysis in studying the epistles. In fact, as Hays writes, "the agenda for the interpretation of Galatians during the past twenty years has been set by…Betz's Hermeneia commentary…(see, e.g., the commentaries of R.N. Longenecker and B. Witherington, which seek in various ways to correct, refine, and expand upon Betz's analysis of the rhetorical structure)." This vol. is aimed at scholars, and most pastors should look to other commentaries for help with the text and message of Galatians. [*WTJ* Fall 83; *TJ* Spr 80; *JBL* 100.2 (1981)]. For a critique of rhetorical approaches see Kern, *Rhetoric and Galatians* (CUP, 1998).

Bligh, J. ‡ 1969. A huge commentary by an English Roman Catholic. Not of much use in my view. [*JBL* 89.1].

Boice, James M. (EBC) 1976. Helpful for pastors, but didn't really add much to the discussion from an academic point of view. This was a tool for expositors interested in communicating Paul's message. See Rapa.

Bring, Ragnar. ET 1961. "Oriented in the direction of Lutheran dogmatics" (Carson).

✓ **Burton, E.D.** ‡ (ICC) 1921. One of the best and fullest entries in the old series. For detailed, close exegesis academics still use Burton, but I doubt that many pastors will be willing to dig through these pages. A number of his theological conclusions are fundamentally wrong-headed. Students should not miss the valuable appendix (p.363ff).

☆ Calvin, John. *Sermons on Galatians*, 1557–58, ET 1997. A welcome new translation of the Reformer's lengthy sermon series (671pp), published by Banner of Truth. Note: the old 16th century Golding translation has, I believe, been kept in print by Old Paths Publications. [*CTJ* 11/98; *SBET* Aut 99].

F Carson, D.A. (Pillar).

Cole, R. Alan. (TNTC) 1965, rev. 1989. Useful, handy, but undistinguished.

✓ Cousar, Charles. ‡ (I) 1982. Evangelicals often do not find the critical works on a book like Galatians to be as troublesome as elsewhere. Higher critical issues do not tend to color the interpretation quite as much because there is agreement on the unity of the letter and Paul's authorship. Cousar is one of the stronger vols. in the series. [*Interp* 7/83].

F De Boer, Martinus C. ‡ (NTL).

F deSilva, David. [*M*], (NICNT). The author's Vita lists this as due in 2010.

✓ **Dunn, James D.G.** ‡ (BNTC) 1993. Dunn is a Pauline scholar of immense stature with a special interest in the Apostle's theology of the law. He pushes hard what he calls "The New Perspective on Paul," *BJRL* 65 (1983). I disagree with his interpretation of Paul's argument in Romans and Galatians (i.e., that Paul was opposing himself, not to confidence in human merit and works righteousness, but to Jewish exclusivism). This full commentary (400pp)—and far more scholarly than might first appear—is definitely to be consulted for papers, but I believe the pastor should look elsewhere for a trusty theological guide through Galatians. Students should note his companion vol.: *The Theology of Paul's Letter to the Galatians* (Cambridge, 1993) [*JBL* Win 95; *SJT* 51.2]; "it would be hard to think of a better introduction to the new perspective on Paul than this book" (Rosner). Two evangelical appraisals of Dunn's theology worth mentioning, alongside the numerous books referenced above under "Pauline Studies," are Silva's article, "The Law and Christianity: Dunn's New Synthesis," *WTJ* Fall 91; and Hagner's article, "Paul and Judaism, The Jewish Matrix of Early Christianity: Issues in the Current Debate," *BBR* 3 (1993): 111–130. [*WTJ* Fall 95; *RTR* 9/94; *JETS* 9/98; *SwJT* Fall 97].

✓ Edwards, Mark J. (ed). *Galatians, Ephesians, Philippians* (ACCS) 1999. [*RelSRev* 4/00; *EvQ* 7/02].

✓ Esler, Philip F. ‡ (New Testament Readings) 1998. [*Scripture Bulletin* 1/99; *RB* 108.1 (2001); *BibInt* 9.1 (2001)].

Fee, Gordon. (PentC) 2007. I have yet to see this 280-page book. According to the publisher's blurb, Fee set out to write a commentary "as if the Reformation never occurred." Hmm. Another book description gives an additional indication that Fee was attempting a fresh reading: there are only 11 works in his bibliography. But if it's Fee, it is probably worth reading. [*JETS* 6/09].

☆ **George, Timothy.** (NAC) 1994. Take a close look at this! There is much to appreciate about this theologically astute, traditionally styled commentary (463pp). This is a good guide for the pastor since it is so focused on Paul's message. George is a fine Reformation scholar (church historian). He is of far greater assistance to the expositor than to the exegete, for he is less engaged with NT scholarship. There is solid exegesis here, though. [*WTJ* Fall 95; *EvQ* 10/96; *Them* 10/97; *JETS* 9/98; *CRBR* 1995].

F Greene-McCreight, Katherine. (Brazos).

Guthrie, Donald. (NCB) 1969. This is a model of clarity in the way it expounds Paul's line of thinking. There is not a wasted word, no sidelights. Guthrie shows that he has the gift for distilling things down and explaining the theology here. This also means that he is not so penetrating as others. [*RTR* 5/70].

Hansen, Walter. (IVPNT) 1994. I have not used this work of 212pp, but it has received some praise as a fine work in its class. Earlier he published "a very valuable monograph" (Silva) on Abraham in *Galatians: Epistolary and Rhetorical Contexts* (1989). In his briefer interaction with the New Perspective, he "finally sides" (Hagner) with its opponents. See Hansen's more recent work on Philippians. [*WTJ* Fall 95 (Silva); *JETS* 9/98 (Hagner); more critical is *Chm* 109.1 (1995)].

✓ **Hays, Richard B.** ‡ (NewIB) 2000. This contribution by a big-name scholar is quite valuable and takes up some of Martyn's views, which Hays considers so important. Of course Hays is a major force among Pauline scholars in his own right—see his dissertation, *The Faith of Jesus Christ* (1983, 2nd ed 2001 [*Evangel* Aut 03]), and a favorite book of mine, *Echoes of Scripture in the Letters of Paul* (1989). Hays has a good annotated bibliography on pp.196–98. Though brief (165 large pages), this may come to be considered among the very best of the recent commentaries on Galatians, especially for those pastors who don't have time for huge vols. like AB. Both exegesis and "Reflection" are superbly done and stimulating, even for one like me who disagrees on a number of issues. By the way, don't be too quick to follow Hays' argument for πίστις Χριστοῦ as a subjective genitive; see Roy A. Harrisville, "Before ΠΙΣΤΙΣ ΧΡΙΣΤΟΥ: The Objective Genitive as Good Greek," *NovT* 48.4 (2006): 353–58, and Cranfield's cautionary essay (pp.81–97) in the book *On Romans* (1998). For fuller discussions one can look up the Dunn-Hays dialogue in the 2001 edition of the dissertation and then consult *The Faith of Jesus Christ: Exegetical, Biblical, and Theological Studies* (2010), edited by Bird and Sprinkle [*Them* 7/10 (Silva)].

Hendriksen, William. (NTC) 1969.

Jervis, Ann. [𝓜], (NIBC) 1999. [*Interp* 7/00; *Chm* Win 00; *RTR* 4/01].

☆ **Lightfoot, J.B.** 1865. Hard to believe, but a strong case can be made that this often reprinted work is still among the richest commentaries around. Carson sells it short when he writes that Lightfoot has been mined so thoroughly that he hardly adds anything to more modern treatments. It continues to be mined because it is an enduring classic. Students and pastors could gain from mining it too; the exercise would be a lesson in appreciating the worth of classic commentaries. For an assessment of Lightfoot's contributions to scholarship, see *Evangel*, Summer 1989. Note his companion works on Philippians, Colossians-Philemon.

✓ **Lührmann, Dieter.** ‡ (ContC) ET 1992. One of the somewhat recent German commentaries (Lutheran), though not as full as many of the other scholarly works on this list (168pp). Lührmann concentrates on theology and does not provide us with a technical, historical and linguistic commentary. The Germans no longer dominate Pauline studies like they once did. [*WTJ* Fall 95; *SJT* 49.4 (1996)].

MacArthur, John. 1987. Useful for its pastoral concern and passion for proclamation, but students should look elsewhere for help with difficult passages. See further comments under Matthew.

✓ Machen, J. Gresham. *Notes on Galatians*, 1972. Fragmentary but incisive. The student could learn much about exegesis here. Machen takes a "North Galatian" view.

☆ McKnight, Scot. (NIVAC) 1995. McKnight's mentors have been Dunn and E.P. Sanders. This is a fine homiletical commentary from that perspective. However, some of us think that, according to the New Perspective, Galatians' argument has a much narrower application than the traditional interpretation and is more or less confined to pastoral problems in the 1st century. In other words, Dunn's thesis makes applying Galatians today difficult. McKnight is the NT editor of the series. [*JETS* 3/98; *Ashland Th Journal* 29 (1997)].

McWilliams, David B. (Mentor) 2009. Edifying, Reformed exposition.

✓ **Martyn, J. Louis.** ‡ (AB) 1997. NT specialists were waiting for this one. Hays calls it "a work of provocative scholarship, unmatched in its penetrating insight and theological depth by any NT commentary of our generation." That's overdoing it, but this AB gains such high praise because it, somewhat like Barth's work on Romans, is a theological treatise in its own right. Martyn understands Galatians to be "the reproclamation of the gospel in the form of an evangelistic sermon" (p.22). He develops Käsemann's "apocalyptic gospel" idea and points to 4:3–5 as "the theological center of the letter" (p.388). The grace of God is understood as operating more on the grand, cosmological scale (God's "invasion" in the Cross), and less on the level of the individual (the dominant Protestant emphasis ever since Luther). He downplays "forensic" elements in the book. Some reviewers, e.g., Carson, believe that Martyn's exegetical judgment can frequently be called into question. He is not for the average pastor, but scholarly types will find Martyn fascinating reading. [*JR* 4/00; *ExpTim* 5/00; *Interp* 10/98; *CBQ* 4/99; *PSB* 21.1 (2000); *JSNT* 75; *AsTJ* Spr 02; *JBL* Sum 00; *RBL*; *DenvJ*].

✓ **Matera, Frank J.** ‡ (SacPag) 1992. Cousar, also a commentator on this Bible book, gives Matera's vol. very high marks. Those wanting a moderately critical reading of Galatians from the Roman Catholic perspective should look this up. Matera essentially follows Dunn's views on the heresy of the Jewish missionaries. I usually read Dunn rather than Matera. [*ExpTim* 3/93; *Interp* 4/94; *CBQ* 10/94; *CRBR* 1994; *ExpTim* 8/08].

F Moo, Douglas. (BECNT). Moisés Silva once had the contract.

☆ Morris, Leon. 1996. Accessible, useful and dependable. This is not unlike Morris' Romans commentary in both style and worth. This vol. will not spark great excitement, but it does the job of providing the pastor with solid phrase by phrase exposition. It is a standard commentary format with good attention paid to details like word study. Morris is of less usefulness to NT students. [*Them* 2/00; *SBET* Spr 97].

✓ Nanos, Mark D. (ed). ‡ *The Galatians Debate*, 2002. Students will gain much from consulting this collection of 23 articles and from the lengthy bibliography. [*RelSRev* 10/03; *JTS* 10/04; *WTJ* Fall 03; *RTR* 4/04; *TJ* Fall 04]. There is also a published dissertation by Nanos: *The Irony of Galatians*, 2001 [*HBT* 12/02; *JETS* 3/03; *JBL* Sum 02; *Interp* 7/03; *ExpTim* 2/03; *JR* 10/02; *JTS* 10/05; *JSS* Spr 04; *BibInt* 12.4].

Ngewa, Samuel. (Africa Bible Commentary Series) 2010. I regret that I have not yet been able to use my senior colleague's book.

F Oakes, Peter. (Paideia).

Perkins, Pheme. ‡ *Abraham's Divided Children* (NT in Context) 2001.

✓ Plumer, Eric. *Augustine's Commentary on Galatians: Introduction, Text, Translation, and Notes* (OUP) ET 2003. [*EuroJTh* 15.1].

Ramsay, W.M. *A Historical Commentary on St. Paul's Epistle to the Galatians*, 2ⁿᵈ ed 1900.

Rapa, Robert Keith. (EBCR) 2008. I have not yet used this (94pp). I know the author did a dissertation on *The Meaning of "Works of the Law" in Galatians and Romans*.

Riches, John. ‡ *Galatians through the Centuries* (BBC) 2008. [*CBQ* 4/09; *JSNT-BL* 2009; *ExpTim* 7/09; *Interp* 7/10; *EuroJTh* 18.1].

Ridderbos, Herman. (retired NICNT) 1953. Replaced by Fung and long o/p. Though insightful and theologically astute in its day, this commentary suffered on account of it brevity. [*WTJ* Spr 54]. You can get his more mature reflections in *Paul: An Outline of His Theology*, referenced previously under "Pauline Studies."

F Schreiner, Thomas. (BHGNT).

F Schreiner, Thomas. (ZEC).

✓ Silva, Moisés. *Interpreting Galatians*, 2001. This fine book is nearly identical to a 1996 issue, *Explorations in Exegetical Method: Galatians As a Test Case* [*JETS* 9/99]. I had expected it to be preliminary to a forthcoming BECNT, but see Moo above. [*Them* Spr 03; *SwJT* Spr 03; *BBR* 14.2].

Tenney, Merrill C. 1950.

F Tuckett, Christopher M. ‡ (ICC–new series). This is a reassignment after the sad news of Graham Stanton's death in 2009; Galatians was to have been Stanton's *magnum opus* in retirement.

F Van Voorst, Robert. (ECC).

F Vickers, Brian. (NCCS). The author teaches at Southern Baptist Theological Seminary in Louisville.

F Wakefield, Andrew H. (S&H).

✓ **Williams, Sam K.** ‡ (ANTC) 1997. Compact. Has received some rather favorable reviews as a lucid, non-technical presentation of the conclusions of important critical scholarship. Williams treats the Apostle's arguments as "matters of opinion— Paul's opinion," and argues that his "polemical charges provide an unreliable basis for characterizing the aims and motives of these Jewish-Christian missionaries" (p.25). I wish he had more sympathy with Paul and his gospel. [*Interp* 7/98; *CBQ* 10/98].

☆ **Witherington, Ben.** *Grace in Galatia: A Commentary on Paul's Letter to the Galatians*, 1998. See my comments under 1 Corinthians. [*Interp* 7/99; *RelSRev* 4/00; *RB* 108.1 (2001); *JSNT* 76].

F   Witherup, Ronald D. ‡ (CCSS).

F   Wright, N.T. (THC). Hints at Wright's approach to Galatians are given in "The Letter to Galatians: Exegesis and Theology," in *Between Two Horizons: Spanning New Testament Studies & Systematic Theology* (2000).

—ɯ—

EPHESIANS

★ Chapell, Bryan. (REC) 2009. Creative, clear, and polished sermonic material on the epistle Dodd once termed "the crown of Paulinism." While the theological exposition is fine, preachers may appreciate President Chapell's illustrations and application most of all. An excellent vol. to set alongside Ryken's REC on Galatians. Students will show less interest in this, unless it's homiletics class, in which case they will learn much. Other fine expositions for the preacher are Boice, Calvin's *Sermons*, Ferguson, Hughes, Lloyd-Jones, Mackay, and H.C.G. Moule.

★ **Lincoln, Andrew T.** ‡ (WBC) 1990. His published dissertation on Ephesians, *Paradise Now and Not Yet* (1981), led us to expect great things. And this is a great commentary, but unfortunately Lincoln changed his mind on Pauline authorship and became more critical after completing his doctoral work at Cambridge. The value of this commentary is somewhat vitiated for evangelicals by his denial of Pauline authorship. He uses some space in this huge work of 550pp distinguishing the theology of Ephesians from that of the genuine Paul. Honestly, it is hard for me to figure why the arguments he adduces for a deutero-Pauline setting convinced him; they do not strike me as strong. Mainly for the advanced student and scholarly pastor, who will also enjoy Lincoln's *Theology of the Later Pauline Letters* (CUP, 1993). The average pastor, I predict, will not be able to appreciate and put to good use the full wealth of data and scholarly argument here. Most evangelicals will hold that Thielman and O'Brien (perhaps adding Hoehner), without Lincoln, provide more than enough exegetical guidance. [*WTJ* Fall 92; *CBQ* 1/93; *EvQ* 4/93; *RTR* 9/93; *JBL* 113.2 (1994); *Them* 1/92]. N.B.: In a series preaching through Ephesians, I found that Robinson on the Greek text gave me more sound guidance per hour invested. Yes, the scholarly student will not want to be without Lincoln for detailed exegesis, but many pastors who give the Scriptures the highest credit-rating and who are time-pressed might prefer Robinson, which is sadly o/p.

★ **O'Brien, Peter T.** (Pillar) 1999. This is the average pastor's first choice, especially if one prefers a forthrightly evangelical commentary upholding Pauline authorship. That is not to say that O'Brien is always to be followed; along with most major interpreters (Calvin, Mitton, Lincoln, Best) I take διὰ πιστεως in 2:8 as referring to our faith, not Christ's faith/faithfulness. This book is of the same quality as his vols. on Colossians–Philemon and Philippians. O'Brien built well on Lincoln. I am glad his treatment is fuller than Bruce, which had previously been the evangelical standard. At 536pp it is fuller, too, than most others in the Pillar series. [*RTR* 12/00; *SwJT* Fall 00; *RelSRev* 7/00; *Them* Spr 01; *JSNT* 6/01; *JETS* 12/01; *Evangel* Aut 02].

★ Snodgrass, Klyne. (NIVAC) 1996. The author is a veteran evangelical NT scholar, teaching at North Park Theological Seminary in Chicago. He knows Ephesians like the back of his hand and is well qualified to guide the expositor through the text to relevant contemporary application. His selection of quotes, both to help along exposition and to help push application, is often superb. This vol. will speak to the pastor's mind and heart. I am very glad for Snodgrass's emphasis upon "union with Christ." Still, I judge Stott a better, safer theological guide through Ephesians, especially for discussion of election. Snodgrass understands election in terms of "God valuing us" (p.59)—he tries to backtrack on p.64 and deny that personal merit or accomplishment pertain to divine election. When he protests so much for human freedom and responsibility and when he asserts a corporate view of election (à la Barth, Torrance), conservative Reformed folk will not want to follow him. Many will feel he is fighting shy of Paul's teaching.

★ Stott, John. *God's New Society: The Message of Ephesians* (BST) 1979. Almost 300pp. This has the same qualities as his vol. on Galatians—don't miss it! Stott is remarkable for drawing from the best of previous works. Through his expositions, he is a pastor to pastors. [*JETS* 6/80].

★ **Thielman, Frank.** (BECNT) 2010. Appreciating the previous publications of this Beeson Divinity School professor and PCA minister, I eagerly awaited this major exegesis (520pp) and anticipated it being a top pick. Hoehner can be daunting for busy pastors, and this proves handier for students and expository preachers working through the Greek text. Thielman's strengths are deep learning in rhetoric and ancient literature (the classics and the Church Fathers), judicious interaction with the best, latest scholarship on Ephesians, discussion of the circumstances that prompted the letter (building well on Trebilco), and theological exposition. (I expected robust and widely-ranging theological discussion after seeing his 2005 *Theology of the New Testament: A Canonical and Synthetic Approach*.) Thielman is surprisingly readable and accessible for a commentary with in-text citations and so much Greek. Here is more reason to sit up and take notice: Moo writes in a blurb, "This commentary will join Hoehner and O'Brien as the first references on Ephesians to which I turn." For students and pastors exegeting the original, this would be the smart first purchase. See also Larkin for a handy, most thorough and current guide for coming to grips with syntactical questions in the Greek text.

✧ ✧ ✧ ✧ ✧ ✧

Abbott, T.K. (retired ICC) 1897. Covers Ephesians and Colossians. Not all that remarkable even decades ago, Abbott can be safely ignored. See Best below.

F Arnold, Clinton E. (ZEC). Here he will build upon his CUP monograph, *Ephesians: Power and Magic* (1989), which I regard as very important reading for students.

✓ **Barth, Markus.** ‡ (AB) 2 Vols., 1975. An amazingly full (850pp) and rigorous treatment, this has a predictable theological *Tendenz*, and follows some lines of thought suggested by his father's work. These volumes were once classed as indispensable to the advanced student and scholarly pastor, and will hold your interest. Argues for Pauline authorship and so is more conservative in some ways than Lincoln. [*WTJ* Fall 75].

F Baugh, Steve. (EEC).

Beare, Francis W. ‡ (IB) 1952.

✓ **Best, Ernest.** ‡ (ICC–new series) 1998. Along with Lincoln, this is an all-important detailed exegesis of the Greek text from the critical camp which denies Pauline authorship. Best comes from Northern Ireland and a Presbyterian theological background. Students will surely consult this, but few pastors will consider purchasing Best to be money well spent. [*JTS* 10/99; *NovT* 41.2; *Interp* 4/99; *CBQ* 10/99; *RTR* 4/99; *SwJT* Spr 00; *RelSRev* 1/01; *EvQ* 10/01; *JETS* 6/01]. As with other recent commentaries in ICC, Best's vol. has been abridged and issued in pb (2004) [*JSNT-BL* 2005]. For further reading, see his *Essays on Ephesians*, 1997 [*JSNT* 72].

☆ Boice, James M. 1988. I found this to be a very useful book of sermons.

✓   Bratcher, R.G., and E.A. Nida. (UBS) 1982.

☆   **Bruce, F.F.** *The Epistles to the Colossians, to Philemon and to the Ephesians* (NICNT) 1984. Replaced E.K. Simpson's weak half-vol. entry in the series from 1957. Bruce's sensible, well-informed commentary spends about 200pp on Ephesians. Previously this NICNT was a recommended purchase, but O'Brien has taken its place. [*RTR* 5/85; *JETS* 6/86; *Them* 1/86]. Bruce also published an earlier exposition, which was more popular in its appeal (1961).

       Caird, G.B. [*M*], (New Clarendon) 1976. Covers the "Prison Epistles" (Ephesians, Philippians, Colossians and Philemon) with lucid, incisive comments in brief compass. Similar in character to Houlden but much better. The spirit of criticism here is quite mild; he upholds Paul's authorship of both Ephesians and Colossians. No brief work on the Prison Epistles competes with Caird.

☆   Calvin, John. *John Calvin's Sermons on Ephesians*, ET 1973. This is a separate vol. from the commentary. "For the homilest an excellent purchase" (Childs). Over 700pp of penetrating exposition. Especially helpful for preaching through the packed theology in chs. 1–3. In previous eds. of this guide I have recommended this for purchase.

       Cohick, Lynn. (NCCS) 2010. The author now teaches at Wheaton College, Illinois. I have yet to see this 190-page book.

F   Dockery, David. (NAC).

       Donelson, Lewis. ‡ *Colossians, Ephesians, 1 and 2 Timothy, and Titus* (WestBC) 1996. [*RelSRev* 7/97; *Interp* 1/98].

       Eadie, J.A. 1883. This sturdy old work, which comments on the Greek text, is cited several times by Markus Barth.

✓   Edwards, Mark J. (ed). *Galatians, Ephesians, Philippians* (ACCS) 1999.

☆   Ferguson, Sinclair B. *Let's Study Ephesians*, 2005. On the popular level I have not found anything better for either group Bible studies or devotional reading (205pp).

       Foulkes, F. (TNTC) 1963, rev. 1989. Not outstanding but a good value. [*JETS* 6/92].

F   Fowl, Stephen E. ‡ (NTL). Fowl is more conservative, but in this series I expect a pseudonymity position.

       Gurnall, William. *The Christian in Complete Armour*, 1662–65. A Puritan classic on Ephesians 6 and a rich example of "experimental" (practical) divinity. Add it to your library as a devotional work. John Newton paid Gurnall's tome the highest compliment when he said that if he might read only one book beside the Bible, he would choose this. You should note that Gurnall has been recently updated in more modern prose and published in paperback by Banner of Truth Trust. [*WTJ* Fall 59; *Chm* 107.2 (1993)]. I have also seen a Hendrickson reprint announced.

☆   Hendriksen, William. (NTC) 1967. More helpful to the preacher theologically than exegetically.

F   Hendrix, Holland. ‡ (Herm). At one time G.W. MacRae was said to have the contract.

☆   Hodge, Charles. (GS) 1856 original. Of good value theologically and for understanding the Apostle's train of thought. Banner of Truth issued a hb reprint in 1964, followed by a 1980 Baker Books pb edition. In 1994 it was edited for inclusion in the Crossway Classic Commentary series (see below). I believe I prefer Hodge to Hendriksen.

☆   Hodge, Charles. (CrossC) 1994.

☆   **Hoehner, Harold W.** 2002. Rivals Markus Barth as the fullest, most detailed commentary ever written on Ephesians (about 900pp)—and less accessible for that reason. I term this Hoehner's *magnum opus*; it is the fruit of many years of intense study. He provides a solid, dependable, (older style) grammatico-historical exegesis of the Greek text and (in smaller measure) a reverential theological exposition. For decades to come, this will be a useful tool on the desk of a bookish pastor. For a briefer Hoehner commentary, see below. Note that this was selected in previous editions as a recommended purchase, but Thielman's volume displaces it, especially for those preferring a shorter exegesis. The scholarly preacher planning a full expository series will make this purchase. Students ought to read Hoehner's 60-page defense of Paul's authorship. [*Them* Sum 04; *JETS* 12/03; *JSNT* 9/04; *SBET* Aut 05; *RelSRev* 1/04; *BBR* 16.1; *Interp* 1/05; *ExpTim* 3/09; *DenvJ* 1/03; *Anvil* 21.3].

Hoehner, Harold. (CorBC) 2008. Hoehner, Harold. (CorBC) 2008. In this multi-author volume Hoehner covers Ephesians; Philip Comfort treats the Philippian and Thessalonian correspondence; and Peter Davids well covers Colossians and Philemon. See above the huge Hoehner work, once recommended, of which this provides a profitable distillation.

Houlden, J. Leslie. ‡ (Pelican) 1977. See Caird above.

☆ Hughes, R. Kent. (PTW) 1990. See under Mark.

Kitchen, M. ‡ (Read) 1994.

Klein, William W. (EBCR) 2006. I have not seen this commentary yet.

Kreitzer, Larry. ‡ (Epworth) 1979. This is highly praised and a bit like Stott, except it comes from the critical (deutero-Pauline) side.

☆ Larkin, William. (BHGNT) 2009. Larkin's 196-page handbook guides the student through the problems and nuances of the Greek text (linguistics and syntax). It is done so expertly, and in such a detailed fashion, that even the Greek professor would use it as a reference. See Larkin under Acts.

✓ Lightfoot, J.B. 1904. See under 1 & 2 Thessalonians.

☆ Lloyd-Jones, D. Martyn. 1974–82. Among bookish pastors this 8-vol. exposition needs no commendation. "Eminently worthwhile, but only if you read very quickly" (Carson). [*JETS* 6/82].

F Long, F.J. (RRA).

MacArthur, John. 1986. See Matthew for my perhaps too-harsh review of this series of sermonic/expositional vols.

✓ **MacDonald, Margaret Y.** ‡ *Colossians and Ephesians* (SacPag) 2000. Of note because of her social-scientific approach to these epistles, which she blends with more traditional historical critical discussion. She takes the standard critical line on introductory matters. [*Interp* 10/01; *ExpTim* 3/02; *RelSRev* 10/03; *ExpTim* 8/08; *BSac* 7/10].

Mackay, John A. [*M*], *God's Order*, 1953. Often this vol. can be picked up second-hand. It is one of the more thought-provoking expositions I have seen. Mackay (pronounced "Mc-eye") was President of Princeton Seminary (1936–59). Readers will catch his enthusiasm for Ephesians, both because "to this book I owe my life" (p.6) and because of the epistle's ecumenical vision.

✓ Martin, Ralph P. ‡ *Ephesians, Colossians, and Philemon* (I) 1991. Already in the mid-1970s Martin had published his verdict that Ephesians is deutero-Pauline, and I wonder if he, as NT editor for WBC, influenced Lincoln to adopt the same position. Martin long taught at Fuller Seminary, then briefly moved back to his native England and the University of Sheffield, before closing out his teaching career at Fuller. He is best known for editing and writing for the Word series (*2 Corinthians* and *James*), and for his several works on Philippians. Though Martin is a prominent Pauline scholar, his theological exposition here in Interpretation is a little too brief (156pp) to compete with other fine works now available to pastors. Martin's theology is more conservative than his position on matters of introduction and historical setting. See also his works on Colossians. [*CRBR* 1994; *CBQ* 7/93; *BSac* 1/93].

✓ **Mitton, C. Leslie.** ‡ (NCB) 1981. A packed, moderately critical commentary which denies Pauline authorship. Mitton is a useful work in the hands of the discerning student. Prior to the publication of Lincoln, Best, and Schnackenburg (in ET), Mitton's commentary was much more important to consult for understanding the standard critical approach. He also wrote *The Epistle to the Ephesians: Its Authorship, Origin and Purpose* (Clarendon, 1951), which still stands as perhaps the classic presentation of the arguments for the epistle being a post-Pauline production. For the student wanting some well-grounded, orthodox response to the critical position, there is a compact answer in the NT introductions by Donald Guthrie and Carson/Moo, a fuller defense in O'Brien and Hoehner, and a full-length monograph by van Roon (listed below).

☆ Morris, Leon. *Expository Reflections on the Letter to the Ephesians*, 1994. In the same style as his *Reflections* vols. on John's Gospel, this 240-page book clarifies the meaning of the text, brings out contemporary application, and includes some illustration. [*JETS* 9/96].

✓ **Muddiman, John.** ‡ (BNTC) 2001. This provocative work of 338pp by an Oxford scholar challenges the critical consensus on authorship. Muddiman contends that Ephesians is an authentic letter, but edited and expanded much later in the 1st century. The exegesis (which offers his own translation of the Greek) is penetrating and valuable, and I aver that it should be better known in the USA than it is. [*JTS* 10/02; *Interp* 4/03; *ExpTim* 8/01; *JR* 7/02; *RelSRev* 7/02; *RTR* 4/07; *RB* 7/05; *Anvil* 19.4].

✓ Murphy-O'Connor, Jerome. ‡ *St. Paul's Ephesus: Texts and Archeology*, 2008. See the companion vol. under 1 Corinthians. Advanced students will benefit from perusing this. [*JETS* 3/09; *CBQ* 7/09].

Olyott, Stuart J. *Alive in Christ* (WCS) 1994.

Patzia, Arthur. [𝓜], *Ephesians, Colossians, Philemon* (NIBC) 1990. This Fuller Seminary professor believes Paul probably wrote Colossians, but not Ephesians. Not a bad value for your money in pb (300pp).

✓ **Perkins, Pheme**. ‡ (NewIB) 2000. A succinct (115-page), perceptive, well-written commentary from the critical angle. Perkins also did Mark in this series, and the vol. on Ephesians for the Abingdon NT series; see next entry. [*Sewanee Theological Review*, Easter 01].

Perkins, Pheme. ‡ (ANTC) 1997. [*Interp* 7/98; *CBQ* 10/98; *RelSRev* 7/98].

☆ **Robinson, J. Armitage**. 2nd ed 1904. This is a true classic. "The old standard English commentary of Armitage Robinson has held up quite well, and is actually more useful than Westcott who is always impressive" (Childs). This entry in the old Macmillan series has three parts: an exposition; the Greek text accompanied by extensive exegetical and philological notes; and 80pp of useful essays and text critical notes. This vol. was reprinted by Kregel back in 1980, by Lutterworth in 2002 (Britain), and by Wipf & Stock in 2003. If you love your Greek NT, want to build a larger and high-quality commentary collection, and find a copy of this, buy it! If you're unable to locate a copy, rely upon the Lincoln, Hoehner, and Thielman analyses of the Greek text, and compare with O'Brien's conservative exegesis.

✓ **Roon, A. van.** *The Authenticity of Ephesians*, ET 1974. This masterful dissertation is favorably reviewed in *WTJ* Fall 77 (by Lincoln, no less!) and *EvQ* 10/77. As an older, in-depth defense of Pauline authorship, it was probably the best. Though somewhat difficult to read in its English dress (the translation isn't the best), it is worthwhile reading for the student.

✓ **Schnackenburg, Rudolf.** ‡ ET 1991. One of the most important scholarly commentaries—alongside Barth, Best, and Lincoln. It was Childs' first choice, but that was before Lincoln came out. Perkins says Schnackenburg provides a "particularly helpful analysis of the logical flow of the letter" (p.366). This Roman Catholic scholar is best known for his studies and commentaries on the Johannine literature. [*ExpTim* 3/93; *JBL* 104.2 (1985); *EvQ* 1/96].

Simpson, E.K. (retired NICNT) 1957. See Bruce above.

F Slater, Thomas B. ‡ (S&H).

Stoeckhardt, George. ET 1987. A 19th century, conservative Lutheran work by a productive scholar.

✓ **Talbert, Charles H.** ‡ *Ephesians and Colossians* (Paideia) 2007. Talbert is a highly respected NT critic who teaches at Baylor and serves as a General Editor for this nascent series. Ephesians and Colossians may have been taken together here because of the many thematic similarities (literary dependence questions), and also because many scholars, Talbert among them, view the two as pseudonymous. The exegesis is compact and very well-informed. [*ExpTim* 9/08; *RelSRev* 3/09; *DenvJ* 4/08; *JETS* 12/08; *JSNT-BL* 2009; *BBR* 20.1; *CBQ* 7/09; *Interp* 4/09].

✓ Trebilco, Paul. ‡ *The Early Christians in Ephesus from Paul to Ignatius*, 2005. A massive historical research (826pp) which aids the biblical scholar in background studies, though Trebilco discounts the usefulness of the epistle for his own work. This was republished by Eerdmans in 2007 [*CBQ* 7/10].

F Turner, Max. (NIGTC). Should be quite good, perhaps rivaling Lincoln, Hoehner, Best, and O'Brien.

F Turner, Max. (THC).

Uprichard, Harry. (EPSC) 2004.

F Webster, John. (Brazos).

✓ **Westcott, B.F.** 1906. Will always be consulted as a careful, dependable work. One of the very best of the older works. See also Robinson above.

F Williamson, Peter S. ‡ (CCSS) 2009. [*RelSRev* 36.2].

☆ **Witherington, Ben.** *The Letters to Philemon, the Colossians, and the Ephesians* (SRC) 2007. The Methodist author's stunningly prodigious output continues with this nearly 400-page addition to his project of Socio-Rhetorical Commentary. Since there is scholarly disagreement over, and so much to say about, the rhetorical form and intention in these particular Pauline epistles, Witherington's work here is notable. One student of classical rhetoric, Harrill (in *CBQ*) says Witherington's thesis that Paul adopted "an Asiatic style" is absurd because no such thing existed; but I have seen references to an Asian school/style in Quintilian (*The Institutio Oratoria*, 12.10.16–19) and elsewhere. The basic interpretive approach of this commentary is like that of his other works: Romans, Corinthians, Galatians, etc. [*RTR* 12/08; *CBQ* 10/08; *JSNT-BL* 2009; *BTB* 2/10; *RevExp* Win 09; *Anvil* 26.3-4].

F Wolfe, Paul. (NAC).

Wood, A. Skevington. (EBC) 1978. See Klein above.

✓ **Yoder Neufeld, Thomas R.** [*M*], (BCBC) 2002. This Mennonite commentary is 400pp and seeks to hold to a mediating position in the critical debates; he seems to land more on the pseudonymity side. Yoder earned his Harvard PhD with a dissertation on Ephesians and the armor of God image, so perhaps ch. 6 is where he has the most to say. [*JETS* 9/04; *Interp* 4/03].

NOTE: Pastors will benefit from reading T. David Gordon's article, " 'Equipping' Ministry in Ephesians 4?" in *JETS* 3/94; cf. Sydney H.T. Page, "Whose Ministry? A Re-appraisal of Ephesians 4:12," *NovT* 47.1 (2005): 26–46.

PHILIPPIANS

★ **Fee, Gordon.** (NICNT) 1995. A prodigious Pauline scholar, Fee produced an excellent vol. to replace Müller's then 40 year-old work. Like his hefty commentary on 1 Corinthians in this series—of which he is now General Editor—this work on Philippians is very full (528pp). Even after this NICNT publication, I still prefer O'Brien's vol. for both detailed exegesis and theology. However, Fee has more application, is more accessible to beginning students, and somehow seems more attractive in its layout. A pastor's first pick, not to be confused with Fee's briefer IVPNT work listed below. Fee and O'Brien work well together. [*CBQ* 7/97; *ExpTim* 3/96; *EvQ* 7/99; *JETS* 3/98; *WTJ* Spr 96; *Interp* 7/97; *RTR* 9/97; *JTS* 10/98; *RelSRev* 7/97; *Anvil* 17.1].

★ **Hansen, G. Walter.** (Pillar) 2009. I have had little opportunity to use this full (355pp) and readable commentary by a Fuller professor and noted Paul scholar. What I have read, however, is remarkably clear and mature scholarship. He believes the dominant themes in the epistle are the gospel of Christ and the community in Christ (p.30). Hansen, in his treatment of 2:5–11, comes to sounder theological conclusions than his colleague Ralph Martin, in my opinion. Coming to 3:9, which is important in the debate over the New Perspective, Hansen supports the more traditional reading of both "my righteousness" (gently critiquing Dunn and Wright) and "faith in Christ" (critiquing Hays). As Carson writes in the Editor's Preface, readers benefit from the insights of a seminary professor who previously served as a pastor and missionary. Just to note, Hansen wrote the Galatians vol. for the IVPNT. [*Them* 4/10; *Chm* Aut 10].

★ **O'Brien, Peter T.** (NIGTC) 1991. This is the best technical commentary on this book and should be your first choice (close to 600pp), if your Greek is good and your interests are more scholarly. It more than measures up to the standard set in his WBC vol. on Colossians-Philemon. O'Brien is soundly Reformed theologically, exegetically perceptive and very thorough. Oakes [*BSB* 9/97] is right to say "the proliferation of detail sometimes makes it hard to see the wood for the trees" in this "magisterial" work, while "Fee keeps the wood very clearly in view." (Note: O'Brien, Silva, Fee, and N.T. Wright—see his article, referenced below—are in essential agreement regarding the *kenosis* passage, all of them accepting the Harvard research done by Roy W. Hoover.) [*WTJ* Fall 92; *CBQ* 1/93; *JBL* Fall 93; *RTR* 9/93; *JETS* 9/95; *Biblica* 75.1 (1994)].

★ **Silva, Moisés.** (BECNT) 1992, 2nd ed 2005. A superb, compact commentary which, in the 1st edition—either WEC in 1988 or the reformatted BECNT in 1992—was my first choice before NIGTC and Fee's NICNT came out. Silva shows a sensitivity to language and employs sound hermeneutical principles (his specialty is semantics). Though widely read and interacting with most of the literature, he always keeps Paul's line of thought in view. In other words, he isn't always distracting the reader with side issues or a severely academic focus on minutiae. There is a humble tone to this commentary which is appropriate for a work on Philippians, but at the same time it briefly expounds Paul's themes in a grand way. I always read O'Brien and Silva together. The 2nd edition is almost 300pp; there is no major rewrite. [*JETS* 12/90; *EvQ* 10/91; *ExpTim* 3/90; *Them* 10/90; *TJ* Spr 94; *CRBR* 1991; *JSNT-BL* 2006; *ExpTim* 5/06].

★ Thielman, Frank. (NIVAC) 1995. Could be considered one of the very best in the NT section of the series. See Motyer, Lloyd-Jones, Carson, and Boice below for more expositional help.

✧ ✧ ✧ ✧ ✧ ✧

✓ Barth, Karl. ‡ ET 1962. As one might expect, this is a perceptive theological treatment in brief compass. And there is a "40ᵗʰ Anniversary Edition" from WJK.

✓ Beare, F.W. ‡ (retired BNTC) 1959, 3ʳᵈ ed 1973. Often consulted, but not so valuable as some think. His construal of the book's editing is unbelievable. And now it has been replaced in the series by Bockmuehl.

F Belleville, Linda. (NCCS). The author teaches at Bethel College (IN).

☆ **Bockmuehl, Markus N.A.** [𝓜], (BNTC replacement) 1998. A major, conservatively critical interpretation for students to consult. Bockmuehl can be compared with the recommended commentaries above in helpfulness to the pastor; if this were the only book you had on Philippians, you would be well-served. The discussion of such matters as partition theories is conducted at a high level. Contains a good measure of theology, and, as noted by Carson, his treatment of the hymn is excellent. This author has done a careful and oft-cited work on *Revelation and Mystery in Ancient Judaism and Pauline Christianity* (1990). See Beare above. [*RelSRev* 10/99].

☆ Boice, James M. 1982. This has been updated by Baker Books to be based on the NIV text.

Briscoe, Stuart. *Philippians: Happiness Beyond Our Happenings*, 1993.

Bruce, F.F. (NIBC) Originally 1983. Like Martin's Tyndale work, this is handy. It is perceptive, to the point, and rather brief (probably too brief to aid pastors much).

Caird, G.B. [𝓜], (New Clarendon) 1976. See under Ephesians.

☆ Carson, D.A. *Basics for Believers: An Exposition of Philippians*, 1996. Among the very best, most substantive pastoral expositions. Others on the same list include Lloyd-Jones, Boice, and Motyer. Preachers, buy this!

F Cassidy, Richard T. (Paideia). This vol. will include Philemon.

✓ **Collange, Jean-François.** ‡ ET 1979. A provocative commentary. Lots of sparkle, but not so dependable in its exegetical judgment. This was one of Martin's favorites because of its "Gallic verve and élan." More critical in its view of authorship and composition; Collange, in a manner similar to Beare, tries to understand the epistle as a mixed-up composite of three letters.

Comfort, Philip. (CorBC) 2008. See Hoehner under Ephesians.

Cousar, Charles B. ‡ *Philippians and Philemon* (NTL) 2009. The author is an esteemed professor emeritus at Columbia Theological Seminary. I regret to say that I found his work surprisingly slim, with less than 90pp on Philippians and about 10 on Philemon. He mentions an illness in his foreword, and I wonder if that may help explain why this work is perhaps half the length we would expect from this series. Cousar had earlier published a commentary on Philippians in the series "Reading the New Testament" (2001). This cannot be classed as a reference tool. [*RBL*; *ExpTim* 6/10; *JSNT-BL* 2010].

Craddock, Fred B. ‡ (I) 1985. Craddock is best known for his work in the area of homiletics; he is less a NT specialist. This work is only 84pp. [*JETS* 6/87].

✓ Edwards, Mark J. *Galatians, Ephesians, Philippians* (ACCS) 1999.

☆ Fee, Gordon. (IVPNT) 1999. Though very well done, this cannot compare with Fee's NICNT. Leave this for the Sunday School teacher. [*Chm* Win 00; *Them* Spr 01].

Flemming, Dean. (NBBC) 2009. See under series. [*JETS* 9/10].

☆ **Fowl, Stephen E.** [*M*], (THC) 2005. This theological interpretation, which is full (254pp) and very readable, will be welcomed by students and pastors alike. I found it to be among the more winsome books on Philippians I have used. There is adequate exegetical scholarship undergirding his theological and ethical reflections (centered on the American context). Yet there are theological questions issuing from the text, especially 2:5–11, that the author does not adequately address. Fowl has an evangelical background—he studied under Hawthorne—and now teaches theology at Loyola. He leans toward a reader-response approach to hermeneutics. This was the first or second vol. released in the series. [*EvQ* 10/07; *RTR* 4/07; *CBQ* 10/06; *Them* 10/06; *Interp* 7/07; *JSNT-BL* 2007; *RB* 4/07; *RelSRev* 9/08; *Pro Ecclesia* Win 09; *JTS* 10/09; *Anvil* 24.4].

☆ Garland, D.E. (EBCR) 2006. One of the most insightful brief (85-page) commentaries on Philippians I have run across. This is bound in a vol. (Vol. 12) treating Ephesians to Philemon.

F Guthrie, George. (ZEC).

F Hamm, Dennis. ‡ *Philippians, Colossians, and Philemon* (CCSS).

☆ **Hawthorne, Gerald F.** (WBC) 1983; revised and expanded by Martin, 2004. Before WEC/BECNT, NIGTC and NICNT came along, Carson wrote that this is "probably the most serviceable commentary." Hawthorne put us all in his debt by his painstaking work, and Silva definitely builds on Hawthorne. However, his independently-minded exegesis at times left me wondering if he was trying too hard to say something new. His theological exposition of the Philippians "Hymn" in ch. 2 did not satisfy me. The 1983 vol., like WBC as a whole, is geared for scholars and diligent students. But now we have "what is virtually a new work" (p.xii) with Martin's thorough rewrite. The revised edition is much longer (about 360pp vs. 262pp). I have not been able to make a close comparison of the two, except at two points: the new bibliographies are marvelous and Martin occasionally may retain Hawthorne's original section of "Explanation" while adding a section of his own thoughts, where the two of them differ—see, e.g., the "Application" of the hymn (2:5–11) on pp.132–34. [*WTJ* Fall 84; *RTR* 5/84; *JBL* 104.4 (1985); *EvQ* 4/85; *JETS* 12/83; *ExpTim* 3/08].

☆ Hendriksen, William. *Philippians, Colossians, and Philemon* (NTC) 1962. Not one of his strongest efforts but still trusty for many pastors.

F Holloway, Paul A. ‡ (Herm). Koester once had the contract.

✓ **Hooker, Morna.** ‡ (NewIB) 2000. As with Perkins on Ephesians, this is a succinct (80-page), insightful, and well-written commentary from the critical angle. [*Sewanee Theological Review*, Easter 01].

☆ Hughes, R. Kent. (PTW) 2007.

F Hunsinger, George. (Brazos).

Kent, Homer A., Jr. (EBC) 1978. Skip this and go to Garland's EBCR.

☆ **Lightfoot, J.B.** 6th ed 1881. Still one of the most valuable works on Philippians. See Silva's introduction for a fine review of this vol.'s worth. Lightfoot treats the Greek text, but his interpretive comments have been heavily edited for a popular audience in the Crossway Classic Commentaries edition (see below).

☆ Lightfoot, J.B. (CrossC) 1994.

☆ Lloyd-Jones, D. Martyn. 2 Vols., 1989–90. This exposition would be a very wise addition to the pastor's library. Not nearly so long as his other works (e.g., his 8 vols. on Ephesians), which may be a plus. This has recently been reprinted (1999) by Baker in a one-vol. pb: *The Life of Joy and Peace: An Exposition of Philippians.* I came very close to including the cheaper edition among my recommendations for purchase.

Loh, I.-J., and E.A. Nida. (UBS) 1977.

Marshall, I. Howard. (Epworth) 1991. This preacher's commentary would have been very, very useful, had it been more available in North America.

☆ **Martin, Ralph P.** [*M*], (TNTC) 1959, rev. 1987. A handy vol. for pastors. The earlier edition is not to be disdained or discarded; Martin was more conservative then. See also Martin's NCB below and his rewrite of the Hawthorne WBC.

✓ **Martin, Ralph P.** [*M*], (NCB) 1976. Takes a rather different approach to the letter than TNTC: more academic and technical. Carson notes that his interpretation of 2:1–11 has been influenced for the worse by Käsemann's "Odyssey of Christ" idea. [*EvQ* 10/77]. Later he would write that Christ's *kenosis* "entails a suspension of His role as the divine Image by His taking on an image which is Man's" (*A Hymn of Christ*, 196), and I reject this. Martin's just cited vol. on ch. 2 was originally a monograph, published by Tyndale House, intended for scholars entitled *Carmen Christi* (1967, rev. 1983). The later version is *A Hymn of Christ* (IVP, rev. 1997), which examines the hymn at great length. The 1983 edition is reviewed in *EvQ* 10/85. Further research on the topic by various scholars is presented in *Where Christology Began: Essays on Philippians 2,* edited by R.P. Martin and B.J. Dodd (1998). Finally, see Hawthorne above for Martin's latest contribution to Philippians studies.

Melick, Richard R., Jr. *Philippians, Colossians and Philemon* (NAC) 1991. Fits well into the series and meets its aims (384pp). [*EvQ* 1/94; *ThTo* 10/93; *JETS* 3/96].

☆ Motyer, J. Alec. (BST) 1984. Motyer builds on his 1966 book, *The Richness of Christ.* Apposite comments with a good deal of practical worth. Recommended for the expositor. In early editions of this guide, I recommended this for purchase, but I now prefer Thielman in this category of expositional commentary. [*JETS* 3/85].

Müller, Jac J. (retired NICNT) 1955. Brief, aged, and wasn't stellar to begin with. This work was once noted because Müller's dissertation examined *The Kenotic Theory in Post-Reformation Theology* (1931). Note: printings of this work prior to 1984 included his work on Philemon for the series. This commentary has now been replaced by Fee.

✓ Oakes, Peter. *Philippians: From People to Letter*, 2001. A most important, fresh investigation of the social setting. [*EvQ* 1/05; *BTB* Win 05; *Anvil* 20.2].

Osiek, Carolyn. ‡ *Philippians, Philemon* (ANTC) 2000.

Plummer, Alfred. 1919. You can ignore it at this point.

✓ Reed, Jeffrey. *A Discourse Analysis of Philippians,* 1997.

✓ **Reumann, John.** ‡ (AYB) 2008. Tragically, this professor of NT and Greek at Lutheran Theological Seminary in Philadelphia died mere months before his massive (800-page) technical commentary saw publication. Because of size, this will probably prove to be a work consulted by students/scholars on specific pericopae, but read in full by very few. It is extremely dense. I look forward to seeing interaction with it in forthcoming works by Holloway, Still, and Wright. [*Interp* 10/09].

F Still, Todd D. *Philippians and Philemon* (S&H). This author is an evangelical.

Sumney, Jerry L. *Philippians: A Greek Student's Intermediate Reader*, 2007. Reading this would be like a Greek refresher course for many pastors. The author wrote the Colossians vol. for the prestigious NTL. [*RelSRev* 9/08; *JSNT-BL* 2009; *Anvil* 26.3–4].

✓ **Thurston, Bonnie B., and Judith Ryan.** ‡ *Philippians and Philemon* (SacPag) 2005. I have not had much opportunity to use this 290-page work. Vining says, "No new ground is covered in these commentaries." There is well-informed exegesis from a critical Catholic perspective; theological conclusions are drawn with some tentativeness. [*CBQ* 1/07; *Interp* 7/06; *JSNT-BL* 2006; *RB* 10/05; *RelSRev* 1/06; *ExpTim* 2/06; *BSac* 7/07].

✓ Vincent, M.R. ‡ (ICC) 1897. Treats Philemon too.

F Wagner, J. Ross. (BHGNT).

F Watson, D.F. (RRA).

☆ **Witherington, Ben.** *Friendship and Finances: The Letter of Paul to the Philippians*, 1994. See the reviews of his other commentaries under 1 Corinthians. This fine vol. on Philippians comes from the Trinity Press "NT in Context" series, and can be recommended to students and studious pastors. [*JETS* 12/96; *SBET* Aut 96].

F Wright, N.T. [*M?*], (ICC–new series). Whiteley was earlier slated for this. While waiting on Wright, students of the NT would be smart to digest, maybe even photocopy, the author's important study of the kenosis passage: "ἁρπαγμός and the Meaning of Philippians 2:5–11," *JTS* 37 (1986): 321–52.

F Zerbe, Gordon. (BCBC).

NOTES: (1) See I.H. Marshall, "Which Is the Best Commentary? 12. Philippians," *ExpTim* 11/91; and (2) Todd D. Still, "An Overview of Recent Scholarly Literature on Philippians," *ExpTim* 119.9 (2008): 422–28.

COLOSSIANS

NOTE: Since it is now customary in most series to treat Philemon together with Colossians in the same vol., I have marked with a [P] those works which follow the pattern. That custom has arisen, you may know, because Philemon was resident in Colosse, and Onesimus is mentioned in both epistles.

★ **Dunn, James D.G.** [*M*], (NIGTC) 1996. [P] Dunn is a prolific Pauline scholar, having published major commentaries on Romans, Galatians, the Pastorals, and here Colossians. This 400-page vol. rivals O'Brien as a first-rate technical work on these epistles. Students will want both side-by-side. Evangelical pastors will prefer O'Brien and Moo. Dunn sits on the fence with regard to authorship of Colossians; he seems to describe the epistle as deutero-, but not post-Pauline. His assertion regarding the theological problem at Colosse—a forceful Judaism—is "the most striking contribution of the commentary" (Achtemeier). His previous journal article on the topic was "The Colossian Philosophy: A Confident Jewish Apologia," *Biblica* 76 (1995): 153–181. See my comments on his past work under Pauline Studies, Romans, and Galatians. [*Them* 1/97; *JETS* 3/99, 6/99; *JBL* Win 97; *JTS* 4/97; *CTJ* 4/98; *Interp* 1/98; *CBQ* 7/97; *Chm* 112.4 (1998); *RelSRev* 7/97].

★ Garland, David E. (NIVAC) 1998. [P] The author now teaches at Truett Theological Seminary, Baylor University. He also contributed the Mark commentary to this series, the 2 Corinthians vol. to NAC, and an in-depth exegesis of 1 Corinthians to BECNT. Not only does Garland frequently provide good homiletical direction, he also interacts with much recent scholarship, including Dunn and Barth-Blanke, and thereby helps the student who makes this purchase. Among these recommendations, my counsel to pastors is start with Moo, then buy O'Brien or Garland next depending on whether you want more exegetical or expositional help. Other leading pastoral/devotional books would be Hughes, Thompson, Lucas.

★ **Harris, Murray J.** (Exegetical Guide to the Greek NT) 1991. [P] This was to have been the first in a proposed 20-vol. series of guides to exegeting the Greek NT. Harris's 300-page work seemed to bode well for the series as a whole, if it ever really got off the ground. I finally concluded it wouldn't. However, in 2009 B&H

took it over from Eerdmans and will attempt to revive it. Few books could be better for encouraging the pastor to get back into his Greek NT and begin mining out the riches there. This vol. includes structural outlines, incisive exegetical comments on grammar and rhetoric, and some good homiletical suggestions from the original. Harris has also published a major commentary on 2 Corinthians. [*WTJ* Spr 93; *CBQ* 10/92; *ExpTim* 3/93; *JETS* 9/95; *CTJ* 11/92].

★ **Moo, Douglas J.** (Pillar) 2008. [P] It is great to see an up-to-date and high-quality exegetical commentary on Colossians from the evangelical ranks. The fact that this comes from a veteran scholar in Pauline studies makes it all the more welcome. Students will be glad for the interaction with more recent literature. There is no question that this thorough work is the pastor's and student's first pick (471pp). His NICNT on Romans is also a first pick. [*JETS* 9/09; *Them* 4/10; *Presb* Spr 09; *ExpTim* 9/09; *CBQ* 4/10 (Arnold); *JSNT-BL* 2010].

★ **O'Brien, Peter T.** (WBC) 1982. [P] One of the very best in the series and used to be the best on this book. (Now see Moo.) O'Brien's is a model commentary on the Greek text, though some quibble over a lack of text critical help. Dunn rivals this work. For a commentary on the Greek text, my preference for O'Brien over Dunn is slight. Note that the latter's bibliography is far more valuable to students. Reports are that O'Brien is to be revised by Clinton Arnold for a 2ⁿᵈ edition of this WBC. [*WTJ* Fall 84; *RTR* 1/83; *EvQ* 1/85].

Abbott, T.K. (ICC) 1897. See under Ephesians. Wilson now replaces Abbott.

Appéré, Guy. *Mystery of Christ* (WCS) 1984.

✓ Arnold, Clinton E. *The Colossian Syncretism*, 1995. This evangelical study proposes that the heresy opposed in the Letter to the Colossians was not incipient Gnosticism (1ˢᵗ century "Gnosis" teaching) nor a philosophical tradition, but rather a regional, syncretistic folk religion which had adopted certain elements of Judaism. A work of note for all NT students. But there are such diverse views among scholars! Besides Arnold's vol. and the standard commentary discussions of the issue, students should see W.A. Meeks and F.O. Francis (eds), *Conflict at Colosse*, rev. ed 1975; Richard DeMaris' *The Colossian Controversy: Wisdom in Dispute at Colosse*, 1994; Troy Martin's *By Philosophy and Empty Deceit: Colossians as Response to a Cynic Critique*, 1996; and Thomas Sappington's *Revelation and Redemption at Colosse*, 1991.

✓ Barclay, John M.G. ‡ (NT Guides) 1997. [P] A superb entry in the series.

Barclay, William. ‡ *The All-Sufficient Christ*, 1963. Quite a study to get the pastor thinking. Different from the "Daily Study Bible."

✓ **Barth, Markus, and Helmut Blanke.** [*M*], (AB) ET 1994. A major work, following Barth's two-vol. AB set on Ephesians. Their commentary on Philemon is published in ECC. This vol. on Colossians is essentially a mid-1980s piece of work. Using the maxim, *in dubio pro reo*, they urge that Pauline authorship be upheld (p.125). Students should certainly consult Barth-Blanke, along with O'Brien, Dunn, Wilson, Lohse, etc.

F Beale, Gregory K. (BECNT). [P]

Bird, Michael. (NCCS) 2009. [P] The author teaches at Highland Theological College, Scotland, and co-edits the series with Craig Keener. [*JETS* 9/10].

Bratcher, R.G., and E.A. Nida. (UBS) 1977. [P]

☆ **Bruce, F.F.** (NICNT) 1957, rev. 1984. [P] See under Ephesians. Up until the 2001 edition of this guide, Bruce's vol. was always recommended for purchase. It remains a smart buy, but not a top pick. Just as good on Colossians as on Ephesians.

Caird, G.B. [𝓜], (New Clarendon) 1976. [P] See under Ephesians.

Carson, H.M. (retired TNTC) 1960. [P] The theology drawn out is healthy and strong (conservative Reformed Anglicanism), but the exegesis does not probe to any depth. It served its day well, and now it's Wright's turn. Pastors can ignore Carson, but should not toss it out of the church library.

F   Cassidy, Richard T. (Paideia). [P]

F   Cranford, Lorin. (S&H).

Davenant, John. (GS) 2005. The Puritan author of this large work (900pp) was a professor at Cambridge; he presents the learning of his age (1579–1641). This commentary is not easy to use. [*RTR* 4/06].

Davids, Peter. (CorBC) 2008. [P] See Hoehner under Ephesians.

Deterding, Paul E. (Concord) 2003. I have hardly used it. At 200pp it is one of the briefest entries in the series—by comparison the Philemon vol. is nearly twice as long.

Donelson, Lewis. ‡ *Colossians, Ephesians, 1 and 2 Timothy, and Titus* (WestBC) 1996. See Ephesians.

✓   Gorday, Peter (ed). *Colossians, 1–2 Thessalonians, 1–2 Timothy, Titus, Philemon* (ACCS) 2000. [P] [*SwJT* Sum 01].

F   Hamm, Dennis. ‡ *Philippians, Colossians, and Philemon* (CCSS). [P]

✓   **Hay, David M.** ‡ (ANTC) 2000. There are quite a few technical and large-scale Colossians commentaries. This is more accessible as an exegesis (182pp) from the critical angle. Overall, this is a very competent work, scholarship-wise, which fulfills the aims of the series, but it is not stellar. Theology is my main problem, as he pushes "the notion of cosmoswide salvation" (p.63). [*CBQ* 10/03; *Anvil* 18.2].

Hendriksen, William. (NTC) 1965. See under Philippians.

F   Holmes, Michael, and Cathy Wright. (BHGNT). [P]

Houlden, J. Leslie. ‡ (Pelican) 1977. See under Ephesians.

☆   Hughes, R. Kent. (PTW) 1989. One of the best expositions available. See under Mark.

F   Jeal, R.R. (RRA).

Johnston, G. ‡ (retired NCB) 1967. [P] Quickly replaced; see Martin.

✓   Kiley, Mark. ‡ *Colossians as Pseudepigraphy*, 1986. Presents in full the arguments for the more critical position. We note in passing that even Kümmel, the old standard critical Introduction in Germany, upheld Pauline authorship of Colossians.

✓   **Lightfoot, J.B.** 2nd ed 1879. [P] Often reprinted. Another classic like his commentaries on the Greek text of Galatians and Philippians. This work continues to be consulted by scholars; e.g., Dunn's NIGTC cites Lightfoot about as much as any other commentator. For Greekless readers there is the Crossway Classic edition (below).

☆   Lightfoot, J.B. (CrossC) 1997. [P]

✓   **Lincoln, Andrew T.** ‡ (NewIB) 2000. This 115-page commentary is especially of note because of the author's past work on Ephesians, the sister letter to Colossians. Lincoln tentatively concludes that Colossians, too, is deutero-Pauline (pseudonymous). [*Sewanee Theological Review*, Easter 01].

✓   **Lohse, E.** ‡ (Herm) ET 1971. [P] Still among the leading technical commentaries coming from the critical camp. An exegetical mine for the specialist. As is typical of German scholarship, Lohse denies Pauline authorship of this letter. Deadening and too dense for pastors. [*JBL* 89.4 (1970) and 91.4 (1972); *ThTo* 30.2].

☆   Lucas, R.C. (BST) 1980. [P] Even if one disagrees with Lucas's ideas about the doctrinal problem Paul was facing in Colosse, there is still a lot here to stimulate the preacher to think practically. There are only 7pp on Philemon; by comparison Garland has 83pp.

MacArthur, John. 1992. [P] See my review of the series under Matthew. [*BSac* 1/95].

✓ **MacDonald, Margaret Y.** ‡ *Colossians and Ephesians* (SacPag) 2000. See Ephesians above.

Martin, Ernest D. (BCBC) 1993. [P] Praised by D.A. Carson.

☆ **Martin, Ralph P.** [*M*], (NCB) 1974, rev. 1981. [P] Quite good for the exegete, though this work has declined in value with the passing of time. [*EvQ* 1/75]. You could also profitably look up his more popular exposition which is entitled, *Colossians: The Church's Lord and the Christian's Liberty* (1972). See also the next, more recent entry.

✓ Martin, Ralph P. ‡ *Ephesians, Colossians, and Philemon* (I) 1991. [P] With little hesitation, he denies Pauline authorship of Ephesians. For Colossians, his "persuasion is to stay with Paul's authorial responsibility for the letter, though with some hesitation" (p.98). See under Ephesians.

Melick, Richard R., Jr. (NAC) 1991. [P] See under Philippians.

✓ **Moule, C.F.D.** [*M*], (CGTC) 1957. [P] Has a well-deserved reputation as a fine exegetical tool for working with the Greek. Will be consulted for a long time. More conservatively critical. Moule was one of the greatest NT exegetes of his time.

F Pao, David W. (ZEC).

Patzia, Arthur. (NIBC) 1990. [P] See under Ephesians.

✓ **Pokorny, Petr.** ‡ ET 1991. Published by Hendrickson. Denies Pauline authorship and is a significant scholarly work for students to note. [*JBL* Spr 93; *JTS* 10/92; *CBQ* 10/92; *Them* 4/93].

F Seitz, Christopher. *Colossians* (Brazos). Seitz is an OT specialist with a keen theological mind.

✓ **Schweizer, Eduard.** ‡ ET 1982. "One of the best in the series [see EKK in this guide's "Introduction," and also "Commentary Series" section]; and this work combines full knowledge of the relevant literature with some down-to-earth exegesis" (Carson). Fairly useful to the studious pastor, though it should be noted that Schweizer rejects Pauline authorship. I bought this years ago in a pb edition and found it rich, but it is less important now. [*ExpTim* 3/83].

✓ **Sumney, Jerry L.** ‡ (NTL) 2008. The author teaches at Lexington Theological Seminary and did his doctorate on Paul at Perkins School of Theology (SMU). His commentary on Colossians is about 300pp and argues, as one might expect from this series, that the letter is pseudonymous. But along the way he seems tentative about his conclusion and dates the epistle remarkably early (62–64). This is a major work in a prestigious series. I have not yet had occasion to review it carefully. [*JETS* 9/09; *CBQ* 10/09; *ExpTim* 1/10; *JSNT-BL* 2010].

✓ Talbert, Charles H. ‡ *Ephesians and Colossians* (Paideia) 2007. See under Ephesians.

☆ **Thompson, Marianne Meye.** [*M*], (THC) 2005. [P] This is considered a thoughtful, well-researched, and well-written theological commentary. Though Thompson is a more critically-oriented evangelical, her conclusions on introductory matters are solidly conservative. I regard this as one of the best recent works on Colossians. See also her fine work on 2 Corinthians. [*CBQ* 7/07; *JETS* 12/06; *JSNT-BL* 2007; *RB* 4/07; *RelSRev* 1/07; *BTB* Win 08; *JTS* 10/09; *Anvil* 24.3].

Thurston, Bonnie. ‡ *Reading Colossians, Ephesians & 2 Thessalonians: A Literary and Theological Commentary*, 1995. These three letters are grouped together, apparently because of the common critical view that they are pseudonymous.

Vaughn, Curtis. (EBC) 1978. Better than others in this vol.

✓ **Wall, Robert.** (IVPNT) 1993. [P] This professor at Seattle Pacific also authored commentaries on Revelation for NIBC and on James. This little vol. (225pp) brings out the relevance of these epistles for the Church today, but, in general, I find this series too expensive in hb for what it has to offer. Wall, a Dallas Seminary graduate (ThD), has taken an interest in Canonical Criticism, co-authoring the Sheffield vol., *The New Testament As Canon: A Reader in Canonical Criticism.* [*RTR* 5/94; *CRBR* 1994].

Williams, A. Lukyn. (Cambridge Greek Testament for Schools and Colleges) 1907. [P] Use Moule instead.

✓ **Wilson, R. McL.** ‡ (ICC–new series) 2005. [P] Though there is the expected wealth of detail in this ICC, some regard Wilson's work as deficient as a thorough and authoritative exegesis. I view it as fully meeting the usual ICC standards but not being one of the strongest vols. in the series. While this is among the most important reference works for students to consult, pastors will find mid-level works by Moo and Thompson and the technical exegeses of O'Brien, Dunn, and Harris more useful. Wilson rejects the Pauline authorship of Colossians in an understated British sort of way. His discussions of Gnosticism and the Colossian Hymn are important for students. [*CBQ* 7/07; *JETS* 3/07; *Interp* 1/08; *NovT* 50.1; *ExpTim* 11/06; *EuroJTh* 16.1].

☆ **Witherington, Ben.** *The Letters to Philemon, the Colossians and Ephesians* (SRC) 2007. [P] See Ephesians.

☆ **Wright, N.T.** (TNTC) 1986. [P] This commentary deserved the rave reviews it received when it first appeared. Those familiar with the high caliber of this scholar's work will not be disappointed here. I read this all the way through and recommended its purchase until 2005. Wright has some strong views and should not be used on its own. Wright's work retires H.M. Carson in the Tyndale series. Note: compare O'Brien and Wright on the "Colossian Heresy"; I think the former is closer to getting it right. No doubt this pb is one of the best buys on Colossians. [*Them* 1/88; *RTR* 9/87; *EvQ* 7/88; *Chm* 101.4 (1987)]. There is another, more recent popular treatment by Wright called *Paul for Everyone: The Prison Letters* (2002).

NOTE: Nijay Gupta, "New Commentaries on Colossians: Survey of Approaches, Analysis of Trends, and the State of Research," *Them* 35.1 (2010).

—ɯ—

1–2 THESSALONIANS

★ **Fee, Gordon.** (NICNT replacement) 2009. In light of the quality of his past work (e.g., 1 Corinthians, Philippians in NICNT), I expected this could be a recommended purchase, and it is. Though there is a disappointingly brief introduction—compare the 11pp here (on two epistles even) with his 55pp in Philippians—Fee makes up for that lack with a disciplined focus on the text and sober, thorough, penetrating exegesis. There is a good, satisfying measure of theological reflection. I suspect that less study went into this NICNT commentary than Fee's Philippians and 1 Corinthians vols. See Morris below. This is now my top pick for a pastor's exegetical reference. Those with a strong interest in eschatological debates may be disappointed with Fee's downplaying of such issues; such readers may repair to a giant dissertation, on the longer letter at least, by David Luckensmeyer, *The Eschatology of First Thessalonians* (2009). [*JETS* 6/10 (Weima); *RBL* 7/10 (Aageson); *JSNT-BL* 2010; *Them* 7/10].

★ **Green, Gene.** (Pillar) 2002. I used to term Green "the Morris NICNT for a new generation" (though Green does not have the same focus). It is well-done, thoroughly evangelical, careful in its exegesis, and is pitched at pastors, rather than specialists. This has been a good place for pastors to start (less in-depth is Beale). Students will value the bibliographies and probing exegesis. On the negative side, as Howard Marshall points out [*Them* Spr 04], there is less exposition and biblical theology than pastors want; also the emphasis on patron-client relations seems overdone. Prior to Fee's appearance, I said that Thessalonians lacked an obvious "pastor's first choice" that is sufficiently well-rounded to guide the pastor in the areas of both detailed exegesis and theological exposition, but I added that this is very good as a middle-level work. [*RTR* 8/03; *JETS* 9/03; *ExpTim* 11/03; *RelSRev* 10/03; *Chm* Spr 04; *Interp* 1/05; *NovT* 46.4; *DenvJ* 1/03].

★ Holmes, Michael. (NIVAC) 1998. One of the more successful in the series at meeting the stated aims. Preachers are so well served by Stott and Holmes! [*CTJ* 4/99].

★ **Malherbe, Abraham.** ‡ (AB) 2000. This vol. is a very, very important work for students, with more dependable exegesis than some of the other brilliant AB commentaries (e.g., Martyn on Galatians and Elliott on 1 Peter). Prior to this major commentary, Malherbe had published a good bit on Thessalonians already; see especially his Fortress work, *Paul and the Thessalonians: The Philosophical Tradition of Pastoral Care*, 1987. The author is Professor Emeritus of NT Criticism and Interpretation at Yale. His commentary will cheer many evangelicals by its defense of the second letter's authenticity. There is much else to praise here. Malherbe sticks to the task of close exegesis, and the scholarly standards are exceedingly rigorous. His conclusions tend to be conservatively critical. The commentary is even fuller than its 500pp might indicate; there is nary a wasted sentence for the student. Specialists interested in Paul's socio-cultural context and his "church rhetoric" will find this work to be invaluable. On the issue of rhetorical analysis, Malherbe concludes that "Paul made extensive use of the conventions of discourse used by philosophers who aimed at the moral and intellectual reformation of their listeners" (p.96). Scholarly pastors will learn much here, even as they wish there were a little more theology and a few less citations of other ancient literature. Many pastors will prefer the more manageable, more accessible Beale or Witherington. [*CBQ* 4/02; *JETS* 9/02; *JBL* Sum 02; *ExpTim* 1/02; *Biblica* 83.1; *NovT* 44.4; *JR* 4/04; *RelSRev* 1/03 (2 lengthy reviews); *DenvJ*].

★ Stott, John. *The Gospel and the End of Time* (BST) 1991. This is an excellent complement to Bruce's more exegetical work. All of Stott's expositions are worth the money. This 200-page commentary also has an inductive study guide at the end which a pastor or lay leader could put to good use in a Bible Study group. Stott draws from a number of major commentaries (hadn't seen Wanamaker, though), but one reviewer would have been glad for interaction with more current scholarship (e.g., Malherbe's 1987 book). [*EvQ* 4/95].

★ **Wanamaker, Charles A.** [*M*], (NIGTC) 1990. Since 1993 this was Carson's first pick, though I wonder if he buys Wanamaker's reversal of the letters' order. A perceptive commentary which uses some of the newer critical methods on the text (especially social scientific research). Long on rhetorical analysis, but sometimes short on theology. Wanamaker should definitely be consulted, but the work seems marginally less valuable to the preacher than Bruce's more traditionally-styled commentary—yet with Stott and Holmes on hand, that is not so serious a problem. For a more accessible and up-to-date socio-rhetorical commentary, see Witherington. [*JBL* Sum 92; *CBQ* 1/92; *Interp* 10/92; *RTR* 5/92; *JETS* 9/95; *CTJ* 4/92; *Biblica* 73.3 (1992)].

F   Adams, S.A. *A Linguistic Commentary on 1 and 2 Thessalonians*, 2011? To be published by Brill.

F   Ascough, R.S. (RRA).

☆   **Beale, Gregory.** (IVPNT) 2003. This is very well done and ably mixes exegesis and theological exposition, pointing ahead to application today. As with his outstanding work on Revelation, Beale gives special attention to the OT background of the NT text. I would have no quarrel with anyone who thinks this deserves a place on the list above. If a pastor could buy only one book, this would work well. [*EvQ* 7/05; *JETS* 6/05; *Them* 4/06; *RelSRev* 4/06; *ExpTim* 2/05; *Evangel* Sum 06; *Anvil* 22.2].

✓   **Best, Ernest.** ‡ (BNTC) 1972. One of the most valuable commentaries in the series. More advanced students will appreciate this penetrating work, though it explains the English text (RSV). This is a standard work to consult, and students may note that the 1977 and 1979 revisions only added to the bibliography. It is not entirely satisfactory on the issue of the authorship of 2 Thessalonians, but Best does assume both letters came from Paul's hand (in conjunction with his fellow workers). It is disturbing to me to see how scholarship has moved decisively in the last 30 years in the direction of rejecting the authenticity of the second epistle. Fuller discussion than Bruce. This scholar has produced a *magnum opus* on Ephesians in the ICC. [*JBL* 93.2 (1974)].

    Bridges, Linda McKinnish. ‡ (S&H) 2008. It seems the main assumption governing this work is "that the believers in Thessaloniki were artisans who lived, worked, and worshiped in their workshop" (p.8) and that these letters address a predominantly male community and betray an androcentric viewpoint. Bridges suggests that "a feminine perspective is absent, either by force or ignorance." The purpose of her commentary, then, is to take up "the challenge of creating new worlds of meaning that will be more inclusive and available to all the readers" (p.12). Bridges follows the critical line in treating 2 Thess as pseudonymous. The feel of the work is odd. On the one hand it can be intensely personal and even autobiographical. On the other, it can be rather inaccessibly academic; e.g., the Introduction begins with a lengthy quote from that famous theorist of dialogism and intertextuality, Mikhail Bakhtin. This vol. is less useful than some others in S&H as a theological exposition for pastors. [*CTJ* 4/10; *Interp* 1/10 (Weima)].

☆   **Bruce, F.F.** (WBC) 1982. This has long been among the most useful commentaries for the student and pastor reading the Greek text. It is marked by Bruce's characteristic thoroughness (though I wish it were longer), carefully weighed comments on the text, and good historical sense (always his forte). Silva's first choice, though I find I want a supplemental theological exposition alongside. Compare with the fuller NIGTC. Bruce's former student Seyoon Kim will revise this for a 2ⁿᵈ edition; when that new edition appears it may well move back up to the recommended purchase category, where I had it from 1990–2005. [*JBL* 104.2; *JETS* 6/83; *RTR* 1/84; *EvQ* 1/85; *Chm* 101.1 (1987)].

☆   Calvin, John. (CrossC) 1999.

    Cara, Robert. (EPSC) 2009. By a professor at RTS Charlotte.

    Comfort, Philip. (CorBC) 2008. See Hoehner under Ephesians.

    Denney, James. (EB) 1892. Long a mainstay in the pastor's library and still useful for sermon preparation, if read along with a careful exegetical work like Wanamaker, Bruce, Green, etc.

F   Donfried, Karl P. ‡ (ICC–new series). Also worth noting for students' sake are Donfried's collected essays on *Paul, Thessalonica, and Early Christianity* (2002) [*JTS* 10/03; *ExpTim* 6/04; *RelSRev* 1/05]; and the excellent Donfried/Beutler edited vol. entitled *The Thessalonians Debate* (2000) [*CTJ* 4/01; *RelSRev* 4/01; *JTS* 10/01].

    Elias, Jacob W. (BCBC) 1995. Accomplishes the aims of the series.

F   Farrow, Douglas. (Brazos).

✓ Findlay, G.G. (Cambridge Greek Testament for Schools and Colleges) 1904. Was reprinted in 1982 by Baker. Reprints do not always indicate value, but Findlay has held value and is one of my favorite older commentaries. The author earlier did the more accessible Cambridge Bible for Schools and Colleges (1894).

✓ **Frame, J.E.** (ICC) 1912. Still useful for fuller research. Carson, I believe, may underestimate its worth.

✓ **Furnish, Victor Paul.** ‡ (ANTC) 2007. The reputation of the author led me to expect a high-quality exegesis, and I have not been disappointed. For a compact (204pp), critical exegetical commentary, you can't do any better; this is especially true of 1 Thessalonians (his commentary on 2 Thess. is too brief at 40pp for my liking). Furnish is a deeply learned, mature Pauline scholar. He believes the evidence indicates that 2 Thess is deutero-Pauline, but is open to interpreting the letter as authentic. See his strong AB contribution on *II Corinthians*. [*Interp* 7/08; *RelSRev* 9/08; *JSNT-BL* 2009].

F Garland, David. (NCCS). This prolific Baptist author teaches at George W. Truett Theological Seminary (Baylor) in Texas. See further comments on Garland under 1 Corinthians and 2 Corinthians.

✓ Gaventa, Beverly Roberts. ‡ (I) 1998. Judged to be a success, but it cannot be a first choice. Though a thin vol., there is much packed into it for the expositor. Disappointingly, she decides 2 Thessalonians is deutero-Pauline. [*NovT* 41.4; *Interp* 4/99; *RelSRev* 10/99].

✓ Gorday, Peter (ed). *Colossians, 1–2 Thessalonians, 1–2 Timothy, Titus, Philemon* (ACCS) 2000.

F Grant, James H. (PTW). The author pastors Trinity Reformed Church in Rossville, TN, and has recently completed the manuscript for this exposition.

Hendriksen, William. (NTC) 1955. Now bound with the Pastorals. See my comments there. Long a mainstay for Reformed pastors.

Hiebert, D. Edmond. 1971. A full-length exposition which numbers of pastors have found helpful. Strongly Dispensational.

✓ Jewett, Robert. ‡ *The Thessalonian Correspondence: Pauline Rhetoric and Millenarian Piety*, 1986. This argues that the letters were written to counteract an over-realized eschatology.

F Johnson, C. Andrew. (THC).

F Johnson, E. Elizabeth. ‡ (NTL).

F Koester, Helmut. ‡ (Herm). This Harvard professor is radically critical.

✓ **Lightfoot, J.B.** *Notes on the Epistles of Paul*, 1904. Students who are unaware of this resource will be glad to discover it. Lightfoot and his friends, Westcott and Hort, had planned to write a series of commentaries on the Greek text of each NT book. Though several were published, they did not live to see the series' completion. Several of Lightfoot's commentaries were in progress when he died, and these are included in this 325-page work. The commentaries cover 1 and 2 Thessalonians (complete), 1 Corinthians 1–7, Romans 1–7, and Ephesians 1:1–14. This vol. has been reprinted along with the three famous vols. on Galatians, Philippians and Colossians-Philemon.

☆ **Marshall, I. Howard.** [*M*], (NCB) 1983. I think this was one of Marshall's better efforts earlier in his career, though an exegetical commentary in shorter compass. He self-consciously builds on the foundation of Best and also discusses Trilling's influential German work (combating Trilling's arguments for pseudonymity). This work is highly recommended and mildly critical. [*WTJ* Spr 85; *Them* 1/85; *JETS* 12/83].

Martin, D. Michael. (NAC) 1995. It came as a bit of a surprise to me, considering the Southern Baptist character of the series, that Martin cannot find a Pre-Tribulational rapture in Thessalonians. Neither can I. The author teaches at Golden Gate Baptist Seminary. Wanamaker calls this 300-page commentary a work of solid scholarship, but it is not first-rate. [*BSac* 1/98; *Them* 1/97; *RelSRev* 10/97].

F Marxsen, Willi. ‡ (ContC) 1979–82, ET ? Childs says the German original "offers a brilliant exegesis from the far left." I am doubting this will ever appear. The NT section of ContC has been stalled since the early 1990s.

✓ **Milligan, George.** 1908. A great scholar's treatment of the Greek text in the venerable Macmillan series. Milligan has long been consulted as a valuable resource. He was more critical in his day but did not reject the authenticity of the second epistle (p.xcii).

Moffatt, James. ‡ (Expositor's Greek Testament) 1910.

Moore, A.L. ‡ (NCB) 1969. Too brief to do much good; now replaced in the series by Marshall.

☆ **Morris, Leon.** (NICNT) 1959, rev. 1991. Morris also has a shorter, more popularly styled work in the Tyndale series (listed below), but this is to be preferred as the more thorough and scholarly of the two. Regrettably, with the NICNT the 1991 revision was not extensive; in fact I did not even bother to buy the 2nd edition. In 1993 this vol. was George Knight's first choice for the pastor. Because Morris is more balanced between exegesis and exposition than WBC or NIGTC, I used to consider this a good first purchase, but now Fee and Green have taken Morris's place. See Fee above for the replacement.

☆ Morris, Leon. (TNTC) 1957, rev. 1984. See NICNT above. [*JETS* 12/85].

✓ Nicholl, Colin R. *From Hope to Despair in Thessalonica: Situating 1 and 2 Thessalonians*, 2004. [*JETS* 6/05; *Them* Sum 05; *JR* 10/05; *ExpTim* 5/05].

✓ Paddison, A. *Theological Hermeneutics and 1 Thessalonians*, 2005.

Palmer, Earl. (Good News Commentary) 1985. Can be ignored.

Plummer, Alfred. 1918.

✓ **Richard, Earl J.** ‡ (SacPag) 1995. A high quality, major critical commentary, sensitive to rhetorical matters and "focused on philology," which should certainly be consulted by students. The author teaches at Loyola and believes the second letter is deutero-Pauline. As Fee points out, Richard is remarkably the "only significant commentary in English over the past century and a half that has tried to make sense of this letter as a forgery" (p.237). [*EvQ* 4/99; *JBL* Win 97 (Weima); *CBQ* 10/97; *SwJT* Spr 99; *RelSRev* 4/97].

Smith, Abraham. ‡ (NewIB) 2000. About 100pp from an African-American professor at Andover-Newton. Doubts Paul wrote 2 Thess. Smith does not probe deeply enough to help students much, and the critical orientation makes this NewIB commentary less suitable for evangelical pastors. [*Sewanee Theological Review* Easter 01].

F Still, Todd D. (Paideia).

Thomas, Robert L. (EBC) 1978. Dispensational and not so penetrating, but perhaps better than some others in the series. Thomas later completed a major two-vol. exegesis of Revelation. See the EBCR and EEC below.

Thomas, Robert L. (EBCR) 2006. I have not had opportunity to use this as yet.

F Thomas, Robert L. (EEC).

Ward, Ronald A. 1973. A helpful exposition with good study behind it. This was more highly valued by pastors back in the 1970s and 80s. See Ward on the Pastorals below.

F   Weima, Jeffrey A.D. (BECNT). This able conservative scholar now teaches at Calvin Seminary, and I eagerly await his commentary. Advanced students may wish to consult the Weima/Porter Brill vol., *An Annotated Bibliography of 1 and 2 Thessalonians*, 1998.

Whiteley, D.E. ‡ (New Clarendon) 1969. One of the better works in the series.

☆   Williams, David J. (NIBC) 1992. Have not had opportunity to use it much, but only scanned it. It certainly appears to be competent and well researched. Quite handy, too, at about 150pp. This competes with Morris' TNTC as the "best bargain" pb for the student. [*CRBR* 1994 (Wanamaker, negative)].

☆   **Witherington, Ben.** (SRC) 2006. This prolific scholar's work on Thessalonians is clear, accessible, fairly full (286pp), and provides a fresh socio-rhetorical interpretation. He is practiced at producing such commentaries. Note that he disagrees with Malherbe for giving prominence to epistolary rather than rhetorical considerations (p.17). See Witherington's earlier work on Matthew, Mark, John, Acts, Romans, Corinthians, Galatians, etc. This vol. on Thessalonians appears to be among the best so far. [*CBQ* 10/07; *JTS* 4/08; *JSNT-BL* 2007; *RelSRev* 4/07; *ExpTim* 7/07; *DenvJ* 1/07; *NovT* 51.4 (Burke); *Anvil* 25.1].

NOTES: (1) Sean A. Adams, "Evaluating 1 Thessalonians: An Outline of Holistic Approaches to 1 Thessalonians in the Last 25 Years," *CBR* 8.1 (2009): 51–70. (2) Stanley Porter, "Developments in German and French Thessalonians Research: A Survey and Critique," *CurBS* 7 (1999): 309–34.

—⚏—

THE PASTORAL EPISTLES

★   Hughes, R. Kent, and Bryan Chapell. (PTW) 2000. A fine piece of work, not only for its sure-footed exposition, but also for the guidance it provides the pastor toward appropriate application. Good research stands behind this commentary, though they constantly misspell the name Torrance. How they managed to consult and cite Mounce (also published in 2000) is remarkable. Though students and scholars probably won't spring for this, preachers will. The student who would prefer an exegetical rather than homiletical commentary should look at Marshall's ICC, Johnson's AB, Quinn (Titus), and Kelly.

★   **Knight, George W.** (NIGTC) 1992. This 540-page commentary was once my first pick. It is careful, dependable theologically, contains a good defense of Pauline authorship, and provides a probing, phrase-by-phrase exegesis of the Greek text. Conservative through and through, Knight in places pays more attention to theological exposition and practical-pastoral concerns than some other entries to the series (e.g., Ellingworth on Hebrews). However, the method is far more exegetical than expositional. This work is the fruit of many years of study in the Pastorals, going back to his dissertation on the "Faithful Sayings" in these letters (published 1968). One is glad for all the interaction with the Ridderbos Dutch commentary. For more high-level discussion of the Pastorals, their authenticity, and their place in the canon, see also the Porter and Wall articles in *BBR* 5 (1995) and 6 (1996). [*ExpTim* 1/95; *Them* 5/94].

★   **Mounce, William.** (WBC) 2000. This huge vol. (cxxxvi + 600pp) by a former Gordon-Conwell professor has been worth the wait. Though Mounce gives us a detailed, scholarly exegesis of the Greek text, he aims more to benefit the pastor and the Church than the academy. He is alert to pastoral concerns and questions. He seems to believe, as I do, that the Scriptures belong to the Church and that theology is best done in the Church context. In short this is a useful and satisfying work, though not always an easy tool to use. On conservatives' "big issues" he takes friendly positions, stalwartly defending both the authenticity of the letters and a traditional reading of Paul's instruction regarding the role of women in the Church. He arrives at his positions through disciplined exegesis and weighing all the evidence. The handling of the Greek text shows the attention to detail and carefulness one would expect from a fine NT grammarian. Scholarly pastors, especially the frugal ones, will probably want to buy this first for study of the Greek, but they will also want Marshall, Knight, and Johnson's AB ready at hand for exegesis. [*JETS* 6/02; *BSac* 7/02; *Evangel* Aut 02; *Anvil* 20.2].

★ Stott, John R.W. *Guard the Gospel: The Message of 2 Timothy* (BST) 1973; *Guard the Truth: The Message of 1 Timothy and Titus* (BST) 1996. Everything you would expect of Stott. I wish that here in the USA IVP would combine the two vols. in one, as IVP did in Britain. [*Chm* 112.1 (1998)].

★ **Towner, Philip H.** (NICNT) 2006. Here we learn that Towner was not in full agreement with Marshall on the authorship issue (see Marshall below). He tentatively upholds the authenticity of the letters (pp.83–88). His discussion of 1 Timothy 2:8–15 is influenced by Bruce Winter's scholarship on the "new Roman woman" [*JTS* 10/05], and he critiques both the complementarian and feminist arguments (he is egalitarian). He wants to jettison the label "Pastoral Epistles" because it tends to encourage a "corpus mentality" among interpreters and obscure the individuality of each letter. Theological reflection is a strong point of this NICNT, though he does not venture as much into application issues as he did in IVPNT (see below). Towner builds upon his fine dissertation and his IVPNT work. He has worked so long and carefully on these epistles and has produced such a full (886pp), well-rounded, and insightful commentary, that many will want to make this their first pick. Marshall calls it "arguably the finest and most useful commentary based on the English text of the letters (with adequate discussion of matters Greek in the footnotes)." [*CBQ* 7/07; *BBR* 17.2; *JTS* 4/08; *JSNT-BL* 2007; *NovT* 49.2; *RB* 10/08 (Murphy-O'Connor, hypercritical); *ExpTim* 6/07; *RelSRev* 7/07 (Malherbe); *JETS* 9/08; *BSac* 7/08].

✓ Arichea, Daniel C., and Howard A. Hatton. (UBS) 1995.

☆ Barcley, William B. *1 & 2 Timothy* (EPSC) 2005. By a professor at RTS in Jackson. Directly serves the preacher with its focus on the message and on application. Easy to read. Some may balk at spending $30 (Amazon) to buy this 315-page exposition; other stores carry it for much cheaper.

✓ Barrett, C.K. ‡ (New Clarendon) 1963. Insightful in brief compass.

✓ **Bassler, Jouette M.** ‡ (ANTC) 1996. Better than Houlden or Hanson. Perfect for students who want to consult a probing critical exegesis but don't have time to tackle the new ICC, Quinn/Wacker, or another dauntingly full work. Bassler rejects the Pastorals as authentic Pauline epistles. [*RelSRev* 1/98].

F Beale, Gregory K. (ZEC).

F Belleville, Linda, Jon C. Laansma, and J. Ramsey Michaels. *1 Timothy, 2 Timothy, Titus, Hebrews* (CorBC) 2009. Bound together, Belleville is responsible for 1 Timothy, Laansma takes II Timothy and Titus, and Michaels comments on Hebrews.

✓ Bernard, J.H. 1899. Reprinted in 1980 by Baker in their "Thornapple" series.

☆ Calvin, John. (CrossC) 1998.

✓ **Collins, Raymond F.** ‡ (NTL) 2002. The first vol. in the series, this is a major mid-level (400-page) commentary from a renowned professor at Catholic University of America. The introduction's conclusions are mainstream critical, denying Pauline authorship (these epistles are said to be a later interpretation of the true Paulines). Collins shows interest in rhetorical features and the links the Pastorals have with other Hellenistic literature. He scarcely interacts with other commentaries. (Here is one case where a lack of a modern author index does not handicap the reader.) C.K. Barrett rates this as excellent. The chief difficulty here is the anticipated audience; students will want more interaction with other scholars' views and preachers will desire more discussion of the theological message, with hints at contemporary relevance. [*JTS* 10/04; *CBQ* 4/03; *JETS* 9/03; *BSac* 4/05; *ExpTim* 9/03; *ThTo* 4/04; *Interp* 1/05; *RelSRev* 10/03 (Malherbe); *BBR* 14.1 (Marshall); *CurTM* 8/05].

✓ **Dibelius, M., and H. Conzelmann.** ‡ (Herm) 1966, ET 1972. Long the standard critical commentary for exegetes, Dibelius/Conzelmann has a mine of information for the advanced student, especially on the Greco-Roman literary backdrop. Highly critical and, of course, rejects Pauline authorship. There is little here for the pastor. [*ExpTim* 10/73; *Interp* 1/74].

Donelson, Lewis. ‡ *Colossians, Ephesians, 1 and 2 Timothy, and Titus* (WestBC) 1996. He made his mark in scholarship with *Pseudepigraphy and Ethical Argument in the Pastoral Epistles* (1986).

✓ **Dunn, James D.G.** ‡ (NewIB) 2000. At 105pp, this commentary has insights but does not intend to compete with full-length technical commentaries. Dunn sits on the fence regarding authorship, but seems to lean toward a position similar to Marshall's. He argues that "pseudonymous writing would be attributed to the originator only if it was deemed to be an appropriate elaboration or extension of the original" (p.780)—a separate discussion of this issue can be found in Dunn's article on "Pseudepigraphy" in IVP's *Dictionary of the Later New Testament and Its Developments*. This NewIB work includes some wise and responsible application. [*Sewanee Theological Review*, Easter 01].

Earle, Ralph. (EBC) 1978. Covers 1 and 2 Timothy. Not so valuable. See Köstenberger for EBCR.

Easton, B.S. ‡ 1948. Finds some genuinely Pauline material, but is essentially liberal in its approach.

Ellicott, C.J. 3rd ed. 1864. An old classic which most have forgotten.

Fairbairn, Patrick. (GS) 1874. Reprinted every decade or so, most recently by Banner of Truth.

☆ **Fee, Gordon.** (NIBC) Originally 1984, 1988. An excellent accessible commentary which is fuller than many in the series. Very insightful, even if his interpretation of a couple important passages is disappointing. "Fee has worked hard at building a more or less believable 'life setting' that ties the contents of these three little books together" (Carson). In brief compass, this surpasses Kelly (barely) and Guthrie as the best commentary. It needs to be said that Fee is not as valuable now as I once considered it (I recommended its purchase until 2009); quite a number of evangelical commentaries have appeared over the last 20 years. [*JETS* 12/91].

✓ **Fiore, Benjamin.** ‡ (SacPag) 2007. This critical Catholic exegesis is not as full (253pp) as some other vols. in the series and not so strong on theological reflection. It is strong in the area of rhetorical/literary research, which makes sense since the author trained in the classics. He rejects Pauline authorship. Malherbe regards this as "a splendid contribution to Sacra Pagina." [*CBQ* 1/09; *Interp* 1/09; *ExpTim* 8/08; *RelSRev* 3/09 (Malherbe)].

Gealy, Fred D. ‡ (IB–Exegesis) 1955. Once made some contribution. He regards the letters as pseudonymous. With all the new commentaries over the last couple decades, you can safely ignore Gealy.

F Gloer, W. Hulitt. ‡ (S&H).

✓ Gorday, Peter (ed). *Colossians, 1–2 Thessalonians, 1–2 Timothy, Titus, Philemon* (ACCS) 2000.

☆ **Guthrie, Donald.** (TNTC) 1957, rev. 1990. Most valuable for its sturdy defense of Pauline authorship, but one can get that in his massive NT introduction. Generally speaking, Guthrie is quite useful, offers an insightful and accurate exegesis, and would be a wise purchase on the part of the pastor.

✓ **Hanson, A.T.** ‡ (NCB) 1982. Previously he also published *Studies in the Pastoral Epistles* (1968) and wrote the vol. for CBC. Quite critical. [*ExpTim* 12/84].

Harding, Mark. ‡ *What Are They Saying about the Pastoral Epistles?* 2001.

Hendriksen, William. (NTC) 1957. Now bound with the commentaries on 1 and 2 Thessalonians. Has long found a place on the bookshelf of Presbyterian and Reformed pastors. Hendriksen still provides some good theological guidance. See my review of NTC as a whole in the "Commentary Series" section above.

Hiebert, D. Edmond. (EBC) 1978. Covers Titus and offers some help to pastors, but not students. See Earle.

Houlden, J.L. ‡ (Penguin) 1976. Has been reprinted in Britain by SCM (1989). Has some insights—more than you might expect from such a short work. Argues the critical line.

F Hutson, Christopher R. (Paideia).

☆ **Johnson, Luke Timothy.** ‡ *1 & 2 Timothy* (AB) 2001. Johnson, a conservatively critical Roman Catholic scholar, upheld Pauline authorship in his esteemed introduction, *The Writings of the New Testament: An Interpretation* (3rd ed 2010). This vol. on Timothy is a bracing challenge to the "conventional wisdom" that the Pastorals should be treated together as a body and that they are pseudonymous. Need I say that evangelicals are delighted with this shot across the bow of critical scholarship? The liberals, by contrast, are not pleased [*JR* 1/03]. Johnson's exegesis is well-done, so well-done that the scholarly pastor will want to buy this to use alongside the new ICC, WBC, and NIGTC—all "musts" for the student. See Quinn below for the companion AB vol. on Titus. [*ExpTim* 8/01; *CBQ* 4/02; *JETS* 6/03; *NovT* 44.2; *HBT* 6/02; *RelSRev* 7/02; *JBL* Spr 02 (Towner); *TJ* Fall 02 (Yarbrough); *BibInt* 10.1 (Marshall); *DenvJ*]. Students should note that this commentary, at least on the correspondence with Timothy, supersedes Johnson's fine 1996 pb vol., *Letters to Paul's Delegates: 1 Timothy, 2 Timothy, Titus* ("NT in Context" series) [*Interp* 7/98; *SwJT* Spr 98].

Johnson, Luke Timothy. ‡ (Knox Preaching Guides) 1987.

Karris, Robert J. ‡ (NTM) 1979.

☆ **Kelly, J.N.D.** [*M*], (BNTC) 1963. Definitely one of the best in the series. This has been reprinted in the past by Baker in their "Thornapple" series. Kelly used to be my first choice and should still be considered for purchase; he has an outstanding grasp of the milieu of the 1st century Church. He also upholds Pauline authorship with surprising vigor. [*WTJ* Spr 65].

F Kidd, Reggie M. (BECNT). Kidd is Professor of NT at RTS Orlando. His dissertation for Duke University entitled, *Wealth and Beneficence in the Pastoral Epistles*, has been published in the SBL Dissertation Series. This should be a careful, incisive commentary on the Greek text, but will it appear? See Porter for a conflicting report.

☆ **Köstenberger, Andreas.** (EBCR) 2006. Well-done and a marked improvement over the older series. Many pastors will gravitate toward this dependable guide. Students will look at this as a quick reference, if they don't have time to delve into the very lengthy technical exegeses of Marshall, Quinn, Mounce, Towner, etc. Köstenberger also edited *Entrusted with the Gospel: Paul's Theology in the Pastoral Epistles*, 2010 [*Them* 7/10].

Krause, Deborah. ‡ *1 Timothy* (Read) 2004. A feminist interpretation, hostile to "Paul" (i.e., Paul's interpreter in this pseudonymous letter) and to what she alleges are apostolic attempts to misuse authority to control or silence others. [*JTS* 4/06; *Interp* 10/06; *JSNT-BL* 2005; *RelSRev* 1/06].

✓ Lea, Thomas, and Hayne Griffin. (NAC) 1992. A full exegesis and exposition (352pp), reasonably well done, which argues for the authenticity of the letters.

☆ Liefeld, Walter L. (NIVAC) 1999. Very fine work, but I judge it to be not as successful as Stott or Hughes-Chapell. Pastors should take a closer look at this. Egalitarian. Marshall [*BSB* 3/01] praises it highly, for "Liefeld provides excellent preparatory material for preachers." [*BSac* 4/02; *Evangel* Aut 02].

☆ Lloyd-Jones, D. Martyn. *I Am Not Ashamed*, 1986. Contains 11 challenging sermons on 2 Timothy 1:21.

✓ **Lock, W.** [*M*], (retired ICC) 1924. An acclaimed commentary on the Greek text during its time. It is still useful, but eclipsed by newer exegetical works. Lock tentatively upheld Pauline authorship. This has been replaced by Marshall.

MacArthur, John. *1 Timothy*, 1995; *2 Timothy*, 1995; *Titus*, 1996. The strength of this series of expositions lies in practical insight and bold application rather than in careful exegesis. Many pastors and Sunday School teachers will find it useful. See further comments on the series under Matthew.

F Malherbe, Abraham. ‡ (Herm).

☆ **Marshall, I. Howard.** [*M*], (ICC–new series) 1999. Called "splendid" by C.K. Barrett. On this enormous project Marshall had the assistance of Philip Towner, who taught for a year at Covenant Seminary. The exegesis is masterful and will be influential for decades to come. The more academically inclined pastor will certainly want to buy this. Marshall and Towner have some sympathies with the traditional position on authorship, and "have tried to present the message of the letters as they are ostensibly meant to be understood, as letters from Paul to Timothy and Titus" (p.xiv). Still, they—Marshall in particular—reject direct Pauline authorship and propose that authentic Pauline materials were edited after the apostle's death. The use of the term pseudonymity, with its commonly attached nuances of deceit/fraud, is avoided (p.84); Marshall prefers "allonymity" instead. Second Timothy is viewed as having a more patent Pauline character and as providing "the spur for the writing of the subsequent two letters" (p.86). They read 1 Tim. 2 as prohibiting public teaching of men by women, but conclude it is also a time-bound text (relevant only to the immediate 1ˢᵗ century situation addressed by the author). Whatever may be my disagreements with Marshall and Towner on interpretive cruxes, I treasure this 869-page vol. The price used to be prohibitively high in hb, so I recommended Mounce or Knight for pastors who are scouting for a commentary on the Greek text. Advanced students and the best-trained pastors (with a generous book allowance) will purchase the ICC in pb and make constant use of it as they read the Greek text. [*NovT* 42.3; *ExpTim* 5/00; *EvQ* 10/01; *JTS* 10/01; *JETS* 9/01; *BSac* 4/02; *JSNT* 9/01; *Evangel* Aut 02].

Montague, George T. [*M*], (CCSS) 2008. A brand-new series published by Baker which is easily accessible. This vol. is about 250pp and assumes the letters are from Paul (p.23). One critical reviewer recommends Fiore instead, because of the "traditionalist bent" (Beavis) of this work. [*JETS* 6/10; *CBQ* 7/10; *RelSRev* 9/09].

Moule, H.C.G. *The Second Epistle of Timothy*, 1905. This devotional commentary concentrates on the message of the book and its application to the heart. Long treasured by preachers.

Ngewa, Samuel M. (Africa Bible Commentary Series) 2009. The main strength here is warm, clear pastoral exposition (466pp) focusing on the questions and needs of the African Church. See also the author's expositions of John's Gospel and Galatians. [*JETS* 6/10; *CBQ* 7/10].

✓ Oden, Thomas C. [*M*], (I) 1989. Covers the Pastorals in 192pp. A pleasant surprise (for this series) was his defense of Pauline authorship. This well-known Drew professor of theology has been moving in a conservative direction for some time, calling the Church to resist modernity and postmodernity and return to the faith of our fathers,—the Church Fathers especially. You can profitably consult this for theological reflection. [*JETS* 6/92; *Interp* 7/91; *CTJ* 4/91; *CRBR* 1991].

Plummer, Alfred. (EB) 1907.

F   Porter, Stanley. (BECNT). This conflicts with earlier reports on Kidd.

✓ **Quinn, Jerome D.** ‡ *The Letter to Titus* (AB) 1990. A leading critical commentary by a Roman Catholic scholar, this has to be one of the most exhaustive works on Titus ever written (334pp). The accompanying vol. on Timothy has now been published outside AB. Quinn's decision to complete first the Titus commentary reflects his conviction that that epistle was issued prior to 1 & 2 Timothy. Father Quinn suggests that the PE were written as a "third roll" by the author of Luke-Acts, and has the closest of connections to the authentic Pauline tradition. Quinn's work is comprehensive, moderately critical, superb for word studies, and of use to students. I do not judge the ECC Timothy tome below to be as successful as this AB vol.

✓ **Quinn, Jerome D., and William C. Wacker.** ‡ *The First and Second Letters to Timothy* (ECC) 2000. Originally intended for AB, but Quinn's untimely death drastically slowed the production. I was glad, finally, to see the appearance of this 800-page commentary on Timothy. There are a few odd aspects to the tome, however; chief among them for me is the transliteration of the Greek when this lengthy work will be used by very few besides students and scholars. Marshall praises this vol. while calling it uneven in editing; in a more critical moment he termed it "poorly organized and dull" [*BSB* 3/01]. See Quinn above. [*ExpTim* 10/00; *SwJT* Fall 00; *JBL* Spr 01; *NovT* 43.1 (2001); *JTS* 4/01; *CBQ* 1/01; *Them* Spr/Sum 02; *JETS* 9/01; *Interp* 1/02; *RelSRev* 4/01; *Chm* Sum 01; *EvQ* 7/05; *SJT* 60.1].

☆ Ryken, Philip. *1 Timothy* (REC) 2007. Great for pastors. See his similar works on Luke and Galatians.

Saarinen, Risto. ‡ *The Pastoral Epistles with Philemon & Jude* (Brazos) 2008. This vol. has been praised by the likes of I. Howard Marshall for doing "an excellent job of mediating the insights of recent large-scale works in a readable exposition that concentrates on theology, bringing in from time to time the contributions of such expositors as Chrysostom and Calvin." The Pastorals are his main focus, and he regards them as pseudonymous. [*RelSRev* 9/09; *JSNT-BL* 2010].

✓ Simpson, E.K. 1954. This work on the Greek used to be often consulted, owing to the relative paucity of good commentaries on the original text. But since 1990 we have seen a wonderful crop of works published, and Simpson is no longer so valuable.

F   Spencer, Aida Besançon. (NCCS). The author teaches at Gordon-Conwell Seminary in Massachusetts and has published on Paul's literary style and on evangelical feminism.

F   Stanley, Steve. (EEC).

☆ Towner, Philip. (IVPNT) 1994. This scholar wrote his Aberdeen dissertation on the Pastorals under Howard Marshall, published by Sheffield as *The Goal of Our Instruction* (1989)—it is outstanding, by the way. Towner has served as Marshall's research assistant and as a UBS consultant. On his own he has produced a learned and insightful commentary for IVPNT on the message of these books (208pp). Exegetical issues are not passed over. A very fine representative of the series. Both pastors and students should realize that the NICNT (see above) has superseded this IVPNT as a scholarly resource. [*JETS* 12/96].

F   Twomey, Jay. ‡ (Blackwell).

F   Wall, Robert, and Richard B. Steele. (THC).

Ward, Ronald A. 1974. This companion to his Thessalonians commentary has 280 full pages of deep, spiritual exposition. The author was well-trained in NT (University of London PhD) and long served as a pastor in the Anglican Church in Canada.

F   Wilder, Terry. (Mentor).

☆ Witherington, Ben. *Letters and Homilies for Hellenized Christians: A Socio-Rhetorical Commentary on Titus, 1–2 Timothy, and 1–3 John*, 2006. This vol. and its companion on Hebrews, James, and Jude (*Letters and Homilies for Jewish Christians*, 2007) are of the same ilk as the author's many other socio-rhetorical commentaries. They are stimulating, insightful, and useful for exegesis, though I have found them a good bit less satisfying for theological reflection. He is in the egalitarian camp. [*Chm* Win 07; *CBQ* 1/08; *ExpTim* 6/08].

F   Yarbrough, Robert. (Pillar).

Young, Frances. ‡ *The Theology of the Pastoral Epistles*, 1994.

Zehr, Paul. (BCBC) 2010. The author has long served the Mennonite Church in "supervised pastoral education." This is not so much for students.

NOTES: (1) There is important literature on 1 Timothy 2:9–15, a crux in the interpretation of the Pastorals. I cite an important early journal article, that of Douglas J. Moo on "1 Timothy 2:11–15: Meaning and Significance," *TJ* 1 (1980): 62–83. Philip Payne's reply to this article, together with Moo's surrejoinder, was published in No. 2 (1981): 169–222. These represent a learned staking-out of the complementarian and egalitarian positions. Taking the debate to a higher level was the *Christianity Today* "1993 Book of the Year," *Recovering Biblical Manhood and Womanhood* (Crossway Books, 1991). For a full length "hashing out" of the issues in a debate format, see *Two Views on Women in Ministry* (Zondervan, 2001) and *Women in the Church* (IVP, 1995) [*JETS* 9/98; *TJ* Spr 96]. Probably the most influential work from the complementarian side exegeting the 1 Timothy text is *Women in the Church: An Analysis and Application of 1 Timothy 2:9–15* (Baker, 1995, 2nd ed 2005). The best, fullest treatments of the egalitarian position are now Keener's *Paul, Women, and Wives* (1992) and Payne's *Man and Woman, One in Christ* (2009) [*DenvJ* 2/10 (Blomberg)]. (2) I. Howard Marshall, "Some Recent Commentaries on the Pastoral Epistles," *ExpTim* 1/06.

PHILEMON

NOTE: See Colossians.

★   **Fitzmyer, J.A.** ‡ *The Letter to Philemon* (AB) 2000. Most will think the Colossians-Philemon vols. recommended above perfectly suitable for covering this letter's 25 verses. But the preacher wishing to build that "first-class exegetical library" I talk about will want to add this to the Colossians purchases. Fitzmyer is ever the patient, thorough exegete and provides excellent treatment of background matters (though I disagree on Onesimus' plight). Like Dunn and a few others recently, he holds that Onesimus was not a *fugitivus*, "but rather a slave who has been in some domestic trouble with his master Philemon and who has come to seek the intervention of an *amicus domini* (friend of the master) in the hope that he might be restored peacefully to his former status" (p.18). This Roman Catholic scholar also wrote the AB vols. on Luke, Acts, Romans, and 1 Corinthians. [*CBQ* 10/01; *JTS* 10/01; *Interp* 7/02; *SwJT* Fall 01; *RelSRev* 10/01; *BBR* 11.2; *DenvJ*; *ExpTim* 3/10].

Barclay, John M.G. "Paul, Philemon and the Dilemma of Christian Slave-Ownership," *NTS* 37 (1991): 161–86. This article, alongside Nordling's of the same year, presents potent arguments for the traditional runaway-slave interpretation. See also his NT Guides vol. (1997).

✓ **Barth, Markus, and Helmut Blanke.** ‡ (ECC) 2000. An unbelievably big volume (544pp) on a brief epistle. See their AB work on Colossians, which was probably intended as a companion to this commentary. A rich resource for researching the social-historical background of the letter, the Greek text, and the history of interpretation. But do take note that the vol. was so long in production that the research was over 10 years old when it appeared. Will this ever be surpassed in comprehensiveness? I fear that such interpretive overkill tends rather to obscure than to clarify things. [Complimentary reviews are *ExpTim* 4/01; *SwJT* Fall 01; *JETS* 12/01; and *Evangel* Sum 02; more perceptive are *JBL* Sum 02; *Biblica* 83.2; *JTS* 10/01 (C.F.D. Moule)].

✓ Burtchaell, James T. ‡ Philemon's Problem: *A Theology of Grace*, 1973, rev. 1998. This is a difficult book to characterize. It treats matters of ancient slavery, the master-slave motif in Scripture, Paul's Epistle to Philemon, and the theological theme of grace (with application to today). What some people may not know is that the author faced charges of preying on young boys while teaching at Notre Dame; he resigned. [*EvQ* 4/02].

✓ Callahan, A.D. ‡ *Embassy of Onesimus: The Letter of Paul to Philemon*, 1997. The revisionist thesis that Onesimus was no fugitive slave, but rather the estranged brother of Philemon, doesn't fly (see Fitzmyer's critique, pp.19–20). [*CBQ* 10/98; *RelSRev* 4/98].

Cousar, Charles B. ‡ *Philippians and Philemon* (NTL) 2009. See under Philippians.

✓ Felder, Cain Hope. [𝓜], (NewIB) 2000. A good, up-to-date commentary by a professor at Howard University. Felder appreciates evangelical scholarship and addresses the slavery issue with poignancy and good sense. For preachers. [*Sewanee Theological Review*, Easter 01].

✓ Knox, John. ‡ *Philemon among the Letters of Paul*, 1935, 2nd ed 1959. Proffered a much debated revisionist thesis about the letter's circumstances and recipient. Archippus, he says, was the slave-owner, not Philemon, and the runaway slave Onesimus should be identified with the later bishop of Ephesus who is mentioned by Ignatius. Said bishop was a major influence in the formation of the Pauline canon (and the inclusion of this epistle).

✓ **Kreitzer, Larry J.** ‡ (Read) 2008. Nearly 200pp, comprised of history of interpretation, a small commentary, and seven more chapters on quite a variety of topics, including some reception history. [*RBL*; *RelSRev* 12/09].

Müller, J.J. (retired NICNT) 1955. Philemon was originally bound with his Philippians commentary and is now long out of print. Replaced by Bruce.

✓ **Nordling, John G.** (Concord) 2004 This large scale (379-page) Lutheran work reveals deeper learning than some other vols. in the series. He is one of the strongest defenders of the traditional interpretation; see his long article in *JSNT* 41 (1991). As with the Barth and Blanke, I fear most pastors would be wearied and discouraged using such a large commentary on little Philemon. [*EvQ* 10/07].

✓ **Osiek, Carolyn.** ‡ *Philippians, Philemon* (ANTC) 2000. Only 20pp on the shorter letter.

✓ Petersen, Norman R. ‡ *Rediscovering Paul: Philemon and the Sociology of Paul's Narrative World*, 1985. A judicious and important monograph, not a commentary, on the social situation.

Rupprecht, Arthur A. (EBC) 1978. Merely 14–15pp. Now replaced by EBCR.

F Saarinen, Risto. *I–II Timothy, Philemon* (Brazos) 2008.

F Still, Todd D. ‡ *Philippians and Philemon* (S&H).

✓ Stöger, A. ‡ *The Epistle to Philemon* ("The New Testament for Spiritual Reading") ET 1971.

✓ Tolmie, D. Francois (ed). ‡ *Philemon in Perspective: Interpreting a Pauline Letter*, 2010. A large vol. (391pp) of essays issuing from an international colloquium. The lead contribution is "Tendencies in the Research on the Letter to Philemon since 1980" by Tolmie.

✓ **Thurston, Bonnie B., and Judith Ryan.** ‡ *Philippians and Philemon* (SacPag) 2004. See under Philippians.

✓ **Vincent, M.R.** ‡ (ICC) 1897, 5th ed 1955. Bound up with the Philippians commentary.

HEBREWS

★ **Bruce, F.F.** (NICNT) 1964, rev. 1990. Bruce's deliberative, well-reasoned exegesis made this valuable, even as one of the top two choices, for many years. Back in the 1980s conservatives were pretty well agreed that Bruce and Hughes were indispensable and a well-matched pair. The difficulty, as Carson has pointed out, is that the revision undertaken by Bruce was not extensive, and one gained little in replacing the first edition with the revised one. (I must add to Carson, however, that the author does offer his own fresh translation of Hebrews in the later work.) Students now use this less than before. This will eventually be dropped from my list, but not now. For other Bruce commentaries, see Acts and Ephesians. [*JBL* 12/65; *NovT* 34.3; *CTJ* 4/91].

★ **Guthrie, George H.** (NIVAC) 1998. Normally I would not urge students to consult NIVAC for exegesis, but this is an exception. Guthrie has long been doing a "rhetorico-discourse analysis" of this letter and has been concerned to understand "The Structure of Hebrews," which is the title of his 1991 dissertation for Southwestern Baptist Seminary (Brill, 1994; Baker, 1998). That doctoral work has been termed "an invaluable road map through one of the letter's thorniest problems" [*RelSRev* 10/97]. Lane provides in his WBC a fine review of Guthrie's contributions (p.xc–xcviii); I thank my friend, John Turner, for alerting me to the Lane citation. Besides the exegetical help, there is real theological and homiletical worth in the vol. Also on the list of best expositional helps are R. Kent Hughes, Richard Phillips, John Owen, William Barclay, Raymond Brown, John Brown, and Simon Kistemaker.

★ **Hughes, Philip E.** 1977. It is difficult to overestimate the value of this largely theological commentary. It complements Lane beautifully. This used to be my first choice—for pastors, that is. Hughes will be valuable for many decades because he was as fine a theologian as he was a biblical scholar, and you need a penetrating theological commentary on Hebrews. Amazingly, Hughes also had expertise in Church History, and this vol. is highly esteemed for his choice citations of the

Church Fathers. He knows the history of interpretation well, and leads us to draw on those rich resources. Hughes' commentary is nearly 600pp in length, and the theology is in line with the Reformation tradition. The author was an Anglican clergyman who, at the close of his career, taught at Westminster Seminary in Philadelphia. This vol. has been published in both hb and pb; it had been o/p but is now available again. Are there weaknesses? Well, Peter Head points to one [*BSB* 9/06]: "Hughes' interest in reading Hebrews in the light of the rest of the NT may actually blunt his appreciation of its distinctive theological witness." [*WTJ* Spr 79; *RTR* 5/78; *JBL* 9/79].

★ **Lane, William.** [*M*], (WBC) 2 Vols., 1991. If you are desiring an exegetical commentary on the Greek that leaves no stone unturned, this is the best piece of scholarship from the evangelical perspective, arguably the best piece of scholarship from any perspective. A mountain of work—12 to 15 years' worth—went into these vols. Students will naturally wish to consult Attridge, Ellingworth, Koester, etc., but Reformed pastors with Calvin, Hughes, Guthrie, Lane, and O'Brien have all they need. Lane's views on the message of Hebrews are available to a wider segment of Bible students in his earlier *Hebrews: Call to Commitment* (1985). Lane also wrote a fine commentary on Mark. [*CBQ* 1/93; *ExpTim* 5/93; *RTR* 9/93; *Them* 1/93; *WTJ* Spr 94; *CRBR* 1994].

★ **O'Brien, Peter T.** (Pillar) 2010. After completing his trio of commentaries on the Prison Epistles, where he demonstrated exceptional ability in exegeting the Greek, rhetorical interpretation, and theological exposition, O'Brien has produced this dependable commentary. I will even call it brilliant and my "first choice" for the pastor's study. Students will be glad to have all the bibliographical guidance in this 630-page vol. Perhaps those same students might compare O'Brien's approach to discourse analysis with Westfall below. Take Ellingworth's word for it: "I cannot commend this work too highly." I also note that there is noise about an additional O'Brien vol. on "The Theology of Hebrews" in the IVP series "New Studies in Biblical Theology." The theological orientation here is winsomely Reformed. [*DenvJ* 7/10; *Them* 7/10].

✧ ✧ ✧ ✧ ✧ ✧

F   Alexander, Loveday. ‡ (ICC–new series). I expect this is a long way off.

    Allen, David L. (NAC) 2010. After being delayed by the publisher, the 672-page work was recently released. I have not seen it as yet. The author is both Dean and a professor of preaching at Southwestern Baptist Theological Seminary in Texas. Along the way he has also written *Lukan Authorship of Hebrews* (2010).

✓   **Attridge, H.W.** ‡ (Herm) 1989. An enormously learned tome which will, together with Lane and Ellingworth, be a leading scholarly commentary in English for a very long time. Attridge teaches at Notre Dame and has expertise in the areas of Greco-Roman philosophy and Gnosticism. He pays special attention to the structure of the epistle and the rhetorical skills of the author, whoever he was. Use with some discernment. [*Biblica* 72.2 (1991); *JTS* 10/90; *JBL* Fall 91; *CBQ* 10/91; *Interp* 1/92]. Students will benefit from consulting his collected *Essays on John and Hebrews* (2010).

☆   Barclay, William. [*M*], (DSB) 1957. This is a splendid little vol., probably the best in the series.

✓   Bauckham, Richard, et al. (eds). *The Epistle to the Hebrews and Christian Theology*, 2009. The University of St. Andrews has begun sponsoring an annual Conference on Scripture and Theology, which seeks to bridge the longstanding divide between systematic theologians and biblical scholars. This large work (nearly 500pp) is a welcome Conference product, containing as it does such high-quality exegetical and theological essays. Contributors are generally more conservative critics, from Theology and both the OT and NT guilds, as well as several famous evangelicals (I. Howard Marshall and Ben Witherington). [*ExpTim* 5/10; *JSNT-BL* 2010].

☆   Brown, John. (GS) 1862, reprinted 1961. Mainly a theological exposition which shares many of the same characteristics one finds in the Puritans. Brown was a godly and learned pastor and professor in Scotland. Spiritually edifying. See his other works on Romans and 1 Peter.

☆   Brown, Raymond. (BST) 1982. Not to be confused with Raymond E. Brown, the liberal Catholic scholar. This is a helpful vol. which a preacher could put to good use, but not so valuable as some others in the series (notably Stott). Brown isn't as strong as he might be in understanding the connection between the doctrinal and hortatory sections of the epistle. [*WTJ* Spr 87; *JETS* 9/82].

Bruce, A.B. 1899. Reprinted from time to time, this has a theological orientation.

Buchanan, G.W. ‡ (AB) 1972. One of the earlier entries in the series. Though Buchanan is a noted scholar, this isn't one of the stronger works on Hebrews or better entries in the series. It has been replaced by Koester.

✓   Calvin, John. 1551. His brilliant grasp of the theological argument in Hebrews is not to be missed. Remember the strong recommendation to purchase his NT commentaries in the Torrance edition.

F   Carson, Donald A. (BECNT). I don't expect this to appear before 2015.

Cockerill, Gareth L. *Hebrews: A Bible Commentary in the Wesleyan Tradition,* 1999. "Written with the purpose of enabling the Christian in the pew to understand God's message in the book of Hebrews" (p.315).

✓   Craddock, Fred B. ‡ (NewIB) 1998. From a famous emeritus professor of preaching and NT. See Long below.

✓   Delitzsch, Franz. 2 Vols., ET 1868–70. A technical work and part of the exceedingly rich tradition of German commentary on Hebrews over the past 150 years (Bleek, Braun, Michel, Riggenbach, Grässer). In between writing all those masterful volumes on the OT for KD, he found time to write this weighty, incisive commentary. Recommended more for students than expositors. Has been reprinted by Klock & Klock.

☆   **deSilva, David A.** *Perseverance in Gratitude: A Socio-Rhetorical Commentary on the Epistle "to the Hebrews"* (SRC) 2000. This marks a continuation of Witherington's program—apparently an Eerdmans series—to provide (Vernon Robbins-esque) socio-rhetorical commentaries on the NT. This vol. of over 500pp is successful enough that I added deSilva to my own "Buy List" because he's asking and answering some questions not taken up in more traditionally-styled commentaries. He convincingly proposes that "the rhetorical situation of Hebrews (as an address…urging the maintenance of loyalty and obedience) must govern its application and appropriation" (p.242). See what he does with 6:4–8 to get the flavor of this work, which will serve well as a complement to the exegetical treatments by Lane, Ellingworth, Attridge, etc. At points, though, I'm afraid he presses the biblical material into the mold of his patronage thesis (see Motyer's review). His insistence that the epistle's recipients were wavering Gentile Christians does not seem well-founded. My counsel is that more studious pastors consider buying this as a provocative fresh reading. [*ExpTim* 10/00; *CBQ* 10/00; *Interp* 4/01; *JTS* 4/01; *EvQ* 1/02; *Them* Aut 02; *Biblica* 82.4 (Attridge); *Anvil* 18.2 (Motyer)]. His dissertation, now revised, is often cited: *Despising Shame* (1995, rev. 2008).

☆ **Ellingworth, Paul.** [*M*], (NIGTC) 1993. A massive, erudite work (760pp) which should be consulted for papers and, like Attridge, will definitely be of interest to the pastor wanting to build a first-class exegetical library. (Earlier he wrote a 731-page Aberdeen dissertation on Hebrews.) Lane is probably better for pastors, for this NIGTC is more detail-oriented and less theological. The biggest plus is that this patient scholar was able to interact with the findings of both WBC and Hermeneia. Ellingworth's exegesis here is complemented by a briefer 1991 "Epworth Commentary" for preachers. This NIGTC is a very smart purchase for the more scholarly. [*ExpTim* 1/95; *RTR* 9/94; *Them* 1/95; *CBQ* 7/94; *CRBR* 1994].

F Fanning, Buist. (EEC).

☆ **France, Richard T.** (EBCR) 2006. This commentary replaces Morris from the old EBC and is a real improvement. France is especially known for his large-scale, quality works on the gospels.

Gench, Frances Taylor. ‡ *Hebrews and James* (WestBC) 1996. [*Interp* 7/98; *RelSRev* 7/98].

☆ Gordon, Robert P. (Read) 2000, 2nd ed 2008. The author, an OT professor long at Cambridge, here offers a shorter study of Hebrews. Other *Alttestamentler* (OT specialists) have written insightfully on this epistle in the past (e.g., Delitzsch), and Gordon again shows that they have a lot to say. His 2nd edition discusses further the supersessionism controversy and makes the important point that both Judaism and Christianity represent "a significant break with the religion of the Hebrew Bible/ Old Testament." Gordon's study, not really a commentary *per se*, is in a class all by itself. See also his work on Samuel. [*JTS* 10/01; *Anvil* 18.3].

Gouge, William. Reprint of 1866 ed. This huge commentary has a reputation to match its size among lovers of the Puritans. Gouge died in 1653.

☆ Guthrie, Donald. (TNTC) 1983. A fine replacement vol. in the series. Now becoming dated itself. [*EvQ* 1/85].

☆ Hagner, Donald A. (NIBC) 1990. This 278-page book is one of the best in the category of non-technical exegesis and exposition. Hagner is a fine exegete and writes clearly. Certainly worth more than a skim. Added to this commentary is a recent college textbook *Encountering the Epistle to the Hebrews*, 2002, given many warm reviews [*Them* Spr 04; *Interp* 7/03; *RelSRev* 7/03; *JETS* 6/03]; the beginning student would do well to start with it.

F Hahn, Scott, and Mary Healy. ‡ (CCSS).

F Hall, R. (RRA).

✓ Harrington, Daniel J. ‡ *What Are They Saying about the Letter to the Hebrews?* 2005. [*JETS* 9/06; *BTB* Fall 06].

F Hart, David. (Brazos).

✓ Heen, Erik M., and Philip D.W. Krey (eds). (ACCS) 2005. [*JETS* 6/06].

✓ Heil, John Paul. *Hebrews: Chiastic Structures and Audience Response*, 2010. A large (475-page) work with a fresh approach to the intriguing epistle. Heil says (p.2), "This new proposal is distinguished by the discovery of multiple levels of macro- and microchiastic patterns that, in a consistent and concerted way, drive the rhetorical rhythm within the persuasive strategy of Hebrews as 'the word of the encouragement' (Heb 13:22)." The overall thesis may not be convincing, but the parallels are fascinating, illuminating, and worth further exploration.

Héring, Jean. ‡ ET 1970. In his survey Martin might again have referred to Gallic verve when reviewing this quite critical work. See under 1 Corinthians.

Hewitt, Thomas. (retired TNTC) 1960. Well replaced by Donald Guthrie.

☆ Hughes, R. Kent. (PTW) 2 Vols., 1993. See under Mark. This would be a good addition to the preacher's shelf. Compare with Phillips.

✓   Hurst, L.D. *The Epistle to the Hebrews: Its Background of Thought*, 1990.

F   Jewett, Robert. ‡ (NCBC).

✓   **Johnson, Luke Timothy.** ‡ (NTL) 2006. This veteran scholar with a Catholic background has written many of the best NT commentaries from a mildly to moderately critical perspective (see his Luke, Acts, Timothy, and James). Among accessible, middle-length interpretations of Hebrews from the critical camp, this is now the standard work. The commentary emphasizes the theme of discipleship and seeks to trace the influence of Platonism (especially Philo) upon the argument/theology of the epistle. Evangelical readers may be troubled by Johnson's excursus on the Old and New Covenants, where he joins most critics in rejecting any kind of "supersessionism." What is noteworthy is that Johnson contends that Hebrews itself rejects supersessionism, allowing for the continuance of the old way of worship without reference to Christ, viewing the Old Covenant as remaining valid for those in the old camp (but not for those who would return to it?). Students will not find lengthy interaction with the massive scholarship on Hebrews. [*Chm* Aut 08; *CBQ* 4/07; *JETS* 9/07; *Interp* 4/08; *JSNT-BL* 2008; *ThTo* 4/08; *ExpTim* 12/07; *RelSRev* 3/08; *Biblica* 90.3; *HBT* 29.1].

☆   **Kistemaker, Simon J.** (NTC) 1984. Builds on his dissertation, *The Psalm Citations in the Epistle to the Hebrews* (1961). Because of that previous research one might have expected a more scholarly work, but Kistemaker is writing for this specific series. Has real value for the preacher. [*RTR* 9/85].

✓   **Koester, Craig R.** ‡ (AB) 2001. A replacement for Buchanan, Koester must be placed alongside the other recent large-scale commentaries, such as Lane, Attridge and Ellingworth, as a first-rate reference tool. While most interpretations amplify the "superiority of Christ" idea as central to Hebrews, Koester thinks "the purposes of God for his people" is the main theme. This is one of the stronger recent vols. in the AB series. [*JTS* 4/02; *ExpTim* 3/02; *RelSRev* 1/03; *DenvJ* 1/02 (Blomberg)].

Lang, G.H. 1951. Bruce writes in the first edition of his NICNT work, "For drawing out and applying to the conscience the practical lessons of the epistle, Lang has few rivals."

Long, Thomas G. ‡ (I) 1997. Well written. Some might wish he had written more. After a mere 3pp of introduction, he provides 146pp of commentary. Call this a "stand-by"—such a brief commentary does less to help the preacher unlock the riches of this Bible book. In liberal circles, this vol. and Craddock are the usually recommended preacher's commentaries. [*ThTo* 1/98; *Interp* 7/98; *CBQ* 7/98; *RelSRev* 7/98].

MacArthur, John. 1983. See Matthew for a review of the series, of which this was the first vol.

McKnight, Edgar, and Christopher Church. ‡ *Hebrews–James* (S&H), 2004. This vol. is something of an odd blend. First, the seasoned NT scholar McKnight provides an understated commentary on Hebrews (320pp) with much information to help pastors draw their own conclusions. He gives guidance as *you* read and *you* make application. Church (95pp), on the other hand, forcefully reads James with you and makes many specific applications. The two commentaries have a different feel, one more academic and reflective, the other more urgent and preachy. [*Interp* 7/06].

☆   Michaels, J. Ramsey. (CorBC) 2009. See Belleville under Pastorals.

✓   **Mitchell, Alan C.** ‡ (SacPag). 2007. This full (357-page), accessible, critical commentary completes the Catholic series. Mitchell downplays what others see as the Jewish orientation of the epistle, and treats the material as best falling into the genre of homily. Good attention is paid to rhetorical aspects. Sometimes the exegesis, in my opinion, completely misses the point; e.g., despite the following stern verse, Mitchell argues that 10:26 "may mean that attempting any other rites of purification is senseless, since that end has been accomplished by Christ's death." [*CBQ* 4/08; *RelSRev* 7/07; *ExpTim* 8/08].

✓ **Moffatt, James.** ‡ (ICC) 1924. "A strong commentary, but more useful to teachers than to preachers" (Childs). Bold, rigorous exegesis. This was the standard reference work for scholars many decades ago. Still worth consulting, if the student is doing an in-depth exegesis.

✓ Montifiore, H.W. ‡ (BNTC) 1964. Martin has impressive things to say about this work, but it's hard for me to understand why. It is a good commentary, a serviceable commentary for its day, but hardly a first or second choice. Montifiore is moderately critical. [*WTJ* Spr 66].

F Moo, Douglas. (ZEC). As with Carson, I do not expect this before 2015.

Morris, Leon. (EBC) 1981. All in all, not his best day. About 150pp. See France.

F Motyer, Steve. (THC).

Murray, Andrew. *The Holiest of All*, 1894. This famous devotional classic, for all its heart-warming thoughts, isn't so solid in its exegetical base. Not to be discarded, Murray should always be checked against a careful scholarly work like Bruce. Murray ministered in the South African Dutch Reformed Church and was a main proponent of the Keswick "victorious life" teaching. Several other notable devotional gems are: F.B. Meyer's *The Way into the Holiest*, H.C.G. Moule's *Studies in Hebrews*, and Griffith Thomas's *Hebrews, A Devotional Commentary* (each of these shows a Keswick influence).

☆ Owen, John. 7 Vols. 1668–74 (1980 Baker reprint). All the rigor, theological profundity and verbosity you would expect from the greatest scholar among the Puritans. Can be an extraordinarily difficult chore to work through this, but hard work does pay off. This set has been abridged into a one-vol. work and published under the title, *Hebrews: The Epistle of Warning* (pb. by Kregel). More recently published is the Crossway Classic edition (1998). The last mentioned is probably what the average pastor would find most conducive to personal study. Reformed congregations with a tradition of deep Bible teaching would do well to add the CrossC edition to their libraries. [*SBET* Sum 93].

☆ **Pfitzner, Victor C.** ‡ (ANTC) 1997. One of the best in the series. The author, a Lutheran scholar teaching in Australia, gives both a mature and fresh interpretation which demonstrates "that every climactic point in the book is a statement about worship" (Lane). Perhaps Pfitzner's reflections on a Bible-based theology of worship will spur evangelicals to give that topic more thought than they often do. A very fine, compact exegesis, which expertly draws connections between texts. He also uses the older and newer structural studies like Vanhoye and Guthrie. Some evangelicals would say Pfitzner is not always the best theological guide. [*AsTJ* Fall 99; *RelSRev* 1/99].

☆ Phillips, Richard D. (REC) 2006. One of the very best practical/devotional commentaries available. Readers will find it especially rich and thoughtful on ch. 11; Phillips builds on his earlier book, *Faith Victorious: Finding Strength and Hope from Hebrews 11*, published in 2002. The author is pastor of Second Presbyterian Church (PCA) in Greenville, SC. The vol. is quite stocked with helpful material (650pp) for expositors.

Pink, Arthur. 1954. A huge vol. of exposition published for many years by Baker. Verbose but suggestive to the expositor who speed-reads.

Rayburn, Robert S. *Evangelical Commentary on the Bible* (one-vol.), 1989. A rather radical thesis is propounded here. Rayburn argues that the terms "old covenant" and "new covenant" should not be understood as having religio-historical significance, but as describing the religion of legalism and the religion of faith in all ages (B.C. and A.D.). This is no place for a full review, but this much should be said: the author of Hebrews has derogatory things to say about the "old covenant" because after Christ the OT cultus is a closed door. The new age has come in the appearance of a better Prophet and Priest. Adhering oneself to the old economy is *now* the way of unbelief because such an act disregards Messiah's coming and his self-sacrifice. (See Calvin's *Institutes*, II. ix-xi.).

Stedman, Ray C. (IVPNT) 1992. Helpful for communicators, less so for students. Stedman published a fair number of expositions on both OT and NT books. This is probably the least scholarly contribution to IVPNT. [*Chm* 107.4 (1993)].

F Thatcher, Tom. (NCCS). The author teaches at Cincinnati Christian University.

☆ **Thompson, James W.** ‡ (Paideia) 2008. It is hard to find anything more valuable than this in the category of compact (288-page), moderately critical exegesis. Thompson's research on Hebrews goes back to a 1974 dissertation. He is recognized as an expert in detailing the philosophical background to the epistle (more the Greco-Roman than the OT and Jewish background). See Moo's review of Thompson's weaknesses as an exegetical reference for one moving text-by-text. [*ExpTim* 12/09; *Interp* 4/10; *BBR* 20.2 (Moo); *CBQ* 4/10; *JSNT-BL* 2010; *Them* 7/10].

✓ Trotter, Andrew H. *Interpreting the Epistle to the Hebrews* (Guides to NT Exegesis), 1997. Not a commentary, but a fine introduction for students [*JSNT* 75]. A little more recent is Harrington.

✓ Vanhoye, Albert. ‡ *Structure and Message of the Epistle to the Hebrews*, 1989.

✓ Vos, Geerhardus. *The Teaching of the Epistle to the Hebrews*, 1956. This is a true gem. If you plan to do any work on the theology in Hebrews, you would do well to read this rich biblical theological study. Reprinted from time to time by P&R.

✓ **Westcott, B.F.** 3rd ed 1920. Even today this is regarded as a valuable classic; it "remains impressive and is especially rich in Patristic references" (Childs). This would not be an unwise purchase. I believe this is still being reprinted.

F Westfall, Cynthia L. (BHGNT). Her published dissertation, *A Discourse Analysis of the Letter to the Hebrews* (2005), is already a highly useful commentary for advanced students [*Biblica* 88.2; *ExpTim* 8/07].

✓ Wilson, R. McL. ‡ (NCB) 1987. A good entry, but in view of the many great works now available you won't pay as much attention to it. Wilson is slightly over 250pp.

☆ **Witherington, Ben**. *Letters and Homilies for Jewish Christians: A Socio-Rhetorical Commentary on Hebrews, James and Jude*, 2007. Stunningly, this marks the completion of his project to comment on the entire NT. [*JSNT-BL* 2009; *DenvJ* 1/08].

NOTES: (1) George Guthrie, "Hebrews' Use of the Old Testament: Recent Trends in Research," *CBR* 1.2 (2003): 271–94. (2) J.C. McCullough has written four valuable articles in *Irish Biblical Studies* surveying Hebrews scholarship; see *IBS* numbers 2, 3, and 16. (3) Cambridge lecturer Peter Head shows himself to be a shrewd judge of the best commentaries on Hebrews as he reviews a dozen of them in *BSB* 9/06.

—ᴍ—

JAMES

★ **Blomberg, Craig L., and Mariam J. Kamell.** (ZEC) 2008. Both pastors and students will warmly welcome this handy (288-page), well-written vol., which leads the reader through grammatical analysis and other matters of exegesis. A strength here is the wise way that the coauthors point out the key questions and problems faced in interpreting James. This is a promising start to the ZEC (see Commentary Series). I will voice a complaint, however, about the number of sections into which the commentary is divided (7). For the weaknesses of the book, see Davids' review. [*JETS* 9/09; *Them* 7/09; *CBQ* 7/09 (Davids); *ExpTim* 2/10 (Hartin); *BTB* 8/10; *JSNT-BL* 2010].

★ **Davids, Peter.** (NIGTC) 1982. Years ago this was the first choice of Childs, Carson and Martin. You should also note that Davids contributed the brief, more popularly-styled commentary in NIBC (1989). NIGTC is of much greater value, especially if one is carefully studying the Greek NT. Davids argues that James the Just received some sort of editorial assistance and that there is some discernable structure to the epistle's argument. Compare with Laws. For student or scholarly pastor, Johnson is more current in scholarship and just as probing and useful, and I regard McCartney as now superseding this good book in several respects. [*JETS* 6/83; *WTJ* Fall 84; *JBL* 102.4 (1983); *RTR* 9/83].

★ **Johnson, Luke Timothy.** ‡ (AB) 1995. Brilliant! A sizable (347pp + indices) work from a more conservative critic with a Catholic background. Johnson should be of great use to those interested in rhetorical criticism; he's proved himself to be a skillful practitioner of the new literary critical approaches. Students should appreciate Johnson's attention to the history of interpretation. While most Bible expositors will bypass Johnson, the scholarly pastor wanting a first-class exegetical library will buy this—my four "musts" are Davids (NIGTC), Moo (Pillar), McCartney (BECNT), and Johnson (AB). In shorter compass (about 50pp), Johnson does "James" in the NewIB. For more on Johnson, see Timothy, Luke, and Acts. [*JETS* 3/99; *Interp* 7/97; *RelSRev* 1/97; *JR* 1/98]. Students can consult his *Brother of Jesus, Friend of God: Studies in the Letter of James*, 2004 [*JTS* 10/05; *SJT* 59.4; *CurTM* 4/05; *ExpTim* 2/05; *HBT* 29.2].

★ **McCartney, Dan G.** (BECNT) 2009. McKnight was once listed for this series, but he is now writing for NICNT (see below). McCartney taught at Westminster Seminary in Philadelphia for about 25 years and is now at Redeemer Seminary in Dallas; he is a very careful, thorough exegete and has a fine theological mind. As one might expect from a WTS professor, the approach is both rigorously Reformed and fresh. McCartney does not simply recycle older views. I consider it well-rounded: "exegetically rewarding, theologically rooted, and pastorally wise" (Schreiner). While pastors will probably still buy Moo's Pillar vol. first, students might well make McCartney their choice. For advanced students of the Greek NT, the bibliography is quite valuable but not as full as I had expected. This fine reference tool (335pp) deserves the warmest of welcomes. See McKnight below. [*DenvJ* 6/10 (Blomberg)].

★ Manton, Thomas. (GS) 1651, 1693 ed. This is, no doubt, a surprise to some. I make no apologies for including this classic of Puritanism. This work has a rich vein of practical theology that a pastor can mine out during an entire lifetime of ministry. Those preachers who prefer a more up-to-date work should probably buy Doriani, Hughes, Motyer, or Blanchard (more devotional), or Nystrom (offering more cultural critique). Note: reading literature from another era and culture can provide the Bible interpreter with a different perspective. Manton often helps at points where we may have 21st century, American blinders on. Cheaper and more accessible than the GS edition is the CrossC pb version (1995) [*SBET* Spr 97].

★ **Moo, Douglas.** (Pillar) 2000. This commentary builds upon and supersedes the 1985 TNTC work; it is about twice as long and is a fresh interpretation of the epistle. After a well-written, satisfying introduction of about 45pp, readers are treated to some 210pp of careful exegesis and theological reflection. Moo's thorough knowledge of Romans leads to some expert discussion of the differences and similarities between the two letters—an issue pastors often wind up explaining in their teaching ministry. (Johnson as well has some learned discussion of the topic.) Moo, however, reads James on its own terms and does not fall into the trap of interpreting the epistle by reference to Paul. I am glad for the interaction with Johnson's superb recent work in AB. This has been, hands down, the first choice for the evangelical pastor, but it now has competition from McCartney and the forthcoming McKnight. [*Interp* 1/01; *RTR* 8/00; *SwJT* Spr 01; *CBQ* 4/01; *Them* Spr 04; *EvQ* 10/03; *JETS* 9/02; *Chm* Aut 01; *BBR* 12.1 (Davids); *Evangel* Spr 02].

F   Adam, A.K.M. (BHGNT).

✓   **Adamson, J.B.** (NICNT) 1976. This is a good work which didn't have the best scholarly reception. Carson summed up the problem when he described the commentary as "disproportionately dependent on Hellenistic parallels at the expense of Jewish sources." One need only compare Adamson with Davids on a few passages to see Carson's point. Adamson has made his contribution to scholarship—perhaps not in the commentary so much as in his monograph, *James, The Man and His Message* (1989). In that 500-page work he answers his detractors [*CRBR* 1991; *WTJ* Spr 91; *JETS* 6/92; *Evangel* Sum 92; *Chm* 104.2 (1990); *TJ* Spr 89 (McKnight, glowing)]. Note that Adamson will be retired by McKnight's replacement vol.

F   Allison, Dale. ‡ (ICC–new series).

F   Baker, Bill. (THC).

✓   **Bauckham, Richard.** [*M*], *James: Wisdom of James, Disciple of Jesus the Sage* (NT Readings) 1999. This fresh reading of James' epistle is well worth consulting, both by students interested in exegesis and the structure of the letter (influenced, he says, by "Jewish wisdom instruction") and by preachers who are eager to apply the message to hearers' hearts and lives. Bauckham is conservatively critical. Don't miss this (256pp). If it were not rather pricey at $45, then it could be heartily recommended for purchase. [*JTS* 4/02].

☆   Blanchard, John. *Truth for Life: A Devotional Commentary on the Epistle of James*, 2nd ed 1986. I would like to have included this book among the recommendations above. Its 400pp are eminently practical, good food for the soul, and directly serve the preacher in his task of applying Scripture to life. [*EvQ* 10/84].

✓   Bray, Gerald (ed). *James, 1–2 Peter, 1–3 John, Jude* (ACCS) 2000. This vol. is fascinating reading and instructive for all who wish to study how these epistles were first interpreted by the Church. There are fresh insights and remarks to ponder on nearly every page (xxx + 288pp).

Brosend, William F. [*M*], *James and Jude* (NCBC) 2004. The author follows Vernon Robbins' socio-rhetorical approach. I have not had much opportunity to use this, but I note that it is getting good reviews. Brosend takes a conservative stance, arguing that these two letters are well treated together as written by Jesus' half-brothers. [*Interp* 1/07; *JSNT-BL* 2005; *RelSRev* 1/05; *ExpTim* 10/05].

✓   Burdick, Donald W. (EBC) 1981.

Cheung, Luke L. *The Genre, Composition and Hermeneutics of James*, 2003.

Chilton, Bruce, and Jacob Neusner (eds). *The Brother of Jesus*, 2001. Essays from an SBL consultation.

✓   **Dibelius, M., and H. Greeven.** ‡ (Herm) 1964, ET 1976. A standard exegetical tool from the critical camp. This is for specialists and advanced students. By its critical and atomizing approach the commentary does injustice to the tone and message of James, stripping this vibrant book of all theology, and, for me anyway, losing all sense for connection of thought in the epistle. Dibelius/Greeven is not of much use to the pastor. The German original was the 7th ed. KEK from 1921, and it was subsequently revised and expanded up to 1964. [*JBL* 85.2].

☆ Doriani, Daniel. (REC) 2007. A very worthwhile homiletical commentary to use after having carefully done one's exegesis. The author taught NT at Covenant Seminary and now pastors in St. Louis. As expected, then, Doriani's exegesis is well-studied and dependable. [*JETS* 6/08].

Gench, Frances Taylor. ‡ *Hebrews and James* (WestBC) 1996. [*Interp* 7/98].

F George, Timothy. (Brazos).

F Green, Joel B. [𝓜], (NTL).

☆ Guthrie, George. (EBCR) 2006. Quality, concise (75-page), accessible evangelical exegesis from a scholar who has published important work on Hebrews.

✓ **Hartin, Patrick J.** ‡ (SacPag) 2003. Far deeper scholarship is in evidence in this vol. (319pp) than in most other Sacra Pagina vols., which tend to wear their learning lightly. This work by a Roman Catholic may be compared with Johnson above. He holds that James of Jerusalem is the author of the material, which was collected and published in one letter soon after his death. Cargal says this "commentary represents 'the state of the art' in research on the letter of James." One of his particular interests is *James and the Q Sayings of Jesus* (1991), originally his dissertation. [*Interp* 10/04 (Johnson); *ExpTim* 6/04; *JETS* 3/05; *CBQ* 10/04 (Cargal)].

Hiebert, D. Edmond. 1979, rev. 1992. An exposition published by Moody. Quite full.

✓ Hort, F.J.A. [𝓜], 1909. This weighty exegetical treatment of the Greek covers most of the epistle—it was left incomplete, ending at 4:7—and was published by Macmillan (xxxiii + 118pp). More conservative in its criticism.

☆ Hughes, R. Kent. (PTW) 1991. See under Mark. Compare with Doriani.

F Jimenez, Pablo. (NCCS). The author is a pastor in Puerto Rico.

Johnson, Luke Timothy. ‡ (NewIB) 1998. For students this commentary should be passed over, in favor of the larger AB, which is a major resource for scholarship on this epistle. Preachers will find some of their proclamation concerns addressed in this 50-page NewIB contribution.

☆ Johnstone, Robert. (GS) 1871. A thoughtful, reverent exposition which many pastors have used.

☆ Keddie, Gordon J. *The Practical Christian* (WCS) 1989.

☆ Kistemaker, Simon J. *James and 1–3 John* (NTC) 1986. [*Them* 4/88].

F Kloppenborg, John S. ‡ (Herm).

✓ Laato, T. "Justification According to James: A Comparison with Paul," *TJ* 18 (1997): 43–84. Counted important reading by several leading evangelical scholars such as Moo and McCartney.

✓ **Laws, Sophie.** ‡ (BNTC) 1980. Perceptive, packed, and highly praised by a number of scholars. In the 1980s Davids and Laws were probably the two most important reference commentaries. This is more accessible than Davids in that she explains the English text. However, she has obviously done her homework in the original. Laws argues for a late date and Roman provenance, which seems far less likely than the setting proposed by Davids, i.e., James addresses Jewish Messianists in the 50s and 60s. Laws' approach also entails a rejection of Jacobean authorship. More critical than Davids. [*ExpTim* 1/81; *JBL* 102.4; *JETS* 9/82; *ThTo* 38.3].

MacArthur, John. 1998. See Matthew for a review of the series. This is one of the better vols. he has done.

F **McKnight, Scot.** (NICNT replacement) 2010. See Adamson above. (Ignore the old report of Verseput doing NICNT.) I am expecting this to arrive in late 2010 and to become a likely top-pick. The report is that it totals 536pp.

☆ **Martin, Ralph P.** [*M*], (WBC) 1988. He probably uses the odd WBC format better than anyone else. In his surprisingly lengthy introduction (100pp), Martin has some very interesting rhetorical analysis of the letter. This commentary is a success, even if you don't buy into his idea of a two-stage compositional history (p.lxxvii, trying to balance the Greek style and Palestinian flavor). I admit to being irritated when Martin attributes so much to some "enterprising editor," even questioning that James intended a letter to be sent, and then declares that we cannot tell whether the editor succeeded in his publishing venture, whatever his purposes. Besides such introductory issues, I am more trusting of Davids' exegetical judgment in commenting on pericopae. As always, Martin's bibliography is superb. For more scholarly types. [*WTJ* Spr 92; *EvQ* 10/92; *RTR* 9/90; *CBQ* 10/91; *Them* 4/91; *Chm* 105.2 (1991)].

 Maynard-Reid, Pedrito U. ‡ *Poverty and Wealth in James*, 1987. An Orbis issue, "organized according to its exegesis of select passages…that just happen to have the sharpest ideological edge and the greatest sociocultural implications" (Brosend, 25).

✓ **Mayor, J.B.** [*M*], 3ʳᵈ ed 1910, 1913. Another mammoth work in the old Macmillan series. Advanced students should try to obtain a copy of this work if they can. Mayor did for James and 2 Peter-Jude what Selwyn did for 1 Peter, except with less flair. Mayor is deeply learned, conservatively critical in the old British tradition, and treats the Greek text in detail.

✓ Mitton, C.L. ‡ 1966. A stimulating expositional commentary, unfortunately o/p. This is better than his Ephesians commentary. Mitton posits a Palestinian milieu and points to a date in the 50s.

 Moffatt, James. ‡ (Moffatt) 1928. Covers the General Epistles. Moffatt was always liberal, deeply learned, and scintillating at the same time.

☆ Moo, Douglas. (TNTC) 1986. This superb commentary is Moo's earlier effort, which I once recommended for its exposition which complements the more exegetical NIGTC entry. Contains a great deal of practical and pithy comments, besides astute scholarly judgment. This vol. is superseded by Moo's Pillar commentary.

☆ Motyer, J. Alec. (BST) 1985. Lives up to the standards of the series. Blanchard, though more diffuse, is just as useful as Motyer to the preacher. In editions of this guide prior to 2001, Motyer was always a recommended purchase. Still a smart buy for two main reasons: it is an inexpensive pb and Motyer's OT expertise gives him special insight into the letter's theological background. [*JETS* 3/87].

☆ Nystrom, David. (NIVAC) 1997. The author's forte is ancient history and contemporary cultural critique, not NT scholarship. While the literature cited in "Contemporary Significance" sections is current, Nystrom uses little periodical literature and seems largely dependent upon Davids, Laws, and Martin in researching the "Original Meaning." He does helpfully draw from the Caird/Hurst *New Testament Theology* (1994). In short, this vol. provokes preachers to make application but is weak in the exegetical foundation laid beforehand.

F Osborne, Grant. (CorBC).

 Painter, John. ‡ *Just James: The Brother of Jesus in History and Tradition*, 1999. A helpful "sourcebook for the study of the letter of James" (Brosend). [*Anvil* 17.3].

F Painter, John, and David deSilva. ‡ *James and Jude* (Paideia). Painter is responsible for the James commentary while deSilva does Jude.

✓ **Perkins, Pheme.** ‡ *First and Second Peter, James, and Jude* (I) 1995. Covering all four letters in about 200pp makes this commentary a bit too thin at points to help its intended readership. By contrast the Tyndale series treats these letters in 638 total pages. Another problem noted by reviewers—ironically in the direction of inaccessibility—is the more academic orientation which renders it perhaps less serviceable than other "Interpretation" vols. to those without a solid scholarly background. [*JETS* 9/97; *ThTo* 1/97; *Interp* 4/97; *CBQ* 10/96; *CRBR* 1996].

Plummer, Alfred. *General Epistles of St. James and St. Jude* (EB) 1891. Still cited in the literature.

Reicke, Bo. ‡ (retired AB) 1964. Covers Peter and Jude as well, but the comment is spread too thin to make it very worthwhile. Rejects Jacobean authorship. The series' editors have replaced this work. We now have Johnson on this epistle, Elliott on 1 Peter, and Neyrey on 2 Peter/Jude.

Richardson, Kurt. (NAC) 1997. The author teaches at Gordon-Conwell, and his commentary is full enough at 272pp to accomplish some good. The exegesis tends to be weak, however, and I predict you will much prefer Moo's Pillar vol. This is not one of the stronger contributions to the series. [*BSac* 10/99].

✓ **Ropes, J.H.** ‡ (ICC) 1916. Though students will find the best help on technical issues in Mayor, Dibelius/Greeven, Davids, Martin, Johnson, and McCartney, they could consult Ropes and Hort too. Those older commentaries retain some value and are cited in the more recent works. Ropes is more critical than Hort or Mayor and argued for pseudonymity.

Ross, Alexander. (retired NICNT) 1954. Replaced by Adamson. Carson spoke of it as "a book warmly devotional in tone but offering no serious help in the difficult passages."

Sidebottom, E.M. ‡ (NCB) 1967. Covers Jude and 2 Peter too, but in my estimate it is too brief to do much good. Would likely have been replaced, if the series had continued.

✓ Sleeper, C. Freeman. ‡ (ANTC) 1998. Some reviewers are calling this 150-page, compact exegesis a success, but it does not compete with the likes of Davids, Moo. [*Interp* 7/01].

☆ Stulac, George. (IVPNT) 1993. A practical exposition of some 190pp by a PCA pastor in St. Louis. I have not had opportunity to examine it closely, but some give it high marks, not so much for scholarly penetration, but for pastoral insight and an earnest humble "spirit" which is in line with the epistle's tone. Students will need to look elsewhere for exegetical helps. [*Chm* 109.1 (1995)].

Tasker, R.V.G. (retired TNTC) 1957. A brief, perceptive work replaced by Moo.

Taylor, Mark Edward. *A Text-Linguistic Investigation into the Discourse Structure of James*, 2006.

F Wachob, W.H. (RRA).

✓ **Wall, Robert W.** *Community of the Wise: The Letter of James*, 1997. Exceedingly full (335pp) for the series of which it is a part, Trinity Press's "The NT in Context." (Contrast Sloyan's 76pp on John's Epistles in this series.) Wall describes his intention: "my work seeks to expose a layer of meaning by mining the text within the context of scripture itself—a canonical *Sitz im Leben*" (p.1). This is a fine contribution. [*Interp* 7/98; *DenvJ*].

✓ Webb, Robert L., John S. Kloppenborg (eds). ‡ *Reading James with New Eyes: Methodological Reassessments of the Letter of James*, 2007.

Webber, Randall C. ‡ *Reader Response Analysis of the Epistle of James*, 1996.

☆ **Witherington, Ben.** *Letters and Homilies for Jewish Christians: A Socio-Rhetorical Commentary on Hebrews, James and Jude*, 2007. The introduction and commentary on James stretch over 170pp.

NOTES: (1) Ruth B. Edwards, "Which Is the Best Commentary? XV. The Epistle of James," *ExpTim* 6/92. (2) Todd Penner, "The Epistle of James in Current Research," *CurBS* 7 (1999): 257–308.

1 PETER

★ Clowney, Edmund. (BST) 1989. A favorite of mine. His exegetical decisions are well considered, and his theological interpretation is very valuable. One of the best informed entries in the series. He was a communicator too (former President of Westminster Seminary and Professor of Homiletics and Practical Theology). This work is interesting from start to finish; you can read it straight through. Compare with McKnight, who is stronger in NT scholarship. [*Evangel* Win 89; *JETS* 12/92; *RTR* 1/92; *CTJ* 11/90; *Chm* 103.3 (1989)].

★ **Davids, Peter.** (NICNT) 1990. My first choice among mid-level works. The earlier James commentary led us to expect a lot, and those expectations were not disappointed. This is an ideal commentary: careful exegesis, superb theological reflection, thorough yet pithy. As I was preaching through 1 Peter myself, Davids was the most lucid and helpful in wrestling with the cruxes: 3:18–22 and 4:1, 6. [*CRBR* 1992; *Them* 1/92; *CBQ* 7/92; *Evangel* Sum 92; *NovT* 35.3].

★ **Jobes, Karen H.** (BECNT) 2005. "Thankfully manageable in size (ca. 350 pages...), this is nonetheless a major critical commentary" (Green) from the evangelical camp. Jobes has done much work on the Septuagint (Westminster PhD) and has contributed the Esther vol. to NIVAC. The up-to-date bibliography and interaction with recent technical commentaries will make this a fine reference vol., advantageous to students. Her special contributions, besides the solid exegesis, are: a proposal that the recipients were converts, possibly from Rome, displaced to Asia Minor; assessment of the LXX background; and a research of the quality of the Greek. Pastors can benefit much from the fine exegesis. [*CBQ* 4/06; *JETS* 3/07; *JSNT-BL* 2006; *NovT* 49.4; *BSac* 10/07; *ExpTim* 5/06; *BBR* 19.3 (Hafemann)]. Students will consult Jobes alongside the major heavyweight commentaries of Achtemeier, Elliott, and Michaels, with more than a nod to Selwyn, Goppelt, Kelly, and Feldmeier.

★ McKnight, Scot. (NIVAC) 1996. The author is an editor of the NT series and here contributes a model commentary for it. See NIVAC under "Commentary Series." Almost 300pp.

★ **Schreiner, Thomas.** *1, 2 Peter, Jude* (NAC) 2003. One of the best vols. in the whole NT series. Though Schreiner gives a very good study of 1 Peter, with plenty of bibliographical help for students, I have valued this vol. even more for 2 Peter and Jude because of the long-standing lack of evangelical exegetical commentaries on that portion (Davids and Green have now supplied that lack). Preachers will appreciate the author's clarity, exegetical good sense, and focus upon theological exposition (more or less Reformed). Blomberg rightly says, "If someone could afford only one commentary on these three letters together, then this is the obvious one to choose, with no close rivals." [*RelSRev* 4/04; *JETS* 12/04; *BSac* 10/05; *DenvJ* 1/04 (Blomberg)].

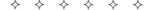

☆   **Achtemeier, Paul J.** ‡ (Herm) 1996. A significant publication which is of greater interest to the NT academic than the average pastor. This 400-page entry in the series argues for pseudonymity and a date between 80 and 100. I find Achtemeier's work more theologically sensitive than most others in the series. (The theology drawn out is more conservative than the critical conclusions on introductory matters.) Students are advised to take notice of this vol. in their research writing; it is now to be regarded, alongside Elliott's AB, as *the* leading full-scale critical commentary available. The advanced student or scholarly pastor could put this superb work to good use; I prefer it to Elliott, Michaels, and Goppelt because of Achtemeier's sensible, sure-footed, and even masterful exegesis. I also predict this vol. will have a long shelf-life. [*JETS* 6/99; *JBL* Spr 98; *WTJ* Fall 96; *Interp* 1/98; *CBQ* 1/98; *SJT* 51.3 (1998); *RelSRev* 7/97].

    Adams, Jay E. 1979. A popular commentary which digs into the theology and may be worth skimming.

    Bartlett, David L. ‡ (NewIB) 1998. This 90-page exposition, from a Yale professor of preaching, dates the book near the close of the 1ˢᵗ century.

✓   **Beare, F.W.** ‡ 1947, 3ʳᵈ ed 1970. Beare immediately followed Selwyn and put forward a rather more critical interpretation of the epistle. Scholars remember him for his proposal that we read 1:3–4:11 as a "baptismal discourse" (pp.25–27), but today it is hard to find anyone who believes the letter springs from a homily or liturgy. All discussion of 1 Peter since 1947 has taken as its starting point these two rigorous works. Beare denies Petrine authorship in this most valuable of all his commentaries.

☆   Bentley, Michael. *Living for Christ* (WCS on 1 & 2 Peter) 1990.

✓   **Best, Ernest.** ‡ (NCB) 1971. Useful for reference, but not nearly as important as his work on Thessalonians for BNTC or on Ephesians for the revised ICC. Best denies the authenticity of this letter.

✓   **Bigg, C.A.** ‡ (ICC) 1902. Still quite useful for its technical work. Covers Jude and both epistles of Peter. Defends Petrine authorship of the first letter, but rejects 2 Peter as pseudonymous.

✓   Blum, Edwin A. (EBC) 1981. Insightful and clear, but too brief to compete with the other works listed.

✓   Boring, M. Eugene. ‡ (ANTC) 1999. Boring argues for pseudonymity and is not the safest theological guide to the epistle. As he presses his case for universalism, he takes issue with other writers such as Achtemeier.

✓   Bray, Gerald (ed). *James, 1–2 Peter, 1–3 John, Jude* (ACCS) 2000. See James above.

    Briscoe, D. Stuart. *When the Going Gets Tough*, 1982. Twenty fine sermons on 1 Peter.

    Brown, John. *Expository Discourses on First Peter*, 3 Vols., 1866. A huge Calvinistic work that is rich and suggestive theologically for anyone willing to wade through it. Somewhat in the Puritan vein.

✓   Campbell, Barth L. *Honor, Shame, and the Rhetoric of 1 Peter*, 1998. Compare with Martin's understanding of rhetoric and structure.

☆   Charles, J. Darryl. (EBCR) 2006. This author contributes the commentary on 1–2 Peter and Jude. Earlier he did 2 Peter and Jude in BCBC.

    Craddock, Fred. ‡ *First and Second Peter and Jude* (WestBC) 1996. The expositor may learn a lot here, but students will turn to more exegetical works. Craddock is agnostic about authorship but favors the pseudonymity position. [*CBQ* 4/97; *RelSRev* 10/97].

✓   Cranfield, C.E.B. [*M*], (Torch) 1960. Covers both of Peter's epistles and Jude. It is insightful and penetrating, as one would expect from Cranfield. There was also an earlier work on 1 Peter (1950) which was eclipsed by this entry. Fairly mild in its critical stance on 1 Peter.

✓ Dalton, William J. ‡ *Christ's Proclamation to the Spirits: A Study of 1 Peter 3:18–4:6*, 1965, rev. 1989. This is certainly one of the most important monographs published on this epistle over the last 50 years. Most commentators (e.g., Davids, Achtemeier, Boring, and Michaels, but with an odd twist) follow his interpretation.

F deSilva, David. [*M*], (ECC).

F deSilva, David. [*M*], (RRA).

F **Donelson, Lewis R.** ‡ *I & II Peter and Jude* (NTL) 2010. Announced as 336pp.

F Dubis, Mark. (BHGNT).

✓ **Elliott, John H.** ‡ (AB) 2001. This commentary is huge in size and erudition. Few know the literature on the book of 1 Peter as well, or have contributed so much to contemporary Petrine scholarship as Elliott. He argues for pseudonymity and takes a heavily sociological approach. His earlier work is *A Home for the Homeless: A Sociological Exegesis of 1 Peter, Its Situation and Strategy* (1981, rev. 1990). I cannot agree with Elliott that the "aliens and strangers" were literally homeless; this is a case where sociological research should not trump Biblical Theology. See Achtemeier above. Advanced students will lean hard on Elliott for bibliographical help. [*CBQ* 10/01; *NovT* 46.3].

✓ **Feldmeier, Reinhard.** ‡ *The First Letter of Peter: A Commentary on the Greek Text*, 2005, ET 2008. I was glad finally to see this 317-page Baylor University Press issue. Davids is the translator, and when a productive scholar takes time out to do a translation project, we expect there is good reason. German readers should note that the ET is a revision of, and improvement on, the original edition. Horrell says Feldmeier "offers much insight in a short space" (*1 Peter*, p.29), and Hagner calls it "an exceptional commentary that is not only brilliant academically, but one that is also edifying." On the authorship issue he tentatively concludes that the weight of evidence is against the Apostle Peter (p.38). [*CBQ* 1/10; *ExpTim* 7/09 (Horrell)].

F Glenny, Ed. (EEC).

☆ **Goppelt, Leonhard.** ‡ 1978, ET 1993. This valuable volume from the *Kritisch-exegetischer Kommentar* has been translated and published by Eerdmans. This work is of immense help to the scholar for its technical and theological discussion. The commentary is probably most notable for its sociological approach. Goppelt, along with just about all the German NT scholars, rejects Petrine authorship. Because sales were not so strong, Eerdmans was once selling the overstock at a good discount. [*JBL* 100.1 (1981)]. Goppelt is well known for his useful two-vol. NT theology, published in German 1975–76 and in translation 1981–82.

F Greaux, Eric. (NCCS). The author teaches at Winston-Salem State University in North Carolina.

☆ **Green, Joel B.** (THC) 2007. The author, now gone from Asbury and teaching at Fuller, here delivers a fresh exegesis with extended theological reflection on the epistle's contribution to NT Theology. As with Marshall on this same epistle, the author's Methodist convictions are not so much on display. Along with Fowl on Philippians, this is one of the best vols. in the developing THC series. For a probing critique see G. Green. [*RTR* 12/08; *CBQ* 10/08; *ExpTim* 1/09; *JETS* 12/08 (Gene Green); *JSNT-BL* 2009].

☆ **Grudem, Wayne.** (TNTC) 1988. Sought to produce a more independent work and was quite successful in delivering fresh insights. Morris, the general editor, made a wise choice in Grudem, who gives good attention to theological questions. Compare with other commentaries on "preaching to the spirits in prison." In the first six editions of this guide I urged readers to purchase this book. [*WTJ* Fall 89; *JETS* 6/91; *CTJ* 4/90].

F   Hafemann, Scott. (Pillar).

Harink, Douglas. ‡ *1 & 2 Peter* (Brazos) 2009. I have not seen this but guess it is a widely-ranging, lively, and provocative theological interpretation, directly challenging many traditional evangelical views—a book not unlike his *Paul among the Postliberals* (2003). [*ExpTim* 9/10].

☆   Helm, David R. *1 & 2 Peter and Jude* (PTW) 2008.

Hiebert, D. Edmond. 1984. A lengthy commentary which seeks to be both exegetical and expositional. Has some attractive features, but not as penetrating as some other works. Dispensational. [*JETS* 9/85].

☆   **Hillyer, Norman.** *1 & 2 Peter, Jude* (NIBC) 1992. Clear and useful for its size (300pp)—"both concise and incisive even in its exegesis of difficult verses" (B. Campbell). The approach here is thoroughly evangelical. Call this a bargain. [*RTR* 1/96; *Them* 1/96; *CRBR* 1994 (Davids)].

F   Horrell, David. ‡ (ICC–new series). A portion of the preliminary research is published in Horrell's expert overview of recent scholarship in the "NT Guides" vol. on 1 Peter (2008) [*ExpTim* 5/09; *JSNT-BL* 2009; *RelSRev* 9/09; *BTB* 8/10]. There was an earlier (1998) commentary, aimed at assisting preachers, on The Epistles of Peter and Jude in the Epworth series [*Anvil* 17.3].

✓   Hort, F.J.A. 1898. Though fragmentary and covering only 1:1–2:17, this work is worth noting for its exegesis (see Michaels, p. x). Intended for the old Macmillan series.

✓   Hunter, A.M. [*M*], (IB) 1957. I find he always has something profitable to say, but few ministers make use of IB anymore. Takes a more conservatively critical approach.

F   Keating, Daniel. ‡ *First and Second Peter, Jude* (CCSS).

☆   **Kelly, J.N.D.** [*M*], (BNTC) 1969. Valued by all scholars and by studious pastors, this commentary covers both of the epistles of Peter and Jude. This is a judicious work by a renowned authority on the Early Church. Unfortunately he follows the critical line on the authorship of 2 Peter. Has been reprinted by Baker in the "Thornapple" series as well as by Hendrickson Publishers. [*JBL* 89.4 (1970)].

☆   Kistemaker, Simon J. *Peter and Jude* (NTC) 1987. Though not profound, this will serve the pastor as a sturdy theological guide through these very theological epistles. Strongly supports the stance of believing scholarship regarding the authenticity of both 1 & 2 Peter. His exegetical decisions are well-grounded and clearly explained. Schreiner has done us a similar service more recently. [*WTJ* Fall 89; *CTJ* 11/90].

✓   Knight, Jonathan. ‡ (NT Guides) 1995. For a quick survey of scholarship.

Leighton, Robert. 1693–94. This classic work of full theological exposition is extremely valuable to the pastor willing to work through it. Was reprinted by Kregel in 1972. Leighton (500pp) has been edited down and included in the Crossway Classic series; see below.

☆   Leighton, Robert, and W.H. Griffith Thomas. *1 & 2 Peter* (CrossC) 1999.

✓   Luther, Martin. 1522–27. His commentaries on the Catholic Epistles are available in both a 19th and 20th century translation. The single vol. published by Concordia (1967) is the one to possess, if you wish to purchase the work, though the earlier one is serviceable. Do not expect to find a commentary on the Epistle of James— the "epistle of straw," as the Saxon Reformer termed it—in this vol.

MacArthur, John. 2004. See Matthew for a review of the series.

☆   **Marshall, I Howard.** (IVPNT) 1991. Marshall is general editor and his work always carries a weight of scholarship. This is a very, very fine book, satisfying in its exegesis and contemporary application. There is a great deal more substance to this work than one might suppose looking at its slim size—reminds me of Cranfield. I would even go so far as to say this would be an excellent first purchase for a pastor. [*CRBR* 1992].

F   Martin, Troy. (NIGTC). He will build upon his 1990 dissertation, *Metaphor and Composition in 1 Peter*.

☆   **Michaels, J. Ramsey.** [𝓜], (WBC) 1988. A remarkably learned work which advances the scholarly discussion a good ways. This was Carson's and Silva's first choice in years past. Though I dislike Michaels' fence-sitting in the introduction (pp.lxii-lxvii), I am impressed with his erudition and was greatly helped in my understanding of 1 Peter by this commentary. Surprisingly, Michaels wants to argue that the evidence supports both Petrine authorship and a date in the 70s—a view earlier put forward by A.M. Ramsay. Advanced students especially will want to purchase this, but compare with Achtemeier, Selwyn, Elliott, and now Jobes (who was able to interact with all the previous scholarship). [*JTS* 40.2; *WTJ* Fall 89; *JETS* 12/91; *Them* 1/92; *CTJ* 11/90; *Chm* 104.1 (1990); *CRBR* 1990 (Elliot, too negative)].

Miller, Donald G. [𝓜], *On This Rock: A Commentary on First Peter*, 1993. Mainly a theological exposition designed to appeal to a wide audience.

Moffatt, James. ‡ (Moffatt) 1928. See under James. Moffatt upheld Petrine authorship (dictated to Silvanus).

Mounce, Robert H. *A Living Hope*, 1982. Covers both epistles of Peter. This popularly-styled commentary is appreciated for its warm-hearted tone, clarity, and its thoughtfulness.

F   Newman, Carey C. ‡ (S&H).

Nisbet, Alexander. (GS) 1658. Covers 1 and 2 Peter, and this Puritan surprisingly wasn't verbose. Banner of Truth mercifully came to our rescue by resetting this classic in modern typeface.

F   Osborne, Grant. (CorBC).

Perkins, Pheme. ‡ (I) 1995. See James above.

F   Powers, Daniel. *1 & 2 Peter, Jude: A Commentary in the Wesleyan Tradition*, 2010.

Reicke, Bo. ‡ (AB) 1964. See under James. Argues for Petrine authorship through Silvanus.

✓   Richard, Earl J. ‡ *Reading 1 Peter, Jude, and 2 Peter: A Literary and Theological Commentary* (Reading the NT) 2000. This work of nearly 400pp is published by Smyth and Helwys but not in their S&H series.

☆   **Selwyn, E.G.** [𝓜], (Macmillan) 1946. This was a magisterial work in its day and continues to be consulted by all engaged in serious study. Reprinted in Baker's "Thornapple" series back in 1981. In spots I find it marginally more useful than WBC for working through the Greek. I used to recommend Michaels' WBC above because it is fairly up-to-date and discusses Dalton, and because Selwyn is now o/p and rather difficult to obtain. Selwyn defends Petrine authorship but through Silvanus. [*WTJ* Fall 47]. See also his valuable, lengthy 1964 essay on "Eschatology in 1 Peter," in *The Background of the New Testament and Its Eschatology* (Dodd *Festschrift*).

✓   **Senior, Donald**, and Daniel Harrington. ‡ *1 Peter, Jude, 2 Peter* (SacPag) 2003. Jude and 2 Peter are treated by Daniel Harrington. More critical positions—all three epistles pseudonymous—are assumed regarding authorship issues. (Does this not serve to diminish St. Peter's place in the Early Church?) This is both learned and accessible as a commentary reference, but it does not break any new ground really.

The authors are both in the top rank of American Catholic scholars. [*ExpTim* 5/04; *RelSRev* 1/04; *JETS* 12/04; *Interp* 4/05].

Skaggs, Rebecca. *1 Peter, 2 Peter, Jude* (Pentecostal Commentary) 2004. [*ExpTim* 4/06].

✓   Talbert, Charles H. (ed). ‡ *Perspectives on First Peter*, 1986.

✓   Walls, A.F., and A.M. Stibbs. (retired TNTC) 1962. Walls contributed the introduction and Stibbs did the commentary. This work has been replaced by Grudem and can now be ignored.

Waltner, Erland, and J. Daryl Charles. *1–2 Peter, Jude* (BCBC) 1999. Waltner writes on 1 Peter in this good vol., perhaps the most conservative in the NT series thus far. See Charles above. [*Interp* 1/01; *JETS* 9/01].

F   Watson, Duane F., and Terrance Callan. ‡ *1 and 2 Peter* (Paideia). Watson will contibute the work on 1 Peter.

✓   Webb, Robert L., and Betsy Bauman-Martin (eds). ‡ *Reading First Peter with New Eyes: Methodological Reassessments of the Letter of First Peter*, 2007. [*ExpTim* 8/08; *BibInt* 18.1].

F   Wilkins, Michael. (ZEC).

☆   Witherington, Ben. *Letters and Homilies for Hellenized Christians, Vol. II: A Socio-Rhetorical Commentary on 1–2 Peter*, 2008. A much fuller work (400pp) than some of his recent vols. on the epistles. I have not been able to review this as yet.

NOTE: Mark Dubis, "Research on 1 Peter: A Survey of Scholarly Literature Since 1985," *CBR* 4.2 (2006): 199–239.

—〰—

2 PETER

NOTE: Since it is now customary in most series to treat Jude together with 2 Peter in the same vol., I have marked with a 'J' those works which follow the pattern. For works treating Jude but not 2 Peter, see the Jude section below.

★   **Bauckham, Richard J.** [𝓜], *Jude, 2 Peter* (WBC) 1983. [J] The first choice of Carson, Silva, Martin, and Childs. Simply put, this has been regarded as the best exegetical commentary on the Greek text of 2 Peter/Jude in any language. Nelson indicates that a revision is in the works (2011?); for this reason it might be best to hold off purchasing the 1983 edition. Readers should be apprised that Bauckham rejects Petrine authorship. (The order of books in his title indicates his conclusion that Jude came first and 2 Peter is literarily dependent.) For a conservative assessment of Bauckham's thesis that 2 Peter is "testamentary writing" and his arguments for pseudonymity, see Davids and G. Green. This vol. is very useful to students and to scholarly evangelical pastors, who will likely conclude that the author's theology is healthier fare than his historical criticism. (He is regarded as belonging to the critically oriented wing of British evangelicalism, and so I have marked him as "mediating" or [𝓜].) Compare to Neyrey. [*EvQ* 7/85; *RTR* 9/83; *JETS* 3/84; *TJ* Fall 84; *Them* 9/85; *JBL* 104.3].

★   **Davids, Peter H.** (Pillar) 2006. [J] This scholar has a well established reputation as a commentator on the General Epistles; his works on James and 1 Peter have both exegetical merit and rich theological exposition. This vol. has a learned discussion of the relationship between the two epistles, concluding (with Bauckham) that Jude came first and 2 Peter shows signs of literary dependence. At the same time he says Bauckham's case for pseudonymity is "not proven." Davids' exegesis is scholarly—more scholarly than some other Pillar works (e.g., Kruse)—and reliable, and his theological discussion is a great help to both students and preachers. Students will keep Bauckham and G. Green close at hand, but pastors will wisely make this their first pick. [*BBR* 18.1; *Chm* Win 07; *RTR* 12/07; *CBQ* 10/07; *JETS* 9/07; *JSNT-BL* 2007; *RelSRev* 7/07; *ExpTim* 5/07; *DenvJ* 5/07; *BSac* 10/08; *Anvil* 25.1].

★ **Green, Gene L.** (BECNT) 2008. [J] This can be put alongside Davids as a dependably conservative work on two epistles for which we earlier had little in the way of evangelical exegesis besides E.M.B. Green. This vol. is especially strong in discussing the historical, cultural, and intellectual background. He helpfully reopens debate of the Bauckham thesis that 2 Peter is testamentary literature, suggesting that a testamentary section (1:12–15) does not make the whole letter such. This 420-page work is a boon for evangelical students, and more studious pastors will buy this as a supplement to Davids and Moo. [*DenvJ* 1/09; *JETS* 3/10; *CBQ* 7/09; *ExpTim* 6/10 (Davids)].

★ Lloyd-Jones, D. Martyn. *Sermons on 2 Peter*, 1983. There is probably nothing better to get a sense for the power of this epistle when preached by one with full confidence in the authority of the Holy Scriptures. These 25 sermons were originally delivered in London's Westminster Chapel in 1946–47, immediately after the apocalyptic horrors of World War II. Still more homiletical help is available in Helm, Lucas/ Green, Nisbet and the two CrossC vols. listed below.

★ Moo, Douglas J. (NIVAC) 1996. [J] Moves so well and wisely from exegesis of the ancient text to discerning the contemporary message that lazy pastors might be tempted to let Moo do all their work for them. I used to say this vol. should be the model for the whole NT series. Note that Moo also does Romans for this series.

Adams, Thomas. *A Commentary on the Second Epistle General of St. Peter*, ca. 1633. This huge Puritan classic was reprinted by Soli Deo Gloria in 1990.

Barnett, A.E. ‡ *The Second Epistle of Peter* (IB) 1957.

F   Bateman, Herb. (EEC). [J]

☆   Bentley, Michael. *Living for Christ* (WCS on 1 & 2 Peter) 1993.

✓   **Bigg, C.A.** ‡ (ICC) 1902. [J] See 1 Peter above.

✓   Blum, Edwin A. (EBC) 1981. See 1 Peter above.

✓   Bray, Gerald (ed). *James, 1–2 Peter, 1–3 John, Jude* (ACCS) 2000. See James above.

☆   Brown, John. *Parting Counsels: 2 Peter Chapter 1* (GS) 1856. Has a Puritan flavor to it—Spurgeon called him "a Puritan born out of due time"—and provides much commentary on the theological message. Reprinted by Banner in 1980. Brown has other full expositions of Romans, Hebrews, and 1 Peter.

F   Callan, Terrance. ‡ (RRA). [J] See also his joint work with Watson on 1 and 2 Peter in Paideia.

☆   **Charles, J. Darryl.** (EBCR) 2006. This author contributes on 1–2 Peter and Jude. See Waltner below for an earlier Charles commentary. I would use this more recent commentary instead of BCBC.

Craddock, Fred. ‡ (WestBC) 1996. [J] See 1 Peter above.

✓   **Cranfield, C.E.B.** ‡ (Torch) 1960. [J] See 1 Peter above.

F   Davids, Peter H. (BHGNT). [J]

F   **Donelson, Lewis R.** ‡ *I & II Peter and Jude* (NTL) 2010.

F   Ericson, Norman. (CorBC). [J] He was once slated to deliver the BECNT.

☆   Gardner, Paul. (Focus on the Bible) 1998. [J] One of the best in the series with excellent exegesis in the background. (Gardner once taught NT at Oak Hill Theological College in London.) Pastors can benefit from the theological exposition, and I cannot think of a better book on these letters to put in the hands of an eager lay Bible student.

☆   **Green, E.M.B.** (TNTC) 1968, rev. 1987. [J] A sturdy defense of the authenticity of 2 Peter, together with a solid exegesis. This is a fine little commentary from a prominent evangelical preacher in the Church of England; for so long in conservative circles it was the standard work on 2 Peter/Jude in pastors' and churches' libraries, in part because there was hardly anything else. In the first six editions of this guide, I listed this as recommended for purchase. Reformed folk will note his Arminianism in the interpretation of 2 Peter 3:9. See Michael Green's other well-received works on Matthew's Gospel. [*WTJ* Fall 69].

F   Hafemann, Scott. (NIGTC). [J]

F   Harink, Douglas. *1 & 2 Peter* (Brazos), 2009. I have yet to see this.

    Harvey, Robert W., and Philip H. Towner. (IVPNT) 2009. [J] Announced as 249pp. Reports are that the late Harvey was mostly responsible for 2 Peter and he offers mainly a devotional reading. Towner then offers a solid exegesis of Jude, but one which can be challenged, according to a reviewer, when it "repeatedly makes the assertion that the letter is a missional document intended to offer hope to Jude's opponents" [*JSNT-BL* 2010]. I have not had a chance to review this. [*JETS* 9/09 (Davids)].

☆   Helm, David R. *1 & 2 Peter and Jude* (PTW) 2008.

    Hillyer, Norman. (NIBC) 1992. [J] See 1 Peter above.

    James, Montague Rhodes. (Cambridge Greek Testament) 1912. [J]

F   Keating, Daniel. ‡ *First and Second Peter, Jude* (CCSS).

☆   **Kelly, J.N.D.** [*M*], (BNTC) 1969. [J] See 1 Peter above. Many would argue this is still among the very best general treatments of 2 Peter. Kelly's writing is a model of clarity, and I have used him extensively over the years.

☆   Kistemaker, Simon J. (NTC) 1987. [J] See 1 Peter above.

✓   **Kraftchick, Stephen.** ‡ (ANTC) 2002. [J] I have not used this 190-page commentary. It is given a good review by Davids [*CBQ* 7/03]. The critical stance will be off-putting for many evangelicals. [*RelSRev* 7/03; *JETS* 9/03].

☆   Leighton, Robert, and W.H. Griffith Thomas. *1 & 2 Peter* (CrossC) 1999. An edifying exposition for the Church. For Jude see the Manton vol. in the series.

☆   Lucas, R.C., and Christopher Green. *The Message of 2 Peter and Jude* (BST) 1995. [J] Dick Lucas, a famous British evangelical Anglican, also contributed the BST vol. on Colossians. [*RelSRev* 10/97].

    Luther, Martin. *The Catholic Epistles*, 1522–27. [J] See 1 Peter above.

✓   **Mayor, J.B.** [*M*], *Second Peter and Jude,* 1907. [J] A companion to Mayor's James commentary and Selwyn's encyclopedic First Peter in the Macmillan series, with the same exhaustive approach to grammatico-historical exegesis; few stones are left unturned. Advanced students are encouraged to look this up. Mayor denies Petrine authorship, but he is less dogmatic than many critics on the issue ("there is not that chasm between 1 and 2 Peter which some would try to make out," p.civ). The Macmillan work is reprinted from time to time. Note too that Mayor has a fine old 70-page commentary on Jude in the *Expositor's Greek Testament* (1897).

F   Mbuvi, Andrew. (NCCS). [J] The author teaches Shaw University Divinity School in North Carolina.

    Moffatt, James. ‡ (Moffatt) 1928. [J] See James above.

    Mounce, Robert. 1982. See 1 Peter above.

✓   **Neyrey, Jerome H.** ‡ (AB) 1993. [J] In its close exegesis of the Greek text, this commentary is said by some to compete with WBC as a first choice for scholars, but does not supersede Bauckham. I have found Bauckham to be a shrewder, more balanced exegete and a much better guide into the theology of these epistles. Some of the conclusions in this AB replacement for Reicke are far-fetched. A Catholic professor, Neyrey follows the critical line—arguing both letters are pseudony-mous—and the commentary is close to 300pp, including introduction and indices. Students will value this for its bibliography and for its application of the methods of social-scientific research, though the arrival of several major commentaries (2003–) makes this AB less important to students than was the case a few years ago. [*Interp* 10/95; *JBL* Sum 95].

Nisbet, Alexander. (GS) 1658. See 1 Peter above.

F   Pearson, B.A. ‡ (Herm). [J]

Perkins, Pheme. ‡ (I) 1995. [J] See James above. Gene Green finds much of value here as a theological exposition of 2 Peter/Jude [*BSB* 12/03].

F   Powers, Daniel. *1 & 2 Peter, Jude: A Commentary in the Wesleyan Tradition*, 2010.

✓   **Reese, Ruth Anne.** [*M*], (THC) 2007. [J] The author, a professor at Asbury Seminary, gives almost as much space to Jude as to 2 Peter. She earlier published *Writing Jude: The Reader, the Text, and the Author*, 2000. Reese pursues a canonical reading of these books and avoids taking positions on the higher critical issues. I find her theological reflection careful and thought-provoking yet deficient, starting as it does from a definition of theology itself (see p.3) which neglects divine revelation and is largely anthropocentric. Her approach seems tied to a more postmodern way of thinking, e.g., the idea that our beliefs in community are the source of our knowledge. Her work represents one of the few attempts to interpret these two epistles using contemporary literary theory. Note that Davids says the commentary on 2 Peter "is significantly weaker than her work on Jude." [*CBQ* 4/09; *RelSRev* 9/08; *JETS* 9/08 (Davids); *JSNT-BL* 2009; *ExpTim* 7/09 (Davids)].

Reicke, Bo. ‡ (AB) 1964. [J] See James above.

✓   Richard, Earl J. ‡ *Reading 1 Peter, Jude, and 2 Peter: A Literary and Theological Commentary* (Reading the NT) 2000. [J] This work of nearly 400pp is published by Smyth and Helwys but not in their S&H series.

☆   **Schreiner, Thomas.** *1, 2 Peter, Jude* (NAC) 2003. See under 1 Peter. Excellent. Though Schreiner gives a very good study of 1 Peter, with plenty of bibliographical help for students, I used to value this vol. even more for his treatment of 2 Peter and Jude because of the lack of evangelical exegetical commentaries on that portion. For so long we had little more than Michael Green's slim Tyndale vol., and Green does not interact with much scholarship in his exegesis. I spoke of this NAC in 2005 as the average pastor's first choice for a mid-level exegesis and exposition of 2 Peter and Jude. With the recent appearance of both Davids and Gene Green, Schreiner is not the standout work that it was. It remains, however, a smart purchase for its quality, coverage (Three epistles at low cost), and sound theology.

✓   Senior, Donald, and **Daniel J. Harrington**. ‡ *1 Peter, Jude, 2 Peter* (SacPag) 2003. [J] Harrington is responsible for the latter two epistles. See 1 Peter above.

Sidebottom, E.M. ‡ (NCB) 1967. [J] See James above.

Skaggs, Rebecca. *1 Peter, 2 Peter, Jude* (Pentecostal Commentary) 2004. [*ExpTim* 4/06].

✓   Waltner, Erland, and **J. Daryl Charles**. *1–2 Peter, Jude* (BCBC) 1999. [J] Charles has previously done much work on both 2 Peter and Jude and makes a decent contribution here. Though not a major commentary, this has been a good reference for students because of its date (more current bibliography) and the research which lies behind the work. I will quickly note in passing Gene Green's disappointment with this commentary [*BSB* 12/03]. See Charles' more recent EBCR above. See also under Jude below. [*Interp* 1/01; *JETS* 9/01].

✓   Watson, Duane F. ‡ (NewIB) 1998. [J] Not of great account in my opinion, and better on Jude than on 2 Peter. Greek students will probably learn much more from his

Duke dissertation: *Invention, Arrangement, and Style: Rhetorical Criticism of Jude and 2 Peter* (1988), which began to establish his reputation as a leader in the field of rhetorical studies on the NT.

F   Watson, Duane F., and Terrance Callan. ‡ *1 and 2 Peter* (Paideia). Callan will contribute the work on 2 Peter.

F   Webb, Robert L. (NICNT). [J] Originally this was to be a joint work with Peter Davids (for Davids see Pillar and BHGNT above). Webb has his PhD from Sheffield and now teaches at McMaster University. There is a foretaste of his interpretation of Jude in "The Use of 'Story' in the Letter of Jude," *JSNT* 31.1 (2008): 53–87.

F   Webb, Robert L. (RRA). [J]

☆   **Witherington, Ben.** *Letters and Homilies for Hellenized Christians, Vol. II: A Socio-Rhetorical Commentary on 1–2 Peter*, 2008. A much fuller work (400pp) than some of his recent vols. on the epistles. I have not been able to review this as yet.

THE EPISTLES OF JOHN

★   Burge, Gary. (NIVAC) 1996. Highly praised by a number of my pastor friends. This is a good addition to the other recommendations—all strong on exegesis and theological exposition—because of its fuller discussion of how John's Letters might best be applied today. Burge has some good exegesis, too, but that is not the main value of his commentary here. He is unsure whether the Fourth Gospel and John's Epistles come from the same hand. *DenvJ* makes Kruse, Yarbrough, and Burge its top three picks. [*JETS* 6/99].

★   **Kruse, Colin G.** (Pillar) 2000. Prior to Yarbrough, this commentary was valuable as probably the best recent evangelical exegesis. (There has not been much competition, and thus the eagerness for Carson's forthcoming work.) The pluses of this vol. are its confidence in the authority of God's Word, its spiritual insight, its succinctness and manageable size (250pp), and its distillation of much current scholarship. (There is substantial interaction with the trio of Brown, Schnackenburg and Strecker.) On the negative side, the commentary is thinner on 2 & 3 John (32 of 184 total pages of commentary). I feel that a fuller commentary would have been beneficial at points; by comparison Moo's Pillar vol. on James has over 200 pp of commentary. Kruse argues for authorship by John the Apostle. "Dependable" is the right adjective here, even though Collins is correct in pointing out instances where Kruse follows the NIV and should have paid much closer attention to the Greek (e.g., aspect theory, abundant use of μένω). Pastors working without the Greek could probably start with Kruse, but those delving into the original will prefer the guidance provided by Yarbrough. [*RTR* 12/00; *Interp* 4/01; *SwJT* Spr 01; *EvQ* 7/03; *JETS* 12/01; *Chm* Aut 01; *Presb* Fall 05 (Collins); *Evangel* Spr 02; *Anvil* 19.3].

★   **Marshall, I. Howard.** (NICNT) 1978. This is a splendid commentary, though some of us take issue with Marshall's forthright Arminianism. (He is a Methodist minister, long on the faculty of the University of Aberdeen, and now regarded as the elder statesman of evangelical NT scholarship in Britain.) He writes with the pastor in mind, and this has been the evangelical classic that pastors have used for 30 years alongside Stott's gem. The introduction disappoints some conservatives in that he states his uncertainty about the author's identity. At least he believes that the three came from the same hand. This vol. is still valuable to students for its full survey of introductory issues—Smalley refers his own readers to it (1984, p.xxi). Well worth obtaining; years ago this was my own first purchase on John's Letters. Marshall has also written magisterial commentaries on Luke and the Pastoral Epistles, and a fine compact Tyndale vol. on Acts. [*WTJ* Fall 79; *JBL* 99.4 (1980); *EvQ* 4/79].

★ **Stott, John R.W.** (TNTC) 1964, rev. 1988. This is probably the best in the series. I used to go so far as to recommend the expositor purchase Stott first, and that remains good advice. You will use it the rest of your life. Of course, students need a tool which is in-depth and which interacts with current scholarship. [*RTR* 5/89].

★ **Yarbrough, Robert.** (BECNT) 2008. Sterling. This vol. replaces Smalley on my recommended list and is now my top pick for both pastors and students. The author is a PCA minister, who trained under Howard Marshall at Aberdeen, headed the NT Department at TEDS, and co-edits this series. He recently returned to Covenant Seminary. The exegesis of the Greek is both carefully thorough (464pp) and aimed at the exposition of the theological message. I welcome his attention to the history of interpretation, with special place given to Augustine, Calvin, and Schlatter (one of his favorites). Students appreciate the interaction with well-sifted, modern Johannine scholarship, while preachers find help—more than usual in BECNT—as they seek to discern the pastoral implications of the text. After the rehashing of the Martyn/Brown thesis in so many commentaries, it is refreshing to read this one. He plows a different furrow. (Carson will do the same.) Foster suggests that Yarbrough and Lieu are well paired, since the former's weak spot (2–3 John) is precisely where Lieu is strongest. [*JETS* 9/09; *DenvJ* 1/09; *RBL*; *CTJ* 11/09; *BSac* 7/10; *ExpTim* 8/09 (Foster); *TJ* Spr 10; *CBQ* 7/10].

☆ **Akin, Daniel L.** (NAC) 2001. This approximately 250-page commentary is similar to Kruse in some respects (especially the intended audience of pastors). It is solid, reveals substantial research on the part of the author, and would be a worthwhile purchase for pastors. Akin is President of Southeastern Baptist Theological Seminary. [*Them* Sum 04; *JETS* 9/02; *BSac* 7/03].

F   Anderson, Paul N. (THC).

     Barker, Glenn W. (EBC) 1981. Haven't used it.

✓   Black, C. Clifton. ‡ (NewIB) 1998. A little over 100pp of solid scholarship.

✓   Bray, Gerald (ed). *James, 1–2 Peter, 1–3 John, Jude* (ACCS) 2000. See James above.

✓   Brooke, A.E. ‡ (ICC) 1912. Remains somewhat useful as a reference on technical questions.

☆ **Brown, Raymond E.** ‡ (AB) 1982. *"Commentaire monumental"* (Bonnard)! Brown was a Roman Catholic who taught at Union Seminary in New York for many years. Only for the advanced student and specialist. See also Brown's commentary on John's Gospel—the epistles were not written by the evangelist, he argues. This is by no means a conservative work and it is too full (800 jam-packed pages) for the average pastor. Still, the commentary is self-recommending as an enormously learned tome and a high point in Johannine scholarship. Quite influential is his argument (building on Wayne Meeks' 1972 article, "The Man from Heaven in Johannine Sectarianism") that these Epistles reflect controversy in the "Community of the Beloved Disciple" over the proper understanding of the Johannine tradition. Though I do not buy this argument, in some ways I prefer Brown to the more conservative but less rigorous Smalley. Advanced students and academically-inclined pastors might invest in this, if they want more than Yarbrough and are impatient for Carson. [*JBL* 103.4].

☆ Bruce, F.F. 1970. An excellent, brief commentary that is very much to the point. Were it not for Stott, this might be considered the best popular exegetical work. Now bound with Bruce's work on John's Gospel.

Bultmann, Rudolf. ‡ (Herm) ET 1973. One of this scholar's last publications. Quite slim (115pp plus bibliography), radically critical, and not all that influential at this stage, though at one time it was. Don't bother with it, unless you are an advanced student deeply engaging the question of where Johannine scholarship has come from. Bultmann has now been replaced in the series; see Strecker below.

✓ **Burdick, Donald W.** 1985. One of the largest evangelical works on John's Epistles. Has a number of good points and is a good value in pb, but this cannot be among the top choices. Now o/p. Note: this work should be distinguished from his earlier and much briefer work (also) for Moody Press.

☆ Calvin, John, and Matthew Henry. *1, 2, 3 John* (CrossC) 1998.

Candlish, Robert. *1 John* (GS) 1866. A full exposition by a 19th century Scottish pastor and professor. It is good to see the work get a new lease on life by being added to the GS series. [*SBET* Fall 95].

F Carson, Donald. (NIGTC). This will be cause for celebration and will likely become a first choice, at least for students and those pastors who are comfortable with their Greek NT. Carson's exegetical skill and gift for theological interpretation are well-known. This forthcoming vol. and Yarbrough may do for the Epistles of John what Carson and Köstenberger do for the Gospel of John.

Culy, Martin M. *I, II, III John: A Handbook on the Greek Text*, 2004. This brief guide (155pp) is published by Baylor and guides the student through the basics of lexical and grammatical analysis. [*EvQ* 1/07; *JSNT-BL* 2006; *ExpTim* 9/06].

F Derickson, Gary. (EEC).

Dodd, C.H. ‡ (Moffatt) 1946. An old classic with all of Dodd's brilliance, but from an Evangelical perspective the theology is atrocious. "Wildly out of sympathy with the text," says Carson.

☆ Findlay, G.G. *Fellowship in Life Eternal*, 1909. A devotional classic, justly famous, to which pastors have turned again and again. The same can be said for Law's book below. Findlay only treats 1 John.

✓ Grayston, Kenneth. [𝓜], (NCB) 1984. Challenges the usual conclusion of modern scholarship that the letters are a good bit later than the Fourth Gospel. Grayston is cited today mainly for that original theory. Of interest to students rather than pastors. [*JETS* 9/85; *ExpTim* 12/84; *Them* 1/86; *EvQ* 1/87].

✓ **Haas, C., M. deJonge, and J.L. Swellengrebel.** (UBS) 1972, rev. 1994. Marshall had high praise for the first edition: "an extremely valuable book, useful to all students and not merely to Bible translators." The revised edition is 214pp.

Harris, W. Hall. *1, 2, 3 John: Comfort and Counsel for a Church in Crisis*, 2003. A Dallas Seminary professor contributes an exegetical work (292pp) on the Greek text, published by Biblical Studies Press. I have not seen this vol. which is praised in Glynn's *Survey*.

Houlden, J.L. ‡ (BNTC) 1973. Retains some value, but it is not worth poring over, at least not in its 1973 edition. I have yet to see the 1994 revised edition Carson mentions. [*JBL* 94.4 (1975)].

☆ Jackman, David. (BST) 1988. An exposition which builds on Stott's TNTC (first edition). More useful to the expositor than to the student.

F Jobes, Karen. (ZEC). See her previous work on Esther and 1 Peter.

☆ Johnson, Thomas. (NIBC) 1993. A fine work of about 180pp which is more up-to-date than Stott with regard to NT scholarship and more exegetical, but is not quite as helpful to the expositor. For a compact exegesis, Rensberger is more rigorous and critical. [*Chm* 108.1 (1994); *CRBR* 1994].

Jones, Peter Rhea. (S&H) 2009. The vol. is said to be 312pp in length and the product of a mature pastor and former seminary professor (McAfee School of Theology). This may be one of the better contributions to the series.

☆ Kistemaker, Simon J. (NTC) 1986. See under James.

Köstenberger, Andreas J. *A Theology of John's Gospel and Letters*, 2009. See under John's Gospel.

✓ Kysar, Robert. ‡ (Augsburg Commentary) 1986. [*JETS* 6/90].

☆ Law, Robert. *The Tests of Life*, 1909. See Findlay above. Stott mined this work and uses Law's idea that 1 John encourages readers to test themselves whether they have true life in Christ (tests of love, doctrine, obedience). You will find Law more valuable than Findlay.

✓ **Lieu, Judith M.** ‡ (NTL) 2008. This reasonably full work (336pp) stands in the top rank of critical commentaries and seems especially welcome because there have been few excellent exegeses published by either the critics or evangelicals since the mid-1980s. The author was able to build upon two notable scholarly monographs: *The Second and Third Epistles of John: History and Background* (1986) and *The Theology of the Johannine Epistles* (Cambridge, 1991) [*CRBR* 1993]. She has presented some wise caveats regarding the dominant Brown thesis, and has emerged as a major authority on this literature. (Lady Margaret's Professor of Divinity at Cambridge, Lieu has been president of the Society of New Testament Studies.) The "book description" gives her central thesis: "Each letter shows how an early Christian author responded to threats against authority by recourse to the correct teachings of the faith and a proper understanding of the relationship between Jesus and God. Together, these letters argue for a bond of unity among believers, based on fidelity to the truth of God." In line with the critics' consensus, she believes 1–3 John exhibit no signs of knowing the Fourth Gospel. [*JETS* 9/09; *ExpTim* 8/09; *Interp* 7/09 (Kysar); *JSNT-BL* 2010].

☆ Lloyd-Jones, D. Martyn. *Fellowship with God* (1993); *Walking with God* (1993); *Children of God* (1993); *The Love of God* (1994); *Life in God* (1994). This sermon series is well worth consideration. I am very glad that the publisher, Crossway, has put it all in one cheaper, fat (736-page) vol., entitled *Life in Christ* (2002).

F Ngewa, Samuel. (NCCS). The author has long taught in his native Kenya and has previously published lengthy expositional commentaries on John's Gospel and the Pastorals.

✓ **Painter, John.** ‡ (SacPag) 2002. Painter's vol. is to be valued especially for its lengthy introduction—over a quarter of the 410-page vol.—and for his interpretation of the epistles as reflecting a polemical situation within the Johannine community. He dialogs with Brown a good bit in the technical "Notes." This is more of a literary and historical commentary than a theological one. Preachers will likely not find much to assist them here. [*CBQ* 10/03; *Interp* 7/03].

F Parsenios, George L. (Paideia).

Plummer, Alfred. (Cambridge Greek Testament) 1886. Reprinted from time to time. But if you want one of the older works, pick up Westcott.

☆ **Rensberger, David.** ‡ (ANTC) 1997. This is among the leading compact critical exegetical commentaries and shows the influence of Brown's thesis. Of special interest to students. More directed toward meeting the expositor's need is the next entry. [*Interp* 1/99].

Rensberger, David. ‡ (WestBC) 2001. A slim vol. of only 130pp, this work probably will not be a preference among evangelicals because of its critical theological orientation. Rensberger is sometimes out of sympathy with the text, and his adoption of the Martyn/Brown thesis, I find, makes application of the epistles' message to-day more difficult. [*Them* Spr/Sum 02; *ExpTim* 8/02; *SwJT* Spr 02; *RelSRev* 4/02].

F   Root, Michael. (Brazos).

Ross, Alexander. (retired NICNT) 1954. Now replaced by Marshall and long o/p.

✓   **Schnackenburg, Rudolf.** ‡ 1984, ET 1992. Like his fellow scholar, Brown, Schnackenburg is a critical Roman Catholic who has produced in-depth commentaries on both the Gospel of John and the Epistles. Both scholars moved left since they first began commenting on the Johannine Literature, the late Brown more so. Schnackenburg was also more conservative to begin with. This exceptionally fine scholarly work, translated out of the German (Herders series), is 302pp. This is Childs' first choice and is given high marks by Carson, who is presently working on these epistles. Schnackenburg will find his way into more students' hands than pastors'. I bought it. [*Interp* 1/94; *JETS* 9/96; *BSac* 7/93].

F   Schüssler Fiorenza, Elisabeth. ‡ (WestBC).

✓   Sloyan, G.S. ‡ *Walking in the Truth: Perseverers and Deserters—The First, Second, and Third Letters of John*, 1995. A very slim work in the series "NT in Context."

☆   **Smalley, Stephen S.** [𝓜], (WBC) 1984, rev. 2007. A solid, respectable vol. by a scholar at home in the Johannine literature. A great deal was to be learned from the 1984 work, which began to show its age. Though I preferred the huge work by Brown in some ways, I was always convinced that Smalley was more useful to the pastor, in part because the WBC was more manageable at half the length. Students appreciated Smalley for his extensive interaction with the many works available in the early 1980s on these epistles in all the languages. It is happy news that there is now a thoroughly revised edition (xxxi + 376pp). At the same time, I regret that he pushes the Johannine Community interpretation like he does. In the Revision he "remain[s] convinced that the Johannine corpus…enshrines the history of a volatile community, gathering in some sense around John the Apostle, the Beloved Disciple, and that it is possible to trace the story of his church from the Apocalypse, through the Gospel, and thence to the Epistles" (viii). I wish he had taken opportunity to interact with Strecker, Klauck, and Kruse in the new edition. See Smalley under John's Gospel and under Revelation. This was Silva's first choice years ago. Yarbrough replaced this on my recommended list. Expect Carson's forthcoming vol., too, to become more valuable as a guide for the scholarly pastor into the intricacies of the Greek text. [*WTJ* Fall 86; *RTR* 9/85; *JBL* 106.1 (1987); *EvQ* 4/87; *JETS* 3/86].

✓   Smith, D. Moody. ‡ (I) 1991. This author has long been a noted contributor to Johannine scholarship, and some students may wish to consult this shorter work—I wish he had written twice as much. Smith also has a commentary on John's Gospel. Do note the next entry. [*CRBR* 1993].

F   Smith, D. Moody. ‡ (ICC–new series).

✓   **Strecker, Georg.** ‡ (Herm) 1989, ET 1996. This replacement vol. for Bultmann in Hermeneia is a translation of a rigorously, radically critical vol. in the EKK and extends to somewhat over 400pp. Strecker studied under Bultmann at Marburg. Compare this commentary with Schnackenburg. Advanced students will use this, but not pastors. [*JETS* 6/99; *JTS* 10/97; *Biblica* 74.1; *JBL* Win 00].

Thatcher, Tom. (EBCR) 2006. This replaces Barker in the earlier EBC. I have not used Thatcher.

Thomas, John Christopher. *1 John, 2 John, 3 John* (Pentecostal Commentary) 2004. [*ExpTim* 4/06; *Anvil* 22.4 (Smalley)].

☆   Thompson, Marianne Meye. [𝓜], (IVPNT) 1992. This useful, 168-page commentary was written with the pastor in mind, including both exegesis and application (with preaching-style illustrations). The interpretive work has good research behind it, but the application (often the truly hard work of preaching) is not as useful. Perhaps she comes off sounding too much like an academic. A solid representative of the series. [*Them* 5/94; *Chm* Spr 95].

F   Wahlde, Urban C. von. (ECC). This is announced as a three-vol. set, and the first release (2010?) is *The Gospel and Letters of John, Vol. 3: The Three Johannine Letters.*

F   Watson, Duane F. ‡ (NCBC).

F   Watson, Duane F. ‡ (RRA).

✓   **Westcott, B.F.** 1902. "A classic of lasting value" (Childs). Comments on the Greek text, and would not be an unwise purchase. Pastors of the last three generations have relied heavily on Westcott, which is reprinted quite often. The latest reprint, I believe, is Wipf & Stock in 2001, and the vol. is not o/p.

F   Williamson, Rick. *1, 2, & 3 John: A Commentary in the Wesleyan Tradition*, 2010.

☆   Witherington, Ben. *Letters and Homilies for Hellenized Christians: Vol. 1: A Socio-Rhetorical Commentary on Titus, 1–2 Timothy, and 1–3 John*, 2006.

NOTES: (1) D. Moody Smith, "The Epistles of John: What's New Since Brooke's ICC in 1912?" *ExpTim* 120.8 (2009): 373–84. (2) There are two review-essays by Klaus Scholtissek in *CurBS* 6 (1998) and 9 (2001), and they pay special attention to German works.

JUDE

NOTE: See "2 Peter" above.

✓   Bauckham, Richard J. [*M*], *Jude and the Relatives of Jesus*, 1990. Quite important as a follow-up to the masterful WBC vol. on 2 Peter/Jude.

☆   Benton, John. *Slandering the Angels: The Message of Jude* (WCS) 1999. I have not seen this, but it is said to be about 190pp in length, which is substantial indeed for this epistle.

    Brosend, William. ‡ *James and Jude* (NCBC) 2004.

✓   Charles, J. Daryl. *Literary Strategy in the Epistle of Jude*, 1993. An evangelical work. See Waltner under 2 Peter & Jude.

    Jenkyn, William. *Jude*, 1652. Manton self-consciously built on this Puritan work, which he regarded as exceptional. Jenkyn has been reprinted in the past.

☆   Manton, Thomas. *Jude* (GS) 1658. Extends to almost 400pp in typical Puritan fashion. Those who readily profit from Puritan writings are encouraged to purchase this beautifully bound vol., reprinted in 1989. "Full of deep application," says *Evangel* Sum 90. A scaled-down, modern language version of Manton's Jude is the Crossway Classics edition of 1999.

F   **Painter, John, and David deSilva.** ‡ *James and Jude* (Paideia). See James above.

    Plummer, Alfred. *General Epistles of St. James and St. Jude* (EB) 1891. Still cited in the literature.

    Reese, Ruth Anne. ‡ *Writing Jude: The Reader, the Text, and the Author*, 2000. This dissertation, with its reader-response criticism, led to the THC commentary on 2 Peter and Jude. [*BibInt* 12.4]. I confess I learned little here about Jude as Reese invited much reflection on "the openness and possibilities of language" (p.158). There seemed to be more Barthes, Foucault, Freud, and Lacan than NT study.

☆   Saarinen, Risto. *The Pastoral Epistles with Philemon & Jude* (Brazos) 2008. See under Pastorals.

✓ Wasserman, Tommy. *The Epistle of Jude: Its Text and Transmission*, 2006. A stunningly thorough study of text-critical issues. [*CBQ* 7/07; *BBR* 18.1; *JSNT-BL* 2008; *NovT* 50.3; *ExpTim* 5/07; *Them* 5/08]. Earlier there was Charles Landon, *A Text-Critical Study of the Epistle of Jude* (1996).

Watson, Duane F. ‡ *Invention, Arrangement, and Style: Rhetorical Criticism of Jude and 2 Peter*, 1988. See under 2 Peter.

✓ Webb, Robert L., and Peter H. Davids (eds). ‡ *Reading Jude with New Eyes: Methodological Reassessments in the Letter of Jude*, 2008. [*ExpTim* 7/09; *JSNT-BL* 2010].

☆ **Witherington, Ben**. *Letters and Homilies for Jewish Christians: A Socio-Rhetorical Commentary on Hebrews, James and Jude*, 2007.

REVELATION

NOTE: I hesitate to make strong recommendations of commentaries on this Bible book. There is an enormous range of interpretations, and one's own eschatological convictions can strongly influence value-judgments. Some key approaches are (1) preterist: Revelation points to its immediate historical context and is mostly already fulfilled; (2) historicist: Revelation predicts the whole course of Christian history; (3) futurist: Revelation is primarily fulfilled in the final events of history—there are both simpler and wildly extreme interpretive positions here; (4) idealist: Revelation is a symbolic portrayal of the struggle between God and Satan. Also, there are a good many scholars today who, in emphasizing the apocalyptic genré, argue that Revelation is more an encouragement and witness to Christian endurance in the face of imperial Roman and cultural pressure/persecution. I believe you can best use this section of the guide if you know my position. While taking the prophetic character of the book very seriously (1:3), I cannot take a strictly futurist approach. The highly symbolic character of the apocalyptic genré present here—which ironically 'conceals' as much as it 'reveals'—makes me very cautious about details and inclined to sympathize somewhat with idealist interpretations. Still, I am compelled by my own exegesis of Rev. 20 to take a Historic Premillennial (i.e., post-trib) stance. I have tried to evaluate the works available without much reference to my own convictions. As it falls out, two of the five full-length recommendations are Amil, two are Premil, and one is hesitant to decide. All have been highly praised by scholars of every stripe. All are notable for their sensitivity to the book's tension between Apocalyptic and the prophetic tradition, both of which impacted 1st century Jews and Christians. Those who are unfamiliar with Apocalyptic and its significance are urged to digest Leon Morris' little vol. entitled simply *Apocalyptic* (Eerdmans, 1972) or George Ladd's article in the revised ISBE. (For more in-depth study there is a bibliography above, following Daniel.) It is best to avoid the plethora of fanciful works which view Revelation as a forecast of imminent world events (esp. in the Middle East), seemingly written for 20th and now 21st century Americans, with no relevance to the Early Church. Would that more people heeded the ancient advice of Irenaeus: "It is...more certain, and less hazardous to await the fulfillment of the prophecy, than to be making surmises, and casting about for names that may present themselves" (*Against All Heresies*, 5.30.3). I admit to having strong views against the sensational fiction which has been so popular the last three decades. Here is a challenge for all of us to take to heart: "If responsible interpreters do not make the effort to set forth the message of Revelation in terms that are faithful both to Scripture and to our own times, this task goes by default to others" (Boring, p.59).

★ **Beale, G.K.** (NIGTC) 1999. His published dissertation led us to expect a fine piece of work, and this is a treat, especially for those who love their Greek NT. Probably to be regarded as the best, most exacting evangelical exegesis! A pleasant surprise is that Beale provides a good bit more theology than we are used to receiving from this series. He takes a modified idealist approach. The best feature of this work is its treatment of Revelation's OT background; I expected this. (In my humble opinion, though, Beale fails to do full justice to the influence of Ezekiel.) Compare with Aune's set. Some pastors may be scared off by the size of this tome (1200pp). The price is steep as well. [*Them* 2/00; *TJ* Spr 00; *JBL* Spr 00; *WTJ* Spr 00; *Biblica* 81.3; *Interp* 1/00; *RTR* 12/00; *RelSRev* 7/00; *HBT* 12/02 (Aune)]. Students will want to note another of Beale's titles, *John's Use of the Old Testament in Revelation* (Sheffield, 1998).

★ Johnson, Dennis. *The Triumph of the Lamb*, 2001. This is a very suggestive exposition with an Amillennial perspective and with a sensitivity to biblical theological themes, anticipated in earlier Scripture and developed in Revelation. (Goldsworthy and Poythress use a similar approach.) I expected this would be good, but it's far better than I had even hoped. For another very useful Dennis Johnson commentary, see Acts.

★ Keener, Craig S. (NIVAC) 2000. This vol. of 576pp shows great insight and learning—the modern author index extends over 9pp, while the index of "Other Ancient Sources" is 16pp. (Keener previously wrote the *IVP Bible Background Commentary*.) In the exegesis sections ("Original Meaning"), there is much interaction with the recent commentaries of Aune and Beale. Theologically, he likes to "cut the difference" between Premillennialists and Amillennialists. This is a work for both students and expositors. Though there is not always the maturity of reflection and synthesis one finds elsewhere in NIVAC, Keener does well in stimulating the preacher to think hard about the extraordinarily complex move from interpreting Revelation responsibly to applying the book's message helpfully. He was given a most difficult task and did it well. Though a strong partisan on some theological points, Keener here is very fair to various schools of interpretation. [*RelSRev* 7/03].

★ **Mounce, Robert.** (NICNT) 1977, rev. 1998. Used to be the most scholarly of the evangelical works I suggested for purchase. The first edition was the result of 15 years' intensive research on the book, and with the revision "a good piece of work has been turned into an even better one" (I.H. Marshall). This or Osborne would be my first choice for pastors. In Beale's tome we have a good up-to-date commentary on the Greek, but this commentary by Mounce contains in the notes some close exegesis of the original and some text criticism for those who don't want to take out a bank loan to purchase NIGTC or the three-vol. WBC. Mounce takes a historic Premillennial position, but is fair and appreciative in dealing with the Amillennial point of view. [*CTJ* 13.2; *JBL* 9/79; *EvQ* 7/78, 7/99; *TJ* Spr 00; *RelSRev* 4/01].

★ **Osborne, Grant.** (BECNT) 2002. Very well done and more accessible than one might think for a commentary on the Greek text. The expositor who feels intimidated by the size and scholarship of Beale might take a small step down and buy this instead. Like Mounce, Osborne offers a Premillennial interpretation of ch. 20 (expected of a TEDS professor), but is a model of fairness is dealing with other positions. [*RTR* 8/04; *Them* Spr 04; *JETS* 12/03; *Interp* 4/04; *SBET* Spr 03; *RelSRev* 10/03; *CTJ* 11/04; *ExpTim* 5/06].

★ Stott, John R.W. *What Christ Thinks of the Church*, 1958, rev. 1990. A slim vol. on the letters to the churches which is suggestive for pastors. Those interested in more expositions of Revelation 1–3 can look up Barclay (1957—different from DSB) or, even better, Marcus Loane's book called *They Overcame* (1971). Surely the best historical study on these chapters is Colin Hemer's *Letters to the Seven Churches of Asia* (1986), which superseded the old work by W.M. Ramsay. More critical is Roland Worth, *The Seven Cities of the Apocalypse* (Paulist Press, 1999).

✓ Alford, Henry. *Alford's Greek Testament*, 1875. A seminal treatment which caused the Premillenarian ranks to swell in the 19th century. Alford continues to be quoted by today's commentators, especially his argument on the two resurrections in vol. IV, p.732.

✓ **Aune, David E.** ‡ (WBC) 3 Vols., 1997–1998. From his journal articles I anticipated that this would be thorough, very scholarly, moderately critical, and have a few idiosyncratic views. I guessed right. Go to Aune and Beale for first-rate commentaries which will long serve the academic world; I believe you will judge Beale to be the better balanced and more judicious. Also, Beale is far more interested in theology. Aune by contrast joins with those who "bracket theology" (p.xlviii). Boring considers the commentary's most helpful contribution to be where Aune shares "his vast knowledge of the Hellenistic world and its literature." This three-vol. work (nearly 1600pp) is quite a foil to Beale who emphasizes rather the OT background of the Apocalypse. One could wish for more in the introduction on "history of interpretation." Need I say this is more of a scholar's reference set than a tool for the working pastor? Students can make excellent use of his vol. of essays listed previously under Apocalyptic Literature. [*ExpTim* 11/99; *RelSRev* 10/98, 7/00 & 10/00; *Biblica* 79.4 (1998); *JTS* 10/99; *NovT* 42.2; *Interp* 7/00; *Chm* Spr 01; *JETS* 9/00 (unsatisfactory review)].

✓ Barr, David L. ‡ *Tales of the End: A Narrative Commentary on the Book of Revelation* (The Storyteller's Bible, 1) 1998 [*RelSRev* 7/00]. See also the collection of essays in *Reading the Book of Revelation: A Resource for Students*, 2004 [*JSNT-BL* 2005; *CBQ* 10/04].

Barr, David L. (ed). *The Reality of Apocalypse*, 2006. Students interested in cutting-edge rhetorical analysis, genre, intertextuality, and ritual studies will want to look up this vol. of SBL essays. [*ExpTim* 8/08].

✓ Bauckham, Richard. [𝔐], *The Theology of the Book of Revelation*, 1993. [*JETS* 9/97; *CBQ* 7/94]. Coming out about the same time was his book of essays, *The Climax of Prophecy: Studies on the Book of Revelation* (1993), which Ian Paul termed "perhaps the most significant English-language work on Revelation in recent years" [*BSB* 9/06].

☆ **Beasley-Murray, George R.** [𝔐], (NCB) 1974. Brilliant and mildly critical, with more of a stress on Apocalyptic than prophecy. This "richly suggestive" (Martin) commentary offers a historic Premillennial interpretation of ch. 20. In early eds. of this guide I always recommended buying both NCB and NICNT. Unfortunately, this good book has become harder to find. [*EvQ* 7/75].

✓ **Beckwith, I.T.** 1919. One of the better old scholarly commentaries. More conservative than Charles' magisterial set. Still to be consulted for work in the Greek text.

✓ **Blount, Brian K.** ‡ (NTL) 2009. The author, who previously served as a pastor and as a professor at Princeton Seminary, is now President of Union Seminary-PSCE in Richmond. He writes as a moderately critical scholar who sees connections between the courageous faith of the early Church, with her non-violent protest against Roman idolatry and injustice, and the experience of African-American Christians. Regarding historical setting, he dates the book to *ca.* 95 and contends that persecution under Domitian was, at the time anyway, a real, but as yet largely unrealized, threat to the Christians in the empire. [*Interp* 7/10; *ExpTim* 2/10; *JSNT-BL*

2010]. Earlier Blount gave us a politically-engaged reading in *Can I Get a Witness? Reading Revelation through African American Culture*, 2005 [*ThTo* 1/06].

Boring, M. Eugene. ‡ (I) 1989. Treats Revelation in 240pp. A careful and well received exposition which is widely used in more liberal pastoral circles. Professor Boring is especially fond of the universal salvation idea. [*Interp* 4/91; *CRBR* 1991].

✓ **Boxall, Ian.** ‡ (BNTC) 2006. This is a solid replacement for Caird's stellar vol. There is a tendency in NT scholarship to downplay any severe Roman persecution as the contextual key to the message of Revelation (e.g., see Thompson's ANTC). Boxall gives greater weight to that pressing concern within the faithful community. The author is a more mildly critical, Oxford scholar. [*JETS* 9/07]. A previous publication was *Revelation Vision and Insight: An Introduction to the Apocalypse*, 2002.

✓ **Bratcher, R.G., and H.A. Hatton.** (UBS) 1993. A fairly full vol. of 352pp, called "invaluable" by Thompson. [*CRBR* 1995].

✓ Brighton, Louis. (Concord) 1999. The author is emeritus professor of NT at Concordia Theological Seminary in St. Louis. This is a full-scale commentary (673pp) from a conservative Lutheran perspective. I have not seen it.

Brooks, Richard. *The Lamb Is All the Glory* (WCS) 1986.

✓ Buchanan, George Wesley. ‡ (Mellen Biblical Commentary) 1993. A huge scholarly commentary of nearly 700pp, which pays special attention to Revelation's relationship to other texts. Students may never see this o/p book (originally $140) without recourse to inter-library loan. [*SwJT* Spr 98].

Bullinger, E.W. 1909. A large work reprinted by Kregel in 1990—why I don't know. It deserves to be buried. Though a scholar of some repute long ago, Bullinger and his "ultra-dispensationalism" were vigorously rejected by Dispensationalists: Ironside called it "an absolutely Satanic perversion of the truth."

✓ **Caird, G.B.** ‡ (BNTC) 1966. Similar to NCB in its interpretive approach, but slightly more critical. Caird's commentary has been one of the most highly regarded works on Revelation. He was an incisive exegete indeed. The drawback is that it is now so dated. [*JBL* 86.2 (1967)].

F Carson, D.A. (Pillar replacement). I expect this is a long way off. See Hughes below.

✓ **Charles, R.H.** ‡ (ICC) 2 Vols., 1920. The extraordinarily learned Charles produced an enduring classic with this mine of technical information for students. Though it will be consulted for scholarly work even long into the new millennium, the set "has nothing to offer the preacher" [*BSB* 9/06]. Charles interprets Revelation using all his background studies in Daniel, the OT Apocrypha, and Pseudepigrapha. See also Swete.

✓ Chilton, David. *The Days of Vengeance*, 1987. This large commentary delivers a Postmillennial exposition with a "Reconstructionist" flavor. He's not generous in his handling of opposing viewpoints, and his dogmatism in dating the Apocalypse prior to Jerusalem's Fall (AD 70) flies in the face of too much evidence. Still, there is real theological insight in this commentary and presses the overall point that Christ's ultimate victory ought to mean everything to the Christian today. Chilton wrote regularly for *World* magazine and seems to have substantially moderated his theonomic views before his untimely death.

✓ Collins, Adela Yarbro. ‡ *Crisis and Catharsis: The Power of the Apocalypse*, 1984.

Court, J.M. ‡ *Revelation*, 1994. This is an introduction, not a commentary, useful for reviewing developments in scholarship (especially continental European).

F deSilva, David. (RRA).

✓ **deSilva, David A.** *Seeing Things John's Way* (SRC) 2009. A fairly large-scale commentary (416pp), focused upon "The Rhetoric of the Book of Revelation" (the subtitle), and aiming to explain the relevance of the Apocalypse to the 21ˢᵗ century Church. The strength of this Ashland Seminary professor's work is, as some might expect, more in the academic area of rhetorical analysis. I find it less helpful for pulpit concerns of theological reflection and application. For more on where he positions himself regarding rhetorical approaches to Revelation, see "What has Athens to Do with Patmos?" *CBR* 6.2 (2008): 256–89. For an earlier commentary by deSilva, see Hebrews.

    Durham, James. 1658. This is a full, 1000-page exposition which will be treasured by lovers of the Puritans. Recently reprinted by Old Paths (2000). Spurgeon recommended Durham's gospel "savour" more than his lines of interpretation. This author's work on Song of Songs has also been brought back into print, but by a different publisher (Banner of Truth). [*CTJ* 11/01].

F   Fanning, Buist. (ZEC). This scholar embraces Reformed theology and teaches at Dallas Seminary. I expect there will be good discussion of the Greek (he is fine linguist), but how will he nuance his eschatological position?

✓   **Farrar, Austin M.** ‡ *The Rebirth of Images,* 1949; *The Revelation of St. John the Divine,* 1964. The latter is a penetrating, provocative commentary first published at Oxford's Clarendon Press, still useful to consult though not a reliable guide. Caird says Farrar "first opened my eyes to John's use of the imagination and taught me to see in him both an exegete and a supreme literary artist" (p.v).

F   Fee, Gordon. (NCCS). The author taught at Regent College, has written many commentaries, and is editor of the NICNT series.

✓   **Ford, J. Massyngberde.** ‡ (AB) 1975. One of the most startlingly eccentric commentaries—on a Bible book that has had its share. She says Revelation is the product of John the Baptist and his circle and is a decidedly Jewish Apocalypse, pre-Christian in parts. Wild and woolly ideas! Advanced students may wish to consult her work for its references to the DSS (many references incorrect, according to Carson) and Church Fathers. Ford will not be doing a revision of this work, as had previously been reported; Yale will replace this with a new commentary by Koester. [*JBL* 9/76].

F   Friesen, Steven J. (Paideia). Earlier he wrote the well-received *Imperial Cults and the Apocalypse of John: Reading Revelation in the Ruins* (OUP, 2001), which one can read alongside Kraybill.

    Glasson, T.F. 1965. Published by CUP.

☆   Goldsworthy, Graeme. *The Gospel in Revelation,* 1984. I cannot think of a better book for Bible study groups than this 160-page theological guide. The author has an excellent background in biblical studies, especially the OT, and here uses the key of Biblical Theology to unlock the riches of Revelation. He makes the truths of Scripture exciting and practical for the Christian life. See also his book, *Gospel and Wisdom: Israel Wisdom Literature in the Christian Life.*

    González, Catherine Gunsalus, and Justo L. González. ‡ (WestBC) 1997. [*RelSRev* 10/98, 7/00].

    Gregg, Steve (ed). *Revelation: Four Views—A Parallel Commentary,* 1997.

    Guthrie, Donald. *The Relevance of John's Apocalypse,* 1987. This fine book of lectures moves beyond the fine points of exegesis and questions of Revelation's meaning for the future to examine the practical relevance of the book for the Church today.

F   Hamilton, Jim. (PTW).

✓   **Harrington, Wilfred.** ‡ (SacPag) 1993. Covers this Bible book in 271pp. This commentary exemplifies some of the best contemporary Catholic scholarship and is worth consulting by the student. Compared with some other vols. in the series, this early commentary is brief. [*SwJT* Spr 95; *CRBR* 1994; *ExpTim* 8/08].

☆ **Hemer, Colin J.** *The Letters to the Seven Churches of Asia in Their Local Setting*, 1986 (2001 reprint in pb). Hemer gave us a great piece of historical scholarship which also serves the expositor's needs. Reading this may prompt the preacher to plan a seven-week series. See Stott above and Worth below. [*EvQ* 1/02; *SwJT* Spr 02; *RelSRev* 7/03].

☆ Hendriksen, William. *More Than Conquerors*, 1939. One of his first books and has a different scheme of interpretation: recapitulation. This exposition has long been a favorite in Reformed circles. Preterist.

☆ Henry, Matthew. (CrossC) 1999.

✓ Hort, F.J.A. [*M*], *The Apocalypse of St. John I–III*, 1908. Rigorous exegesis; it is a pity he was unable to complete it.

☆ **Hughes, Philip E.** (Pillar) 1991. About 250pp, this theological exposition is suggestive from the Amillennial angle, but not up to the standard he set in his Hebrews commentary. I think you will prefer Hughes to Hendriksen. This has greater stature among evangelicals than among critical scholars. For even better Amillennial expositions, see Dennis Johnson and Kistemaker. Eerdmans let this go o/p; see Carson above for the future replacement. [*WTJ* Fall 92; *EvQ* 7/92; *CTJ* 4/91; *CRBR* 1992].

Johnson, Alan F. (EBC) 1981. One of the best in the NT section of EBC and has 200pp which are packed with information. Historic Premillennial interpretation. This is now revised and updated in EBCR below.

☆ Johnson, Alan F. (EBCR) 2006. The length of the new work is similar to the old. This remains one of the most useful shorter evangelical exegeses.

Johnson, Darrell W. *Discipleship on the Edge: An Expository Journey through the Book of Revelation*, 2004. The author teaches Pastoral Theology at Regent College and here offers 412pp of sermonic material.

✓ Kiddle, Martin. ‡ (Moffatt series) 1940. Continues to be consulted by scholars working on Revelation. An in-depth work, but not as valuable as its length (450pp) might imply.

✓ Kik, J. Marcellus. *Revelation Twenty, An Exposition*, 1955. There are not many Postmillennial commentaries, and this one is in the classic Postmil. mold. See also his *Eschatology of Victory*, 1971. Some may be interested in a Postmillennial work from the Reconstructionist camp and should consult Chilton.

☆ **Kistemaker, Simon J.** (NTC) 2001. This highly theological, Amillennial exposition has been used as a textbook at RTS Charlotte. I salute Professor Kistemaker for finally completing this Baker series, which has proved its usefulness to the Church. It was a huge task he undertook. [*Them* Aut 02; *JETS* 3/03; Interp 1/03].

✓ Knight, Jonathan. ‡ (Read) 1999. [*ExpTim* 1/00; *Them* Spr 01; *WTJ* Spr 02].

F Koester, Craig. ‡ (AYB). This will be a replacement for Ford, written by the author of Hebrews in this series. Koester has one of the best critical introductions in print: *Revelation and the End of All Things*, 2001.

✓ Kraybill, J.N. ‡ *Imperial Cult and Commerce in John's Apocalypse*, 1996.

✓ Kuyper, Abraham. ET 1935. Full (350pp) and one of the better Amillennial works for the pastor. Heavily theological, which one would expect from the great founder of, and theology professor at, the Free University of Amsterdam.

☆ **Ladd, George E.** 1972. Relative to NCB and NICNT, Ladd has a greater stress on futurist aspects. But I hasten to add that he is famously a proponent of Historic Premillennialism, not Dispensationalism. Many of his writings deal with eschatology. (Building very much on Ladd's foundation is the recent Blomberg/Chung [eds], *A Case for Historic Premillennialism*, 2009 [*Them* 7/09].) This is a dependable commentary, a Premillennial favorite, with a sharp eye for theological themes. Lots of preachers love this one and Wilcock's BST. [*WTJ* Spr 73; *EvQ* 1/75].

LaHaye, Tim. *Revelation Unveiled*, 1999. Popularizing old-style Dispensationalism. Because of the author's name recognition, this has sold like mad. See Michaels below.

MacArthur, John. 2 Vols., 1999–2000. See Matthew for a review of the series. Strongly Dispensational.

✓ Malina, Bruce J., and John J. Pilch. ‡ *A Social-Science Commentary on the Book of Revelation*, 2000. Published by Fortress Press. The authors take up many issues and interpretive methods scarcely used in more traditional commentaries. I found the appendix helpful for getting a quick view of the structural development of the Bible book and some of its more significant literary features. The main line of interpretation (John as an Astral Prophet) is weird and forced. [*JR* 10/01; *RelSRev* 7/03].

Mangina, Joseph L. (Brazos) 2010. I have yet to see this book.

Mauro, Philip. *Things Which Soon Must Come to Pass*, 1925. A hefty conservative commentary often reprinted.

☆ **Michaels, J. Ramsey.** [*M*], (IVPNT) 1997. The author is a well known scholar who has also published a fine introduction entitled *Interpreting the Book of Revelation* (Baker, 1992) [*CRBR* 1994]. The popularly styled IVPNT commentary is well done; I would like to see it get into the hands of many people who might be tempted to get their eschatology from the "Left Behind" series. Here is a taste from *Interpreting*: "The purpose of preaching from Revelation is to evoke first wonder and then faithfulness to the slain Lamb, not to explain the book away or reduce it to a blueprint of the future. The preacher's task is to stand out of the way and let the book's images do their work" (146). Michaels joins those who view Apocalyptic as an inadequate genre identification for Revelation. [*RelSRev* 7/00; *Chm* Win 06].

Minear, Paul. ‡ *I Saw a New Earth*, 1968. Listed mainly for the value of its bibliography. [*JBL* 89.4 (1970)].

✓ Moffatt, James. ‡ (Expositor's Greek Testament) 1910.

☆ **Morris, Leon.** (TNTC) 1969, rev. 1987. One of the best informed works in the series and Amillennial in its interpretation. Fine introduction and 210 pages of insightful, crystal clear exposition with more stress on the prophetic tradition. In early eds. of this Guide I included this on my recommended purchase list. Note Morris' helpful slim vol. on *Apocalyptic* (1972).

✓ Moyise, Steve (ed). ‡ *Studies in the Book of Revelation*, 2001. [*Them* Aut 03; *JTS* 10/03].

F Mulholland, M. Robert. (CorBC).

✓ **Murphy, Frederick J.** ‡ *Fallen Is Babylon: The Revelation to John* (NT in Context) 1998. Nearly 500pp in length, this is definitely a reference book for students. Still, it is accessible to a broader audience interested in literary readings of biblical texts. [*RelSRev* 7/00].

Newell, William R. 1935. See under Romans. This was perhaps the favorite exposition among Dispensational pastors before Walvoord was published.

F Patterson, Paige. (NAC). We can expect a Dispensational work

Pieters, Albertus. 1950. A notable commentary in the preterist tradition.

☆ Poythress, Vern. *The Returning King: A Guide to the Book of Revelation*, 2000. This pastoral and theological exposition is especially notable for its clarity in presenting the recapitulation scheme of Amillennial interpretation and its gracious spirit in interacting with other positions. It also introduced me to the author's fascinating idea of "counterfeiting." This P&R issue is a good addition to either pastors' or church libraries. I imagine that the book got its start in Poythress' "Notes on Revelation" in *New Geneva Study Bible*, 1995, one of the best sections in that Nelson project.

Prigent, Pierre. ‡ *Commentary on the Apocalypse of St. John*, ET 2001. A huge (717pp) and deeply learned work which gives much attention to both the historical background and the Apocalypse's indebtedness to the OT.

✓ Ramsay, W.M. *The Letters to the Seven Churches of Asia*, 1905. Another of William Ramsay's excellent historical-archaeological studies, but now dated. See Hemer (above) and Worth (below).

Ramsey, James B. (GS) 1873. This posthumously published exposition only covers the first 11 chapters.

☆ **Reddish, Mitchell G.** ‡ (S&H) 2001. A readable, critically-informed exposition in the Baptist tradition, this 512-page work is given a very warm review by Aune. The author teaches at Stetson University in Florida. The retail price of nearly $60 will probably keep it off many pastors' shelves. [*RelSRev* 7/03].

Resseguie, James L. [𝓜], *The Revelation of John: A Narrative Commentary*, 2009. From Baker Academic. While insights abound, I am not convinced of the hermeneutical approach to this Bible book. Compare with Barr's *Tales of the End*, and take note of Resseguie's earlier scholarship in *Revelation Unsealed: A Narrative Critical Approach to John's Apocalypse* (Brill, 1998). [*Them* 11/09; *JETS* 6/10; *ExpTim* 2/10; *JSNT-BL* 2010].

✓ **Roloff, Jürgen.** ‡ (ContC) 1984, ET 1993. Useful, but unfortunately not as thorough as most others in the series (250pp). There is less interaction with other points of view than one might hope for. This is not a technical work (i.e., a comprehensive historical and linguistic commentary) and is quite accessible, even to well-educated lay folk. [*PSB* 15.2 (1994); *Interp* 4/95; *SwJT* Spr 95; *SJT* 49.3 (1996)].

✓ **Rowland, Christopher C.** ‡ (NewIB) 1998. Probably the most significant contribution to this vol. (XII). Rowland is an Oxford professor who writes with flair in an essay style. He is renowned as an expert on the place of apocalyptic in Judaism and early Christianity; see *The Open Heaven* (1982). His introduction includes a fine overview of the history of interpretation (especially some little-known British movements and liberation theology), the use and misuse of the Apocalypse. Note that biblical scholarship is not the emphasis here, and that Rowland scarcely ever interacts with evangelical works. He believes the Book of Revelation leads us to resist the idolatries and demands for compromise issuing from the dominant culture, wherever we may be, and to put our hope in a sovereign God. Actually, a better book for preachers may be Rowland's 1993 "Epworth Commentary."

F Schüssler Fiorenza, Elisabeth. ‡ (Herm). Will proffer a highly technical exegesis and a liberationist-feminist interpretation. Students might note her book of essays entitled, *The Book of Revelation: Justice and Judgment* (1985, rev. 1998), and her brief 1991 commentary, *Revelation: Vision of a Just World*, both of which outline her "perspective from below" and show her interest in rhetoric. (I am assured by a former student of hers that it is Dr. Schüssler Fiorenza, not Dr. Fiorenza.)

Seiss, J.A. 1909. A lengthy Dispensational work which was reprinted many times.

Skaggs, Rebecca, and Priscilla C. Benham. (PentC) 2009. Earlier, Skaggs contributed the vol. on Peter & Jude in this series. [*ExpTim* 6/10; *JSNT-BL* 2010].

☆ **Smalley, Stephen S.** [𝓜], 2005. Subtitled "A Commentary on the Greek Text of the Apocalypse" and published by SPCK (IVP in North America), this full (597pp) and densely-packed vol. contains much interaction with other scholars' writings. Smalley has concentrated for decades on the Johannine literature and knows it well. He interprets Revelation as "a creative and coherent drama" in two acts

(1:9–11:19; 12:1–22:17) and as a unity authored by John the Apostle (= the Beloved Disciple) shortly before AD 70. This is a very good book for both students and academically-minded ministers. A few reviewers allege that the book has a more traditional feel, paying less attention to cutting-edge social scientific and rhetorical approaches. Like Osborne, it is a more accessible commentary on the Greek than Aune or Beale. The general approach is more or less idealist. [*JETS* 12/06; *JSNT-BL* 2006; *BTB* Win 07; *BSac* 7/07; *ExpTim* 8/06].

F Stallard, Mike. (EEC).

✓ **Sweet, John P.** ‡ (WPC, now TPI) 1979. A highly acclaimed vol. which was lengthier than others in the now defunct Pelican series. Though Sweet is starting to show its age, I continue calling this one of the best briefer commentaries on Revelation. [*JETS* 6/80].

✓ **Swete, H.B.** 1906. A classic comparable to Beckwith and the more liberal Charles. Swete is a careful, in-depth study on the Greek text and is still useful. Reprinted occasionally.

Tenney, Merrill C. *Interpreting Revelation*, 1957. An introduction to the issues facing the expositor and to the various schemes of interpretation. Premillennial.

F Thomas, John Christopher, and Frank Macchia. (THC).

✓ **Thomas, Robert.** *Revelation 1–7* (intended for WEC?) 1992; *Revelation 8–22*, 1995. The 2 vols. are 524 and 690pp respectively and compose a massive exegetical commentary from the Dispensational perspective. Though somewhat more moderate than Walvoord (in openness to other views), it still presses the literal interpretation much too hard—"The proper procedure is to assume a literal interpretation of each symbolic representation provided to John unless a particular factor in the text indicates it should be interpreted figuratively" (p.36). I believe only those sharing Thomas's doctrinal commitment will give it a high grade. On the plus side, Thomas gives copious citations of others' works and views, sometimes approaching being a catena or chain of extracts. This is a valuable reference for students. [*WTJ* Spr 93; *BSac* 4/94, 7/96].

✓ **Thompson, Leonard L.** ‡ (ANTC) 1998. From an expert on the historical background of Revelation. (See *The Book of Revelation: Apocalypse and Empire*, 1990 [*JR* 1/92], which sparked a resurgence of interest in social setting.) This is among the best compact commentaries from the critical camp (190pp). Some of us disagree with him when he gives a positive reassessment of Domitian's reign, arguing that Revelation was written to a community living in peace and that there was no persecution setting. [*RelSRev* 7/00].

☆ Trafton, Joseph L. (Reading the NT) 2005. I like this book. It is subtitled "A Literary and Theological Commentary" and contains good insights from a conservative angle.

✓ Wainwright, Arthur. ‡ *Mysterious Apocalypse*, 1993.

F Wainwright, Geoffrey. (Brazos).

Walhout, Edwin. *Revelation Down to Earth: Making Sense of the Apocalypse of John*, 2000. The author is a retired Christian Reformed Church minister. He writes that his commentary "explains this difficult book of the Bible from a pastoral point of view" (p.1). It is a thoughtful personal reading, foregoing much interaction with scholarly literature, except when he discusses the structure of the Apocalypse.

☆ **Wall, Robert.** (NIBC) 1991. Fairly full for the series at over 300pp. The reviews are a bit mixed. [*WTJ* Spr 93; *EvQ* 10/97; *Them* 4/96; *CRBR* 1994].

✓ Walvoord, John F. 1966. To see what old-style Dispensationalists do with the book you could consult this work, which has been a standard Pre-tribulational commentary.

I cannot recommend it as a guide to interpreting Revelation. These days, when I want to read the Dispensational interpretation of a passage (and have the time), I look up Thomas instead. Walvoord tends to be irritatingly dismissive of all other approaches.

✓   Weinrich, William C. (ed). (ACCS) 2005. [*JSNT-BL* 2007].

☆   Wilcock, Michael. (BST) 1975. Different type of interpretation, but most stimulating for anyone preaching or teaching through this book. A very smart purchase. I am tempted to place this above among the recommended purchases. [*EvQ* 4/76].

F   Williamson, Peter S. ‡ (CCSS).

Witherington, Ben. (NCBC) 2003. This launched the new series, with Witherington himself serving as General Editor. As might be expected in light of his past work, the author here pays attention to both historical backdrop and socio-rhetorical analysis. He writes that "John is what Eusebius was later to call a 'chiliast,' a believer in a thousand-year reign" upon the earth (p.291). I have not used this commentary enough to justify a recommendation. Students will appreciate his bibliographical guidance on pp.51–64. [*ExpTim* 9/04; *RelSRev* 4/04; *JETS* 3/05; *Interp* 7/05; *CBQ* 4/09; *JSNT-BL* 2005; *Anvil* 22.1].

✓   Worth, Roland H. *The Seven Cities of the Apocalypse and Roman Culture*, 1999; *The Seven Cities of the Apocalypse and Greco-Asian Culture*, 1999. See Hemer above.

Yeatts, John R. (BCBC) 2003. This book and the series come from the pacifist tradition. [*Interp* 4/04].

NOTES: (1) Ian Paul, "Ebbing and Flowing: Scholarly Developments in Study of the Book of Revelation," *ExpTim* 119.11 (2008): 523–31. (2) Michael Naylor has reviewed the recent scholarship on "The Roman Imperial Cult and Revelation," *CBR* 8.2 (2010): 207–39.

Bargains for a
Bare-Bones Library

These choices will, I hope, provide the "average" student or pastor with the best resources, given an extremely limited budget. The following might be termed "best bargains," though few would be a first choice if one had plenty of shekels to spend. Or you might think of these as "emergency purchases," where, say, you really want a Genesis commentary for a new Sunday School class on the Life of Abraham but only have about $10–15. I have chosen for the most part one volume commentaries in paperback with an evangelical perspective. (Believing scholarship should, I think, be given a priority in building a personal library of restricted size.) The choices also tend to be exegetical rather than homiletical in their aim. Something to consider: it could be that with scarce resources you would be best off buying a commentary series or two on CD-ROM. Since commentaries are often sold at a discount in entire sets, you also might consider building your library around a series, like the Tyndale OT and NT Commentaries. In this list, names appear in the order of preference—perhaps with cost as a leading consideration—where the connectives "and" or "or" are used.

GENESIS	**Hartley** (NIBC) or Kidner (TOTC)
EXODUS	**Bruckner** (NIBC) or Enns (NIVAC); *Bruckner is more critical, Enns more expensive and expositional.*
LEVITICUS	**Harrison** (TOTC); *Hess (EBCR) is far superior in a vol. covering Genesis to Leviticus.*
NUMBERS	**Wenham** (TOTC)
DEUTERONOMY	**Wright** (NIBC)
JOSHUA	**Hess** (TOTC); *The NIBC pb vol. covers Joshua-Ruth.*
JUDGES/RUTH	**Block** (NAC); *Judges and Ruth covered in one hb; you can't find a good cheap exegesis. For a theological exposition, see Davis (Judges) and Atkinson (Ruth).*
SAMUEL	**Baldwin** (TOTC); *The best quality deal would be to get Gordon second-hand.*
KINGS	**Provan** (NIBC)
CHRONICLES	**Selman** (TOTC)
EZRA/NEHEMIAH	**Kidner** (TOTC) or Allen (NIBC); *Clines (NCB on Ezra-Esther) would be a good choice.*
ESTHER	**Laniak** (NIBC) or Baldwin (TOTC) or Firth (more expositional); *Jobes (NIVAC) would cost you a bit more money*
JOB	**Wilson** (NIBC) or Andersen (TOTC)
PSALMS	**Broyles** (NIBC) or Kidner (TOTC)
Proverbs	**Hubbard** (WCC); *Other option is Kidner (TOTC)*
ECCLESIASTES	**Hubbard** (WCC) — *with Song of Songs in one pb vol.; 2nd option is Kidner (BST)*

SONG OF SONGS	**Hubbard** (WCC)— *with Ecclesiastes in one pb vol*; *2nd option is Carr (TOTC)*
ISAIAH	**Motyer** (TOTC)
JEREMIAH/LAM.	**Longman** (NIBC) or Harrison (TOTC)
EZEKIEL	**Tuell** (NIBC) or **Stuart** (WCC); *Tuell is not conservative, but offers the most and best exegesis for the money. The bargain for theological exposition is Wright.*
DANIEL	**Baldwin** (TOTC) or Longman (NIVAC, for a few more dollars)
MINOR PROPHETS	**McComiskey (ed) in one vol.**; *On a single Minor Prophet, probably buy TOTC.*

MATTHEW	**France** (TNTC) or Mounce (NIBC)
SERMON ON MT.	**Stott** (BST)
MARK	**Hurtado** (NIBC) or Cole (TNTC)
LUKE	**Evans** (NIBC) or Morris (TNTC)
JOHN	**Kruse** (TNTC)
ACTS	**Marshall** (TNTC) or Stott (BST); *Williams (NIBC) and Longenecker (EBC) are good too.*
ROMANS	**Stott** (BST)
1 CORINTHIANS	**Morris** (TNTC); *Bruce's NCB on 1 & 2 Corinthians was once a super bargain, now o/p.*
2 CORINTHIANS	**Kruse** (TNTC)
GALATIANS	**Jervis** (NIBC) or Cole (TNTC, more exegetical), or Stott (BST, expositional)
EPHESIANS	**Stott** (BST)
PHILIPPIANS	**Fee** (IVPNT) or Martin (TNTC); *Fee's NICNT is really worth the extra money.*
COLOSSIANS	**Wright** (TNTC) or Lightfoot (CrossC)
THESSALONIANS	**Beale** (IVPNT) or Williams (NIBC) or Morris (TNTC); *Pastors may prefer Stott.*
PASTORALS	**Fee** (NIBC) or Kelly (BNTC) or Towner (IVPNT) or Guthrie (TNTC)
PHILEMON	***See Colossians commentary incorporating Philemon***
HEBREWS	**Hagner** (NIBC) or D. Guthrie (TNTC)
JAMES	**Davids** (NIBC) or Moo (TNTC)
1 PETER	**Hillyer** (NIBC, on 1–2 Peter, Jude = cheapest) or Grudem (TNTC); *Cf. Schreiner*
2 PETER/JUDE	**Hillyer** (NIBC, on 1–2 Peter, Jude = cheapest) or Green (TNTC); *Cf. Schreiner*
1–3 JOHN	**Stott** (TNTC) or Johnson (NIBC); *Students may prefer the exegetical NIBC.*
REVELATION	**Morris** (TNTC) or Michaels (IVPNT); *The latter is a little more money.*

—ᵚᵚ—

An Ideal Basic Library for the Pastor

These choices will, I hope, provide the "average" student or pastor with the best resources for a basic library, given a typical (?) budget. I sought to pick works that young pastors could grow into, rather than grow out of (because not engaging the text deeply enough). I wish to clarify that this is only a beginning library, restricted to two commentaries per Bible book, and balanced between detailed exegesis and theological-practical exposition. In the case of certain Bible books, I have mentioned works that would be complementary or perhaps preferred by the more advanced student or scholarly pastor. Names appear in the order of preference where the connectives "and" or "or" are used. Believing scholarship should, I think, be given a priority in building a personal library of restricted size. I have selected a few more technical works (using original Hebrew or Greek) for the NT than OT, since pastors tend to use them more.

— Old Testament Commentaries —

GENESIS — **Wenham and/or Mathews** (exegesis), **then Walton** or Ross (exposition)

EXODUS — **Stuart** (exegesis) **and Enns** (exposition), then add Childs (if you are more academic).

LEVITICUS — **Wenham** or Rooker, then Gane (exposition); *Compare Hess. Hartley could be added for close work with the Hebrew.*

NUMBERS — **Ashley** or Wenham (for the frugal); *Add Milgrom for detail work, while Duguid offers lots of expositional help.*

DEUTERONOMY — **McConville and Wright**

JOSHUA — **Hess and Howard**; *Pastors will add Hubbard (NIVAC) for expositional help.*

JUDGES — **Block**; *Advanced students will add Butler, while pastors may want an exposition.*

RUTH — **Hubbard**; *Add Bush for detailed exegesis of the Hebrew text. Preachers should consider Ulrich.*

SAMUEL — **Firth** (exegesis), **then Arnold** or Brueggemann (exposition); *Add AB and/or WBC for more detailed exegesis and textual criticism. Preachers should consider Woodhouse and Davis.*

KINGS — **Provan and House**; *Scholarly types will want to add Hobbs and consider AB and Sweeney.*

CHRONICLES — **Selman** (evangelical), **then Japhet or Williamson** (if you are both scholarly and serious about studying Chronicles); *Advanced students working on 1 Chron. will "invest" in Knoppers. To focus more on 2 Chron., pick up Dillard. Pastors look at Pratt, Hill for expositional help.*

EZRA/NEHEMIAH — **Williamson and Kidner** (as a conservative counterbalance)

ESTHER   **Jobes, then Baldwin** (conservative exegesis) **or Bush** (more technical exegesis of Hebrew); *Advanced students find a trio of Jewish scholars stimulating: Levenson, Berlin, and Fox. Pastors love Firth (exegetical conclusions and theological exposition).*

JOB   **Hartley or Habel**; *Hebrew students will want to add Clines, while preachers will want expositional help from the likes of Balentine, Wilson, Derek Thomas, and Hywel Jones.*

PSALMS   **VanGemeren and Mays,** then Wilson (exposition); *Kidner is great for just starting out; advanced students will gravitate toward WBC, Goldingay, and ContC.*

PROVERBS   **Waltke and Hubbard** or Ross; *Longman serves well as a one-vol. treatment. Advanced students may buy Fox and Waltke together to start off.*

ECCLESIASTES   **Bartholomew** (exegesis), **and Hubbard** or Kidner (for exposition); *Either Fredericks or Longman is a top pick if you agree with him. Seow, Fox, and Murphy are top-notch for scholars.*

SONG OF SONGS   **Hess or Estes or Longman**, or Carr (less expensive); *Scholars appreciate Murphy, Keel, Exum.*

ISAIAH   **Motyer** (1993) **and Smith or Oswalt** (NICOT); *Add an exposition like Brueggemann or Webb; Calvin is a big help here, too. The studious will appreciate Childs and Wildberger.*

JEREMIAH   **Thompson** or Huey, **then Fretheim/Brueggemann/Dearman** (as an expositional help); *The choices among evangelical works are not so clear for Jeremiah; some of the best are older (NICOT and BCBC), and some of the newer are not the best. Students should start with AB, Hermeneia, and Allen's OTL. Scholarly pastors should buy AB first and quickly add a theological exposition (not Lundbom's area of interest).*

LAMENTATIONS   **Garrett/House** or Provan (less expensive); *Students will also want access to AB and OTL.*

EZEKIEL   **Block, then Duguid**; *Zimmerli and Greenberg are invaluable from the critical angle, but will be best appreciated by academic types.*

DANIEL   **Longman and Goldingay** (add conservative counterbalance like TOTC)

MINOR PROPHETS   **McComiskey set; Dearman** (Hosea); **Stuart** (Hosea–Jonah); **Robertson** (Nahum–Zeph); **Taylor and Clendenen** (Haggai and Malachi); **Boda** (Haggai–Zech); *Pastors will add Gary V. Smith's NIVAC on Hosea/Amos/Micah and Bruckner on Jonah, Nahum, Habakkuk, Zephaniah. Students will want to add a few gems like Paul on Amos (Herm), Sasson on Jonah (AB), Meyers/Meyers on Haggai-Zechariah (AB), and Hill on Malachi (AB).*

— NEW TESTAMENT COMMENTARIES —

NEW TESTAMENT   **Calvin's Commentaries** (Torrance Ed.)

MATTHEW   **France** (NICNT) or **Carson, then Hagner** or Nolland (*for detailed Greek exegesis*)—one of the pair should be France or Nolland (as newer works); *NT aficionados, with ambition to do a PhD in that field, need a rich uncle to buy them the sets by Davies/Allison and by Luz. For more expositional help see BST and NIVAC.*

SERMON ON MT.	**Guelich, then Lloyd-Jones** or Stott (for exposition and application)
MARK	**Stein and/or France** (Greek text, but very accessible), **then Garland** (exposition); *Students will also want WBC. If the pastor thinks Stein and France too demanding, buy Pillar.*
LUKE	**Bock** (BECNT) **and Green**; *Students will want access to Marshall and Fitzmyer. Preachers will add an exposition to this mix, say a Wilcock or Hughes. L.T. Johnson is strong, but I regard Stein as the best purchase for the pastor who can only afford a single volume.*
JOHN	**Carson, then Köstenberger** (Greek text) **or Burge** (NIVAC, for exposition); *Advanced students will also look at Keener, Barrett, and Brown for detailed exegetical help. Expect a massive NICNT from Michaels in 2010.*
ACTS	**Peterson** (Pillar) **and Bock** (Greek text), **then Stott** (exposition); *For the true scholar the Barrett set will be maybe a first or second purchase. Look for WBC, NIGTC.*
ROMANS	**Moo** (NICNT) **and Cranfield** (ICC) **and Stott**;
1 CORINTHIANS	**Garland** (builds on Fee) **or Fee, then Blomberg** (practical exposition) **or Thiselton** (exhaustive on the Greek text); *It's hard to pass by Fee, even if you disagree. Expect a stellar Pillar volume in late 2010.*
2 CORINTHIANS	**Barnett** (NICNT) or Garland, **then Hafemann** (exposition) **or Harris** (Greek text).
GALATIANS	**Longenecker** (not entirely satisfactory) **or Bruce, then Stott** (exposition); *Fung or George are good for expositors (if your Greek isn't up to WBC).*
EPHESIANS	**O'Brien, then Stott** (exposition) **or Thielman or Lincoln** (for Greek text…but do note that Lincoln pushes a deutero-Pauline interpretation); *Hoehner's 2002 volume is also excellent.*
PHILIPPIANS	**Fee** (NICNT) **and O'Brien** (Greek text), **then Thielman** (for exposition); *Hansen is fine.*
COLOSSIANS	**Moo, then O'Brien** (Greek) **or Garland** (expositional help); *Wright in short compass; add Dunn for scholars.*
THESSALONIANS	**Fee or Green, then Stott** (for preachers) **or Malherbe or Wanamaker** (for Greek text);
PASTORALS	**Towner** (NICNT) **and Mounce** (WBC), **then Stott** (for exposition); *Marshall and Knight are indispensable for work with the Greek text.*
PHILEMON	***See Colossians commentaries incorporating Philemon***
HEBREWS	**O'Brien, then Lane** (WBC for Greek exegesis) **or Guthrie** (for exposition); *Scholars also prize Hermeneia, NIGTC, and AB.*
JAMES	**Moo** (Pillar) **and McCartney** (Greek exegesis); *Scholarly types might make Johnson's AB a first or second purchase, and pastors will want an additional expositional help. Look for a large NICNT from McKnight in late 2010.*
1 PETER	**Davids and Jobes** (Greek), **then McKnight** (exposition); *Scholarly pastors would like to add Achtemeier and Michaels, perhaps Elliott too. If the pastor can only afford one vol. on Peter and Jude, buy Schreiner.*
2 PETER/JUDE	**Davids** (Pillar), **then Green** (BECNT for Greek exegesis) **or Moo** (exposition); *If you're the scholarly type, plan to acquire Bauckham—either the 1983 edition now or the 2nd ed. later.*

1–3 John   **Yarbrough and Kruse, then Burge** (exposition); *Look for Carson's NIGTC (a likely first choice). Advanced students will relish Schnackenburg, Lieu, and Brown.*

Revelation   **Mounce** (1998), **then Keener** (exposition) **or Beale** (for detailed exegesis of the Greek text); *Osborne is also superb and could be substituted for Mounce, especially by those who are working with the Greek text.*

— Old Testament Research Tools —

1. *BHS*, but note that one replacement (among several projects), *Biblia Hebraica Quinta*, is already appearing. Pastors struggling to stick with their Hebrew might consider *A Reader's Hebrew Bible* (Zondervan, 2008) [*Them* 7/09; *EuroJTh* 18.2].

2. *HALOT* (2 vol. "Study Edition") [*Them* Aut 02], for those quite serious about Hebrew; otherwise buy Holladay's lexicon. Students should consult the Sheffield *Dictionary of Classical Hebrew* [1993–] in the library [*CBQ* 4/09].

3. *New International Dictionary of OT Theology and Exegesis* [*JETS* 6/99; *ExpTim* 1/00; *Chm* 112.1 (1998)].

4. The Waltke/O'Connor Hebrew Syntax-Grammar [*JSS* Aut 91; *CRBR* 1992] or the more concise Arnold/Choi, *A Guide to Biblical Hebrew Syntax* (Cambridge, 2003) in pb [critiqued in *HebStud* 2005; *VT* 55.4; *ExpTim* 3/05].

5. High-powered Bible study software. Gone are the days when I recommended a concordance to the Hebrew OT by Even-Shoshan (all Hebrew) or Kohlenberger & Swanson [*JSOT* 84] (for those with only basic Hebrew).

6. *Old Testament Exegesis* (4th ed. 2009) by Douglas Stuart.

7. OT Introductions by Longman/Dillard, 2nd ed. 2006 [*JETS* 3/97], Childs, and Harrison (who has information that is hard to find elsewhere).

8. OT Survey by LaSor/Hubbard/Bush (1996 ed.) [*JSS* Spr 00].

9. OT Histories by Provan/Long/Longman [*RTR* 8/06; *BSac* 7/05; *CJ* 10/05] and Merrill (2nd ed. 2008) [*TJ* Spr 09].

10. Consider King/Stager, *Life in Biblical Israel*, 2001 [*Them* Sum 03; *WTJ* Spr 03; *Interp* 1/03; *JETS* 12/04; *JNES* 7/07; *DenvJ* 1/02 (Hess); *Evangel* Sum 03], if you will in fact read the beautiful book.

11. Among OT Theology books, which I argue are possibly the most helpful volumes on a preacher's shelf, I can recommend House (1998); Martens' *God's Design* (2nd ed 1994, 3rd ed 1998); and Robertson's *The Christ of the Covenants*. Stimulating from the more critical side are Goldingay's set (2003–09) [*Chm* Win 07; *CBQ* 4/05, 11/07; *JTS* 10/05, 4/09; *JETS* 6/05; *Them* Win 05; *BSac* 7/06; *Interp* 4/06, 4/08; *TynBul* 57.1; *ExpTim* 1/05; *SJT* 63.1 (Chapman, Brueggemann); *Anvil* 22.3 (Moberly); *DenvJ* 4/08 (Hess)]; the liberal/postmodern Brueggemann (1997) [*Them* Aut 99; *Interp* 1/99; *CTJ* 4/00; *JETS* 12/99; *TynBul* 57.1]; and classics by Eichrodt (ET 1961–67) and von Rad (ET 1962–65). Regrettably, I was less impressed with Waltke's huge 2007 effort as an OT Theology—especially when Ruth and Ecclesiastes together get about as many pages as "Prophets" (pp.805–27) and "Prophetic Books" (pp.828–49); on the plus side Waltke gives much attention to what he terms NT intertextuality [*JETS* 3/09; *BSac* 4/09; *VT* 60.1; *Them* 7/09].

Scholarly Students Will Likely Want To Add:

12. Reference works on Hebrew grammar such as the Gesenius volume and perhaps *A Biblical Hebrew Reference Grammar* by van der Merwe/Naudé/Kroeze as well [*JETS* 9/01; *JSS* Aut 01], while they use Joüon and Muraoka (2006) in the library [*Heb-*

Stud 2007]. Serving well as a classroom text and as a reference is *Williams' Hebrew Syntax*, Ronald J. Williams, 3ʳᵈ ed, rev and expanded by John C. Beckman (Toronto: University of Toronto Press, 2007) [*HebStud* 2008].

13. A copy of the LXX, plus the Liddell & Scott Greek Lexicon: Abridged. To be consulted in the library is Muraoka, *A Greek English Lexicon of the Septuagint* (2009)—"an indispensable tool for everyone who studies the Septuagint or works with it in any way" [*JAJ* 1.1].

14. An Aramaic grammar (we are spoiled for choice here): Alger Johns' *Short Grammar of Biblical Aramaic* (1972); or Frederick Greenspahn, *An Introduction to Aramaic* (2ⁿᵈ ed 2003) [*JETS* 9/01; *JSS* Spr 03, Aut 06; *HebStud* 43; *VT*, 55.1; *ExpTim* 12/04]; or Steinmann's *Fundamental Biblical Aramaic* (2004) [*JETS* 6/05]; or Franz Rosenthal, *A Grammar of Biblical Aramaic* (Harrassowitz, 2006); or Elisha Qimron, *Biblical Aramaic* (Bialik Institute, 1993).

15. *TDOT*.

16. Three useful histories are Bright (3ʳᵈ or 4ᵗʰ ed.); Shanks (ed), *Ancient Israel: From Abraham to the Roman Destruction of the Temple*, rev. 1999 [*DenvJ*]; and the more critical Miller/Hayes, *A History of Ancient Israel and Judah*, 2ⁿᵈ ed 2006 [*JSOT-BL* 2007].

17. *The Face of Old Testament Studies*, edited by Baker/Arnold [*Chm* Spr 06].

18. One last item not to be missed is Greidanus' *Preaching Christ from the Old Testament: A Contemporary Hermeneutical Method* (Eerdmans, 1999), "of interest to biblical theologians as well as preachers" [*JSOT* 89 (2000); *Interp* 4/00; *Chm* Sum 00; *EvQ* 10/01; *CTJ* 4/01; *Anvil* 19.1].

— New Testament Research Tools —

1. Either the UBS *Greek New Testament*, 4ᵗʰ ed., or the Nestle/Aland *Novum Testamentum Graece*, 27ᵗʰ ed.—on the differences see *NTS* 4/96, and *ExpTim* 1/96. Some pastors struggling to stick with their Greek might consider *The UBS Greek New Testament: A Reader's Edition*, 2007 [*Them* 4/09], or *A Reader's Greek New Testament* (Zondervan, 2ⁿᵈ ed 2007).

2. Bruce Metzger's *A Textual Commentary on the Greek NT*.

3. The BDAG Greek Lexicon (2000) [*JTS* 4/03; *JETS* 12/03; *JBL* Win 01]. (I continue to find BAGD useful as well.)

4. *NIDNTT* (also condensed into the one-vol. *NIV Theological Dictionary of NT Words*) or the one vol. *TDNT*.

5. A solid intermediate-advanced Greek grammar (like Wallace's *Greek Grammar Beyond the Basics*, which is easier to use than the old standard Blass/Debrunner/Funk).

6. High-powered Bible study software, instead of a recent concordance to the Greek NT. The expensive print editions one might use in the library are Bachmann/Slaby (De Gruyter) and Moulten/Geden/Marshall (6ᵗʰ ed) [*NovT* 45.2; *Them* Spr 03; *BBR* 14.2; *JETS* 3/03; *Anvil* 20.1; *CurTM* 4/06]. If one's Greek is rusted-out, then see Kohlenberger/ Goodrick/Swanson.

7. *New Testament Exegesis* (4ᵗʰ ed. 2010) by Gordon Fee.

8. NT Introduction by Carson/Moo (2ⁿᵈ ed 2005) [*Chm* 107.4 (1993); *CRBR* 1994; *ExpTim* 1/08; *Anvil* 24.1]. Just to note, Guthrie (revised 1990) has information difficult to find elsewhere. Newer and slightly more critical works by Powell (Baker, 2009) [*JSNT-BL* 2010] or deSilva (IVP, 2004) [*Them* 1/06; *Chm* Spr 06; *Anvil* 22.3] could perhaps be added afterwards for their narrative and rhetorical interests. While still evaluating the content, I am impressed with the beautiful presentation in Köstenberger/Kel-

lum/Quarles (B&H, 2009) [*SBET* Spr 10 (Marshall); *RBL* 8/10 (Hartin)], which Hartin has described as "a masterful piece of work that interacts fairly with modern biblical scholarship." Finally, I will be interested to see Hagner's upcoming work, to be published by Baker.

9. NT History volume by Paul Barnett: *Jesus and the Rise of Early Christianity* (1999) [*TJ* Spr 03]. Alternately one can pick up a copy of the F.F. Bruce classic: *NT History* (1969). Witherington was not playing to his strength in his *NT History: A Narrative Account* (2001) [*Them* Aut 02; *JETS* 3/03].

10. NT Theologies by Ladd (Revised 1993), Thielman (2005) [*JETS* 9/06; *Them* 4/09], and I.H. Marshall (IVP, 2004) [*Chm* Spr 07; *CBQ* 7/05; *BBR* 18.1; *JETS* 12/05; *Them* 10/05; *Interp* 1/06; *SJT* 62.1; *RelSRev* 1/05; *ExpTim* 1/06]. Compare Schreiner (2008) who uses a thematic approach in an often inspiring manner [*Them* 4/09; *RelSRev* 3/09; *JETS* 3/09 (Blomberg); *CBQ* 10/09; *JSNT-BL* 2010 (Oakes)].

11. Among content surveys, the set by Craig Blomberg (*Jesus and the Gospels*, 1997, 2nd ed 2009; *From Pentecost to Patmos*, 2006) [*Chm* Win 07], and Luke Timothy Johnson's *The Writings of the NT* (‡, 3rd ed 2010) are hard to beat as introductions to the NT literature, as opposed to introductions to NT scholarship.

Scholarly Students Will Likely Want To Add:

12. Brown's NT Introduction [*JBL* Spr 99; *CTJ* 11/98].
13. *The Face of New Testament Studies*, edited by McKnight/Osborne [*Chm* Spr 06].
14. Barrett's *The New Testament Background* (Rev. 1989), or the user-friendly Elwell/Yarbrough (ed), *Readings from the First-Century World* (1998).
15. Perhaps Dunn's set *The Making of Christianity* (2003–).
16. N.T. Wright's *The Resurrection of the Son of God*.
17. Aland's *Synopsis Quattuor Evangeliorum* [*NovT* 29.2].
18. The Louw/Nida *Greek-English Lexicon*, based on semantic domains (UBS, 1989).
19. Metzger's *Text of the NT* (3rd ed 1992, 4th ed 2005 [*JTS* 10/06 (panned); *JETS* 12/06; *NovT* 48.2]), or the Alands' *Text of the NT* (2nd ed 1989).

— Research Tools For The Whole Bible —

1. At least five good translations of the Bible, in addition to the venerable KJV. The most useful to me are specific editions: *NIV Study Bible*, *ESV Study Bible* [*Them* 4/09], *HarperCollins Study Bible* (NRSV with Apocrypha), *Tanakh* (NJPS, the 1985 Jewish translation, especially in *The Jewish Study Bible* edition of 2004), RSV, and *New Jerusalem Bible* (Catholic translation using "Yahweh"). I find I refer only occasionally to the New Living Translation (NLT). I consider *The Message* to be far too loose a paraphrase. [For reviews of the ESV specifically, see *RTR* 8/03 (critical); SwJT Sum 02; *Anvil* 20.4; the large articles on translations in *ExpTim* 4/03, 10/03; and Leland Ryken, *The Word of God in English: Criteria for Excellence in Bible Translation* (Wheaton: Crossway, 2002), reviewed in *VT* 57.1.]

2. An analytical concordance, even an old one, still comes in handy.

3. *New Bible Dictionary*, then buy the *International Standard Bible Encyclopedia* (Revised).

4. *New Dictionary of Biblical Theology* [*EvQ* 7/04; *Them* Aut 01; *CTJ* 11/03; *JETS* 12/02].

5. A good atlas: perhaps the Currid/Barrett *Crossway ESV Bible Atlas* (2010); *The New Moody Atlas of the Bible* (2009) by Beitzel [*Them* 11/09], *The Zondervan Atlas of the Bible* by Rasmussen (rev. 2010), or *The IVP Atlas of Bible History* [*CBQ* 10/07]. Another excellent reference is the *Oxford Bible Atlas* (4th ed 2007). A slightly different,

impressive work is Beitzel (ed), *Biblica, The Bible Atlas: A Social and Historical Journey through the Lands of the Bible* (2007). If you can afford it, you could buy either the Aharoni/Avi-Yonah *Carta Biblical Atlas* (4ᵗʰ ed 2002) or Rainey/Notley, *The Sacred Bridge* (2006) [*BBR* 17.1], both of which are excellent for inter-testamental Jewish history, too. For a cheaper epitome of Rainey/Notley, see *Carta's New Century Handbook and Atlas of the Bible* (2007) [*BBR* 19.3]. Another large expensive work is Pritchard's beautiful *Harper Atlas of the Bible*. University libraries will likely have the exquisite *Tübinger Bibelatlas* (2001) and Princeton's *Barrington Atlas of the Greek and Roman World* (2000). My personal favorites are Currid/Barrett (2010), Beitzel (2009), and either of the Rainey/Notley works.

6. Geerhardus Vos's *Biblical Theology* is still a brilliant, seminal read.

7. The more scholarly will certainly save up to buy the *Anchor Bible Dictionary* (1992), which I usually prefer to the more recent *New Interpreter's Dictionary of the Bible* (2006–09).

8. Kevin Vanhoozer, *Is There a Meaning in this Text?* [*JETS* 12/01; *JBL* Fall 01], should be required for any evangelical seriously wrestling with contemporary literary theory and the denial of determinate meaning in texts.

9. Thiselton's *Hermeneutics: An Introduction* (2009) and the 2004 revision of Klein/Blomberg/Hubbard, *Introduction to Biblical Interpretation*.

10. *Dictionary for Theological Interpretation of the Bible*, edited by Vanhoozer [*CBQ* 10/06; *TJ* Fall 07; *Interp* 1/07; *ExpTim* 11/08; *SJT* 62.2; *DenvJ*; *JSOT-BL* 2007].

The Ultimate
Reference Library

An unfortunate fellow once quipped, "If my ship ever comes in, there's sure to be a dock strike." This list gives my choices for a first-class exegetical library, were my ship ever to come in. Money is of no concern here, scholarship is. The emphasis is less on expositional helps and more on comprehensive and detailed technical works from a variety of perspectives which will appeal to, or stimulate, the scholarly pastor, advanced student, and specialist. I am concerned to put an evangelical treatment or two up front and will separate the conservative and critical works with a dash. Works are generally listed in order of preference within the divisions of conservative and critical works, but that's not to say I don't prefer the first critical work listed to the second or third evangelical work (e.g., I'd buy Milgrom on Numbers after getting Ashley). I have attempted to keep the number of works to 8–10 per book. I admit that this dream list has been inspired by "Appendix B" in Longman's 1995 commentary survey. It's fun to dream.

— Old Testament —

Old Testament	Calvin, Keil & Delitzsch
Genesis	Wenham, Hamilton, Mathews, Waltke — Westermann, Sarna, Alter, Brueggemann
Exodus	Stuart, Enns — Childs, Houtman, Sarna, Fretheim, Propp, Dozeman
Leviticus	Hartley, Wenham, Rooker, Kiuchi, Gane — Milgrom, Gerstenberger, Levine, Balentine
Numbers	Ashley, Wenham, Cole, Harrison — Milgrom, Olson, Levine, Knierim-Coats
Deuteronomy	McConville, Wright, Craigie, Christensen (2001) — Weinfeld, Miller, Tigay, Nelson, Driver
Joshua	Howard, Hess, Hawk, Woudstra, Hubbard — Butler [*M*], Nelson
Judges	Block, Butler, Webb — Schneider, Boling, Lindars, Niditch, O'Connell, Moore
Ruth	Hubbard, Bush — Campbell, Nielsen, Sakenfeld, Sasson
Samuel	Firth, Youngblood, Gordon, Tsumura, Bergen — Klein, McCarter, Anderson
Kings	Provan, House, Wiseman — Hobbs [*M*], Cogan/Tadmor, Sweeney, Walsh, Brueggemann
Chronicles	Dillard, Selman — Japhet [*M*], Knoppers [*M*], Klein, Williamson [*M*], Johnstone, McKenzie
Ezra/Nehemiah	Fensham, Kidner — Williamson [*M*], Blenkinsopp, Klein, Clines
Esther	Bush, Jobes, Laniak, Baldwin, Firth — Berlin, Levenson, Fox, Clines
Job	Hartley, Wilson, Andersen — Clines, Habel, Gordis, Balentine, Janzen, Pope

PSALMS	Craigie, VanGemeren, Goldingay [𝑀], Tate, Allen, Wilson — Kraus, Mays, Hossfeld-Zenger, Gerstenberger
PROVERBS	Waltke, Van Leeuwen, Longman, Hubbard — Fox, Murphy, Perdue, Clifford
ECCLESIASTES	Bartholomew, Longman, Kidner — Seow, Fox, Murphy, Crenshaw, Krüger, Whybray
SONG OF SONGS	Hess, Garrett, Longman, Gledhill — Murphy, Exum, Keel, Fox, Bergant
ISAIAH	Motyer, Smith, Oswalt — Williamson, Wildberger, Goldingay/Payne, Goldingay (*Message*), Beuken, Childs, Baltzer, Seitz, Westermann, Sweeney, Koole
JEREMIAH	Thompson, Huey — Lundbom [𝑀], Holladay, Fretheim, Allen, Stulman, Brueggemann
LAMENTATIONS	House, Provan — Hillers, Berlin, Renkema, Dobbs-Allsopp, Westermann
EZEKIEL	Block, Duguid — Zimmerli, Greenberg, Joyce, Darr, Allen, Hals, Cooke
DANIEL	Baldwin, Longman, Hill, Young — Goldingay, Collins, Lucas [𝑀], Montgomery
THE TWELVE	Sweeney
HOSEA	Dearman, Stuart, McComiskey — Andersen/Freedman, Macintosh, Mays, Wolff, Ben-Zvi
JOEL	Dillard, Stuart, Allen — Wolff, Crenshaw, Barton
AMOS	Smith, Stuart, Carroll R (2002) — Paul, Andersen/Freedman [𝑀], Wolff, Jeremias
OBADIAH	Raabe, Stuart, Niehaus, Allen — Wolff, Renkema, Barton, Jenson, Watts, Ben-Zvi
JONAH	Stuart, Alexander, Nixon — Sasson, Wolff, Trible, Limburg, Jenson
MICAH	Waltke, Allen — Andersen/Freedman [𝑀], Wolff, Hillers, Mays, Jenson, Ben-Zvi
NAHUM	Longman, Robertson, Patterson, Christensen [𝑀] — Roberts, Spronk, Floyd
HABBAKUK	Robertson, Patterson — Andersen [𝑀], Roberts, Floyd
ZEPHANIAH	Robertson, Motyer, Patterson — Sweeney, Berlin, Vlaardingerbroek, Roberts, Ben-Zvi, Floyd
HAGGAI	Motyer, Taylor, Verhoef, Merrill — Meyers, Wolff, Petersen, Floyd
ZECHARIAH	Stuart (F), McComiskey, Boda, Klein, Merrill — Meyers, Petersen, Conrad, Floyd
MALACHI	Hill, Clendenen, Stuart, Verhoef, Merrill — Petersen, Glazier-McDonald, Floyd

— NEW TESTAMENT —

NEW TESTAMENT	Calvin's Commentaries (Torrance Ed.)
MATTHEW	France, Carson, Hagner, Nolland [𝑀], Keener — Davies/Allison, Luz
SERMON ON MT.	Guelich, Lloyd-Jones (for theology) — Betz
MARK	Stein, France, Evans, Guelich [𝑀], Edwards, Gundry, Witherington — Collins, Marcus, Boring, Moloney, Hooker, Cranfield [𝑀]
LUKE	Bock, Green, Marshall [𝑀], Stein, Nolland [𝑀] — Fitzmyer, Bovon, Johnson

JOHN	Carson, Köstenberger, Keener, Michaels, Ridderbos — Barrett, Brown, Schnackenburg, Lincoln, Smith
ACTS	Peterson, Bock, Walton (F), Witherington, Marshall — Barrett, Fitzmyer, Johnson, Pervo, Haenchen, Conzelmann
ROMANS	Moo, Schreiner, Murray, Osborne, Lloyd-Jones — Cranfield, Dunn, Jewett, Käsemann, Wright, Fitzmyer, Keck, Stuhlmacher
1 CORINTHIANS	Thiselton [*M*], Garland, Fee, Ciampa/Rosner (F), Witherington — Barrett, Fitzmyer, Hays, Collins, Robertson-Plummer, Conzelmann
2 CORINTHIANS	Harris, Barnett, Witherington, Hafemann — Furnish, Barrett, Thrall, Martin, Matera
GALATIANS	Longenecker, Bruce, Lightfoot, Luther — Betz, Dunn, Martyn
EPHESIANS	Thielman, O'Brien, Hoehner, Robinson — Lincoln, Best, Barth, Schnackenburg, Muddiman
PHILIPPIANS	O'Brien, Fee (NICNT), Hansen, Silva, Bockmuehl [*M*], Hawthorne — Reumann
COLOSSIANS	O'Brien, Moo, Thompson — Dunn, Wilson, Barth/Blanke, Schweizer, Sumney, Lohse
THESSALONIANS	Fee, Wanamaker, Green, Marshall — Malherbe, Richard, Best
PASTORALS	Mounce, Towner (NICNT), Knight, Fee, Kelly — Marshall/Towner [*M*], Johnson on Timothy (AB), Quinn on Titus, Quinn/Wacker on Timothy, Dibelius/Conzelmann
PHILEMON	Nordling — Fitzmyer, Barth/Blanke, Kreitzer
HEBREWS	Lane (WBC), O'Brien, Ellingworth, Hughes, deSilva, Bruce, Guthrie — Attridge, Koester, Johnson
JAMES	McCartney, McKnight (F), Davids (NIGTC), Moo (Pillar), Blomberg/Kamell — Johnson (AB), Martin, Laws, Mayor
1 PETER	Jobes, Davids, Michaels, Selwyn, Schreiner, Grudem, Kelly — Achtemeier, Elliott, Goppelt
2 PETER/JUDE	Davids, G. Green, Moo, Hafemann (F) — Bauckham, Kelly, Neyrey, Mayor
1–3 JOHN	Carson (F), Yarbrough, Kruse, Marshall, Stott — Brown, Schnackenburg, Lieu, Smalley [*M*], Strecker
REVELATION	Beale, Osborne, Mounce, Smalley, D. Johnson, Hemer, Thomas[1] — Aune, Caird, Boxall, Charles

—◊—

OMNIA IN GLORIAM DEI

---

1 I believe there is need to include at least one Dispensational commentary (especially in light of how many millions follow that theological system), and Thomas is the most scholarly.

About the Author

John Frederick Evans is a lecturer at the Nairobi Evangelical Graduate School of Theology in Nairobi, Kenya.

A native of North Carolina, Rev. Dr. Evans grew up in Indiana as the son and grandson of Presbyterian ministers. He served as a pastor in the Presbyterian Church in America (PCA) before moving onto the mission field in 1997. He served in Zambia until 2007, then for one year in Namibia before moving to Kenya in 2009.

Dr. Evans and his wife Elizabeth have three children: Martyn, Beth, and Daniel. He enjoys music, running, playing tennis, and wildlife photography.

EDUCATION: The Stony Brook School (Stony Brook, NY), Diploma with High Honors, 1981 • Calvin College (Grand Rapids, MI), B.A., 1984 • Columbia Biblical Seminary & Graduate School of Missions (Columbia, SC), grad studies, 1984–85 • Covenant Theological Seminary (St. Louis, MO), M.Div. *magna cum laude*, 1989; Th.M., 1995 • Universiteit van Stellenbosch (Stellenbosch, South Africa), D.Th., 2006 • University of Cambridge (Cambridge, England), 2005, post-doctoral studies 2010.

About Doulos Resources

Our goal is to provide resources to support the church and kingdom, and to build up and encourage the pastors and leaders within the church. Our resources follow the model of Ephesians 4:12— "to prepare God's people for works of service, so that the body of Christ may be built up." We produce books, curricula, and other media resources; conduct research to advance our goals; and offer advice, counsel, and consultation. We are Reformed and Presbyterian, but not exclusively so; while we do not lay aside our theological convictions, we believe our resources may be useful across a broader theological and ecclesiastical spectrum.

Our goal with *A Guide to Biblical Commentaries & Reference Works*, as with all of our resources, is to offer well-edited, high-quality, and useful materials at an affordable price that makes our resources accessible to congregations and members of the church.

If you are interested in ordering additional copies of *A Guide to Biblical Commentaries & Reference Works*, or to order other materials that Doulos Resources offers, please visit our website: www.doulosresources.org. If you are ordering in quantity for a church or other ministry, contact us to inquire about a discount for quantity orders.

Doulos Resources Contact Information:

U.S. Mail:
195 Mack Edwards Drive
Oakland, TN 38060
USA

Telephone:
(901) 451-0356

Internet:
website: www.doulosresources.org
e-mail: info@doulosresources.org

CPSIA information can be obtained at www.ICGtesting.com
Printed in the USA
LVOW01s1411091014

408060LV00004B/11/P